'Christina Stead has long needed a good biographer, and here she is. Hazel Rowley is no pedant, boring the reader with a maze of footnotes, nor does she use her subject to focus her own needs, and the result is a fine and balanced book.'
Doris Lessing, *The Independent* (London)

'Hazel Rowley, in this splendidly detailed account, supplies the narrative that makes sense of the novels' angry, many-voiced, impatient, digressive brilliance. Hazel Rowley, who is as patient and tactful as Stead was impatient and savage, has portrayed her "monster" with exemplary clarity (and charity).'
Lorna Sage, *Times Literary Supplement*

'Neither [Stead's] life nor her art ran smoothly, and it is the measure of Hazel Rowley's achievement in *Christina Stead: A Biography* that she dodges none of the difficulties, while managing to produce an exceptionally readable and enjoyable book.'
Anne Chisholm, *The Observer* (London)

'Hazel Rowley's book can hardly be faulted for its sympathy and intelligence. It is unlikely to be bettered.'
James Wood, *The Guardian* (London)

'It's a hell of a life that Hazel Rowley has on her hands. It is to the credit of the biographer that she makes the reading of Stead's life, which has its pits of negativity, both willed and suffered, a profoundly moving experience. This is biography of the highest order, as finely organized as anything by Ellmann and with a command of narrative tempo that will put it on the shelf next to Marr's *Patrick White* as one of the finest biographies ever written about an Australian.'
Peter Craven, *The Age* (Melbourne)

'*Christina Stead: A Biography* will, I'm sure, in time become one of those stories from Australian literary life, which simply have to be read by anyone interested in Australia's intellectual and social history, in the literature of the English-speaking world, and in the biographer's art at its most consummate.'
Robert Dessaix, *24 Hours* (Sydney)

The Miegunyah Press

The general series of the
Miegunyah Volumes
was made possible by the
Miegunyah Fund
established by bequests
under the wills of
Sir Russell and Lady Grimwade.

'Miegunyah' was the home of
Mab and Russell Grimwade
from 1911 to 1955.

Christina Stead

Christina Stead
A Biography

Hazel Rowley

THE
MIEGUNYAH
PRESS

THE MIEGUNYAH PRESS
An imprint of Melbourne University Publishing Ltd
187 Grattan Street, Carlton, Victoria 3053, Australia
mup-info@unimelb.edu.au
www.mup.com.au

First published 1993
Revised edition published 2007
Text © Hazel Rowley 2007
Design and typography © Melbourne University Publishing Ltd 2007

National Library of Australia photos in photo insert pages: Christina Ellen Stead, 1904 (vn3704503); Christina Stead, 1937 (an24717059); Christina Stead, 1983 (an23501688).

Cover designed by Pfisterer + Freeman
Text designed by Alice Graphics
Typeset by Megan Ellis
Printed in Australia by Ligare

National Library of Australia Cataloguing-in-Publication entry

Rowley, Hazel.

Christina Stead: a biography.

New ed.
Bibliography.
Includes index.
ISBN 9780522854060.

1. Stead, Christina, 1902-1983. 2. Women authors,
Australian – 20th century – Biography. I. Title.

A823.2

Contents

Prologue

IT WAS THE interviews Christina Stead gave late in life that first aroused my curiosity. 'I'm a good-natured person,' she would insist. 'I don't expect anything, because I don't care. I take everything as it comes.' The façade she displays is brusque and pragmatic. Her rhetoric is scientific—influenced, she would always say, by her naturalist father. 'When you're a little girl and you look in an aquarium and you see fish doing this and that … you don't criticise and say they should do something else. And that's the way in which I was brought up.'

This detached persona seems scarcely reconcilable with Stead's fiction, repeatedly described by critics as 'savage' and 'furious'. In her two autobiographical novels, *The Man Who Loved Children* and *For Love Alone*, Stead's fictional counterparts plan murder and suicide. And Stead often said she invented nothing in her fiction—neither characters nor plots. I found myself wondering about the person behind the mask.

Virtually the whole of Stead's writing life—forty-six years in all—was spent in the northern hemisphere. She left Sydney as a young woman of twenty-six; she returned aged seventy-two, a figure of international repute, rivalling Patrick White as the finest writer Australia has produced.

No major writer of any nationality has been more cosmopolitan than Christina Stead, with her genius for portraying disparate locales, voices and expressions. Joyce in exile remained quintessentially Irish; D. H. Lawrence abroad, grumble as he might about his homeland, remained unmistakeably English. Stead was Australian in the sense that restlessness and travel are an Australian tradition. Culturally, she was as adaptable as a chameleon.

A child of the Edwardian era, she came to maturity during that period of cataclysmic change straight after the Great War, before radio and jet travel transformed communications. She arrived in England in 1928, and Wall Street crashed the following year. The movements of Stead and her companion Bill Blake would reflect those of a tide of expatriates. They were in Paris at the same time as James Joyce and Gertrude Stein, the doyens of 'modernism'. They were in the United States when John Steinbeck's *The Grapes of Wrath* was celebrated as the great proletarian novel. When leftwing solidarity gave way to the Second World War and its tragic aftermath, the Cold War, Stead and Blake fled McCarthyist America for Europe.

Wherever she was, Stead's internal baggage went with her, but its dead weight was something she hid from others. 'Why does anyone want to know about the life of a writer?' she once asked. 'The writer is usually engaged in telling the story of other people's lives.'[1] Her curiosity about other people was unquenchable. She was fascinated by ordinary lives and the extraordinary passions that propelled them along. But she was the least reliable of sources when it came to her own life. In later life, she destroyed all the drafts of her manuscripts and most of her private papers, diaries and intimate correspondence.

Stead would sometimes say she had no need to write an autobiography; she had already written it in her books. But her fiction is reality transmuted. Her fictional *alter egos*, Louisa, Teresa, Lydia, Persia, Laura—all with names ending in *a*, like Christina—are idealised Christinas. None of *them* is hanging in Stead's gallery of monsters. Those were modelled on her family and friends. But just like Victor Frankenstein's creation, Stead's monsters partly represent her own shadow side.

No one knew better than Stead that life itself is a narrative. She was happiest when she was turning life into story. As she once wrote: 'The true portrait of a person should be built up as a painter builds it, with hints from everyone, brush-strokes, thousands of little touches.'[2]

I

Ocean of Story

JULY 1902 – AUGUST 1917

ＩN CHRISTINA STEAD'S memory, her mother was a dim vision of pale skin, dark eyes and long dark hair lying across a pillow on a high brass and lacquer bed. She herself, dressed in a red twill dress, was swinging on the bedpost, singing to her mother, who had always liked her singing. It must have been morning, for the sunlight filtered through the front window of their whitewashed cottage. Suddenly the nurse, an ugly old woman, told her to go away and stop annoying her mother. The little girl looked at her mother, who said: 'Yes, go, Chrissie.'[1]

Filled with a sense of betrayal, the child left the room. She was fingering the panelling of the door, not knowing why she had been sent out, when her aunt came along: 'What are you doing there—spying?' Although she was only two and a half, the child knew what was meant. Her aunt shooed her away. Seventy-seven years later, Christina Stead was still angry.

Christina Stead never made much consciously of the loss of her mother, though she did once say, comparing herself to a guttercat, that she had not trusted anyone since she was two.

After her mother's death, she became her father's special girl. David George Stead was a zoologist, brimming with stories about the marvels of the natural world and its strange inhabitants. In the evenings, with the light falling from the streetlamp through the open slats of the venetian blind and his foot on the packing case on which his daughter slept, he would tell his tales. 'And it went on and on, night after night, for more than two years.'

Among the last things Stead wrote was a tender piece reconciling her to the 'unusually gifted man' whom she had reviled in her most famous novel, *The Man Who Loved Children*. It was her father, she acknowledged, who had taught her to swim in the 'ocean of story'.[2]

Christina Ellen Stead was third-generation Australian. She liked to think her family history was shaped by literature. In *Great Expectations*, published in 1861, the convict Magwitch is transported to Australia, where he makes his fortune in sheep. In 1862, Stead's paternal grandfather, an avid reader of Dickens, packed his bags, farewelled his family in Kent and boarded the *Hotspur* for the three-and-a-half-month voyage to Sydney. He was sixteen years old. Whether or not fiction played so decisive a role in Samuel Stead's destiny, Australia did offer an opportunity for hard-working tradesmen to break out of the English class system. By the time Samuel Stead came to Sydney, gold had paved the way for a boom in the Australian economy that was to last for thirty years. Samuel did not make his fortune, but he was enterprising and found employment with a firm of building contractors, later setting up his own business in North Sydney. Late in life he joined the Dickens Society, and as a child, Christina was occasionally taken to see her grandfather perform at socials, where he would recite from the novels, joyfully impersonating Scrooge, Nicholas Nickleby, Quilp and Fagin.

At the age of twenty-two, Samuel Stead married 19-year-old Christina McLaren. Scottish born, she had come to Australia as a baby with her newly widowed mother. Samuel purchased a small plot of land on Walker Street, a winding street not far from the harbour in St Leonards (now North Sydney), where he built a two-storey weatherboard house. There Christina produced seven children by the time she was thirty-two. One daughter, May, died in infancy, leaving three boys and three girls: Sydney, Samuel, Christina, Jessie, David and Florence.

Grandfather Samuel—with twinkling eyes, moustache and a dashing dark red handkerchief—was a 'freethinker', as atheists were then called, who occasionally took snuff and enjoyed a glass of port. He belonged to the Order of Odd Fellows, the oldest of the several orders of British lodges transplanted to Australia, committed to ideals of brotherhood, democratic sharing of responsibility and mutual financial assistance.

His wife, Christina, by contrast, was a kind-faced but plain woman, with an austere, world-renouncing piety. As a member of the Plymouth Brethren, a nonconformist Protestant sect, she regarded smoking, alcohol, dancing, gambling and the theatre as vices.

David George was born on 6 March 1877. He was a handsome boy, with thick yellow hair, soft blue eyes and a happy nature. According to his daughter Christina he actually shone: his 'pale blaze' dazzled people. If his older siblings still entertained sentimental ideas about 'Old England', David responded to the country of his birth like Adam in Eden: 'Australia was his prolific and innocent garden.'

Despite their mother's puritanism, the Stead household was cheerful and musical, with frequent family singsongs around the piano. When they sang in the evenings in the front room with the lights on and the blinds up, passers-by would stop in the street to listen.

One terrible night in the winter of 1893, Christina, their mother, died of an angina attack. She was forty-four. David, who was sixteen years old and particularly close to his mother, was devastated. He vowed to keep her rules of life.

> He never went to the theatre or to concerts; he abhorred dancing, because
> of the contact of bodies; he did not allow kissing or embracing in the home,
> nor endearments, nor cajoling, which he thought led to degrading habits
> of mind.

David George held a strange mixture of both parents' views, with passionate fervour. He was an atheist, like his father, and so committed to atheism that he refused to enter a church. Yet he was a puritan, like his mother, and just as firm about never letting a drop of alcohol pass his lips.

All three boys left school at the age of twelve. David was apprenticed to the Sydney rubber-stamp maker Karl Faulk, where he learnt to pride himself on his decorative lettering. But his passion had always been nature. In his late teens he attended a zoology course at Sydney Technical College, where he boiled down and mounted a cat and a dog that would stare at his children from glass cases. And he became an active member of the New South Wales Naturalists' Society, a group of committed amateurs. In 1898, at twenty-one, he joined the Linnean Society of New South Wales, the professional naturalists' body. By 1900 he had several short articles published by the prestigious British Linnean Society.

———— ✼ ————

David's lively younger sister Florence—who had her father's beautiful voice and taste for acting—went to work at fourteen as a seamstress in the workrooms of David Jones, the fashionable department store. It was through Florence that David met Ellen Butters, an embroideress, whom he married on 17 August 1901, the year Australia was formally declared an independent nation.

Twenty-five-year-old Ellen Stead came from an ardently devout family, but her wedding was not a religious service: the 24-year-old groom was adamant about that. He even tried to forbid his wife to pray. Ellen's father, equally headstrong, banished his daughter and her new husband from the family home. Ellen's brother Duncan later claimed that she visited her mother and siblings secretly, and was bewildered by the strange world into which she had married: 'snakes in the copper and creatures everywhere and she not allowed to pray'.[3]

Two months after her marriage Ellen was pregnant, and it was in their two-roomed cabin on Kimpton Street, Rockdale, south of the city, that Christina Ellen Stead was born on 17 July 1902, the year that Australian women gained the right to vote in federal elections. Grandfather Butters refused to speak to his daughter or look at his grandchild.

In the next year or so, the family moved to Oakleigh Villa, a whitewashed house with a stone verandah and picket fence, standing alone on a rutty road leading to Rockdale station. David Stead set up his menagerie in the back garden. He kept venomous black snakes, and a diamond snake, whose erratic eating habits he noted with interest. But his special interest was fish. David Stead's expertise in this area was acknowledged by the NSW Fisheries Commission, who gave him a job in May 1902, despite his lack of formal qualifications.

Christina Stead liked to think she looked like her mother, but the one surviving photograph of Ellen Butters shows little resemblance. In the solemn studio photograph, Ellen is in her early teens: a comely adolescent with docile brown eyes, full lips, a long dark plait and a white communion book in her lap. She is wearing a prim dress with a high neck, leg-of-mutton sleeves and a fur collar clasped by a large, ornate brooch. She looks timid, submissive—the daughter of an authoritarian Victorian father.

As a child, Christina was very fair and had several of her father's features, though in her, unfortunately, they did not form the same harmonious blend. Her father was tall and strongly built. In photographs he has the air of a man who knows he is handsome. His large forehead, prominent nose and resolute chin give him a proud, self-confident bearing. His daughter had the same imperious presence.

In the family it was said that Christina looked like her father's sister Jessica—something she hated to hear, not because Jessica's appearance was unpleasing, but because she had remained an 'old maid', a fate Christina regarded with horror.

Christina was two and a half when Ellen was rushed to Prince Alfred Hospital, Camperdown, with acute appendicitis. It is likely, given Stead's vague picture of her mother ill in the front bedroom, that she had been ill for some time. Was she pregnant again? Did she wonder whether she was being punished for ceasing to pray? After eighteen days in hospital, Ellen Stead died on 9 December 1904, and was buried in the General Cemetery at Rookwood. She was twenty-eight.

After Ellen's death, David's younger sister Florence moved into Oakleigh Villa with her 18-month-old daughter Gwendolin. In some unpublished notes, Christina Stead writes:

> When my mother died I was so young that I did not miss her; I lived with a sprightly goodlooking pair of young people, a loving brother and sister, my father David and my aunt Flo, and I had a little girl to play with, my aunt's baby daughter. The house was gay and full of music. My father whistled, imitated birds, hammered, sawed and took photographs; my aunt sang, ran the sewing machine; they told us innumerable stories about real and imaginary people.

The arrangement suited everyone. The previous year Florence had married a doctor, Hugh Walker-Smith, whom she had met in an amateur repertory company, but it was a marriage on paper only. For the time being, she was only too pleased to be housekeeper to the brother she so admired. David Stead provided the financial support, enabling Florence to stay at home and look after the two girls. Years later, Christina Stead would fondly inscribe books to her 'sister-cousin'.

In Stead's overtly autobiographical novel *The Man Who Loved Children*, good-hearted Aunt Bonnie, stage-struck and always bursting into song as she goes about her housework, creates a scandal within the self-righteous Pollit family by becoming pregnant outside marriage. Florence Walker-Smith was certainly pained by these revelations.

Christina was to have a lifelong respect for kind, open-minded 'Auntie Florrie', who knew 'it took all sorts to make a world'. Her talents as a mimic, pianist and singer brought her occasional small parts in musicals, but she had no opportunity to develop her gifts and, as a deserted wife, she was to lead a life of drudgery as a seamstress and domestic servant. But she cultivated a sweet fortitude: 'Well, it is Kismet, isn't it? A merry heart goes all the way.'

As a father, David Stead was in his element. He saw himself as an educator of the masses, particularly children. Before breakfast, he would carry his daughter around his study and ask her to name in turn the various solemn faces whose photographs hung around the room: James Cook, Cuvier, Buffon, Darwin, Huxley. After this came the photographs of fish. Christina was expected to know the Latin names for their body parts and the botanical names of plants. Later, she would find foreign languages comparatively easy. And her memory was exceptionally good.

The menagerie in the backyard grew bigger: the tortoise was obliged to bear the weight of small passengers; there were guinea-pigs, mice, rabbits, a duck, an echidna and, of course, the snakes. David and Florence read the girls the children's classics: *Alice in Wonderland*, *The Water Babies*, Hawthorne's *Tanglewood Tales*. The supreme moment for Christina was bedtime, when she had her father all to herself. Gwen had a cot in her mother's room; Christina slept in her father's room on a packing case containing treasures, real and imagined, that he had collected: a 'crocodile head with a bullet hole over the left eye', an ivory whale tooth, a giant Japanese spider-crab, dried human heads, a snake's skeleton and 'the kneecap of some monster extinct millions of years before'.

Her father told her stories of the outback, about the first Australians and their corroborees, about 'brave canoe-sailors, men washed away by wind and current', tales of Krakatoa and Mauna Loa, volcanoes that blew people's heads off, convict ships, Captain Cook's travels, Charles Darwin's voyages in the *Beagle* and extinct monsters—triceratops, mastodons and giant kangaroos—that used to roam the mud swamps among the cycads. Infused with her father's passion for the Australian continent, she was filled with a 'curious feeling … of terrestrial eternity, a sun that never set'. Although her mother was dead, she did not think of death as a horrible personal doom. She knew it was necessary for evolution to take place.

When her father left her, to talk to his sister in the kitchen, the room was still alive with voices. The little girl's head was filled with a clamour of 'interminable, stupid conversations'. The pieces of furniture—her father's double bed, the rug, the fireplace—talked to each other. The chest of drawers would say: 'I am so heavy, full of old clothes, the drawers squeak in and out', and the floorboards would chime in: 'What about us? We have your weight, you're crushing us.' She went to sleep amid these dialogues.

Looking back, Stead later thought it strange that the pieces of furniture were so 'morose' and 'grumpy'. Since she could not remember her father or her aunt ever voicing discontent, she surmised that the complaints of the furniture reflected her own dissatisfactions.

An unpublished draft by Christina Stead describes a little boy who in every way resembles her, confronting a recurring morning drama. He is placed on a high chair in front of a plate of lumpy oatmeal that he stubbornly refuses to eat.

> 'He must sit there till it's eaten,' his father would say gaily but firmly as he
> ran for the tram … In the evening, an enquiry was made. 'If he won't eat it
> for breakfast it must be given to him for lunch. We must break his will.'

Christina Stead's early memories were all associated with a sense of rejection, which she attributed to her physical unattractiveness. In all her stories about her childhood, she is acutely conscious of personal appearance. Her father, she writes, was an 'extremely handsome man'. Her mother, her Aunt Florence and Gwen were pretty. She was not.

This burning sense of her own plainness was reinforced by her father. That his eldest daughter was not endowed with good looks was a source of chagrin he made no attempt to conceal. He was obsessed with appearance himself. Worse, he expounded the theory, flattering to himself, that appearance reflected character: his own handsomeness and fairness were the outward signs of his goodness and innocence.

In *The Man Who Loved Children*, Stead says of Sam Pollit: 'Like many a handsome body, Sam was not only revolted by deformity and plainness but actually saw essential evil in it.' To David Stead, plainness was a kind of deformity.

—— ✺ ——

Then came the catastrophe that was permanently to undermine Christina's security. By 1906, her father was becoming well known in scientific circles. An extraordinarily energetic man, he gave lectures, wrote scientific articles and newspaper columns on a vast number of nature subjects. He had published two monographs, *Crustaceans, Ancient, Modern and Mythical* and *Fishes of Australia*, each with splendid photographs, and was already at work on a third, *Edible Fishes of New South Wales*. His work entailed quite a bit of travelling: he was often away for a few days, inspecting oyster leases and the stocking of rivers and dams, checking the position of sewage farms. But then he took to being away on Saturday afternoons and not coming home until long after Christina had gone to bed.

He had met Ada Gibbins through her father. Frederick John Gibbins was known as 'the Oyster King' of the northern rivers, where he owned dozens of leases. He also owned pearling luggers in Torres Strait, timber mills at Terrigal and a wharf at the foot of Market Street, where the timber from the family mills was shipped for storage in his Sussex Street warehouse. Gibbins warmed to David Stead and invited him to meet the family. While Stead had no personal fortune, his future did seem promising. Whether or not Frederick Gibbins encouraged the unlikely courtship between David Stead and his youngest daughter, known in the family as 'Tott', he did nothing to deter it.

One Friday evening, when Christina was four, her long fair hair was put in rag curls that she had to sleep on all night. The next afternoon, wearing her best dress and hat, she went with her father by tram to the neighbouring district of Arncliffe, from where they took a pony trap along the old, convict-built Wollongong Road to a handsome two-storey mansion on the hill. They were visiting a lady whom Christina was told to call 'Auntie Tott'.

The lady had black hair, olive skin, dark eyes and long fingers. Her skirt was very full, her waist quite tiny. Next to the house was a small orchard. 'You can run about and stay here till I call you,' her father told Christina. Later, they had tea and cakes in the house, served by the maid. French windows opened onto the tessellated verandah, where an ancient Mexican parrot sat on its perch and shrieked.

———— ✿ ————

Ada Gibbins, the youngest of eight surviving children, had been born in 1879 at the family home in Kent Street in the heart of the city. Six years later, the family had moved to Dappeto, the mansion on the hill.

Frederick Gibbins, born in 1841, was the only son of a convict called John Gibbins, who arrived from England in 1829, at the age of eighteen, sentenced to fourteen years' transportation for theft. It was John Gibbins, more than anyone in Christina Stead's own family, who, like Magwitch, transformed himself from felon to successful businessman. His son Frederick had further increased the family fortune.

Ada was greatly attached to her indulgent father. 'Old Dad', as his numerous grandchildren were to call him, was a handsome, lively man, very much in the Edwardian mould. Ada's mother, Catherine ('Old Mum'), was a strongly built woman with snowy hair pulled back in a bun, and blunt, no-nonsense speech that shocked Christina when she was a little girl.

Ada had her mother's fine eyes but none of her practicality. At a small private finishing school in the Blue Mountains, she had learnt the ladylike accomplishments she would need in a world of visiting cards and 'At Homes'. She also painted watercolours, sang in a thin quavery voice, played the piano weakly and prided herself on delicate embroidery—something she was to teach Christina.

By 1906, the year she met David Stead, Ada was twenty-seven, stuck at home with her parents and an older brother who drank too much. There was nothing to do: housework and cooking were done by servants.

David Stead wanted a wife. And, by the time she met David, Ada must have been seriously worried about her marriage prospects. It seems, from the beginning, to have been a marriage more of convenience than of love. David Stead was probably charmed, initially, by Ada's dark eyes and society girl coquetry; he certainly liked and admired her father. Ada was doubtless attracted by David's looks, and perhaps his energy and enthusiasm seemed to offer a remedy for her own boredom.

In an unpublished sketch based on her stepmother, Christina Stead refers to an earlier engagement that had been broken off, leaving 'Pitti' heartbroken and close to a nervous breakdown. When 'Ewan', a young naturalist, proposes to her, she is at first relieved. She accompanies him on several naturalists' expeditions and although too prettily dressed for that group, she charms people. Ewan, however, is astonished by her ignorance: she does not even know what stamens and pistils are. Quite soon Pitti begins to find Ewan's unbending ways oppressive: he disapproves of the novels she devours, disapproves of alcohol, disapproves of God himself. She runs away to relatives. When she tells her aunt she does not love her fiancé, the aunt retorts: 'Do you want to be left on the shelf?' Christina would always claim that her stepmother was married off by her father, Frederick Gibbins, against her will.

The wedding was held on New Year's Day, 1907. The Gibbins family would have liked a large church wedding. This time, David Stead was prepared to compromise to the extent of agreeing to a religious service— but no church. The Anglican rites were performed in the drawing room at Dappeto. It was pouring with rain. Christina sat near the temporary altar in a Swiss muslin dress and a large white hat. Her father wore a new suit and the bride a dress of cream brocaded satin, with a veil of Brussels lace. After the ceremony they adjourned to the dining room, where a feast was spread out on the long oak table. That afternoon, Christina acquired her third mother in four and a half years.

David Stead's second marriage brought about a dramatic change in his circumstances. The benevolent Frederick Gibbins made available to the couple a substantial colonial mansion, a mile away from Dappeto, which he had bought in 1890 and rented out. For the next ten years, David and Ada Stead were to live there rent free, with their ever-expanding family.

The district was still almost rural. Lydham Hill, as the Steads called their home on the knoll, was one of the original houses, dating from the 1850s.[4] Built of local sandstone, it comprised four large rooms, each with pink and black Italian marble fireplaces, and two sloping attic rooms upstairs. The kitchen and washrooms lay across a flagstoned yard. The front of the house looked out to the Pacific through the headlands of Botany Bay, Cape Banks and Cape Solander.

It was a fine life for children. In the mornings, the front windows of Lydham Hill were drenched in sunlight; in the evenings, playing at the back of the house, the children would watch the sun disappear behind the Blue Mountains in a crimson and orange blaze. Cool sea breezes tempered the humidity of summer, though in winter the coal fires never quite warmed the large rooms.

The house was on three-and-a-half acres of land, which included two paddocks, an old orchard and a belt of pines and camphor laurels. It was an idyllic playground for children, and the outbuildings—the former stables, coach house and servants' quarters—were ideal for David Stead's collection of stuffed animals, bones and artefacts. Two large Japanese turtles lived in a well in the courtyard; cages contained snakes, possums and injured birds; a tall aviary housed a boobook owl and kookaburra, finches and budgerigars. Two emus, Dinnawan and Mundoey, acquired as striped chicks, ran around in one of the paddocks. Occasionally they would escape, stalk along the gravel drive and swallow whatever lay on the kitchen windowsill.

In later years, in Paris, London and New York, some small thing would trigger Christina Stead's memory of this house and the 'whole landscape of childhood' would rise up before her, leaving her almost breathless with nostalgia. She would 'hear the eucalypts rustling at old Lydham' and smell the pungent smell of 'the cockchafer beetles, burnished gold, falling from the boughs'.[5] From Paris she told a friend:

> You know those nights when for some reason all you did when a little child rushes back over you: I did not get a wink of sleep, thinking of the time we built nests in the pine-needles and flapped round pretending to be starlings … or hid in the kangaroo grass pretending to be prince and princess.[6]

'My stepmother was kind to me until her first child was born, and then I was the outsider.'[7] Christina was always acutely conscious that she was different from the other children, a semi-orphan. Within ten years Ada had six of her own children. The four boys were named after famous scientists; the girls, more modestly, after the women in the family. David Darwin arrived on 4 October 1907, Catherine Ada on Christmas Day 1908, Frederick Huxley in June 1911, Doris Weeta (an Aboriginal name for a spotted bower-bird) in October 1913, Samuel Kelvin in February 1915 and Gilbert Jordan in October 1917.

Christina now called Ada 'mother', but Ada never let her forget that she was the daughter of another woman. Gwen Walker-Smith remembers her cousin as a difficult, stubborn child, often sullen; Ada tried to impose her ideas, and Christina resented her from the beginning. Ada was short-tempered, often sarcastic, with a dry sense of humour and a tendency to exaggerate. Although she could be very amusing when she was relaxed, she was anything but easygoing. Caught in the crossfire of allegiances, David Stead found it more comfortable to appease his wife. (In *The Man Who Loved Children* Sam Pollit tells Henny, Louisa's stepmother, reproachfully: 'I taught her not to coax me or kiss me, or climb on my lap as the others do because in the beginning it made you so angry.')

Christina thought it 'very natural' that her stepmother did not like her—let alone love her. She saw the fault as her own: even a real mother would find it hard to love *her*. Unconsciously she may have believed that her own mother had left her because she was bad: such feelings are not unusual in children whose parents have died. At another level, she was angry about being deserted. It is a small step from being unloved to believing oneself unlovable. And those who feel rejected have an uncomfortable way of making sure they really are. As a writer, Christina was to become an observer, a professional outsider.

Stead had a vague memory of Ada as she was one year after her marriage: 'a beautiful dark, thin young lady in a ruffled silk dressing gown, mother of a very large red infant in a ruffled bassinet, receiving in state a company of very beautiful young ladies, all in their best dresses'.[8] But Ada Stead's pampered upbringing in no way equipped her for the life she would lead. She was pregnant, on average, every second year, and although in the Lydham Hill years they usually had a servant to help, there was too much for one servant to do. There were clothes and sheets to be turned in the copper and squeezed through the mangle. There was ironing, done with heavy flatirons; there was mopping and sweeping, polishing and darning. There were beds to make, the wood stove to stoke, meals to cook.

Florence Walker-Smith lived with them on and off, between paid domestic positions, and she and Gwen visited often. If she was able to, Florence would come and help when Ada was ill or about to give birth. The other helper was Christina, whom everyone called 'Peg'. Her father, who gave all children nicknames, had decided that his ruddy-skinned daughter was 'Pig Face' or 'Piggy'. Kindly Aunt Florence, horrified, had insisted on changing this to 'Peg' or 'Peggy'.

Since her father saw no need for it, Peg did not make an appearance at school until the unusually late age of seven. At Bexley Public School the teachers were shocked to discover that Christina, a big girl for her age, was still 'unlettered'. The dilapidated primary schoolhouse, down the hill from the Steads' house, gathered in boys and girls from dwellings scattered around the district. Looking back, it pained Stead to remember how the poorer children were ostracised and humiliated.

After school, Peg would be sent to fetch milk from Dappeto. This meant crossing pastures, jumping over foul gutters, trying not to slip on the muddy, unpaved streets. She was terrified by a boy from one of the farmhouses who often waylaid her, and she dreaded spilling the milk on the way back. In the family she already had a reputation for being clumsy—'always in the wars'.[9]

Once she learnt to read, Christina could escape alone into another world. Every Saturday, she walked a mile and a half into Bexley and spent her pocket money on books, which cost a penny each. Her favourites were the Brothers Grimm and Hans Christian Andersen. Later, she would read these to the children at bedtime.

David Stead liked nothing better than to entertain young children. His own favourite book as a child had been Joel Chandler Harris' tales of Uncle Remus, Tar-Baby and Br'er Rabbit, and he was an adept at Uncle Remus-speak. A letter he wrote to his children in 1922 ended: 'Luv to evryboddie and all be goode. Thoes who duz thare dutie ar luvly wuns thay will get some frottie and some kurren bunz. From DadPad the Boald.' David Stead's other linguistic model was the American comic writer Artemus Ward. Though this endless wordplay could be tiresome at times, it was at least an imaginative lexical system David Stead taught his children to explore.

Sunday, he decreed, was 'Funday'. (Study on that day was outlawed, to the bitter resentment of his eldest son, David Darwin.) 'Funday' was organised by David Stead, King of the Kids. For his own children, and any of the neighbourhood children he could enlist, David Stead invented stories, thought up exuberant games, initiated magnificent adventures.

He was a great walker, and liked to take Christina on long walks, saying it would make her grow. She would always remember and resent her father for one fifteen-mile walk along the coast from Rockdale to Cronulla—'nearly killing me'.[10]

At weekends, there were visits to Dappeto. Stead, who would read 'shoals of detective novels' in her life, was grateful when these authors left the scene of the crime to the reader's imagination, for Dappeto would always be the setting she imagined. The house had all the appurtenances of a detective novel: French windows giving on to lawns, flowerbeds, windows with drainpipes, numerous stairs, rooms contiguous and adjoining, balconies.

She would spend hours examining the bibelots and pictures at Dappeto. Over the chimney, opposite her place at the table, was an oil painting in a heavy gilt frame. It showed a table on which were arranged 'globulous heavy grapes', fruits and flowers, and plumy, bloody, disembowelled birds and fish with a knife stuck in them. Even its name was mysterious: did *Still Life* mean there was still life in the fish and birds?

A dominating character, charming, energetic and imaginative, David Stead was the major influence in Christina's life. He was her father, her own blood; unlike Ada, he loved her. Indeed, he talked a great deal about love, in an abstract sort of way. At times they were close companions: both were bursting with ambition, both shared a lively curiosity about the world, a vivid imagination, an interest in language, a love of story and jokes. By the time she was in her early teens, it was his daughter who was David Stead's confidante, not his wife.

Committed to imparting to the community a love of nature and through that, a belief in goodness and justice, David Stead's substitute for religion was Nature. He saw himself as an apostle of 'Right, Justice and Truth' (his words) and he wanted his children to follow in his path. He was always saying that he loved 'humanity and the mass more than anything else'. People were fundamentally good; the wicked were merely insufficiently educated. As an adult, Christina Stead realised he would have made a good minister among puritanical, earnest New World dissenters.[11]

One of the early and most outspoken conservationists in the country, David Stead co-founded the Wildlife Preservation Society of Australia—

the precursor of the Australian Conservation Foundation. In 1910, on the strength of his books and articles, he became one of the youngest Fellows ever elected to the British Linnean Society. The same year, at thirty-three, he was promoted within the Board of Fisheries to Superintendent of Fishery Investigation—all without high school education.

A born teacher, he was a willing and popular speaker, illustrating his talks with lantern slides. A favourite with audiences, one that Christina came to know well, was 'Giants and Pygmies of the Deep'. He often took her to lectures and naturalist expeditions, hoping to encourage her interest in science. She would meet entomologists, geologists, botanists. 'They bored me to death,' she said later. 'Unbearably prosy' characters, they were 'always correcting each other about some trivial matter, like the name of a beetle'.[12]

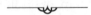

Though he gave so much time and energy to children, David Stead was not a loving or supportive father. He would romp and tease and call the children affectionate names, but they could never quite please him. When David Darwin came second in French one year, his father's only comment was, 'Why not first?' The following year, when he did come first, his father merely shrugged and said, 'Of course, from a son of mine!'[13]

What 'the man who loved children' really loved—more than the children as individuals—was the power to form young minds. He was against compulsory schooling: he would have preferred to educate his children himself. He had very definite ideas, on which his children endured endless diatribes. There was no God. Cats and dogs carried disease. Alcohol was evil. Doctors were fools. Make-up was vulgar. Ada accepted the taboo on alcohol, keeping only a bottle of medicinal brandy in the house. Doctors came to the house for births, and Ada called the doctor when the children were seriously ill, but sometimes at the cost of a domestic row. If the children ventured a different viewpoint, their father would retort, 'Under my roof you do as I say.' The children made a joke of his horror of hydatids (larval tapeworms), which he told them were carried by cats and dogs. It became a comic danger cry in their games: 'Watch out, hydatids!'[14]

In Christina Stead's ironic terms, her father was 'part of the Huxley-Darwin reasonable-rational nature-agnostic mother-of-all-things-fresh-air-panacea eclectic-socialist universal-peace-manhood-suffrage-and-vegetarianism of the English breed, inheriting from the eighteenth century age of light and Jean-Jacques ...'[15]

But all this was based on prejudice as much as reason. He objected to his Australian-born children learning subjects like French and history, steeped as it was in the dubious legends, class divisions and 'bloodstained scroll' of 'wicked old Europe'.[16] He proclaimed the equality of all peoples, but disliked Jews (whom he called moneylenders) and did not think much of the French, despite the benefits of the Enlightenment. Publicly, he espoused the rights of women, but his letters to the family were spiked with misogynist remarks. (Women, he believed, should be pretty, wholesome and domesticated; too often they were conniving and manipulative.[17]) He wanted his children to do well at school, yet he was jealous when they did. 'He was conscious of the fact that he didn't have any academic qualifications whatsoever,' said Thistle Harris, his third wife, 'and it acted as a frustration to him all his life. I think it affected his whole personality.'[18]

Conflict between David Stead and his children began when the children reached the age of dissent, and Christina was the first to do so. During her adolescence, alongside her love and admiration for her father went an anger that verged on hatred. It would not have helped, her brother David comments, that her father regularly called her 'a lazy fat lump'. (She was big-boned, but never fat.) In *The Man Who Loved Children*, Louisa Pollit, a young adolescent, has to endure constant jibes about her size. 'When she walks she wobbles,' says her father observing her. 'Take your fat belly out of the sink,' says her stepmother, seeing Louisa slop dishes about, wetting her dress. Whether or not everyone called Christina a 'barrel of lard' as they do Louisa, Stead once wrote to friends: 'Always I felt like a cripple. Do we all? Why is it? I have never been a cripple—and I thought it was because my father thought I was ugly.'[19]

The David Stead counterparts in Christina Stead's fiction have a sadistic streak. In the short story 'Uncle Morgan at the Nats', Uncle Morgan, Chairman of the Naturalists, goads his 3-year-old niece to put her hand in the fire. He is 'training the child to obey'. The story was essentially true: David Stead had apparently tried to persuade 3-year-old Gwen to do just that. In *The Man Who Loved Children*, Louisa Pollit, at eleven, has started to have doubts about her father and to resist him. Sam Pollit is bewildered and disturbed by this new turn of events: 'I'll break that miserable dogged spirit of yours,' he tells her. He boasts that he knows her inside out: 'You are myself.' In fact, though he pries into his daughter's private diary and tries to prod her inner thoughts, he is far from understanding her. In his frustration, he attempts to colonise not only her mind but her body. Playing with the children one day, he joins mouths with his baby son and pushes chewed food into his mouth, explaining to the others that parent birds do this to their nestlings. He then calls over his adolescent daughter.

> She got up and came to his side, rather shyly. 'Right here!' Surprised, she came closer. Mottled with contained laughter, he stretched his mouth to hers, trying to force the banana into her mouth with his tongue, but she broke away, scattering the food on the floor and down the front of her much spotted smock, while everyone clamoured and laughed. Sam himself let out a bellow of laughter, but managed to say, 'Get a floor cloth, Looloo-girl: you ought to do what I say!'

Christina Stead claimed this was also based on fact.[20]

The Stead children learnt from an early age that their father was not someone you could trust. With him you had to be on your guard: he set you up, challenged you, humiliated you when you least expected it. Games often ended in tears.

When Christina was twelve years old, her father submitted a scheme for a deep-sea trawling industry to be run by the state government. There was a severe shortage of fish in the Sydney shops, and David Stead drew the government's attention to the huge variety of edible fish in the coastal waters off New South Wales.

Trawling at that time was virtually unknown in New South Wales. Labor Premier William Arthur Holman was enthusiastic: he was eager to establish government-owned industries. In June 1914, David Stead was sent by the Department of Fisheries to Britain, Europe and the United States to purchase and equip three modern steam trawlers and to enquire into methods of fish distribution and canning. He took with him a collection of 131 specimens of New South Wales fish as a present to the British Museum.

He sailed at the end of June 1914, and was in France when war broke out in August. His letters to his children from France and Norway reveal the extent of his obsession with female beauty:

The Parisienne is splendid—she is lithe, she is supple, most graceful and beautifully formed. If a man never noticed women anywhere else he would notice them in France and specially in Paris … So many of the faces are so beautiful too—without make-up, of course—and, in very many cases, even where there is make-up, in the fashionably dressed women, it is done so artistically, as to reduce its offensiveness to a minimum.

In Stavanger, David Stead was arrested by the beauty of Norwegian women:

Many of the girls are so pretty, with lovely flaxen hair (the real thing) and blue eyes and loveliest of complexions, with mostly 'peach' and, sometimes, 'apple' cheeks. And *this is very wonderful*: there are hardly any really plain girls in Bergen, Hangesund or Stavanger … . Sunny dispositions are everywhere apparent in nice clean honest faces of both sexes … I hope our Australian governments will do all they can to attract suitable people from among these splendid industrious coastal Scandinavians to our continent … The infusion of such splendid blood into Australia can only bring benefit to our posterity and present population.

Not only did David Stead worship beauty: he would have liked to rid the world of ugliness. How could he expect his eugenic enthusiasms to be shared by his 12-year-old daughter, to whom this letter was principally addressed, painfully conscious as she was of her plainness?

David Stead's attitude reflected the period, in which there was much theorising about the 'racial' superiority of the Nordic peoples. A personal friend and self-made man whom he greatly admired was David Starr Jordan (1851–1931), the world's leading ichthyologist, the first President of Stanford University, who openly advocated eugenic practices. As Director of the World Peace Organisation, he was the foremost exponent of the dysgenic significance of the Great War: it violated the process of natural selection by killing vast numbers of the able-bodied male population, leaving the physically or mentally unfit at home to perpetuate the race. His ideas were elaborated in his book *The Blood of the Nation, A Study of the Decay of Races through the Survival of the Unfit* (1920).

Starr Jordan visited Sydney a couple of times. Christina remembered him well, as one of the few visitors to the house at Bexley—'a tall imposing man with a broadbrimmed hat and dark clothes'.[21] In David Stead's autograph book, he wrote a maxim from Emerson that impressed

Christina: 'The world stands aside to let pass the man who knows whither he is going.'

David Stead was away from Sydney for almost the whole duration of his wife's fifth pregnancy. One postcard to Ada has survived. Written in late February 1915 from Boston, the message was a few dull lines about the picture on the other side; there was no 'dear Ada' and no 'love David', no concern about her health. Yet earlier that same month she had given birth to Samuel Kelvin.

The Man Who Loved Children contains a violent Oedipal melodrama written by 13-year-old Louisa for the occasion of her father's fortieth birthday. There are just two characters in *Tragedy of the Snake-Man*: Anteios and his young daughter, Megara.[22]

Megara tells her father that in his company she feels guilty, yet she knows she is innocent. He, with his 'rascally wiles', ravishes her peace of mind, her solitude. Now she shares her solitude with a stranger called hate. 'If I could, I would hunt you out like the daughters of King Lear.'

'Horrible,' cries Anteios. 'What a she-devil!'

The daughter begins to choke; she feels herself being strangled. The stranger is a snake and he has turned, she realises, not on her father but on her.

> MEGARA: (Shrieking) I am dying. You are the stranger. You are killing me.
> Murderer! Murderer! Mother!
> ANTEIOS: I am only embracing you. My beloved daughter. (But he hisses.)
> MEGARA: Mother, father is strangling me. Murderer! (She dies.)

Stead was thirty-six when she wrote this in her dingy New York apartment, and though it is presented as a piece of Louisa's juvenilia, Stead knew she was plunging into her own unconscious.

In *The Man Who Loved Children*, Henrietta Pollit screams that she has had enough of having babies, scrubbing floors, putting up with her husband's 'vile animals' and his 'everlasting talk, talk, talk, talk, talk'. On another occasion, Sam Pollit, expatiating upon love and goodness, tells Louie that he has sacrificed his whole life to nature and mankind. She starts to scribble something down, and he imagines she is taking notes. When he bends over her shoulder to look, he reads: 'Shut up, shut up, shut up, shut up, shut up. I can't stand your gassing, oh, what a windbag, what will shut you up, shut up, shut up.'

Sam Pollit, of course, is 'terribly hurt', and instead of reflecting even for a moment on his own behaviour, the all-loving Sam flings at her:

> What is the matter with you? You're mean and full of hate ... I think of love and you are all hate. Sitting there you look like some mean cur in the street, whining and snivelling ... What can I do with a girl like you? You have no looks ... I don't understand you.

The Man Who Loved Children recreates the fierce tension in Christina Stead's relationship with her father: the admiration, disappointment and anger on her side; the double binds and contradictions on his. With her stepmother it was easier: Christina never expected anything from her, and was surprised by their brief interludes of mutual sympathy. 'They ... made an etching out of me,' she wrote later, explaining the bitterness that marks the novel. 'I am deep-bitten.'[23]

Brolga, Kooraga and Gunundaal, the three trawlers that David Stead had bought in Hull and christened with Aboriginal names, arrived at Port Jackson in April and May 1915. The State Trawling Industry was officially established in June, with David Stead as General Manager. 'For five lively years,' writes his daughter, 'we had nothing but trawling and fishing talk.'

For David Stead, who called himself 'a state socialist', this was the ideal opportunity to bring together his scientific expertise and his social idealism. Brandishing the slogan 'Fresh food for the people', he set out to provide cheap and wholesome food for the less wealthy. His was a grandiose vision: he assured the government of a regular, cheap fish supply and a profit within the first twelve months. The Municipal Fish Market and the state-owned fish shops would eradicate the 'grasping middlemen', he claimed. His lack of diplomacy soon created enemies.

His dream was quite realistic. Wartime Australia suffered from low wages and a high cost of living, and the waters off Botany Heads were in fact an untapped source of nourishing food. He was right: the coast of

NSW proved to be among the best fishing grounds in the world. Out of the trawling nets came John Dory, snapper, whiting, flathead, leatherjackets, barracouta, ling, silver dory, skate—many of which the public had never seen. Premier Holman recalled later: 'The newly obtained catches appealed to the public imagination like miraculous draughts, and people came literally in their thousands.'[24] By 1917, four more trawlers, built in the Sydney dockyards, were added to the fleet.

But trouble was brewing. The fishermen, out for days at a time, went on strike for Sundays in port. David Stead was caught between being a strike-breaker and supplying fish for the people. Stead wrote:

> My father, a staunch Labour man, who believed in the people, in the good of man, attempted to break the strike by getting helpers from the office and shops, from our family and among friends, to scale and gut, to save the fish which lay then at the docks. There was great enthusiasm I remember: he was satisfied with this activity and everyone 'pitching in', 'lending a hand' (one of his favourite jolly ideas).[25]

War conditions made it difficult to import machinery: the launching of the other trawlers was delayed and the Australian-built vessels ended up costing far more than the imported ones. But the fundamental problem was political: the State Trawling Industry posed a threat to private interests. Although David Stead argued that a young socialist industry was not supposed to make a profit, that it was for the people, his enemies made much of the alleged financial losses, using them as an excuse for what Christina Stead later described as 'shocking crass attacks, both on the government, its ministers and on him personally'.[26]

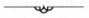

By her early adolescence, Christina knew she was going to be a writer. Writing was something she was good at, something she loved to do; it was a means of shining, of feeling better about herself. When she was eleven, she won the district essay competition for a piece on the life cycle of a frog, thus spawning her writing career very much in the shadow of her father.

At twelve and a half, she had been sent to Kogarah Intermediate School, something between a vocational school and an academic high school for girls. She was there only a year before St George Girls' High was opened, in February 1916, and the girls were transferred to the new school, a rambling old villa beside an orchard. The institution's small size made it seem like a private school. Nine teachers, all with university degrees, taught 143 students.

Christina liked to stand out, and made an ostentatious display of her writing. In a world in which David Stead made everyone into his satellite, it was a useful defence to act the same way by writing fiction, playing God in creation. She achieved notoriety with a poem called 'Green Apricots', which made mock of a new teacher who rebuked the girls for stealing unripe apricots from the orchard. The final stanza read:

> Who is it, on the hanging bough
> Green apricots once saw, and now
> Finds them scattered, lying low,
> And goes at once, to make a row?
> Green apricots!

In later years, Christina Stead greatly regretted her 'malicious poem'. She would never forget that the teacher was almost driven from the school by the hostility of the girls, without anyone quite knowing why she was so disliked.[27]

By contrast, the poems she wrote to her English teacher were without the cruelty—though just as public. Everyone in the class knew that Peggy Stead had a crush on Miss Paradise, and was writing what she grandiosely referred to as her 'Paradise Cycle'. Wildly ambitious, she intended the cycle to comprise hundreds of poems in every conceivable form and metre. Angela Carter was later to comment that Stead 'was, from the very beginning … a writer of almost megalomaniac ambition'.[28]

Writing had become a means of attaining power over others, and resisting their power over her. By writing—and showing her writing to others—Christina could reduce people by ridicule or raise them to great heights. It was an important and lasting discovery.

Within the ten years they lived at Lydham Hill, Ada Stead was transformed from an elegant young spitfire into a querulous, frazzled and embittered shrew, who took out her frustration on the children—particularly her stepdaughter. Her fictional counterpart Henrietta Pollit ('Henny') undergoes the same drastic metamorphosis: 'The dark lady of the ruffles had disappeared and in her place was a grubby, angry Henny, who, after screeching, and crying at them all, would fall in a faint on the floor.'

Gwen Walker-Smith and David Darwin well remember the fainting fits. Without any warning, Ada would fall straight down in a rather shocking way—on her face, side or back. Somehow, miraculously, she never broke a bone. Christina, horrified at first, gradually became used to it and would run for a pillow and let her stepmother lie there, very pale, until she came to herself.

Ada had had these momentary seizures since childhood: she may well have suffered from *petit mal* epilepsy, which was hard to diagnose. But over the years, David Stead came to regard her fainting spells, fairly or not, as a spoiled woman's trick. The rest of the family also came to suspect they were at least partly self-induced. 'Sometimes she would get into a state and throw herself on the floor,' says Gwen Walker-Smith, who conjectures that it was probably her aunt's way of 'getting away from things'.[29] (Ada used to say as much herself.) 'She was an emotional woman, very unhappy, and under great strain with all those kids.'

As a child, Gwen Walker-Smith was aware of the tension in the air when David and Ada were together. Her aunt, she recalls, 'had no idea how to manage on a limited budget. To get away from the children she would go to town and buy things the family could ill afford.' David Stead's Public Service income did not go far among six children, and they relied on 'Old Dad' not only for the free house, but also for extras, such as wages for the servant. Ada's visits home—she found gracious Dappeto and conversations with her earthy mother a welcome retreat these days—invariably resulted in a small handout. Back at Lydham Hill, looking tired and worn, she would console herself with endless cups of tea and games of patience. The piano was rarely touched, except when Florence Walker-Smith came to stay.

Later in life Christina Stead was not without sympathy for her stepmother. 'She married the wrong man, that's all,' she would say, 'and that's extraordinarily difficult.'[30] In *The Man Who Loved Children*, Henny, mad with frustration, talks of going back to her family and taking the children with her. Ada Gibbins no doubt made the same threats. But the reality was that a wife's situation completely lacked legal protection. A husband was not legally bound to provide for her future or for their children's; wives had no rights either in the guardianship of the children or in the distribution of the family's accumulated wealth. Ada was virtually a prisoner in her own house—a situation her stepdaughter saw very clearly in later years: 'Cells are covered with the rhymes of the condemned, so was this house with Henny's life sentence, invisible but thick as woven fabric.'

———— ❧ ————

David Stead's scientific ambitions for Christina were more typical of a father's for a son; he certainly did not have the same aspirations for his other daughters. She was good at science at school, eager to impress her father. But since she was a daughter and not a son, David Stead was dismayed that she was not prettier. His deep ambivalence, transmitted to Christina, meant that the scientific meetings did not at all achieve the desired effect.

> What repelled me, it's shameful of me, but it's true, is the women used to dress very plain: long plain skirts, hair way back, in a bun, and I couldn't stand it. Not for me!
> ... I made up my mind at the very earliest age that I would not be a scientist: I intended to have nice dresses and to get married, and I very soon observed that these earnest women were either not married, or were married to men that seemed to me very old and very homely.[31]

'If women are to cultivate the sciences they must remain celibates for life,' opined the *Bulletin*, the radical, republican journal, in 1888. This view of professional women was just as prevalent two decades later, and the social stigma attached to unmarried women was as strong in the Stead household as anywhere else. David Stead's sister Jessica—the aunt whom Christina was said to resemble—was an unmarried 'pupil teacher' (as infant teachers without formal training were called), and an object of pity and disdain within the family.[32] Older schoolmistresses belonged in a grievous category of 'old maids' and 'dessicated virgins'—for those who married were obliged to leave the service. It did not warm Christina to the teaching profession.

———— ❧ ————

> INTERVIEWER: 'It has been said that [*The Man Who Loved Children*] is perhaps the greatest book about family life that's ever been written. It is

certainly the most powerful evocation of what it's like to live in a family
that I've ever read.'
CHRISTINA STEAD: 'That's a terrible criticism, isn't it?'
INTERVIEWER: 'Terrible criticism?'
STEAD: 'Of family life.'[33]

Written in New York when Christina was in her thirties, the novel for
which she is now best known was no hymn to her father, nor to family
life. On the latter, Stead agreed wholeheartedly with the pessimistic
Strindberg. In later life, she freely acknowledged the fact that the Pollit
family was based on her own family. She even admitted—though she was
always cagey about her feelings—that writing the book caused her intense
emotional distress. She would then revert quickly to a pragmatic stance
that disclaimed the singularity of her own case: 'Most children live through
great tragedies and they grow up and they're just normal and ordinary ...
It strengthens their character.'[34]

Stead's public matter-of-factness contrasts starkly with the cauldron
of seething emotions in the novel itself. At the time of its publication,
in 1940, critics would complain that the novel was overwhelming. Mary
McCarthy protested: 'The reader is put in the position of the awestruck
children listening in their beds to a nightlong family quarrel.'[35] Clifton
Fadiman found Sam Pollit nerve-shattering: 'You're ready to scream at him
as if he were not a character in a book but a man in your living room.'[36]
New York Times critic Charles Poore exclaimed: 'In the end one is not so
much inclined to ask mercy for the family but mercy for the reader.'[37]

Randall Jarrell was one of the few to find the novel's overbearing quality
a strength:

> *The Man Who Loved Children* makes you a part of one family's immediate
> existence as no other book quite does. When you have read it you have
> been, for a few hours, a Pollit; it will take you many years to get the sound
> of the Pollits out of your ears, the sight of the Pollits out of your eyes, the
> smell of the Pollits out of your nostrils.[38]

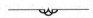

At the time of writing, Stead commented that the novel had 'a plot derived
from, although not exactly mirroring, our home in the early days, not the
procès-verbal, but the dramatic truth'.[39] In other words, it represented the

emotional truth—her own. She was conscious then that her novel was both 'true to life' and an artistic construction, that it was not just a matter of what she put in: it was also a matter of what she left out.

In later life, Stead would deny the gap between the 'dramatic truth' and reality. 'I was brought up by a naturalist, and I *am* a naturalist,' she would say, implying (in the tradition of nineteenth-century realist writers) that hers was the impartial, objective gaze of the empirical scientist. For her, she made clear, there was no difference between snakes and people: she observed life, she took notes, and she wrote about what she saw. She went so far as to insist that she had recreated her family life exactly, once claiming she had written the truth 'word for word'. It was a bizarre stance for a creative writer to take, one which disowned the complex process of fictional transformation.

What her claim does indicate is a desire for control altogether reminiscent of her father's. David Stead was always saying that he worshipped 'truth'. He meant *his* truth: he interpreted the world largely according to his own needs. His daughter made the same claim about *The Man Who Loved Children*: it told the truth. 'They were so much alike,' says Gwen Walker-Smith of Christina and her father. 'That was the clash.'[40]

———— ⟊ ————

Like the fictional *alter egos* she would later create (Louisa in *The Man Who Loved Children* and Teresa in *For Love Alone*), Christina as an adolescent was full of passionate, romantic yearnings intensified by a sense of outrage. Books were her solace, her refuge and her companions. They nourished a sense of self-worth that her daily existence could not provide. As a reader she could identify with both the heroes in fiction and the writers who created them. She read voraciously, re-reading favourite authors constantly and learning lengthy passages by heart.

She had a marked penchant for the fantastic, the ghostly, gothic and grotesque. The sumptuous and erotic mediaeval world of *Arabian Nights*, which she read in Richard Burton's famous translation, coloured her imagination for life. In her own fiction, she would not be able to resist occasional images of genies bowing their way out of snuff jars in smoky spirals.

She liked old tales and legends. The stories in her mother's King James Bible (which her father had kept, despite his hostility to religion) were

wonderful. And the scientific books in her father's library were full of true
adventure. She would always admire the writing in Darwin's *Origin of the
Species* and *Voyage of HMS Beagle*. One book that particularly haunted her
was on venereal disease, with poems by the insane and stories about nuns
who dreamt that the Devil jumped over the wall into the convent. She also
read the bush ballads and stories of Henry Lawson, Banjo Paterson, Steele
Rudd, members of the 1890s 'stockwhip and wattle-blossom school'.[41]

The family was 'full of Dickens', and Christina read every one of his
novels, even though for the most part her own father disapproved of novels.
When she changed the children's sheets, Christina would find concealed
in the linen cupboard romantic novels from the local library. They did
not interest her, but she was amused that Ada took no more notice of
David's puritanical prejudices than she did. Books, in his view, should
not treat 'unsavoury subjects'. He would have thoroughly disapproved
of Strindberg's bitter short stories about marriage, yet they enthralled his
daughter, who saw Strindberg as the only writer to tell the truth about
families. In time, her filial revolt would go much further. Not only did she
read novels with 'bad subjects': she was to spend her life writing them.

She treasured *Peer Gynt*, Ibsen's drama about a dreamer and wanderer,
and learnt long passages from the William Archer translation by heart.
And it was with something akin to rapture that she discovered Milton,
Byron, Tennyson and Keats: her early poetry shows the influence of English
Romanticism. For her fifteenth birthday her father gave her the complete
works of Shelley. She loved *The Cenci*, and her alter ego Louisa vigorously
identified with Beatrice:

> ... I, alas!
> Have lived but on this earth a few sad years,
> And so my lot was ordered, that a father
> First turned the moments of awakening life
> To drops, each poisoning youth's sweet hope.

But her great love was Shakespeare. Later she would claim (doubtless an
exaggeration) that as an adolescent she read the family's battered tome of
his *Complete Works* from beginning to end every year.

By this time the family assumed that their dreamer would be a writer,
though they were too preoccupied with their own struggles to pay her
scribblings much attention. As an adult, Christina Stead was grateful
that she had been left alone to develop in her own way. When she saw

precocious American children being 'prodded and puffed' by their parents, she thought the result disastrous.[42]

At school Christina was not an outstanding student. Her ambition lay elsewhere. In the NSW Intermediate Certificate examination for which students sat after two years of high school, her results were an A for art and Bs for English, History, French, Botany and Maths. It was November 1916; she was fourteen and a half, the legal age for entering the work force, and the age at which most pupils, especially girls, left school.

That summer, in January 1917, 'Old Dad' died. The Gibbins family vaguely knew that Frederick Gibbins' investments in the Lake George Gold Mine had failed, but only now did they learn of the extent of his debts. Dappeto and Lydham Hill, the genteel family homes, would have to go under the hammer.[43] It was a shattering blow to David and Ada Stead. The last thread to fine bourgeois living had snapped. Ada had not only lost the father she loved; she had lost all connection to the life for which she had been brought up.

It was probably their bleak financial prospects that made David Stead suggest to Christina that she take up an apprenticeship in journalism. She was aghast: she wanted to be a writer, not a journalist—especially not a female journalist, confined to the women's pages. Her father must have been halfhearted about the idea himself, for he soon agreed to her staying on for the two years it would take to finish school.

To her dismay, Ada found herself pregnant once again. David Stead had to look for a new house at the same time as an embarrassing public inquiry was being held into the State Trawling Industry. Premier Holman supported him, but Holman too was under a political cloud, and partly for the same reasons: he was a threat to private industry. According to H. V. Evatt, Holman's biographer in 1942, Holman was principally destroyed by a 'systematic campaign of political vilification'.[44] This was to apply equally to the State Trawling venture.

David Stead found a house at Watson's Bay. Today the area is prime Sydney real estate; in 1917, it was a sleepy little village with fishermen's shanties, boatsheds and fish nets drying in the sun. Still surrounded by large areas of bushland, it was a favourite Sunday picnic spot for city dwellers. Not until the 1920s, with the advent of the family car, did the farther eastern suburbs become popular residential districts.

The weatherboard house at No. 10 Pacific Street, one of the few two-storey houses in the area, was dilapidated. In parts its external walls and wooden floors were quite rotten. It had been built by 'Captain Jack', a retired master mariner, in the mid 1880s. David Stead, a good handyman, would be fixing it up, with the help of his boys, for years to come. They moved on 31 August 1917, just six weeks before Gilbert Jordan (named after Starr Jordan) came into the world.

The children loved the sprawling ramshackle house that fronted straight on to the harbour and was within a short walk of the Heads. Standing on the sandstone boulders at the edge of the natural swimming pool at the end of the garden, they saw fish glide past. Looking up, they saw a wooden jetty, yachts, a dredge, motorboats. They were in their element. So was their father. For Ada, who disliked the sea and detested the smell of fish and seaweed, it was a terrible wrench. From elegant Lydham Hill to this unpretentious, reeking bay!

Christina had just turned fifteen. When she was not reading or writing, she was composing in her head. Wonderful, solitary hours were spent describing things to herself, and improving upon the description. She was training herself to see small details, to hear the exact rhythm and cadence of dialogue, to observe the external world, to be aware of internal conflict. 'How blunt our senses are,' one of her characters would exclaim, 'how many thick veils hang between us and the world. How will we ever refine our eyes to see atoms and our ears to hear the messages of ants?'[45]

Twenty-one years later, in *The Man Who Loved Children*, Christina Stead would re-create the atmosphere of the day they moved to Watson's Bay:

> Henny heard the men moving in some heavy thing, and heard her husband say wearily, 'Looloo-dirl, make some cawf!' The reek of weeds forever damp and of the brackish water came up to her and the smell of the ground under the veranda. It had rained slightly in the night. Louie, who pretended not to hear Sam's call, came in a dawdle round the house and leaned against the veranda post behind the vines, chewing a grass stalk. She was droning to herself and presently she droned clearly, 'Oh the waterskin crawls shorewards; and the leprous sky scales earthwards, from the musical moaning channel, to the dirty margin. It was halfwater; the surface was dull, and the sky was windy.'
>
> At that particular moment, Henny awoke from a sort of sullen absence and knew what was happening; her heart was breaking. That moment, it broke for good and all.

'Stop that rot,' she cried madly to Louie, startling her out of her wits, 'I never heard such damnfool tommyrot. Go and get the coffee. A big lumbering sheep, and on a day like this, she holds up the veranda post.' Louie, with tactful soft-footing, disappeared from behind the vines, and presently Henny heard her saying,

'I say, Dad, this gas won't turn on; it's jammed.'

The men trundled backwards and forward and puffed. Louie soon came to the veranda with a cup of tea for her mother (Henny's heart would not stand coffee), 'Mother, Daddy says, Where do you want things put?'

'What the devil do I care? Put them on the orchard and make a bonfire of them. Put them where you like,' she ended, less ungraciously. 'Is it my home? It's your father's idea. Do what you like; all I want is a place to lie down, and get me a bed for Baby. Tell him I am not going to lift a finger to fix up his stinking tenement: the animals have better cages. Go on now, don't stand there staring.'

Louie, not at all offended, and now observing more closely the many defects of the old house, the hanging window cords, unlatchable latches, and sunken floors, went in to say, 'Mother says put everything where you like.'

Sam, only too pleased, at once hallooed and whistled for the gang of children and consulted their tastes. It was not hard to suit most of them.

Calling her fiction the 'truth' was the adult Christina Stead's way of controlling her universe, then and there as well as for posterity. After she had written *The Man Who Loved Children*, either out of revenge or through a fusion in her imagination, she used to refer to her father in letters and conversation as 'Sam'.

When she sat at her typewriter at the age of thirty-six to write about her family, it was she at last—not her father—who had the whip hand over her childhood.

2

Embarkation for Cythera

———— ❦ ————

SEPTEMBER 1917 – APRIL 1928

A FEW METRES FROM their tall, weatherboard house, which David Stead named Boongarre, after an Aboriginal chief who had lived in the area, ocean liners from all over the world—Shanghai, Naples, San Francisco, London—anchored in the harbour awaiting quarantine inspection. Christina's bedroom was upstairs at the back of the house; from her window she could see the ships in the harbour 'lighted like a Christmas tree', and the 'great subtropical moon' that hung over the water like a lantern.[1] She liked to lie in bed listening to the boom of ocean rollers against the cliffs. Even though Boongarre was protected under the hill, the spray from the surf would reach their roof.

The children swam for nine months of the year. To Ada's dismay, the house was always full of sand brought in by the children. There were mice too, and occasionally rats would come up from the waterfront. On summer evenings, large black cockroaches scurried along the footpaths and the kitchen benches. In front of the house, the garden ran down to the harbour; at the water's edge, several sandstone boulders formed a natural pool. When the young children were playing in the water, someone would always have to stand on 'Pegler Rock'—the biggest of the boulders—and watch out for sharks. As young boys, David and Fred scoured the rockpools for crabs and little oysters, which their father made them boil because of typhoid. In the early years, they paddled around in an old rowboat; when they were older, they would sometimes go out with the fishermen, coming back with fish that Ada then had to cook, though the smell made her feel queasy. Once they caught a twelve-foot blue pointer shark, lurking in shallow water within fifty feet of the house. This caused considerable excitement, and their father, enthusiastically discoursing on the many virtues of fish oil, got them to boil down its liver in the laundry copper. It was one of his madcap ideas: after several hours, the shark's liver had yielded four gallons of oil, but the terrible stench pervaded the whole neighbourhood and the copper would never be the same again.[2]

Christina had lost her childhood fairness: her long hair was light brown now, and usually tied back in a ribbon. A tall, big-boned adolescent, with keen grey-blue eyes, she had developed womanly curves early. But she had a rather ruddy complexion, a stubborn-looking jaw and buck teeth. She was definitely no beauty.

She was happiest in her own world, where her imagination had free rein. She liked to walk up the hill and sit among the boulders and pines at the cliff top, describing to herself a view that never failed to delight her—a scene she would later portray lyrically in her two Australian novels, *Seven Poor Men of Sydney* and *For Love Alone*. Her first publication, a sonnet called 'The Hill', appeared in the school magazine when she was sixteen, and begins:

> I stand upon a hill—on either hand
> Lie darkening waters. At my feet, the sea
> Clothed with faint mists that steal upon the land,
> E're yet the moon has risen, roars sullenly.[3]

Along the clifftops, the place known as 'The Gap', an indentation in the cliffs where the sea pounds the rocks with hellish ferocity, was the city's favoured suicide spot. Christina used to contemplate the desperation of those who threw themselves over the cliff and worry that the bodies would be dashed open on the shale platform below instead of finding a more gentle death in the foaming ocean. Michael Bagenault, in *Seven Poor Men of Sydney*, taking a last determined step towards the edge of the cliff, is stricken (too late) by the same thought: 'What if I should fall upon a rock?'

Christina knew that women threw themselves over The Gap because they were pregnant outside wedlock. On summer evenings, when she walked home down the hill and through the park, she would hear groans and strange cries emanating from the bushes and tangled scrub. She was fascinated, curious and vaguely repelled. Her fictional counterpart Teresa, in *For Love Alone*, imagines herself walking through 'a strange battlefield ... with sounds of the dying under the fierce high moon'.

<hr/>

Despite the beauty of the bay, life at home had become 'atrociously wretched'.[4] They were poor these days: it was a struggle to clothe the family and maintain the house at a respectable standard, and to a certain extent Ada had given up. At thirty-eight, she had six children under ten and a difficult adolescent stepdaughter. There was no longer any money for domestic help. And Florence Walker-Smith had found employment in a home in the bush, which to her dismay, meant that Gwen had had to be sent to relatives.

Ada, bitter about the wretchedness of her situation, rarely even spoke to her husband. When they did talk, there were sharp words, and sometimes dramatic rows. David Darwin recalls his mother hitting his father with rage on more than one occasion; he never saw his father hit back.

David Stead had no idea how to deal with wilful adolescents. Christina was fifteen now, and seeing his authority slipping, David resorted to taunting and belittling her, making invidious comparisons with other girls, pretty girls, *nice* young ladies. Gwen Walker-Smith remembers her cousin's frequent 'withdrawn almost sullen silence'.

But there were good moments, happy times, and these made Christina feel guilty for feeling so often resentful and angry. She was at her best with the younger children, inventing stories and games, taking them on walks, mothering them. At Christmas time, she devoted hours to making presents and preparing surprises for them. More than sixty years later, her sister Weeta, recalling this distant past, declared Christina 'the most wonderful sister any young girl could have wished for'.[5]

<hr/>

Three days after moving to Watson's Bay, in September 1917, Christina began at Sydney Girls' High School, the oldest and most prestigious state girls' high school in New South Wales. The 45-minute ferry-steamer trip via Parsley Bay, Neilsen Park and Garden Island, past hills covered in red roofs and the grey towers of the Rose Bay convent in the distance delighted her. On summer mornings, she would gaze across the glaze of the water and imagine the heat smoking on the distant hills. The task she had set herself as a future writer was to describe the smallest details with the accuracy of a miniature painter. Observation was a challenge she took seriously.

From Circular Quay, she walked past the shipping offices and warehouses, up a mild incline, past the colonial government buildings on Macquarie Street, to the red brick school on the corner of Elizabeth and Market Streets. The austere schoolhouse, previously St James's School, had been designed by the famous convict architect Francis Greenway and built by convicts in the 1820s. A dingy and cramped two-storey building, with a small asphalted yard shaded by two large Moreton Bay fig trees, it was enclosed by a high stone wall that added to the impression of a prison; but the girls developed a strong affection for the old building, in which lessons were punctuated by the clattering of trams and honking of motorcars.

Christina Stead was one of the first pupils to record 'no church' under 'Religion' in the Admissions Register.[6] She liked to be different. One of her classmates recalls an incident that occurred the following year, in November 1918, when the girls were about to attend thanksgiving services for the end of the war:

> We stood in groups according to denominations and the Church of England group was nearest the foot of the stairs. We were waiting for Miss Garvin to lead us over to St James. She came down the old stairs, … buttoning her gloves, passed a severely scrutinising glance over us and finally to the tall girl standing aside said, 'Why are you not with one of the groups?' In a deep hoarse voice Peggy Stead answered, 'I am an atheist.' Miss Garvin looked at her for two seconds and then said, 'Oh? Well, just get over here with the Church of England group and come along.'[7]

The atheism came, of course, from David Stead; so did Christina's political sympathies. With a father who called himself a 'state socialist', Christina had grown up proud of Australia's working-class heritage and labour tradition. Australia, with its old-age and invalid pensions, maternity

allowances and female suffrage, enjoyed an international reputation for
social reform. However, the Great War was producing a new conservatism.
The tide of loyalty to the Empire meant that labour organisations, which
opposed conscription, were regarded as traitors. The Bolshevik Revolution
in 1917 would further polarise Left and Right: it gave conservative
newspapers a new menace: the Reds. Christina Stead had great respect for
her progressive history teacher, Miss Barnes, who had the girls discussing
the *Communist Manifesto*.

It was the era of patriotism. At the cinema, silent newsreels of 'battleships
loaded to the gunwales with cheering soldiers dipping victoriously
through freshening seas' were accompanied by rousing nationalist music.[8]
'Anzac' and 'Gallipoli' had become emotionally charged additions to
every Australian schoolchild's vocabulary. At Sydney Girls' High, the girls
knitted socks for the men fighting on the Belgian front and filled boxes
with Christmas comforts for 'our men in France'. They brought things
from home and set up stalls in town to raise money. The school magazines
of 1917 and 1918 were filled with rhetoric about the 'noble deeds' of
the 'glorious Allies', and included a Roll of Honour—names of fathers,
brothers and sons who were serving the Empire.

Christina Stead was sub-editor, then editor, of those patriotic issues
of the school magazine, yet she herself was no war patriot. Her father
was a committed pacifist: so was she. Thirty-seven when war broke out,
David Stead condemned it as mass murder: he was hardly likely to join
the 40 per cent of Australian males aged between seventeen and forty
who volunteered for the Imperial Forces. To the family's horror, his sister
Jessica sometimes stood on Macquarie Street handing out white feathers
to able-bodied men passing by.

More than 60000 Australians died in the war. No army in the Empire
suffered losses in greater proportion. War memorials commemorating the
dead sprang up in every small town. Christina's age group was too young
to lose fiancés, but the girls were well aware that the pool of potential
husbands had shrunk.

Christina was in the third-year tug-of-war team in 1918, but she was not
much interested in sport, absorbed as she was by her studies, her reading
and writing. She enjoyed all her classes, and did well. English, with Miss

Ethel Gretton, was her favourite subject. She prided herself on being good at French, too, and she would be grateful for those school *dictées* when called upon, as a secretary in London and Paris in the late 1920s, to write letters in French. Later she claimed that her whole view of life was formed by Guy de Maupassant, the profoundly pessimistic nineteenth-century naturalist writer whom they studied at school. Inspired by the sobriety and simplicity of Maupassant's writing, Christina borrowed all the French books she could lay her hands on from the Sydney Municipal Library: from Rabelais to Chateaubriand, Hugo and Zola. The naturalism of Zola, who claimed that writers should develop the meticulous observation of scientists, would be an important influence on her own writing. And she 'fell overboard' for Balzac, a lifelong passion.[9]

George Henry Lewes' two-volume biography of Goethe affected her profoundly. Goethe, like Balzac, was more than a literary genius: his wide-ranging interests included morphology, genetics and foreign languages. The wartime mood was venomously anti-German, and German was not taught at her school; nevertheless, Teutonic culture, with its *Sturm und Drang* and High Romanticism, had great appeal for a passionate, rebellious adolescent.

Since the school did not have its own library, the girls were regularly issued with two library tickets from the Sydney Municipal Library. Christina collected them from girls who did not want theirs and would call in at the library after school with ten or more tickets. Classmates remember her as 'literature mad'. In the evenings, she would sit in her room with a pile of books on each side of her: to the right the books to be read, to the left those already consumed. Her brother David recalls her reciting lengthy tracts of Byron's 'Battle of Waterloo'.

Christina was intensely interested in the major and minor passions 'running in the undergrowth of poor lives'. While still at school, she decided that her first book would be called something like *The Lives of Obscure Men*. The idea would grow on her: the title of her first novel would be *Seven Poor Men of Sydney*. In the late 1940s, she briefly toyed with the idea of compiling an Encyclopaedia of Obscure People, a subversive *Who's Who*.[10]

Stead's last year at school, 1919, was one her generation would never forget: the terrible Spanish influenza, which raged worldwide, took 10 000 Australian lives in eight months—a death rate as high as for an equal period in the war. New South Wales schools closed for several weeks.

That year, Peggy Stead was sole editor of the school magazine (though modesty, it seems, prevented her from including any of her own writing) and one of seven senior prefects elected by the staff. She was happy at Sydney Girls' High, and developed a certain confidence, though she did not have a close friend and ate lunch by herself. But everybody in the class knew about her crush on Tempe Datson. Blonde and blue-eyed, outstanding at schoolwork and athletics, Tempe was extremely popular. Peggy was always scribbling sonnets for Tempe. At the time, Tempe laughed at them and privately tore them up, embarrassed. It was something she would come to regret.

Tempe remembers her admirer as 'plain looking', with no interest in clothes. 'Peggy was rather odd. You wouldn't want to make friends with her.' Because Tempe lived nearby, in Double Bay, she was sometimes invited to Boongarre for a meal, but her relationship with Christina remained distant. Tempe's impression was that the Steads had a 'happy home life', though Peggy did not seem to like her stepmother much. To Tempe, Mrs Stead seemed 'pleasant' and Mr Stead 'an interesting man, with a fine build'. Peggy was evidently very proud of him.[11] David Stead, for his part, was charmed by the polite and smiling Tempe Datson. When she left on a trip for Europe in 1935, aged thirty-three, he was at the quay to see her off.

It was less easy to be proud of his own plain and sullen daughter who somehow had a knack of arousing hostility in people. Was it the strong jaw and contemptuous air? Was it the clumsy, attention-seeking behaviour? The poet and community activist Mary Gilmore met Christina through David Stead when Christina was in her late teens, and would remember her later as a 'lank-haired pallid-faced anyhow-dressed girl'. In 1936, when Gilmore read *The Salzburg Tales* and was struck by its 'genius', she mused that she would never have thought 'that girl' would have attained such heights.[12]

There were only four years of high school in those days with the Leaving Certificate, a state examination, at the end. Stead sat the exam in November 1919 and did well: Honours in English, A for Botany and Bs in French, Maths I and II and Modern History. Her results won her an Exhibition to the university, a scholarship that paid her fees and an allowance for books, but Latin was a prerequisite for a Bachelor of Arts, and so Stead was officially 'unmatriculated'. Kogarah High had probably not offered Latin, but it is surprising that she was not encouraged to take it up at Sydney Girls' High. It seems that Stead had not thought of going to university until her third year of high school: she took Latin in her last year, hoping to pass the supplementary examination early in 1920, but she was unable to catch up four years' work in one. She would have been accepted for a science degree, but she had no desire to become one of those dreaded creatures with a long black serge skirt and bun. There were two options left to her: a year's scholarship for secretarial training at a business college, or a two-year Teachers' Training Scholarship. She opted for Teachers' College. She hated the idea of being any kind of schoolmistress, but teachers' training at least meant she would be paid £50 a year to study for two more years, though afterwards she would be bonded to the Education Department for a minimum of five years. The year Stead began at Teachers' College, 1920, the pay for female teachers was increased to four-fifths of the male salary.

Along with the other young female teachers-to-be, Christina Stead, at seventeen, had to sign a contract with the Department of Education, stating that she had no intention of marrying until her bond was either paid back or worked off. No wonder the teaching profession was irrevocably connected in Christina Stead's mind with being *unmarried*. 'It was a rather terrible prospect,' she admitted.[13]

———— ༜ ————

The striking figure—half Jesus, half Samson—who straddles the opening of *For Love Alone* is Andrew Hawkins, modelled once again on David Stead.

> Naked, except for a white towel rolled into a loincloth, he stood in the door-way, laughing and shouting, a tall man with powerful chest and thick hair of burning gold and a skin still pale under many summers' tan. He seemed to thrust back the walls with his muscular arms; thick tufts of red hair stood out from his armpits.

He is complacently boasting to his two adolescent daughters that his beauty has attracted many a woman. 'Inward and outward beauty', he explains, 'strike one chord.' Looking at them, he muses aloud: 'What a strange thing that I didn't have lovely daughters. I who worship beauty so much!' When 19-year-old Teresa explodes with anger, his taunts ring out:

Look at her! Pale, haggard, a regular witch. She looks like a beggar. Who would want her! What pride! Pride in rags! Plain Jane on the high horse! When she is an old maid, she'll still be proud, and noble. No one else will count!

Such taunts were a constant refrain in Christina Stead's own adolescence. Like Teresa, she appeared cold and indifferent, but in fact her father's poisoned arrows hit their mark.

> There was a glass pane in the breast of each girl; there every other girl could see the rat gnawing at her, the fear of being on the shelf. Beside the solitary girl, three hooded madmen walk, desire, fear, ridicule.

Christina was made to understand that finding a man was something to which she could scarcely hope to aspire. As she said later: 'We were brought up to be pretty and catch men. I wasn't pretty and they didn't think I'd catch one.'[14]

Stead's relationship with her disapproving, coaxing father ebbed and flowed. She hated him, she loved him; she resented him, she pitied him. For years she was his confidante. The Oedipal tensions were further intensified when David Stead told her, in 1919, that he had fallen in love with a schoolgirl her own age.

Sixteen-year-old Thistle Harris had recently joined the New South Wales Naturalists. Thistle was pretty, passionate about botany, sweet-natured and full of admiration for David Stead, who at forty-two was in his prime. Christina, who often went on the Naturalists' excursions and knew Thistle, was shocked. It seems that David Stead decided the romance was too outrageous to pursue, though he continued to hanker after his young friend. The following year, Thistle Harris, who was studying botany and zoology, bumped into Christina in the university grounds. Thistle said 'Hello Peg'. The response, she recalls, was a frosty 'Good afternoon, Miss Harris'.

Christina's feelings toward her father were further complicated when he lost his job early in 1920. For several years, as Manager of the State Trawling Industry, he had been the target of calumnious attacks by the conservative Opposition in Parliament. He was accused, quite unfairly, of 'fishing out' the waters, of gross mismanagement. There were vicious notices in the newspapers, blackmail, public and private pressure. Christina Stead recalled:

He would sit at the table when the morning papers came containing attacks upon him and he would in detail explain what was wrong, what the lies and fables were ... 'Write to them,' we would cry, the young ones, too, 'write to the papers, tell them.' ... Then he would sit back, saying nothing, looking exhausted and defeated.[15]

Early in 1920, the Royal Commission into the State Trawling Industry praised David Stead's hard work, scientific knowledge and enthusiasm, but came up with the verdict that David Stead was 'first and foremost a scientific man', not a business manager. He was relieved of his post. In time it was decided that he would lose all claims to superannuation. It was a bitter turning point in his life.

He was not to have regular work for almost two years. In September 1921, under the pseudonym 'Dinnawan, the emu, the king of the plains', he began a weekly series called 'The Great Outdoors' for the children's section of the *Sunday Times*. The jauntily written articles—featuring Nundaba the Snake and Mi' Poo' Yoo the mullet—were addressed to a character called Every-boy.[16] In David Stead's universe, girls had a secondary place.

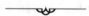

Christina Stead started at Sydney Teachers' College in February 1920. The new redbrick building had been opened that month in the grounds of Sydney University, but the two institutions were quite separate and different worlds. The 850 trainee teachers at the college were mostly women, and the lecturers mostly men. In university circles it was generally accepted that Teachers' College Scholarship holders were a class below university Exhibition holders.

In her second year, 1921, Stead scored distinctions in two subjects, Education & Logic and Ethics Psychology, and credits or passes for the rest. Her execrable handwriting was considered a problem for a teacher. Another was her weak speaking voice, and the following year she would be given special tuition in voice production. Her final mark, at the end of the two-year primary teaching diploma, was a 2A.

Stead co-edited the college magazine, *The Kookaburra*, and a poem of hers, 'The Gentle Supervisor', published in the college magazine of 1921, shows she had not given up the habit of adulatory poems. This one was humorous and aimed at a male lecturer. The same issue contained a second poem by Christina E. Stead, as she now signed herself, various humorous columns that suggest she projected herself as something of a college wit and a four-page short story, 'The Key of the House of Shadows'. Evidently she no longer suffered from undue modesty as an editor.

Only the story, 'The Key of the House of Shadows', indicates unusual talent. Set in an old French town, it is told by a first-person narrator in a confidential, anecdotal style reminiscent of Edgar Allan Poe. Like his stories, the narrative moves quickly from the everyday world into the realm of the fantastic and horrific, juxtaposing naturalistic and supernatural elements.

It was possibly after reading this story that Stead's art teacher, a young woman engaged to be married, suggested that Stead write a book of short stories that she would then illustrate. Stead was enthusiastic, and took the idea seriously. She rose at dawn to write, before leaving for college on the ferry.

The following year (she was still attached to the Teachers' College), she won a small Teachers' College prize for her poem 'In the Great Hall', which paid lyrical tribute to the university's 'hushed hall' with its 'tendrilled arches'.

At the end of Stead's second year at Teachers' College, in December 1921, David Stead left for Singapore to take up a year's appointment as Special Fisheries Commissioner in British Malaya. He needed the salary badly, but he also liked to think he would be contributing to 'the great international work' that was 'some day, going to make all men brothers'.[17]

He wrote to the family once every month or two, whenever a boat was about to depart for Australia, and several of his letters have survived. They give an interesting insight into his relationship with Christina at the time—a relationship that was likely to have been improved by distance. It was to 'Pegler', now nineteen, that David Stead wrote most fulsomely, and it was to *her* letters that he most looked forward.

David Stead's health suffered from the tropical climate. Normally such an energetic man, in Asia he struggled with headaches, insomnia, fever and terrible lethargy. He was lonely and homesick and at times felt close to physical breakdown. Unlike most of his white associates, he never allowed himself the relief of alcohol. He wrote to Christina:

You see a lovely vista of palms and wonderful trees—and it is too hot to go for a walk ... Then you see a lovely sheet of water; but it is too hot to go out on it. Because it is TOO HOT everywhere. The heat wilts you like a soft leaf—just like a pumpkin leaf goes in our place on a very hot day in Sydney.[18]

In *The Man Who Loved Children*, two letters from Sam Pollit in Malaya are taken almost word for word from a long, humorous letter David Stead wrote to Christina from Singapore in July 1922. He had just visited a Chinese Buddhist Temple. The 'burning of joss sticks and firing off of crackers' was 'a great way of worshipping', he told her with joyful irreverence. 'You get something for your money.' He described the torture scenes on the walls of the temple ('terrible pictures showing what will befall the unbeliever who flouts the gods') with great relish, admitting that he had originally intended the letter for Weeta, but 'I know you love blood-and-thunder'.

Other letters reveal David Stead's hortatory, messianic side, and he was generous with praise when it came to himself:

Most ... people are extraordinarily unobservant. It is the same in Australia, and it is the same everywhere in the world that I have travelled in. Is it any wonder then that I am solitary. I do all my rambles in the cities of the world exactly as I did my rambles up and down the coast and in the fastnesses of mountains and gullies in my beloved Australia—alone.

David Stead believed passionately in social justice and rights for native peoples (he felt especially strongly about Australian Aborigines): in Singapore he once refused to sit on an official platform where there were no native representatives. It is striking that he teased the natives in the same paternalistic sort of way he used for his children. From Pagi Pagi he wrote to 'Pedler':

You should see my Indian stenographer laugh when I joke about his 'color'. Sometimes I tell him I can't see him he's too dark. The other day I stopt [sic] suddenly in the middle of dictation to say that I thought I saw his soul, notwithstanding the pigmentation (rather 'heavy') of his skin. And yet he says that my presence ennobles him & has given him a new view of honor and right. They are not used to human feeling from 'superiors'.

For all his 'Pedler dear', there is, in David Stead's letters, a peculiar lack of tenderness and empathy. In his solipsistic world, his dreams for his children were mere extensions of his dreams for himself. He seemed to have no sense of his eldest daughter as a *different* person, with her own anxieties, emotional needs and torments. This made it very difficult for her (especially as she had no recourse to a loving mother or even close friends) to establish a healthy sense of her own, separate identity.

When Sam Pollit, in *The Man Who Loved Children*, outlines to the children his hopes for the unity of mankind, a system that he says could be called 'Monoman' or 'Manunity', Louisa says drily, 'You mean Monomania'.

Christina's letters to her father have not survived, but it is clear that she had her own excitements and turmoils that year. She was to have gone out teaching, but was saved from this dreadful prospect by her psychology lecturer, Gilbert Phillips, who had observed her interest in the subject and arranged for her to be his research assistant.

Intelligence testing was then attracting intense interest and was being used internationally to determine differences between women and men, whites and blacks, and social classes. The French psychologists Binet and Simon had devised tests intended to single out 'dull' children. Stead's job was to go round to various government schools testing children individually. She had to present them with a set of problems, verbal and pictorial, and determine their intelligence quotient by calculating their alleged mental age against their actual age.

Several years later, Stead would have a character in *Seven Poor Men of Sydney* criticise the Binet-Simon tests on the grounds that they appeared to demonstrate that poor children were 'ten per cent, below the average, middle-class children at par, and rich children ten per cent, above the average'.

Christina had enrolled for Psychology II at the university that year, as a non-matriculated student, taking it as a non-degree subject. This course in experimental and abnormal psychology complemented her research. Professor Tasman Lovell even gave lectures on Freud, which were very popular with the students. Stead scored a bare pass, but it at least afforded her the opportunity to mix with university students.

Lucy Firth also studied Psychology II that year, and by September Christina was occasionally staying over at her house—presumably to save herself the trip to Watson's Bay after lectures or union debates in the evening. Lucy was twenty-nine, almost ten years older than her fellow students. Coming from a poor background, she had worked for some years before enrolling at the university. Christina was embarrassed by Lucy's primly dressed, old-maidish style, but Lucy was a serious student and an interesting woman. She was taking history, philosophy and psychology, and nearly every year she would come equal first. That year, once again, she shared the Psychology II prize with her friend Walter George Keith Duncan.

Lucy Firth would be 'Miss Haviland' in *For Love Alone*, an admirable but pitiful figure: a young old-maid. Her name has cruel echoes of Miss Havisham in *Great Expectations*. Keith Duncan (as he called himself) was to be the model for Jonathan Crow, the young man in *For Love Alone* with whom Teresa fell in love.

Keith Duncan (whom his friends, with the Australian passion for abbreviation, called 'Dunc') was nineteen, a year younger than Christina, when she first set eyes on him in 1922. Goodlooking in an intense, nervous sort of way, he was dark-haired and lean, with a narrow face, a broad, agile mouth and brown eyes that would flash behind his glasses with righteous conviction.[19] Yet photographs from the time betray an uneasy, anxious look behind his casual boyish poses.

As a second-year undergraduate, Duncan was just beginning to take part in the university debates that—along with his consistently outstanding marks—would make him a well-known campus figure. The university newspaper, the *Union Recorder*, frequently refers to his eloquent, melodramatic rhetoric. But the debates' secretary was not uncritical. After one performance came this note on Duncan: 'The speaker should try to overcome his incoherency of thought, and also realise that sarcasm is a dangerous weapon, which needs skilful handling.'

For Love Alone, which depicts this period in Stead's life, is a powerful evocation of a young woman in a permanent state of sexual desire. It is made to seem only too natural in this 'fruitful island of the sea-world'; everyone suffers 'the torments of the southern sun'. Girls ripen early in the Antipodes. The sun, violent and relentless, has a sexual force. Teresa,

half-maddened by the noon heat, would experience a 'torment of desire
... as the sun mounted'.

The novel conveys a lasting impression of the sheer sensuality of
summer in Sydney. Nature dominates; the physical aspect of life cannot
quite be contained. In the scorching heat, people smell like foxes; young
women's new-washed hair gives off a 'scent of little woodland beasts'.
When Teresa, 'a powerful, full-blooded young woman', walks home late
one evening, past the murmurs of lovers in the park, it is full moon and
high tide, the sound of cicadas fills the bay, and people are sitting 'in their
moist warm gardens, talking and hitting out at the mosquitoes'. At the
house, Teresa drags on a black bathing suit she has grown out of ('sleek
and fishy to swim in') and splashes around in the water, dreaming about
gently drowning.

This is no fog-bound London adolescence, yet this upside-down society
('winter is in July, spring brides marry in September, and Christmas is
consummated with roast beef, suckling pig, and brandy-laced plum
pudding at 100 degrees in the shade') had adopted the straitlaced
Victorian morality of the Old Country. Australian schoolgirls had to wear
thick cotton stockings and gloves even in blistering heat. And though it
was tacitly acknowledged that young men experience sexual desires, a
nice young lady was not supposed to feel lust as long as she remained
unmarried.

The young women in Stead's fiction toss in bed from the age of fourteen.
In *The Beauties and Furies*, Oliver calculates how many 'loving-nights'
Elvira, married at twenty-one, missed out on from the age of fourteen. One
senses that it was a calculation Stead had made about herself. Fourteen
when she first experienced the 'torment of desire', Stead had to wait until
she was twenty-six before she gratefully surrendered the burden of her
virginity. It meant that she had twelve and a half years in which to imagine,
fantasise and fear the 'night of the senses'. 'Hunger of the stomach can be
confessed,' she would write later, 'but not sexual hunger.' The need to
conceal it made it 'fiercer, madder'.[20]

Stead's wide reading gave her insights, albeit confused, into the ways
of the flesh; as a young girl she had been aroused by the enchantments
of *Arabian Nights*; at school her imagination was further piqued by Zola,
Swinburne, Thomas Hardy, Stendhal's essay *On Love*. Like the fictional
Teresa, Christina knew 'the disorderly loves of Ovid, the cruel luxury
of Petronius, the exorbitance of Aretino, the meaning of the witches'

Sabbaths, the experiments of Sade, the unimaginable horrors of the Inquisition, the bestiality in the Bible, the bitter jokes of Aristophanes and what the sex-psychologists had written'. At university, she read Havelock Ellis, Adler, Freud, Krafft-Ebing. All this produced a potent mix in her imagination. Jottings Stead made when she was planning *For Love Alone* in the early 1940s describe the febrile, masochistic fantasies of a young woman:

> Virgin after being excited is torn by bayonets in her womb: animals trained to flesh-eating, but only the lower parts: woman exposed to lusts of deer, horse, bull, and thus torn to pieces ... women in gaol visited foully by gaoler and greatest criminals ... wasteful man keeps beautiful girl for year or more, letting her see all obscene plays and his acts with other slaves, but she must not taste it, he likes to see her suffer ... girl is tormented by men who do the act coitus interruptus, until she is so wild that she flings herself at their feet, is trampled on, begging for love.

All her life, Stead firmly believed in a link between sexual deprivation and madness: in those virginal years she sometimes feared she was going mad. It was not just the seemingly interminable period of sexual frustration: there was also the dreadful marriage panic. Young women lived with fear and ridicule. What if they were not married at twenty-five or thirty?

> Teresa suffered for herself and the other girls; each year now counted against them; nineteen, and has she a boy-friend? Twenty, and does she like anyone particularly? Twenty-one, now she has the key of the door; she ought to be looking round! Twenty-two already! Twenty-three and not engaged yet? Twenty-four and not even a nibble?

The unmarried woman stood to miss out on everything: sex, love, motherhood and social respectability. For many—certainly for Christina Stead—it seemed a fate far worse than death.

———— ❧ ————

In January 1923, Christina Stead could put it off no longer: she was obliged to take up her first teaching appointment. She was twenty when she began her teaching career at Darlinghurst Girls' School, in the middle of Sydney's inner-city slums, on a salary of £143 per year. (The Public Service Basic Wage for males was set at £193 per annum in September 1923.) After one

week teaching a large class, her voice gave way. The headmistress expressed
concern about the progress of the class. Christina consulted a doctor, who
diagnosed chronic pharyngitis and recommended having her tonsils out.
At the end of February, tonsils still intact, she wrote to the Education
Department asking to be transferred to a position that would relieve the
strain on her voice, suggesting 'work with small groups of subnormals, or
experimental work in psychology'.[21] She was granted a week's sick leave
without pay, and then transferred to Blackfriars Correspondence School,
in the hope that the largely clerical work associated with teaching children
in the outback would suit her better. She remained at Blackfriars until the
end of the year, but her voice was merely a symptom of the real problem,
which was that she detested teaching.

The following year, 1924, Gilbert Phillips came to the rescue again,
and employed Christina at the Teachers' College as a Junior Lecturer in
Psychology, on a salary of £175 per annum.

In July and August 1924, her father was in Honolulu, as part of a
New South Wales government delegation attending the Pan-Pacific Food
Preservation Conference. He came back very excited. After the conference,
he had been in an aeroplane for the first time—US airmen had flown him
right into the crater of the Kilauea volcano. His scientific and eugenicist
friend David Starr Jordan had been at the conference and the two men
had talked about international progress, the future of the Pacific area and
brotherhood between America and Australia. It must have made Christina
more determined than ever to travel herself.

The crisis came in 1925. The Junior Lectureship at the Teachers' College
had been for one year only, and in January 1925 Christina Stead had
to return to primary teaching. She spent part of the week at Glenmore
Road Public School and part of the week at Darlinghurst Public School.
By February, her voice had given out again and she was back at the
Correspondence School. In May, the Education Department established a
'Special Class' at William Street Public School: a class of 'feeble-minded'
children who had been culled out of nearby schools. It was thought that
this work might interest Miss Stead, who had previously expressed interest
in subnormal children and had special training in intelligence testing and
abnormal psychology.

She lasted scarcely five weeks at William Street. It was not that she did not like the children; she did. Two of them, born to syphilitic parents, were deaf and dumb; she thought them 'utterly sweet'. There was a 'wild boy', with whom she tried the standard ploys she had learnt in educational psychology, and a nice adolescent boy who tried terribly hard ('like the clerk in Russian literature') but was no good at anything and he knew it. And there was a beautifully dressed little girl ('like something from a German opera') who looked 'absolutely pure and sweet' but had no brain at all. There was nothing Stead could do to help them; they never made any progress, and she found it unbearably sad. In truth, she found teaching—any sort of teaching—so depressing that she was close to a nervous breakdown. Years later, she would say, 'I didn't have the nervous strength. I have plenty of nervous strength for books. But all those little shrimps, no … I couldn't do it'.[22]

The problem was not the demands on her time, the preparation, the unruly children or her weak voice. It was more that she had a complete psychological block. From the day she had signed up with the Education Department and assured the administrator that she was not thinking of getting married, Christina had been terrified by the spectre of becoming 'an old maid of a school-ma'am'.[23] As she walked through the school gates in the mornings, every fibre in her body rebelled. She had taught for only eighteen months but she had reached breaking point.

In *For Love Alone*, the teaching treadmill appalls Teresa, who sees female teachers as 'being condemned to servitude for life'. The unmarried ones, she observes, seemed to 'go queer'. Her panic and desperation have reached the point of physical nausea.

> As soon as she caught sight of the school buildings in the morning, their dirty yellow, and heard the bell, the shrieks, the boots rushing across the asphalt; as soon as she smelled that thick oily and dusty scent which school buildings alone give out, human grease and neglected corners, old varnish and urinals in the heat, the little oils from lunches in paper and boot polish, old stuffs ironed at home with the soap still in them, the dirty heads; that huge, fat, sickening smell that poured down the street, on every side, and seeped from outside into the purer dust of the closed schoolroom—as soon as she saw it and smelled it, that illness to which she was condemned for life, until she was sixty, when a woman is not a woman, she began to float in her misery, not to walk. She forgot her feet and yielded herself to a kind of delirium of horror.

That year Christina, determined to get out of teaching as soon as she could, had been going to an evening class in stenography. She was now quite determined to travel abroad, and she had been told that a secretary could find work overseas, whereas a teacher could not. To be a secretary in the city, in an office surrounded by men doing business, seemed bliss compared with being stuck in a classroom surrounded by female teachers jaded with 'kid-whacking'. But she was trapped—under bond to remain in the teaching service until 31 December 1927.

By mid June 1925, Christina could take it no more. She had had enough of being 'Miss Stead' at the front of the room, chalk in hand. On the morning of Thursday 18 June, instead of going to William Street, she went to Central Station and took a train to Gosford, up the coast. She was fleeing to her kindly Aunt Eva and Uncle Charles, her dead mother's relatives who had a citrus orchard in Narara.

Teresa does the same in *For Love Alone*. She flees to Narara. And in the train she feels a surge of elation: she has broken away from the treadmill, done something for herself, something daring and courageous, for the first time. 'She had never felt so well in her life. She could hear laughter, from the hills shouldering off their forests, from the rivers slipping away down.' She tells herself this is only the first stage of a larger, grander, more perilous journey.

A few days later, David Stead arrived in Narara and persuaded Christina to come home. But Christina had made her point: by running away, risking a humiliating dismissal from the Education Department, she had made her father and stepmother understand that her antipathy to teaching was serious, that her mental health was in jeopardy. On 25 June 1925 she applied for two weeks' sick leave. On the medical certificate her doctor wrote that she was suffering from neurasthenia.[24] In a memorandum accompanying it, Gilbert Phillips, her official teaching supervisor, commented 'Miss Stead is at present quite unable to continue teaching. In my opinion she is temperamentally unfitted for ordinary class teaching.' The Education Department granted her a month's leave without pay.

No longer was Stead's voice the problem; now it was her 'temperament'. On 13 July, with only four days of her sick leave remaining, Christina, unable to face the prospect of returning to the classroom, applied for a month's extension. This time, her doctor wrote on the medical certificate that he was strongly urging Miss Stead to give up teaching altogether, that she was 'temperamentally quite unfitted for such an occupation'. Gilbert Phillips used the same phrase: 'temperamentally unfitted for teaching'.

But the leave was not extended, and Stead's time off expired on Friday 17 July. It was her birthday, the day she turned twenty-three. She had fulfilled only two and a half years of her five-year bonded service, and still had to pay back £68. But that day she made a momentous decision. Never again would she stand in front of a class. Never again would she pace the playground on supervision duty; never again would she be found in a teachers' room that smelt of 'hot face powder and sweet tea'.[25]

That very day she wrote to the Director of Education—in scarcely legible handwriting that suggested (whether deliberately or not) a degree of mental derangement—that the Registrar had recommended she ask for permission to resign from the service. Gilbert Phillips, a loyal mentor to the end, supported this: 'In my opinion Miss Stead has genuinely tried to serve the Dept. but her temperament is such that she will never be of use as a class teacher.'

Having faced the ignominy of being seen to have failed, there was the bond to pay back: a debt that would delay her travel plans by at least two years. (The third-class boat fare to England was about £45.) That she was prepared to do this shows the measure of her desperation.

Christina's bond guarantors were Ada Stead and Emma Pattison, Ada's older sister. On 7 October, Ada Stead wrote to the Department, in her elegant, rounded hand: 'As bondsman in the case of Miss Christina Stead, I beg to apply for release from payment of my obligation in view of the fact that Miss Stead resigned solely on account of ill health. A Medical Certificate to that effect is enclosed.' This time the accompanying medical certificate claimed that Christina's neurasthenia made her 'permanently incapacitated' for teaching.[26]

Within a week, the Director of Education, Mr S. H. Smith, wrote back. In view of the evidence of the medical certificates, the resignation of Miss Stead would be accepted without the enforcement of the conditions of her bond.[27]

Christina was not the only member of the family to act impetuously that year. Her father, now forty-eight, had been approached by the New South Wales government to investigate methods of controlling and exterminating the rabbits that were ravaging the New South Wales countryside. Soon after he had been appointed Rabbit Menace Enquiry Commissioner for New South Wales, work took him to Brisbane. On the Friday evening he boarded the train south to visit a 23-year-old friend who was teaching botany (her first appointment) at a high school in Murwillumbah, near the border of New South Wales and Queensland.

Thistle Harris was at home that evening, miserable because it was a long weekend and her fellow teachers had left town, when her landlady came to tell her there was a man to see her. David Stead took her to the pictures. The next day they went camping with friends. It poured with rain and she slept in his arms. On Monday he returned to Brisbane. On Tuesday afternoon, one of the children in Miss Harris' class glanced through the window and said, 'There's a man out there.' He had a big grin on his face.

When Thistle returned to Sydney for the September vacation, the romance became an affair. Her parents were about to separate and she was staying with friends, in freer circumstances than usual. But her father somehow got wind of his daughter's affair with a married man his own age, and before Thistle returned to the north, he 'gave David an earful'. And Ada Stead wrote a couple of letters to Thistle, pointing out 'a few things'.[28] Thistle was persuaded she must have nothing more to do with a married man whose eldest child was her own age, and whose youngest was only eight. She was quite miserable about the decision, but when David sent her letters and parcels she resolutely sent them back. The romance was called off a second time.

David Stead, also much in love, told Christina everything. Some vaguely fictionalised drafts, perhaps intended for a story, suggest that Christina reacted calmly this time. She may have secretly admired her father for throwing himself into his passion, just as she would have liked to do.

By the middle of that year, Christina had a passion of her own to occupy her thoughts. From June 1925, she attended an extramural tutorial class in psychology, held on Monday evenings at the university. The tutor was Keith Duncan. Known for his controversial and outspoken ideas, he had attracted an interesting group of people. Lucy Firth went along. Herman Black, an economics student (later Chancellor of Sydney University) was there. Marie Byles had graduated in law the previous year and was the first woman to be registered as a solicitor in New South Wales. Florence James was a vivacious New Zealander who had come to Sydney five years before and studied at the Conservatorium of Music for two years before deciding to take an arts degree instead. The same age as Christina, she was in her final undergraduate year and active in the Sydney University Drama Society.

Class discussions ranged widely over social and philosophical questions. The object, Herman Black recalls, was nothing less than 'the Reform of the Universe'.[29] At twenty-three, Duncan had the brash confidence of a postgraduate who had topped virtually every subject in his first degree. The previous year he had graduated with First Class Honours and the University Medals in History and Philosophy and now he was doing an MA in philosophy, hoping to win a scholarship to London to do his doctorate there. Stead was very impressed. From a working-class family, brought up in the slums, Duncan's success was due to his own hard work and determination. She felt lazy and undeserving by contrast.

An eloquent lecturer, Duncan liked nothing better than to challenge accepted beliefs and stir up a good argument. He saw himself as a leftwing liberal, not a communist; but like most of the group, he believed at that time that Russia was the hope of the world. In cavalier fashion he blamed imperialism and capitalism for most of the world's ills: the modern wage slave was in a far worse position than the ordinary slave, he would claim.[30] Religion and morality were merely repressive impediments to clear thought. The world's only chance of salvation lay in eugenics, education and 'the scientific spirit'. Unrestricted migration of white races to Australia 'would militate against the solidarity of labour'.[31]

Dora Russell's controversial book *Hypatia*, published that year, proclaimed women's right to sexual freedom and pleasure, attacked marriage and advocated 'free love'. Duncan approved of these ideas, which the group discussed with vigour. Dora Russell's basic tenet was that the true force of creation was love between men and women. Stead wholeheartedly agreed.

Herman Black would later recall Christina Stead in that group as 'a striking, not-very-communicative young girl'.[32] Florence James' first impression was of a 'rather beaky profile and prominent upper teeth, and her characteristic way of speaking—airing strong opinions, yet speaking with diffidence'.[33]

In *For Love Alone*, Teresa goes to Jonathan Crow's discussion group and finds his 'hunger for learning' and world-weary cynicism immensely appealing. She is not the only young woman to find him attractive. His provocative manner, his slum background and academic successes make him 'the gadfly of desire'. Keith Duncan, too, was popular with women: this doubtless became part of his appeal for Christina. In later life, however, she would make caustic comments about this aspect of his personality:

> He had a certain number of girls he kept on a string. Quite different types too ... And he led off with this 'Pity me' routine. You know, 'I come from the slums' and all that kind of thing, and 'I had to struggle hard to get here' ... He was very rich in detail of his struggles. Motherly hearted women—which I regret to say ... we all are—naturally bleed for this kind of struggle.[34]

Apart from Stead's occasional comments, which all reinforce the picture of the tortured relationship painted in *For Love Alone*, we have to rely on the novel for any real insight into the nature of Stead's relationship with Keith Duncan. What is clear is that her passion for Duncan was, from the very beginning, as frustrating as it was nourishing.

In *For Love Alone*, Teresa Hawkins and Jonathan Crow sometimes walk part of the way home together. They arrange occasional outings, and both hope that the other will make some sort of physical move, but Teresa is shy and awkward, and Crow is passive, wary of emotional involvement. His brief moments of warmth are followed by long stretches of coolness. Teresa's emotions are tossed hither and thither, and she believes herself in love.

Around the time that she resigned from the teaching service, July 1925, Stead finished the book of children's stories she had been writing for the past four years. Several were elaborations of stories she had invented as bedtime stories for her siblings—exotic fantasies, probably inspired by the *Arabian Nights*. Her art teacher at the Teachers' College had produced half a dozen illustrations, as promised.

Strangely, Christina was not particularly ambitious about publication; it was her father who submitted the manuscript to George Robertson of the firm Angus & Robertson, Publishers. The reply came on 21 July 1925:

Dear Mr. Stead,

I read and enjoyed Peg's stories. They are remarkable for their language and imagery—in fact they are charming. The trouble is that poetical fantasies like these are too old for young children, and older boys and girls who could, and ought to, appreciate them mostly prefer books of adventure, stories of school life, and so on. I am writing as a Sydney publisher; a London publisher with forty million constituents—or, better still, a New York one with a hundred million—might be glad to have them. Besides, they would have no difficulty in finding an illustrator capable of drawing beautiful princesses, etc.

From your letter, I gather that Peg is quite young, and have no hesitation in saying that she will be heard of in the world of letters one day.[35]

David Stead called in several times to Angus & Robertson's offices seeking further advice, but the publisher was always busy. In October 1925, David Stead wrote again, asking if Robertson would suggest some publishing houses in New York or London. He explained that he was 'the more keen on this because it seems to be really the only thing (this story writing) that Peg is thoroughly interested in'.

The curious thing is that she does not seem to value very highly the actual publication of them; yet I feel sure that if some of her stories were published it would give her a tremendously added interest—not only in such work, but in life generally.[36]

Robertson suggested asking a friend in London or New York to run the gauntlet of publishers, adding that Angus & Robertson would take 200 copies if the book was published in England at six shillings or less.

Angus & Robertson were cutting down their local publications during the 1920s, preferring to reprint English or American bestsellers instead. In 1929, they would reject the joint winners of the *Bulletin* prize: Katharine Susannah Prichard's *Coonardoo* and M. Barnard Eldershaw's *A House is Built*. If Australian writers were lucky, they found an English publisher, since English and American publishers did not republish books published first in Australia. But it was called a 'colonial edition', and they were paid lower royalties, which were nevertheless subject to heavy English income tax.

Angus & Robertson, Australia's only major publishing house, would not publish Christina Stead until 1966—more than thirty years after she had made her name abroad. It was, she would tell Nettie Palmer in 1951, 'disgraceful'.[37] Her first volume of stories was destined never to be published. The manuscript would be lost in France.

Soon after giving up teaching, Stead landed her first secretarial job, with the Sydney architect Mr Weeks. Later she would reflect how kind he was to her, considering the poor standard of her typing.

She had lunch sometimes with Marie Byles and Florence James in the Botanical Gardens, close to their various offices. All three women had a fierce determination to travel, and would spur each other on with their talk of 'getting away'. Each of them had studied the shipping schedules and worked out when she would be able to afford to sail. The venturesome Byles, one of the first women to walk the city streets in trousers, was a keen bushwalker and camper, and had exotic plans to climb mountains in Asia and Europe and to see the world on freighters and cattle-boats. (Later she would write books about these experiences.) Florence James had graduated and was working as a secretary in her father's engineering firm. Not obliged to pay board at home, she was saving money fast and intended to sail in 1927. She was engaged to a Dutchman from Java, a lawyer, but intended to travel around Europe and see something of the world before she settled down. Beautiful and theatrical, Florence could hardly have been more different from Christina, yet they were destined to become the closest of friends.

In May 1926, Keith Duncan, who had just been awarded a Master of Arts degree and the University Medal for Philosophy, was one of four Sydney graduates to win a travelling scholarship to Europe. It paid the first-class return steamship passage and a living allowance of £200 per annum for two years. Duncan was going to study political science at the London School of Economics.

He left Sydney aboard the *Osterley* on 26 August 1926. With him were the three other young men, Ian Henning (going to Paris), Raymond McGrath (heading for Oxford) and John Beaglehole, an historian from Wellington, New Zealand, also going to London. They played quoit tennis, enjoyed the first-class food and occasionally treated themselves to a liqueur at sixpence a head. Four days after leaving Sydney, Beaglehole wrote to his parents: 'We do a good deal of arguing ... The Sydney lads are right willing controversialists.' He added that Keith Duncan knew 'a whole lot about social problems' and had a good sense of humour.

> He is mad on Bertrand Russell at present. Henning says one day 'Who is this Bertrand Russell, anyhow?' Duncan looks at him wonderingly for a moment & then bursts out 'Good God, have you ever heard of Jesus Christ?' He is going to London too which is cheerful.[38]

Christina had to go abroad the hard way—with neither a scholarship nor help from her parents. She told herself reproachfully that she had been lazy at university: as a consequence, she would have to save up and offer herself her own travelling scholarship.[39]

Florence James sailed in August 1927. Shortly beforehand, Marie Byles invited a group of young female friends, including Christina Stead, for a weekend at her parents' cottage at Palm Beach, north of Sydney. Florence James, in high spirits, sprawled on the kitchen table and sang 'O, Shenandoah, I love your daughter'. That weekend would be the inspiration for the opening scene of *Miss Herbert*, written some thirty years later.

Once in England, Keith Duncan wrote to Christina, and for twenty-one months, until Stead's own arrival in London, they corresponded. It is likely that Duncan's letters reflected his behaviour in person: certainly, in *For Love Alone*, Crow's letters contain occasional bursts of warmth that build up Teresa's hopes, followed by messages designed to hurt or humiliate.[40] The fact that letters took six weeks to arrive by boat further added to the ambiguity of their relationship.

The family noticed the blue envelopes on the mantelpiece, waiting for Christina when she got home late in the evening; they were vaguely aware that there was a young man in her life who had gone to England. Christina talked about Duncan a great deal to her cousin Gwen; at weekends they sometimes went on long walks together and Christina would stride along, 'shaking back her unruly hair' and talking in 'high pitched nervous tones' about getting away.[41]

Duncan had headed for the cultural centre of the English-speaking world. To be educated at the London School of Economics by the best minds in England was the aspiration of every budding political economist in Australia. But why did Christina Stead feel she had to leave Australia? She had no place awaiting her in a famous institution. Was it really because of Duncan that she was so obsessed with getting to Europe?

In later life Stead would vehemently protest if anyone suggested she had left Australia because of its cultural inferiority. When the term 'cultural cringe' (meaning Australia's obsequious attitude to England's cultural heritage) was introduced by A. A. Phillips in the 1950s, Stead would insist that the phenomenon had not existed in her day. But it did, and she must have known it. She had already experienced it at the hands of the publishers Angus & Robertson.

It took more than three months for return mail from Europe. In 1920 an Australian crew had broken all records by flying from England to Australia in fewer than thirty days (without radio or weather reports), but regular commercial flights were still decades off. In 1928 the population of Australia was a mere six million and fragmented by the distance and rivalry between the major cities. Australian writers were isolated from one another, as well as from the rest of the world.

Australian literary culture was still far too dependent. Nearly all books and magazines were from England; even American books arrived in English editions—usually several years later. The few good Australian novels were usually out of print in Australia. The only magazine with literary interests, the *Bulletin*, had lost its influence.

The greatest Australian female writer at the time, 58-year-old Henry Handel Richardson, had been living in Europe since 1887: her 1908 novel *Maurice Guest* was set in Leipzig. Miles Franklin, author of *My Brilliant Career* (1901) had gone to America in 1906 and was still living abroad. Katharine Susannah Prichard, author of *The Pioneers*, *Black Opal* and *Working Bullocks*, had left for London at twenty-five and spent several years in England before returning to Australia.

Christina Stead did not know what to expect abroad; she scarcely knew enough about the world to articulate her fuzzy ambitions. But Duncan had left for London; the brilliant students all headed for Europe. With a vague but powerful belief that she had a great destiny, she knew she had to go to see for herself.

It was not 'for love alone' that Christina wanted to follow Duncan to England: she was far more in love with what he represented: wider horizons, the experience of European culture, the flight from a world she instinctively knew to be narrow and parochial. She did want love—she

wanted it desperately—but if it was only love she was after, she could have
found it at home. The proof? Colin Lawson.

She was now working as a secretary in a large hat factory, Henderson's,
just behind Central Railway Station. The hats were made on the premises:
there were showrooms and an office in which Christina worked. One of the
salesmen, Colin Lawson, a lively young man who was passionate about music
and opera, was intrigued by the romantically thin and pale new secretary,
and he began to pay her court. She seemed to care only about literature and
love: he nicknamed her Tosca. On Fridays he sometimes brought her flowers.
Christina found his attentions a great solace, but resisted his overtures. In
For Love Alone, the young salesman Erskine calls Teresa 'La Traviata' and
she, parched as she is for affection, is dangerously drawn to this man who
seems genuinely to desire her. But Teresa tells herself:

> She did not want to love anyone here just when she was going. If she loved
> him, she might stay here—for ever, anchored in the little harbour where she
> was born, like a rowboat whose owner had died and which had never been
> taken off the slips.

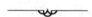

From 1927, David Stead was out of work again. He had written a five-
volume report on the rabbit menace and was writing a monograph on
whales and whaling, and now that radio had become the new state-of-the-
art medium, he was giving some of the first school broadcasts on nature
subjects. Though he kept tirelessly busy, the man who used to leave for
work in the mornings whistling and get off the ferry in the evenings full
of tales about his day now found himself pottering about the house, with
no regular income. His rigid principles remained unbending, even with a
household of adolescents.

Christina would have liked to leave home, and she sometimes toyed
with the idea of taking a room in town closer to the hat factory, but it was
cheaper to stay at Boongarre, even though she paid board and the season
ticket on the ferry was expensive. She stayed out till late most evenings
and after stepping past the motorcycles that were invariably being cleaned
or repaired by David and Fred, she would find her dinner kept warm. Kate,
now nineteen, mostly did the cooking. The boys were earning: Fred was
an apprentice motor mechanic; David was working by day and studying

metallurgy in the evenings at Sydney Technical College. At twenty, he was an angry young man who had not spoken to his father for a whole year. These days, the older members of the family kept more or less to themselves.

No one took much notice of Christina and her strange moods. She looked shabby and neglected, for she did not want to spend her money on clothes: her dresses and stockings were patched. She slept badly and ate badly. The small degree of confidence she had enjoyed in her school years was gone: no longer did her grand future seem at all assured. She was desperate and frightened, afraid of failure. (In *Letty Fox*, the young female protagonist remarks, 'What a beautiful girl says can never really be stupid, whereas with a plain girl one always feels that what she is really saying is, "I am a failure"'.)

Christina had become quite obsessive. So determined was she to save money that she had adopted an asceticism that bordered on masochism. It was a long walk from Circular Quay to the hat factory, but she walked summer and winter, morning and evening, intent on saving the tram fare. In *For Love Alone*, Teresa is the same: she walks everywhere—to the point of utter exhaustion.

> The tram ride only cost twopence, so that it might seem folly to wear oneself out in this way, but she was afraid to give in on any count and in some way the endless walking, walking, meant England. She was walking her way to England.

Each day, Christina rose early and spent an hour or more writing before catching the ferry to work. 'Day of Wrath' was a story she wrote after the *Greycliffe* disaster.[42] In the late afternoon of 3 November 1927, the ferry-steamer SS *Greycliffe*, bound from Circular Quay to Watson's Bay with 125 passengers on board, many of them schoolchildren, collided with a passenger liner bound for San Francisco. The ferry sank immediately—the worst shipping disaster ever to occur inside Sydney Harbour. Divers were recovering bodies for days afterwards. It was a shock to Christina, who imagined the bodies below, 'with a glow on their cheeks still through the green gloom of the deep-water channel'.

On a hot summer day in February 1928, Christina's cousin Ettie was married at Bellevue Hill—a wedding that caused some family trauma, for the bride was pregnant. Christina was there, and to all the world she looked aloof and contemptuous. Only her fiction (*For Love Alone*) betrays the anguish she was really suffering in a world where everyone talked of 'hope chests' and 'Mr Right' and girls being 'on the shelf'. Christina did not want to marry the 'neighbour's son'.[43] She wanted a love that did not shackle her: spiritual companionship, passion, equality, creativity. It was to find this sort of love, she believed, that she had to leave Australia. But she was already twenty-six that year. And going to a new city where she knew no one but Keith Duncan was a risk. What if Duncan rejected her? What if she missed out altogether? As she wrote later:

> There's a glamour of a diabolic, miserable sort attached to wandering, unhappy, uneasy, unkind rebel sons; but what about daughters—daughters who will not conform have no glamour, respect or love: what they have in mind interests no-one. They have no position in society—and what man will ever marry them?[44]

After work in the evenings, Christina was in no hurry to go home, and would usually go to the Public Library on the corner of Bent Street and Macquarie Streets for several hours. She filled her letters to Duncan with discussion of her eclectic reading: Nietzsche, Freud, John Stuart Mill, Edmund Burke's speeches, Frazer's *The Golden Bough*.[45]

For a time she attended evening classes in life-drawing at Julian Ashton's Sydney Art School, but eventually decided she had no real talent for drawing. She was interested in art—particularly the work of contemporary Australian painters: Hans Heysen, Norman Lindsay, Elioth Gruner, Julian Ashton—and made regular pilgrimages to the New South Wales Art Gallery in the Domain. One old-fashioned painting in the European collection haunted her with its sense of entrapment, and she went back and back to gaze at it. *The Sons of Clovis* portrayed two brothers, 'hamstrung, deathly pale, floating bound on a barge down a ghastly grey river'.[46]

Stead's first novel, *Seven Poor Men of Sydney*, would reflect her own desperation in her twenties in Sydney: all the characters are constrained—physically, psychologically or economically. All, without exception, suffer from a 'vermicular pain' in their head and bowels—the pain of intense loneliness.

'One must have chaos in one, to give birth to a dancing star.' Stead delighted in the poetry of Nietzsche's aphorisms and learnt substantial passages of *Thus Spake Zarathustra* by heart. In Nietzsche, the philosopher who claimed that God was dead and that conventional morality stultified and repressed the individual, and that 'noble-minded and aspiring people' often 'undergo their severest trials in their childhood', Stead found consolation and inspiration. Would she be one of the *Übermenschen*, with the courage to rise above the general 'herd' and bear the burden of her freedom in a joyful, Dionysian affirmation of life?

Nietzsche's 'free spirit' is a 'youthful soul' who repudiates his fetters and chains, experiencing a 'rebellious, arbitrary, volcanically erupting desire for travel, strange places, estrangements'.

> A will and desire awakens to go off, anywhere, at any cost; a vehement dangerous curiosity for an undiscovered world flames and flickers in all its senses. 'Better to die than to go on living *here*.'

To Christina Stead this must almost have seemed a personal message. Once the 'free spirit' had broken away, Nietzsche promised, his creativity would bloom.

> It seems to him as if his eyes are only now open to what is *close at hand* ... What a good thing he had not always stayed 'at home', stayed 'under his own roof' like a delicate apathetic loafer![47]

Just as Nietzsche condemned the 'loafer' who stayed at home, so did Stead. Although she would always describe herself as a writer who observed without judging, in her early fiction there is a clear sense of *winning* or *failing* in the game of life—and an implicit moral judgement. In an interview for the *Australian Women's Weekly* in 1935, seven years after leaving Australia, Stead would claim that whereas some people become 'wanderers', others 'stew all their lives in their own juice and ferments'.[48]

Women who find Nietzsche's philosophy an inspiration for their own lives are to some extent obliged to read him against the grain. His wanderers are unequivocally male and his opinion of women unapologetically low. Nietzsche was the inspiration behind the avant-garde Sydney magazine *Vision*, which so excited Stead when it appeared in 1923 and 1924.[49] *Vision*'s celebration of passion and sexual freedom liberated her turgid imagination. Edited by Jack Lindsay, Kenneth Slessor and Frank C. Johnson, and influenced by the artist Norman Lindsay, Jack's father, it was

Dionysian in its bohemian intoxication with life and love, post-Romantic in its literary tradition, and close to Dadaism and early Surrealism in its youthful rebelliousness.[50] But this rebelliousness was decidedly male.

Vision poets Kenneth Slessor and Christopher Brennan perpetuated the misogynist tradition of the peregrinating male hero who needed to flee the domestic hearth. In Brennan's poem 'The Wanderer' (not published in *Vision*, but which Stead certainly would have read), the hero, 'driven everywhere from a clinging home' is eager to 'spread the sail to any wandering wind of the air'.

But it was also in *Vision* that Stead met a powerful counter-myth, which offered her sustenance as a woman. Kenneth Slessor's poem called 'The Embarkation for Cythera' (after Watteau's painting) was published in the February 1924 issue, and the idea of the journey to Cythera, 'that port of love' where 'lovers twine/darkly with naked thighs', would become a key 'animating myth' in Stead's life and work.[51] Cythera, mentioned in no less than four of her novels[52], symbolised a place where she could fulfil her 'secret desires', a place where the expression of love was not taboo and where women's talents, unregimented and unconstrained, could burst forth with a 'primeval force'.

Christina Stead well knew that the stakes were far higher for the free spirit who was female. Among her unpublished papers are notes, probably dating from when she was writing *For Love Alone* in the early 1940s, which spell this out explicitly:

> Although there isn't a woman alive who … is not perfectly aware of the ignominy, detestation, and social death that awaits her if she does not conform, there are a lot of women who cannot conform. The refractory spirit is in them.[53]

The female rebel, 'inspired secretly or openly by her own glory or strength', will throw off her 'miserable training'. But left to her own resources, with no one to guide her, she acts awkwardly. 'It takes years before she knows what kind of human being she is: in the meantime she acts roughly and clumsily, like a young bird in which the nest-building instinct is not yet shaped.'

It was 28 March 1928, a cool Wednesday morning in late summer. The *Oronsay*, a Royal Mail Steamer of the British Orient Line, was preparing for departure at No. 7 wharf, Woolloomooloo Bay.

The whole family had gathered there to see Christina off. She was travelling to London, third class. As one of the 'steerage' passengers, her name was not among the passengers listed in the *Sydney Morning Herald* that day.

Weeta sobbed as they said their final farewells. Christina, dressed in a summer dress and broad-brimmed hat, had dry eyes. When the ship pulled out and the streamers eventually snapped, Uncle Sam drove the children round to South Head, near Watson's Bay, where they excitedly held up a large white sheet.

Standing on deck, scanning the coast, Christina was awed by what she knew to be a momentous moment in her life. She did not know that she would never see her father or her stepmother again. Nor her favourite brother, Fred. And that she would eventually return to Australia as a grey-haired, famous writer. But she sensed that her own life—her *creative* life—was just beginning. She might not be happy in her future life, but she had done what she had to do.

3

Port of Registry: London

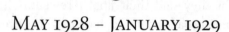

MAY 1928 – JANUARY 1929

IT WAS AN unusual voyage. Unlike Keith Duncan, Christina Stead did not play quoits in the fresh sea air. Nor did she enjoy a shipboard romance, as Florence James had done. Her only friend was a nightwatchman. In the daytime, she slept.

The *Oronsay* had just left Perth when a young alcoholic heiress tried to throw herself overboard, delirious with drink. The ship's doctor, anxious to avoid a recurrence, asked for volunteers from third class to look after his first class patient. The job entailed preventing the stewards from supplying the woman with gin.

Stead came forward. She told herself she would fatten up on the rich first class breakfasts she was given at the end of her shift—a great improvement on the steerage fare of stewed apricots and tea. She would describe the furtive cabin-visiting and petty dramas of the A- and B-deck microcosm in her autobiographical short story 'A Night in the Indian Ocean', written in Paris a year or two later. In this, Stella, the young volunteer nurse, is shocked by, but feels sympathy for the pitiful woman lying in bed in diaphanous chiffon, craving alcohol (which she had been given by her mother to keep her quiet as a child) and the embraces of a man—any man. When Stella confides that she has a male friend in Europe, the heiress advises her bitterly: 'If you get a chance, marry him. Take my tip. Don't wait and don't you live with him without marrying him. It doesn't pay. I know men.'[1]

Stead's nights were spent fetching the heiress water, rubbing her feet and keeping her amused. When her patient was asleep, she would go on deck and sit with the old watchman, who would bring them coffee from the bridge. It was his last trip; he was about to retire. He told his young friend that she would have to work for six months in England before becoming eligible for the £1 a week dole, and if she could not find work in London, she would be welcome to stay with him and his wife in their cottage on the coast while she looked around there. His words made Stead anxious: she had never even considered that she might not be able to find work.

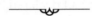

The ports of Colombo and Aden were a glimpse of Asia, the rugged mountains of Calabria Stead's first view of Europe. As the ship emerged from the Straits of Messina around midnight early in May 1928, she was on deck to see Stromboli's fiery fountain erupt into the moonlight. There were brief calls in Naples, Toulon and Gibraltar—then the last leg northwards.

Stead's youthful imagination had been inflamed by the Continent, not England, that 'cloud-sunk … adamantine island chained to the shifting bank of the Channel'.[2] Yet she must have been moved by the first view of the country her grandparents had left. For young colonials, the chalky cliffs of Dover symbolised much more than the excitement of arrival, the culmination of six weeks on the water. At school they had studied Shakespeare, Dickens, Keats; most were more familiar with British than Australian history and better acquainted with the names of English plants and trees than with indigenous flora.

But a great weight hung on Stead's shoulders. This voyage was also symbolic, and spelt success or failure. It was only partly about escape, flight from her family: it was also a quest, a quest for love. As the ship chugged into Tilbury, Stead probably felt too numb with anxiety to be excited.

Disembarking from the *Oronsay* into the bustle and noise of Tilbury docks on 5 May 1928, the new arrivals were faced with a depressed economy.

After ten years, England had still not recovered from the First World War. Unemployment was more than 10 per cent. The industries on which the nation had relied before 1918—coal, iron and steel, shipbuilding and textiles—were precisely those now in decline, and exports were down. The nine-day general strike in May 1926 had polarised the country and left the working class bitter—a bitterness exacerbated by legislation in which the Tory government attempted to clamp down on compulsory trade-unionism and strikes.

The population of Greater London had increased almost 10 per cent during the 1920s, as country people drifted to the city looking for work. Inner city boarding-house districts were congested, and there was chronic overcrowding and poverty in the East End. Already in 1919 a Select Committee on London Traffic had declared conditions intolerable. Before the war, motorcars had been the privilege of the rich; now the middle class aspired to a family car. Traffic lights had not yet been introduced in London, nor had driving tests: fatal accidents were legion. Pollution from cars added to the dismal effect of grime and smut from coal-burning domestic chimneys.

May 1928 saw the female voting age in England lowered from thirty to twenty-one. Women were breaking out—Christina would have her hair bobbed that year. *Lady Chatterley's Lover* and Radclyffe Hall's novel about Sapphic love, *The Well of Loneliness*, came out that year, though both were banned immediately in England. Virginia Woolf's 1928 essay, *A Room of One's Own*, discussed the plight of the female writer in a country where women earned less than men and still did not have anything like equal educational opportunities.

Australian writers have frequently described how the surge of intoxication they experienced on first seeing Dover was superseded, at least initially, by numb shock. When 18-year-old Ethel Richardson—the future Henry Handel Richardson—arrived from Melbourne with her mother and sister in 1888, she was dismayed by the ugliness and filth of Tilbury and 'the miles on miles of dismal slums' through which the train travelled to the sooty terminus.[3] When Jack Lindsay arrived from Sydney in 1926, he was hardly able to believe that people 'could live in such a dwarfed and sootied world'. He felt betrayed. 'To have come so far for this.'[4]

There is no record of Stead's first impression of England. Her first letter to her cousin Gwen, dated 12 June 1928, after five weeks in England, conveyed neither awe nor horror. London was 'something like Sydney', she remarked dully. 'I have to pinch myself so that I won't take everything for granted.' By July she was admitting that traffic-infested London would be 'unbearable' were it not for the many little squares 'with millions of light fluttering leaves'. It was as well that she arrived in the spring: Stead would always detest the bleak northern hemisphere winters. And when she left London for Paris, after nine months, she would describe London as 'crooked, narrow, mean, dirty and ill-conceived'.[5]

We have little information about Stead's first few months in the northern hemisphere. Although she wrote to her family, the letters have not survived. Only the sporadic letters she sent to Gwen and Florence Walker-Smith were lovingly preserved.

In *For Love Alone*, Christina Stead's fictional counterpart, Teresa, met from the boat by Jonathan Crow, quickly sees that the gap between them has widened. After twenty months in England, Crow is more worldly and self-assured. His voice is 'firmer, more melodious' (though his 'rasping, assertive, complaining tones were there, as before'). Handsome in his fine clothes, 'he could have any woman for the asking', Teresa thinks to herself. She, on the other hand, is a 'friendless girl', too thinly clad for the cold English spring. Aware how thin and worn she looks, she shrinks from Jonathan's gaze.

Keith Duncan was acutely conscious that the English looked down on colonials, and his friends were mostly Australians, New Zealanders and Boers; nevertheless, being a postgraduate at the London School of Economics lent him a certain status. He was hearing lectures by the great minds of the day: Arnold Toynbee, Sydney Webb, George Bernard Shaw, Bertrand Russell. The latter was his idol: the historian John Beaglehole, his room-mate, wrote home that Duncan followed Bertrand Russell round 'like a dog'.[6]

Duncan was fortunate to have Professor Harold Laski as his doctoral supervisor. The newly appointed Professor of Political Science was in his mid thirties, a brilliant, witty speaker, and a prominent figure in the British Labour movement. He blended certain Marxist views with his Labour sympathies, but his traditions were firmly Benthamite and Liberal, and his influence on Duncan, whose thesis was on the evolution of the philosophy of Liberalism in England, was profound. Open house was held at the Laskis' on Sunday afternoons. There his postgraduates would meet anyone from cabinet ministers, trade union leaders and Indian nationalists to American playwrights. Duncan and his friends declared Laski 'friendly and companionable enough to be a colonial'. As a Jew and a leftwing radical, Laski knew what it was to be an outsider.

Though this stimulating cultural environment gave Duncan a new air of confidence, he was still the angry young man he had always been. Christina, sounding distinctly sceptical, described him in her first letter to Gwen:

> He has a thorough-going indignation for (what he conceives to be) all forms of oppression, depression, impression, repression, suppression, compression and (irrational self-) expression, in short for all forms of everything which does not represent (what he conceives to be) Liberty and Justice.

Keith Duncan shared a large room at 21 Brunswick Square in Bloomsbury with the historian John Beaglehole. Stead found a room ten minutes away, in a working women's clubhouse at Cartwright Gardens, a *demi-lune* of boarding houses overlooking one of London's 'providential squares'.[7]

Anxious not to deplete her savings, Stead did not even give herself a few days to look at London's landmarks before she set about finding work. At the first employment agency she was told of a position at Strauss & Company, a grain exchange business requiring a secretary with a good knowledge of French. She was put off by the pay: £2 10s a week—less than she had been earning in Australia. (Duncan and Beaglehole's scholarship money was £4 a week, and they considered themselves 'poor students'.) Moreover, when she heard that the agency claimed the first week's pay, she left the office in disgust.

By the end of that day, she had traipsed all over town and discovered that all agencies charged the first week's wage, and that the wages offered by Strauss & Co. were higher than anywhere else. She had also realised the extent of unemployment in London and that secretaries who knew French were alarmingly plentiful. Feeling foolish, she presented herself again at the first agency at opening hour the next day. Miraculously, the job had still not been filled: two applicants had been turned down. She took a bus to the City and hurried nervously through the maze of narrow streets clutching a map and a book.

Strauss & Co.'s office was in St Mary Axe, not far from London Bridge and the Tower of London. The Associate Manager who interviewed her was a short, genial New Yorker in his early thirties, who had only just arrived in London himself. Years later, Stead recalled her first impression of Mr William Blech: 'I thought he looked nice ... Very nice. I thought he looked marvellous. So pure. What girls think! But I wasn't wrong, really.'

She got the job. All her life, she remained dumbfounded by this piece of luck. 'I must have looked like a dead duck. But I think the clincher was—Bill told me years afterwards—that I looked so shy and at the same time serious. I was carrying a book of Bertrand Russell. And I think that got him. So he engaged me.'[8]

William Blech, who disliked the English and their condescending manner towards Americans, was pleased to be employing an Australian. This particular colonial (he told her afterwards) seemed to have something about her.

***

By mid June, after six weeks in London, Stead was able to tell her Aunt Florence that Piccadilly, Pall Mall, St Martin-in-the-Fields and St Paul's now seemed like her 'own backyard'. 'Tired of hearing all the great monuments of London lauded indiscriminately', she had 'approached them with a gauche irreverence', she admitted, but found St Paul's 'glorious and august', even with its coating of filth. Her domicile at No. 33 Cartwright Gardens was just 'five minutes from where Carlyle used to live and seven minutes from where the Protector's daughter is buried'.[9]

Nevertheless, her daily life was 'not intensely exciting', she told Florence Walker-Smith. In truth, her relationship with Duncan was tense and upsetting, but this was not something she chose to divulge to any members of her family.

She wrote that she had spent 'a thoroughly delightful evening' at Keith Duncan's, with John Beaglehole and a visiting New Zealand woman. They had listened to Duncan's assortment of new gramophone records—from Wilhelm Backhaus and Fritz Kreisler to The Mikado and Lilac Time—and had passionate discussions. 'However,' she allowed herself to add dolefully, 'all the jollifications are spread out evenly over quite a long period.' Duncan was going to rumbustious postgraduate orgies at which his friends dressed up, danced around lamp-posts and gave mock speeches. She was not invited.

One Sunday afternoon, she found her way through the 'subterranean tubes, corridors, lanes, subways, arteries' of the Underground and spent three hours at the National Art Gallery, emerging 'with a head full of Venuses of dubious virtue'. But sightseeing on her own made her feel rather forlorn. 'At one moment you feel grand to be there on your own and seeing the sights and treading historic grounds and smelling historic smells and the next you feel like some small sort of insect crawling about miserably waving its antennae ...' She remained the daughter of a naturalist.

Her new job was 'really delightful', and she was using her school French.

> Yesterday I had to write my two very firstest letters in French and of course I was positive they would both be wrong and would have 'de' and 'pour' in the wrong places, etc. I positively blushed from timidity—but no! they were both right. Wonderful luck. I was quite pleased, but I am feeling rather shaky now in case I can't keep up my reputation.

William Blech, her immediate boss, was unlike anyone she had ever met.

> I have a boss who knows (the names of, at least) Europe's uncrowned heads and obliges me with discourses on every subject under the sun at a moment's notice and even in the middle of dictation, and is not too proud to give me
>
> 1. all the bibliographies I require for
>   a) music
>   b) economics
>   c) literary criticism
> 2. his assistance when the Managing Director goes too fast or too Roumanian.
> 3. his blessing when I have an appointment (early) at the hairdressers.
> !!!!!!!!

The incredulous exclamation marks are hers. Mr Blech seemed to her extraordinarily brilliant, erudite and compassionate. Not at all the typical investments manager, he was a Marxist. Short and rotund, he had the energy and vitality of a 'small Vesuvius'.

The Managing Director was also an astounding character. Alfred Hurst, born Avrom Hersovici, even managed to surpass Blech's energy. A Sephardic Jew from Romania, Hurst had come to England as a boy, gone to school in London's East End, begun his career as a runner for a grain company and now possessed a substantial fortune.[10] A 'short giant' with 'a great skull, bull neck, prizefighter's shoulders, gorilla's chest, thick waist and fleshy limbs'[11], he, like Blech, was to thread his way through Christina Stead's future and into her fiction.

Eager to improve her French systematically, Stead responded to a newspaper advertisement by a private tutor. She paid the young Frenchman for several sessions in advance and met him in the visitors' room of his Bloomsbury boarding house. At the third meeting he suggested they go dancing at the Russell Hotel. She refused; her interest in him was confined to learning French. He did not turn up for the next lesson and soon afterwards she received a postcard from Switzerland. She never heard from him again. After that, she enrolled in a French class at Hugo's, the language institute, and enjoyed the lessons immensely.

She was lonely, but she was not bereft of company. Her elderly cousins lived at Streatham Common, on the southern outskirts of the city. Great Aunt Emma, Uncle Cecil and their two unmarried daughters, Winnie and Jessie, were old-fashioned but welcoming and kind. David Stead had written, asking them to keep an eye on Christina.

Soon Christina made a friend her own age. They possibly met while sightseeing. Francette Hubert, from Asnières-sur-Seine, near Paris, was in London to learn English, and worked as a secretary in a shipping office in the City. It was with Francette, full of enthusiasm for tourism, that Christina visited the London landmarks. Beside her French friend, who knew far more about European art and history, Christina felt ignorant and naive. 'Vous êtes une poire, une poire,' Francette would say, shaking her head in disbelief.[12]

They taught each other French and English idiomatic expressions. It was decided that Christina should speak French and Francette English, and they would correct each other. Christina told Gwen:

> Francette has taught me quite a lot of infamous expressions which I must never use outside of Montmartre and then only when disguised. And I have taught her that she must never say 'My God' which is innocent in French

but scandalous in English: ... that one must not say 'at thirty, one is blown-up' when one means 'one is in full bloom.'

Over the next few months, she grew very fond of Francette's 'yellow head, her artistically painted little Mongol face ... her little temper, her great kindness, her sunny wit and enormous understanding of the heart'. It was agreed they should meet in France the following spring.

Francette had come to London on a romantic 'wild goose chase'. Christina was beginning to think she had too. Their favourite subject was the ways of the heart, a subject about which the French woman could talk with considerably more experience than Christina. It was probably Francette who recommended De L'Amour, Stendhal's meditations on the perversities of love, infatuation, jealousy and feminine pride that so delighted Christina. And when Francette went home, just before Christmas, she sent Christina the illustrated edition of Pierre Louÿs' erotic novella Aphrodite. Re-issued that year in a new underground edition, it contained a chapter censored from the 1896 original, and the frontispiece was a series of bold engravings of organs in highly explicit amorous postures, which Stead declared 'finely vignetted'.[13] Stendhal and Louÿs were both mentioned in the novel she had just started to write.

Francette Hubert would be the inspiration for Francesca in The Beauties and Furies, who proclaims: 'One should do anything for love.'

At the end of For Love Alone, Teresa, having just seen Jonathan Crow, that teaser of women's hearts, pass her in the street, sighs bitterly: 'It's dreadful to think that it will go on being repeated for ever, he—and me! What's there to stop it?'

For Love Alone, written in 1942–43, is fiction, though autobiographical. However, Stead would always talk as if the novel were a sequel to The Man Who Loved Children, with Teresa an unproblematic representation of herself as a young woman and 'Jonathan Crow' merely a pseudonym for the man himself. Crow was easily identifiable by those who knew Keith Duncan.[14] His appearance, working-class background, manner of speaking: these details were deliberately true to life—and this gave an illicit punch to the bits Stead made up. The fictionalisation of her past gave her real power: the power to re-cast reality.

By insisting that her autobiographical novels, *The Man Who Loved Children* and *For Love Alone*, were 'the truth', Stead tried to have things both ways: she wanted the liberty of invention and the authority of non-fiction. The temptation, of course, was to make herself look better and Keith Duncan worse—if not for her own satisfaction and revenge, then for the sake of the story: a young woman finding love and independence against the odds. A good story was always more important to Stead than the facts: even within the novel, James Quick, the New Yorker based on William Blech, enjoys tossing his conversation with Jonathan Crow about in his mind afterwards, 'improving and depraving it' to tell Teresa. As the contemporary American writer Nora Ephron puts it:

> Fiction at the very least ... is a chance to rework the events of your life so that you give the illusion of being the intelligence at the center of it, simultaneously managing to slip in all the lines that occurred to you later.[15]

Some details in the novel are invented; others are 'improved and depraved'. One obvious change is that Stead has Teresa Hawkins arriving in London in 1936, not 1928, as she herself had—a change she made in order to bring in events surrounding the Spanish Civil War at the end of the novel. To collapse together events that in reality occurred years apart seems a small thing, but it necessarily entailed fracturing the novel's autobiographical truth: Teresa's psychological state at the end of the novel does not reflect Christina's after the same period of time in London.

However, even if details are invented or distorted, scattered clues extraneous to the novel suggest that it gives a good impression of the sort of torment Stead suffered in her first few months in London. Unfortunately, nothing more than scattered clues is available.

For Love Alone is a brilliant study of thwarted sexual desire. Teresa's attraction to Jonathan Crow, unrequited, is dangerously close to a 'mortal fascination'. 'Do any of us know what we are doing in sex?' muses the sapient James Quick at one point. Great emphasis is placed on Jonathan Crow's seductive appeal. A whole array of women in Sydney and London fall for him. With his dark looks and his 'strange dark eyes' (a Lawrentian touch), Crow appears to Teresa 'very virile'. She is attracted by his long mobile mouth, his capacious hands. Above all, she is captivated by the sound of his voice, which 'altered all the time and was full of natural devices, slurring, drawling or sharp, keen notes, an irresistible burring of affection, soft laughs and pauses of self-blame'. Her first impression of him as 'a dark axe-faced man' had long since faded.

Teresa is never able to predict Crow's mood; he is 'sardonic and naive, cruel and gay, tender and cold' in one breath. One minute he stirs her by the depth of his feeling for suffering humanity; the next he talks flippantly about his friends' sordid sexual abuse of a housemaid. He presents himself as a passionate advocate of women's rights, and at the same time he vilifies women incessantly, denouncing them as parasites hellbent on luring a male to the altar. His talk of sexual equality—though Teresa does not yet see this—is entirely self-interested: 'modern women' are supposed to practise 'sexual freedom' without ensnaring their men.

He wants to take her to bed—or rather, he wants her to take him to bed—but without emotional ties. Teresa misses the implications of the hints he drops and believes he is still a virgin suffering from the same physical torment as herself. She can see that he desires her at times, but he also seems as timid and awkward as she when it comes to making overt advances. So far is she from understanding the real nature of this power struggle with a misogynist that when Crow kisses her on the lips, soon after her arrival in London, she takes this for a declaration of love.

> His lips were warm. She had always heard, on the ferry going to work, that the proof of real love was the kiss, that a man who received a kiss with cold lips from his wife began to think of divorce. A little smattering of ferry-lore, garbled like this, was all she knew of love in practice. Therefore, her first thought was, on receiving this extraordinary kiss, 'He loves me after all.'

Jonathan's rare embraces are clumsy and rough; mostly he refrains from touching Teresa altogether. Sexually passive, he is also wary—understandably so—of her romantic expectations. His secret affair with the servant-girl in his house (which the reader sees; Teresa doesn't) is altogether less loaded, for she cannot exert any rights nor entertain the slightest expectations of any future with her 'gentleman'.

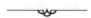

Keith Duncan had a summer job as a tutorial class lecturer in the university extension program in Oxford. He talked of having an early joint-birthday celebration before he left: his birthday was 11 July and Christina's just six days later. Stead told her Aunt Florence:

> We are going to have a cake with 51 candles. It is all arranged—you see, he is 25 and I am 26, so *we* are really 51! Creeping old age doth grasp us!

The party was not mentioned in her next letter, written on Keith Duncan's birthday, and perhaps it had never taken place. Stead merely remarked, 'Keith is tutoring at Oxford and having a gloriously lazy time in dazzling sun, he says—which makes me painfully envious'.

One week later, Christina told Gwen, 'It makes me feel wicked that I am not always as happy as a lark with all your kind thoughts'. She was writing to Gwen from the office. Mr Blech had 'tootled off to Paris' for five days, 'partly on business', and there was not much work for her to do. She did not mention the other reason for her boss's visit to Paris: his wife and 8-year-old daughter were living there, and he crossed the Channel as often as possible to see them. The letter continued:

> Heaven! I am tired, I could sleep for a week ... I get tireder and tireder, although I have not much office work to do. But the fact is that it is the sitting still and the waiting and the doing-nothing that knocks one out, *if* all the time one is sitting still, etc. one's head goes running on and running on about nothing in particular ... When I get near bedtime, I am consumed with a desire as bad as any described in the most harrowing novel by the most able author, but it is only to go to sleep. I don't think I shall ever get up off this chair, for instance: I think it would be charming to go on for ever, dreaming ... and get deeper and deeper in the flood of oblivion until saturated, when I should like to go to sleep, like mad Ophelia, singing silly songs.

Stead was easily carried away by words, and the allusion to able authors indicates her self-consciousness in regard to her art. But there was more to this than the literary pleasure of describing a near-trance. It is a curious cry in the dark from someone who normally took great care to appear cheerful. She knew that her words were likely to cause concern, for she added, by way of feeble reassurance: 'Don't get alarmed: I went to bed late last night, that's all.'

It was auto-hypnosis that Stead was describing—a state, Freud and Breuer claim, that occurs in people prone to habitual reveries if they have suffered protracted anxiety. An all-pervasive desire to sleep, to blot out the world, is also a common symptom of depression.

Stead is likely to have been musing on the parallels between the scorned Ophelia and herself. Keith Duncan had rejected her. It must have seemed to the 26-year-old Stead that the three hooded madmen—desire, fear, ridicule—were crowding in on her.

The degree of Stead's desperation can be gauged from her apparent conviction that she was going to die. Later in life, she readily alluded to this romantic notion, without ever elaborating. She recalled that she occupied the long, lonely summer evenings of 1928 writing a novel—'under such stress' that she 'never expected to write another book'.[16] But she had resolved to leave something behind her.

At first she had hammered away on an old Corona borrowed from Duncan, but she soon bought her own typewriter with her savings. The title of her novel was *Death in the Antipodes*. Later—with Dickens' *Seven Poor Travellers* in mind—she would call it *Seven Poor Men of Sydney*.

During the summer and autumn of 1928, Stead reached a nadir of self-loathing. In Sydney, she had eaten little and walked to the point of exhaustion; now she resumed her old habits. When Florence James saw her early in November for the first time in eighteen months, she was shocked at how thin she was. Every morning Stead walked from Bloomsbury to St Mary Axe; every evening—until she became 'too feeble for it'—she walked home. Later, she would comment: 'I didn't realise the connection between my walking and this continued privation and my feelings.'[17]

Christina Stead, wary and self-contained, very rarely discussed her emotions in letters. It is to her fiction that we must turn for clues about her inner life.

In both *For Love Alone* (written *about* this time) and *Seven Poor Men of Sydney* (written *at* this time), Teresa and Catherine eat badly—mainly buns with cups of tea. Both are virgins, lonely and desperate, physically fidgety and verging on manic.

In the avowedly autobiographical novel *For Love Alone*, written fourteen years later, Teresa is jilted by Jonathan Crow. She is close to a nervous breakdown: when she climbs into bed, 'the strange orchestra with fifes and tympani' begins to beat and gets 'louder and more furious each night'. Rejected by the man for whom she crossed the world, her voyage to England now strikes her as 'a buffoon Odyssey'. She is, she tells herself, 'a detestable thing, an ugly, rejected woman'. Crow's rejection of her is perfectly understandable: 'Who could love me? Do I love myself? Then why should he?'

She resolves to die, but is not quite ready to kill herself. 'Impulsive bloody suicide is a coward's death,' she tells herself. A more 'honorable suicide' would be to work herself to death. That way, she would have time to finish her 'testament'.

An extraordinary piece of writing—especially for its layers of self-reflexivity—is Teresa's Introduction to her novel. Here she describes herself spending those 'long pale evenings of the northern twilight' writing. Her testament, *The Seven Houses of Love*, depicts 'the ages, a sacred seven, through which abandoned, unloved women passed before life was torn out of their clenched, ringless work-worn fists'.

Teresa has also written some notes: 'A System by which the Chaste can Know Love'. These notes portray in a tone of feverish lyricism a woman's life as a metaphor for sexual intercourse. In the first house, the word 'love' carries 'floating ideas' that will cause the young girl 'physical warmth, a naive joy'. In the second, the adolescent girl imagines 'scenes of festive and dark violence'. In the third, she experiences 'yearning lust'. And so on. The sixth house, 'Heaven and Hell', is her experience of love as tyranny and humiliation. The seventh house is 'the last star'.

> To die by the last effort of the will and body. To will, the consuming and consummation. To force the end. It must be dark; then an extraordinary clutching of reality.

The Seven Houses of Love is the fiction within the fiction. In reality, Christina Stead was writing *Seven Poor Men of Sydney*, which contains the very same themes. Catherine and her half-brother Michael each contain something of Stead herself: each grapples with madness and suicide.[18] Certain passages in the novel come close to being paeans to death.

Catherine, who describes herself as 'insupportably lonely', romanticises madness: 'I am terribly unhappy: my heart is bursting, that is why I have to go mad.' Michael struggles against madness: 'Am I going cuckoo? Is this how it starts? No wonder they shriek out, madmen, if it feels like this.'

Brother and sister are obsessed with suicide. Walking by the harbour one stormy evening, Catherine calls out, half to herself, half to her companion:

> 'Come, sweet sea!' She added: 'Come sweet death, I mean.' She lay back on the grassy slope, sopping wet. 'That is the sort of death I would like, to go down in the swilling storm-waters, ough, guff, gubble, gup, and you're drowned: that death I could die a thousand times.'

This is, once again, death as orgasmic dissolution. Michael thinks of suicide, but decides 'he could not let the waters close over him without first knowing the sweet profound experience of cleaving to a loving woman's flesh and sinking into oblivion with her'. In the end (having experienced sexual rapture), he leaps over the notorious 'Gap' and sinks into oblivion in the sea. The imagery of abysses, drowning, sleeping and leaping is consistently sexual.

Madness; suicide. Why does Stead impose such a tragic quietus on her shadow selves? In a novel about pent-up sexual desire, cruel loneliness and frustrated aspirations, madness and suicide are seen as a means of regaining lost power and reasserting selfhood. By *writing* about madness and suicide, Stead could assert herself vicariously, through her characters. Ironically, by writing the novel, she was working herself not to death, but back to life.

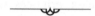

William Blech was curious about the young man his secretary mentioned from time to time. He found himself wondering what kind of man attracted her. Keith Duncan, who knew how much Christina was impressed by her boss, the Marxist investments manager who seemed to know something about everything, was equally intrigued. Duncan was planning to go to the United States to pursue postdoctoral research, and he welcomed the opportunity to meet a New York intellectual. Some time in the autumn, when he returned from Oxford, a meeting was arranged—without Christina.

'Bill came back with very negative opinions,' Stead recalled later. He apparently probed Duncan about his feelings for Christina, and the disdainful Duncan had let drop that Christina thought herself a writer. Back at the office, Blech asked his secretary whether he might see something she had written. One Friday, she handed him her work in progress, *Death in the Antipodes*.

> He took it away one weekend. We weren't friendly—well, we were friendly, but we weren't close. And he brought it back and he looked at me, he had beautiful brown eyes, … and he looked at me with absolute astonishment when he sat at the desk opposite me. He called me in from my little typist den and he said: 'It has mountain peaks.'[19]

Whenever she told people that she met William Blech within a week of arriving in London, Christina Stead would say she had won the great prize in the lottery. She had a keen sense of the guiding hand of Fate, and she always believed their meeting to be pure serendipity.

When she wrote to Gwen Walker-Smith early in September 1928, though Stead did not mention Blech, his presence loomed large between the lines. It was his opinions she was airing, and the letter was suffused with a new joy and confidence.

> I understand the only place to live on the Continent (of great towns) is Bruges, which is all 16th century horsefairs, great patron bourgeois merchants, religious processions and steeples. I don't like London: I have a good mind to try Bruges, therefore: but how! I feel like a bird which has just learned to fly. I wish to explore the universe of stars!

The next letter to her cousin, four closely typed pages, was written in mid October: the beech trees in Cartwright Gardens were shedding their leaves. Once again, the letter spoke of everything but the man who was rapidly becoming the focus of Christina's attention. She had been to concerts conducted by Sir Thomas Beecham and Sir Henry Wood. (She does not say with whom she went.) Beecham impressed her with his 'charming manners' towards the musicians: 'he beckons them up like lambs and brushes them back like daisies and smiles ineffably in the soft sweet passages'. At the Proms, Sir Henry Wood was 'woolly and playful'.

Several characters in the novel she was writing were printers, Stead told Gwen, and so she was studying the history and mechanics of printing. She was also musing on spiritual matters. She had just read *Apologia pro Vita sua*, Cardinal Newman's account of his spiritual development; *Commonsense Theology* by the agnostic rationalist C. E. M. Joad and A. N. Whitehead's philosophical treatise on symbolism. Moreover, she was still persevering with Bertrand Russell's *The Analysis of Mind*, the book she carried at her job interview.

'I live a very circumscribed life,' she told Gwen, 'so that I am ashamed to write about it.'

In *For Love Alone*, Teresa finds herself tripping into work with new enthusiasm for life. She tells her boss: 'You light up everything when you explain it. The world has changed for me since I knew you.'

Christina told Mr Blech: 'I love to hear you talk. It helps me forget.'[20] Blech too found himself curiously drawn to his secretary. He was probably inviting her to concerts with him. And on two or three occasions in October he arranged to meet her at Lyons Corner House in Tottenham Court Road, to talk after work.[21]

For Love Alone was written more than a decade after the failed romance with Duncan. Though she believed she had worked herself into a state of sympathy with her character Jonathan Crow—several passages are narrated from his point of view—Stead's anger was intact. Indeed, if the second half of the novel is weaker than the first, it is because Stead had an overriding ulterior motive: to take revenge.

A brief glimpse at the imagery used to portray Crow reveals the degree to which the portrait was artistically heightened. His very name betrays the author's hostility. But it is in the final chapters of the novel that his comeuppance is delivered. His condemnation not just by Teresa but also by the affable James Quick intensifies the force of the authorial axe.

Before he meets Crow, Quick reads an essay by him on the biological and social differences between the sexes and races. Appalled by its racism and misogyny, Quick surmises that Crow is 'a dim-witted, dim-faced, bobbing pedant'. In a subsequent chapter, Quick sits in the Tottenham Court Road Corner House, waiting to meet Crow for the first time:

> He had not been watching long before he noticed a shrewd and unscrupulous-looking man in his thirties, who strolled round the stands and looked sharply at him, perhaps a private dick, he thought. The man was swarthy, oak-complexioned, with a hammered-out distorted and evil face and a syncopated rolling walk which looked like the business stroll of the second-rate spottable spy.

This is the stuff of detective fiction, negative to the point of caricature. The two men find a table and talk. Quick, true to his name, gets the measure of his rival within minutes. He is struck by Crow's 'shrewd, hard look and twisted, canny smile'. Further conversation confirms his hunch:

> … an ambitious small-town man, sly, ignorant but a cudgeller of faculty cabals, a wit-picker, a notion-thief, a man bound to get on, a paste-and-scissors scholar, of the kind that often makes a name for himself by writing forewords to great works.

Our final glimpse of Jonathan Crow comes at the end of the novel. It is dusk. Teresa, out walking with James Quick, sees a 'peculiar, sliding, fumbling figure' go by. They pass under a streetlamp; in this light, the figure has the bluish tinge and unshaven lantern jaw of expressionist caricature. Then Teresa recognises him. She feels 'a pang as if faced by a murderer. The vile-faced man, the bent-backed man, walking crowded with all the apparatus of melodrama was Jonathan Crow!' He is every bit the exaggerated villain of Victorian melodrama whom audiences love to hiss.

In 1987, aged eighty-three and terminally ill with cancer, Professor W. G. K. Duncan, very bitter about Christina Stead, recalls the rapidity with which she transferred her affections from him to *Mr Blech*, as he calls him, with mocking emphasis. 'Frailty, thy name is woman!' he mutters drily, unwittingly echoing Stead's own many borrowings from *Hamlet*. He himself could never have done that, he says.

> 'Christina must have been very lonely,' I say.
> 'That's no excuse. Loneliness is no excuse. It was so quick.'
> 'But you were probably quite cold towards her,' I suggest.
> 'That's true.' He nods.

It is February 1987, mid morning. The air has the desert dryness of Adelaide summers. We are in the Helping Hand Home, in the leafy tranquillity of North Adelaide, the gracious old district favoured by the university establishment. Professor Duncan and his wife Dorothy have recently moved in here, to rooms on separate floors.

He is sitting at a table by the window, in baggy flannel trousers and a waistcoat—as if he had walked out of a photograph from the 1920s. Were it not for the heat we could almost have been sitting in his student room in Bloomsbury. He is a little deaf. I have to raise my voice.

He has silver hair, a narrow face, and behind his heavy glasses, large brown eyes that fix me intently. He has no intention, he says, of talking about 'that woman Christina Stead'. His eyes flash over the top of his glasses. He tells me she is guilty of 'gross misrepresentation', that in her books she says things about people that are not even erased by that person's death, things that will never be forgotten.

And then we talk about Christina transferring her affections with undue haste. He pauses, looks out at the garden, and mutters: 'If that's what women are like, God preserve me from them!'[22]

———— ∿ ————

Was Stead guilty of 'gross mis-representation'? Literary critics today argue that writing can never be a representation, a mirror to life; realist literature is merely a set of literary conventions to which we have become so accustomed that we are no longer aware of the immense gap between writing about life and life itself. Though it is by writing oneself that one becomes acutely conscious of this gap, in interviews Stead regularly made the opposite claim: her fiction reflected reality almost exactly. This claim would have been even more offensive to Keith Duncan than the novel itself. Though there is considerable sympathy for Crow in Part One of *For Love Alone*, Stead's portrait of Jonathan Crow is ultimately not generous; but this really matters only when art claims to be life.

Duncan's outrage is understandable. Take Jonathan Crow's affair with the London housemaid. If Stead invented these details, Duncan was made to look guilty by association; if the story was true, he would have been horrified to see it in print. Either way, he lost.

If Duncan chose never to say anything about the novel, it was no doubt because he preferred not to draw attention to a portrait that was both false and uncomfortably accurate. Paradoxically, the fiction became even 'truer' than it intended. In the novel, published in 1944, Crow is described as 'the sort that climbs slowly but successfully on his undangerous stupidity ... to be head of his department'. Had the novel been published seven years later, this sentence would have been defamatory, for in 1951 Duncan was appointed Professor of History and Political Science at the University of Adelaide.

Dr Hugh Stretton, Duncan's colleague at the University of Adelaide, and someone who knew him well in his last thirty years, comments:

> Duncan was an odd, interesting man, cold but very strongly committed to unexceptionable good causes (civil liberties, lifelong education for everyone, good public libraries). He was a total chauvinist husband, but capable of very hard-working, self-effacing kindnesses to a few friends and favourite students ... I could see plenty of psychological truth in the Crow portrait. But it is vengeful, without much compassion for his internal emptiness or respect for (what turned out eventually to be) the very active, genuine reformer that he became.[23]

Several months passed before Stead contacted Florence James, whom she had first met at Sydney University, and who was now living in London, working as a freelance journalist. Christina would not have wanted to share her misery over Keith Duncan with her, especially as they had other friends from the university in common. Florence James had no difficulty attracting men (she had already broken off her engagement to the Dutch lawyer from Java), and would only have inflamed Christina's burning sense of failure.

But by late October, Christina's life had taken a turn for the better, and she dispatched a note to Florence proposing lunch and a Saturday afternoon concert at Queen's Hall, where Elizabeth Schumann was singing. A few days later, James wrote to her mother:

> The concert was delightful, mostly German lieder, and she has an exquisite voice. Afterwards we met Chris's chief who was also there and he bore us off to tea, which incidentally took about two hours. Mr. Blech is a German Jew and what he hasn't read or doesn't know about in art, literature and music seems almost negligible—not that he's a particularly discerning critic although a very opinionated one—but marvellously stimulating company. Christina and I walked back here afterwards and cooked supper on my gas ring: she's a very nice girl and I'm hoping to see more of her.[24]

Stead enjoyed the evening too, for five weeks later, in early December, she wrote to Florence James with another proposition. She was renting a large room at the corner of Cartwright Gardens and Marchmont Street for six months, while the owner, an artist, was in South America. Would Florence like to share it with her?

It was 'very superior accommodation', James recalls. The doors and windows were painted black with scarlet knobs; cushions of every shade were strewn around. A china cupboard contained fine willowpattern dishes; there was even a disappearing washstand. Florence told her mother:

> I'm thinking seriously about it. Christina would be an ideal companion, except that one would have to keep one's eye on her, she's the least businesslike of mortals, and is always trying to take more than her fair share of any burden. In the first place she says 10/- a week for me. Now I know she's paying 28/- and as she's out from 8 to 6 every day when I have the

room to myself, half shares is the least I could contemplate ... Christina, by
the way, is in the midst of writing a novel.

The room was expensive for one person; by comparison, Keith Duncan
and John Beaglehole were paying 17s 6d a week each for their shared
room in Brunswick Square.

The following Sunday, 16 December, Florence packed up and took the
first instalment of her belongings round to Marchmont Street, where she
found Christina and Francette Hubert cosily drinking tea in front of the
fire. Francette was shortly to return to France.

The three went to the Cartwright Gardens clubhouse for lunch, then
Christina accompanied Florence to her old room in Chelsea and they
transported a large chest to Bloomsbury by threading a walking stick
through the handles and taking one end each.

Now that she was happier, Christina was consciously trying to fatten
herself up. Whereas Florence saved money by cooking on their gas ring,
Christina paid 15s a week for breakfast and dinner at the clubhouse.
Florence explained to her mother, 'Christina is a slim creature and needs
feeding'.

Florence James and her friends were lively, interesting women, whose
company did Christina good. She wrote to Gwen:

> Florence is a Sydney girl whom I met once or twice before coming over,
> but I never thought I should be sharing my dearest secrets with her in a
> Bloomsbury square, and my Jewish buns and my Yiddish godfather.[25]

They shared clothes as well as secrets. That is, Christina borrowed from
Florence, who had brought some smart clothes from Sydney. Florence
recalls Christina trying on one of her evening dresses. It was a perfect fit,
but Christina had only walking shoes to wear with it.

Christina liked domestic elegance. She was very proud of a lace
tablecloth she had bought, and whenever they had guests she would bring
out pretty napkins and dishes. Florence liked to drink her tea, bohemian-
style, out of a mug; Christina would fuss with cups and saucers. They were,
James points out, rebelling against very different family backgrounds: she
had had fine china at home; Christina had not.

'I am atrociously tired, I know not why.' It was early January 1929. Dense 'pea-soupers' regularly cast London in 'a graveyard gloom'. But Stead's fatigue was no longer due to depression. She told her aunt Florence that the sleeping arrangements were to blame. There was only one bed in their new room, and she and Florence were taking it in turns, week about, to imitate 'St Simeon Stylites and Other Celebrated Martyrs' by sleeping on a wooden trunk with a chair at one end and a suitcase at the other. She joked: 'I am further guided along the path of godliness ... by the landlady never having found it necessary to instal a bath.' For their ablutions, performed behind a screen (Florence was amused by Christina's extreme modesty), there was a basin with a pull-down lid and a bucket beneath. Fetching water involved a trip downstairs.

In fact, the cause of Stead's exhaustion was not the bed; nor was it work on her novel, which had slowed down in recent weeks. It was simply that her life was in utter turmoil. That morning, 9 January 1929, only seven months after she had stepped ashore in England, a telephone call had come from Mr Blech, who was in Paris for a few days. He was making arrangements to return to work in Paris in a few weeks' time. Would she join him as his secretary? When she wrote to Gwen that afternoon, Stead was dancing on a highwire: 'I have been shouting Banzai, Halleluia and other Hebrew sounds ever since, because he is a very nice fellow and Paris sounds fine to me.'

Her family must have been very curious by now about the 'very nice fellow' to whom Christina only ever referred in her letters as 'Mr. Blech' or 'my employer'. The many typing mistakes in her letters did not suggest top secretarial skills: was it purely for business reasons that Blech wanted her in Paris? Though Christina remained non-committal, near the end of her letter came this astonishing morsel:

> My employer tells me that I have no idea how to dress and I will look a different woman when properly dressed (frankness is charming), so I have a soft anticipatory thrill and feel those voluptuous stirrings and those plenitudes we all feel when we consider the sort of woman we could be if we had the right climate and care.

At first, Christina herself did not know what to make of this sudden and dramatic turn of events. Among her unpublished papers are notes about this period that reveal her complete lack of confidence in her own charms:

Because Bill though separated from his wife was not divorced, when he asked me out, he also asked my room-mate, a splendidly built handsome girl … so that for some time I thought he had fallen in love with her, until one concert conducted by the then young and promising conductor John (later Sir John) Barbirellis [sic], when he sparkled and I felt dreary and let down and upon returning home my room-mate said: 'If you ever treat him that way again, I shall refuse to go with you. In any case it's no fun playing gooseberry.' I thought her modest and shy, that she was wrong; but she was right.

William Blech, a tornado of energy, was swirling both women off their feet. He would turn up with a friend and they would go as a foursome to the theatre, concerts and restaurants. For Christina and Florence it was an introduction to an entirely new world. One evening they would go to a seedy-looking little Soho restaurant known only to the *cognoscenti*; the next they would be ushered inside the plush Café Royal on Regent Street. Florence James well remembers the animated conversation and laughter. The men chose the food, and the men paid.

Sometimes it was Stead's Managing Director, Alfred Hurst, who made up the foursome. A married man with children, he was an inveterate Don Juan: he had a luxurious bachelor flat at No. 14 Park Lane, Mayfair, for romantic assignations. For the time being, however, William Blech was living there, and all parties were back in their own rooms at the end of the evening.

Christina must have been rather shocked by the libertine world in which she found herself, but she was also dazzled by Bill's worldliness. Her notes continue:

Bill, though not much older than me, behaved like a father to me: to him, coming from the brilliant city of New York, I was an apt and interesting but almost ignorant outlander, almost a child, almost a savage, and he eagerly, with sparkling, continuous wit and information, did his best to educate me … He loved to impart, and he did it gaily, affectionately, without pedantry …[26]

With her avid curiosity, sense of fun and love of language, Christina Stead must have been an exciting and appreciative companion for William Blech. Finding herself with two Jewish bosses, she had already plunged into a study of Jewish culture. With her Christmas bonus from the office she bought an English–Yiddish grammar book and taught herself smatterings of Yiddish. In her lunch hour she liked to walk to Whitechapel, the Jewish East End area, and wander around the vast network of lanes trying to decipher the Yiddish signs. On wet days she would sit in the library in the Mile End Road and read about Jewish legend in the *Encyclopaedia Judaica*—material that she later worked into *The Salzburg Tales*. Blech was proud of his Jewishness; so was Stead.[27]

'You will of course have sized up the situation,' Florence James told her mother in a long and colourful letter dated 23 January 1929, 'I'm basking in reflected glory from Christina as far as Mr. Blech is concerned.' She added: 'It's really a delightful situation for she's such a modest soul, quite unused to being made a great deal of fuss of.'

The previous fortnight, Florence explained, had been a frenzy of social activity. One evening, Christina had come home from work 'with dancing eyes' and told her to get dressed quickly as Mr Blech had managed to get tickets for Artur Schnabel's piano concert and they were going to dinner first. The evening was concluded at Verrey's in Regent Street, 'a very elegant café'. The following Tuesday, Blech took them to the Pro Arte String Quartet; on Thursday, he and a friend, Mr Kempner, came round to the flat; on Saturday, they saw *Thérèse Raquin* at the Q Theatre. On Sunday, Blech took Christina to Cambridge for the day. On Monday morning, Christina and Florence, exhausted, vowed they would go to bed straight after the delivery of the Australian mail in the evening.

> Behold, we'd finished reading it when the bell rang. Two gentlemen to see us. Mr. Blech and Mr. Kempner in full evening dress. 'How long will it take you two girls to change, and we'll do a night club!' Well, the two girls didn't take long to change! We disported ourselves in the Piccadilly Hotel ... We really had a delightful evening, and thoroughly interesting.

On Friday they were to have dinner at Mr Blech's flat in Park Lane, followed by a string quartet, then a nightclub. When the time came, Mr Kempner was in bed with flu, so the nightclub had to be cancelled. Florence told her mother: 'Mr Blech's so thoroughly smitten himself he's anxious to wish the rest of the world into a state of similar beatitude.'

In mid January, in Cambridge, at the lectern of a famous church, William and Christina exchanged their first kiss. The following Sunday, they made an excursion to Canterbury, through countryside white with snow.[28]

In *For Love Alone*, Stead has Teresa and James Quick spend a day in Canterbury. Coming back on the evening train, through countryside 'white with young moonlight', Teresa is 'miserable and maddened' by Quick's frenzied passion. Quick, holding 'the near-fainting Teresa in his arms', talks blithely about their 'union'. He tells her, more dramatically than sensitively, that he wants them to become lovers, continuing:

> 'If the law says I am married, I will make you my back-street wife.' Yes, even if she would not live with him as his wife but was afraid of public opinion 'as so many nice girls are' he would take care of her, get her a room somewhere, furnish it, and come to see her.

Quick eagerly rushes on:

> He would bring her books, music, take her to concerts, theatres, if she wished, send her to the university—make a woman of her, make a brilliant woman of her, the sort of woman who in all ages had charmed men, the Montespan of the age ... He was a stepping-stone, he told her; she would be a Staël, a Récamier, a Catherine II. He would take her to Paris, and elsewhere, no one who knew her now would know her then; he would make her over entirely.

Faced with this awesome prospect, Teresa, understandably, feels overwhelmed, no longer quite her own person. Moreover, she has serious misgivings:

> In all this storm of words he had only mentioned marriage once and then in a dubious way. She wanted to go to the Sorbonne—but to be a back-street wife, to give with one hand and take with the other—not that!

Christina Stead would have been every bit as loath as Teresa to become a 'back-street wife', a mistress. She did not want a lover to be a stepping-stone; she wanted a husband. Yet it is likely that William Blech's initial propositions did not include actual marriage. Though he seems to have blurred this point when talking to Christina, he was not formally separated from his wife. He was a proud father; his wife was Jewish and beautiful, and though their relationship was not fulfilling, they had reached some sort of *modus vivendi*. His mother, who was also financially dependent on him, thought the world of Mollie, his wife. He knew the havoc it would cause if he divorced and broke up the family. His daughter Ruth was the age his elder sister had been when their own father had abandoned them: he well remembered the misery that ensued. Blech was a progressive, a feminist even, but in his world wealthy financier friends kept mistresses. The wives, provided they were adequately cared for financially, accepted the situation.

Years later, Stead told a friend: 'Dear Bill said once to me in the beginning of things that he would like to be to me what G. H. Lewes was to George Eliot.' She joked: 'I was not very pleased, because G. E. was not a pretty girl.'[29]

FEDERAL BUREAU OF INVESTIGATION

This case originated at New York City.

Date when made: 2/2/44.

Character of Case: Internal Security.

Title: WILLIAM JAMES BLECH, with aliases: William Blake, William J. Blake, William James Blake, George B. Collingwood, George S. Kent.

SYNOPSIS OF FACTS:

Subject was a Single Taxer at the age of 15 and acted in Democratic Party at 18. Protested America's entry into First World War. From 1919 to 1926 he was connected with private banking in Wall Street and wrote for the 'Magazine of Wall Street'. From 1926 to 1934 he engaged in banking activities in Paris and London.

... Friends and associates of subject label him 'intellectual Communist', 'a fellow traveller', and 'cynical capitalist' but all maintain he is not dangerous. Subject reported to have profound admiration of and respect for Russia and is great student of Communist theory.[30]

Born in St Louis on 28 July 1894, William James Blech was the second child of German parents, who were among the two million Jews to migrate to the United States between 1870 and 1914. His father, Gustavus Maximilian Blech, a doctor, was born in Strasburg in 1867; his mother, Rosa Sachs, was born in the Baltic seaport of Riga in 1869. When she was young, her family, well-to-do and liberal German Jews, had moved to St Petersburg then Königsberg, where, family legend has it, one of the four brothers was physician to the Tsar.[31] Certainly, the family belonged to the small minority of privileged Jews in tsarist Russia. But during the 1880s and 1890s new laws prohibited Jews from owning or renting land outside towns or cities; quotas restricted their entrance into the *gymnasia* and the universities. Pogroms—organised massacres of Jews—were deliberately provoked by the tsarist government, in some 600 villages and cities, to divert the discontent of the Russian peasants into racial hatred and religious bigotry.

Rosa Sachs was eighteen when she sailed past the Statue of Liberty in 1887, joining two of her brothers in New York. Small and squat, with large brown eyes, she read and spoke five languages fluently and played the piano well. She soon married Dr Gustavus Blech, another recent immigrant. But the marriage was a bitter disappointment: they were not well off and Gus was an incurable womaniser.[32] In 1891 Rosa gave birth to a sickly girl, Jenny. Three years later, she bore their only son, named after the influential American philosopher and psychologist William James.

William's first five years were spent in St Louis, Missouri. An industrial city on the west bank of the Mississippi, it contained a large German community that had left Europe after the failure of the 1848 revolution. The community was active and enterprising, boasting four daily German newspapers and several German 'Kindergartens'. Jenny and William did not learn English until they started school.

When William was five, the family moved to Chicago, and it was in that port and railway city that Gustavus abandoned them. Rosa, who clung ferociously to bourgeois respectability, found herself tarnished with the disgrace of divorce. Gustavus remarried; before long his cheques stopped coming. In desperate straits, Rosa decided to move with her children to New York, close to her brothers.

They settled in the slums of lower east Manhattan, and Rosa told people she was widowed. The Lower East Side, the area south of Houston and east of the Bowery, was, at the turn of the century, an impoverished ghetto of European Jewish immigrants, where Jews from all the Yiddish-speaking centres of Europe lived in clusters according to their nationality. Henry Roth, in his novel *Call It Sleep* (1934) paints a memorable picture of this tumultuous corner of Manhattan, with its 'avalanche of sound' in which the screams of babies, bickerings of mothers, bawling cries of hucksters and yowling of cats blended with the clattering of horse-cars, honking of automobiles, banging of garbage cans, the cacophony of small industries and the boat horns on the East River. Because of the heavy Jewish migration of the early 1890s, the dark tenement houses were dangerously overcrowded and sanitation was wretched. In the stifling summer months, roofs, fire escapes and sidewalks were converted into sleeping quarters. In 1899 the Board of Health noted the mounting incidence of tuberculosis, the 'White Plague', in the city. In 1903, at the age of twelve, Jenny Blech died of tuberculosis. William was only eight at the time, and his sister's death marked him deeply—both his character and his politics.

In the hurly-burly of the New York slums, William became his mother's protector and adviser. While she taught the piano (her pupils were wealthy daughters from the neighbouring affluent areas where her brothers lived), William, left in the home of one or other of his uncles, would amuse himself by reading whatever was around: encyclopaedias, medical and legal books, dictionaries. One of his teachers, amazed by the boy's extraordinary wealth of information, cited Oliver Goldsmith's lines to describe him:

> And still they gazed, and still the wonder grew,
> That one small head could carry all he knew.[33]

Although he was something of a prodigy at school, William had to go to work at fourteen. A benevolent family friend, John T. McRoy, a Scottish engineer who had amassed a fortune through various inventions, employed him as his runner and secretary. McRoy, a socialist and philanthropist, helped establish several talented boys on Wall Street.[34] From being a Wall Street runner, 19-year-old William Blech moved into an office on Wall Street—a not altogether rare transition for bright working-class boys at the time.

The overthrow of the Tsar in February 1917 was greeted with loud rejoicing in immigrant families and in the American press, both Left and Right. (The conservatives preferred a government run by businessmen to the feudal Romanovs, and rightly assumed that the new government would pursue the war against Germany more vigorously.)

Colonel Gustavus M. Blech, surgeon-general in the Medical Reserve Corps of the US Army, was horrified when his son, who was called to serve the forces in August 1917, declared himself a conscientious objector to the war. (They saw each other briefly then, for the first time since Gustavus left the family, and would not meet again until the 1930s, in Chicago.)

Young Blech was influenced by the radical socialists who denounced it as a capitalist war that espoused national patriotism rather than international working-class solidarity.

Twenty-three-year-old William Blech went underground in Boston. Most Americans regarded conscientious objectors as traitors, but his girlfriend, Mollie Grossman, a progressive and a suffragette, worked as a secretary to keep them both. The two had known each other since childhood when they had attended the same public school and William had sometimes gone to Mollie's in the afternoon. Mollie, from a well-off Russian-Polish Jewish family, had completed high school and proceeded to study French and German at Hunter College. The young pair eventually gave in to family pressure and married in New York on 13 October 1918.

During the 1920s, Blech worked on Wall Street—some of the time employed by Alf Hurst, who came briefly to New York from Scotland to set up a grain business. Blech attended extramural evening courses in history and economics at Columbia University, and wrote articles on stocks and bonds for *The Magazine of Wall Street*.

Their daughter Ruth was born on 30 April 1921. Six years later Mollie Blech, who had long harboured a dream to go to France, chaperoned a niece across the Atlantic to seek medical treatment. She took Ruth with her. When William joined them, after seven months, his talkative little daughter greeted him in French.

Throughout the 1920s Americans, taking advantage of the favourable exchange rate and lower steamship fares, had flooded into the artistic capital of Europe. In 1927, William Blech, who had developed transatlantic financial contacts, worked in a private American bank, the Travelers' Bank, on the fashionable Place Vendôme. Like his wife and daughter, he loved Paris. In the evenings, after dinner, the family would stroll to a nearby café. Ruth, who could rarely be persuaded to go to bed before 11 pm, would drink sweet pomegranate grenadines and enjoy the attention of the people around, while her parents drank cup after cup of coffee. She remembers a world of talk and music. Her father had built up an impressive record collection and friends would come to the apartment to listen to music. Ruth was very proud of her papa. And he was devoted to her.

William and Mollie had drifted into an affectionate but distant relationship. They had been married for nine years now, and were accustomed to spending time apart. Mollie, a modern woman, used to say that marriage stifled individuality. In the United States, she had sometimes taken Ruth and gone for several weeks to the luxurious kosher hotel her mother ran in the country, leaving William to his long hours of work and his political meetings in the evenings.[35] And she and Ruth had packed up and left for France without him. So it did not seem strange that William, eager to spend time in Europe's financial capital, should go to London early in 1928 to work in Alf Hurst's London and Scottish grain exchange business. It was a temporary arrangement and he promised the family he would make regular trips across the Channel to see them.

And then, one day in May, when spring was in the air, a young Australian woman walked into the office clutching a book by Bertrand Russell, and applied for a job.

4

La Parisienne

L ONDON WAS BITTERLY cold that year. Household pipes were frozen. In the icy streets a constant procession of muffled people carried jugs of water. By the time the milk was plucked from the doorstep in the morning, it had turned into ice cream.

On a Friday afternoon in that bleak February of 1929, Christina Stead scrolled the office notepaper into her typewriter. It was her last complete week at the St Mary Axe office: the following Friday she would be leaving England. At the top of the letter she typed her new address.

Care Travelers' Bank,
20 Place Vendôme,
PARIS,
France. 8.2.29
Dear Gwenyth,
The above address will be mine next week, so will you please address your letters as above in the future? …

I have been wondering if you have been feeling much better since your holiday and have not been troubled any more by the weakness, and headaches you last wrote me about. What you want is a long holiday say six weeks in duration, a sea-voyage, a voyage to Paris, a voyage to see your cousin. I want to see you: can't you come over here to see me? I don't see why my entire family should desert me and go and live in the Antipodes. Please let me have a short note, in any case, and let me know how you are.

This is only to be a short note, too, because I am getting ready to go to Paris, where I will work with my present manager, Mr. Blech, in a new banking office associated with the Travelers' Bank, which is a very flourishing association, an American bank under a most able American, a friend of Mr. Blech. You may have heard by this time that I am going to marry Mr. Blech (his name is William James Blech, and I call him Wilhelm). Wilhelm is a German Jew of American upbringing, small, very loquacious, very astute in business and literary affairs and art, highly educated and original: he is 35, has a white skin with black hair and beautiful brown eyes, has small, delicate hands: a small head square-set like a Teuton as to the back, with a curious Mongolian forehead and high cheek-bones, the lower face, Teutonic. He is a South German, his family coming from Karlsruhe. The family is intellectually distinguished and his cousin is Dr. Leo Blech, Director of the Berlin State Orchestra. His father is a distinguished surgeon in the U.S. His chief characteristics are his marvellous humanity which melts stones and metals, and his brilliant eyes which shine out of his face, sometimes in a startling way, when his skin is looking particularly white.

Wilhelm and I are going to Fontainebleau for a short vacation before we start work in Paris, as we are both weary of the dirt and cold here, and we both have warm blood in our veins. Wilhelm's previous marriage is not yet dissolved, but as he has actually separated from his wife I am going to live with him in the meantime. I love him dearly and he loves me very dearly, which is a strange thing to me, but which is sincere. He wins the heart of every one of my friends, so that I would have you believe too in the essential firmness and sincerity of our relation. You will perhaps be offended by the fact that I will live with him before we are married, but I hope you will not. I do not even wish him to marry again at all, if it is better for his career not to do so, but he loves a home and he loves children, so that he is very anxious to marry me as soon as possible. We will not have any children for a couple of years, according to our present feelings, not because we don't want them but because we want to become firmly established in Paris, and have a good financial background first. Also, I am thinking, I should like to go about Europe a bit and there are various things I should like to work at first. However, I am looking forward to some hopeful future when my little Gwen will come and visit Wilhelm and me in Paris, and I hope it is not a very distant future. I want to import quite a few of my relatives and it means that Wilhelm and I will have to work our fingers to the bone. Wilhelm is thoroughly Hebraically tribal in the matter of relatives.

I am throwing away all my clothes as not being good enough for Wilhelm, bless his heart, and I am very nigh naked. My friend Florence James has gone out today to get me some lawn underlinen and some lawn for a nightdress she is going to make me. We go to Fontainebleau (it may be Montigny-sur-Loing or Barbizon, which are just outside Fontainebleau) on Friday morning next, by the 'Golden Arrow' express and arrive at Fontainebleau about 6.30. My beloved Wilhelm has all sorts of crazy notions about what he is going to do to my appearance when we get to Paris—such and such a wave, and such and such an eyebrow shave, and such and such a rouge and this perfume. I ask him if he expects me to cook his omelettes aux fines herbes if I have to get myself up to this extent, but his one object in life is to see what sort of a Parisienne he can make of me. I tell him I will be a perfect 'sight' but he says ... he will then take me out to Australia to see what the relatives think of his highly polished Christina. He is planning a trip to Australia with me in about five years: it *may* come off. Isn't it delightful though? You don't know how happy I am—I am only lacking in one thing, my Gilbert and the rest, my Gwen and the rest.

With much love,

Peg

(or as some people like to say Christina Blech)

Things had moved extraordinarily fast in recent weeks. It was only a month ago that her boss had rung from Paris inviting her to work there as his secretary and it had only become clear around that time that he had a romantic interest in her. Now the talk was of marriage. Christina could at last tell her family about her relationship with Mr Blech.

She had been cautious at first, not accustomed to being loved. It was not something she could trust easily, and she was aware that to William Blech, with his European-American heritage, effusive, passionate words came easily. But she was at last convinced of his sincerity. He wanted to marry her, he talked about children, he wanted to meet her family.

She embroidered a bit in her letter to Gwen. This was perfectly understandable, given what she was announcing: that she was about to move in with a married man. She polished up Blech's credentials and made the romance appear less flurried and the divorce more imminent than they really were. It is likely that Blech had touched up the facts when he told them to *her*. In reality, he was not formally separated: his wife and daughter (Stead had not mentioned the daughter in her letters home) were expecting him home again soon. It is true that Gustavus Blech was a distinguished surgeon in the States, but he was an absolute stranger to his son. William *was* 'highly educated', but he was an autodidact, like David Stead, with neither secondary nor tertiary qualifications. (Blech often fudged this point.) Stead—revealing her own prejudices—liked to portray her future husband as more German than American; however, Blech had not set foot in Europe until the previous year. Like many immigrant children born in the New Country, his German, though more or less fluent, was full of grammatical mistakes. For a year Stead persisted in calling him 'Wilhelm', but she would eventually stop trying to deny his American side. All his American friends called him Bill, and so, in the end, did she.

Despite her libertarian protestations that she did not mind whether she married her 'beloved Wilhelm' or not, Stead was actually dreading the family's reaction. She fully expected them to be 'troubled if not outraged'. When their letters arrived twelve weeks later, she was taken aback. 'I did not trust them enough,' she told Gwen. 'As it is Mother has been very kind indeed and Dad also, and also the family in England.' Since her father had always expressed the standard prejudices about Jews, Christina particularly appreciated Ada's encouraging comment that Jews were reputed to be good to their wives.[1] The only sour note came from Aunt Jessica, Stead's maiden aunt in Sydney, who declared that she was ashamed that any woman in the family could conceive of living with a married man.[2]

William Blech certainly led Christina to understand that she would be 'Madame Blech' before the end of the year. When they left England, Florence James told her mother: 'They are hoping to be married quite shortly.'[3] In truth, Stead was far more sensitive about her marital status than she made out to Gwen. She badly wanted to be married. She was no Dora Russell, who disapproved of conventional legal marriage and upheld free love (though even Russell ruled out 'poaching on another's preserves').[4] Neither was she a Simone de Beauvoir who was just then joyfully entering into a *union libre* with Jean-Paul Sartre (though she too would have preferred to marry him). Stead was not a 'New Woman'. To her, it was not marriage that represented a form of female bondage; it was spinsterhood. And rationally, she was quite right: the 'free woman' risked a great deal. Rebecca West, who had had an affair with the already-married

H. G. Wells and became pregnant by him, had learned the hard way that an unmarried mother was 'the most outcast thing on earth'.[5] Christina Stead would always firmly hold the view that committed love (ideally marriage) was a wonderful liberation for women.

Marriage is an all-important goal for Stead's young women. Near the end of *For Love Alone*, Teresa, now living with James Quick, looks out of the train window and realises that her struggles have ended, that she has 'reached the gates of the world', and that 'the first day lay before her'. And at the end of *Letty Fox*, Letty, who has finally found a husband, declares:

> It's a question of getting through life which is quite a siege, with some self-respect. Before I was married I had none; now, I respect not only my present position, but also all the efforts I made, in every direction, to get here … The principal thing is, I got a start in life; and it's from now on. I have a freight. I cast off, the journey has begun.

Before the happy couple left London, Blech took Stead's female friends to a final celebratory dinner in Soho. Stead finished up at the office on Wednesday, 13 February, with one day to shop and pack. She and Florence made a brisk excursion through the snow to buy her an evening dress. On Friday, 15 February, at 11 am, the honeymooners left London on the luxurious *Golden Arrow*.

They stayed at the Hôtel de l'Aigle Noir in Fontainebleau, a former private residence with a grand entrance court. It was across the road from the palace, the country residence of the kings of France and Napoleon's favourite domicile. From there the Black Eagle had set off, incognito, for the island of Elba.

Mid February. Fontainebleau was covered in snow, under a radiant sun. The forest was half hidden in a ghostly mist and the palace fountains had snap-frozen in mid fall. The 'ice world' was like a fairytale stage décor; it left a powerful impression on Stead, who made it the setting for a passionate episode in *The Beauties and Furies*. Her fictional honeymooners take a room in the Hotel of the Black Eagle and walk in the frozen palace grounds.

It was probably on Sunday that Blech and Stead took a bus through the forest to the mediaeval town of Moret. Like the fictional honeymooners, Oliver and Elvira, they wandered past the ruined abbey and 'improbably romantic houses' arm in arm, smiling into each other's eyes. 'They were so in love that afternoon that they returned from Moret by taxi and pulled down the blinds to stop even the winter sun from coming into their room.'[6]

'This is your feast of life beginning, your new adolescence,' Oliver tells Elvira, in *The Beauties*. 'You will not miss any nights now: every one will be gemmy with bright lights and loving eyes and stars and kisses.' Autobiography has crept into the fiction where it does not belong: the fictional Elvira Western, married for the past seven years, has not been deprived of loving eyes and kisses. It was Stead herself who had been missing out on these; and although Oliver is modelled partly on Keith Duncan, in this scene he sounds very like the exuberant William Blech.

Christina Stead had had to wait until she was twenty-six and a half before she finally experienced 'the night of the senses'.[7] *Her* imprisonment (as she saw it) had lasted twelve and a half years. Later, Christina would say that their 'anniversary' was 17 February (though since she and William liked to combine it with a Valentine's Party, it came to be 14 February).[8] This must mean that though they arrived in Fontainebleau on the Friday evening, they did not actually make love until Sunday, 17 February.

Emotions probably ran high. Stead was deeply in love with William Blech; but she was sleeping with another woman's husband, and the risk she ran should not be underestimated. And if Blech had not fully realised the enormity of his responsibility before, he must have realised it then. He must have dreaded the anguish ahead, the inevitable confrontations with Mollie. In *For Love Alone*, when the married James Quick eventually has his precious Teresa in his arms all night, he moans in his sleep and weeps, foreseeing that 'there was no solution but a bitter one'.

Christina Stead had expected to love Paris. She did. Snow lay piled under the trees and blocks of ice floated on the Seine, but the cafés were full, their terraces glassed-in against the cold, and their stoves burning bright. She loved the old apartment houses, with their ornamentation in stone and iron, and the grand and imposing boulevards. The people all seemed chic. Stead would capture her poetic first impressions of Paris in *The Beauties and Furies*, which pays tribute to that 'garden of lovers, joy of youth, nest of revolution, city of the thrice-fired blood!'

Paris seemed to her a wonderful place to be a woman. On her first morning there, she and Blech were having breakfast at the Lutétia in the Latin Quarter when three men and a woman came in. The woman was plain and spinsterish, but Stead was struck by the gallant way the men behaved towards her and by the woman's grace and confidence. She concluded that French males seemed to know how to bring out the charm in every woman, however lacking she might be in conventional beauty. This, for the daughter of David Stead, was a revelation.

Wilhelm treated her with great chivalry: she found herself being 'fed, sunned, dressed in grand chic, petted, educated, loved, indulged, taken (intelligently) all over Paris, musiced, champagned, cabareted, zooed'.[9]

'My beloved is coming back from London tomorrow evening,' she wrote to a Watson's Bay acquaintance, Nellie Molyneux, at the end of her first week in Paris. 'I must go and have my hair waved, or else buy some flowers to put in the salle à manger.' She was revelling in being the wife—a role she had feared she might never have the opportunity to play.

> He is a ridiculous person, but how lovely!—He would first of all go to London for a week, for he has a lot of business to transact; then he decided he could do it in four days, then in three, then he said he would return to me on Sunday, but now he rings me this morning that he will come back tomorrow at midday, and he only left yesterday at midday! He is most kind to me, and loves me very much: it is surprising to me and I am not used to such a romance, but I am really very happy.[10]

Stead, who would never regard herself as worthy of love, looked upon her happiness with grateful wonder. In early April, she wrote to Nellie again, and this time she pretended to be complaining about her lot:

> I never get any opportunity to do any exploring by myself—I have seen some parts of Paris inside-out, but always under the wing of Mr. Blech, who is a marvellous raconteur, rapporteur—a great memory and ingenuity and enthusiasm—and who will not leave my side for even two hours. I was never so lived with in my life: the result is that everything rushes past me in a dream—anecdotes, histories, tableaux, epigrams, dramas, obscenities: I see nothing with my own eyes. Mr. Blech also cannot stand still: he is the prince of intermittent vulcans: the only way I can appreciate a thing … is to hang over it for an hour, mope, mingle and maunder in an epileptic state which would give him the yellow jaunder if such should be his fate … Well,

it is only by appealing to his most powerful emotions that I can get him
to stand still for one minute to look at the Sainte-Chapelle, the Bridge of
St. Geneviève, the Sacré Coeur or the river Seine as it softly floweth. After
one minute of standing stock still in the name of love, fatherhood and
Paradise, he bears me onward, while I am left with one-sixtieth of a vision.

She added happily: 'You hear the lover's complaint; the troubles of a person
too happily husbanded, garnered, threshed out and shot into a sack in the
best season of twenty-six years.' She was jubilating in her metamorphosis
from the raw Australian-grown product into a highly polished 'Parisienne'.
And if we stretch the metaphor a little (as she probably intended), it
seems she was enjoying her sex life.

But her complaints were not entirely ironical. She *was* feeling rather
overwhelmed by her new life. Two of the young women in her fiction,
Teresa in *For Love Alone* and Emily Wilkes, in *I'm Dying Laughing*, have
whirlwind courtships, and both are slightly uneasy about their new
happiness. Emily tries to explain this to her husband Stephen:

'I guess I'm not happy living the perfect romance,' she said to him; 'it's my
training; it's too good; I'm an unbeliever; how can it happen to Emily the
Dope?'

'But it can. You'll get used to it. You'll learn.'

He began to talk about their future—we'll do this, we'll try that, we
won't have any children at first; I have a daughter and that's enough. I'll take
you to the best hairdressers and *couturières*, we'll get rid of your freckles,
if you like. On the way back to the hotel, he bought her a large box of
chocolates.

He did everything with such gaiety, such inner and outward grace, she
felt like a pleased child and yet she did not quite like it.

'It's because I'm used to the battle of life,' she said to herself.

In those first years in Paris, very much in love, Christina Stead was the
happiest she would ever be. But she knew better than most people that
happiness is a highly precarious state. The shadow side of love is fear of its
loss; she would always feel the tug of these tensions.

At first they rented a small apartment in the rue Mesnil, near the Place Victor Hugo, a fifteen-minute walk from the Champs-Elysées and a short bus trip to the office at No. 9, Boulevard Haussmann. The American & Foreign Discount Corporation, as it was called, was associated with the Travelers' Bank, but ten minutes away by foot. Stead enjoyed walking past the exclusive fashion houses—Cartier, Worth, Paquin, Houbigant.

The Travelers' Bank, a private American bank, speculated on the foreign exchange market and dealt in securities on the stock and commodities markets. Patronised by wealthy South Americans, English and French aristocracy, and playboys and gamblers from around the world, its greatest asset was its Managing Director, Bertrand Coles Neidecker, known to his friends as Peter Neidecker. A handsome man, with irresistible charm, he was 'a free and easy, devil-may-care chap', a gambler by nature, who revelled in risk and adventure. Yet somehow people instinctively trusted him. During the war, when he was in the American Air Force in France, he made money by selling American telephone books to Germans wanting to know the addresses of relatives in New York so they could write to them for money. In 1923, knowing nothing about banking, he had opened the bank in Paris, initially getting it off the ground by giving exceptionally good rates of exchange to American soldiers. Now it was a thriving family business, with Peter's two brothers, Aubrey and George, as nominal co-directors.

The working day began for Blech and Stead at 10 am and ended soon after 8 pm when the New York Stock Exchange closed (at 3 pm New York time). Lunch was usually a leisurely two hours; occasionally, in the late afternoon, they would go out again for a hot chocolate or a glass of port. Stead, as secretary, typed letters in French and English and sometimes worked at the cable switchboard, telegraphing transfers to New York. Unlike Blech's, her workload was light, and after the first few days, when she conscientiously looked around for more work, she used her free time for personal letters, making notes and writing. Peter Neidecker, aware that she was using bank time in this way, appears to have been quite lenient. His attitude is likely to have been that of Jules Bertillon, his fictional counterpart in *House of All Nations*, who admires successful writers just as he admires successful bankers—as talented con people. For Bertillon, art, like banking, is a comfortable way to get oneself fed by the rest of humanity: 'a rather delicate little trick for getting jam'. The price of Neidecker's indulgence towards Stead was the hard work he extracted from Blech.

In the evenings they frequented the artist-and-expatriate cafés on the Left Bank—the Dôme, the Coupole or the Select on the Boulevard du Montparnasse. After some months they moved to the Left Bank themselves, renting a flat near the Panthéon. Stead loved the French cafés with their shining nickel and brass bars and cheery waiters. They were, she quickly realised, ideal loitering places for a writer wanting to know more about the lives of Parisians. She was convinced that it was no coincidence that in Germany, France and Austria, all famed for their culture, the café was a central focus of artistic and literary life.

They rapidly got to know people: Blech was infinitely gregarious. Despite their admiration for the French, most of their friends were Americans—often of European descent. In their two worlds, financial and cultural, they straddled the Atlantic.

Many of their friends eventually would work their way into Stead's fiction. Samuel Putnam lived just near the Dôme and supported his wife and 3-year-old son by translating from French, Portuguese, Italian and Spanish for a Chicago publisher.[11] With Ezra Pound (whose views were becoming uncomfortably 'pre-fascist'), Putnam edited the *New Review*, a quarterly published in Paris and distributed in New York, which reported on European and American literature, arts, radio, cinema and photography. Cocteau, Ford Madox Ford, James Farrell, Boris Pasternak, Beckett and Henry Miller all appeared in the magazine. Sam Putnam was more immersed in Parisian bohemia than most of their friends and Stead enjoyed the stories he told. One evening, a year or two previously, Sam and Riva Putnam had given a party for Jean Cocteau and Ezra Pound at the Café de l'Odéon; a fight broke out in the homosexual contingent; one hit another with his stiletto heel; another American friend (Eric Townsend) intervened, braining the aggressor with a carafe. Stead noted the details in her diary.

Eric Townsend was a wealthy loafer from Baltimore in his early forties, who spent his days drinking on the *terrasse* of the Deux Magots and lived off cheques sent from home. While other Americans were talking about the stock exchange, the daily *Herald-Tribune* crossword puzzle or places to eat, the inebriated Townsend would tell Stead wonderful stories, most of them risqué. (She often missed the point.) Slightly deaf, he spoke in a low 'threadbare voice' she called 'Prospero's whisper' and paused only to dip his moustache into his Pernod. Stead was to model several minor characters in her fiction on Townsend.[12]

Another eccentric friend, who lived partly in Paris and partly in New York and worked at times for the Travelers' Bank, was Frederick Sard, a brilliant, unstable character, 'a great show off'. He would make vast quantities of money and live the 'high life like a sheik', then lose it all.[13] A Marxist, he believed, like Blech, that Russia offered the salvation of the world. Like Marpurgo, his fictional counterpart in *The Beauties and Furies*, he was a lover of music and widely read, expressing himself in tortuous phrases.

Surrounded by voluble people, Stead prided herself on being 'that precious thing; a good listener'.[14] One of her café acquaintances, she told Gwen, was a handsome Jewish woman of Spanish origin, Rhoda de Pinto.

> She spends the hours telling me all about her lovers, of which there has been a large number: as I cannot riposte with tales about mine, I simply listen and acquire an enormous stock of information about other people's history: which is a talent one polishes to a high degree in Paris.

But there was an art to drawing people out:

> Don't think it is easy to be a good listener: if you let the person spill the beans too early, she will have a grudge against you for a few days, feeling that you encouraged her to give herself away. Don't imagine I try to be a clever kid, but the fact is something takes people here: they will divulge their life histories within half an hour of meeting a person: a café has an 'Open Sesame' effect.[15]

Stead was always making notes: she wrote down striking anecdotes, jokes, snatches of dialogue in French or English; she copied out phrases from political screeds that appeared on the hoardings. Letters from friends and family were chronologically filed in manila folders (a different dossier on each person); she cut out interesting newspaper items. The stuff of fiction was life itself. Like her character Marpurgo, she sniffed up details 'with the animal delight of a dog reconnoitring fenceposts'.

She saw herself as a word-stringer only on paper, and was hugely impressed by the verbal skills of the French. 'In the cultured French circles, the ability to spin words, to reverse, invert, pervert and controvert ideas and to divine character makes every foreigner sit back in surprised (and often ashamed) silence.'[16]

Not every foreigner sat back in silence. Not William Blech. At first, Stead herself was held back, if the conversation was in French, by her self-consciousness about her accent and grammar. 'Willy, on the other hand, blunders gaily ahead, raises and lowers his voice dramatically, smiles seraphically, and is radiantly successful, sans grammar, sans accent—but with a genius for expression which is his very particular talent.'[17] She was unduly shy about her own French: she wrote French well from schooldays and soon spoke it fluently, with only a light accent. She had a talent for languages: over the years she would learn quite good German and an impressive smattering of Russian, Italian and Yiddish.

Expatriate artists, particularly Americans and white Russians, formed a large and visible presence in Paris in the 1920s. The city was rivalled only by Berlin as the literary and artistic capital of Europe. In the autumn 1928 issue of *Transition*, displayed in the bookshops when Stead and Blech arrived, various American expatriates explained why they chose to live in Europe. They spoke of American puritanism, the repressive work ethic, the tastelessness of American mass culture, subservience to the god-dollar and indifference to the spirit and intellect. Gertrude Stein declared:

> America is now early Victorian very early Victorian, she is a rich and well nourished home but not a place to work. Your parents' home is never a place to work it is a nice place to be brought up in.

The anti-realism, irrationalism and experimentation that had been sweeping Europe since the war were now finding their expression in English language and literature. In Paris, James Joyce and Gertrude Stein were the doyens of modernism: Joyce's 'Work in Progress' regularly appeared in *Transition*. His friend and fellow countryman, Samuel Beckett, was in his early twenties and just starting out as a writer in Paris.

By the time Stead and Blech arrived, at the tail end of the period of expatriate euphoria, Ezra Pound, Hemingway and F. Scott Fitzgerald had left and Gertrude Stein no longer held her salon, though she and Alice B. Toklas still lived in the rue de Fleurus. But the poet Natalie Barney still held a Friday afternoon salon in her rue Jacob apartment, where French and American writers could meet over tea and cakes. Samuel Putnam, a regular visitor, relished the heady atmosphere of wit and abandon there. (William Carlos Williams was amazed by the sight of Barney and her lesbian friends dancing by moonlight around the temple of Eros she had erected in the garden.[18]) Janet Flanner continued to link New York and Paris with her fortnightly 'Letters from Paris', published in the *New Yorker*.

The many 'little magazines', which published experimental work that would not normally find an outlet elsewhere, were badly affected by the devaluation of the dollar later that year. In most cases they folded. The most important, *Transition*, survived for another decade. Proclaiming the 'Revolution of the Word', it promoted all that was new in the arts. Founded in 1926 by Eugène Jolas, an American citizen brought up in France, the quarterly was filled with discussion of the current 'isms': German Expressionism, Dadaism, Surrealism, Vorticism, Futurism. Joyce and Stein featured regularly, alongside translations of André Breton, Thomas Mann and Kafka. Stead and Blech followed the *Transition* debates with interest.

An important focal point for expatriate writers was Sylvia Beach's English-language bookstore, Shakespeare & Company, at No. 12 rue de l'Odéon, in the sixth *arrondissement*. Neat and girlish-looking in her severely tailored suits, Beach was a modest, helpful presence. Her greatest claim to fame was to have published *Ulysses*, in 1922, after it had been refused by English and American publishers. The book was still banned in English-speaking countries, so that tourists and expatriates thronged to buy it, hoping to smuggle it back past Dover and New York customs officials. The Continent was less censorious: a German translation had appeared in 1927 and the French translation, *Ulysse*, appeared in February 1929, the month Blech and Stead arrived in Paris. Because other books banned in English-speaking countries were available at Shakespeare & Company—the unexpurgated Florence edition of *Lady Chatterley's Lover*, for example, and Radclyffe Hall's 1929 lesbian novel *Well of Loneliness*— Sylvia Beach had developed a reputation she did not care for, as a promoter of eroticism. In fact, her bookshop merely reflected the greater liberalism of French culture.

It would be Sylvia Beach to whom William Blech turned early in 1930, asking for her opinion on another decidedly experimental novel by an expatriate Anglo-Saxon—Christina Stead's *Seven Poor Men of Sydney*.

Coming from a Sydney not yet transformed by European immigration, Stead had never seen anything like the range of foods available in Paris.

She loved to go shopping, filling her canvas bag with a *baguette*, Russian herrings, halva and exotic salads. She and Blech bought cheap, sweet white Burgundy from a dark cellar in their street. Her teetotalling upbringing was now the distant past.

Blech, only 5'3½" and inclined to put on weight, had to watch his diet. He was a very moderate drinker, but he did love food. His real foible was 'cawfee', as he called it: as many as thirty cups a day. Stead, encouraged by Blech, was trying to put on weight—hardly a chore in a place where for a mere Fr. 1.60 she could have a coffee and a large slice of *tarte aux pommes*. She was drinking abundant quantities of sterilised milk, and eating bananas, cakes and cream. Eric Townsend recommended a 'disgusting drink' guaranteed to fatten her up at the rate of four pounds a week: a bar of chocolate, a glass of milk and one raw egg, mixed together.

Paris also had an openness about sex that was often shocking for sheltered expatriate women from puritanical English-speaking cultures. But Christina Stead prided herself on casting off the vestiges of her repressive upbringing as rapidly as possible. She appears not to have flinched at the obscenity in *Ulysses*, and was contemptuous of the 'erudite customs officials' in Britain, America and Australia who placed the book on the censored list. When Malila Slade, an Australian friend of Florence James, contacted her in Paris in May 1930, Stead took her to the Casino de Paris in Montmartre (where the black dancer and singer Josephine Baker used to perform), and though her companion was unable to understand the French jokes, Stead found the spectacle of naked dancing girls 'really very gratifying'.[19] In *The Beauties and Furies*, Elvira goes to the *Folies Bergère* and comments that the 'stageful of beautiful naked young girls, dark, with nipples like raspberries … satisfied you like a good French dinner'. From an early age Stead saw herself as a sexual libertarian.

William Blech could not have expected his wife or mother, now living in Paris too, to welcome Christina Stead's presence in that city—and they did not. Mollie Blech's wrath was directed less at her unfaithful husband than at the 'other woman'. As a little girl of eight, Ruth Blech learnt never to utter Christina's name in front of her mother. And the situation never changed. When Ruth married, in 1953, her husband was warned never to refer to a certain person in Mollie's presence.[20]

Nobody could have anticipated the tragic impasse. Who would have imagined that for twenty-three years Mollie Blech would refuse to grant a divorce? Happiness had come Stead's way at last, but it had a sting in its tail. Occasionally she had the nagging and dismal feeling that she had still not quite managed to secure a husband.

Within their first few weeks in Paris, William Blech introduced Stead to his mother. It was to be anticipated that Rosa Blech, who was very fond of her daughter-in-law and grand-daughter, would not warm to this plain and awkward outsider, this *shiksa* from Australia. Her son ignored the undercurrent of hostility: by early June he was making arrangements for his mother to live in the room next to their apartment and to share meals. Stead, aware of his strong sense of family loyalty, did not feel she could object, but she commented warily to Gwen Walker-Smith:

> Mrs. Blech is a tiny worrying little body, who knows three or four languages (like every blessed Jew I ever met) and is unhappy when she cannot live on the fat and heavy Jewish fare.

She was painfully conscious that Rosa Blech thought her plain, and she suffered from comparison with Mollie. Once, after she had had her hair set badly, she hung back from visiting Rosa, telling Gwen: 'I feel an oddity and I have to go and see Bill's mother who is a charming little person, but has a small head full of private comment, so that I dress up for her while appearing nonchalant.' This was a rare admission: Stead's letters home rarely so much as hinted at the domestic tensions in her life.

Fortunately for Stead, Blech's plan to have his mother live next door fell through on this occasion. Rosa, only sixty, preferred her independence. She thought she might settle in the spa town of Baden Baden in south-west Germany, not far from the French border. In the meantime, she travelled to Riga, her city of birth, to visit relatives.

Letty Fox, written some thirteen years later, gives a good impression of the tensions between the women in William Blech's entourage. Grandmother Fox, closely drawn from Rosa Blech, calls Persia (her son's companion) *die Konkubine*. Whether or not Mrs Blech senior ever applied this unpleasant epithet to Christina, she certainly spoke of her to Mollie and Ruth as *die Schöne* (the beauty), in a tone of lacerating irony.

In late June there was a family crisis when Mollie Blech, dismayed by the turn of events, talked of returning to the United States with Ruth. Stead wrote to Gwen Walker-Smith:

As things are now, it looks as though we must think of going to the States as soon as it can be managed. Wilhelm's little girl is going there with her mother, and Wilhelm is very devoted to her. She is a beautiful and charming little girl, very intelligent with good manners, gay and spoilt in the best way, that is, she is not cranky, but she is uninjured by hardship or bad manners. Her mother is a beautiful woman and has excellent manners, and a very good intelligence.

Only to Florence James did Christina confide her anxiety and resentment. She had no desire to go to the States quite yet; she wanted to immerse herself in French life. But she was not in a position to protest. She felt sure that Mollie Blech, knowing that William would want to be near his daughter, hoped to shake off his Australian mistress by returning to New York. As it happened, Mollie changed her mind and she and Ruth stayed on in Paris.

Stead was very good with young children, but she wisely stayed in the background where Ruth was concerned. William would visit Ruth at Mollie's flat or he would call and take her out—to the zoo, the cinema, a museum. Sometimes he took along 10-year-old Nadine Lewin, the daughter of their Russian-born American friend Lina Lewin, a widow. Nadine recalls that as a young girl she found Christina quite delightful: amusingly eccentric, generous to a fault and a wonderful storyteller.[21]

Stead had fulfilled both her youthful dreams: to be in Europe and to have a loving companion. If ever she had hesitated, that year in Paris, she fell deeply in love with William Blech. There was so much she admired about him: his energy and curiosity, wide-ranging culture and flow of words, his affectionate sociability, his cosmopolitanism, his political commitment.

Heavens, what a Niagara of energy from morning till night: he gets up at eight in the morning, he works, discourses, reads, finds situations for his friends, writes, attends to everything with vivid interest, gets home at midnight, refuses to go to bed until 1.30 or 2.00 because he must read (I generally give up the ghost at 1.30 or thereabouts)—seven days he does this, the eighth day he perishes in his tracks, and we go to bed at 9 p.m. and I heave a great sigh and fall straight asleep (as you can guess). Girl, what a life! But what fun![22]

His friends all use the same expression: Blech's knowledge was 'encyclopaedic'. Nothing was too obscure or trivial for his lively curiosity. Stead was moved to discover that he remembered every detail she ever told him about her family and friends in Australia.

Blech had a beautiful voice, resonant and modulated. A skilled mimic, he would always be performing 'private theatricals'—impersonating, 'in far-reaching tones', characters like Stonewall Jackson, Abraham Lincoln, Alexander Hamilton or Benjamin Disraeli. Stead sometimes worried about what the neighbours might think, but it was 'very good fun'. The element of inventive play, the laughter that she had enjoyed as a child, had come back into her life. She and Bill shared a keen sense of the absurd; they took delight in jokes, silly stories and word games. Each knew how to make the other laugh.

Stead was fiercely proud of her 'small Vesuvius', but there was something else too—something to which she was not at all accustomed. Bill, that soft-eyed, pale-faced man, brought out an extraordinary tenderness in her. There was something childlike and vulnerable about Blech's appearance. No beauty, he was short and plump, with podgy hands. His large brown eyes were set in an unusually white, translucent face; when he was tired he looked green. His dark brown hair was already thinning; his round head sat sturdily on his square shoulders. When he was speaking seriously, his expression was 'earnest, devoted and saddened', leading Stead to remark in her diary: 'Due to his having no hard lines, Bill can look extremely piteous and sorrowful.' Because he did not like spending money on himself, his clothes often looked shabby, frayed, slightly ill-fitting. Whenever he lost weight, his suits became too big for him, accentuating his smallness. When he was anxious or excited, he would pace up and down, twisting his handkerchief into knots and talking to himself.

At weekends, they would take a tram to the countrified outer suburbs and go for long walks. Blech loved to walk, and Stead was also a good walker. Sometimes they took a train out of Paris—to Chartres, Nancy, Burgundy, the Loire Valley. If they were lucky enough to find some 'true sun' (rather than 'the pallid silvery northern variety'), the Australian was delighted. In July, on a brief trip to Bordeaux and Tours, 'Wilhelm's thick white skin' turned light brown. Stead thought this wonderful.[23]

Blech was passionate about music, but he and Stead found themselves going more to the cinema than to concerts: they saw all the new French films as they appeared. The 'talkies' were the new art form, and French cinema—with Jean Renoir, Marcel Carné and René Clair as directors—was impressive. Stead was particularly interested in the use of dream technique and the presentation of the unconscious. Always partial to horror stories, she savoured every minute of *Caligari* and *The Fall of the House of Usher*.

'We are a model ménage,' she told Gwen. 'We live in each other's company from 12 midnight to 12 midnight ... The funny thing is, I am getting more and more used to it: it is always a deeper pleasure—and of course, when he has to go away for a couple of days, and he comes back, we feel as if we had really been separated for months.'

Blech often went on business trips to Rouen, London, Antwerp, Bruges, Ghent. In September, when he went to Germany to meet his mother in Berlin and help her settle into Baden Baden, Stead was truly envious. She had steeped herself, during her adolescence, in translations of Goethe, Schiller, Theodor Storm and Nietzsche; now she was impatient to experience the culture across the Rhine for herself. Berlin, famous for its opera (Brecht and Kurt Weill had just written *The Threepenny Opera*), avant-garde theatre, jazz cabarets and beer Kneipen, was particularly enticing.

Yet the Germans brought out Blech's penchant for caricature. Berlin, he wrote to her, was 'the elephant's testicles'. In Berlin, 'endless shaved heads and 3-ply necks ogle in heavy jazz rhythms at blonde girls'. The descriptions in his letters and the 'recitals' on his return were so colourful that Stead was able to describe Germany to Gwen as if she had been there herself:

> Berlin is the centre of glass-buildings, futurismus, post-futurismus, music, gaiety, night-life, brilliance, heavy philosophy, Jewish genius, strange finance, revolving post-Reinhardt theatres, passionate ideations, heavy Teutonic fantasy, goose-step culture, reverberate beliefs, negations, assertions—of Nature, Sex and Freudianism, Jungism, Adlerism, of Sex, Pollution and Nature, of Sunlight Cures, Heavy Affirmations, the Cult of Cults. It is the hot potatoes. It is Sin: it is the Gaiety. It is the elephant's pyjamas ... Nevertheless everyone agrees there is one drawback to Germany—the Germans: the hard-headed cultivator of Modernismus wears a shaved head, glasses, a 3-ply neck and a tremendous belly.

We recognise the future author of *The Salzburg Tales*—the delight in irony, the heaping up of detail and imagery, the exorbitant lists, the love of parody. The letter also shows how much Stead was influenced by her companion. His humour and ability to bring a scene or a person to life in an avalanche of vivid and inspired images were equal to Stead's own. She would always be a scavenger. If she liked something someone had written or said, she would somehow work it into her own writing.

Later in September, Blech was in London at the time of a sterling scare. He had seen it coming and sold a group of shares short, but London brokers were not keen to do business just then and he decided to leave early. He just had time to take Florence James to *Juno & the Paycock*, Sean O'Casey's play at the Abbey Theatre. He gave her the tickets he had booked for *The Apple Cart*, Shaw's satire on the monarchy, currently causing a sensation in London. Blech's visits were 'bright spots', Florence told her mother.

Blech always made time to visit the London bookshops, and he would return to Paris with a pile of novels and books on economics. Alf Hurst had commissioned him to write a book on grain markets in Britain, which Blech was working on in the evenings. In September, Blech brought Stead *A House is Built*, a novel by two Australians writing in collaboration: Marjorie Barnard and Flora Eldershaw. Stead already knew of Marjorie Barnard, who had attended Sydney Girls' High five years before her, and the novel's success in Australia and England must have acted as a spur.

While Blech was away, Stead saw *Tosca*, *Cavalleria Rusticana* and *The Barber of Seville* at the Opéra Comique, which seemed to her to have perfected traditional stagecraft. 'I only go to the theatre when he is away,' she told Gwen, 'for we have plenty to do when he is here.' On other evenings she would stay in the office and work on her novel *Seven Poor Men* until late, or go home, cook supper and read. She was reading the latest Soviet novels, which Blech and his friends admired. And she was very impressed with Thomas Mann, awarded the Nobel Prize for Literature that year. 'If you really want to make life insipid, destroy modern literature, and crack your brain, and enjoy it violently into the bargain, read *The Magic Mountain*.'

She read D. H. Lawrence for the first time that year, and thought him 'a marvellous man'. *Sons and Lovers*, Lawrence's autobiographical novel that portrayed his Oedipal relationship with his mother, would no doubt have made her reflect on her relationship with her father. In *For Love Alone*, the portrait of her own sexually charged adolescence bears unmistakable traces of Lawrence in vocabulary and imagery.

For Stead the greatest contemporary writer was James Joyce: his flamboyant gift of language was 'the most extraordinary imaginable'. Like Lawrence, Joyce had written an autobiographical novel about a difficult childhood and adolescence from which he emerged as an artist: these would be useful models when Stead came to writing *The Man Who Loved Children* a decade later. But it was *Ulysses* that impressed her most. She re-read it carefully, with the help of 'learned commentary', and appreciated its genius more than ever. Joyce's work-in-progress, published in *Transition*, needed to be read 'with a rhyming dictionary, an encyclopaedia, the grammars of ten languages, and an annotated "crib" ', she told Gwen, adding that the effort was well worth it. In 1932, when she was polishing *Seven Poor Men of Sydney*, she made the bold comment that there was 'no living writer in English ... not indebted to [Joyce's] methods and his vocabulary'.[24]

Not everyone shared her enthusiasm. D. H. Lawrence thought *Ulysses* obscene. Virginia Woolf described it as 'the scratching of pimples on the body of the bootboy at Claridge's'. (She and Leonard Woolf, who ran the Hogarth Press, were among those who declined to publish it.) Some Leftists, such as Blech, regarded *Ulysses* as an admirable mirror of the decay of capitalist civilisation; others condemned it as decadent and counter-revolutionary. Stead's early fiction is influenced by contemporary modernist writing, particularly Joyce. *Seven Poor Men of Sydney* and *The Beauties and Furies* make sudden shifts in tone and register. They also contain the modernist interest in dream and fantasy, references to Freudian psychoanalysis, frequent allusions to other literary works, and speculation about the nature of narrative itself. Critics of Stead's early work often felt compelled to make comparisons with Joyce. Stead had taken a very different path from those writers who stayed in Australia in the 1920s and 1930s, where 'dun-coloured' realism still reigned supreme.[25]

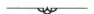

Then came 'Black Thursday', 24 October 1929, the Wall Street crash. It marked the beginning of a world economic crisis that first reached the banking centre of New York, then London, Vienna and Berlin, and was to last more than a decade. Many small investors lost everything; there were suicides among speculators. At first France, with its heavy stocks of gold, was not affected like Britain and America, though the crash immediately hit the Americans in France, whose dollars were devalued. The next few months saw many of these reluctantly head home. Others moved to the south, where prices were lower. Paris would be a less lively place for Stead and Blech in the years ahead.

On a business visit to London in mid November 1929, between the first and second act of *The Three Sisters*, William Blech pressed Florence James to return with him to Paris the following evening. Christina was going through a difficult patch, and she would appreciate having her closest friend with her just now.

For Florence, it meant throwing in her secretarial job at the ANZ Bank in London, but it seemed a good time for a holiday. She had just completed a shorthand course, her boyfriend was causing her anguish and Christina needed her.

The Channel crossing was unusually rough. William, a terrible traveller, could not wait to see the lights of Boulogne. He and Florence had dinner on the train and arrived at the Gare du Nord at 9 pm.

Florence had last seen Christina in February: a blissfully happy woman waving from the window of the *Golden Arrow*. She was nonplussed to find her 'shockingly thin'. In a letter from Paris, she told her mother that Christina had been 'really ill', with an 'inward chill'. She added: 'There have been more complications than I can recount in Wilhelm's domestic affairs—not in his and Christina's love for one another, I have never seen a more beautiful relation.'[26]

The truth was that Christina had just terminated a pregnancy. It had come at a bad time: she and Blech had had to move apart, since any hope of an equitable divorce arrangement was jeopardised by the prospect of Blech being charged with adultery. In the last weeks she had been living by herself, in delicate health and melancholy mood, in a modest hotel in the seventh *arrondissement*.

'I never felt the abortion was traumatic for Chris,' Florence James recalls, 'only a necessity, which she put behind her as quickly as possible.'[27] For Stead, the worst trauma was the domestic situation. She was beginning to wonder whether William really wanted a divorce. Pained by Mollie's unalleviated distress, he had told Mollie that Christina was about to take up a job in Geneva and disappear. Whatever the reason for the lie, it naturally rekindled Mollie's hopes. Christina was now terrified that William would decide to return to his family. Would he think that he had purchased her love too dearly, that it had been paid for with too much cruelty? Would he now be cruel to *her*?[28]

Later in life, she would recall with gratitude Eric Townsend's friendship during these forlorn weeks: he had visited her, brought her food and stayed to talk.[29] (Sadly, she would not recall Florence's sacrifices with equal gratitude.)

Florence could see that William was everything to Christina: 'her friends, her experiences came through him'. Nevertheless, she was surprised to discover the extent of Christina's insecurity. She saw that Blech had 'not painted the real picture' to Christina: he did not seem nearly as determined to divorce as he had originally made out. Not wanting to hurt either woman, he was stringing both along. 'His vacillation was something we couldn't have anticipated,' says Florence.[30]

The two friends shared a tiny double room in the Hôtel Royal Park—which, Florence told her mother, sounded much grander than it was. They ate in a nearby *brasserie*. For the first few days they mostly slept, talked and ate, with Christina working at the office for a few hours each afternoon. After some days, she had regained sufficient energy to take Florence to the Louvre, followed by lunch at the Dôme. They went to the *coiffeur* for a shampoo and set each. And on two or three evenings they went to the cinema.

Christina found the precariousness of her situation intensely painful, but she was not bitter. Among her papers are two unusually intimate diary entries, from 9 and 15 December 1929, which provide a revealing glimpse of her feelings at this time:

> Monday, December 9.
> Saw Eric yesterday, talked about Wilh. and meant to rise early this morning to go early to the office to see Wilh. but could not sleep—angry because Eric said Wilh. would die a beggar and a failure ... Got up, sat with quilt round me near window, saw dark clear sky, stars, suggestive closed facades of French houses, ashamed of fretting ... Fl. sympathetic, don't know why I am so wretchedly badhumored.

William had spent the weekend with Mollie and Ruth, and Christina, dreadfully afraid that he might be enjoying his weekend, had hardly slept. On Sunday, Eric Townsend had invited her to lunch and they had discussed William's personality. The conversation had left her very upset.

> Eric said to me:
> I understand Will, better than you because Will is like me, he will always be a good henchman, he needs someone to make him work: you are different ...

I was indignant, but I could not be angry, what is the use, I was his guest, also prejudiced, also Eric is unsympathetic, I feel a conscious maleness. I said:

It is not so, Wilh. is a brilliant man … If he hears people saying what you say … it depresses him, it does him no good. On the other hand, if he is praised and encouraged, he becomes very gay, exaggerated, but he does very good work.

Townsend retorted that she got on with Bill because she did not ask for much. The whole exchange had got under Stead's skin. On Monday morning, she felt terribly frustrated with herself and her situation.

Miss Wilh. at night with every kind of tenderness and lack … Encouraged myself in case I should find Wilh. not unhappy over his weekend (as it proved); recalled Tchechov's women who lose their lovers through empty lives, resolved to work, great energy to 'work,' but the usual lack.

When she arrived at the office, she found Blech working happily, enthusiastic about writing another book on economics—this time for Peter Neidecker. She herself was a tangle of conflicting emotions:

Told Wilh. about Eric's treachery and detraction, flushed with emotion, only letting off steam. Wilh. content with Mollie at present—a terrible pain to know it, I only hope for them to be unhappy whatever I say; as a result pained and upset. Wilh. started to sketch his book for Pete. We did 4 or 5 pages, Wilh. dictating at top speed, very facile and well-phrased, me making mistakes as usual, Wilh. putting in information which he learned when we were in Bordeaux, and so on—said: 'Wouldn't you wonder where I learned it all, you would never think I would remember all that!'

I said: 'No, you are a wonder, you are like a silkworm that keeps on spinning silk out of its inside.' He kissed me warmly.

She reassured him that those people who judged him had not 'one quarter of his passion, enthusiasm, talent or knowledge'. William left the office pleased with the pages he had written. Left alone, Stead thought about Mollie and wept. At home, she asked herself: 'Why am I so hideous? I would prefer she should be unhappy and lonely than that I should be.' She cried again.

By mid December, the time of the second diary entry, Florence James had returned to London and Stead had moved to the Hôtel du Danemark, close to the Jardin du Luxembourg. Blech had suggested the hotel so that he could see her when he visited his mother, who lived nearby. Rosa Blech had not stayed long in Baden Baden.

The hotel was old, run down and not very clean. The concierge, curious about Christina and her regular male visitor, called her alternately Madame and Mademoiselle. Christina was now sometimes calling Wilhelm 'Bill'.

> Feel much more cheerful as if Bill and I had somehow set up house again. B. says M. cannot sleep at night and I wonder if it is because I delay going to 'Geneva': nobody can be happy: I am just about as happy as possible at present, as I see Bill and have free time. The Montparnasse quarter suits me, not so lonely: had breakfast at Dôme, jam omelette and coffee: interesting rugged and sharp faces.

Threatened by the loss of Bill's love, she was conscious of being powerfully in love with him. Her diary is full of admiration for him. When Eric Townsend ('anti-semitic at heart, partly out of a shadowy kind of jealousy of Bill') provocatively suggested in conversation with Bill that Germany could do without its Jews, Bill argued 'with splendid and creative rage'. That evening Bill 'came home', and they had supper at an American bar near her hotel. He reminded the waiter of something he had forgotten to charge them for and Stead, 'very sentimental', almost cried at the 'perfect goodness of his heart'.

Stead's fiction, written later, suggests that she came to see all this in a different light. In *The Beauties and Furies* (1936) and *Letty Fox* (1946) Elvira and Persia both miscarry with intent; and both find themselves lying alone and in pain in a hotel room, while their lover is elsewhere, preoccupied with another woman. Elvira develops metritis. Feverish and unable to sleep, she tells Oliver reproachfully: 'You were away when I was in trouble.' In *Letty Fox*, Persia, Solander's mistress, is left to recover in an Antwerp hotel while Solander Fox is in Paris fussing over his wife. Oliver and Solander are both portrayed as chronic ditherers.

'On the female side, I am a little lonely,' Stead admitted.[31] She missed Florence. In Sydney she had hankered after male company; now she moved in a world of men: bankers, businessmen, artists—primarily friends of Bill. Her banking novel, *House of All Nations*, set in Paris in 1931–32, portrays this man's world: there is not one significant female character in its 800 pages. The women are background figures—wives, mistresses, daughters.

At Christmas the fountains were again frozen over. Stead found the general mood of gaiety, the millions of lights, the snow and rain exhilarating. Eric Townsend and his French girlfriend Suzanne invited them for a traditional turkey dinner.

Townsend aroused ambivalent emotions in Stead: she liked him and disliked him. He made her angry, yet she sought out his company. She rationalised this apparent contradiction to herself by saying that the study of personality was her private passion, and that as a writer, she needed to enter into the mind of people unlike herself. But there was clearly something else too. Her conversations with Townsend suggest a rivalrous sparring (each professing to know Bill better than the other) reminiscent of David Stead's claims to omniscience. In *The Man Who Loved Children*, Sam Pollit maddens his daughter Louisa by claiming that he always knows what she is thinking, or that they are one person:

> 'You will be all right, Looloo,' concluded Sam, kissing her good night. 'You are myself; I know you cannot go astray.'
> 'I won't be like you, Dad.'
> He laughed, 'You can't help it: you are myself.'

David Stead shared Pollit's inability to recognise other people as separate entities, with minds of their own. And it may well have been this colonising tendency that caused his eldest daughter to become so self-contained, secretive and private. It also left her with the desire to do to others what was done to herself: to try to clamber inside their skin, to control them by taking over their very voice. Fiction provided the perfect justification.

Stead projected herself as a serious and ambitious writer. In September 1929, after eight months in France, she told Gwen Walker-Smith, 'I am still struggling with a novel. If it comes through satisfactorily it ought to be saleable in Australia and I hope will make me a little money.' Yet interviewed in her old age, Stead would vehemently deny that she was ever ambitious. She even claimed that the entire impetus to publish *Seven Poor Men of Sydney* came from Bill, who allegedly took the manuscript to Sylvia Beach without her knowledge.

It is unlikely that Blech showed the manuscript to Sylvia Beach without telling Stead. He gave it to Beach early in 1930, several months before Stead left for Salzburg; Beach was encouraging and urged Stead to find an agent in London. A friend took on the job of hawking the manuscript round London. But publishers were not willing to risk such an unconventional first novel. In May 1930, one publisher rejected it on the grounds that it was 'fantastic and digressive', but said he would consider a revised version. Stead was bitterly disappointed but uncompromising, believing it 'impossible to revise it, and artistically a mistake to attempt it'. Blech did persuade her to revise several very clotted pages before submitting it to a second publisher. This was probably the Hogarth Press, for in late June Florence James wrote to her mother:

> I have been reading Christina's manuscript. It came back from the Hogarth Press with a little note that it was not their type of book. I doubt if she will get it published in London, it is so amazingly original and outspoken that only a very courageous firm could touch it. The ms. as it stands has a number of faults, but the thought behind and the prose are so uncommon and beautiful that I think Christina's literary gift one of the most amazing I have met.

By the time Stead returned from Salzburg in September, the manuscript was with a fourth publisher. She reported to Gwen that all were in agreement: 'it has power but is not very easily read'. American friends suggested she send them a copy of the manuscript so they could try New York publishers as well, but this would have involved typing the whole manuscript out again. Understandably, Stead hesitated.

Since no early draft of the novel survives, we do not know how different it was from the published version.[32] The novel depicted the struggles of young city workers in the depressed Sydney of the 1920s, and Florence James thinks that the Sydney setting was considered 'of too narrow an interest', but the main problem was likely to have been the way the novel juxtaposes conventional realism with the poetic and hallucinatory, which has always disconcerted readers. The characters are not yet the rounded portraits they would become in Stead's later fiction. She was a word-drunk young writer, and the novel contains some indulgent over-writing.

But it has a peculiar brilliance. The poetic exuberance of *Seven Poor Men*'s style has a James Joyce quality. Its description of stormy, moonlit Sydney nights and tormented, restless characters has something of Emily Brontë or Dostoevski. And certain haunted passages call to mind Poe or Baudelaire. In later years, the Australian critic Dorothy Green would comment that this first novel of Christina Stead's was a path-breaker in terms of Australian literature: 'It was *Seven Poor Men of Sydney*, rather than any early Patrick White novel, which broke free from kitchen-sink realism into the world of poetry, without losing touch with the ground.'[33] At the time of its publication, Australian critics were too intimidated by its eccentricity to realise the significance of its innovations.

With this first novel, Stead insisted that the characters were 'not actually drawn from life'; they were 'like most characters, crystallisations of various types of men and women'. In fact, there are aspects of herself in both Catherine and Michael. Tom Withers was inspired by Eric Townsend, her Paris friend. The only truly admirable character was Baruch Mendelssohn, modelled on Bill Blech.

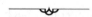

'I'm blessed if I can get down to another piece of work: I have half a dozen themes but no backbone.'[34] By the summer of 1930, Stead was feeling demoralised. Her domestic situation was as difficult and unresolved as ever: she was still living by herself in a hotel, with visits from Bill. Publishers had not shown much interest in her novel. At the Travelers' Bank, she had accumulated two years' worth of holiday, six weeks in all, and she was keen to go away somewhere. Sadly, it would have to be on her own. In August, Mollie Blech's mother was due to visit from the States, and Bill felt he had to be around. He had built up Mère Grossman as a powerful Jewish matriarch, who was crossing the Atlantic 'to fortify a wronged offspring'.[35] He persuaded Stead that it would be better if she left Paris while his mother-in-law was in town and suggested she go to the Salzburg Festival—a chance for her to experience Germanic culture at first hand.

Stead arrived in mid July and found Salzburg and its surroundings 'indescribably romantic'. In a rare handwritten letter (when she had a typewriter, she even typed postcards), she drew ornate little sketches of the local costume for Gwen, pointing out the lace, embroidery and colours.

The festival began on 1 August, with Hugo von Hofmannsthal's *Jedermann*, a modern re-working of the mediaeval English miracle play *Everyman*. Directed by Max Reinhardt, it was an open-air performance in front of the Cathedral. Stead took careful notes. She went on long walks by herself and on organised excursions to the surrounding lakes and border towns; she enjoyed the little puppet theatre in Salzburg (the first time she saw puppets), but she was lonely and anxious. It was the longest period she and Bill had been apart and his letters—brief, jovial and hastily penned—did not do much for her tranquillity of mind. 'Enjoy yourself without regard to money,' he told her paternally, 'and see if you can get in with a good crowd at the centre of Salzburg's life.' Another begins: 'Chris dear, pardon for a *very* hurried note. (Oh dear I will be late for the Duchess.)'[36] Stead had found the Alice in Wonderland joke amusing on previous occasions, but this time she must have wondered whether the Duchess was Bill's wife or his mother-in-law.

On 5 August, she told Gwen she was 'badly missing Wilhelm' and had almost decided to go home early, on 21 August—after Gluck's *Iphigenia in Aulis*. She said 'almost' because the decision was not entirely in her hands. Indeed, Blech wrote entreating her to keep to the original plan: she should leave Salzburg on 20 August, spend a week in Munich and arrive in Paris at the end of the month. 'Do please follow any dates as they will be the best all around.' She wrote that she was fed up with the constant rain and wet feet, but her hint fell upon deaf ears: 'Leave me to grapple with actions and obligations while you meditate the humid eternities in excelsis.'

Mollie, he wrote, was reproaching him for his 'hard' and 'inflexible' attitudes. He added: 'If she knew what my marriage to you will mean to me, she would be in a different state, so I treat her with jocular silence.' This was probably not entirely reassuring to Stead.

Evidently she was trying to sound cheerful, for in his letter of 19 August, Blech wrote: 'Awfully glad to hear that your many, many qualms have disappeared in Salzburg. Mountain air and absence from me is in all ways gut.'

Mollie and Ruth now planned to leave for the United States in late October. This time, Bill was not intending to follow—at least not immediately. 'I have begun a gentle search for lodgings for your good self pending lodgings for our good selves,' he told Stead, who had given up her hotel room to save money.

Blech's letters were bantering and loving, but they were neither intimate nor passionate. In his large, round, sloping hand full of emphatic underlinings, he joked that he wanted her happy and fat: 'Are you, or are you not spending the last fortnight in an orgy of fattening. Remember a skinny girl means <u>divorce</u>, a fat girl <u>perpetual love</u>.' The letter was signed: 'Heavy affection, Wilhelm.' In another, signed 'William James Cook', he declared: 'I love you, dirty little merino, and Watson's Bay waste wool refuse.'

Soon after her return to Paris, Stead went away again—possibly once more to remove herself from the scene of domestic crisis. This time—a rather surprising arrangement—she met Bill's mother at Aix-les-Bains and they spent a week on the Riviera. To Gwen she wrote warmly of the 'unmoderated colors and dazzling days' in Nice and Monte Carlo. The Mediterranean coast reminded her of Australia, without suffering from Australia's insularity. She would have liked to live there permanently—a view shared by many expatriates.

In November Stead went away yet again by herself—this time returning to Fontainebleau and the Hôtel de l'Aigle Noir. She was thinking of setting a romantic scene in this place and wanted to make notes, but it was a sad place to be—full of poignant memories. The town and forest were desolate under a heavy grey winter sky: it rained incessantly, the trees were naked and it was dark by 4 pm. There were no tourists—just soldiers from the artillery school. It was almost two years since their honeymoon sojourn there and Stead was still not married to the man who had first made love to her in that very hotel.

After attempting a walk through the forest early in the week and sitting for several hours on a wet tree trunk to read, she went back to the hotel and put herself to bed. She had caught a cold. Her mood was bleak.

'Fontainebleau is the only argument against communism,' she wrote to Gwen. 'It seems unlikely that anyone but a lord glutted with pride and riches would spend the money to build a thing so exquisite and ornate.' She added that it was a poor argument nonetheless—'a drop of grease in a fire'.

In Bill Blech's company, she had come to see herself as a communist sympathiser, and she tended to parrot his views. ('Wilhelm believes ... that next year the first serious blows will be felt by the capitalism of the world arrayed seriously for the first time against the successful communistic state of Russia. ... It is marvellous that Soviet Russia has put itself into a position to frighten the whole of Europe in so short a time since the revolution.') It was Blech's view that Australia, wracked with unemployment, should repudiate her debt from the Great War, and Stead tried to persuade her cousin of this:

> Australia got hooked into a war she didn't want and had nothing to do with: she lost a lot of youth and much money, and now when she has difficulty in paying her 'debt' she gets no thanks but hard words from the old country. Maybe you think it unpatriotic, but actually that is how most foreigners regard it: they regard the Empire as a sell, especially for the colonies which are sold.

Three years later, she was no longer the parrot; she had intelligently absorbed Blech's Marxist framework and made it her own. 'How does a small minority oppress a large majority?' asks Baruch in the novel, and both *Seven Poor Men* and *House of All Nations* go some way towards answering his question. Stead's first novel also dramatically takes up the torch for Australian independence from Britain. Just as young people need to be freed from parental bonds, so, the novel implies, Australians need to work out their own destiny without the interference of the old country.

At the same time, the creative characters in *Seven Poor Men* know they must break away from Australia and become 'wanderers'. They need to breathe a different air. Now that she was ensconced in the heart of Europe, Stead was more aware than ever of Australia's parochialism. She told her cousin, somewhat tactlessly, that a Sydney woman she met in Paris was 'all that there is of Australian, plus a strong accent, simple, colonial, unsophisticated'.

In an interview with the *Australian Women's Weekly* in 1935, soon after the publication of *Seven Poor Men*, Stead's ambivalent attitude towards Australia, both nostalgic and patronising, is striking:

> It is perhaps obvious that I have not forgotten Sydney during my absence— the climate, the importance of the Labor Movement in everyone's daily

life; the type of society which is near to being a one-class society, the importations into social and national life from England.

To me, of course, this Australian society, even as it stands, is much preferable to English society, hideous with its class divisions, evident even in the Labor Movement here.

... I may not return to Australia, but I am glad I sprang from that raw, fresh and unhistorical society.[37]

Leaving Australia and leaving her family had been the same thing, and there is a sense in which she conflated the two. *Seven Poor Men* depicts parents in an extremely negative light: Michael Bagenault is overjoyed when he discovers that the father whom he has often wished dead is *not* his father, and that he is illegitimate, gloriously fatherless.

Stead may well have thought that by travelling across the world, she too had cut the ties with her father. However, while her first novel must have hurt David Stead, it also owed him a considerable debt. Near the end of the narrative is an extraordinary speech by Kol Blount, a long monologue about the 'continent of mystery' they inhabit. A lyrical description of Australia in the dim anteglacial past, Australia as the undiscovered Terra Australis, Australia as the unconquered land of Aborigines, then Australia after white settlement, it brings to mind the enthusiastic David Stead and his stories about the country he loved.

That was the trouble: she still loved David Stead. His occasional letters, with their wonderful descriptions of nature, were a living reminder to Christina of her father's unusual powers of observation and talent for expression—gifts he had generously showered upon her in childhood. At some stage, she destroyed her father's letters. Two short extracts are all that remain. These she had cut out and pasted onto a sheet of paper, with other notes for an unpublished novel, *The Wraith and the Wanderer*. The first extract she used almost verbatim in the draft of her novel.

Thursday mg.

This morning before breakfast while clearing up the front path, I came across a most lovely example of the St. Andrew's Cross yeepi. It looked most beautiful. Do you remember it? A beautiful symmetrical concentric lined web, on a small scale, with the misty pearly cross on it, the spider splayed on the cross. The early mg. sun was shining through the dark meerschaum legs and the beaut. banded body—the web dotted with little beads of dew and tiny beads of insect stickfast. Dadpad.

The second extract is interesting for other reasons:

> Grand easterly gale blowing this morning. I have just been up to the Gap, but could not stop long because of the glare on the surf (I have dreadful trouble with the glare—much worse than it used to be. With thick, lowering conditions, such as to-day, the glare is much worse than in bright sunlight). It is a magnificent sight, looking out to sea—as far as one can see. I was thinking of you and wished so much that you could see it again, instead of being stuck in that stuffy rue Jean Bart, among those more than stuffy people.[38]

Was David Stead serious about 'stuffy rue Jean Bart'? Sixteen years before (when his family was stuck in stuffy Sydney), the same man had written ecstatic letters from Paris, full of the glories of the French capital. It was precisely this egotism—in the guise of concern—that Stead would depict in *The Man Who Loved Children*. Somehow, her father's experience was always more valid, more precious, than anyone else's.

David Stead was fifty-two now, and his eyes were troubling him. However, from all that distance, he still had the power to upset and irritate Christina, filling her with resentment and compassion.

'Overcote', in *The Salzburg Tales*, is a story by a 50-year-old public stenographer about her father—an atheist and a sentimental but mocking man. During the narrator's childhood, he took up with another woman, who was fifteen at the time. Now, as an older man, her father remains manipulative:

> We never go near our father … You can't forgive the things he does … He can write a good letter, too: but I can't read his letters any more, they are so touching, you almost begin to be sorry for him, and they are so insincere: he is all the time laughing up his sleeve at you if you come; and he cries if you stay away …

After two and a half years away, Stead was beginning to feel a stranger to the family. Her father's romance with Thistle Harris had resumed around the time Christina left Australia. Thistle, missing him badly, had written to David. This third time, they were not going to be put off. In 1930, Ada had moved out of Boongarre and gone to live with her cousin Rachel Davis, at The Entrance. She wrote to Christina less these days. David Stead and the girls wrote occasionally, but everyone was so 'ridiculously discreet' that Christina never had much real sense of what was going on.[39] She worried about her stepmother. And she was conscious that the younger children had acquired quite different personalities by now: she no longer knew them.

Interestingly, she cared a great deal about her image in the family's eyes. Christina admitted to her Aunt Florence her great propensity for tearing up letters. She told Gwen that she had written her Aunt Florence 'a very rubbishy letter from Bordeaux' that she hoped would go astray. 'I was hot, blinded, newly and very badly coiffed, tormented by peanutsellers and rugsellers.'

Far more upsetting than a plague of peanutsellers was to have her hair badly set. Though she believed that in Paris she had learnt to dress in a way that suited her build, and that this gave her new confidence, she was as painfully self-conscious as ever. In this respect too, David Stead's influence was not eradicated by mere distance.

———— ⚬ ————

At the beginning of 1931, Blech had found a pleasant modern apartment on the rue Jean Bart, near the Luxembourg Gardens and the Montparnasse cafés. After having lived apart for more than a year, he and Stead moved in together again. Christina was intensely relieved. Mollie and Ruth had made a temporary trip to the United States and were now living in the South of France.

With *Seven Poor Men of Sydney* doing the rounds of publishers, Stead had begun a novel loosely based on Keith Duncan. As indicated by its rather shrill title, *The Young Man Will Go Far*, she had lost nothing of her hostility. (Later, scarcely less sarcastic, it became *The Travelling Scholar*, then *The Beauties and Furies*.) Blech had seen Duncan on one of his trips to London, and Christina was able to report to her cousin: 'Keith Duncan … is still hanging on to various scholarships in London and expects to get others to take him to the States.'

The novel was abandoned, but remnants reveal it to be an early working of the material in *For Love Alone*. Oliver Gillybrand, a precursor to Jonathan Crow, is twenty-three, dark, poor and a 'new-minted bachelor of arts' at Sydney University. He goes for long walks with Sara, a young writer. Then he wins a travelling scholarship to England. They write to one another.

———— ⚬ ————

Early in 1931, *Seven Poor Men of Sydney* was conditionally accepted by Peter Davies, a 34-year-old London publisher. Having had a burst of success the previous year with Frederic Manning's novel *Her Privates We*, set on the Somme Front, Davies was partial to Australians. But his conditions were stringent: not only did he want Stead to revise the novel but he also wanted another novel from her *before* he published *Seven Poor Men*. The idea was to attract readers to the new author with a less unconventional book.

On a visit to Paris in March 1931, Davies arranged to meet Stead and Blech at Philippe's, an exclusive restaurant near their office. The long lunch was pleasant: Stead would remember that first meeting fondly. It was a moment for celebration: she had been writing with publication in mind since the age of twenty-one—eight years. She had been quietly determined, not impatient, but now she was anxious to be published. Stead would always be grateful to Peter Davies for taking her on as a young and unknown writer.

Davies struck her as extremely English, cultivated and kind: 'I am sure he has never offended anyone in the whole of his life.' His passion for literature was such that he appeared to be in the business more for love than money. His catalogue was 'a record of his personal tastes and fancies ... almost a profession of faith'.[40] She had vaguely heard of his connection with Peter Pan, but timidly refrained from broaching the subject at their first meeting.

Peter Llewellyn Davies, she would discover later, had had a tragic life and loathed his association with the boy who never grew up. Ever since J. M. Barrie's play had opened in London in 1904 and Barrie had claimed that all five Llewellyn Davies boys were models for his young hero, they had been a target of public curiosity. But it was the third son, Peter Pan's namesake, who was assumed to be the real model. At Eton he was teased incessantly about it. Fiction and fact had merged in a sinister way when their father and mother died in 1907 and 1910, leaving behind five young boys—now truly 'the lost boys'.

The eldest son, George, was killed in Flanders in 1915. Peter fought at the Somme and won the Military Cross in 1918, but came home with emphysema and severe depression. In 1921, the youngest brother, Michael, was drowned. When Peter Llewellyn Davies established his publishing house in 1926, it was under the less conspicuous name of 'Peter Davies Ltd', but the English newspapers had duly announced: 'Peter Pan

Becomes Publisher'. And when, on 5 April 1960, Peter Davies would end his life by throwing himself under a train in the London Underground, the event made headlines in English and American newspapers: 'The Boy Who Never Grew Up is Dead'.

In Philippe's that day, it was decided that Stead should aim to complete another book by the end of August—six months hence. Back in London, Peter Davies wrote to confirm the terms of the contract. He enclosed a £50 advance and a friendly note to Blech asking him to make sure that Miss Stead did not overwork.

When Gwen also admonished her cousin not to work too hard, Christina, touched, wrote a frivolous reply—on Café de Flore writing paper to emphasise her point:

> I really never do a stroke of work and Paris is a holiday ... Bill read your kindly adjuration to me, not to overwork myself, and he is busy laffing and holding his sides at the idea. He is more than rude!

Bill Blech added his round handwriting to the bottom of the letter:

> I note in your letter a touching solicitude for your poor Peg, with counsel for her not to overwork herself. Allow me, politely but firmly, to indicate that labour has been alien to her experience for three years. Piracy and not labour is the mechanism by which she extracts hard French cash. W.J.B.

'So Wilhelm says!' Christina scribbled in the margin.

Neither of them was exactly slothful. That particular Monday evening, they had arranged to meet after work, at 8 pm, at the Régence, a chess café opposite the Louvre. Blech, coming from the bank, got there late; the stock market was more than usually bearish that day. Stead, who had been writing in the office and forgotten the time, arrived later still. They lingered there a while listening to the classical quartet playing in the corner, observing the scene and making up stories about their fellow drinkers. Then they walked home in the rain, past the beds of red, white and blue hyacinths in the Tuileries gardens, across the Seine with its shimmering lights, to the rue Jean Bart, where 'Bill discoursed for about an hour and a half, as usual on everything under the sun'. Then they 'sallied forth again' and sat in the Flore until well past midnight. It was there that they wrote to Gwen.

After signing the contract with Peter Davies in April 1931, Stead set herself a punishing writing schedule of 4000 words a day, determined to finish the next novel by the end of August. She gave it the Nietzschean title of *The Wraith and the Wanderer*[41], and remaining fragments reveal it to be autobiographical material—material that Stead would re-work in later novels. Sally, the protagonist, sees herself as a 'clumsy ugly duckling'. As an adolescent, made restless by the sultry Sydney nights, she falls in love first with her English teacher then with a girl in her class and composes sonnets for both. Richard Lovelace is an early portrait of Oliver Fenton and Jonathan Crow.

'I am not a born writer,' she told Gwen, 'but I must say that when I have actually launched myself, I get the profoundest and most passionate satisfaction from writing.' She admitted that life itself never quite lived up to her expectations and made her 'fretful'.

The problem with life outside fiction was that it was beyond her control. There were frustrations, domestic worries. In March 1931 she made a business trip to London for the Travelers' Bank and stayed with Florence James, who wrote home: 'It has been a sheer delight having her here, I wish she could stay and we could set up house together again—she is the one out of all my friends that I know nothing can change.' But on Sunday night, the eve of her departure, Christina suffered what she thought was an appendix attack. On Monday morning, she looked ill and was nervous about making the Channel crossing. Florence persuaded her to see a doctor, who told her that she could manage the trip back, but that she should have her appendix removed as soon as possible.

On a second business trip in June, she lunched with Peter Davies in Soho and handed him four chapters of *The Wraith and the Wanderer*. And she had another attack. This time, the doctor thought the problem was probably 'nervous' and that the operation could wait. Stead notes in her diary around this time:

> Bill goes south next week and will return with family: says Mollie is becoming even softer and more dependent: find the situation distracting and will endeavour to make trip to Chartres for purposes of novel during their sojourn in Paris.
>
> Feel complete happiness with Bill and cannot understand (temperamentally) all these hitches, although endeavour to understand all

for sake of not questioning Bill. Have moments of acute despair remembering past and Mollie's refusal to free us.

It was not just the deadline for her novel that was causing her anxiety.

5

In the Phantom Buggy

JUNE 1931 – JULY 1935

S OME TIME IN 1931, Blech and Stead moved from their office in the
Boulevard Haussmann to the Travelers' Bank at No. 18 rue de la
Paix, where Stead, to her delight, was given a plushly furnished
office all to herself. From this vantage point she continued to make notes
on characters and conversations within the bank.

Our best insight into the Travelers' Bank comes from *House of All
Nations*, Stead's fourth book, begun in 1935, after she had left Paris. The
novel, set in 1931–32, has as its background the terrifying rise of Hitler,
the Japanese attack on Manchuria, the demise of Ramsay MacDonald's
Labour government in England and Hoover's overthrow by Roosevelt in
the United States. The financial world is in a state of alarm. Austria's largest
bank, the Creditanstalt, has collapsed; Germany is in severe economic
trouble; and in September 1931 England goes off the gold standard.

Later in life, Stead freely admitted that she had based the fictional Banque
Mercure on the Travelers' Bank, adding that it was as close a picture as she
could paint without running into libel problems. It was in 1931, during
those difficult times, that Peter Neidecker, the director, began to lose his
nerve. ('I want to scram,' says Jules Bertillon, his fictional counterpart.
'Now is the time to shut up shop.') But the bank was saved by a sudden
windfall and Neidecker, the passionate gambler, was able to pride himself

on making money in a dissolving world. Somehow his bank managed to
stay afloat when all around the financial titans were crashing. As Michel
Alphendéry (the character based on Bill Blech) puts it nervously:

> We're in the phantom buggy with him. We're riders of the storm: all of
> us together with him in this phantom bank, built on misery, shining out
> of mire, solid in an earthquake, soundproof in thunder, a living lightning
> conductor: an accident in capitalism.

In the novel, the Banque Mercure collapses at the end of 1932; the
Travelers' Bank would manage to keep going until July 1935.

------ ꙮ ------

Peter Neidecker's charming, roguish ways fascinated Stead. He would
appear in three of her early works, and Jules Bertillon, the director of the
bank in *House of All Nations*, is the most seductive character in her gallery
of rogues.[1] All three fictional portraits of Neidecker are fundamentally
warm, and yet morally and politically Neidecker stood for everything
Stead allegedly despised. What she and Blech admired were his bursts
of generosity, his boyish enthusiasm, his inventive mind and humorous
American language, his sheer recklessness. He was a man who would be
sure to 'go out looping the loop'.[2]

Throughout her life Stead would find herself haunted and obsessed
by certain individuals, who attracted and angered her at the same time.
They were the people on whom she based her major fictional characters,
and they were, without exception, charming and manipulative, highly
articulate, energetic, humorous. Indeed, ambivalence was the motor
behind Stead's most powerful writing.

Her liking for such characters was reinforced by Bill Blech, who, by his
own admission, had a tendency to have 'crushes' on men.[3] From 1929, for
six years, Blech, too, fell under Neidecker's spell.

------ ꙮ ------

Stead went to London on two more business trips, in January and June
1932. There may have been other trips as well. In *House of All Nations*, it
is Adam Constant who is sent to London as a representative of the bank.
Constant, a minor but significant character in the novel, is a 24-year-old

bank clerk, a committed Marxist who plans to leave soon for Red China.[4] Jules Bertillon and his brother William do not inform him properly about the business he is to do, but he knows it is probably shady. In London, as he visits brokers, bankers and financial journalists, he feels foolish.

> He bit his lip and set out once more on the weary lope, upstairs and downstairs, into all sorts of little offices, and grand upper storeys of banks, to face surprised kindly little men, who treated him with a coddling air as if he were a rather advanced five-year-old and they had to amuse him till the policeman arrived to take him home.

Adam Constant also plans to write a novel about the bank, and his words can be read as an encoded statement of Stead's own intention:

> There are no men in this bank ... only an infection of monsters with purses at their waists that we wait upon and serve ... My dream is that one day I will get them all down, I will leave them on record. I want to show the waste, the insane freaks of these money men, the cynicism and egotism of their life ... Although, of course, there are plenty of living intelligences among them, sidetracked talents, even warm breasts, perspicacious men amongst them, but all, all compliant and prostituted.

What is striking is that the moral message, even here, is highly ambiguous. Are these men 'monsters' or 'warm breasts'—pimps or prostitutes? (The whorehouse analogy is reinforced by the title, *House of All Nations*, which refers to an exclusive Parisian brothel patronised by the international élite.) Despite his forceful statements, for a Marxist Adam Constant is strangely attracted to these 'perspicacious men' and 'sidetracked talents'.

Constant's ambivalence reflects the equivocation within the narrative itself. Readers are ultimately uncertain as to whether the novel is a hard-hitting exposure of international stock manipulation or a playful and indulgent satire. But no wonder Stead equivocated: Bill Blech was one of the pimps.

Another was Alfred Hurst—Henri Léon in *House of All Nations*. Hurst the wealthy wheat broker, the 'Grand Jew', as Stead called him, would occasionally come over from London or Antwerp and treat Bill and Christina to expensive dinners, shows and cabarets. At the end of 1931, he was courting Florence James and trying, unsuccessfully, to persuade her to accompany him to Paris for Christmas with Christina and Bill. No one could have been more committed to the game of profit making than

Hurst. Bill Blech once commented: 'The best you can make of a bargain with him is the worst of it.'[5] Yet Hurst liked to call himself a socialist, and he was friendly with Labour ministers in high places. Prime Minister Ramsay Macdonald had even written a preface to Hurst's book on the grain trade in Great Britain, *Bread of Britain*, published in 1930. Entirely written by Bill Blech (without acknowledgement), it was a thoughtful exposition of the farm relief question and policies of price-fixing, and a sustained plea for state control of the British grain trade, and had been widely praised by reviewers for its 'clearness and impartiality'.

***

On the basis of the four chapters Stead had handed him in June 1931, Peter Davies announced *The Wraith and the Wanderer* among the forthcoming books in his Autumn and Christmas catalogue, giving the publication date, a little optimistically, as November 1931. He heralded it with exceptional trumpeting.

THE WRAITH AND THE WANDERER
by Christina Stead

Miss Stead is an Australian by birth; she is still in her early twenties [sic]; she lives in Paris; and she has written a first novel to which it seems quite impossible to deny the quality of genius. It is an altogether extraordinary book, displaying the *macabre* imagination of an Edgar Allan Poe, the descriptive fervour of a Herman Melville, the loftiness of vision, in certain passages, of a Dante. Yet so far from being in any sense imitative, it is a highly original and extremely modern story. To describe it is almost an impossibility. It is a book to be read and read again with increasing admiration.

But the August deadline went by and *The Wraith and the Wanderer* was not finished. Stead had struck problems: it is likely that she still lacked the requisite emotional distance from her own childhood to be able to write fiction about it. And that winter her progress was further delayed by illness.

On a business trip to London in January 1932—this time staying at the prestigious Grosvenor, her expenses paid by the bank—she once again became quite sick, and decided it must be the poisonous smog and dismal atmosphere of London. But the London doctor had been right in the first place, and her troublesome appendix was removed some time in the spring of 1932.

It was around that time that she decided to abandon the novel, which was not going anywhere. This decision would not have been made lightly. She was very aware of time passing. In July she would turn thirty, and she had made no progress since she signed the contract with Davies a year ago. Her first book, contingent upon a non-existent second book, still awaited revision.

She needed to produce something fast, and for some time she had been thinking she would like to write more short stories. She loved bizarre tales, fairy tales, folklore and legend, the *Arabian Nights*, the stories of Poe, Hawthorne, E. T. A. Hoffmann. Her plan, extremely ambitious, was to attempt a tale cycle in the variegated manner of Boccaccio's *Decameron* and Chaucer's *Canterbury Tales*. Her group of characters would meet in the Capuchin woods overlooking Salzburg and entertain one another with strange stories from all over the world.

Stead wrote the first draft of *The Salzburg Tales* at great speed, working on it during the day at the bank and in the evenings at home on the kitchen table. The stories she liked best were those inspired by Jewish folklore—dangerous subject matter in those anti-semitic times, she joked.[6] Surrounded as she was by Jewish friends and their self-deprecating humour, she allowed herself the indulgence of ironic stereotypes: the 'Centenarist' (so-called because he organises centenary festivals to commemorate the births and deaths of great composers of music), the only Jewish storyteller, has 'a dark craft profile, like an ancient Venetian, with a long, pointed nose and thin lips'. But all the characters in *The Salzburg Tales* are caricatures, and the Centenarist, a mystic and learned soul, has the great virtue of being 'as full of tales as the poets of Persia'.

The first draft of *The Salzburg Tales* was written in a state of high creative excitement. Stead was revelling in her talents, writing with a new buoyancy and confidence, allowing her wit and imagination full play. One or two of the four stories set in Australia had been written in Sydney almost a decade before. Now Stead reconstructed them from memory, the early manuscript having been lost in Paris.

The revision was painful: she cursed her 'terrible vice' of correction, which would often involve six or seven re-typings. After a day of hammering at the typewriter, she felt 'dead to the imaginative world'.[7] In all, it took her just more than a year to write the book. She sent off a first batch of stories to Peter Davies in March 1933 and the rest of the manuscript in August that year.

'Bill and I are wondering where we can fly to,' Stead told Florence James anxiously in April 1933. They were frightening times. In January, a beer-hall agitator—Adolf Hitler—had been named Chancellor of the Third Reich. Late in February came the Reichstag fire. Hitler, declaring it a communist plot, had dissolved Parliament, arrested thousands of communists and socialists, suspended civil liberties and silenced opposition parties and trade unions. In March, the Reich had established a concentration camp at Dachau. April saw a national boycott of all businesses owned by Jews, and draconian measures announced against Jewish men living with Aryan women.

In May the books were burning. Works by Heine, Marx, Freud, Einstein and Stefan Zweig were thrown into the flames, along with the works of non-Jewish radicals—Brecht, Heinrich Mann, Erich Maria Remarque. Leftwing intellectuals and prescient Jews were beginning to flee the country; many headed for Paris.

The literary world now talked about 'revolutionary literature'. In this threatening atmosphere, many writers—Stead included—believed they had moral responsibility. In December 1933 she noted, 'Gide and all the writers of merit and intelligence have gone into the revolutionary camp'.[8] André Gide, a patrician figure in French literature, had surprised everyone when he embraced Soviet communism in the struggle against fascism. Another celebrated extra-Party 'fellow-traveller' was the brilliant André Malraux, the same age as Stead, who won the prestigious Goncourt prize that year for his novel *La Condition humaine*, set in revolutionary China. Stead admired its passion, drama and psychological acuity.

By the end of 1933, business friends were returning from Germany with sinister reports of massive re-armament. In France too, Stead observed, there was 'naked preparation for war'. She was horrified to learn that French armament makers were selling huge supplies of armaments to Germany.[9]

The Travelers' Bank was a cynical microcosm in a cynical world and by 1933, Stead and Blech felt increasingly uncomfortable about working there. Somehow the bank had continued to totter along with remarkable success, despite regular crises. Neidecker, of course, was not alone in his corrupt approach to banking in those years, when anything that made a profit was considered good business. Tax avoidance, managerial secretiveness, lax accounting and bogus companies were standard practices.

Operating in a depressed world economy, the Neidecker brothers and Bill Blech performed as stock-market bears, gambling on a falling market. Blech was one of the Paris bears who helped to ruin the swindler Ivar Kreuger by driving down the prices on Kreuger's securities, and forcing him to go deeper into debt to support his own stocks and bonds. The Swedish Match King shot himself in September 1932. Blech's strategy brought the bank a major windfall, allowing it to continue to operate with the appearance of solvency.[10] Blech, who himself did very well out of the venture, took the view that Kreuger ('a poor smelly vulture pierced by the arrow of deflation'[11]) deserved all he got. The fact is, however, that pierced tycoons drag innocents down with them.

Apart from lucky speculation within the law, the Travelers' Bank kept afloat by means of highly illegal balancing—or *contre-partie*—operations. Much of its business was not genuine: the transactions were simply book entries resolving themselves into what were in fact bets on the stock market against the bank's clients. In short, the bank was a 'bucket house': the bucketeers financed their transactions with outlays from clients.

For tax evasion and to cover transactions carried out by the bank against the operations of some of its clients, Neidecker had set up various branches abroad—on the Riviera, in Brussels, Amsterdam, London and New York.[12] He also floated a number of bogus companies, such as the London Reserve Insurance Co. Ltd, in which Bill Blech employed Florence James Heyting for a few hours each week. (In September 1932, Florence had married her original fiancé, Pym Heyting, the Dutch lawyer.) Operating from a splendid office in Bush House at the top of Fleet Street, Florence was paid a nominal wage to forward mail. Christina explained in a letter: 'The idea is that the L.R.I. is a concern doing business in London and which has just started business with the Bank.' She added: 'Please destroy this letter.' It is plain that she was perfectly aware of the illegality of the proceedings.

Shortly after her marriage—possibly prompted by her husband, who disliked Bill Blech—Florence James became uncomfortable about 'the cloak and dagger style' of business proceedings. One letter from the Travelers' Bank instructed her to forward any messages in a sealed, blank envelope to Miss Stead and to place this envelope inside another addressed to Mr Blech at No. 10 rue Jean Bart, with no reference to Miss Stead on the outside envelope. When Florence expressed disquiet to Christina, Stead told her it was because of her unmarried status that she had instructed the bankers to leave her name off correspondence. Their sense of propriety had made them come up with 'the ridiculous plan of the inner envelope.'

By 1933, Bill Blech had lost his taste for wild-cat schemes of speculative investment that, as a Marxist, he could only view as 'pure theft' and 'titanic pickpocketing'. He often talked of leaving the bank and 'going bolshevik'.[13]

The most detailed picture of Blech in the whole of Christina Stead's fiction is the portrait of Michel Alphendéry in *House of All Nations*. A warm portrait, it is by no means idealised. Alphendéry has sold his soul— at least for a time. Why does he remain in a job he detests? Partly out of fear of poverty (he has an 'army of dependants'), partly out of misguided loyalty to his employer and partly out of inertia. Even Jules Bertillon, observing his frequent fits of gloom, asks him why he does not go and join the communists if that is what he wants to do.

> He felt unspeakably melancholy. Jules had recommended him to give up this mad and detested life and join his real friends. But Michel could not contemplate leaving Jules yet … He went to a workers' meeting that evening and gave one hundred francs to the collection, immediately after felt extremely gay and lighthearted, and came back to the bank the next day without a thought of leaving and everything went on as before.

Alphendéry—like every other character in the book, including the narrator—is in the sway of Jules Bertillon, a princely figure, 'fragile, tall, elegantly dressed'. Lighthearted, debonair and daredevil, he runs the bank 'like a booth in a bazaar'. 'It's easy to make money,' he says. 'You put up the sign BANK and someone walks in and hands you money. The façade is everything.' Portrayed as an avatar of Mercury (the god of trade and commerce), Bertillon is not only full of cunning, he also seems blessed with Mercury's winged sandals. ('I'm just a gilded pickpocket and, believe me, a pickpocket has to have twinkling ankles.')

Bertillon respects his brilliant investments manager, Michel Alphendéry, the mastermind behind many of the bank's most successful ventures, yet he exploits him and makes no bones about it. He tells Alphendéry that his preferred employees would be either dopes or communists.

> Dopes are grateful to you for keeping them because they're dopes and communists because you know they're communists ... Look where you stand with me, Michel. You are a sort of limited power of attorney; you have the right, also, to buy and sell stocks, bonds, gold, commodities, transfer them in or out as you wish; you sign checks, you accept accounts, you make decisions. But you're not a director, you haven't got a contract, and I could turn you out tomorrow if I wanted to ... Why is it you're not ambitious and you don't try to steal my job? Because you're a communist. You despise me. You wouldn't let your friends see you standing in my shoes.

Throughout 1933, Stead was revising her short stories and driving herself hard, typing until late at night. She was tired and thin again. Blech lay awake till the early hours and groaned in his sleep. He was expected to manage the bank by himself for up to a month at a time while Peter Neidecker went to the US on business or took off with his family on their yacht, *Etoile Filante*, to sun himself in the Balearic Islands. Because Blech's financial know-how and flashes of brilliance had more than once saved the bank from ruin, he could rarely be spared. Stead was incensed that Neidecker, 'the idlest fellow of an idle world', could not see that Blech needed a holiday. In November 1933, she wrote to Florence James:

> I was so mad this morning thinking of the miserable twelve days taken last year—our only vacation, that I started to rouse on Bill, for I remembered that it was only by staging a scene last year that I got him to move. He promised to talk the whole business over tomorrow afternoon with Pete.

Three months later they had still not had a holiday.

> There is now no chance of our getting away for some time.
> An unexpected happening on Saturday leaves Bill with a great deal of responsibility for at least a month, if not much longer. It is horrid and I nearly cried with mortification and anxiety about Bill's health.

In March 1933, when Peter Davies set eyes on the first half of *Tales in the Capuchin Wood*, as Stead called her book of short stories at that time, he was dismayed. He had already announced *The Wraith and the Wanderer* in his catalogue and now, in its place, he was confronted with short stories every bit as unconventional as *Seven Poor Men of Sydney*. Considering this too great a business risk, he again asked Stead to write something else. But this time she put her foot down, and insisted she would produce nothing else before *Seven Poor Men of Sydney* was published. Peter Davies agreed to go ahead.

The publication date for *The Salzburg Tales*, as they became, was January 1934. Peter Davies arranged American publication with D. Appleton-Century later that year. During the waiting period, Stead began to lose confidence. She declared herself 'quite dissatisfied with the kindergarten style of *The Salzburg Tales*' and told Florence James that she wanted to write about something 'richer and stronger' than 'this old backwoods stuff'. She had several projects in mind: a love story set in Paris, a novel about the bank and a novel about the passions of women, their 'struggles for domestic and economic position' and 'the distortions imposed by society and physical inferiority'. The seeds of *The Beauties and Furies*, *House of All Nations* and *For Love Alone* were already planted in her mind.

'Her ladyship decided not to "free" us after all! What a training in patience!' Mollie Blech had appeared to be on the brink of consenting to divorce, and then she changed her mind. For Christina it was a cruel blow. She wrote the bitter news to the newly married Florence James in March 1933:

> Mollie is still on the theme, 'though you don't love me, you owe it to the child to live with me, especially now that your salary may be cut down' so you see a divorce is not in the air with that lady. Bill is extremely tired of the ridiculous discussion and either wants to get her off to America finally, or to go to England himself. He even spoke of going to Australia, this week, or South Africa, but it is all nebulous, till we know what is going to be done.

More than half of Bill Blech's earnings were going to his wife, daughter and mother. From September 1931 10-year-old Ruth Blech had boarded at Beacon Hill School, Bertrand and Dora Russell's experimental school in England. It suited Mollie's progressive, anti-authoritarian ideas, and Ruth had loved it there[14], but after a year Bill could no longer pay the exorbitant fees. He and Mollie had talked of sending her to school in Germany for a year to learn the language, but by 1932 it was no longer a suitable place to send a little Jewish girl. Instead, she was sent to a boarding school on the outskirts of Paris—chosen because it appeared to be the only one in the whole of France where the children could have regular baths. Despite their passion for France, Bill and Mollie remained very American.

Bill's mother had been living in a small apartment near the Buttes-Chaumont park. At the end of the year, to save Bill's money, she moved into a hotel in the rue Jean Bart, and spent most of the day in their crowded apartment, eating with Bill and Christina, and not retiring to her own quarters until the late evening. 'It is not a very satisfactory arrangement either for her or us,' Stead told Florence James, 'but the best we can do until we know what we are going to do.'

> She is a very sweet person, has no faults at all, except that she has a permanent weakness for describing potato pancakes, meatballs, stuffed salmon etc. at all hours of the day and year.

Christina was taking German lessons in secret to surprise Bill at Christmas, and for practice, she was laboriously translating a 1929 communist book, *Illustrierte Geschichte des Bürgerkriegs in Russland*. Her long-term aim, perhaps inspired by their translator friend Sam Putnam, was to get a firm grip on German and Russian, in addition to French, in the hope of earning money as a translator of fiction.

The other motive for learning German was to understand Rosa Blech better. The old lady spoke a patois peculiar to herself: German broken down to something resembling Yiddish—a language she had developed to communicate with the old ladies she met in the park, where she would sit and talk for hours. She resorted to this language whenever she wanted to say something to Bill that she did not want Christina to understand. To add to the difficulty of communication, Rosa Blech had trouble understanding Christina's soft voice and non-American accent. Christina complained to Florence:

> I am almost hoarse, for I have to repeat everything I say three or four times. You may think I have a colonial accent, but to her it's pure glottal abstraction: I am trying to learn American for moments of urgency, but I am not too good at it.

One of the stories in *The Salzburg Tales*, 'The Little Old Lady', portrays the tension between a querulous old German-speaking woman and her son Paul's female companion. At the Opéra Comique together, the old lady tells her about Paul's ex-wife:

'I never saw such a pretty little girl. Twenty years they knew each other, and loved each other, before they were married: it was a real romansch. They were little playmates together.'

Paul's betrothed was silent.[15]

In letters Stead regularly complained of fatigue—insomnia was to be a problem all her life. A tense, restless person, plagued by anger and self-recrimination, she was what she called a 'waker and dreamer'.

She would often lie awake and think about her family in Australia, her childhood. Sometimes these were nostalgic memories of 'the old, old days' when she played with her cousin in the kangaroo grass and pine needles of Lydham Hill. More often, they were painful memories.

These days, letters from home arrived at intervals of three months or so. From her father came the usual 'rhetoric about the sun, the sea, prosperity, the light of human progress and other dreamy notions'.[16] From the others came letters about 'fishing and swimming and taking in the washing', depending on the writer. (The domestic letters were from Percia Stead, her brother David's wife, whom she had never met.) Ada, now living with her son Fred and his wife Mavis in the Blue Mountains, wrote only rarely. Thistle Harris had moved into Boongarre, and because she was living with a married man, the Watson's Bay locals tended to shun her. (Harris, recalling this period later in life, says she minded less than David did.) Sixteen-year-old Gilbert had run away from home, stowing away on a ship, and nothing had been heard of him since August 1933.

In December 1933, Alfred Hurst visited Paris, and over a luxurious meal at Prunier's, tried to persuade them to join him in Antwerp where he had a successful grain business. For the first time since Stead had known him, this restless womaniser seemed to be in love. In Brussels he was living with Mitzi, a German woman, pretty and smart, who had divorced her husband for him. Were it not for his family commitments in England, he told everyone, he would marry her. From his house in Brussels, he motored to work each day in Antwerp, his grain business was flourishing, and he had a hotel-flat in Antwerp where Bill and Christina could live free of charge. Blech thought the offer tempting for a year or so, but Stead wanted to move back to London—smog or no smog.

She had had enough of being on the periphery of the English-speaking world: her English syntax was beginning to sound French. Much as she loved France, Stead felt a foreigner there. 'You can't write about foreigners,' she asserted. 'They write better about themselves.'[17] The English were less foreign to her, though she needed to become better acquainted with contemporary British literature and politics. In London, she hoped to be able to earn money by freelance journalism.

Heavy snow fell in Paris just before Christmas and the bitter cold was 'like a slug on the head'. Blech, who hated the cold and felt 'villainously fatigued', wanted to head south for Christmas. Stead wanted to stay put and work.

The Salzburg Tales were published in England on 18 January 1934 to considerable acclaim. Unlike most first books by young writers, it was given lengthy reviews in all the prestigious papers, sometimes by well-known reviewers. The collection was generally deemed remarkable, auguring a dazzling future for this 31-year-old Australian writer with her startling imagination and cosmopolitan sophistication.

In Australia, with its almost wholly naturalistic short-story tradition, the collection seemed highly eccentric, yet when the British edition arrived in Australia, reviewers were enthusiastic. The first copies sold out rapidly and interested readers had to wait weeks for additional supplies to arrive from England. Stead's family, who had been forwarded advance copies, sent congratulations. ('They are all a little *cagey* in their criticisms,' Stead told Florence James. 'I think they are waiting to see what the critics say before they commit themselves.')

In the United States, where the book was published by D. Appleton-Century in September 1934, the reviews were almost all positive. The most outspoken in his praise was the up-and-coming Clifton Fadiman, who announced in the *New Yorker* that Miss Stead's tales were 'far better than the *Decameron*'.

Stead had based a number of the characters in her tales, and the storytellers themselves, on people she knew. She wondered what their reactions would be. Though the portraits were embellished, with many details wholly invented, the individuals concerned had no trouble recognising themselves, and their reactions were mixed. Some were quite upset. Stead's portraits would never be exactly complimentary: that was the problem.

'I sit here,' Stead grumbled, 'and hear nothing on earth but Nazis, stockmarket, and stockmarket, Nazis, Stavisky and the air units, air units and Stavisky.'[18] She and Blech had been alarmed by the outbreak of violence in Paris in February 1934. The Stavisky crisis, the biggest of a succession of scandalous frauds involving corrupt politicians, brought to a head public disgust with the failure of the Radical Socialist Party to cope with severe economic deterioration and rising unemployment. Alexandre Stavisky, a stockbroker of Russian Jewish origin, had engaged in large-scale international operations, selling worthless bonds. During investigations, Stavisky was found dead, and it was discovered that his activities were known to certain government ministers. On 6 February, which came to be known as 'bloody Tuesday', there was a mass demonstration with all political factions in the Place de la Concorde. Police fired on the angry mob, killing seventeen and injuring hundreds in the bloodiest street battles since the Paris Commune of 1871. After this, Edouard Daladier's socialist government resigned.

Fear of a rightwing *coup d'état* and the prospect of France succumbing to the fascist madness that was gripping Italy and Germany brought the left factions together. A 24-hour general strike was held on 12 February. A United Front meeting against fascism was planned for 27 May. These events would form the background of *The Beauties and Furies*, set in Paris in 1934.

Stead wrote to Florence James on 16 May: 'The cops have been ordered to "observe order", that is, use their batons with great severity. The city has been over-garrisoned and over-policed for months. We are quite miserable here.' Blech, like many others, believed civil war could well break out within six months. It forced a decision: they resolved to leave Paris and the bank in June. Most of their American friends had gone home. Those who had clung on after the dollar fell were now fleeing before the war clouds burst.

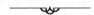

Stead was hard at work again, this time revising *Seven Poor Men of Sydney*; Peter Davies wanted the completed manuscript by May 1934. A demanding task, it meant going back to a manuscript begun five and a half years earlier, in a quite different frame of mind. In bleak moments she felt the manuscript was a 'frost' and unworkable, but Blech kept her to her task. Davies had given some editorial guidance: he wanted cuts and some elaboration; she was to try to flesh out the characters and improve some of the speeches. To capture the characters' Marxist rhetoric, she was reading Marxist theory and questioning Blech about political economy. Several of the characters were printers: on a trip to London in March 1934, she visited a printing works and took detailed notes.

At the beginning of May, Stead stopped work at the bank to devote herself to finishing the book. She was aiming to complete it by mid June 1934, before they left Paris. It would not have helped her tranquillity to discover she was once again in a state she wryly described to Florence James as 'a Malthusian sickness to which I have been susceptible in my time'. Her letter revealed neither regret, self-reproach nor self-pity: she merely wrote that she had been 'rather sick for some days'. Bill took her to Reims for the weekend to recover. She thought it quite the 'airiest and prettiest town in France'.

Beyond coy allusions to a 'little operation', Stead wrote nothing about her terminations—neither in letters nor her fiction. Did she really want a child? Early in 1934, Florence James Heyting, who was thinking about children herself, had asked Christina about her plans in this regard. Christina had just become a highly successful published author, and was beginning to envisage a future without children.

> I seem to be too tired to think of them at present: they may eventuate this year, but I must admit the truth, I do not yearn for them: my ideas have turned to other channels, or else I am so used to the present family regime that I think it well enough.

However, three months later, after the abortion, she told Florence that children were on the cards: 'We are waiting for England or some other semi-permanent settlement, but we won't wait long, only a few months.' And six months later again, she told Florence (now pregnant) that Bill was talking of a child after she finished *The Beauties and Furies*. 'Bill says when *this* is done we will have a baby: you know I hae ma doots.' When Florence gave birth to a daughter (christened Julie Christina) on 16 July 1935, Christina wrote that she felt 'fearfully jealous'. But in the next few years, when Florence was absorbed with her two young daughters, Christina would privately disparage her as a suburban wife and mother.

The Beauties and Furies, written the following year, in 1935, does not suggest maternal longing. The pregnant Elvira cannot decide whether to keep the baby she has conceived by her lover Oliver, but it is striking that Elvira never sees motherhood as creative, though she has no other interests in life. She envies her husband and lover their work, their 'self-expression', and tells Oliver:

> 'Since I bore life in me I feel a will growing in me. But the will is the infant. When he is born, he will just leave me like an old skin. I shall be the same as before, limp, aimless.'

One afternoon, Elvira, feeling sick, suddenly decides she 'can't go through with it', and a woman friend takes her to the *sage-femme*. Afterwards, she is in pain for several days, but feels no regret. Nowhere in Stead's fiction is there a joyous picture of maternity.

Blech did talk from time to time about having children, though this might have been to please Christina. They told themselves they were waiting for the divorce to come through; they were waiting to be settled somewhere; they were waiting for Stead to finish her next novel. The issue of children—like the issue of the divorce or where they would live—would remain unresolved until Christina's age put an end to their vacillations.

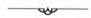

Having given notice on their apartment at No. 10 rue Jean Bart, they were due to leave Paris on 15 June 1934. The large electric gramophone, the 700 or so records and books were packed up and dispatched by a supplier, to be stored by Florence and Pym Heyting in their large new house in Belsize Park, until Blech and Stead found a flat in London.

Seven Poor Men of Sydney appeared in October 1934, just ten months after *The Salzburg Tales*, and Stead had her first experience of an avalanche of negative criticism. Reviewers tended to compare it with the short stories, always to the detriment of the novel. Everyone was in awe of its brilliance and 'originality', but to many, the novel lacked depth and coherence. In Australia, the *Bulletin* announced a 'dazzling book by a Sydney girl'; the reviewer thought it 'diabolically clever', but rambling. Stead found the reception very disappointing.

> Nobody likes it very much: no doubt they will like the following ones in a harmonious crescendo of dubiety and slam: can't be helped. As long as Davies or some other keeps publishing I can hope to strike it lucky one day.[19]

Stead and Blech left Paris in June 1934. By October they had installed themselves, their furniture and possessions at No. 78 Chiltern Court, Baker Street, on the seventh floor of a modern block of flats, with spectacular views of Westminster, Regent's Park and the city spires. This time, Rosa Blech was living with them.

Stead had wanted to be back in London, but had not anticipated that Mollie and Ruth would also be back in London that June after a second brief trip back to the States. The situation was as distressing as ever. Florence James recalls that Christina was tense whenever Bill went to visit Mollie, and would go to the cinema for diversion, sometimes asking Florence James' German au-pair girl, a Heidelberg graduate, to accompany her. One evening, the girl rang Florence saying she would be staying out later than expected because Christina was in a terrible state.

The domestic turmoil was probably the reason for Blech and Stead's decision to return to Paris. Blech had not yet formally severed his connection with the Travelers' Bank, and so they went back to Paris and to the bank, leaving Rosa Blech and most of their worldly possessions in the London flat.

It suited Stead for the time being, since she was setting her work in progress, *The Travelling Scholar* (later *The Beauties and Furies*), in Paris. She was working hard, hoping to finish the novel by early the following year. As a pick-up, she was 'scoffing arsenic'. A Swiss doctor in Paris had prescribed 'arsenyl', along with tincture of belladonna, a herbal mixture, for stomach troubles that she had feared might be an ulcer. She liked the taste of the belladonna, which calmed her nerves and helped her sleep. The doctor told her no one of nervous temperament should be without it. From now on, she made sure she was not.

That she was completely immersed in the writing of *The Beauties and Furies* is evident from her letters during this period, which have the same lightly decadent atmosphere, visionary images and playful humour. She wrote to Florence James:

> Imagine what I did yesterday evening: waiting for Bill in one of the grander rooms of the Bank (I have my own little one but it is rather cold) I discovered the box of cigars of some friend of Pete's and in an access of boyish immorality began to smoke one: after not more than eight puffs I began to float, my head began to spin, my throat to have a sort of convulsion and my eyelids to flutter down. With due haste I opened the window: below, the corner of the rue de la Paix and the rue Daunou and a young gent of Argentine aspect in an automobile: the young man signals and I though groggy, close the window and think—'that's how one sin leads to another and souls are eventually lost, or, how puffing leads to necking.' ... What ogres men are though: the way they drink, smoke cigars and sink in debauch and still come up fresh and smiling!

In the novel, Marpurgo, an inveterate cigar smoker, declares cigars very important for spiritual adventures.

To Stead's dismay, Bill Blech spent Christmas 1934 in London with Ruth and Mollie, who were shortly to return to New York. Stead tried to console herself, and with the half-advance she had received for the American edition of *Seven Poor Men*, she took a friend out to dinner, gave some money to the red press, and bought 'two slap-up hats' and a grape purple dinner dress. But none of this could make up for being left alone in Paris during the festive season. On Boxing Day, she wrote to Florence James, 'I haven't heard from Bill, and neither has anyone here, but I suppose he is surrounded by multitudinous Grossmans.' She added, fervently: 'I hope (against hope) that we will set our house in order this coming year.'

She and Bill had been together five years now, and in some respects nothing much had changed.

———— ∽ ————

The political situation in Paris was still fraught with tension: police stood four or five deep at some street corners. Stead and Blech were relieved to have their flat in London so that they could 'jump over the channel at a moment's notice'.[20]

Stead had returned to a half-written manuscript, begun in 1930. Then called *The Young Man Will Go Far*, it was a portrait of Keith Duncan, but set in Paris. Now she called the novel *The Travelling Scholar*, and with the aim of making the portrait kinder, she was making the fictional character Oliver Fenton an amalgam of Keith Duncan and Frank Manuel. Both were bright young scholars who considered themselves leftwing radicals.

Dr Frank Manuel, a historian, was in Paris on a postdoctoral scholarship to work in the archives. He became a friend. One evening Stead accompanied him to a meeting of revolutionary writers. He asked Stead to collaborate with him on a project on the Saint-Simonian period in France, 1836–48, when the peasants felt threatened by the introduction of threshing machines. The project was dropped, presumably because Stead soon left again for London, but it may have given her the idea of exploring the effect on artisans of the mechanisation of the lace industry. To find out more about the machines, the designing of lace and lace-dyeing, she made an excursion to the lace museum in Calais.

Stead described her new novel as a 'sexual drama'. The novel is set in Paris in the first few months of 1934, during the political troubles. Mrs Elvira Western has been swayed by the ardent entreaties of her young lover Oliver to leave her respectable, eminently sensible doctor husband in London and join Oliver in Paris; he is there to write a doctoral thesis on the French workers' movement. Dark, melancholy Elvira is a sort of sleeping beauty whom Oliver fancies he has woken just as the thorns were closing in on her. Her only rival as beauty and muse is Paris itself.

At the beginning of the novel, adventure is in the air: Elvira is leaving for Paris, the 'garden of lovers'. The novel closes with Oliver on the train going back to England. Elvira has already gone back to her husband. For all their halfhearted attempts, neither Elvira nor Oliver (their names suggest mirror-images) are real 'wanderers'. They remain 'becalmed off Cythera'.

The only positive character is Coromandel Paindebled, daughter of antiquarians who live in the rue Jacob, in Saint-Germain—a precious enclave of artisans whose values are out of joint in the modern world of commercially minded entrepreneurs and vandals. Passionate about her work as a book designer, Coromandel commands a fertile, chaotic inner world. An independent woman sexually and economically, she sleeps with Oliver, whom she at first finds charming. (He has not told her about Elvira.) When she realises, before long, that he has a 'flabby soul', she brushes some earth from her hands, literally, and with this gesture metaphorically brushes Oliver from her life.

―――――――◁◁▷―――――――

In the spring of 1935, Blech and Stead returned to the Chiltern Court flat in London. Mollie and Ruth were back in New York. Blech was still involved with the Travelers' Bank, but from a distance, which he preferred. Stead was trying to finish *The Beauties and Furies*.

In April, Peter Neidecker was summonsed to court and accused by a half-commission man of fiscal fraud and breach of trust. The bank records were investigated. Neidecker's passport was confiscated, but he was released on bail.

A few weeks later, early in May, Peter Neidecker urgently summoned Bill Blech to Paris. From Paris, Blech wrote to Stead, explaining that a 'fanatical blackmailer' was laying charges against the bank and that he was 'not even moved by bribery'. Blech was loyal to Neidecker to the end. And yet, even if Neidecker did not give Blech exact information about the bank's reserves (or lack thereof), Blech had always known that the bank was operating in quicksand, and he was certainly implicated in the bank's shady transactions over the years.

After four days of 'sheer horror' in Paris, Blech, exhausted by the bank's recent dramas, went south, as planned, for a few days in Barcelona, followed by a health cure in Madrid. From the Hotel Colon in Barcelona he wrote that he was 'much too worried about dear old Pete to be in the frame of mind to appreciate the city'. But he was still able to appreciate the 'madly beautiful' Spanish women.

From Chiltern Court, where she was cooped up with Bill's mother, Christina wrote Bill loving letters.

> It was beautiful today outside. I made a solemn resolution to join the 'Proletarian Club of Round-Walkers' or 'The Promenaders of the Hammer

and Sickle' or whatever there is that enables me to go into the country walking on Sundays in summer.

She finished, teasingly: 'How am I going to get through the night with no Bill? A lot you care, with your madly-beautiful.'

A week later, she was feeling wistful: 'I hope that when you're quite well, strong and fit again that we can have a more united life ... It would be pleasant if we had a real home where we knew we would stay for five or ten years, where we could have some ground and a large library.'

After two weeks, Christina, with only one letter from Bill, was feeling even more forlorn. (Due to the mule-speed of the Spanish mail, his letters would arrive after his return.)

Dear wee, hurry up and write, or I will be forced to begin to look hungrily at London's toiling millions of ginks, which I should be loath to do, but my breast is as empty as a turned-out tin of peaches: you are not domestic, you never turned out a tin of peaches, so you don't know the feeling ... Wow! I aint got a guy, I aint got a letter. I aint got nuffin.

In London, Blech rapidly made new friends—mostly communist journalists associated with the *Daily Worker* and the *Left Review*, established in 1934 and already the most influential of the Left magazines. These friends would call in to discuss politics with Blech, filling the flat with all sorts of American and English regional accents—and plenty of smoke. After the relative isolation of their last years in Paris, Blech and Stead rejoiced in the company of these 'drifting talents', mostly men—unaffected, easygoing and adventurous.

The last chapters of *For Love Alone* describe the atmosphere at the Chiltern Court flat in that spring of 1935:

Many men came to see them in the little flat in the court off Fleet Street, more men than women, many unmarried or libertine, picaresque, amiable, floating men. They came first to see James Quick who had the American's political fervour and the Marxist's political sophistication, who saw Whitehall from the American viewpoint and the White House as from the State House of some Middle-Western State. These men first loved the man and then his woman.

Patrick and Anne Dooley wrote for the London *Daily Worker*. Patrick, an Irishman and a union organiser, regularly spoke at communist rallies; Anne was a thin, nervous Tynesider, whose accent was a source of endless fascination to Stead. Eamon MacAlpine, an ex-IRA man, now worked for the Consolidated Press in London. Under the byline Frank Pitcairn, Claud Cockburn wrote for the *Daily Worker* in London, the *New Masses* in New York and *Pravda* in Moscow. And for the past two years he had been editing an influential mimeographed newsletter, *The Week*, famous throughout Europe. Another frequent visitor to the flat was Ralph Fox, who discussed political and economic questions with Blech for hours at a time.

By now, Stead had decided that she was very partial to the company of men. After five and a half years in Paris in Blech's company, she had acquired a greater ease with people and a certain cosmopolitan refinement. The previous year, she had published two books, and she was generally considered to be a rising literary star. She spoke French fluently and had a good smattering of German. At thirty-two, she felt better about herself than she had ever done in the past.

A contemporary photograph shows her with bobbed hair parted in the middle. The eyebrows are arched, the eyes sharp and observant, the lips full; she looks challenging, somewhat defiant. When Nettie Palmer, the Australian writer, met Stead on the train to Paris in June that year, she was quite discomfited by the younger woman's elegance and worldly air. Palmer could detect no trace of Australian accent in Stead's singsong voice.

Always restless, always passionate, Stead now began to flaunt her interest in men. If anything, Blech seems to have encouraged her. Perhaps he understood that her need for men's affirmation was an almost desperate need to be found physically desirable. Certainly he prided himself on a free-thinking liberalism that encompassed open marriages. He himself does not appear ever to have dallied with other women—apart from Mollie. But his fierce and affectionate brotherly relationships may well have reinforced Christina's own preference for men.

In *For Love Alone*, one man stands out among the cluster of characters who would come to the flat to talk to James Quick. Harry Girton is 'an Oxford graduate, a radical pamphleteer who lived in a distant seedy suburb with his swarthy-browed and sullen mistress-wife'. A shabbily dressed man with 'dark gold hair', his 'easygoing smile' and lingering gaze appeal to many women: he 'had loved much'. Girton is one of Stead's archetypal wanderers:

> At the back of his mind was the firm intention of getting away, wandering out, and amusing the soul of his soul by picking his way through a very alien land, like Hudson, like Lawrence, like Burton.

Teresa and James Quick are drawn to Harry Girton 'as driftwood is sucked in by waters rushing downwards round a hidden reef'. Teresa is fascinated by the stories that circulate about Girton's wild and dissolute personal life. His image begins 'to lure her, growing on her in her sleep'. The attraction she feels for this man—more than six feet tall, broad, with 'shapely limbs' and 'splendid oval blue eyes'—is strongly physical. 'Differently from any other man till then, it was of his body that she dreamed.'

> He looked at her and a storm of the uplands blew round her ears, she reeled and felt half-mad with love, and kept thinking to herself: 'It comes again, it does not die with marriage, it is not over once for all ...' Now she really felt a woman.

Harry Girton is based on Ralph Fox, a handsome, restless Halifax man, with a pale face, fine nose and gentle grey eyes.[21] Two years older than Stead, he was a passionate political activist, a committed writer and journalist, and a restless wanderer. In Fox's novel, *Storming Heaven*, his hero describes his strange thirst: 'I feel I must wear my feet out seeing this world, finding out why people do what they do, why they are what they are.'

Fox was the black sheep in his conservative, middle-class family. At Oxford, his studies ranged from the French Encyclopaedists to Oriental Languages. In 1920, at the age of twenty, he had helped establish the Oxford branch of the Communist Party of Great Britain. That same year, he travelled to the south-east of the Soviet Union, a region ravaged by famine in the wake of the White Russian armies, and was impressed by what he saw of the Soviet system. His first book, *People of the Steppes* (1925), and his only novel, *Storming Heaven* (1928), were based on his experience in Russia.

In 1925 Fox went to Moscow and worked for the Communist International, where he met an English woman, Madge Palmer, a fellow activist, whom he later married. He was back in England for the General Strike of 1926, but returned to Russia in 1929 and spent three years as librarian at the Marx-Engels Institute in Moscow, active in the Russian

Communist Party. While in Moscow, he worked through vast amounts of archival material for a biography of Lenin, published in 1933. Since being back in England, he had written short books on the British class struggle and on British imperialism, and regular articles for the *Daily Worker*, the *Sunday Worker*, *New Writing* and *Left Review*, which he co-founded.

Fox read widely in English, French and Russian literature, and was currently writing a book on Marxism and literature, *The Novel and the People*. The Indian novelist Mulk Raj Anand described Fox as one of the most versatile men he had ever met:

> ... a person who could talk about the bronzes of the Tang dynasty and of Kuo-min-tang politics, of Spanish conquistadors and of the origins of the caste system, of contemporary English poetry, of the Chinese novel and of the new novel in Europe, all in one afternoon.

Stead could hardly fail to be impressed.

The year 1935, in which the Nuremberg laws stripped German Jews of their citizenship and rights and Mussolini invaded Ethiopia, was a year of solidarity for the literary Left. The Popular Front, officially launched by the Comintern (the Communist International) in Moscow, urged Left factions to form a solid block against fascism. With the aim of forming a broad Left alliance, communist parties throughout the Western world organised writers' leagues and writers' congresses. From now on, 'fellow travellers' and even liberals (previously regarded with contempt) were encouraged to participate.

The First International Congress of Writers for the Defense of Culture, a mass meeting of intellectuals against fascism, was held at the Salle de la Mutualité in Paris from 21 to 25 June, attended by an imposing collection of literary luminaries. Among the French contingent were Aragon, Gide and Malraux; the Germans, now living in exile, included Brecht, Heinrich Mann, Anna Seghers, Alfred Döblin, Robert Musil, Johannes Becher and Egon Kisch. It was a gathering of people 'for whom fascism was a personal insult', as Maxim Gorki wrote from Russia, in a telegram excusing his absence.

There were few radicals among prestigious British writers. In the spirit of the Popular Front, the congress organisers invited liberals Virginia Woolf,

Rebecca West, E. M. Forster and Aldous Huxley. The two women did not attend. Afterwards Huxley would privately complain that it was five days of 'endless Communist demagogy'.[22]

The English delegation largely comprised associates of the *Left Review*. Christina Stead's invitation to join the British delegation as their secretary probably came from Ralph Fox, who was on the organising executive. After all, *Seven Poor Men of Sydney*, her novel about struggling workers strangled by their material circumstances, contained solid Marxist dialogue.

John Strachey, a Marxist theorist of international stature, was another delegate. He had just returned from a political lecture-tour in the United States that the US government had done its best to prevent. Amabel Williams-Ellis (Strachey's sister) and playwright Montagu Slater were editors of *Left Review*. James Hanley, a former seaman, was generally considered Britain's best proletarian novelist. Pearl Binder wrote for *Left Review*; Shelley Wang was a revolutionary Chinese poet living in England; and Herbert Read, the future art critic, had just written the novel *The Green Child*. Travelling with the group, but representing Australia, were Nettie Palmer and an unknown, John Fisher.

Nettie Palmer, fifty that year, was a significant figure on the Australian literary scene. She was energetically trying to promote interest in national writing at a time when poor publishing conditions and a lack of cultural journals meant that Australian literature was at a low ebb. Her broad reading in European and American literature gave her an assured and independent voice in Australian letters: her 1924 book *Modern Australian Literature 1900–1923* had been the first systematic critical study of its kind.

Palmer had found *Seven Poor Men of Sydney* singularly haunting. Earlier that year she had commented: 'To read [Stead's] book is to spend your time in the company of an exhilarating author, who is probably a genius ... Whatever road she may take, we shall never be willing to lose sight of her.'[23] In Paris, in April, she had been to Sylvia Beach's bookshop and seen in the window—alongside Shakespeare, Hemingway, Gertrude Stein, Whitman and Thackeray—Christina Stead's *Salzburg Tales* and *Seven Poor Men*. She was curious to meet the author in person.

Some of the English contingent had arranged to travel to Paris together on the boat-train on Friday 21 June: the congress was to open that evening. In her diary Nettie Palmer recorded her first impression of her 32-year-old compatriot:

Christina Stead came in light-foot and assured, perfectly dressed, tailored and supple, gloves-bag-hat, shoes, all dark blue. She carried nothing superfluous, except perhaps the newspaper her husband handed in to her at the last moment. —'Hm-m. Bill's idea of a newspaper,' she said to me as the train began to move: she smiled, half-guilty, but I felt as if it were her idea of a newspaper too. It had some name like *The Economist*.[24]

Nettie Palmer jotted other impressions in her notebooks. As the train was about to leave, she noticed 'a middle-sized youngish man planting his typewriter and his casual suit-case in the rack'. When he spoke to his fellow passengers, she observed 'a hint of Yorkshire in his accent'. This, Stead proudly informed her, was Ralph Fox, who had written a novel about his travels over ground trodden by Genghis Khan, and as a reporter for the communist press, made regular trips between London and Paris. Palmer learnt that he was thirty-five and a talented linguist—'probably the best French speaker of us all'.

The Australian women sat opposite John Fisher, whom Stead thought 'a real Australian bush boy'. As the train 'glided through early summer landscape down to Newhaven', Palmer asked Stead about her work. At Newhaven they joined the boat and went down to the saloon for a meal described by Nettie as 'a last, stern specimen of England'. From Dieppe, they travelled by train, third class, to Paris.

> Summer had suddenly appeared in full strength—there were poppies all through the wheat and dazzling sun. Christina said we'd never have enough frocks in our own suitcases, lucky we'd arrived just in time for the midsummer sales. But where were we going to stay in Paris for the six days?

Nettie Palmer was at a complete loss to know what to make of the 'elegant' and 'poised' Christina Stead. She could not match the author of *Seven Poor Men of Sydney*, that novel full of wild poetry and potency, with this sophisticated woman who seemed so concerned about clothes. How could this 'secure woman of the world' have written about the 'smells of Woolloomooloo' and 'the breakers of the Pacific against the Gap'? Did she really care about political causes? The bits of the puzzle simply did not seem to fit.

Stead's question about accommodation must have been addressed to the group generally, for she very much hoped to stay in the same hotel as Ralph Fox and his friends; she was devastated when Nettie Palmer knew of a hotel where the landlady had been very pleasant on her previous visit. Stead and Shelley Wang found themselves bustled into a taxi that Nettie Palmer directed to the Hôtel des Grands Hommes in the Place du Panthéon.

That evening Nettie Palmer steered the little group to the Foyer des Etudiants for a cheap but hearty dinner. Although Stead had already decided that Palmer was bossy, meddlesome and interfering, she was in better humour; perhaps it was the prospect of meeting up with the others at the evening session. She told Nettie she was ravenous and explained that she had been taking medicine with arsenic in it, which sharpened her appetite. Nettie Palmer reflected in her journal:

> I don't know what anyone takes arsenic for, but Christina Stead strikes me as one who has known T.B.—at any rate in the past. She's not so much restless, or fatigued, as insatiable. I notice she often refers to T.B. as a probable element in someone *else's* motives or plan of living: it's nothing rare or abnormal to her. Her face is thin, with high cheek bones, but looks as if it has been thinner. High colour close to the eyes.

That evening, on the platform of the Mutualité, Gide, Malraux, Aragon and Nizan stood in front of the bright red presidential table and raised their right fists to the first bars of the Internationale. André Gide, 'Dean of French letters', gave the opening oration, receiving a rousing storm of applause.

Some four thousand students, workers and intellectuals were gathered together in that 'hothouse atmosphere'; among them liberals, Marxists, Christians, surrealists. All were passionately against fascism, but many found the communist rhetoric off-putting.

Stead's report on the congress in the July issue of *Left Review* is the most emphatic printed statement she would ever make about the political responsibility of writers. She asserted that writers in the contemporary 'embroiled world' were witnessing 'the last corruptions of capitalist decay' and *had* to be concerned with politics. There was no place any more for 'denizens of the ivory tower'. The duty of younger writers was to 'give up their poetic solitudes and soft self-probings to study worldly subjects, enter the political arena, take lessons from workmen and use their pen as a scalpel for lifting up the living tissues, cutting through the morbid tissues, of the social anatomy'.

She admitted this was no easy task, since the disruption of the bourgeois world was inclined to leave the writer, whatever his origin, 'quite at sea'.

———— ✺ ————

Living on the same floor of the same hotel, Christina Stead and Nettie Palmer saw quite a bit of each other during their time in Paris. They did not warm to each other. It was not the most opportune time for them to meet: if Stead had 'high colour close to the eyes', it was probably because proximity to Ralph Fox and other impressive young revolutionaries made her quite heady. Having just emerged from a long period of solitude and hard work, she was feeling a little giddy with it all. Palmer does not seem to have guessed these undercurrents in Stead's life.

Both women could be dogmatic and their views diverged significantly. Though Nettie Palmer read French, German and Greek and believed it essential for Australian writers to keep in touch with the larger world, she and Vance Palmer passionately championed a distinctive Australian national culture, one that was no longer passively responsive to British and European influences. Stead's own literary influences were European, not Australian, and from her internationalist perspective, Palmer's attitude seemed narrow and provincial.

Nettie Palmer insisted the Australians should sit together in conference sessions; Stead—for reasons the least of which was national identity— wanted to sit with the English contingent. It remained a rankling point throughout the five days of the congress.

Politically, the women were at different ends of the liberal spectrum. Both were inspired by the broad Left alliance, but Stead strongly identified with the communist element that perturbed Palmer. In later years, Stead declared Palmer a 'good-natured, school-teacherish woman, totally without flair or imagination'.[25]

On the Sunday, yet another glaring hot day, the two Australian women set out after breakfast for a walk to the Luxembourg Gardens. Stead, Palmer noted in her diary, looked 'lightly elegant'. On their way, they passed masses of police militia in trucks and Stead mused aloud:

> Now *why* are all these gendarmes being sent out in lorries from the barracks to-day? What meeting of the people are they going to break up? Would it be that big communal picnic at St. Cloud? Look, there's another lorry being loaded with them. Who's going to be crushed?

Palmer's diary recounts the conversation in the Luxembourg Gardens. With her customary indifference to tact, Stead apparently told Palmer, who had always felt herself to be rather a plain woman:

My father wanted me to be a scientist like himself. When I was very tiny he used to tell me the names of what interested him most—fishes with frightening faces. It was all right, but when he saw I learnt easily he took me to science meetings. I suppose I was about ten by then. I wasn't frightened of fish with ugly faces, but those science women who didn't know how to do their hair or put their clothes on! I ran away from science forever.

The monologue in Palmer's diary—supposedly Stead's voice—continues in the same vein:

I was determined to make enough money some day to have the right clothes. I must admit that I've got rather a weakness for shoes. And gloves. Yes, and hats. I buy my hats in London, but it does seem a pity not to be able to take one back from Paris now. It's not the best part of the season, though; it's too late.

Nettie Palmer, an astute observer of her fellow-beings, kept a journal throughout her life. In her portraits of people, she liked to cite dialogue, and would write whole slabs of speech in inverted commas, as if she had a tape recorder. But there was an element of deception in this technique.

Fourteen Years, Palmer's published journal, is unfair to herself as well as to Stead, since it omits comments in the unpublished notebooks that portray Stead far more warmly. The conversation about hats is placed in a quite different light by these two qualifying sentences, omitted later:

C.S. is a woman who has read enormously, studied by-ways of mathematics, histories of sorcery or period costume, always consuming them whole. These subjects leak in—so does her economics, her finance.

Also omitted from the published diary are details which show that Palmer reflected—and not ungenerously—on the contradictions she found in Christina Stead:

When she came to England, she carried her few banknotes sewn into her corset. She now has a sense of security with her husband (not wealthy, I gather, but security and a little more), and her books have brought in something—as well as sudden, dramatic fame, in a heady draught.

The fact is, Christina Stead, a magpie in her eclecticism, was as interested in hats as in international finance. She made the mistake, perhaps, of imagining that Nettie Palmer was equally diverse in her interests. The other factor at play is Stead's self-image. It was certainly important to her to be seen as an elegant, fashionable woman, who had been influenced by her years in Paris, and she would have liked Nettie Palmer to carry this image of her, Christina Stead, back to Australia.

Stead's excitement was neither snobbery nor feminine silliness. The truth, which Palmer seems not to have guessed, was that Stead felt terribly insecure about her appearance, and that French clothes *had* liberated her in some small way. Fifteen years later, Stead would tell her sister Kate that in Paris, for the first time, she had found clothing that suited her.

Palmer does not seem to have realised that Christina Stead's was the grab-bag mind of an imaginative writer rather than an intellectual—the kind of mind Patrick White describes as *his*, and for which he, too, was criticised. His defence, in his autobiography, could equally well have been Stead's:

> I knew I hadn't a scholar's mind. Such as I had was more like the calico bag hanging from the sewing-room door-knob, stuffed with snippets of material of contrasting textures and clashing colours, which might at some future date be put to some practical, aesthetic, or even poetic use.

Patrick White adds—and Stead could not have put it better:

> I believe it is this rag-bag of a disorderly mind which has more than anything offended some of my Australian academic critics. For them the controlled monochrome of reason, for me the omnium gatherum of instinctual colour which illuminates the more often than not irrational behaviour of sensual man.[26]

It was a sociable week. The French writers entertained the delegates to lunch at a restaurant on the Champs-Elysées; there were private get-togethers and late 'evening sit-ups', and tea at the Soviet Embassy on the last day. Christina Stead would remember this conference as 'those amazing five days'. Ralph Fox, in the *Daily Worker*, proclaimed it 'one of the most remarkable meetings in the history of the world'.

The return trip to London on Thursday 27 June was a lively affair. Stead, Fox, Amabel Williams-Ellis, Pearl Binder and Nettie Palmer travelled back together, full of the congress. On arrival in London, they discussed sharing a taxi to Hampstead, but Stead pressed them to drop in at her flat, to tell Bill Blech about the congress. Two weeks later, Nettie Palmer visited the flat again:

July 12th, 1935.
Another hot July afternoon. London people, plunging into shorts, seem to feel the pressure of it. I had to go up and see Christina Stead with a message. Up ... A huge building of flats, and hers on the seventh storey—a long corridor from the lift. Lightness, modernity. One room given up to a gramophone with masses of records on shelves, and to a typewriter, with masses of files in pigeon-holes. (Files of *Humanité*, for instance, on account of its *faits divers*, Christina surprisingly said.)

She looked flushed, emaciated, romantic. She had been writing a long, elaborate account of the Paris Writers' Congress, as well as her usual work, and taking it out of herself. Her husband, William Blake, came in, a powerful, rather nuggety dark man, and his mother, a little lonely expatriate from Germany ... Christina would make tea for me, gracefully whisking out pink serviettes, but adventurously, as if making *maté* in honour of a Uruguayan; and offering me some wine as if for relief.

From one window there was a view of Westminster, not only the spires but the parks. A sense of rolling carriages in golden afternoon dust (motors, I suppose). The London season in flower ... They were speaking of Ralph Fox, who comes regularly to read economics with W.B., and what a serious, versatile fellow Fox is. And what a linguist; they declare he can talk Russian with peasants in their villages, and of course he's in Paris every few months making speeches at workers' meetings in the suburbs.

W.B. had a bit of a hangover from too many cocktails somewhere yesterday evening. I happened to mention being to dinner at the fantastic-serious Boulestin's ... 'Boulestin,' said Blake with heavy caution, 'Boulestin's not entirely trustworthy with his *plat du jour*; that can be commonplace. But with someone who knows how to order, as I gather your host did ...'

He's like that—a connoisseur in all the arts, an epicure to whom even Boulestin's is not the last word in cookery. When we moved back to the next room, Christina put on a special recording of 'The Sunken Cathedral'.

Years later, Stead would tell a friend that on the train to Paris, speeding through Normandy on the way to the congress, she was standing in the corridor watching the countryside when Ralph Fox came up to her and said, 'Let's get out at the next station and walk through Normandy. I don't want to go to this conference.' She felt a stab of excitement, thoughts flew through her head, and she did not answer. Two minutes later, another delegate joined them and the moment passed.[27]

If, throughout the congress and the following weeks, Nettie Palmer was struck by Stead's feverish look, it was the look of a woman flushed with love.

In mid July 1935, just as Stead and Blech were establishing a circle of friends in London and beginning to warm to a city neither had ever much liked, the storm cloud that had darkened their existence for some time burst, and the phantom buggy crashed.

The Travelers' Bank had been in trouble for a long time now, with heavy withdrawals and bad speculations. Bill Blech had officially resigned on 3 May 1935.

On Thursday 19 July, the bank in rue de la Paix did not open its doors. A notice informed clients that it would re-open the next day. But the next day the doors remained closed. The French police searched Peter Neidecker's luxury apartment on the Avenue Foch to no avail. Neidecker, his wife Sybil, his three children and his two brothers had disappeared without trace. On Saturday, the police entered the bank, placed it under seal, seized the account books and correspondence and issued warrants for the arrest of the two brothers most involved, Bertrand Coles (Peter) and Aubrey Neidecker. On 22 July, the London *Daily Telegraph* reported:

> The whereabouts of Mr. Coles Neidecker are uncertain. His yacht, the *Etoile Filante*, left Marseilles some days ago, but it is not known whether he was on board.
>
> The bank has associated institutions in France, Brussels, Amsterdam and London. It is reported to have gold reserves in London ...

The names of the banker's wife, Mrs. Sybil Neidecker, and their three children, appeared in the passenger list of a liner that left Havre for the United States last month.

French and English newspapers offered daily bulletins on the mystery. Police searched for the American Scarlet Pimpernel in Paris, London, Brussels, the Riviera and on the high seas. Overseas branches of the bank had also closed. The Director of the London branch, on Old Broad Street, affirmed that liabilities from the Travelers' Bank (estimated at something in the vicinity of £1 300 000) would affect its clients. Frederick Sard, Director of the New York branch, claimed he had had no news of Neidecker and presumed he must be on his yacht.

As a senior employee in the bank until May 1935, Bill Blech was heavily implicated. Fellow bankers in London advised him to leave Europe without delay. He and Christina took two or three days to pack and make passport and visa arrangements. Their friend Jean MacAlpine (little realising what a chore she was taking on) kindly offered to see to the subletting of their flat. Bill Blech, his mother and Christina Stead walked out of the Baker Street flat, leaving behind furniture, books and records, not knowing if or when they would be back.

At the end of July, B. Coles Neidecker was arrested when he tried to withdraw $50 000 from a frozen account in a New York bank. He was released on bail, pending trial. The same day, Aubrey and George Neidecker were provisionally detained when they arrived in Norfolk, Virginia, on a liner that had left France from Le Havre. With them were their mother, Peter's wife Sybil Neidecker and the three children. The French Embassy put extradition orders in to Washington.[28]

Christina, Bill and Rosa Blech fled London, then 'streaked through Ireland' from Dublin to Galway, catching glimpses of peatbogs and 'stormbitten isles'. Without delay, they boarded a boat for the New World.[29]

6

Manhattan Peaks

~~~

JULY 1935 – APRIL 1936

T HE TRIO DISEMBARKED in Boston, among boisterous Irish families emigrating to the New World. After eight years in Europe, Rosa Blech was pleased to be returning to America, which she considered home, having lived there for some thirty-three years. It was where she wanted to die, she told her son.

'After an extensive night-course on American society under C. B. De Mille and Sam Goldwyn', Christina Stead fully expected all Americans to be 'incurably tough, cruel wisecrackers, snipers of the gibe that kills, machine gunners of quickfire backchat'. In notes entitled 'America', in which she describes her first impressions, she writes that she was quickly disabused. The Americans she met were 'slow and genial'. Though they could be funny, they were far from quick-witted. And after Europe, the prevailing 'flatfoot commonsense' of Americans irritated her.

She could see why Boston was the 'immigrant's dream'. She loved the old brownstone districts, with their reminders of the War of Independence and the birth of the Union. The tree-lined streets had carts bursting with summer fruit, flowers and vegetables, in an abundance she had not seen since leaving Australia. The democratic atmosphere also reminded her of Sydney.

The first day in Boston I thought I was in a sort of socialist commonwealth, the policeman in his white shirt-sleeves called my taxi-driver 'buddy', the postman in his blue shirt, the officials of all sorts, amiable and not obsequious: what a change from the brass hats and brass buttons of Europe, I thought.

Though this was the depth of the Depression, America seemed to gleam with a sense of the future, like a 'skyrocket waiting to be let off'. It was the sort of place, Stead mused, that made one wish to live for 200 years to see what would happen next. It struck her as the ideal place to bring up children. And yet the middle classes looked glum. Years later she recalled:

> When Bill and I first landed with his old mother in Boston, … he took us for lunch to some big Boston hotel and, waiting for our food, I looked around and said to Bill in an undertone (not to worry the old lady): 'Bill, has there been a national disaster today? Has the President died? Or what?' But nothing had happened: it was the way the faces of the public struck me—not down-and-outers—but Bostonians having a good lunch.[1]

It did not take long for her to discover the sinister underside to the richest country in the world. Beside Boston's fine bay was the 'rottenest slum' she had ever seen. And on 23 August, when she and Bill stopped to watch a demonstration to commemorate the execution of anarchists Sacco and Vanzetti eight years before, she was shocked by the extreme hostility the police showed the pickets. Was this the Land of Freedom?

They stayed a fortnight in Boston, long enough for Stead to finish revising *The Beauties and Furies* and post it off to Peter Davies. They took a circuitous route, through Washington and Baltimore, to New York, and arrived in August, that notoriously sweaty month, which Stead would portray so vividly in *The People with the Dogs*. It was dawn and still fresh on the water when they approached Manhattan under the Brooklyn Bridge. Stead found the sight of the 'Wall Street main ranges' and the uptown peaks (those 'miles of vertical glass') beautiful beyond expectation.

She and Blech had smiles 'like sunflowers' when they emerged from the offices of her American publishers, D. Appleton-Century. They had called in to collect their mail and found themselves ushered with great conviviality into the presence of high-powered business people, who instantly swung into gear and discussed marketing strategies. They wanted Stead to see reporters and give interviews, write an article on her first impressions of America and produce more of her highly successful short stories. Stead came out calling it 'the land of boundless importunity'.

They learnt later that D. Appleton-Century was practically run by Wall Street; the heads of the firm were financial rather than literary men. 'The firm is liberal-conservative,' Stead wrote to Florence James, 'and I believe more or less strictly Gentile. (You may laugh, but anti-semitism is a very active yeast in this Germanic country. There are plenty of large banking and commercial firms who will not employ a Jew in any position.)'

Within the first month, Radio of America had asked Stead for a copy of her forthcoming novel for a possible radio script. A friend had offered to talk to another friend about a possible scriptwriting job for her in Hollywood. A businessman in insurance, a multi-millionaire with a reputation for toughness, offered Blech work on a commission basis. Blech was sick at the thought of it, and decided he would create a better impression by not jumping at the first offers made. He calculated that he had just enough savings to keep them for twelve months, if necessary. Stead rather hoped he would take some time off: the traumas of the last years had taken their toll. 'He is not at all strong yet,' she told Florence James; 'he has that tired little face that I hate to see.' On a strict diet to lose weight, he occasionally looked quite thin and haggard. 'I feel cheated as if somebody had stolen fifty pounds of Bill away. I like as much Bill as possible.'

<hr>

There was, Stead observed, a fundamental contradiction in the American philosophy of life. In *I'm Dying Laughing*, mostly written in the 1950s, Emily Wilkes probably reflects Stead's own view of the 'American dilemma'.

> You want to be free and break new ground, speak your mind, fear no man, have the neighbours acknowledge that you're a good man; and at the same time you want to be a success, make money, join the country club, get the votes and kick the other man in the teeth and off the ladder. You believe sincerely in Washington, Jefferson, Lincoln; and also know that you'll get your nose bloodied if not worse, if you don't believe in Rockefeller, Mellon, General Motors and Sears Roebuck.

Everything in America seemed to be expressed in terms of money. The snatches of conversation Stead heard in the street were usually about 'bucks' and 'dollars'. In the women's magazines, marriage and divorce were discussed in monetary terms: young women were advised to weigh up the security value of suitors; older women were given advice on coercing ex-husbands for alimony. 'This is horrible, revolting,' Stead groaned. 'Nowhere else is human love discussed in terms of the stock market.'[2]

In *Letty Fox*, a novel set largely in New York in the 1930s and 1940s, Stead would be scathing about the mercenary attitude towards marriage inculcated in American women. A friend writes to Mathilde Fox (modelled on Mollie Blech):

> Nothing is too good for you. You are a wife and a mother. You have given life … We must protect our young. Your husband is obliged to keep you, and if he will not, go to a lawyer, and the lawyer will see to it that he pays, and if he will not, don't be soft, Mathilde, clap him into jail!

In the novel it is a Canadian woman (Pauline) who expresses Stead's own view:

> What luck you have, you American women! Men who pay for everything and don't ask for accounts. Yes, it's Protestantism. The men believe they've done their wives insult and injury by sleeping with them. They must pay forever! … As for the women … they want to get married, naturally. But they behave as if they are disabled for life as soon as they're married. They go in for man-sweating.

After her experience of Mollie Blech's emotional manipulations, Stead was not predisposed to like American women. And after France, she was dismayed by the polarisation of the sexes in America. The worship of the 'baby-face girl' in American films seemed to her to reflect psychological immaturity. In mixed groups, American men tended to exhibit a 'weariness or sense of superiority' towards women, and either talked business or told 'pointless schoolboy antiquated dirty stories'. After a few weeks in the States, Stead told Florence James that she would have to take up tatting or crochet.

> The long hours sitting round listening to the dispersed but emphatic New York prattle, Bill's disquisitions and general vocal thunder will drive me batty or badtempered if I don't have something to fill in the time … My (universally)

clever comments and the studied cunning of my jokes are passed over like sandgrains in the surf ... The result is I get into a state of mute rage, passive murder or heavy sleep. No woman is listened to in New York.

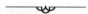

Despite the energetic money-talk encountered in business circles, America in 1935 was a 'stricken nation', as Franklin D. Roosevelt put it. In no other country had expansion been so rapid up till 1929, and in no other country had the economic collapse been so great. When Roosevelt became President in March 1933, during yet another panic in the American banks, he had promised the people a 'New Deal'. In a series of radio addresses—his famous 'fireside chats'—he had outlined his strategy: Relief, Recovery and Reform. His Social Security Act provided financial aid for the unemployed and aged and made provisions for maternal and child health services and public health care, representing a radical break with the traditional American emphasis on self-reliance. The most important part of his program was work relief, which promoted the principle of relief for work done rather than a dole. Vast programs had been set up.

The money to fund the New Deal program was raised by increased taxes. Predictably, it attracted hostility. Stead, extremely impressed by Roosevelt's achievements, was taken aback by what she saw as a peculiarly American hostility towards social welfare recipients. In *I'm Dying Laughing*, Emily Wilkes points out that the virtue Americans made of success had left them psychologically unprepared for the terrible Depression in their country. They had learnt to regard themselves as winners: how could they be losers?

> We're Americans, we can't fail, some sort of covered wagon will get us through; yet we see lean and tattered misery, the banks failed ... dust-storms which used to be farms bowling along the roads covering the corpses of crows and men; and we despair, despair ... We came over in rowboats and founded the USA, we beat the old inhabitants into the dust, we won the West, and now we starve. It isn't right.

Stead had not been excited about coming to New York. They had left behind a pleasant flat, with some fine possessions assembled over the past six years, and good friends. Worst of all, it had been a traumatic and ignominious departure.

At first, she found the city streets ugly; she missed the old buildings of Europe. But it took only three weeks for her to acknowledge that Manhattan had charm. 'There are hundreds of quiet spots, plenty of streets, dark, sweet, romantic, with their own atmospheres, streets like the quiet alleys of Mayfair, like old Paris, like Naples.'[3]

To her relief, Bill managed to organise accommodation for his mother with old German relatives. The arrangement was inexpensive, and Rosa Blech was happy. She was only sixty-six, but had become quite fragile. She would soon have her beautiful long white hair cut short, because her arms were too weak to plait and pin it up every morning. And her mind was wandering badly. 'She has completely forgotten the modern world,' Stead told Florence James, 'and has retreated some thirty-five years into the old days. She doesn't even want to live with Bill now, completely cheerful and rejuvenated in a circle of kaffee-klatsch old girls. This has also made us both more cheerful.'

After installing Rosa, they spent a week with old friends, Sam and Riva Putnam, in their dilapidated timber house near Lambertville, New Jersey. Sam Putnam, their translator friend from Paris days, had been back in the States for two years. He too was shocked to see America in depression, and had become a stalwart communist. For Stead, the brief stay in the countryside was just what she needed after the tension of the previous weeks.

I was a different person out there, mad with energy from morning to night. We came straight back to mad Manhattan and I was dazed the first day and ill for two days after with the nervous shock.

To her, humans were basically animals: they had a natural habitat and suffered when they were removed from it. She considered that her body responded badly to cold northern hemisphere winters and that she was happiest when she spent time in the country.

They found a two-room flat in an old stone house on a quiet street downtown. It was cheap because the street contained factories and warehouses; they were the only residents. Stead liked the large airy rooms, the French windows and the fancy plaster ceilings. Not until darkness descended did they discover that it swarmed with cockroaches.

In the evenings, Stead and Blech went on long walks, observing the ethnic mixes and the street life. One evening, walking along 18th Street, Stead was attracted to a neon sign hanging outside an apartment building that advertised toy and puppet makers. Fascinated, she thought she would like to write a story about puppets. But this meant knowing more about the art of puppetry. She and Blech knocked on the door and introduced themselves to puppeteer Kunz and his wife. The son of a toymaker, Kunz looked a bit like a woodcut puppet himself, Stead fancied. He told them how he had fled from Nazi Germany with his large family of puppets after the burning of the Reichstag.

From Kunz, Stead learnt the principles of marionetting, staging, lighting and stringing. He made them several string puppets. Their favourite was Nello the clown: a little wooden man, thirteen and a half inches high, dressed in a yellow silk pantaloon dress, whom they named after the trapezist Gianello, in Edmund de Goncourt's *Les Frères Zemganno*. Their other favourite was lisping Lucy, who called herself 'Loothy'. Stead became quite skilled at working Nello's eleven strings, and was delighted when children almost believed Nello was real. The Kunzes and their workshop-apartment, bursting with puppets and toys, would be the inspiration for Waldemar and Dorothea Block in *The People with the Dogs*.

Having left all their possessions behind in London, Blech and Stead had no heart for acquiring new things, and they did not intend to settle in New York. For the time being they were making do with one plate, a double saucepan, a milk-measure-plus-lemon-squeezer, a coffee jar and two cups with saucers—all from Woolworth.

At first, because of the bank scandal, Bill insisted that they should keep a low profile. They hardly saw a soul during their first month in New York, and their home address was kept secret from all except a couple of trusted friends. The need for secrecy effectively put an end to any plans on the part of D. Appleton-Century to promote their new author with interviews. 'The three most intimate things have taboo written on them,' Stead told Florence James. 'The dear old Bank which went kerflooey and can't … be dragged into reminiscences, my family situation and my politics.' America was not as broadminded as Europe about unmarried couples, and D. Appleton-Century did not publish communists.

Stead could have done with some publicity: Americans believed in self-promotion. But she was shy, as usual, and felt scarcely presentable. American middle-class women surprised her by their smartness; there was even more good-quality clothing in New York than in Paris. And this business-oriented environment meant that one had to look well dressed to be taken seriously. She and Blech decided it was worth the investment for her to go out and splurge on a smart coat and shoes. The purchases made her feel guilty but better equipped to 'fool the world'.[4]

Stead's last two royalty cheques had gone on London rent and the boat fare to America. Peter Davies, though he now insisted on first names, had not paid an advance for *The Beauties and Furies*. Stead was bitter about this, but too shy to raise the subject. Apart from the small and irregular income from royalties, she had not earned any money since the end of 1934, when she stopped working at the bank for good.

Blech was not finding work. Business was slow, the stock market depressed. After the Travelers' Bank disaster, he was more disillusioned than ever by the world of finance. But he still had a mild interest in the wheat business, and one option was to resort to his old backstop. Alf Hurst was wanting to set up an arbitraging business in Canada; for a while it looked as if they might be leaving for there any day. Blech longed to be back in Europe, but until they heard the outcome of the court case in France, they could not contemplate returning; and with war threatening in Europe and the Pacific, they were better off where they were. Bill even talked about Australia, but the trip was prohibitively expensive, Bill hated travelling and Christina was sure he would not be happy so far from Ruth, his mother and friends.

Mollie and Ruth were also in New York. Bill kept his address secret from them at first, telling them he was mostly in Washington and Philadelphia, looking for work.

Mollie told him she was thinking of a separation. Ironically, Stead felt ambivalent about divorce just then. She was afraid that her resident's status as well as her literary reputation might be affected if she were named in a divorce suit. America was far more puritanical than Europe and her tourist visa, valid for only six months at a time, was somewhat precarious. She told Florence James, her one confidante:

It's my private belief that Bill and Mollie have arranged not to divorce so as not to give Ruth anxiety while she is growing up and at high-school.

I only assume this, but it seems the most logical answer to all the paradoxes of the affair. But I am not discussing anything of this sort with Bill—at least not at present, while he is out of a job and my literary success is not yet established.[5]

Mollie's talk of separation turned out to be as hollow as ever. Two months later, Stead reported wearily:

The lethargic lady makes no move towards divorce. Bill sees the little girl every few days, takes her to the pictures and so forth but does not go up to the apartment and doesn't meet the lady: it seems my coming to the land of the free and the home of the brave was a great surprise to her. I don't know exactly what she's waiting for.

Bill was now forty-one, and he longed to spend his days doing something that really interested him. His private desire was to write—historical books, fiction or non-fiction, that required the research he so loved—but he lacked confidence. He wrote easily, but suspected that good talkers made bad writers. Christina may have pointed out that this was not so of her father; she certainly encouraged Bill to follow his yearnings. The problem was income.

Their unsettled existence made it difficult for her to write anything sustained, and Stead toyed with the idea of a play. She read about a playwriting course, but it was too expensive. ('We couldn't bring ourselves to peel $10 off the pile.') She thought of writing more short stories, and asked Florence James to forward a book left behind in London. Stead had found Georges Polti's *Thirty-Six Dramatic Situations*, in which he outlined the thirty-six plots on which he claimed all literature was based, a great inspiration.

By November, she was making notes for a project that filled her with enthusiasm: a novel about the Paris bank. She had been planning this for years. It was by far her most ambitious project to date. From the beginning, she had high hopes for this novel.

At the same time, Stead was collecting material about her present life for a future novel set in the US. She was fascinated by American social relations. Middle-class New York seemed obsessed with social correctness. When Stead first read the mindless newspaper advertisements and letters in women's magazines, she giggled admiringly, presuming they were a parody, but she soon realised her mistake. She cut out and filed the best ones.

Although she did not know it then, she was already working on *Letty Fox*, a novel published in 1946, which explores and satirises American ruthlessness and conformism, sexual conventions and so-called radicalism.

Blech was sending testimonies about his role in the bank to his lawyer in France. What saved him was that he had rented the London flat in his name. This was taken as evidence that he was officially domiciled in England and therefore not closely associated with the bank at the time of its collapse. It was a fortunate twist of fate, for he had wanted to put the flat in Stead's name for income-tax purposes.

At the end of September Stead and Blech spent an evening with the Neideckers, who were still in New York. 'It was quite a reunion after all these months,' Christina told Florence. 'However, it was purely a friendly call: Bill does not intend to go into business with or through them.' The letter indicated no hint of resentment or anger; she and Bill found Neidecker as charming as ever. He told them the court proceedings were expected to take some time.

> Pete has acted with real gallantry towards everyone ever connected with him, including his two brothers, despite their official positions. As to Bill, he has only been mentioned on a par with the rest of the office-staff, which is perfectly correct as he held no position. In any case, Pete has stated in his evidence that Bill knew nothing of the bank's condition and 'began going away from them from June 1934'. This is a fact and makes things easier for Bill.

According to Peter Neidecker, after Blech's resignation in May 1935, he and his brothers had struggled on a few more weeks, then paid the employees a month's salary and taken flight. Neidecker claimed that he himself had not been aware how little cash was left in the bank, and that his brother Aubrey had not known about certain losses. The books were 'in a perfectly fantastic state'.

In October, when they saw the Neideckers again, Stead asked Peter Neidecker if he would mind her writing a novel set in the Paris bank. He apparently gave her his 'full and glad permission' to write everything she knew.[6] He probably never imagined that she knew as much as she did.

Their first foray into New York 'society' was a large fundraising banquet for the Communist Party held in early October. That evening, Stead and Blech met two genial and passionate men who would become lifelong friends. One was Mike Gold; the other Harry Bloom.

Mike Gold, whom she had met at the Paris Writers' Congress, greeted Stead enthusiastically. (He had read her *Left Review* article, in which she had written about 'irresistible Mike'.) He was in good spirits: on the boat going to the congress he had met the woman he was to marry, a French woman living in America. Years later, Stead would work the shipboard romance into *I'm Dying Laughing*.[7]

In the heady, politicised atmosphere of the mid 1930s, Gold was widely regarded as the embodiment of the Proletarian Hero. Stead described him to her brother as 'the Yankee 'tribune of the people', a local Maxim Gorki, known from coast to coast by lumberjacks and deckhands'.[8] His 1930 bestseller, *Jews Without Money*, a thinly fictionalised portrayal of his childhood in the Jewish immigrant Lower East Side, was generally hailed as a model of proletarian literature.

Born Iztok Isaac Granich, the eldest son of a Romanian father and a Hungarian mother, he had changed his name, unofficially, to Mike Gold, after an old man who had fought in the Civil War on the Union side. Like Bill Blech, Gold had been obliged to leave school in his early teens. A few years later, influenced by the Bolshevik Revolution, his hero John Reed and the journal the *Masses*, he became a communist radical. In 1921 he had joined the editorial staff of the *Liberator*, the sequel to the *Masses*, suppressed by the government because it denounced the imperialist war. In 1926 he became a founding editor of the New *Masses*.

He was forty-two that year, a politically committed writer, a man of action, handsome in an unkempt sort of way and with considerable personal charm. Joseph Freeman, fellow *Liberator* editor, paints this portrait of the younger Gold:

> To us Mike Gold appeared to be the outstanding 'proletarian' of the group. He affected dirty shirts, a big, black, uncleaned Stetson with the brim of a sombrero; smoked stinking, twisted, Italian three-cent cigars, and

spat frequently on the floor ... These 'proletarian' props were as much a costume as the bohemian's sideburns and opera cape ... His assumed *naiveté*, dark, animated face and deep laughter, and his ironic mode of speech won people easily.[9]

Mike Gold married soon after Stead met him, and became (according to a close friend) 'an exemplary paterfamilias'.[10] The transformed Gold would be the model for Jean Frère, the brotherly comrade in *House of All Nations*. Elisabeth, who became Mrs Granich, recalls that in the early days of her marriage Christina seemed 'more than keen on Mike', such that she wondered whether they had once been lovers.[11] Her conjecture is revealing: though probably unfounded, it points to an aspect of Stead's behaviour that was becoming increasingly evident—her flirtatiousness.

Mike Gold introduced Blech and Stead to his friend Harry Bloom, a tall, kind-looking man with small blue eyes and a hearty laugh. Harry (whose original name was Aaron) was born in New York to Lithuanian parents. As a youth, he had been active in the Industrial Workers of the World, the IWW (popularly known as the Wobblies), an exuberant and lawless section of the socialist Left whose ideology rested almost exclusively on the notion of 'sabotage'. A pharmacist, Bloom ran a drugstore at Brighton Beach, just east of Coney Island, which had a large Russian Jewish community. Because he always seemed to be patching up members of Brighton's warring gangs, his friends called him 'the Doc' or 'the Fixer'.

Observing him that first evening, Stead imagined, in her fanciful way, that he saw himself as Mike Gold's protector. Bloom was hearty and strong, whereas Gold, a diabetic and epileptic, was often ill—though he did not allow this to curtail his activities. Harry Bloom's brotherly loyalty towards men he loved—Mike Gold and later Bill Blech—strongly appealed to Stead. Ever since adolescence she had tended to idealise male friendship: to her, Harry Bloom would always be the 'treue Heinrich', after the faithful servant of the 'Frog Prince' in the Grimms' story by that name.

Stead flirted with both Gold and Bloom. Harry Bloom, a married man with two children, responded equally flirtatiously when his wife was not around.[12] As much as she admired fraternal loyalty, Stead had little sense of loyalty to other women.

In *The People with the Dogs*, Al Burrows is a pharmacist with a 'great joyous melodious laugh', nicknamed 'Al-the-Fixer'. His wife is jealous, and with good reason.

———— ⌇ ————

They were sociable times, those Popular Front years, from May 1935 to the outbreak of the Second World War—and the sense of solidarity was greatly reinforced by the Spanish Civil War. Writers, generally isolated, had never seen the like and never would again. Until the war brought it all to a standstill, there were innumerable fundraising gatherings—rallies, public banquets, parties in people's homes.

The notion of a broad leftwing Popular Front was energetically promoted by communist parties around the world. Just before the Paris Writers' Congress, the American Communist Party had held the First American Writers' Congress in New York. It saw the establishment of the League of American Writers, which was broader and less sectarian in scope than the John Reed Clubs, founded in 1929 expressly to encourage proletarian writers. Stead and Blech would become League members in June 1937.

Soon after the October banquet, Mike Gold took Blech and Stead to the office of the *New Masses*, at No. 31 East 27th Street, to meet the editors. The name, the New Masses, implied a continuity with the old *Masses*, founded in 1911. In fact, its editorial direction had veered away from that of its predecessor. The Masses editors—Max Eastman, John Reed and Floyd Dell—had been lofty romantics, literary radicals who, although socialists, were not prepared to subordinate art to politics. Now John Reed was dead, Dell was a disillusioned bohemian and Max Eastman deplored the way the *New Masses* swam 'in the stream of pro-Soviet fanaticism'.[13]

Though it was not officially the organ of the Communist Party, the *New Masses* was the principal communist weekly in America, and most of its associates were Party members. The magazine's business manager was William Browder, brother of Earl Browder, who was General Secretary of the CPUSA. By the mid 1930s, the *New Masses* had become less sectarian, in the spirit of the Popular Front. Hoping to promote proletarian literature, it had recently published a number of distinguished non-Party writers: Theodore Dreiser, Sherwood Anderson, John Dos Passos, Edmund Wilson, Erskine Caldwell, James Farrell and Ernest Hemingway.

One of the editors whom Blech and Stead met for the first time that day was to become another lifelong friend. The 'neat, limber young man with clear large appraising eyes' they first saw quietly working at his desk in the corner was Stanley Burnshaw, thirty that year and a talented poet and literary critic.[14]

———— ◆ ————

Proletarian literature dominated the literary scene in the mid to late 1930s. It was partly for this reason that Stead was so excited about her Paris bank novel. This novel would be ideologically correct: it would expose the sordid machinations of fraudulent capitalists. Later, she would realise that it was perhaps 'revolutionary' literature, but it was not 'proletarian' literature. From London, she would write to Stanley Burnshaw in October 1936, tongue in cheek:

> Everyone is still waiting with baited breath for *the* left novel. It can't be mine, as there is no member of the lower classes in my bank novel and even—I think this shows the highest moral courage—one of my chief moral heroes is a blueblooded *Count*.

What exactly was proletarian literature? It was a popular term, not confined to the extreme Left, though in the States its main champion was the New Masses. In 1935, Clifford Odets' one-act strike play *Waiting for Lefty* was a Broadway hit and considered good proletarian literature. That same year, Mike Gold and five comrades brought out an anthology, *Proletarian Literature in the United States*. The writers of the future were workers, they declared. In the transition period, de-gentrified middle-class sympathisers were needed to show the workers the way. As subject matter, it was assumed that proletarian writers would certainly be 'more interested in unemployment, strikes, the fight against war and fascism, revolution and counter-revolution than in nightingales, the stream of the middle-class unconscious, or love in Greenwich Village'. (This last was a dig at editor Floyd Dell, who had always maintained that Freudian science and psychosexual themes were as important as the class struggle.)

There were endless battles over critical tenets and judgements. Mike Gold's views were among the more dogmatic. According to him, writers should not invent 'precious silly little agonies': there was drama enough in the 'suffering of the hungry, persecuted and heroic millions'. The new literature must be 'functional' and 'eschew verbal acrobatics'. Condemned were writers of the ilk of Proust and Dostoevski; indeed, Proust was scornfully designated the 'master-masturbator of the bourgeois literature'.[15] He did not fit the ideal of the proletarian writer: a smoking, drinking, robust man who slashed out his sentences with a salty disregard for the niceties of style.

Modernist experimentation, interior monologue, exploration of the unconscious were well buried in the leftwing rhetoric of the 1930s. It is probably no coincidence that *House of All Nations*, written in this atmosphere, is Stead's most 'male' book: there is no sense of a woman's world behind the scenes or a female writer behind the narrative. In the 1930s, successful female writers wrote like men. Among the women associated with the *New Masses* was Josephine Herbst, an intrepid reporter (she was to report from Spain during the Civil War), whose novels were praised by Hemingway. Genevieve Taggard's poetry spoke of the necessity for self-discipline, the need to master the passions. Ruth McKenney, who was nine years younger than Stead and later became a close friend, would be ashamed of her popular stories about her family, such as *My Sister Eileen*, published in 1938, but proud of the nonfictional *Industrial Valley* (1939), about the struggles of the Akron rubber workers. Stead would admire her proletarian epic *Jake Home* (1943), about a communist labour organiser who tours the country to campaign on behalf of Sacco and Vanzetti.

The standard proletarian novel formula was a conflict between capitalists and workers, which nearly always ended in defeat for the workers but brought about the politicisation of several worthy characters. Neither John Dos Passos' USA trilogy, which showed the degradation of character in modern materialistic America, nor Theodore Dreiser's *Tragic America*, with its hopeful belief in socialism, was considered a good model. But finally, in 1939, *The Grapes of Wrath* would not only win Steinbeck the Pulitzer Prize; according to the *New Masses*, it possessed all the qualities of good proletarian literature. Steinbeck had personally experienced duststorms and tenant farmers and tractors and automobiles and hoovervilles and cotton picking and fruit picking, and he wrote with an understanding of economic forces. The book even had the unusual virtue of optimism; Marxist critics were continually bemoaning the pessimism of most proletarian novels.

Christina Stead's own writing scarcely exemplified swift action, clear form and the eschewal of verbal acrobatics, yet she spoke up for the vigour and ideology of proletarian literature. Like the indomitable Blech, like most of their friends, she was quite persuaded that good writing went together with socialism. To some extent it was more a matter of peer pressure than personal conviction. Privately she told Stanley Burnshaw that 'party politics cramps a poetic mind'.[16] But in the 1930s, whenever she wrote for a communist readership, Stead used the standard rhetoric.

From today's perspective, the communist rhetoric of the 1930s may seem extraordinarily naive. But as it was the prevailing discourse among Stead's friends and associates, she found it almost impossible to stand aside from it. 'Proletarian literature', very much a 1930s' product, would virtually die with the advent of the Second World War.

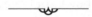

At the beginning of November 1935, Stead and Blech moved to a large, handsomely furnished room, upstairs, in a brownstone house in Brooklyn. Remsen Street ended on the Esplanade, from where there was a glorious view of the Wall Street pinnacles across the East River. The French owner of No. 34 was choosy about her tenants, several of whom were young Princeton graduates, but was very welcoming when Blech (always the house-hunter) told her that his wife was an 'English writer'. Stead would always speak French with the landlady.

She was busy making notes on her banking novel. This involved character sketches of all seventy-two characters. With Bill's help, she filled pages with Peter Neidecker's characteristic remarks. She sketched the different intrigues to be woven into the narrative. Based on the real thing, she drew up an intricate plan of the structure of the fictional bank, its branches and associated companies. She wrote all these notes in French, with the idea that it would help her recapture the atmosphere of Paris. This might explain the occasional lapses into French syntax, which several critics would observe.

At weekends, they saw friends. Once they visited Harry and Ruth Bakwin, wealthy friends from their Paris days, who had a large country estate with a private lake at Kitchawan, up the Hudson River. Harry Bakwin (the 'Doctor from New York' in *The Salzburg Tales*) was the Chief Pediatrician at New York's Bellevue hospital; he and his wife were art connoisseurs and had a private gallery in their New York home.

Another time they took the bus to Lambertville and stayed again with the Putnams. This time, the atmosphere was tense: Sam Putnam was showing the effects of a recent drinking binge, and Riva was upset. The couple invested all their hopes in their son, now ten. Stead would describe the domestic situation, the alcoholism and the prodding of the child, something she vehemently disliked, in her story 'The Right-Angled Creek'.

By December, they knew enough people to host a large party on Christmas Eve. Stead bought more glasses from Woolworth and their landlady lent them jugs and bowls, but they could not bring themselves to skimp on their Christmas tree. The Norwegian spruce tree touched the thirteen-foot ceiling and they decorated it with childlike zest.

Christmas in New York was splendid. It had snowed and the white streets were aglow with lights and Christmas trees. Fifth Avenue was 'like a Hans Christian Andersen fairy-tale'. Sixty thousand destitutes were given a Christmas dinner at the city's expense. In stark contrast was the conduct on Wall Street. Bill, who was perhaps briefly employed on contract work, came home and told Christina all about it. Christina, much amused, passed the details on to Florence James:

> On Christmas Eve, all is blue in Wall Street. Every house offers 'wassail' (it is called) to its customers and friends. … It is your duty to go round and drink the wassail of the houses you know: otherwise they think … that you aren't a right guy. Dear little Bill had about eleven whiskies in the course of the day, but his hard-drinking friends (they finish off every afternoon with highballs) had notched up about 47 apiece when he left. Bill arrived home precisely at five (his appointed hour), ineffably gay, twinkling, seraphic, but perfectly steady, knowing what time it was, and with a load of goods for the party. I realised he had character!

They spent Christmas Day with the Bakwins, at Kitchawan. The lake had frozen over and Harry gave Stead her first lesson in ice-skating: 'I looked nice enough in borrowed gear, but did I bump!' She walked in the snow and amused herself with jigsaws and patience, while the others endlessly played bridge. Harry Bakwin drove them home in a snowstorm— 'a ghostly ride at midnight'.

Life in New York frustrated them both. Blech's old friends now seemed like 'stick-in-the-muds' to him after his years in Paris, and the Wall Street world no longer held the least attraction. Stead felt isolated among people who seemed to talk about nothing but business or politics.

In the New Year, she felt thoroughly depressed when she received the proofs of *The Beauties and Furies* from London. Even at this late stage, Peter Davies was wanting major changes. She rationalised that Davies had reservations about everything she had ever written. With every manuscript, his 'little fake compliments' had been accompanied by a 'library of objections'. She now believed he had made her re-write far too much: not only had it set her progress back at least eighteen months; it had also made her books mere 'rehashes'.[17]

There was still no publication date for *The Beauties and Furies*, and no advance. When Florence James had commented, six months earlier, that Davies lacked business acumen, Stead had defended him loyally: he had picked her 'out of the gutter'; he had arranged the contract with D. Appleton-Century. But now she complained bitterly.

Stead was greatly cheered by a letter from Nettie Palmer, who mentioned that Rebecca West had publicly praised her originality as a writer. This provoked in Stead a rare admission of her ambition.

> Although I am very sensible of the approval of Rebecca West and the others, I hope it means nothing yet: I hope to do very much better than anything I have yet done, I am very simple-minded, I only want one thing, I thirst to do something so good that there will be no denying it on anyone's part.

Further on in the same letter, she allowed herself an equally rare outburst of frustration and bitterness:

> I'm very grateful to you for sometimes passing on remarks like that of Rebecca West: although I hope to do better, it encourages me a bit, for I really put some gristle into the 'Seven Poor Men' and my New York friends haven't even read it: they are mostly fairly well off … but they expect me, out of love and friendship, to give them my books! And I don't. I can't. So they pass the fact that I write up in silence, perhaps feeling slightly injured even that I haven't sent them my books, and sit and talk the whole evening about the stock-market or whatnot. It makes me simply furious: not that I expect to be an object of interest, but not ever to be able to talk about

literature, or characterisation or any of the purely professional subjects that absorb a writer![18]

Later that month, Stead was asked whether she would act as first reader of unsolicited manuscripts for the *New Masses*. There was no payment, but Stead was curious to see behind the scenes at the magazine, and willingly agreed. Editor Stanley Burnshaw remembers her sitting quietly at her desk reading manuscripts several days a week. She kept it up for a couple of months. By the third week she was bored by the re-hashed themes: boss-exposures, unemployment-suicide, hunger and poverty stories.

The winter was fierce that year, the coldest Stead had ever experienced. It gave her 'sleeping sickness'; Blech, thinner now, looked blue, and moped and coughed. Stead insisted that there was 'no question of his traipsing through the snow and mud of the streets looking for business'.[19] He suggested they pack up and head south.

They spent five weeks in February and March in South Carolina and Alabama. The South, too, was wet and cold. Under grey, lugubrious skies, 'fearful dismal swamps' stretched for hundreds of miles, crossed by swollen, muddy rivers. But there was occasional sunshine—one day they even went without coats—and Blech's health began to improve.

Stead loved the first buds of spring, the magnolias in bloom, the scarlet-crested birds. But she was horrified by the 'race-hatred' that hung 'like a black pestilential cloud over the whole south'. While the negroes dressed in rags and suffered from skin diseases and bone deformations from malnutrition, the whites looked corrupt and decadent. A once-off splurge, a meal at Henry's, the most exclusive restaurant in Charleston, South Carolina, allowed Stead to observe the behaviour of the white élite, and she was repelled by the plantation owners, with their large 'whisky-drinking, lynch faces' and 'clear rockcrystal blue eyes'.[20]

It may have been while she was in the South that Stead read *Gone with the Wind*. Set in Georgia during the Civil War, a celebration of the white middle class, the novel—to Stead's disgust—won the Pulitzer Prize that year. It was to be the fastest-selling novel yet published in the United States, with a record of 50000 copies sold in one day.

D. Appleton-Century suggested to Stead she should aim more for the female market and include some sex in her next novel.

The most vigorous promoter of Christina Stead in America was Clifton Fadiman. An editor at Simon & Schuster, he was the *New Yorker*'s regular book critic, and at the age of thirty, already well known for his wit and incisive criticism. Early in the spring of 1936, Blech arranged a meeting. Fadiman suggested drinks at the Lafayette, a popular watering-hole for intellectuals.

They got on well. Blond and softspoken, Fadiman was mature for his age and confident in his judgements. In passing, he told them that he considered Malraux the best of the younger French writers. He asked them if they knew Ralph Fox: 'a born tale-teller with a great future in novels'. Christina Stead he called a 'genius', but predicted she would need four more books to make her name.

In his eighties, Clifton Fadiman could still recall their meeting clearly:

Bill had, over the phone, asked me to look out for a short Jewish man who would never win a beauty prize (or words to that effect). The description was accurate enough. But it did not prepare me for his non-stop and brilliant talk, his iconoclasm, and a kind of aggressive charm. It did not take him long to tell me about himself—that he was a cosmopolitan, a Marxist, and that his father was the only Jewish general (could it have been colonel?) in the United States army. At that time (I was young and innocent) I thought him a genius, for he dominated—and coruscatingly—the conversation, whereas Christina seemed passive and mouselike, though only by comparison. In retrospect, Bill seems to me now, though a remarkable man of high energy and trenchant wit, to have been cast in a pattern one met frequently in the Thirties. Horace Liveright, Maxwell Bodenheim, Ben Hecht and many others typified it: lively minds flawed by a vein of exhibitionism that verged on charlatanism—though Bill was not guilty of the latter.

Christina was tall (though perhaps only so in contrast to Bill, who was shorter than I, and I am only 5'8"), bony, with a worn, somehow sad face. She looked older than her years ... But—and this is pure subjective conjecture and you need not take it seriously—the most salient fact about her was that her face and figure (she was simply *not* a handsome or pretty woman) were at war with what I really believe was her deepest wish—to be loved romantically, almost in the nineteenth century tradition. I know nothing about women's clothes but during the few times we met, surely no more than 5 or 6 in all, I noticed that her costume had something overdone and baroque about it, trailing laces, fichus, extras of one sort or another, as if she were using decoration to compensate for the plainness of her face. Somehow I think of her colors as purple and yellowish white.

I do not remember our conversation but I suppose it revolved around the two matters that engrossed many literary folk in the Thirties—sex and political radicalism. Christina and Bill were clearly free spirits on both counts. Their views (mainly voiced by Bill, a professional talker) influenced and tempered my own comparative innocence.

They made it clear that they were Balzacian heroes, ready like Rastignac to conquer the world of thought, perhaps of action. Of Christina Bill remarked, quite casually, 'She hopes to be the greatest of modern novelists.' (These may not have been his exact words.) Christina, whose manners were perfect (Bill's were not) nevertheless did not dissent.[21]

It was an important meeting for all three; for Bill Blech it was a turning point. Fadiman listened with rapt attention to his stories and admonished him to write them down. He told Blech that one of the directors of Simon & Schuster had a blueprint for a modern Monte Cristo novel and was looking for someone to write it—someone unusually erudite, with a firm grasp of modern finance. Fadiman was convinced that Blech was the man. He invited them to his apartment to meet M. Lincoln Schuster.

He was right. Max Schuster *was* impressed. A note in Schuster's publishing files states that Blake (as Americans all called him) seemed to be the 'man of destiny' for the book.[22] He asked for an outline of the projected novel.

It was probably on the same occasion that Schuster, who had liked *The Salzburg Tales*, offered Stead a contract for her next three books. She felt honoured and excited. Rumour had it that Simon & Schuster never put out a book that sold fewer than 10 000 copies.

What followed was sweet indeed. D. Appleton-Century, on being told of the Simon & Schuster proposal, offered Stead unusually high rates to renew her contract with them. Simon & Schuster then matched the Appleton offer: $500. Stead did not hesitate. Appleton wrote asking her to reconsider. It was all very satisfying, and Stead was pleased to be less dependent on the 'slopoke in England'. In case Davies did not want to renew her three-book contract with him, Simon & Schuster offered to arrange something with the leftwing London publisher, Victor Gollancz.

A royalty cheque for *The Salzburg Tales* arrived from England: Stead gaily blew it all—£1.15s—on a dinner with Bill, Stanley Burnshaw and his wife Madeline. Hard up though they were, she and Bill, generous by nature, loved nothing better than a good meal with friends. Peter Davies renewed his contract, sending a cheque for $250, which mostly went on clothes for both of them. Stead was beginning to feel optimistic about the future.

The Beauties and Furies came out in America in late April 1936, one week before its English launch. Reviewers were nonplussed. Some were put off by its 'verbal showiness', others by the strange mixture of the real and the fantastic, others by its lack of an obvious message. Harold Strauss commented in the *New York Times Book Review*: 'We are forced to praise in Miss Stead's work everything that we would ridicule as stilted, overambitious and pretentious in a less gifted writer.' The erudite allusions and love of words reminded him of Joyce.[23]

It was Clifton Fadiman, more than anyone either side of the Atlantic, who praised *The Beauties and Furies*, pronouncing it Stead's 'finest book to date'. It was flawed, he averred, like all her books. 'Yet it discloses such streaming imagination, such tireless wit, such intellectual virtuosity that I cannot see how anyone who reads it carefully—and there is no other way to read it—can deny Miss Stead's position as the most extraordinary woman novelist produced by the English-speaking race since Virginia Woolf.'[24]

7

'A Harmless Affair'

———— ❦ ————

June 1936 – August 1937

HE TRAIN TRACKS out of Algeciras run perpendicular to the coast. In the distance, across the Strait of Gibraltar, are the ashy mountains of Morocco. It is early June 1936: the heat is already gathering for the day. At the dilapidated railway station, hammers and sickles decorate the doors and shutters. A tall fair rather red-faced woman and a short dark olive-skinned man struggle onto the railway platform, hot, flustered, with too many bags over their shoulders. Foreigners. The porter with them has several large trunks on his cart. Altogether there are thirteen pieces of luggage. 'Millionaires,' mutters the banana-seller looking on.[1] Stead and Blech had left New York at the end of May, taken a ship to Gibraltar, and had just crossed the small bay to Algeciras, on the Spanish mainland. From there they travelled north to Ronda in a light antique train.

The ancient town of Ronda was perched on a narrow rock plateau in the Sierras. Between the craggy cliffs was a gorge a thousand feet deep, etched by the river Guadalevin and crossed, at different heights, by a graceful Moorish bridge and a sturdy Roman one. Stead was delighted by the views, the mountain weather ('cool in the shade, sunstroke out of it'), the peasant women in their black shawls, the laden donkeys plodding up and down the precipitous trails.[2] Late afternoon thunderstorms would bring a burst of rain—brief relief from the hot, dry weather.

Stead had had little more than a month to enjoy *The Beauties and Furies* in the New York bookshops before she and Blech had left for Spain. Despite the threat of war, they planned to stay in Europe. Blech had not found work in New York; in Spain he was to set up a business for Alf Hurst.

That political 'troubles' were expected soon had been obvious even in Gibraltar, already a refuge for land-owning families in flight. Ronda, Stead observed, looked 'ripe for a second Red October'. In the past, the town had been run by the landlords and was known as 'the little Vatican': now it had a communist mayor and the *ayuntamiento* (the local council chambers) buzzed with political discussions among workers and peasants. White walls were daubed with slogans painted in large red letters: '*Viva la Revolución!*' '*Viva la Republica*', and 'Death to the priests and the friars!' The local churches, monasteries and convents were covered with insults; many had been destroyed. Stead had no sympathy with the priests who hurried by nervously, looking 'ugly, bloated, out of countenance'.[3]

General elections in February 1936 had brought the republican People's Front into power; since then Spain had been in turmoil. The government was weakened by concerted opposition from landowners, monarchists, the Catholic middle class and the military. For months, the country had been paralysed by strikes and intimidated by a wave of political murders.

On their walks in the cool of the evening, Blech and Stead observed workers congregating in the fields for political meetings. Others walked along the rooftops, ostensibly cleaning and weeding, but more likely, looking for positions to site machine guns. Stead was reminded of *La Condition humaine*, in which Malraux described the days before the Chinese revolution, when militia men were pacing the roofs to keep watch.

Spain was still quite feudal. The large rural estates were owned by wealthy aristocracy, often absentee landlords, who treated their labourers like slaves. In the face of the current sweeping agricultural reform these landlords were abandoning their estates and emigrating to Portugal and France. Alf Hurst's plan was for Blech to buy an abandoned olive estate while they were cheap and to set up a business.

In *House of All Nations*, the novel Stead would draft in Spain, Henri Léon (modelled on Hurst) talks enthusiastically to Michel Alphendéry (Bill Blech) of his plans for investment in Spain:

'I'm for the people. If they look like putting any sort of order down there, I'm going down. I'm going to buy an estate there. Not too big. And I'll go to the government and I'll say, "Friends, I'm friendly to your cause, I believe in you: I want to put my money in your country. It's a grand country, and I like the women." (That'll move a Spaniard's heart!)' The genial gust blew round them. 'How would you like to be in olives, Alphen? I'll buy a small olive plantation down near Malaga.'

Alphendéry, a man who regularly spoke at workers' meetings and gave money to the French Communist Party, is not at all shocked by his friend's unseemly opportunism. On the contrary. He is excited by the prospect of following the bullfights. There are certainly no heroes in Stead's fiction.

Bill Blech too liked Spain and bullfights, and Ronda's Plaza de Toros was world famous. Did he worry about reconciling Alf Hurst's latest money-making venture with the aspirations of the struggling Spanish people's *Frente Popular*? The new Republican government, striving to bring about agrarian reform in a country racked with poverty and under-nourishment, did not need the incursion of foreign capital, with profits going out of the country.

Blech was running out of money. He had several dependants— including Stead now, who could not live off her small royalties. He urgently needed an income.

His poor health had been a refrain in Stead's letters for years, and like many of their contemporaries, they set great store by a 'change of air'. The five weeks in the American South apparently had not been enough of a break, for on their return Stead told Florence James: 'We are wondering if Bill, for the good of his soul, oughtn't to take a whole year off in a hot climate—provided that I sell anything at all on this new novel and that my new contract turns out as expected.'

Why was Blech so 'exhausted'? Stead used the word often, about both of them. In all probability, Blech's problem was mild depression. For years he had felt frustrated and handicapped by the need to provide for three dependants, and limited by his lack of formal education. If he had hung on at the Travelers' Bank for six and a half years, it was due partly to inertia, but mostly to a lack of real options. In New York, he could not bring himself to return full-time to the cut-and-thrust world of finance. His friends considered him 'brilliant', and when he was interested in something he had extraordinary reserves of energy. But at present he was suffering from torpidity. He had freed himself from the quicksands of the Travelers' Bank only to become dependent once more on the goodwill of Alf Hurst. His situation was profoundly humiliating, and Stead felt it keenly.

At the end of *House of All Nations*, after the bank's collapse, Alphendéry tells a friend: 'I've given my whole life to this sterile business. I'm not a boy any longer ... Maybe I'll get out of it some day.' This was Blech's own fervent hope. He wanted to get on with his Monte Cristo novel, to try his hand at writing. Many an author has dreamt of making a fortune, then retiring somewhere idyllic to write. For Blech, Alfred Hurst's wildcat schemes still seemed to offer this faint hope. That was why he and Stead were in Spain.

The Travelers' Bank court case was under way in Paris, which meant that Blech ran a degree of risk being back in Europe. As a precaution, he had changed his name, unofficially, to Will Blake. His mother, daughter and friends had been asked to write to him under that name, at Florence James' address in London. The only people to be told their Spanish address were Florence, who was forwarding their mail, and Alf Hurst. Before he left New York, Bill had told Mollie that he and Christina were sailing to Europe via Mexico in order to procure a divorce. (Mexican divorces, though not cheap, were notoriously easy to obtain.) Bill was hoping to discourage Mollie from following them to Europe.

Once again, they were involving Florence James in cloak-and-dagger games. Christina asked her to forward all letters addressed to Will Blake to 53 Calle de Espinel, where they were living, and all letters addressed to Christina Stead or William J. Blech to the Ronda Poste Restante. And would Florence herself please address all future letters to Mr and Mrs W. Blake? In the envelope, Christina enclosed letters from Bill to his mother and daughter, to be posted from England.

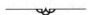

It was soon clear that there was no question of doing business in Spain. Fortunately, their circumstances were eased by cheques from America. Stead was sent $250 by D. Appleton-Century as royalties from previous books and $500 by Simon & Schuster as an advance for her next three books. On the strength of this, she and Blech decided to spend the summer in Ronda, writing.

Once established in their comfortable lodgings, Stead plunged into her banking novel. She had been mulling it over for years and making notes for months: now she was ready to write. Telling herself that in New York she had done no serious writing for almost a year, she worked at a furious pace. She had great hopes for this novel, to be published by New York's most enterprising publishing house. 'It looks exciting enough in its rough state,' she wrote to Florence James in mid July, 'and I hope Simon & Schuster will make a hit with it.' She was enjoying writing 'off the bat'. This time, she resolved, she would forgo the agony of endless revision.

In Ronda, Blake (as he would call himself from now on) made a start on his Monte Cristo novel. Inspired by that magnificent setting, he made the hero of *The World is Mine* a Spaniard: Don Cristóbal Pinzón becomes the richest man in the world, yet he is determined to destroy the capitalist system. The story ends in 1936 with the ignominious death of the hero in Ronda: his remains are thrown into the Guadalevin, at the bottom of the gorge. This melodrama mixed financial intrigues and spirited adventures with high philosophy and Marxist economic theory. The first chapters were largely written in cafés, where Blake could observe the life around him. For him there was no beginner's block; he wrote as easily as he talked. Stead, quite envious, told Stanley Burnshaw, 'Bill is a born novelist: he dashes ahead, no going back, no scratching out. It's a gift.'[4]

They were living in a tailor's house in the Calle de Espinel, a narrow, lively street in the ancient merchant quarter. Their two rooms overlooked an inner courtyard where young women sat sewing by hand, singing as they worked. The day began with a breakfast of *churros, bunuelos*, oranges and roasted coffee. Between mid morning and early evening it was too hot to venture out. Stead closed the long shutters and typed. The lack of distractions was ideal: it reminded Stead of a Spanish convent (before the political troubles).

She was plunged in the world of her characters. 'To me they certainly now exist and converse with each other inaudibly, in my mind, even when I am thinking of something else', she wrote in her diary.[5] In the evenings, she and Bill would discuss the personalities who had worked in the bank. Bill also wrote out for her a summary of the relevant political and financial events between May 1931 and July 1932.

Years later, Stead would claim that she wrote *House of All Nations*—800 pages in all—in six weeks in Spain. Ronda, she would say by way of explanation, was her ideal habitat: a dry climate, on a rock base. In fact, though she worked furiously at the first draft in the Calle de Espinel, the novel was not finally completed until the following summer—a year later.

House of All Nations was an extraordinarily ambitious novel. Stead's fourth book was far more realist than anything she had yet written; this time, she was determined to curb her excursions into the fantastic. She wanted it to be a revolutionary novel, a novel that exposed the paltry schemes of capitalist rascals. It was a world she knew well: just as Steinbeck had lived with the 'oakies', she had lived among bankers.

Her inspirations were Dickens' *Oliver Twist*, Thackeray's *Vanity Fair*, Tolstoy's *War and Peace*, Balzac's *Comédie humaine*, Malraux's *Les Conquérants*—panoramic novels loaded with characters and fast changes from one scene to another. She was also interested in contemporary novels that had been influenced by cinematic techniques. (*House of All Nations* has 'scenes' rather than chapters.) For good cinematographic writing, she turned once again to *Ulysses*.

The realist writers Stead read for inspiration worked meticulously from life, from historical material, such that their novels were also sociological documents. Dos Passos' *42nd Parallel*, which she admired, was only semi-fictional—the sort of novel, Stead wrote, 'which seems to arise from the fright the novelist gets when he looks at the "New York Times" and feels he is a poor second to it'.[6]

Nevertheless, *House of All Nations* goes beyond conventional realism. For Stead, the extraordinary always lurked behind the ordinary. She even managed to weave her magical threads, her Arabian Nights flights of fancy, into the tough tapestry of international finance. Her characters engage in sparkling dialogues, gags and aphorisms, and our lasting impression of the bank is as a 'palace of illusion'. As Harold Strauss was to put it, in the *New York Times*:

> One should not suppose that Miss Stead has turned her back on fantasy. If the elements here are realistic, their assemblage is a crazy-quilt of impressions and associations ... If her knowledge of private banking, of bucketeering and grain options, of foreign-exchange speculation and account gathering, of stock manipulation and politico-financial intrigue is little short of miraculous, she scatters the bright fragments of her information across the skies of her novel in the disorder of star dust.[7]

———— ❧ ————

Stead liked the heat and the deep retreat: in Spain there were no distractions, no friends, no telephone calls. The only problem for her, as a light sleeper, was that the Andalusians came to life at night. Eventually she fell asleep, her head full of the Paris bank, but she would be woken at 6 am, when the animated political discussions finally ended and the apprentices left for their Maestro's atelier. Blake found the heat trying, and the concentrated protein diet of southern Spain—mainly 'ironclad' chickpeas—did not agree with his stomach. After three weeks he fell sick and when he improved, they decided to head north.

They spent two days in Madrid. Stead disliked the city, but appreciated the Prado museum. From there they spent four or five days in San Sebastian, a Basque fishing port on the Bay of Biscay, at the foot of the Pyrenees. To their astonishment, though it was early July and the middle of the tourist season, most of the hotels were firmly shuttered. The locals advised them to move on to Fuenterrabia, between Spanish Irun and France. Once there, they put up at the Hôtel de France, which sheltered a number of wealthy Spaniards who felt safer close to the border.

The day before Christina's birthday, 16 July, there was a rather sinister incident. Bill had gone out to buy Christina perfume, when Republican police flagged down the bus in which he was travelling. The passengers were told to step outside. Bill was singled out and made to stand apart from the others. Eventually, after some interrogation, they let him go. Only afterwards did he realise that he resembled José Maria Gil Robles, the rightwing leader of the Spanish Catholic Party whom the police were after. (Robles in fact had fled to Biarritz the day before.)

On 17 July, a military uprising led by General Francisco Franco broke out in Spanish Morocco. It was not announced on Madrid Radio until 18 July, by which time the revolt had spread to the mainland. Within forty-eight hours the whole country was involved in civil war.

There is no mention of a political crisis in Stead's letter to Florence James on 18 July. Although the government announced insurrections in many of the provinces, it claimed to have the situation well in hand. The north coast was firmly in the hands of the Republicans. Red republican flags flew from the houses and cars; hammers and sickles were daubed over walls and the voice of Madrid radio loudly crackled: 'Viva el Frente Popular'. Young Republican males, dressed in overalls or ragged corduroy trousers, raced around in highpowered cars requisitioned from the wealthy, their hunting rifles propped on the back seat. Raised clenched fists had become the universal salute.

By the end of July, the bucolic summer sojourn was over. Fuenterrabia was darkened at night to avoid air raids, and a 9 pm curfew put an end to evening strolls. Swimming and fishing were prohibited in the resort town. With the fishermen no longer going out, Stead and Blake were embarrassed to be eating precious food supplies. And it had become clear to them that the Hôtel de France was run by monarchist conspirators.

They no longer enjoyed their retreat. There was no news about the recepion of *The Beauties and Furies* in England, and Bill had not heard from his mother. At the end of July, they asked the Republicans at the *ayuntamiento* for safe-conducts to cross into France. Since they had not been required to register their foreign money in Gibraltar, they decided to hide it in a toothpaste tube to secrete it across the border.

They were rowed across the Bidassoa River, the border between France and Spain, in a dinghy called *Lulu*. In France, they were detained for several hours, along with other refugees. Eventually they were released. Stead opened the toothpaste tube. All was well.

They took a bus to St Jean-de-Luz, where a bank teller told them Fuenterrabia was 'thick with corpses'. 'E. A. Poe couldn't do so well,' Bill commented to Christina.[8] They still had no inkling of the seriousness of the situation. Just days after their departure, the Andalusian poet Garcia Lorca would be executed by Franco's insurgents. Six weeks later, San Sebastian would fall to the fascists.

On 1 October 1936, Franco was declared chief of the Spanish state by his followers; he was soon to be recognised as such by fascist Germany and Italy, who gave extensive support to the military insurgents. Young German pilots bombed Spanish civilians from brand new Junkers and Heinkels. With limited backing from the Soviet Union, the Spanish Popular Front government relied on untrained international volunteers and outdated armaments.

He was not Gil Robles, certainly, but Bill Blake had his own reasons for wanting to travel incognito through France. In St Jean-de-Luz they obtained visas for Belgium, and Blake worried that the police might be at the Gare d'Orléans to greet them. It was a nervous trip from St Jean-de-Luz to Paris. At the station Stead rang Blake's lawyer, who was able to tell them that Blake had not been mentioned in any plaint. When they arrived in Belgium on 30 July, with their thirteen pieces of luggage (including linen, books, manuscripts, marionettes and a coffee pot), they felt fatigued but 'honeymoonish' with relief.[9]

In Antwerp, Stead and Blake moved into Alf Hurst's suite in the large, ultra-modern Century Hotel. Since Alf was shortly due to arrive from London, Blake tried to find them a flat. One landlord looked him up and down and remarked that he hoped '*Monsieur*' was not '*Israélite*'.[10] Others implied it. Fortunately, when Alf arrived, he moved into his small Flemish-style house in nearby Brussels, and they were able to stay on at the Century.

Hamburg, located in Nazi Germany, had lost business to Antwerp: the Belgian free port was flourishing. Alfred Hurst's grain business, at No. 9 rue des Douze Mois, was thriving. When Hurst was in Antwerp, he performed wonders with his 'magic voice' and the five telephones on his desk. When he was away, approximately one week in two, business would drop dramatically and Blake could catch his breath. 'Alf is full of life and business,' Stead told Florence James, 'and if he did not occasionally take trips to England and elsewhere would prostrate Bill. Himself too! After a day's Napoleoning, he has to sink into bed at 9 p.m.'[11]

Bill Blake was underpaid: he and Stead had no illusions about that. Jacques Coe, a New York financier who knew him and Hurst well, is convinced that this was always the case when Blake worked for Hurst. 'Bill got a salary from Alf, but there is no doubt he was worth ten times this to Alf.'[12]

All too easily, Stead would also find herself caught up in Hurst's exploitative 'little schemes'. He expected her to do small typing and translation jobs as tokens of friendship, she told Florence.

> He is really a darling fellow in intimacy, full of charm, although a rogue in the way he tries to steal from my writing-time to get all his odd jobs done, to avoid paying a salary to another typiste. (He thinks to work a little blackmail, quite innocent blackmail; he employs Bill—at a stenographer's salary—and he thinks that to keep Bill's job, I will do a lot of little friendly jobs on the side! What a transparent little scheme: you really can't dislike him for it.)[13]

Could she not? Her anger was scarcely concealed beneath the coy display of affection. The problem was that she and Blake were too dependent on Hurst's goodwill to complain.

A decade later, Stead wrote *A Little Tea, A Little Chat*, in which Robbie Grant is an extremely negative portrait of Alf Hurst. For the moment, though, Hurst was Henri Léon in her Paris banking novel. Léon has a smile like a 'sudden sunrise' and a 'beautiful husky voice', and though he employs his friend Michel Alphendéry 'at as low a salary as possible', he is also capable of occasional acts of generosity—'almost unprecedented in the business world'.

Though she knew Alf Hurst could be a 'mean bastard', Stead remained loyal to him until the late 1940s, when she wrote *A Little Tea*. In 1941, Blake would give Hurst a copy of his American Civil War novel *The Copperheads*, writing on the flyleaf: 'To my best friend and true brother, Alfred H. Hurst.' And in 1944, Christina Stead would inscribe a copy of *For Love Alone*: 'To Alfred H. Hurst—our lifelong friend and one brother.'[14]

Stead was not enthusiastic about Antwerp. The autumn sky was as 'blue as skimmed milk'. She thought the Belgians ugly and overweight. ('I feel practically a beauty, but I prefer to be among beauties.'[15]) At least Antwerp was largely French-speaking. And in the cafés, women enjoyed an even greater freedom to sit alone than in Paris. The town was also only fifteen minutes from the Dutch border, in case of a German invasion.

Stead plunged straight back to work, regretting that their moves had caused her to lose time and momentum. Their only friends were Alf Hurst, his Austrian lady-love Mitzi and his office-manager, Edgar Lallemand, half Walloon and half Flemish. Lallemand was Jewish, an active communist and interested in a wide range of literature. Stead was delighted to discover that he had not only read Joyce and D. H. Lawrence but that he had even heard of her American poet friend Stanley Burnshaw.

Stead and Blake could not make any definite plans. Their future depended largely on Hurst, who was waiting for the outcome of a court case in Liverpool before deciding what to do with his London and Antwerp businesses. He still intended to open a business in Spain, provided the revolution went to the government. That plan also involved waiting. He talked, too, of buying several small self-supporting estates in England or

France, one of which Blake and Stead could make their home. Blake liked the idea of a cottage on an acre or so of land near Ely, in England, or perhaps in Normandy or the Dordogne.

Stead said nothing when Blake talked of living in France again: she now wanted to settle in an English-speaking environment. She had become heartily tired of their wanderings and Bill's confusion. He disliked dull Antwerp; at times he voiced a regret that they had not gone to New Mexico with Mike Gold, or back to the Putnams' country place near Lambertville in New Jersey. At other times he regretted that they had gone to America at all: it had been a waste of money and time. 'Poor fellow,' Stead wrote in her diary. 'Our life is madly disordered; I feel he is beating his wings in a dark room.'[16]

Privately she was pinning considerable hope on her new novel, fervently hoping it would bring in the money they needed, that it would be a turning point in her literary career. The bank was a 'wonderful subject' and she was excited to be writing in a 'new mode'. She told Florence James a second time that she had 'the comfort of knowing that S. & S. really push a book when they bring it out'. At the very least, she trusted the novel would have a 'succès de scandale'.

Blake, always eager to explore new surroundings, organised excursions to the country on Saturdays and Sundays. But Stead was not feeling at all receptive to the charms of Belgium. She felt terribly restless, unusually sexually skittish. Was it the diet, she wondered? The grey skies? The 'nervous indoor life'? Was it because nearly all the characters in her current novel were men? (She had been rather shocked to realise this.) In her solitude, she was keeping a diary, which she intended to destroy later. In mid August 1936, she noted: 'Pepper in entrails, heart beating, small appetite and general wretchedness and no relief to date.' In late August she and Bill spent a weekend at Liers, a 'delightful town' with a 'Hans Andersen clock tower'. But Sunday was a disaster: 'Walked much, I unbearably irritable and Bill very angelic.' In early September, the monotony of the endless business talk around her was temporarily relieved by a visit from Ann and Patrick Dooley, communist friends from London. Stead found it 'a breath of salt air' to talk to people interested in books.

By day, Blake was selling guilders, buying Belgian francs, buying Winnipeg wheat and selling it in Liverpool; in his spare time he worked on his Monte Cristo novel. In September, when Hurst spent a week with his family in London for Yom Kippur, Blake had a week off to work on his book.

He was, Stead noted, 'excited and entirely rejuvenated'. In the Rocher de Cancale, a Spanish café in the old quarter, he read her the first three chapters. Stead pronounced them a 'sort of cross between Shakespeare's worst moments, Coningsby, Laurence Sterne, and what you will: in other words, pretty good'.

But Blake, working intensely, was constantly tired, and Stead did not find this easy to accept. In her diary, she alluded cryptically to her sexual frustration. Though she had intended to destroy it later, thirteen close-typed pages have survived. Sixteen lines of it are written in an elaborate mono-substitution code. A second version of the diary also survives, in which all the intimate details have been suppressed, the code passages have disappeared and some names are disguised. The new version is 'artful', somewhere between reality and fiction. It even has a title referring, obliquely, to Bill: 'First Days of a Modern Monte Cristo'.

The two different versions indicate not only that the original was meant to be destroyed, but also the trouble Stead took to cover up certain truths and to create personal myths. Nobody, not even Bill, was to have access to her inner self, since her childhood her one sacred place. In her fiction, reality was transformed into something she could control.

Significantly, Teresa, Stead's fictional counterpart, also resolves, early in her relationship with James Quick, to keep her thoughts to herself. In a delightful moment of 'unchecked intimacy', she had once tried to explain to him her complicated feelings about their relationship. For Quick this truth-telling was terribly threatening. He went 'so cold, that she felt the warmth dying out of his breast'.

She realised her mistake, with a pinching of the heart, and at once abandoned the thought of telling him the truth about her love:

> She resigned herself now to playing a part with him, because she loved him, and in order to give him happiness. She felt the fatigue of life, believing like so many young women that she had found out the truth, which was that man and woman cannot be true companions for each other. But she did not wish to confide in a woman. What woman knew more than she did? … She thought that each day would be a step farther into the labyrinth of concealment and loving mendacity.

Reality and fiction merged in Stead's 'labyrinth of concealment'. Her study of cryptography and use of code, her constant use of initials or fictional names in her diary and even in letters, the wholesale destruction of her papers in later years: all this shows how she protected her privacy with a desperate ferocity. When she talked about her life to friends or in interviews, it would be in the form of *story*, a refracted reality, a kind of legend.

The accidental survival of Stead's original diary allows us a rare glimpse of her private thoughts. Seven years into her relationship with Bill, she had become quite impatient. She was angry about Mollie, angry about Bill's interminable waverings and frustrated by their wandering lifestyle.

All these years wandering chiefly due to fear [of] her retributive raids, search for work which will allow us luxury of keeping her to annoy us, etc. We waste his money, lose homes, books, split friendships, have no circle: everything I write is in vacuum, he continues to work at worthless jobs. Yet will not make up his mind to cut the painter ... Even the experiences we have are no good to us: no time to consolidate them, no place of repose and the ridiculous perennial question of M. He has illusion that M will 'try to get a job' while money is still coming to her easily ... 'If Mollie comes over here, we will leave for a few weeks'!!!! M knows very well the power of a tenacious attitude towards this conciliation and retreat, and there we stand where we were five years ago.

She reflected that they could have been leading 'a happy and useful life' and Bill would not have aged so fast. As it was, at forty-four he was easily fatigued and his face was lined—'with hollows whenever weary'. When she tried to discuss Mollie with him, he would say: 'Oh, C, let's discuss it another time' or 'Are you going to start bothering me too? I'm going to get rid of you!' ('Tired joke', she noted in brackets.)

The diary sections written in code are flawed, with numerous mistakes, but so is her normal typing. Only able to be deciphered by decoding experts, the code passages express frustration about her lack of sexual activity, to which she attributes her 'severe headaches'. 'CWU WIJKWFWAT BNLDU JU LRBC MQKL ACWU BFWLJAD; KSQ VWTWVDV KDVU FJQEDFY QDUGNIUJKFD.' ('His inability comes as much from this climate; our divided beds largely responsible.') In code, she mentions her 'passion for Ralph Fox'.

A brief passage not in code indicates that her anger was also (as usual) anger with herself, mixed with self-pity.

In general am complicated ass ... yell mighty loud when my feelings are hurt, otherwise do what tractor could do better. The whole summer gone—

Spain, Antwerp—while I twiddle indoors on typewriter—gone mad. Result, my skin is dry, I am thin and a virtual misery: I haven't as much voice as a new shoe and my dreams are puerile … Charming outcome of the sturm-und-drang of 17.

Perhaps Stead had received a letter from Ralph Fox on 17 July or 17 August. Elsewhere she notes, in her usual cryptic style, 'Can't keep wolf from door: two or three days post and there he is, upsets me'. In mid September, she writes: 'In evening wanted to go on a bust, but how, where: don't know how to bust, understand Ralph Fox's occasional bust, poor varmint; my life too regular for an artist.'

One week Stead suffered a 'terrible depression' and could not work at all. She wept and raged, threatened to throw in her writing and told Bill that six years of her life had been 'a martyrdom to arbitrage'. As a result, he agreed they should move to London as soon as possible.

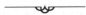

It was autumn and the light in their room at the Century Hotel was becoming too weak to type by. Stead was greatly relieved when they left for England in mid October, though the duration of their stay depended on Alf Hurst's court case. It turned out well: he won it. This meant that he could keep up the London business and employ Blake there.

House-hunting began again. At the end of the first day they went to sleep exhausted in their own downy bed at the MacAlpines. (The 'Macs' and Florence James had been storing their furniture ever since they had fled to the States more than a year before.) They had a pub dinner in Swiss Cottage with Florence James and Pym Heyting, her solicitor husband, but the Heytings had moved house that day and were tired. The dinner was not a success.

The next day, Eamon MacAlpine took them round in his car looking at flats. Soon they were ensconced in a 'postage-stamp flat'—one room with an alcove off the living room as a bedroom—at Red Lion Court, off Fleet Street. (This is the flat Teresa and James Quick share in the last chapters of *For Love Alone*.)

One of Stead's primary reasons for wanting to return to London was Ralph Fox. When she had left London in July 1935, she was very much in love with him, and her passion had not dissipated. Whether she and Blake had heard from him in the intervening fifteen months is not known, but she had certainly heard about him from their mutual friends. She and Blake had been back in London only a few days when they bumped into him. It was a Sunday. They were coming out of Lyons Corner House in Tottenham Court Road, their old haunt, when they saw him crossing the street with a pretty young woman. He seemed embarrassed when they greeted him. It was obvious to Stead that the pair were lovers. Not revealing her feelings this time, she noted in her diary: 'R. tired, hair greying, slight paunch, badly dressed, talking of "getting old" but this is no doubt merely to excuse his slight bulge. Tendency to make satirical remarks about everybody, due no doubt to fatigue.' Ralph Fox told them he was planning to leave for Spain in a few weeks—to fight in the International Brigade.

The Spanish Civil War had become the focus of a world in crisis. A crusade in which the issues were unambiguous, this war against fascism encapsulated the hopes, fears and theories of all liberal-minded people. Blake's friend Claud Cockburn was in Madrid, reporting for the *Daily Worker*. In London, there were pro-Republican rallies, pro-Republican manifestoes, and pro-Republican cultural events. Jack Lindsay's play *On Guard for Spain* was playing at the recently formed Unity Theatre. In their first week in London, Pat Dooley rang to invite Blake and Stead to a fundraising meeting for Spain at which he was speaking.

The fight against evil was temporarily focused on Spain, yet fascism was also stirring in London. Early in October, Sir Oswald Mosley and thousands of his blackshirted, jackbooted supporters had smashed windows, looted shops and assaulted Jews in London's East End.

One Thursday evening in late October, Eamon MacAlpine was visiting Stead and Blake when Ralph Fox phoned to say he was on his way round. 'Mac', a brash Irishman, ex-IRA, and now (Stead noted in her diary) 'a decayed revolutionist', disliked Fox and said, 'I'm blowin',' but he stayed another hour, vigorously running down Fox and his Stalinist politics. Mac was critical of the current purges in Moscow and Stalin's refusal to send adequate troops and munitions to Spain. He had not liked the way Fox had gloated over the execution of one-time leading Bolshevik Zinoviev, shot in August 1936 (along with fifteen others) by Stalin's firing squad. During this tirade from Mac, Stead shut the door and window, afraid that Fox would arrive and overhear him. When Fox arrived, with his girlfriend in tow, Mac brushed past them in the hall with such an air that Fox remarked to Stead: 'I don't think he likes me.' The notes in Stead's diary continue with false ingenuousness:

> Lousy evng. No milk, kitchen in mess, two men talk war all time and leave girl and me on side. Myself feeling nervous and unstable, don't know why. Fox a slightly unstable type himself, voice changes considerably, demeanour, criticisms of men and women, as his confidence rises and falls. He has great charm.

Fox's girlfriend was Ann Dubrowski, a militant union organiser in the needle-trade. The details of that disturbing evening would be worked into *For Love Alone*, with more openness than in Stead's diary.

Fox called several times at the flat after that. He would sit and talk to Bill; Christina would listen, make coffee, observe and admire. Fox's biography of Genghis Khan had appeared that spring, widely praised for the thoroughness of its research into Mongolian history as well as for its colourful writing. He was currently writing a book on Marxism and literature, *The Novel and the People*. Like his American counterparts at the *New Masses*, he advocated socialist realism and a simple prose style, but he was less doctrinaire. He did not believe that revolutionary novelists should restrict themselves to portraying heroic characters. Why not villains? He would like to see a modern novel with a great business man, a Rockefeller or Krupp, as its focus. Stead, immersed in the revision of *House of All Nations*, would have been consoled by this.

To Stead's astonishment, Ralph Fox told her he had been wanting to write his autobiography and the history of his native town Halifax for years; he had simply not yet decided how to cast it. Excited by this talk of autobiography that liberated an impulse she had so far dutifully repressed, Stead hardly slept. Though she did not know it yet, the conversation with Fox had planted the seeds of her next novel, in which she would plunge back into her own childhood.

Christina Stead would remain obsessed with Ralph Fox for the rest of her life. Over the next decade, she portrayed him, always in shadowy form, in three novels and a short story. His fictional counterparts, paradigms of the Nietzschean 'free spirit', are figures of exceptional physical magnetism— and all are burdened with an ugly, jealous wife. The very names of two characters—Adam Constant (in *House of All Nations*) and Luke Adams (in *Letty Fox*)—suggest that for Stead, Fox represented 'the eternal Adam'— the original man. Letty Fox's surname was also a tribute to him.

Stead's posthumously published short story 'A Harmless Affair' closely resembles the Harry Girton episode in the last chapters of *For Love Alone*. In both narratives, a passionate woman (Lydia/Teresa) enjoys a cordial married existence, but marriage has awakened in her a potent awareness of her own sexuality. She develops an overwhelming passion for a virile writer and man of action (Paul Charteris/Harry Girton) who is about to go away and fight in China/Spain. Attracted by his melting smile and shabby clothes (a sign that he is 'revolutionary' and 'honest'), she is even excited by the rumour that he is a heartbreaker. He visits the house often and talks politics with her husband. When once they find themselves alone, they are self-conscious, nervous. She sees him to the door and suddenly tells him that she will go away with him. He smiles at her with his knowing smile.

In *For Love Alone* the two spent a night together and shortly afterwards, Harry Girton leaves for Spain. As he bids farewell to Teresa, he says: 'If I don't come back, remember me. Do my work for me, fill my place, be me.'

'A Harmless Affair' is closer to actuality. Lydia falls in love with the handsome Charteris, but then she and her husband Tom go away for two years. When they return they meet him unexpectedly. He is with a young woman (Rosetta), an activist, and is embarrassed to see them. He looks untidy and pale. Lydia thinks to herself: 'This is the man I nearly lost my head over.' But he starts to drop in at their flat again and her obsession mounts once more. The romance is not consummated; it remains 'a kind of dream'. He returns to his jealous wife, but this relationship is tormented and he tells people he is off to China: 'What have I to stay here for?' Eventually he goes away and is killed.

One of Stead's most sensual pieces of writing, 'A Harmless Affair' is about *desire*. The affair remains 'harmless'. (The irony of the title is powerful, for her longing for this man has taken over Lydia's whole existence.) When he comes to the flat, she is almost in a trance:

> He seemed so potent, full of manly strength that she felt like fainting: she seemed to get a little delirious although she had not drunk very much, and began to think that he was all honey, all roses, and so on. She found that she had moments of absence, when she heard nothing of what was going on, but only heard beautiful words about him, 'His limbs gather passion as the bees

honey and I am the hive ...' Her feeling this evening was so powerful that
she could not believe he did not feel it, that Tom did not feel it, it seemed
to have thickened and made fluid the air.[17]

Lydia tells herself (just as Teresa does) that this man resembles her
temperamentally and physically, though he is a male and 'rather handsomer
and sweeter'.

When he leaves for the front, Lydia regrets 'that she had not known
Paul's love' and bitterly regrets 'not having in her body a child of this dear
and intimate man'. When, some months later, he is killed in action, she is
devastated.

> For quite a long time, perhaps two years or three, she knew that if the
> choice had been lying in his Chinese grave with Paul or living her happy,
> unclouded and fertile life with Tom, she would have taken a long time to
> choose and what would have been the choice?

Bill Blake's daughter Ruth believes that Stead and Fox did spend a night
together; she seems to remember her father telling her, years later, that
the two had gone away together for a weekend and that it had been a
difficult time for him.[18] On the other hand, it is possible that Ruth Blake,
who typed the final manuscript of *For Love Alone*, was confusing fact and
fiction. With Christina Stead, this was easy to do.

When she was writing the last chapters of *For Love Alone* (in 1942), Stead
wrote to Bill Blake: 'I believe last night I dreamed about every eligible man
I have ever known—when I woke up I could remember clearly—Ralph
Fox, Jack Goodman, (you of course)—all very nice, affectionate, friendly
to me, no sex.'[19] If there *had* been any sort of affair with Fox in 1936, Bill
Blake had not been told about it.

Almost forty years later, Stead told Ron Geering, her literary executor,
that she regretted the episode with Harry Girton at the end *of For Love
Alone*. 'It was silly of me—but I went ahead and put in that Harry Girton
thing—which I should not have—it didn't happen and probably hurt Bill
terribly—you can't believe it—but I didn't think of that!'[20]

In her old age, she would often feel guilty about Bill, but there would
have been no reason to lie to Ron Geering about Ralph Fox. Stead liked

to project an image as a woman with a certain past, a woman who had been much loved. She was unlikely to deny an affair with Fox had she had one.

All we know for certain is that Ralph Fox was the passion of her life. He was someone who never disappointed her. He never grew old. With him she was free of the ambivalences and anger that characterised her relations with others. His premature and heroic death in Spain allowed her to transport this passion into the realm of myth.

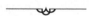

For an author who wrote so lyrically about the anguish and joy, pain and ecstasy of sexual desire and sexual frustration, Stead was exceptionally reticent when it came to writing about the raptures of physical love itself.

The power of 'A Harmless Affair' comes from the portrayal of 'cruel desire', and in the last chapters of *For Love Alone*, Teresa's desire for Harry Girton similarly builds to a crescendo. For weeks he has been teasing her with his surprise visits and lengthy absences. How does Stead portray the eventual consummation of their passion? Teresa and Harry manage to get away in a train together, heading for different destinations via Oxford. Once there, the pair spend the afternoon lamely sightseeing—too inhibited to do anything else. Finally, they go to a seedy tavern in the suburbs (*his* suggestion) and sit downstairs in the bar, listening to the radio with workers from the town. At long last, they timidly announce to one another that they are tired.

> They went upstairs with a candle to a small back bedroom with raftered ceiling and an extraordinarily thick mattress, made of lumps of various materials and without buttons. There was a painted wooden washstand with floral china and the privy was a shanty in the yard; but the room, the halls, and the stairs, as they saw when they walked out in the moonlight across the flagged yard, were wide, bare and clean. Though they were tired, each did his best to please the other and Teresa strove to prove that she was no child at love. At first they wanted to go to sleep but the whole night passed before they slept and for hours they were as close as creatures can be. The sun rose in a clear morning and the light fell on the bare boards through the thickly curtained windows. Teresa got up quickly and dressed. The business of the

night was over and she had never stayed late in bed in her life. She had a feeling of order and modesty in rising early and making everything tidy.

The climax of the novel's last two chapters is summed up in two sentences. The passage is starkly unromantic, with the lovemaking reduced to 'the business of the night'. The surroundings are tawdry. We are conscious that these lovers are merely doing what scores of others have done before them, in the same shabby room. Even the moonlight is glimpsed only as the characters make their way to the privy.

It is interesting that although she has tried to seem sexually experienced, Teresa is actually quite repressed. The passage is focalised through her: it is she who thinks of their lovemaking as 'the business of the night' and who needs to re-establish her feeling of 'order and modesty' by rising early, dressing and 'making everything tidy'. Throughout the whole episode, she behaves as if she were wishing to prove something—to herself, to Girton, to Quick. The sexual desire that overwhelms her like 'a blow' comes when she *thinks about* Girton (beforehand and afterwards)—not when she is actually with him.

On 28 November 1936, Ralph Fox wrote his will, leaving his personal belongings and any monies accruing from his books to his wife, Madge Elizabeth Palmer. The war in Spain was dangerous: Franco was intent on capturing Madrid. There had been fierce fighting and terrible massacres. Churches had been turned into prisons and there were air raids daily. On 1 December, 5000 Germans would land at Cadiz to join Franco.

Two other young combatants from the Communist Party who left at the same time as Fox were poet John Cornford and novelist and Marxist literary critic Christopher Caudwell. Both would be dead within two months.

From Albacete—the town between Madrid and Valencia where the new recruits received what little training was available—Ralph Fox wrote to his friend Harry Pollitt, General Secretary of the British Communist Party. They urgently needed more recruits, he told him. He himself was anxious to stop cooling his feet in that dull place and get to the front line. 'What is happening here is really the greatest thing since 1917. Victory means the end of Fascism everywhere sooner or later, and most likely sooner.'

Fox left Albacete, with 150 or so other Britons, in late December 1936. Part of a French battalion, they were shockingly unprepared. Their guns were nineteenth-century German revolvers; they did not even have tin hats for protection. The battalion headed south-west, where a critical situation had developed near Cordova in Andalusia: Franco's Nationalists were attempting to cut the road to Madrid. Major Gaston Delasalle, who headed their Marseillaise batallion, planned to create a diversion by taking the village of Lopera, held by Nationalist forces. It was a thoroughly incompetent decision. On the night of 3 January 1937—a freezing winter night—he gave the order to attack. Total confusion reigned. His men found themselves running into a wall of fire. Ralph Fox and John Cornford were both killed. The news was in the British papers the next day.

Inevitably, Fox was compared with Byron, who had also died at thirty-six among craggy hills and shattered olive trees—in Byron's case, fighting for the liberty of the Greeks. Spain was a hero's war: one of Fox's comrades-in-arms described him later as 'very dashing' in his black beret, black leather coat and large revolver.[21] Tributes flooded in to the *Daily Worker*. A memorial meeting was held in the Friends' Hall. *Ralph Fox. A Writer in Arms*, a book written that year in his memory, contains glowing comments from friends all over the world.

Along with Amabel Williams-Ellis and Montagu Slater, the editors of *Left Review*, Christina Stead wrote a memorial letter. As good communists, they strove to justify Ralph Fox's death in terms of the ends for which he fought, and they took up Fox's own call to arms in inflated revolutionary rhetoric:

> We write this letter in the belief that such sacrifices, although almost unspeakably tragic, are not vain, and that the writers of England, writers and citizens, must step in and try to fill the places of these men, both by serving, themselves, in the cause of political and intellectual liberty, and by making known the careers and purposes of the dead. Ralph Fox spent his manhood and talents in the love and service of liberty.

It was the first war Stead had ever supported, and her attitude contrasted sharply with Virginia Woolf's after she lost her nephew, Julian Bell, in the same war. A generation older, Woolf simply saw it as a crying waste.

The Spanish Civil War would rage for a further two and a half years, costing more than a million lives. And in the end Franco was victorious. Evil triumphed after all. It made Ralph Fox's death more 'unspeakably tragic' than ever.

In striking contrast to Stead's stolidly revolutionary public response to Fox's death was her semi-mystical private one. For her, the Supernatural always hovered in the shadow of the material world. She firmly believed in the hand of Destiny. In later life Stead would say that when she first travelled to England, she was—unbeknown to either of them—travelling to William Blake. In the same way, it was her absolute conviction that she was *fated* to cross paths with Ralph Fox. It was with a 'singular feeling of destiny' that she believed his physical and spiritual restlessness mirrored her own temperament, that they were twin souls.

At the time of Fox's death, she experienced a telepathic connection with him. In the mid 1940s, sitting in a restaurant in Gramercy Square, New York, Stead would tell her friend Edith Anderson about a sequence of prophetic dreams she had around the time of Ralph Fox's death. (Edith understood them to have been lovers.) On two nights she dreamt that Ralph Fox was standing on the far side of an open trench, staring at her. On the third night the open trench was there but Ralph Fox was not. Anderson, young and extremely impressed by Stead, was convinced by the story: 'I no more doubted her psychic powers than I doubted she was the greatest living writer in English.'[22] Stead attributed great fatidic significance to dreams; it took her some time, in the mornings, to shake off their shadow. And she strongly believed in telepathic communication at the hour of death. In *Seven Poor Men of Sydney*, written several years before Fox's death, Kol Blount has a series of visionary dreams at the very time his friend Michael plunges over a cliff.

As well as her three dreams about Ralph Fox, Stead would tell friends how she lost consciousness at the time of Fox's death. She brought it up again in a video interview when she was seventy-eight. With obvious emotion, she tells her interviewer that a friend with whom she had 'a curious connection' had gone to the Spanish Civil War. She and Bill were living at the time in a little flat near Fleet Street.

> Bill and some journalist were chatting. I had a shower and sat down on the floor. For some reason I fell asleep, dead asleep, for two to three hours. I passed out really, and I never do. And it was at this very hour that this man was killed in Spain.

She concluded mysteriously: 'There are plenty of stories in life you can't tell—and that's one.'[23]

Stead's passion for Fox brought back the mystical intensity of her youth. Despite her admiration for reason and the Enlightenment, Christina Stead was a convinced Romantic, who prided herself on her sixth sense. Her mystic leanings disconcerted Bill Blake, a die-hard rationalist, but he recognised it as part of her creative imagination.

⁓

Soon after they had arrived in London, at the end of October 1936, Stead had sent *House of All Nations* off to Simon & Schuster in New York. That winter, Clifton Fadiman, her editor, came on a business trip to London and discussed the manuscript with her. To Stead's despair, he wanted major revision. It was the very thing she had dreaded and she resented Fadiman's suggestions as much as she had resented Peter Davies'. One page of Fadiman's editorial notes survives, written in his assured, breezy style. The notes are extremely detailed and also encouraging: he praises the 'stuffed carp scene' as 'one of the great comic scenes in English literature', but adds: 'You overwhelm the reader, just as the Hallers overwhelm poor Rac[camond]. Condense.' It is his constant message: cut and condense. Stead agreed to some cuts. Privately, she was convinced that Fadiman was speaking from ignorance: he knew nothing about banking.

She had lost her momentum completely. Everything seemed pointless. She wrote to her brother Gilbert, now aged nineteen:

> Why are we here? We really don't know. We went to Spain and we got here. First, the rebellion broke out; then Bill was offered a sort of trinkgeld job in Antwerp, then we couldn't stick that city of the marshes and the only other thing to do was to come to London. We don't like it and we don't want to be here.[24]

It was an age of heroes—and Stead greatly admired people like Ralph Fox and André Malraux. Yet her new novel had none. She had wanted it to be a revolutionary novel, and now she felt a little besmirched by its cynicism. She told Gilbert:

> My new novel is ... about banking and full of crooks. I hope to wash my soul white as snow after this dousing in soot, by writing an innocent book

about something or other, but I haven't yet thought up a pure subject ... I would like to go out to grass, like Nebuchadnezzar ... If Bill didn't want to run from England so fast, I might tackle an English working class town (or Welsh), but I'm afraid I won't have the time to do it. There's very little else to my life ... I'm still like a typist. I type from foggy morn till sooty eve, year in, year out ...

She was interested, too, in writing a novel about a 'revolutionary type', but it was the *psychology* of a revolutionary that interested her more than his actual deeds. What made someone into a political revolutionary? What sort of psychological impulses were at stake? She tended to think of people as *types*: Alf Hurst was the 'Don Juan type' or the 'Napoleon type'; Keith Duncan was the 'bachelor type'. (She did not know that in 1934, back in Sydney, Duncan had married Dorothy Anderson, an English woman he had met while teaching in the extramural summer program in Kent in the 1920s.) In her liking for taxonomy, Stead was as much a naturalist as her father.

Stead's curiosity about revolutionaries had been a motive for working at the *New Masses*. She had made notes about Mike Gold and would continue to do so over the next few years. When Stanley Burnshaw wrote from New York describing the bitter factionalism among the *New Masses* associates, Stead answered that this was typical of the Left. She added dutifully, 'And I say this as a good Stalinist.' Would he please tell her more? she asked him. 'I have an insatiable thirst for rounding out the details, also the fulfilment of personality.'[25]

Blake wanted to spend spring and summer in Normandy, or else go to Hollywood to look for work. In the end, they went to Montpellier. In this romantic old Mediterranean town surrounded by vineyards, both finished revising the novels they had begun with such zeal a year earlier in Spain.

Stead signed her novel with an uncharacteristic little flourish: 'Montpellier, France 1937'. In early June, Blake proudly wrote to Mike Gold: 'The strangest thing has happened, Mike. I have written a book, lazy, spouting Bill Blech.'

It is so charlatan, lousy, fako, that at night, when I sleep I expect the Heeby-Jeebies on horses to tweak my nose above my pillow to punish me for my crimes. But who knows. John Dumm Public may like it, and I be able to buy Clam chowders for friends.[26]

By the summer of 1937, a mass exodus from Europe had begun. It was clear that war was coming. Hitler constantly reiterated Germany's need for more territory—*Lebensraum*. Himmler, head of the SS, had established a new concentration camp at Buchenwald for enemies of the state. Franco was tightening his grip on Spain.

Blake had sworn he would rather live in Patagonia than go back to New York. And Stead, having written almost nothing during their year there, declared that 'the whole spirit of New York is opposed to the creative mind'.[27] Yet in July 1937, they left Cherbourg on the SS *Aquitania* bound for New York City.

8

The Battleground of Life

SEPTEMBER 1937 – SEPTEMBER 1939

AT THE BEGINNING of September, Stead and Blake were installed in an apartment at No. 403 W. 115th Street, at Morningside Heights, the Columbia University district. 'It is on a narrow ridge between Harlem and the Hudson and is full of churches, belfries, parks and of course the Campus, so there is plenty of air and not too many barrack-apartment-houses', Stead told Florence James. She felt reasonably positive now about being back in the US. It was at least an English-speaking environment, and unlike England, it was removed from the arena of war. New York was full of European refugees, many of them well-known intellectuals and literary figures. And there were things she wanted to write about American society, which still managed to amaze her.

Rosa Blech was living with them again. Quite weak by now, she never ventured beyond the local block and seldom played her small upright piano. To Stead, Rosa was 'still the kobold she always was, asking her million questions a day about the minutiae of life and uttering the inevitable wise-saws'.[1] But Rosa liked New York, and Stead hoped she might be better humoured than she had been in Paris and London.

But she was worse. Christina alluded to the household tension in a letter to her sister Kate, though she described it, in the vaguest possible terms, as a structural problem. 'The couple situation is a very odd one and the mother-son relation is a very odd one, and they simply don't mix.'[2]

In fact, Rosa's wandering mind had become quite paranoid, and many of her private terrors were associated with her son's de facto companion. Above all, she would tell people that the 'shiksa' was starving her, hoping to finish her off.[3] Stanley Burnshaw remembers Stead telling him the hurtful things Rosa Blech would say. She pretended to shrug at them, but Burnshaw sensed her pain.

Not only did Rosa talk about Christina behind her back: she would do so in front of her too—in her German-Yiddish mishmash.

> She used to hold conversations with Bill at breakfast, say, and when it came to concern me, she would break into this *mysterious* language (and the shiksa has a good many amusing conversations written down, from this source).[4]

Stead, who understood German by now, never let on that she could follow the conversation. She wrote down several exchanges between Rosa and 'Vill' (as Rosa called William). In Stead's thinly fictionalised notes, 'Mrs. Segal' speaks a jumble of German, Yiddish and English—a language sprinkled with clichés and muddled references to literature, particularly Shakespeare. Relentless in her pursuit of trite details, her main preoccupation is food: what others eat, how things are cooked, where things were bought. She complains about a lack of food in the house. Her life is empty and unhappy: 'Ich get up early. Ich get up at 7.30. Then I go to bed again. Was ist das fur a life: immer in Bett ... Old is no joke.' Her self-pitying refrain is that she has not long to live: 'Nu, what can I do? I am almost to the last chapter. Man muss "Finis" schreiben.' Similar conversations appear in *Letty Fox*, although for the sake of comprehensibility, Grandma Fox speaks a jumbled English, not German.

Forlorn, manipulative characters based on Rosa Blech had already worked their way into *The Salzburg Tales* and *House of All Nations*. The portrait in *Letty Fox*, which Stead would write after Rosa Blech's death, is rounder and more sympathetic. Grandma Fox is a 'queer little thing, sharp, angry, and disappointed'. Frightened of death, lonely and unhappy, she is sure that her friends and neighbours think of her as 'a rag of flesh, carrion, on the dump heap'. To raise herself in their eyes, she boasts about her glamorous European past, inventing stories about her rich daughter-in-law and her talented grand-daughter. But the details are not consistent. Her companions laugh behind her back. By the end of her life she has 'entered that region of personal misery and isolation which seems like madness to others'.

When Bill visited Mollie and Ruth, whom he had not seen for more than a year, he was amazed to learn that Mollie had thought they were no longer married. (He had told her that he and Stead were going to Europe via Mexico for a divorce.) Encouraged perhaps by this strange turn of events, Blake did some contract work for his stockbroker friend, Jacques Coe, specifically to make the $500 for a Mexican divorce. According to Coe, in just one week, Blake wrote a 'brilliant' and meticulous report on Mexican Eagle oil shares, enabling Coe to pull off a major deal with a previously sceptical client and make a spectacular profit.[5] Blake made his $500, but though a Mexican divorce took only about twenty-four hours, and could even be done by proxy, Blake did not go through with it.

Over the next nine years in the States, Blake would do intermittent bursts of contract work for financiers. Alf Hurst was also in New York, and would remain there for the duration of the war. Blake worked on and off at Hurst's Grain Union Corporation, advising Hurst on straddles, arbitrage opportunities and foreign exchange trends. Hurst also did business in Canada, which involved Blake in occasional trips north.

Ruth Blech, now sixteen, was short and pretty, with her father's lively brown eyes and vivacity and the restlessness of both her parents. Her libertarian and unsettled transatlantic upbringing had made her precocious—in fact, quite a handful. As a 'freshman' at Cornell University in upstate New York, she was finding the remote campus exceedingly dull.

Stead would see quite a bit of Ruth during the next nine years. The two never really warmed to each other; their relationship was always awkward. But there were moments of relative closeness. Stead was curious about the aspirations and experience of the younger generation of women. She had emerged from her own repressed adolescence convinced that sexual freedom for women would have a revolutionary effect on the relationship between the sexes. Yet when she talked to Ruth and her teenage friends, she saw that nothing had changed fundamentally. There was far more sexual freedom, but the young women still seemed pathetically eager to please men, and just as hellbent on finding a husband. This was a subject Stead would explore in *For Love Alone* and *Letty Fox*, begun a few years later.

Stead was 'fooshing about', undecided about what to write next. Temporarily bereft of creative ideas, and in need of money as usual, she thought she should try translating for a publishing house, an idea she had nursed for years. With this in mind, she was doing translation exercises with Elisabeth, Mike Gold's French wife. Mike and Elisabeth, who now had a son, lived a block away, in W. 116th Street. They saw a lot of each other.

Bill Blake did not share Stead's disorientation. No sooner had he finished *The World is Mine* than he started work on an undergraduate textbook on Marxist economic theory, and another historical novel. Stead envied his flow of ideas, and admired the liveliness of his writing. 'He has ten times the novelist in him that I have.'[6]

Blake was impatient to see his first book in print. Stead made out that she was 'grey, old and wise' after years of 'long fangdangling' by Peter Davies, but she too was nervously awaiting publication. Her father's pre-publication copy of *House of All Nations*, sent to him in May 1938, was inscribed:

> For my father—
> nearly 350,000 words—
> 104 scenes—
> a book written in the sweat of my brow—
> a hope to do better in the future—
> an unsatisfied ambition—
> all these—
> affectionately, in one binding—
> Pegler. Christina E. Stead.[7]

Clearly, it remained her all-consuming wish to impress her father.

Their books were due out in the summer of 1938. In the meantime, Stead and Blake made plans for the future. He would go to Reno, in Nevada, and get a divorce. They would go to live in a smaller city—Boston perhaps, or even a country town. They would at last make a trip to Australia. Christina's family was pressing them to visit: 1938 was the tenth anniversary of Christina's departure as well as the 150th anniversary of white settlement in Australia. They would perhaps have a child—though Stead, unconvinced, told Florence James:

> Bill is very anxious for a 'Benjamin' but ever since my appendix operation I have had nothing that carried through the first month; I have never been to a doctor since, I am supposed to go now, but I keep putting it off.[8]

Plans were all prefaced by 'If money is to hand', or 'If we make a million'. But Stead and Blake pinned great hopes on 'S & S', as Simon & Schuster was called locally. 'They are the liveliest outfit I ever struck,' Stead told Florence James. 'Something of the Travelers' Bank in them ... everyone worked to death and everyone with figures in their mind's eye.' The comparatively young firm had a dazzling record of best-sellers: they knew how to promote books and it was rumoured that their average sales were 20000 per book. Their current winner was Dale Carnegie's *How to Win Friends and Influence People*: more than 600000 copies had been sold in 1937 alone. Privately, Stead was horrified by the moneymakers and 'success-cynics' in the publishing game. She was aghast when Bill's first manuscript came back from Simon & Schuster's literary editor ('a really charming and decent young man') covered with 'vile' margin comments such as: 'What we want here is some really luscious screwing.' By contrast with the commercial American hype, Peter Davies, with his genuine love of literature and naivety with money, suddenly seemed an 'Olympian character'.

But Stead and Blake, like their other leftist friends, were personally divided when it came to commercialism.

It is no good throwing up my hands in despair because they are simply moneymakers: they are also very anxious to help you make money and get your name about in other fields (it all helps their game) and so, one way or another, short stories or articles and so forth, they will help us out.

When Stanley Burnshaw was sent an advance copy of Blake's novel, he pointed out many defects, but said he thought the book would sell well. It took Bill some time to recover from this 'carper's field day' (as he called it), but Christina thanked Burnshaw warmly: 'I simply rejoice in your affirmations about the book ... I think Bill has the wisdom and affirmation and humanity of a great writer, and all he needs is to take himself seriously.'[9]

Although they hoped for good publicity, Stead and Blake preferred to be out of town for summer, when their books were to be launched. In May 1938, they went to live in the vacant stone-and-weatherboard cottage near Lambertville, New Jersey, temporarily vacated by the Putnams. For Stead, the dry heat in Lambertville was 'like wine'.[10] And Lambertville was close enough for them to make occasional day trips to New York City. She spent her time dreaming, weeding, watching birds, going for walks and reading Tolstoy and 'the old masters'.

The land was originally a berry farm. Now it was overrun and untended. At the bottom of the property, a wooden bridge crossed a trout brook covered with tiger lilies and banks of poison ivy. Stead wrote enthusiastically to Kate about the native birds and plants. One of the great charms of the American countryside for an Australian who had never seen them before were the flashing fireflies.

> The first time I saw them, I held my breath and it was a very tangible enchantment, it was the Midsummer Night's Dream: each spark shot up through the air, or wound about so much like a fairy, and in so many lovely spots—in thick fields of daisies and wind-breaks of pine-trees, through tall weeds and on the tips of tall trees ... that I for the very first time knew that there could be a real emotion and a real marvel behind the idea of fairies. The beavers, squirrels and all the peeping things give rise to the idea of elves and dwarves and now I see the natural origin of the fairies.

Inspired by the brooding wilderness around her, she began a ghost story, 'The Right-Angled Creek'.[11] It has all the gothic trappings she relished in Edgar Allan Poe: nature is all-powerful and out of control; the Lambertville house is haunted by the ghost of an Indian princess (Pocahontas—Poky for short); there is a mad woman, and a sinister death from poison ivy. The suspense builds up. The summer heat builds up. The narrative, lush as the wilderness in which it is set, resembles a Brueghel painting.   ·

Clare and Sam Parsons come to spend summer in their friends' country house, which they soon call 'Poky's Place'. Clare, a nature-lover, delights in the 'rioting insanity' of the place; Sam, a city boy ('a stubby dark man' with a 'resonant Mid-Western voice') tramps up and down the tracks talking to himself, musing on his 'past business relations' and the books he intends to write.

Nature is out of control; so is Laban Davies—'a pathological drunk like Poe', who struggles in vain against his addiction. Davies, a writer and translator, is modelled on Samuel Putnam.[12] That summer, Stead read books on alcoholism, and books about the district, its natural resources and social fabric. Her background research was always thorough.

The setting allowed Stead to indulge her 'premonitions' and 'grisly fancies'. She told Stanley Burnshaw:

Poky is lying low, but we have discovered a large number of fat green freshwater eels in the brook; or rather, I have, Bill won't so much as glance at eels and the like and I believe it's because he won't face the primitive evil in Nature. However, he has glanced at snakes this summer, and probably in a month or two he will come round to the eels too.

Years later, she would tell her editor that the story was 'all true' ('well most of it')—especially the ghost, 'the only one I ever ran into'.[13]

———— ᘒ ————

House of All Nations was launched in New York on Wednesday 8 June 1938. It was attractively presented, with a dust-jacket and title page designed by their friend Philip Van Doren Stern, who was head of the S & S manufacturing department and a novelist himself. The publicity was good. Stead's photograph was even on the cover of that week's *Saturday Review of Literature*, beaming from all the news-stands. A flattering picture, taken around the time she left Australia, ten years before, her long hair is knotted in the nape of her neck, she is wearing a smart tailored jacket, and looks serious, full-lipped, bright-eyed and intelligent. Inside the magazine, the novelist Elliot Paul declared that he was held by the book 'to the highest pitch of excitement'.

Reviewers were impressed that this Australian female writer had managed to familiarise herself with the intricacies of European financial intrigue. Once again, many used the word 'genius'. Everyone admired the book's vitality and energy. In the *New York Times Book Review*, Harold Strauss wrote of Stead's 'miraculous' knowledge of international finance, her 'pyrotechnic imagination' and the 'star dust' effect of her writing. Clifton Fadiman wrote in the *New Yorker* that the novel was 'full of rich comedy, crowded with Balzacian characters, and, despite certain flaws and a tendency to congested detail ... a work of extraordinary talent'.

Peter Davies had bought the shoots from Simon & Schuster, and the novel appeared simultaneously in England. Less widely reviewed in that country, its reception was also less generous. The novel was considered excessive, too detailed, too long.

———— ᘒ ————

Stead had been 'quite, quite sure' that *House of All Nations* would sell 10000 copies—'even if the publishers lay down on it'.[14] She was in for one of the most bitter disappointments of her life. Simon & Schuster, that sparkling firm of literary capitalists, were as dubious as Peter Davies had always been about the selling power of her work.

Stead had never dreamt that Simon & Schuster's commercialism might go *against* her. Indeed, it is extraordinary how much faith she and Blake had pinned on the capitalist machinery. Six months after publication, she still felt thoroughly betrayed by her publishers. She wrote to Florence James:

> The publishers ... thought it was just another 'lady's' maundering novel and only printed 3,000. The superb reception it had here took them by surprise and their first action was to write to me asking me to reduce my royalty because they were losing money, and making a vague threat—otherwise they wouldn't reprint. I fought tooth and nail and found the financial disappointment unpleasant because I had thought I could visit Sydney out of the 'House'. They refuse to reprint more than 6,000 and now have dropped it. I thought of breaking contract— but who is better? Look at my experience with Peter!

In a state of bitter frustration, Stead confronted Peter Davies. She had always been impeccably polite to him; now she told him how disappointed she was with her publishers on both sides of the Atlantic. It would not have helped her case, she told him, that he had told Simon & Schuster he did not much like the novel. Caught out, Davies was obliged to confess— in that Etonian style that Stead had once found charming.

> It was very naughty of Simon, that astute man, to say I told him I didn't like the *House of All Nations*. I can't imagine myself ever saying of any book of yours that I didn't like it, just like that. There are thousands of words in it I love, and all of it I greatly and enthusiastically admire, and none of it do I take to my soul as I do certain passages in *The Salzburg Tales* and *The Beauties and Furies*. And I do not think it a book, or perhaps even the sort of book, which you ought to write if you desire either fame or success. You are certainly the only writer I have ever published to whom the attribute of genius can be applied, so I may very well be wrong in all this, but I can't help thinking it.

He concluded:

> I am truly sorry you aren't happy with S. and S., the more so as I don't know how you are to get away unless there is a loophole in your contract.

Perhaps there is? On the other hand, aside from your personal feelings, I don't think it necessarily follows that anyone else would sell you better. They are generally regarded as first rate 'stunt' publishers.[15]

Stead had grudgingly admired Peter Davies' lack of interest in marketing strategies, but now his words had the same ring as her American publishers.

William Blake's *The World is Mine* was published by Simon & Schuster on 4 August 1938—two months after *House of All Nations*. It was promoted as a best-seller: less than two weeks after publication, sales had reached 6000 copies, and the novel was rated ninth on the *New York Times Book Review* best-seller list. By mid August it was on its fourth printing; by early December it had sold 10 000 copies. Blake was told that it narrowly missed out on a Book of the Month Club nomination: the novel exposed the Church's dubious financial procedures, and the Catholic Church exerted pressure against it.

A flurry of extravagantly positive reviews appeared. Clifton Fadiman paved the way: 'Mr. Blake has certainly ripped off something to make your eyes bug out.' In the *Daily Worker*, Mike Gold called William Blake 'a new proletarian Dumas'. Poet and critic Louis Untermeyer confessed the book had made him 'grin, goggle, check the references, admire, swear softly, gasp and keep on reading'.[16]

A more sober response came from the poet Stephen Vincent Benét, who regretted that Mr Blake had 'larded his melodramatic story with quite so much portentous philosophizing'.[17]

It was rumoured that the novel's larger-than-life capitalist-cum-anarchist hero, Cristóbal, resembled the author, and Blake was not averse to fostering this image himself. Edd Johnson's interview with Blake for the *New York World-Telegram*, on 31 August 1938, is revealing:

[Mr. Blake] was interviewed this morning over a cup of coffee in a drug store at 116th St and Broadway after mysterious arrangements had been made with his publisher to produce him.

He would not divulge his true name, his address or his marital status, although he mentioned that he has a daughter in Cornell, 'who is also a chatterbox,' and referred in passing to 'an interrupted first marriage.'

He appeared at the appointed time and immediately began to talk in rapid sentences. He stirred his coffee furiously as he talked, overturned a pitcher of cream in the midst of a discussion of the 6% of women who are prostitutes and the 27% of men who are loafers.

He was born, he said, of German-Jewish parents in Chicago. His father was an army surgeon, 'a terrible patriot, a regular Prussian.' His mother was a musician. Both were atheists …

His mother and father were divorced and he came to New York with his mother. At 14 he quit high school and got a job as secretary to a wealthy man who liked radicals.

'I was the oratory type,' Mr. Blake said.

At 15 he got a job as statistician in a brokerage company. He spoke German and French fluently, was a mathematical prodigy and an authority on European history before he left school.

He worked in private banks, analyzing earning reports, mapping out financial strategy, advising boards of directors and writing prospectuses for stock and bond flotations …

In the early years of the World War he made his first fortune on borrowed money in commodities, but when President Wilson broke off diplomatic relations with Germany he became 'active with the opposition.' He was not in sympathy with Germany, but violently opposed to the war—a conscientious objector.

'Some of those prison scenes in my book may not have been imagined,' he said, and then quickly changed the subject and refused to be lured back.

His fortune disappeared during the war. At its conclusion he went back into Wall Street, 'working for people who wanted my brains and weren't interested in my politics.'

…

'I am more European than American,' he said. 'I like the European respect for privacy. That is one of the reasons I won't talk about my private life.'

…

He started to write *The World is Mine* while sitting in a café in Andalusia, where the story opens, and drinking sweet wine. He drank sweet wine while writing the 741 pages of the entire novel.

…

Politically, Mr. Blake is an anarchist turned Marxist. Personally, he is a gourmand. Professionally, he is a successful capitalist.

So is his book's hero.

'But it is not a portrait of me,' Mr. Blake hastened to explain. 'The man is a billionaire, the richest man in the world, the symbol of all capitalism. I am not that type.'

He says he is described—'a horrible picture, but an accurate picture'—in *House of All Nations*, by Christina Stead, 'referred to in one clipping as my wife.'

Sipping his sweet Spanish wine as he worked, Mr. Blake splashed out his prodigious story of gold and passion, of intrigue and torture and blood, on a canvas so broad that critics expressed amazement that any man could know so much. Mr. Blake does not share their amazement. He is accustomed to doing amazing things.

'I am a terrific worker,' he said. 'I write 10,000 words a day, and ninety-nine per cent of it stands without revision. I work all the time—twelve or fourteen hours a day.'

William Blake's writing career had enjoyed a spectacular start. He passionately hoped that he had found an alternative to working in finance.

Stead and Blake left Lambertville in the autumn of 1938, and briefly sublet the Burnshaws' house at Croton-on-Hudson, on the outskirts of New York City. (The Burnshaws' baby was due in December, and they preferred to live near a hospital.) Stead was feeling depressed. As well as the bitter disappointment of *House of All Nations*, there had been tragic news from Australia. In August, her brother Fred had been killed by a truck while riding his motorbike. Just twenty-seven, he left behind a wife and two children. No record survives of Stead's response to the news, but the depiction of Leo, Teresa's younger brother in *For Love Alone*, is an unusually tender portrait. Leo, like the characters based on the dead Ralph Fox, is one of Stead's idealised male figures. She makes him that combination she always found so seductive: a revolutionary (he leads a strike at his factory) and a gentle romantic, who plays the guitar and has a soft spot for women.[18] Interestingly, Leo is also inordinately proud of his sister Teresa.

Before his novel appeared, Bill officially changed his name to William Blake. The choice had nothing to do with the famous poet: he had never liked the way English-speaking people pronounced his surname—something like 'Bletch'—and he had been using the name Blake for years. Most people already called him Bill Blake. Perhaps he also wanted to dissociate himself formally both from the father who had never done anything for him and from the *Vaterland* that was vigorously disowning its Jewish citizens.

In August, Stead announced the name change to her brother Gilbert, adding, tongue-in-cheek: 'I don't have to change mine: mine happens to be the world's best literary name, everyone seems to have heard it and no-one forgets it.'[19] She was feeling disillusioned that summer.

The name 'Stead' had its own problems, she told Gilbert. Middle-class Jews often took it for a Danish or Swedish name, whereupon they assumed she was anti-semitic.

> I never heard any such nonsense from working-class Jews, as they're not interested in the trash of 'semitism' but in their work, their union, or whatever it is. You get so tired of this race stuff in crazy Europe, that the only resort is to believe there are no races at all worth mentioning, which is pretty much the truth anyhow.

By June 1942, when a report from Poland revealed that the Nazis had killed more than a million Jews, Stead saw things very differently, and planned to write a novel about the Jews, that 'martyred people'.[20] But in 1938 her impatience had to do with her general attitude to cultural difference. While she had an expatriate Australian's fascination with foreignness and exoticism, she and Blake were too genuinely cosmopolitan to see cultural difference as something that separated people from one another. She was to be equally impatient with the Women's Movement in the 1970s that— as she saw it—polarised the sexes, emphasising their differences. Stead wanted a world in which cultural and biological differences were neither apologetically concealed nor aggressively proclaimed.

Her attitude towards Jewishness reflected that of most leftwing Jews in the 1930s. More concerned to be world citizens than to be regarded as Jews, they advocated assimilation. At the same time, they continued to differentiate between Jews and Gentiles, often at their own expense. In Michael Gold's *Jews Without Money*, the Rabbi, landlord and pawnbroker are treated as egregious villains. In *House of All Nations*, Stead has the Jewish Marxist Alphendéry tell his colleague, 'What is it the Jew doesn't want to lose? Not Judaism, dear Herr Rosenkrantz, but the bourgeoisie, of which he is the archetype, the most concentrated example.'

Bill Blake's anti-Jewish jokes and stories were simply another facet of his self-irony. He and his friends were proud of their Jewishness, just as Stead was proud to have a Jewish partner. According to Stanley Burnshaw, himself a Jew, Bill if anything deliberately cultivated a Jewish style, and nearly all their friends were Jewish. He and Christina liberally used Yiddish expressions.[21]

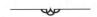

Their Jewish friends at the New Masses officially went along with the Popular Front, but most believed that the true revolutionary was a paid-up member of the communist party. In January 1938, Bill Blake had officially joined the Party, proposed by Mike Gold. But his membership was short lived. He did not have the temperament for party politics at cell-meeting level; his mind was too theoretical. When, having just joined the Upper Broadway branch, Blake received a letter requesting that he attend a New Member Class the following Monday, he told Stead he would try to get out of it. She protested: 'Not the *first* meeting.' Before long, they had left for Lambertville, then Croton, which made attendance at meetings impossible, unless Blake stayed overnight with a friend in New York. He attended meetings intermittently for the rest of that year, then stopped paying his dues. His membership officially lapsed in April 1939. As a 'member at large', he continued to be in great demand as a speaker at political meetings and rallies. Reports of the sensational Moscow trials in the American press did not sway his loyalty to Stalinism.

As a foreign resident in the United States, Christina Stead could not join the Party. She regretted this for one reason only: it would have provided material for the novel she wanted to write about communist radicals. Her commitment was to her writing, not politics. She disliked political meetings, with their endless rhetoric in smoke-filled rooms. However, she did join the League of American Writers, which united writers against fascism, with regular readings, discussion panels and fundraising activities.

Stead was convinced that writers had a political responsibility, but she was impatient with simplistic notions of proletarian literature, and was courageous enough to say so in the *New Masses*. Having offered to review André Malraux's Spanish Civil War novel, *L'Espoir*, which had received mixed reactions from the Left, she turned to Stanley Burnshaw, another 'fellow traveller', for a second opinion. 'Of course, Bill doesn't think much of the calibre of a guy who is not in, but alongside the Party, and so it's no good my breaking up the happy home discussing it with him. I think I understand Malraux: I like him, anyhow; and I think the Party-ites misjudge him.'[22]

Her courage had been fortified by Ralph Fox's widely praised posthumous book *The Novel and the People*, extracts from which appeared in the *New Masses* shortly after his death. Fox was scornful of the 'hardboiled school' of proletarian literature that made fiction into a 'scarcely disguised political tract', and he supported Engels' view that 'the more the opinions of the author remain hidden, the better for the work of art'.

To Fox, celebrating the workers was not as important as depicting characters against their social background, showing them to be determined partly by social forces. 'There is no human character, no emotion, no conflict of personalities outside the scope of the revolutionary novelist.' His conclusion was as Nietzschean as it was Marxist: 'The one concern of the novelist is, or should be, this question of the individual will in its conflict with other wills on the battleground of life.'

These were views congenial to Stead. In her fiction, personal relations were always grounded in the social and economic world. But she did not care to voice her own opinions or take a moral stance. Nor was she interested in presenting heroes and happy endings where there were none. Hers was a universe of contradictions, incongruity and strife. Indeed, the charges of energy in Christina Stead's fiction are generated precisely by the *unreconciled* elements, by individual wills in conflict with other wills on the battleground of life.

Towards the end of the year, Stead was surprised to see an Australian envelope with Florence James' handwriting among a pile of letters forwarded to Croton-on-Hudson. With the threat of war in Europe, Florence had gone back to Australia with her two girls: her husband was joining them later. After ten years in England, Florence's reaction gave Stead 'a palpable notion' of what Australia was like these days. 'Perhaps I shouldn't like it any better than I did before.'[23]

Like most expatriates, Stead's attitude to Australia was ambivalent. She missed the climate and the bush, but shuddered when she thought of Australia's provincialism and isolation. She felt resentful when she considered how little Australians fostered artistic talent, and that, even so, expatriate artists were treated like deserters. In 1938, for the first time, she was featured next to her father in Australia's *Who's Who*, but her talent and contribution to Australian literature had never been celebrated by Australian critics. Entrenched in the realist tradition, they disliked the 'over-luxuriance' of her writing and its elements of modernist experimentation.

In his 1936 book *The Foundations of Culture in Australia*, P. R. Stephensen, who had recently returned to Australia after several years in England, attacked the colony of Australian émigré-writers in London: Jack Lindsay, Henry Handel Richardson, Christina Stead, Frederic Manning and others.

> Had these people remained here, and dealt with the realities of Australia, instead of with the fantasies of European glamour and European antiquity, they would with ease have created a body of Australian literature which, added to that we already possess, would by now have been enough to make Australia's name and quality resound as one of the most highly cultivated and civilised nations upon the earth. But no; the shirkers, they have cleared out, funked their job.

His language was jocular, but the message was serious.

In Australia, critics were obsessed by the need to determine whether books were *Australian* or *Un-Australian*. Of Stead's four novels so far, only *Seven Poor Men of Sydney*, set in her home city, qualified as 'Australian'. Reflecting on the exceptional 1938 harvest in Australian literature, the foremost Australian critic, H. M. Green, paid Christina Stead only grudging tribute:

> The year produced three novels that are outstanding: Christina Stead's *House of All Nations*, Xavier Herbert's *Capricornia*, and Seaforth Mackenzie's *Chosen People*. The first does not really concern us, for its author left Australia ten years ago and settled abroad, and the book is cosmopolitan in tone and subject. But it is difficult to pass it over entirely. Huge, packed, amorphous, it is neither a popular nor an artistic success, but it shows its author to possess a combination of qualities such as I have found in no other writer to-day.[24]

Nettie Palmer tried to retrieve *House of All Nations* for Australian literature by arguing that Stead had written 'an Australian novel of a new genre', pointing out that Stead used occasional Australian phrases and imagery—about gold diggers and surfing. But then Palmer was obliged to admit that Stead used images 'from everywhere else too'.[25]

This pointless debate about 'Australianness' continued until the late 1960s. In the name of cultural nationalism, the debate merely proved the parochialism and defensiveness of Australian culture at the time.

It was eighteen months since Christina Stead had finished *House of All Nations*, and she had only just decided on the subject for her next novel. Almost three years earlier, she had thought she would like to write about her father's life—his upbringing, beliefs and character—but for that project she needed to be in Australia to research the social background. She had been very excited when Ralph Fox confessed his liking for autobiography. Now she decided to write about her own childhood. She would still be writing about her father, but her father as an adult. And for that she could work from memory and personal correspondence.

To avoid the New York winter, she and Blake went to St Augustine, Florida, in January 1939, where Blake researched his novel on the American Civil War, *The Copperheads*, and Stead started to plan *The Man Who Loved Children*. In May, back in New York, they moved into a six-room apartment at No. 152 E. 22nd Street, in the Gramercy Park area. The apartment was large so that 70-year-old Rosa Blech, now in poor condition, could live with them. So could Bill's cousin Jenka, as Rosa's companion.

It was a big step for Stead to decide to write autobiographical fiction. Not only the Left, but Anglo-Saxons generally, tended to deem it self-indulgent to write about one's childhood. Two of Stead's literary models, D. H. Lawrence's *Sons and Lovers* and Joyce's *Portrait of the Artist as a Young Man* were received more sympathetically in Europe than in Britain.

Brought up in the stoic Anglo-Saxon tradition, Stead rarely allowed herself to explore her own emotions. She had majored in psychology and made no bones about being fascinated by the psychology of others, but she was uncomfortable with self-revelation. And she and Blake were fiercely impatient with what they regarded as the self-indulgence of popular psychology. In both *The Beauties and Furies* and *Letty Fox*, Stead ridicules the way psychoanalytic jargon reduces everything to an Oedipus complex or a 'father fixation'. Yet, even if she disliked the Freudian vocabulary, she must have recognised in her struggle with the shadow of her father a classic Freudian scenario.

When she had left Australia a decade earlier, Stead had resolutely left her past behind. Once in the northern hemisphere, she had adopted new ideas, other cultures. Her father was prejudiced against Jews, businessmen and the French; he abstained from alcohol and never went to the theatre or cinema. Christina Stead enthusiastically embraced all these aspects of her new existence. But she had not managed to exorcise the ghost of her father.

Relations with her family in the past ten years had been amicable but distant. In 1938 there had been a flurried exchange of books. Christina sent her father *House of All Nations*. His de-facto wife, Thistle Harris, a botanist, sent Christina and Bill a copy of her *Wildflowers of Australia*. Bill posted off *The World is Mine*, with the inscription: 'To David G. Stead, father of a miraculous daughter and himself highly esteemed by long and indirect knowledge by "William Blake." Wm. J. Blech.'[26]

The picture Christina painted of her father was plainly not wholly negative, yet she was painfully aware that her childhood had left her emotionally scarred. Now, just like Virginia Woolf at a similar age, she felt compelled to write about the figures who had loomed so large in her early years. Six months into writing *The Man Who Loved Children*, she told Thistle Harris: 'I have left it all these years, not able to touch such an autobiographical subject, but last winter I decided to get it off my chest once and for all.'[27] In an interview when she was seventy-five, Stead would say that the novel 'demanded to be written':

> I was quite solitary, although I was very happy with Bill, my husband ... But I was crying every two months and just couldn't stop. I didn't know it then, but it was because of my terrible experiences as a child. Then one day I wrote down everything to clarify my feelings.[28]

Christina Stead was thirty-six when she began *The Man Who Loved Children* in the winter of 1938–39. Virginia Woolf, at forty-four, had found that writing *To The Lighthouse* went some way towards dispelling her parental ghosts. Stead too would say, just two years later: 'It was a great weight off my mind, I ought really to say my soul, writing *The Man Who*—it was as if I escaped from jail, although it may seem savage and mean to others.'[29] At the time, however, plunging into the past brought violent emotions to the surface and caused her extreme emotional distress. The E. 22nd Street apartment was dark and dreary, overshadowed by high rises with factories on the ground floor. Stead felt oppressed by the stonework and brickwork around her. The memories came flooding back. She slept badly. She raged. She wept. Among all that masonry, she was effectively undertaking her own psychoanalysis.

As the novel was being typeset, she told Florence James that writing it had given her 'the jitters'. ('Part of it is taken from my homelife and not very amiable.') She had been 'too down' all these months to write to the family. She still could not write home. It was 'a snake's life', she considered, to shed one's skin as she had done. The choice of image—more evocative of her Sydney childhood than her life in urban New York—suggests she had not shed her skin completely.

Writing about her past made her examine her childhood clinically, from the outside. It crystallised the misery of it all: her father's failure to put himself in her place, his fundamental indifference—an indifference that was part of his charm. As she was writing it, Stead told Thistle Harris that it was one of her aims in life never to see her father again.

> It has been a grand thing for me to get this plucked out of the back of my mind. But, a thing David could not realise, that home was so atrociously wretched and I was so ill at ease as a result that I do not want to see Australia, except on some gilded visit, if I ever get the gilding. Yes, I could live in Victoria, or Queensland, or go out back, say to Broken Hill, that is something I should like to do for a while—but I do not want to see Sydney, nor my family, nor anyone connected with the old days.

Why did Stead write these things to Thistle Harris, whom she scarcely knew? Her long letter to Thistle in July 1939, which reduced David Stead to a case study of egotism, could hardly have been more hurtful about the man Thistle loved. Christina well knew that Thistle might show the letter to David. By aiming her missile indirectly in this way, Christina was hurting both her father and Thistle Harris in one deft move.

Christina had clearly not come to terms with Thistle, who seems to have brought out her sense of rivalry. While writing *The Man Who Loved Children*, she told Thistle she had three more novels brewing.

> I hope I get some backbone and go at it a bit faster than usual, for time draws on and I have only turned out *four* books. It's frightful to think of. Are

you working on another plant book? I hear that this one was written some years ago, but publication was held up.

In *The Man Who Loved Children*, the 'domestic agony' and 'shrieks of madness' Christina Stead experienced throughout her adolescence and early womanhood are condensed into two years. She invented some incidents completely: David Stead never gathered the older children together at the bottom of the stairs to listen to the screams of their mother in labour; nor did Christina write a play for her father's fortieth birthday. The Pollit children are hybrid versions of their real-life models. And unlike Louisa, Christina never gave her stepmother poison—though she fantasised about it.

Samuel Pollit, at thirty-eight, tall, yellow-haired and ruddy-skinned, with 'sparkling, self-satisfied eyes', is a naturalist who left school at twelve and now works for a government department. Henrietta, his highly strung second wife from a wealthy Baltimore family, has black hair and olive skin, and looks like a 'thin, dark scarecrow'. Her sixth child is born in the course of the novel, and 'Henny' excels in bitter diatribes against her lot. Louisa, Sam's daughter by his previous marriage, is a young adolescent, awkward and heavy. Books give her access to a fertile private world.

How true to life are Sam and Henny? Like all fictional characters, they distil and reassign aspects of the people on whom they are modelled. Sam Pollit lacks David Stead's broad erudition, so important a dimension of the real man. And while Henny is Ada Stead at her most wretched and worn, she is also more glorious than her real-life counterpart. Henny's verbal fluency and flights of imagination are not Ada's: these belonged to the stepdaughter herself. Most of Christina Stead's fictional characters are capable of brilliant verbal pyrotechnics; it is not always an accurate reflection of their models.

David Stead's language, on the other hand, did not have to be whipped into thicker cream. Nor was there any need for Stead to exaggerate her father's portrait for fictional purposes. When writing *The Man Who Loved Children*, she was plainly driven by unresolved rage and resentment, but David Stead's real-life character was sufficiently extravagant and infuriating to need no further embellishment. In her old age, Thistle Harris commented that she saw *The Man Who Loved Children* as 'substantially true'.[30]

The writing and revision of *The Man* took Stead a year and a half. No drafts have survived, but a few straggling notes indicate that she prepared for writing with her habitual thoroughness. One page, entitled 'Aunt Josephine', is a character sketch of her dreaded maiden aunt Jessica, noting her expressions, opinions and prejudices. Stead must have typed pages and pages of similar character sketches—always concentrating on the character's voice.

Considerable research was involved in transposing the novel's location from Sydney to Baltimore. Stead and Blake spent time in the genteel districts of Georgetown, Washington. Tohoga House, the Pollits' first grand home, is based on an actual house in the area. (Since David Stead gave things Aboriginal names, Sam Pollit gives his house the Indian name for Georgetown: Tohoga.) Together Stead and Blake explored the shabbier parts of Baltimore, at the head of the Chesapeake Bay, in order to find an equivalent for the house at Watson's Bay. Stead studied local government booklets on trees, subsoil, salinity and the condition of the water in the estuary. It was typical of her ambivalence towards her father that at the very moment when she was writing about the tyrannical upbringing she had endured at his hands, she prided herself on getting the naturalist details right. She also studied local Maryland and Virginia folklore: the story Louisa tells the children, 'Hawkins the North Wind', is based on a Maryland legend.

Why did Stead change the location from Sydney? The explanation she gave later, that it was to shield the family, was not the reason. Already with *House of All Nations*, she had been faced with problems of discretion and libel, yet she had made very little attempt at disguise. She was not at all keen to transfer the setting to America; it was Simon & Schuster who insisted on it, persuading her that it would make the book more marketable for an American readership. Indeed, Stead was so loath to make it an American novel that at first she even contemplated re-writing *The Man Who Loved Children* for Australia afterwards, with Australian settings.

And why did she change the novel's timeframe from the 1910s to the late 1930s? Critic Jose Yglesias suggests that Stead's intention was to give the book contemporary political relevance.[31] But the real reason was linked to the change in location: the America Stead knew was contemporary America—the 1930s; unlike Bill Blake, she was no historical novelist.

It was her good fortune that the Franklin Roosevelt government of the 1930s in many ways resembled the progressive New South Wales government earlier in the century. David Stead had admired that Labor government and its policy of state socialism that enabled him to establish the State Trawling Industry; similarly, Sam Pollit is a 'great partisan of the Roosevelt work plans'.

The spatial and temporal dislocations provided a thorny challenge, to which, several critics maintained, Stead was unable to rise. Mary McCarthy was to comment:

> Though there is a compulsive circumstantiality of detail in the book, the sense of reality is feeble. The action takes place during the Roosevelt administration, when Samuel Pollit is supposed to be between thirty-eight and forty years old; yet all his taste, his slang, and his opinions date from twenty or thirty years earlier; no young New Dealer, for example, would talk about 'Teddy' Roosevelt, or display such a close acquaintance with the works of Artemus Ward ... Some of Miss Stead's most strikingly squalid effects are got from the use of slang that is surely not American but British.[32]

Stead found the revision as tiresome as always. 'Bill had to drag me through the last revision by the hair of my head, I couldn't bear it any more.'[33] Not only was the subject harrowing, but the daunting mass of 'surplus material' and 'surplus drama' kept getting in the way.[34]

Piled up on her work table, as Stead was drafting the novel in their dingy apartment, were her father's writings. David Stead had sent her his small monographs, *Giants and Pigmies of the Deep*, *The Tree Book* and *The Rabbit in Australia* when they were published in the early to mid 1930s. She probably asked him for copies of his newspaper columns and radio broadcasts for schoolchildren about the 'great outdoors' and his travels in Malaya. Presented in the chatty, didactic style he had used with his own children, they were a living reminder of her father's voice. The most important source for Stead were the letters her father had written from Malaya in 1922–23. At the top of a letter from Singapore, written on 20 January 1923, David Stead typed a note: 'Have just re-read this befr sndg [before sending]. Don't be too hard on poor Dad. Remember tht he was sick, tired and nostalgic. Love Dad.'

The surviving letters from Malaya reveal the extent to which Christina Stead used real-life letters in her fiction. Chapter 6 of *The Man Who Loved Children* contains one of David Stead's original letters virtually verbatim. It poses an interesting question: when does 'naturalism' become 'plagiarism'?

In his letters from Malaya, Sam Pollit coincides perfectly with David Stead: the convergence is quite remarkable. By placing her father's letter within *her* novel, Christina Stead had annexed and asserted power over her father's creative product.

Or so it seemed. How must Stead have felt when Clifton Fadiman commented, in his review of *The Man Who Loved Children*, that the novel as a whole did not come off, but that Sam's letters from Malaya were astounding—'extraordinary writing'?[35] It must have seemed to her that she had not, after all, managed to subjugate the shadow of her father. In the very domain in which she struggled to break free from him—her writing—he maintained his power.

Though Stead 'captured' her father in her novel, she would always remain ligated—even at the other side of the world. Perhaps this explains the strange attraction she had felt as a young woman to that painting in the New South Wales Art Gallery—the old-fashioned picture of the sons of Clovis on a barge, bound by their father so they would not inherit his kingdom. Later in life, she recalled: 'I used to look and look at those two boys ... going down the river ... Tied. Hamstrung.'[36]

While she was writing *The Man Who Loved Children*, Stead could not have been easy to live with. Nor was Rosa Blech. The situation at home was 'very painful, almost impossible'. Just one month after they had moved into the large apartment near Gramercy Park, Rosa Blech became ill and was taken to hospital. On 21 June 1939, she died. It was sudden, 'but not too soon'.[37]

In *Letty Fox*, old Grandma Fox is tormented by persecution fantasies. Near the end, she even begins to have suspicions about her beloved son Solander and grand-daughter Letty. But it is her son's companion whom she dreads. Persia, she imagines, is starving her, hitting her, poisoning her, waiting for her money.

In deference to Mollie Blech, Christina Stead did not attend the funeral. In the novel, Persia does. She is escorted by a family friend, and stands in the back row among strangers, unacknowledged by members of the Fox family (even Solander). That *Letty Fox* contains these painful little details about Persia's humiliating situation as Solander Fox's mistress—even if they were not always true of Stead's actual life—is revealing.

Only after Rosa's death did Bill learn that his mother had had a twin sister, who ran off at twenty-one with a Russian officer.[38] Just as Rosa, in her obsession with social respectability, told everyone she was a widow rather than a divorcee, she told no one about her wayward twin. Stead would work these details into *Letty Fox*, and Solander Fox's reaction was probably close to Bill's own:

> 'My heavens,' said Solander, with tears in his eyes, 'don't tell me that my poor little mother concealed all this from me? Poor, poor little thing! What she carried in that little head—what troubles, what disgraces—life is hard!'[39]

Rosa Blech had managed to save $3000, a considerable sum. But though she had lived largely at Bill's expense, she left all her money to her grand-daughter Ruth. As Stead saw it, Rosa's final gesture from beyond the grave demonstrated her hostility towards the 'shiksa'.

Stead and Blake were at last on their own again—'after years of un-ease'. Having leased the large dark apartment for a year, they were obliged to remain there that summer, and felt restless and depressed. Stead agonised over her novel, which seemed to progress 'at a snail's pace'. In addition to her sinus headaches, her regular New York ailment, she suffered from mysterious 'collywobbles'.[40]

Political events reinforced Stead's gloom. September 1938 had Prime Minister Chamberlain signing the Munich Pact, which gave Sudetenland, a region of Czechoslovakia, over to Nazi Germany—a step widely seen as a cowardly appeasement of Hitler. In November 1938, 'Kristallnacht' heralded a new phase of terrorism against Jews throughout Germany. Shops were looted, Jews were murdered and Jewish property henceforth belonged to the Reich. In Spain, during the severe winter of 1938–39, Franco's Nationalists swept to victory. In March 1939, the Germans invaded Prague. In May, Hitler and Mussolini signed a ten-year military alliance, their 'Pact of Steel'. War was imminent.

It was against this frightening backdrop that the League of American Writers held the Third American Writers' Congress in June 1939, a three-day meeting at the New School for Social Research. Shattered by the

Republican defeat in Spain and wary of the temporary peace brought about by the Munich Pact, more than 500 delegates attended. At the opening session on Saturday, 3 June, League President Donald Ogden Stewart challenged authors to fight with pen and typewriter for the defence of civil and cultural liberties in the United States. Thomas Mann, Honorary President, spoke to a capacity audience about the barbarism of the Nazis.

In the fiction session the next day, five writers presented brief papers. Louis Aragon spoke about the social character of the novel; Richard Wright talked about the short novel; Sylvia Townsend Warner discussed historical fiction; Dashiell Hammett spoke about tempo in fiction. Christina Stead spoke about the many-charactered novel, suggesting this was the ideal form of novel for a world in chaos in which the individual felt small.

Blake and Stead were among 400 American intellectuals to sign an Open Letter addressed to 'All Active Supporters of Democracy and Peace'. The letter, dated 14 August 1939, stated: 'The U.S.S.R. was and continues to be "a bulwark against war and aggression".'[41]

Just one week later came the announcement of a Non-Aggression pact between Russia and Germany. Soviet Russia had become Adolf Hitler's ally. The shocking news caused a flood of resignations from the Communist Party and the League—including Thomas Mann. The anti-fascist platform to which they had all committed themselves for the past six years had collapsed. Western communists were faced with their greatest test of loyalty yet. Blake and Stead rallied staunchly to Party policy, and remained active in the much depleted League of American Writers.

The English language acquired a new word from German—to *blitz*. Before dawn on 1 September 1939, the Nazi *Luftwaffe* prepared the way, with massive aerial bombardment, for German tanks to cross into Polish territory. On 3 September, Britain's ultimatum to Germany expired and Prime Minister Chamberlain declared war on Hitler's Reich. France, Australia and New Zealand rallied to Britain's side. The war had begun.

9

Dearest Munx

JUNE 1940 – JUNE 1942

'PARIS HAS FALLEN! We never thought to see that.' It was 15 June
1940. Denmark and Norway, Belgium and Holland had
surrendered to the Nazis and now the swastika was flying on
the Arc de Triomphe. Earlier that month there had been the Dunkirk
evacuation. Stead was horrified: the war was looking grim for Britain and
Australia. Nevertheless, she followed the Comintern line that it was an
'imperialist war' managed by international capitalists and that America
should keep out. The growing 'martial fever' among Americans dismayed
her. 'Dissenters are few. Nothing like the last war.'[1]

The Man Who Loved Children was in the hands of the publishers, Simon
& Schuster. It had taken Stead almost eighteen months—a tumultuous
time emotionally. Next time she would take a different tack, she told
herself, 'less personal, more story and humanity, a broader canvas'.

She and Blake escaped the New York summer in an old cottage at Cape
Cod, 'that seahorse of land' on the blustery Atlantic coast. 'Dirt, sand,
winds, insufficient bedcovers, kerosene stove falling to pieces, you know
the seaside summer holiday,' she told Florence James. She liked the gales
and the Moby Dick atmosphere; Bill did not.

In early October, back in New York, they moved into a brownstone
house in the Old Bowery area, just off Stuyvesant Park. A graceful
staircase, illuminated by the natural light of an *oeil-de-boeuf* in the roof, led

to their sunny apartment on the upper floor, which looked over plantains to the backs of houses and iron fire escapes. The best feature was the large, airy living room with an open fireplace. The kitchen and bathroom were modest, and then there were two small rooms, a bedroom and a study where Blake would work when he was home. (He generally preferred the New York Public Library.) Alone in the apartment most of the day, Stead worked in the living room, and sometimes, when Blake was talking politics, in the bedroom.

The drawback of living near Third Avenue was the noise of the El, the elevated railway, which clattered and screeched on high metal girders from one end of the city to the other. 'El-Hel' was the Rabbinical name for New York, Stead decided.

They would spend the best part of two years at No. 212 E. 16th Street, and despite the noise, Stead was introduced in that house to the real charm of Manhattan life. New York would become one of her favourite cities, along with Paris. It was partly the house, which had a friendly, communal atmosphere. And it was partly the 'people with the dogs', their landlord's extended Russian-American family of dog-lovers.

Their landlord, Asa Zatz, was in his mid twenties. He lived, with his cairn terrier, in a large chaotic room on the second floor. He and his mother, a medical practitioner, had bought the house when his father died in 1935. Dr Zatz had her practice on the ground floor. She died in the spring of 1941, while Stead and Blake were residents. Other rooms were rented out, and there was a communal kitchen in the basement.

Asa Zatz, his communal household and 'Cherry Orchard' family, would inspire *The People with the Dogs*, planned in the early to mid 1940s and written in the early 1950s. In contrast to *Letty Fox* and *A Little Tea, A Little Chat*, Stead's other American novels, *The People with the Dogs* breathes a deep affection for New York. Just as *The Beauties and Furies* is romantic Paris, *The People with the Dogs* is romantic lower Manhattan, 'the last of gaslight New York'.

Manhattan is not wholly idealised in the novel. A murder takes place in the first few pages—though it is a strangely surrealistic incident: most striking is the girl's orange lipstick as she falls, knifed, to the ground. In this city, ambulances squeal past, trains pass overhead with a 'crashing roar', and at the same time, the city is a friendly urban village. The characters walk everywhere, their dogs trotting along beside them; they drop in on friends and 'flop' at each other's places. They eat bagels and *salzstengels*, chicken fat on radish slices, herrings in sour cream, smoked oysters, sweet pickles and cinnamon cakes. They are always on the phone to each other. When Oneida's beloved bull terrier is to undergo an operation, her sisters and brothers and their spouses turn up at the vet's to commiserate.

According to Asa Zatz, Stead invented and embellished characters and exaggerated the extent of the house's communality, but much of the detail in *The People with the Dogs* is astoundingly true to life. He found his own fictional portrait as Edward Massine 'amazing'; Stead had brilliantly captured the way he talked. For him, the experience of reading the novel when it was published in 1952 was 'like being in analysis'. Yet he had no idea, when Stead was living upstairs, that she was even thinking of writing a novel about his family; he merely noticed that she asked a lot of questions.

Zatz's father had written plays. Asa had attended the Yale Drama School, intending to become a director; but, indolent by nature, he found himself drifting into technical jobs like lighting and staging. When the theatre was out, he would visit his actress girlfriend, Florence, and at 2 am or so, he would walk his dog Jock over to Stuyvesant Park.[2]

He would regularly sleep till noon. Almost daily visits were made to his favourite aunt and her husband, Aida and Max Kotlarsky, whose cavern-like apartment was on nearby W. 12th Street. Max, a tall, quiet, witty man, was a concert pianist, who had studied with Artur Schnabel. Tiny Aida, who looked like a 'wide-eyed elfin child'[3], was a talented pianist, though she did not perform. She loved exotic, oriental furnishings and colourful theatrical costume. She loved their country house, deep in the Catskill mountains. Above all, she loved her dogs. Nip and Tuck, pedigree bull terriers, were her surrogate children. She and Max Kotlarsky were to be the models for Oneida and Lou Solway in *The People with the Dogs*.

The title of Stead's novel evokes Chekhov's 'Lady with the Lapdog'. In the nineteenth century, Asa's grandfather, a Russian Jewish émigré, had bought several acres of land near Hunter, in the Catskills. Vaguely inspired by the radical ideals of the Oneida community in upstate New York, he had various cottages built on the estate for his nine children, of whom Aida was the youngest. Family and friends, he declared, would always be welcome there.

At the beginning of summer, when the concert season was in recess, Aida and Max would retreat to this country house. Aida's siblings and their families would move into their cottages. Friends would come to stay— artists, actors, musicians. On occasion, everyone would come together for a meal, with spouses, children, cats and dogs. Stead and Blake would visit several times over the years.

———— ❧ ————

The Man Who Loved Children was published in New York on 11 October 1940. Stead was nervous. It was her most intimate and revealing book ever, and certainly the book that had caused her the most pain. She did not hesitate to call it her 'best book to date'.[4] How would the critics react? She had complied with Simon & Schuster by making it an American novel: would they promote it properly this time?

Simon & Schuster published it with very little fanfare. Four weeks later, Stead told a friend bitterly, 'S & S are disgusted with the book and are doing nothing for it. I should have called it *How to Have Children and Generate People* … I am quitting them.'[5] The book sold slowly at $2.75. Later, when the price was reduced to $1.75, some 5000 copies sold quite quickly.

It was destined to be one of those highly original novels that do not take off at first. Faulkner's *The Sound and Fury* (1929), Nathanael West's *Miss Lonelyhearts* (1933) and Djuna Barnes' *Nightwood* (1936) had suffered the same fate. The moment was unpropitious: people were anxious about the war in Europe and less willing than they might otherwise have been to immerse themselves in a thick novel about the idiosyncratic Pollit family. Publishers and readers were wanting morale-building stories, not tales about flawed characters. By the end of the war, the book would be out of print, along with *House of All Nations*.

The critics, once again, were impressed—with reservations. It was compelling, they said. Miss Stead had 'a theatrical sense of action'. The characters were wonderfully real. But they were 'blighted'. And the novel, they nearly all agreed, was 'remorselessly overblown'.

One of the most positive reviews was Isidor Schneider's in the *New Masses*, which probably did Stead a considerable disservice. Schneider considered the novel an excellent illustration of Engels' *Origin of the Family*. The downfall of the Pollit family was to be attributed to its 'insecure and inelastic economy'. So great was his enthusiasm that he sent his review copy to the Moscow Comintern. Critic Pearl Bell would point out years later, 'With the Marxist imprimatur affixed to Miss Stead's work, no one bothered to investigate the grubby, exhilarating and overpowering reality of *The Man Who Loved Children*.'[6]

One of the few negative reviews was Mary McCarthy's, in *New Republic*. She thought it a 'peculiar, breathless, overwritten, incoherent novel'—much of it 'like an hysterical tirade'. The 'fearful, disordered vindictiveness' in the writing repelled her.[7]

Other critics were also disturbed by the anger ('shrillness') in the novel. Clifton Fadiman, trying to explain the lack of enthusiasm for Stead among some critics, commented that 'women reviewers in particular find her hard to take'. He recognised this prejudice as a double standard on the part of women as well as men.

> Eventually, Christina Stead will impose herself upon the literature of the English-speaking countries. I say 'impose herself' because her qualities are not apt to win her an immediate, warm acceptance. She may have to fight as long and as hard as did Joyce before gaining the suffrage of the majority. Her prose is difficult, often unnecessarily so. Her characters are like so many fiends. Her books are long, perhaps too long. They do not develop one out of the other but are massively solitary. Her humor is savage, her learning hard to cope with, her fancies too furious. Like Emily Brontë, she has none of the proper bearing, the reassuring domestic countenance of a 'lady author.'

Once again, Fadiman predicted that Stead's genius ('the sheer originality, weight, and conscientiousness of her talent') would one day be acknowledged, but he was less impressed with *The Man Who Loved Children* than with *House of All Nations*—and he had been less impressed with *that* novel than with *The Salzburg Tales*. It was extraordinarily discouraging for Stead always to have her past novels celebrated as her 'peaks of achievement'.[8]

Nervous about their reaction, Stead put off sending the family a copy of the novel. She waited two months after its publication in England in June 1941 before sending a copy to Australia. And even then, she sent it to Thistle Harris—whom she scarcely knew. On the frontispiece she wrote: 'To dear Thistle. A Strindberg Family Robinson. In some respects might be considered a private letter to Thistle from Christina Stead.'

How was Thistle to take this? She read the novel. It certainly was not a flattering portrait of the man she loved, but it seems she graciously congratulated Stead on the likeness—adding that she loved David Stead, flaws and all.[9] Christina, who must have wondered sometimes whether she had exaggerated her father's portrait, was jubilant. To Bill, away in Canada on business, she wrote:

Had a letter from Thistle. She read TMWLC and says it is exact—my memory is faultless … 'A monster, an undeveloped personality and a lovable child,' says she. So I hope you now believe your own woman and realise she is not crazy.

To Thistle, she wrote back:

Yes, I feel the characters in TMWLC are very, very real: recreated, but real. I am always surprised at my memory for detail … Sam did really boil a fish for oil (a shark, not a tetrapturus, but I had to make it North American) and Henny really did play cards out of desperation and so on, so on: it did not happen exactly all on one day but what I did is a very real representation of life as it was then. As to the details: I am very happy to hear you say that you recognise them. I did not invent, naturally … I am opposed to inventing in *life*. Life is so strange and we know it so little, that nothing is needed in that direction: we need only study: but real invention is needed in placing, and re-arranging, and re-creating.

Thistle Harris, though she did not say so to Christina, was terribly hurt by the portrait of David Stead. In later years she would admit that she thought the novel 'tremendously cruel'. Strangely, she claims not to know whether David Stead ever read it: 'It's not the sort of thing I could have asked him.' She presumes—since she left it lying round the house quite openly—that he did. But, according to her, they never discussed it. Gilbert Stead insists that his father did read the novel, for they talked about it, and he recalls that his father was shocked that Christina saw things in so black a light.

The brief review of the novel in the *Sydney Morning Herald* in September 1941 would have made it clear to anyone who knew the Stead family that the novel was autobiographical. Considering how American reviewers damned Sam Pollit, David Stead was fortunate that the anonymous Sydney reviewer was so mild.[10] 'At a casual glance,' wrote the reviewer, 'no one could fault Samuel Pollit. His devotion to his family is striking. He is patient with poor Henrietta … and yet, one feels all the time that one must reserve judgement.'

The most striking feature of the *Sydney Morning Herald* review is its schoolmasterly condescension—a familiar tone in Stead's Australian reviews. They talked about her as if she were just a beginner, yet this was her fifth published book in six years. Twenty-five years later, *The Man*

Who Loved Children would be re-issued by Holt, Rinehart & Winston, and hailed by American critics as a 'marvellous neglected novel', a 'long-neglected masterpiece', a 'big black diamond of a book' and 'one of the superb novels of the 20th century'.

———— ✥ ————

Asa Zatz, Stead and Blake's landlord, quickly became a friend. He enjoyed calling in upstairs from time to time for a chat, and Stead and Blake always seemed pleased to see him and would bring out their gallon container of cheap red wine.

> Visiting them was always a treat for me. Can you imagine the conversations one had with them? For some reason they liked me. I suppose I was learning, I was young. That such a young man was their landlord must have been interesting for them. I was crazy about both of them, especially Bill, because of his brilliance. He was the most incredibly brilliant yet unpedantic man you could imagine. It was always worth asking him: 'Hey Bill, what do you think of so and so?'

Zatz found Christina rather forbidding. He remembers her as 'fair, spare and lanky', with 'keen eyes, a jutting jaw and prominent front teeth'. To him, her clothes were drab and oldfashioned—mostly brown skirts and frilly blouses. But she was lively, with a wonderful sense of humour and a 'pleasant giggle'. She loved to hear his jokes and Yiddish stories. (The males in *The People with the Dogs* tell each other jokes almost as a form of greeting.) And she was, he recalls, very interested in a course he attended on cryptography.

Asa was particularly impressed by Blake's vast erudition and extraordinary memory. He remembers one occasion at the house in Hunter when Bill pulled a volume out of the bookcase and challenged him to test his memory.

> [Bill] once told me to give him fifteen or twenty minutes to memorise the details of Gibbon's *Decline and Fall of the Roman Empire*. He really *had* taken in the details! Maybe it was only half the book—I can't remember—but I was amazed! … You'd ask him something and he didn't just give a quick answer … . He told me he hadn't forgotten anything he'd read since the age of eight or something, and I believed him.

In 1940, at forty-six, Bill was becoming known in the US as a Marxian political economist and historical novelist. His book *Elements of Marxian Economic Theory and its Criticism* had appeared the previous year, re-issued shortly afterwards under the title *An American Looks at Karl Marx*. It was lucid, entertaining and selling well as an undergraduate textbook. During 1939, Simon & Schuster had published his second novel, *The Painter and the Lady*, dedicated to the memory of Ralph Fox. Though the novel raised serious questions about the political function of art, it was as 'wildly playful' as the first. By his own admission, Blake tended to view the universe as 'a melodramatic joke of some sixty-legged Brahmin God'.[11]

Asa recalls that Bill, shocked to find him so 'politically illiterate', got him reading Marx, starting him off on *Value, Price and Profit*. When Asa complained it was difficult, Bill retorted that it was the ABC of Marxism, written for workers.

His political curiosity aroused, Asa sometimes went along to hear Bill speak at Party social functions. 'Bill was always the star. There was no stumping him.' Blake was also a skilled fundraiser. 'He'd collect money after the meetings, bully people into forking out.' Among Stead's papers is an admiring note to Blake from the *New Masses* treasurer: 'No one has ever come near you in collection eloquence at an NM meeting.'

A decade later, Stead would write wistfully from Holland: 'I feel such affection thinking back to New York ... I don't grow much attached to anywhere, but I think the New York people were my closest.'[12]

Regular visitors to the flat, Zatz recalls, were Ruth Blech, who 'chatted nineteen to the dozen', Stanley Burnshaw, whom Zatz thought 'a crusty fellow', and Harry Bloom, with his 'wonderful laugh'. Alf Hurst (whom Stead called 'the Great Noise') was often there, but Zatz did not warm to him. Mike Gold and Elisabeth would sometimes drop in: they now had two sons and were living on a single-tax commune, the 'Freeacres Community', in New Jersey.

Around this time, Stead and Blake met Ettore and Jessie Rella. Tall, lanky Ettore struggled to make a living from his poetry and poetic dramas; for the most part Jessie, talented with needlework, supported them.[13] Stead told Stanley Burnshaw that Rella's poetry had 'a free, colourful, intense, masculine style', adding: 'He is a man, as mountain men and mining men and poet men are men.' Rella's exotic background appealed to her; born in Telluride, a silver-mining town high up in Colorado, he had an Albanian father and an Italian mother. To Stead, partial as she was to the exotic, he would always be her 'Albanian friend'.

Another frequent visitor was a man Bill Blake liked to call his brother: 60-year-old Henryk Grossmann. Originally from an affluent Jewish family in Cracow, Grossmann had been Professor of Economics at Warsaw, where he had written a learned treatise on the collapse of capitalism, before leaving in the mid 1920s to work at the Institute of Social Research in Frankfurt. Like most of his colleagues there, he had fled to the US in 1937.

Grossmann's views on political and economic questions were close to Blake's, and the two men would talk until late into the night. Blake had great respect for Grossmann's work, but among his exiled Frankfurt colleagues, now re-grouped at Columbia University, Grossmann was out on a limb. Whereas the Moscow purge trials had left the others thoroughly disenchanted with the Soviet Union, Grossmann remained a committed Stalinist. And theoretically Grossmann was a stalwart of the Old Guard that stressed the economic base, whereas Theodor Adorno, Max Horkheimer, Leo Lowenthal and Herbert Marcuse had become more interested in questions of ideology and culture.

Grossmann never talked about his personal life, and only after the war would Stead and Blake discover that he had left an ex-wife and son behind in Poland. Stead pitied Grossmann in his extreme loneliness. And she enjoyed his old-fashioned Central European gallantry: the hand kissing and bowing. Later she would describe him as 'one of the men who meant something to me'.[14]

Asa Zatz remembers the 'wonderful parties' Stead and Blake used to throw. The small upstairs apartment would be crowded with people eating, drinking and talking. Stead was gracious and smiling, obviously enjoying the role of hostess. She had always prepared marvellous food: curried eggs, Hungarian and German sausage meats with pumpernickel, fresh green salads and potato salads with chives, mixed sour pickles, smoked cheeses. Bill would be somewhere in the room talking and laughing, surrounded by admiring friends. At Christmas, he would dress up as Santa Claus, make speeches and hand out presents to the children.

The female friend who made the greatest impact on Stead during the American years was Ruth McKenney. They were never close—Stead did not allow people access to her vulnerable inner self—but she admired this strange, ebullient woman, extroverted and articulate like Bill Blake. McKenney too was a popular speaker at communist functions. She and her husband Richard Bransten would be immortalised in Stead's novel about revolutionaries, *I'm Dying Laughing*.

Nine years younger than Stead, Ruth McKenney's autobiographical novel *My Sister Eileen* had been a fantastic success in 1938, and Ruth and Eileen McKenney had become part of American legend: Ruth, the bright, lively but unattractive aspiring writer; Eileen, her younger sister, a Celtic beauty who was always falling unhappily in love.

From a working-class Irish-American family in Indiana, the two women had come to New York with Eileen's baby Patrick, and shared a studio apartment in Gay Street, Greenwich Village. Ruth supported them by selling humorous stories to the *New Yorker*. They were happy years— idealised in her autobiographical writings. Her sister, she would write, was the love of her life. 'For ourselves, we just loved each other, fiercely, firm in the conviction that every man's hand was against us.'[15]

McKenney met Richard Bransten in August 1937 and they married, with characteristic impetuousness, just twelve days later. 'It is a good thing we married so suddenly on the first fine tide of joy,' McKenney was to remark, 'for if we had waited around, in some mealy-mouthed way, we should have discovered our contradictions, battled furiously, and probably parted.' Bransten came from a wealthy, conservative California family that disapproved of his radicalism. To placate the family, he used the pen-name 'Bruce Minton' for his political activities.

They made a strange couple. Bransten (his friend Stanley Burnshaw recalls) was 'spectacularly thin' and 'unathletic-looking, with a tension in his expression that could be gloriously dissolved when he laughed'.[16] He suffered deeply from lack of self-esteem. McKenney, short and overweight, completely lacked Bransten's grace. But she did not lack confidence in her own talents.

From the beginning, McKenney and Bransten argued ferociously— usually about money. Though McKenney had always been poor, money, like food and drink, was something over which she had very little control. Bransten, though he despaired about their debts, also lived in a mythological world when it came to money. Their spendthrift ways would horrify Stead and Blake over the years.

Most of the couple's wealth came from Ruth McKenney's humorous writings. In 1940, as sales of *The Man Who Loved Children* limped along,

The McKenneys Carry On went through several reprintings. *My Sister Eileen* became a Broadway hit, and two years later, it was made into a popular film. Over the years, Ruth McKenney continued to churn out best-selling stories about her eccentric family. But she never valued this 'cornmeal mush'[17]; her ambition was to write serious revolutionary novels. Once asked in an interview if the stories about her family were true, she replied: 'Pretty much, only I left out all the real catastrophes. As a matter of fact I had a perfectly horrid childhood.'[18] She and Stead had a number of things in common.

Ruth McKenney's worst tragedy occurred four days before *My Sister Eileen* opened on Broadway. She and Bransten were living in Connecticut. Her sister Eileen had been married for seven months to the writer Nathanael West, author of *Miss Lonely-hearts*, and they were living in Hollywood. The sisters were running up huge telephone bills talking to one another. Then, on 22 December 1940, Eileen and Nathanael West were killed in a car accident, travelling back from a duck-shooting weekend in Mexico. Eileen was twenty-seven, Nathanael West thirty-seven.

It was the tragi-comic duality in Ruth McKenney's life that Stead wanted to reflect with the title *I'm Dying Laughing*.

It was a difficult time for the left. In May 1941, Stead and Blake were among 119 writers to sign the Call to the Fourth American Writers' Congress, a gathering of writers for peace. A strong anti-war statement, it denounced the Roosevelt administration for its warmongering. Among the better-known signatories were Theodore Dreiser, Dashiell Hammett, Lillian Hellman and Orson Welles.

Then came a cataclysmic about-turn. On 22 June 1941, Germany invaded Russia, breaking the Nazi-Soviet Pact. The American Communist Party now called for immediate measures to aid the Soviet Union and its allies against the fascist aggressors. The communist front organisation, the American Peace Mobilization, of which Stead and Blake were members, changed its name to the American People's Mobilization. When the Japanese attack on Pearl Harbor eventually brought America into the war in December, the League urgently called 'on all American writers to put their training, talent, and devotion to the service of our country'.

For her part, Stead was interested in the effect of war on women. She liked the title *Letty Fox: Her Luck*. Letty, obsessed with hunting down a husband, is predatory, like a fox. Stead no doubt thought of Ralph Fox. And friends comment that she liked the hint of bawdiness in the combination 'fox' and 'luck'.

Though *Letty Fox* was not published until after *For Love Alone*, Stead first began it early in 1941. The two novels overlap to some degree. In each, minor characters are based on Stead's father and Aunt Florence. The few remaining pages of an early draft of *Letty Fox* contain characters called Teresa and Jonathan Crow—eventually to be the central protagonists in *For Love Alone*. They became two novels, which British writer and critic Angela Carter would describe as 'thesis and antithesis'. The 'thesis' of *For Love Alone*, set against the background of a Victorian and provincial Sydney, is summed up by Teresa:

> Women had a power to achieve happiness as well—but in what way? Only by having the right to love … It was easy to see how upsetting it would be if women began to love freely where love came to them. An abyss would open in the principal shopping street of every town.

In *Letty Fox*, set largely in New York in the 1920s and 1930s, the abyss *has* opened, and the shopping metaphor has a sinister appropriateness. Young women born in the early 1920s, like Letty, learn to see themselves as marketable products. Told in the first person from Letty's viewpoint, with Letty herself as one of its main objects of satire, *Letty Fox* is a deeply ironic novel about a society that treats sex and love as commodities.

Letty has the misfortune to reach sexual maturity just before the Second World War. The eligible men are soon being conscripted. In the race for males, all women are each other's rivals. The cutthroat, dirty tactics Letty uses to secure herself an apartment in overcrowded Manhattan reflect her strategies for getting herself a man. For Letty, sexual experience is the mark of equality with men: she has more lovers than we care to count. And yet she is as desperate to be married as Teresa, in *For Love Alone*. Even Letty's broadminded father, Solander Fox, never questions his daughter's obsession with making herself 'marriageable'.

For Love Alone leaves readers with the impression that Teresa will go beyond her preoccupation with men and achieve self-fulfilment. *Letty Fox* does not inspire the same optimism. Stead herself would point out later that for all her libertinage, Letty Fox is no 'heroine of feminist freedom'.

> Everyone in the USA understood perfectly that she showed the error of feminine riot! What end was there for her but deterioration, a miserable middle age, desperate abandon, or a total acquiescence with conformity?[19]

Stead offers no solution. Marriage validates women; it also destroys them. Significantly, Persia and Solander, the only positive picture of a couple in the novel, are not married. But Persia is also shown to be vulnerable, for Solander's lawful wife has a hold on him that has nothing to do with love. Stead's conclusion is clear enough: 'It is a real inferno we are born into.'

After *The Man Who Loved Children*, Stead had resolved that her next novel would be less painful to write. But she was becoming aware that anger fuelled her creative fires. As she was writing *Letty Fox*, she told Bill Blake: 'I feel splendid, nastier and more Stead-ish each day.'

Progress on the novel was slow during the summer of 1941. Stead had not yet found a way to shape her mass of raw material, and was feeling tense. To escape the New York humidity and write without distractions, she removed herself in early August to a quiet guesthouse in New Canaan, Connecticut. (Blake, working once again for Alf Hurst, was obliged to stay in New York.) From this 'Department of Old Crocks', as she uncharitably referred to her fellow guests, Christina wrote affectionate, contrite, girlish letters to 'Munx', as she called Bill.

> I miss you very much, but I know it is good for me to miss you and get some work done. I am working, haven't any of that confusion or indecision I have in town.
>
> … I appreciate very well what you are to me; I hope when I get this manuscript finished I will be not so jumpy, a better girl to you; you know I am stuck on you but I certainly am a horror. I'll finish as quickly as I can; the place is a bore of course, and it's a good thing. Try and come the following weekend will you Chick? Love to Alfish who is so very Alfish; I really love the guy.

Four days later she wrote:

> You ought to be strong and you ought to have all the time you need to write a great book, for you have all that Balzac had, except about 100 pounds (less) avoirdupois.

Dear Munx, I don't deserve such a good guy as you, but I am always hoping that a miracle will happen and I will deserve you.

As someone who aimed to transcribe life into fiction, Stead could hardly have set herself a more difficult challenge with *Letty Fox*. The 23-year-old in whose voice the novel is narrated was to be Ruth Blake—an ambitious task for a 39-year-old Australian. In addition to the problem of language and idiom, there was the psychological challenge, for it required at least a superficial identification with Ruth Blake. Would she be able to portray Mathilde Fox—that is, Mollie Blech, whom she had never actually met— through her daughter's familiar gaze? And would she be able to view characters like Mathilde and Grandma Fox (Rosa Blech) from Letty's less critical viewpoint? Could she portray herself—Persia—from Letty's rivalrous standpoint?

Solander Fox, Letty's father, is 'a gay, ribald, talented man', but underneath even his daughter sees that he is 'not very sure of himself'. She also sees that caught between the emotions and claims of his two women—his wife Mathilde and his mistress Persia—he pacifies each by lying to them.

Persia, we learn from Letty, is clever, reads a lot and speaks several languages. Her love for Solander is not based on self-interest, and she placidly puts up with humiliating treatment from his mother. She and Solander lead a nomadic life, always surrounded by hearty male friends— company Persia enjoys, for she has 'a fondness for men'.

Persia—like Teresa, in *For Love Alone*—is Stead's idealised fictional self. But the level-headed Persia, who holds herself aloof from gossip and family crises, could not have written *Letty Fox*.

It seems that Stead carried out her threat to break contract with Simon & Schuster after their indifferent treatment of *The Man Who Loved Children*, for she submitted *Letty Fox* in the autumn of 1941 to Angus Cameron, a distinguished publisher and political radical who worked at Little, Brown & Company. But the pressure to make money prompted her to submit her manuscript too early, and Cameron requested major revision. By November 1941, the manuscript was 'in the deuce of a shape, torn to atoms for a re-do'.[20]

Dismayed by the delay, Stead urgently tried to think of ways of making money out of her writing. In October 1941, she asked Angus Cameron to act as referee for an application for a Guggenheim Fellowship. He willingly agreed. But she soon found herself writing to him again:

Dear Angus,

I feel as if I'm pestering you, but shortness of time makes me do it. Please forgive me. I am told that I ought to have a wellknown American writer to act as reference [sic] as well. I do not know what American writers have read any of my books. Do you know of one who likes one of my books well enough to act as a reference in the same capacity as you will? ... If you know one and could possibly make the request for me, I cannot say how obliged I should be. It would save me a horrible embarrassment: for it is very hard to approach in this way a person one does not know at all. I am now suffering, of course, from my barbarian habits of going nowhere and meeting no one.[21]

Coming from the author *of House of All Nations* and *The Man Who Loved Children*, the tone of the letter is surprisingly helpless. When it came to self-promotion, Christina Stead was dismally bad at presenting herself in the best light. In the end, Angus Cameron managed to organise an impressive list of referees, including the poet Stephen Vincent Benét, critic Clifton Fadiman and Louis Kronenberger, the drama critic for *Time*. Five other publishers and critics agreed to write brief references.

Stead's proposal was to collect legends and contemporary lore from diverse regions in the United States, and to base a cycle of stories upon them in the style of *The Salzburg Tales*. She aimed to use newspaper and oral sources as well as the talents of natural tale-tellers, and pointed out that the Brothers Grimm, Hans Christian Andersen and E. T. A. Hoffmann had all collected folklore in this way. For once she made every effort with the presentation of her application. Usually she would insist that it was content not form that was important, and submitted work typed single-spaced, with numerous errors and crossings out. The Guggenheim application, however, was double-spaced and without a single mistake.

She was not awarded a fellowship. In many ways, the application was ahead of its time: a selection committee nowadays would appreciate Stead's interest in local history and ethnic subcultures. When, in early April 1942, she saw she was not among the list of successful applicants announced in the newspaper, she shrugged at Blake: 'Well, there we are.

I am not a winner and that's sure.' She thought it might be because she was not an American citizen. She even wondered whether the judges were put off by the photo she sent, in which her newly permed hair made her look like a woolly dog. What disgusted her was that most fellowships had gone to academics and critics rather than creative writers. To her poet friend Ettore Rella, whose application had also failed, she wrote bitterly: 'Careful, or even superficial inspection of the Guggenheim lists reveals that it is necessary to be at least a sub-professor at Harvard to get one.'

However, there was money in scriptwriting, and in November 1941, Stead sent Columbia Pictures Corporation the outline of a melodramatic romance: *Was it Heaven or Was it Hell?* Constructed with suitably high and low points to appeal to movie-goers, it was, in rough form, the outline of her next novel, *For Love Alone*. When Columbia Pictures indicated they were not interested in the idea, she began to shape the material into a novel, putting *Letty Fox* aside for the time being.

For Love Alone involved turning again to the past. *The Man Who Loved Children* had ended with the 14-year-old Louisa running away from home to go 'for a walk round the world'. *For Love Alone* opens with Teresa at nineteen. She is recognisably an older version of Louisa, with the same manipulative, self-obsessed father. The setting for the first half of *For Love Alone* is Watson's Bay, Sydney: there would be no compromises with publishers about location this time. The second half is set in London, where Teresa follows Jonathan Crow.

It was fourteen years since Stead had left Australia, and nine years since she had completed *Seven Poor Men of Sydney*. She rejoiced in the chance to write again about Sydney, this time with the perspective of her mature years. Sydney had become if anything more beautiful and exotic in her memory, and Australian society more claustrophobic, vulgar and provincial.

Fourteen years had passed since she had seen Keith Duncan, the man she had followed to England. She had heard nothing during this time, apart from a 1934 newspaper cutting from her aunt with the information that Dr Duncan was the new Director of Tutorial Classes at the University of Sydney. Could she recreate his voice after all these years: the emphatic opinions, the seductive shifts of register, the anger, the self-pity? Years later,

Stead indicated that she became bogged down in letters when writing *For Love Alone*. Though there is no trace of them today, it is almost certain that she kept all Keith Duncan's letters and perused them as closely as she had her father's writings when she created his portrait. Letters were an invaluable reminder of the way people spoke. It is probable that Jonathan Crow's letters to Teresa in the novel contain extracts from Keith Duncan's actual letters—perhaps only vaguely altered.

Never one to back away from bold truths, Stead wanted to portray the repressive sexual attitudes in Australia in the 1920s. Just how courageous she was to broach the subject of female desire is clear from Diana Trilling's review in 1944:

> Miss Stead's heroine not only defies the conventions by being fully developed sexually at so tender an age; she is also improperly outspoken in her fear of spinsterhood. I know no novel, including the novels of Jane Austen, which reveals as frankly as *For Love Alone* the frantic need young women have for a husband and the brutal hypocrisy with which society surrounds their efforts to find one.[22]

Harry Bloom, the radical pharmacist, had left Brighton Beach in 1940 and bought a dilapidated drugstore on Upper Broadway at Washington Heights. Despite the depressed economy, he was turning it into a prosperous business. The family—he and his wife Anne and two children Janet and Michael—lived above the shop.

Harry Bloom and Christina had pursued their flirtatious relationship, first struck up in 1935. Christina found Harry disconcertingly moody—'one minute on the boil, then flat'[23]—but she admired his strength and extraordinary energy. He was funny and engaging, a brilliant raconteur, passionate about politics and an affectionate, loyal friend. He told her he loved her.

Stead's deepest longing was to be romantically courted by men. She had no illusions about this: she once told a friend that her father had been goodlooking and that his success with women made him 'a pain in the neck to his wife; he couldn't stop bragging'. She added: 'I talk too much about my men friends, I know; but that is for the contrary reason—I am so staggered and delighted that they even look at me!'[24]

She was flirtatious: her men friends agree about this. And she thrived on dramas—real or imagined. When Blake was in Canada one time, she wrote to him that Henryk Grossmann was acting as her 'Escort', and that Harry Bloom was jealous.

> Dear Chick,
> ... My Escort turns up next. I wonder at my temerity (in private) in going out cheerfully with the world's leading Marxist, etc. but my Australian brass comes to my aid ... Harry asked (on the phone) if I was lonesome, I said no, I had an Escort. Who? said Harry. I said who. 'Oh, Henry! He's harmless,' says Harry ... I am not being as foolish as I sound.

Bill possibly encouraged Christina's flirtation with Harry Bloom—though if it ever became something more, he was not told about it. Over the years, in letters to Harry, he would call him Christina's 'boyfriend'. Bill himself found Harry extraordinarily lovable.

Anne Bloom was wary of her husband's womanising; Christina was neither the first nor the last of his infatuations.[25] Christina disliked Anne, though they were friendly enough on the surface. To Harry (who rather fostered this image of himself) Christina made it clear that she was sorry he should have a possessive wife who did not understand him.

Harry Bloom's son Michael does not know whether his father and Christina had an affair; he does know that his father was 'not as monogamous as he was meant to be'. He remembers that Christina quite often visited Washington Heights by herself. On one occasion in the early 1940s, when he was in his mid teens, Mike was hanging around when she and his father were talking, and his father eventually told him to go and buy some stamps. Mike flung at him: 'I know! You just want to get rid of me so you can have an affair with Chris!'

Letters from Harry Bloom to Christina after Bill's death are sufficiently intimate to suggest that their relationship was at one time physical. From remarks Christina made in letters to Bill in both 1942 and 1946—remarks that almost certainly understated the case—it is clear she was obsessed with Bloom.

Young Michael Bloom's hunch was probably right: it is likely that Stead and Bloom had some sort of an affair in the early 1940s. During 1942, Stead was writing *For Love Alone*, which ends with Teresa having an affair with *Harry* Girton. Exulting in her sexual freedom, Teresa makes a vow to herself: 'She had learnt from Harry and made up her mind, if the chance came, to learn from others. "I only know one commandment, *Thou shalt love.*"' Stead firmly believed that writers write best about what they know about, that writers need to experience the world, see things, do things. To write about Teresa's affair with Girton, she needed to know what it was like to have an extramarital affair.

Stead (like Teresa) made love and passion into a commandment, yet she would always suffer immense anguish over men. When she discussed the subject with her friend Edith Anderson in 1944, she told Edith that she believed monogamy to be an 'absolute necessity' for writers, since love affairs caused 'tremendous upheavals'.

However, Stead needed upheavals. Love was essential to her wellbeing. She needed to be in love, and she needed to feel loved. Without it, she suspected, her creative juices would cease to flow.

'An acute stage of New-York fatigue' had settled on them. Blake was doing too much, for too little remuneration. Stead was working hard and sleeping little. Her current novel, not yet called *For Love Alone*, was 'spun out of anguished reminiscence'. In a note to Ettore Rella, Stead apologised for their lack of sociability:

> Bill has not written (with all his political work) for many a long day, but he is raring to go and as for me—New York is death to me, the 'El' wins every time and I have made up my mind to get out if it's the last act … We are both so tired that we consider the movies a fatiguing evening and I haven't had a person in for a 'cup of tea' for 500 evenings.

In addition to his political activities and work with Alf Hurst that took him frequently to Canada, Blake wrote articles and reviews for the *New Masses* and still managed to average a book a year. In January 1941, he taught a course in Historical Fiction at the New York Writers' School; early in 1942 he gave lectures on economic history at the newly formed School for Democracy—both 'poor man's schools' established by the Party. Stead tried vainly to protect him from endless requests to speak at rallies—by answering the telephone in a hostile voice or not answering at all.

The League of American Writers had no real function now it no longer opposed the war, but Blake and Stead remained members until it folded in the winter of 1942–43. In the winter of 1941–42, Stead and Blake were both featured in the League's Friday Night Reading Program, along with William Carlos Williams and Richard Wright, whose 1940 novel *Native Son* had made him the leading black writer in the States. Blake read from his recently published American Civil War novel, *The Copperheads*, which was receiving high praise in leftwing circles. Stead read from her untitled work in progress.

The winter of 1941–42 had been mild and the Canadian fur trade slow. Stead told Thistle Harris that Bill and Alf had been working with 'an endearing idiot' with no moral compunctions, who had committed 'catastrophic errors'. It was depressingly reminiscent of the Travelers' Bank.

Hurst was convinced the fur trade would pick up the following winter, especially if the Russian markets, closed because of the war, were to open again. But Blake was tired of Alf's exploitative behaviour, his war profiteering and his manic pursuit of women. (Stead was making notes for a future novel about Alf Hurst: she would call it *A Little Tea, A Little Chat*, his euphemism for sexual conquests.) Blake had had little alternative but to go back into business with Alf: they needed the money. Writing, they now realised, was 'another word for slow-starvation'.[26]

At least Mollie Blech was no longer dependent on Bill. She had not worked all these years, though she was a university graduate, with training both as a teacher and a secretary, but when the United States joined the war, she took a course and became a factory inspector. Ruth Blake was now twenty-one, and with her grandmother's legacy, she was also independent.

Bill Blake had been trying for months to sell the motion picture rights to *The Copperheads*. When he still had heard nothing by the end of April 1942, he angrily terminated his contract with his literary agents, McIntosh & Otis, and decided he and Stead should go to Hollywood themselves. Stead was pessimistic. To her the short-term Hollywood scriptwriting contracts with their ruthless lay-offs sounded 'worse than typhoid'. Blake told her: 'Every situation is a challenge except the boredom of living with Don Juan in a cubicle in a betting office in Wall Street.'

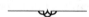

Bill Blake left for Santa Fe, en route to Hollywood, in early May 1942. Stead was to join him within a few weeks, as soon as he had found work. In the meantime, she was to finish her novel, have some work done on her teeth and make arrangements about the apartment.

For ten days before Bill left, Christina lay on her back, while Bill did all the domestic chores. At almost forty, she was pregnant again. And this time, she was trying hard not to miscarry in the first weeks, as she had done several times before.

She and Bill wrote to each other regularly. Tender letters, sometimes passionate, they reveal a strong mutual dependence. Their financial plight was worrying, but Blake was still determined to make money from writing. He had had enough of the likes of Alf Hurst. Despite their trials, he and Stead remained optimistic; almost childishly so. But neither was afraid of hard work.

After his 'crazed employments' in New York, Blake was recuperating in Santa Fe for a few days. It reminded him of Ronda. At an altitude of 7000 feet, he felt strangely euphoric. The weather was cold, but his health was improving, and the countryside was 'enchanting'. Rents and housemaids were cheap. 'If Hollywood does not work out, I think four months here would make you years younger,' he told Stead, finishing, 'I have so much to write about how much I love you, how much more I understand every day what your life is to me ... Ever so much love, Billo.'

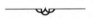

Stead wrote the same day from New York:

> Dearest Munx,
> Our varmint: the creature departed next day and was about one month, that's all. It seemed a pity, why did it have to? ... it would have been so much hope and joy for us. However I am counting that this summer we surely will go at it wholesale and take into account that I don't seem to have any staying powers in that direction. Oh, my back—after lying around for 10 days! ... It touched me so much that you worked so hard for me all that time and really seemed to want it: it is the first time we looked at it this way. Anyhow, no more of this.

Even at her early stage of pregnancy, Stead had excitedly broken the news to Alf Hurst, Asa Zatz, Harry and Anne Bloom. When, shortly after Bill's departure, Alf Hurst rang up, all 'brotherly and anxious' to enquire how she was, she felt such a fool, she told Bill, that she could not bring herself to tell him the sad news. 'He still thinks you a father. It's too stupid.'

Two days later, on Sunday morning, she wrote to Bill that Alf was coming to tea that afternoon, and she would tell him then. To make him feel guilty, she would say that the miscarriage was due to all the work she had been doing. (She could be as manipulative as Hurst himself, when she put her mind to it.) 'I am glad you love me, my darling; I love you, and you know it.'

Bill had been delighted by Santa Fe. 'For the first time I wanted to stay somewhere forever.' However, he soon discovered that his exhilaration was partly due to the altitude. He could not sleep at night. After a few days, he left for Albuquerque, 2000 feet lower. Christina's first letter was forwarded to him there, and having heard the news of the miscarriage by telegram or phone, he was greatly relieved to hear she was all right. 'I had conjured up all sorts of dreads as to bleeding, fever.'

From Albuquerque he took a Pullman coach through the Arizona desert to California, 'a sort of Riviera and Australia'. In Beverly Hills, he was entertained by New York friends, Hy and Reah Kraft. Earlier that year, Blake had passionately defended Hy Kraft's Yiddish comedy *Café Crown* after it had been scathingly attacked by Alvah Bessie, drama critic for the *New Masses*. Hy Kraft was also trying to break into screenwriting.

Blake signed up with Nat Goldstone, a literary agent sympathetic to progressives. 'Half the world's writers, including the most brilliant exiles, are here,' he told Stead. Aldous Huxley was in Hollywood. Bertolt Brecht, Lion Feuchtwanger, Thomas Mann, Leonhard Frank, Oskar Homolka—all refugees from Nazi Germany—were in Hollywood. Everyone was hoping for lucrative employment.

The Screen Writers Guild was 'a real militant Union', Blake told Stead, and the Dies Committee was nosing around. The Dies Committee, named after its chairman, Martin Dies, was officially known as the House Un-American Activities Committee. Formed in 1938, it had already conducted hearings in Hollywood to test the 'loyalty' of film personalities. Now Dies was threatening to hunt out all communists in the film colony.

Alf Hurst visited Christina on Sunday afternoon, as arranged. Kissing her twice on each cheek, he gave her perfume, announcing it was Mother's Day. She could not bring herself to tell him she was not in the family way after all. 'What a lunatic I felt.' She would definitely tell him next time he phoned.

> I sleep relatively well, though dream much, weird long dreams: miss you very much. I love you so much. It is wonderful, after so long … I am so anxious for you to get into the literary game on one side or another: for Alfish, dear old boy, is quite a wash-out for us.

She had told Asa Zatz about her miscarriage, and he was 'as sorry as if it had been his own'. Eventually she told Alf Hurst.

> Alf, a wonderful friend, said, next time I was to remember I am an incubator and if he had known he would have arranged for a maid and a lot more kindly hokum: and we really must have it for between the two of us we would produce a Shakespeare.

She was working extremely hard, hoping to finish her book within a few weeks. Pascal Covici at the prestigious publishing house Viking had expressed a strong interest in it. Covici was known for his communist sympathies, and Viking was already publishing another Australian writer, 30-year-old Patrick White. *The Living and the Dead*, his second publication under their imprint, had appeared the previous year.

Communist Jerome Chodorov, who had written the popular stage version of Ruth McKenney's My *Sister Eileen*, held a welcoming party for Bill Blake on Sunday 17 May in his grand Hollywood house. Some of the guests—screenwriters Albert Maltz, Lester Cole and Herbert Biberman—would become famous in the late 1940s as members of the 'Hollywood Ten'—ten prominent communists tried and imprisoned by the House Un-American Activities Committee.

Blake chatted with Lester Cole about a movie version of *The Man Who Loved Children*. 'He wants Charles Laughton for Sam Pollit and Bette Davis for psychotic Henny.' There was interest too in his own books. 'Herbert Biberman wants to shape *The World is Mine*: he has read it six times.' To Blake's surprise, people seemed most interested in his idea of a movie about the life of George Graham Rice, a glorious swindler, who had written a book called *My Adventures with Your Money*. Things were looking promising.

⟿

'How about the title *It Was For Love Alone?*' Stead was not good at titles, and always sought advice. She had come up with *Spring Tide*, but Stanley Burnshaw, when she told him, had scoffed at that. The present suggestion, proposed by Pascal Covici at Viking, came from a calypso song about Edward VIII's abdication: ' ''Twas for love, love alone, King Edward left his throne.'

Pascal Covici was impressed with the first half of her manuscript, set in Australia. Provided the rest of the book lived up to the first chapters, he had told her, she could consider it provisionally accepted for autumn publication.

Blake was working furiously on a script about Rice, the crooked financier. He was turning down social invitations and not even reading the newspapers. He told Christina: 'I have to look at your picture to know why I am on the job and then I do much better. Write, pliz, for I am turribly lonesome, love Billo.'

It was risky to be working so hard on an uncommissioned script. Sometimes he fell into a panic. Yet it did not seem impossible to live off writing: others could. If between them he and Christina could sell one manuscript a year—the film rights to one of their novels—they would make US$5000 gross ($4000 net after agency and taxes) and could live quite comfortably in the west, where fear that the Japanese might bomb the Pacific coast had caused rents to plummet. For the rest of that summer, he proposed New Mexico. 'Let us make a break for the mountains.'

⟿

In New York, Stead was working hard and living on her nerves. She was talking metaphedrin for bad sinusitis, her constant New York ailment. Her best working time was the evening, when the El was quieter, and she often wrote till 1.30 am. To go to sleep she took half a bromide, but soon woke and lay listening to sirens from boats or factories, wondering whether they were air-raid signals. At night too she was reliving her past: the moist heat of summers at Watson's Bay, the water lapping on the harbour and the frightful scenes at home; the smell of chalk and schoolchildren and her frantic fears; Keith Duncan's discussion group, their letters, her arrival in London and the dark days that followed. She thought again how much she owed to Bill. In her novel, she had James Quick (suitably named) virtually restoring Teresa to life.

The publishers at Viking liked the sexually charged imagery in the first half of *For Love Alone*. 'Old Covici gloated on phone—fairly dripping lechery about some scene where poor Tess is bathing.' From his reading of the first few chapters, Covici intimated that it might make a 'best-seller'.

Stead feared the novel might be 'mawkish'—yet another novel about a female half-deranged by unrequited love—but she was too anxious about money to spend more time on it. She had thrown out 'cartloads of manuscript … all messy dreary talk', but the novel was now going to have to stand as it was. 'Nothing on earth would induce me to revise it.' She told Blake in Hollywood: 'I am not sure, but *think* my book will make a movie.'

Stead went to the pictures with Anne Bloom and was taken aback, coming home, by the beauty of the city in the wartime dim-out. 'Looked like the primeval Manhatto swamp.'

She was not sure whether to sublet the apartment or to give it up. The apartment was 'terribly pretty' with its dappled sunlight and views of trees and birds. She was sorry to be leaving it, despite the El. However, she reasoned, New York *was* expensive—they were paying $75 a month in rent—and a period in the 'Hollywood-Hades' would broaden her experience as a writer.

To Bill she was encouraging. Imitating her father's Artemus Ward language, she admonished him: '*Do not* bust in two tears—you will make out there, I am sure of it!' Be sure to eat liver, steak and salad, she reminded him. And he was not to forget his vitamin pills. 'Christ, Baby, do I miss *you*! Love, mush-mush for ever, Chris.'

Bill assured her:

Your boy bathes every day, does Toofies three times, cuts nails, does not bite fingers, sends laundry regularly, has cheveux shampoinged every week, is shaven and shorn steadily, even bootshined: all to no avail: watches his suits for spots: Mama's boy 100% until Krisht comes here, when owing to the corset of her management I will become Public Slob No. I.

Stead had now plunged into the second part of her novel, set in London. She was trying to work up a feeling of complete empathy with Jonathan Crow, so she could 'gaze' upon him. 'I am just at the point of "giving", I think, & you only give when the sympathy is complete. It is wonderful when it "gives" suddenly: such a relief.'

Sympathy was not quite the right word for her complete immersion in Jonathan Crow. 'His seduction has as much to do with love of women as picking the wings off flies has to do with love of entomology.' She was still angry with this man who had rejected her.

Stead's immersion in her characters, when it worked, generated in her an excitement verging on sexual. She would often liken the creative act to a love affair. Writing about someone aroused similar sensations in her to those of early infatuation: the fascination, the stalking and waiting, the mulling over and musing. At seventy-four, she would tell an interviewer:

> I only write about certain people who strike me in a very peculiar way. It is like a love affair, exactly. I know almost at once: love at first sight … It's nothing to do with observation, it's totally unlike it. It's a reception of some kind of electrical impulse from the other person.[27]

She wrote to Blake that thinking about Jonathan Crow was leading her to consider other 'seducers' she had known: Peter Neidecker, Alf Hurst, Mike Gold—though they did not actually constitute a single type. 'The seducer, of any kind, is not well understood by the rest of mankind: there are several of him, to begin with.' It worried her that her characters were always morally flawed. But she rationalised, 'A truly great character must have meannesses … Look at the private, stupid side of Lincoln!'

Whenever he was beginning to despair about making it in Hollywood, Blake would meet up with a successful 'mogul' and become hopeful again. 'Kingpin Ed Chodorov' was paid $2000 a week for scriptwriting.

'The most touted & best paid writer in Hollywood, the super-odious Ben Hecht' earned $5000 a week—'stopping for 6 months to write awful stories'.

At a communist social function, Blake told the writer W. L. Rivers the story of *For Love Alone*. Rivers was enthusiastic, suggesting Hepburn for the part of Tess Hawkins. ('She is feminist.') And when Blake told him about *Letty Fox* ('the struggles of girls to get married and get men'), Rivers thought 'it would sweep the movies'. Blake, who reported these conversations with childlike credulity, was beginning to think that Stead, with her interest in women, might have a better chance of making it in Hollywood then he had. 'I see that I will soon do the housework while you smoke cigars on the piazza—may it only come.'

In Hollywood he was at last learning something, he told Stead. He was beginning to realise what his uncritical fraternal affection for people like Peter Neidecker, Alf Hurst and Mike Gold had cost him: a great deal of hackwork trying to please and impress them. 'I have pushed off at least 10 incipient male crushes, & all to the good. One lesson learned at last. I will wind up as cool as an Ingres uncle.'

He added: 'But not for oo. The hour approacheth & the bride cometh soon I hope, if I am not to enter Bedlam.'

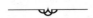

Leo Horney, their dentist from Paris days, had proposed to take out Stead's protruding front teeth. She agreed. An inveterate woman-chaser, Horney joked that she should get herself out to Hollywood fast before some woman got hold of Bill. She teased Bill: 'Has Greta or Marlene got her hooks into you?'

Blake's mood was oscillating violently. On 9 June, he wrote with his usual conviction that everything would turn out for the best: 'I still think that Hollywood is the writer's lifesaver.' Three days later, desolate, he surrendered all decisions to Stead:

At the moment I have no clear indication that I will make a cent here. Selling here is not so easy—*Copperheads*, God no, it would offend the south (they are all convinced that *Gone with the Wind* is the greatest novel ever written & that picture the greatest accomplishment of mankind, incl. Homer). *TWIM*, who cares about Spain now? *The Painter & the Lady*—too psychological ...

But the query is this: do you want to come here & brave it out? There is a high possibility, of course, of our making a living within a reasonable time, certainly our chances are no worse than in N. Y. So decide, anything you do pleases me, for, candidly, life is not worth living except for you: I am a man in love, I have that as my great joy in life, all other things are subordinate, & whatever else this absence has shown me, it has revealed the root of my adult existence.

———— ⟿ ————

June 15, 1942

My dear Munk,

I got your Friday letter in which you say how hard it is to get in—and I know this of course, have seen from your letters what the set-up is. The best thing we can do is go to Santa Fé, get some proper rest, fresh air and working-strength and work at some MSS; and try again. It is much cheaper than living here—we cannot afford this $75 pied-à-terre, with N. Y. scale of expenses. My teeth are nearly finished and Leo will wait for his money, as you know. I have bought two summer suits which will do for anything ... will last for years, and in Autumn and Winter, under a furcoat.

... I am working like a dog on the MS; extraordinary how long it takes to finish. But I suppose they will accept it, with alterations, and if they do I will ask them to advance me a bit of the advance.

... Santa Fé is the best thing. You absolutely must have a rest. I cannot travel this week—wd. not be finished in the beginning; the end is my lunar rendez-vous, unsuitable for travelling—but as it is shorter now I wd. be ready to travel on Monday next. Of course, the MS. must be in first.

... Cheer up, sweetheart. All is not lost. A few months in a Paradise where you can't spend dough, some peace and quiet and good hard work, work—we will feel wonderful. I feel myself full of books. I know this is but the writer's illusion and that each of these books takes inexpressible months to finish—but we will try, Love, Your Christina.

Stead had her own frustrations. She had handed Pascal Covici a large chunk of manuscript and he had insisted that the novel was now long enough, though she planned at least ten more chapters. And he had taken one look at her untidy single-spaced manuscript and said it would have to be re-typed by his office staff at her expense. This was an unexpected financial blow.

She could not decide whether to sublet the apartment (which would mean placing their furniture and pictures at risk, and putting up regulation air-raid blinds) or to pack the furniture up and place it in storage at $8 a month. She was embarrassed to be letting down Asa Zatz, a dear friend. They had not signed a formal lease, but there was a tacit understanding that they would rent for a second complete year—until October. She had put a sublet notice in the *Villager*, but enquirers lost interest when they heard there was no elevator.

The previous day, she had had sharp pains, an old problem that she took to be the aftermath of her appendix. She had spent the day in bed reading Balzac's *The Middle Classes*, and was reminded, once again, how good Balzac was. 'Every word he writes seems to be spoken in my ear ... I know him and I understand him, as a man ... and that is because he is so like you,' she told Blake.

In Hollywood, Blake was selling his soul:

> I have handed the script to an old pimp at the game, who came up today and worked out a plot with me, so banal and so vulgar that it left me shuddering and yet I know that it is the only chance for money.

Two days later, he went with friends to visit Lion Feuchtwanger, the German refugee and author of *Jew Süss*, 'the guy we all chipped in pennies to aid'.

> He has a palace and grounds at Pacific Palisades reminiscent of the Rothschilds and a private library that for the first time made me green with envy.

Blake felt the irony keenly.

Stead was tense, suffering from severe sinus headaches and the high blood pressure she believed she had inherited from her father. She had hoped to finish her novel before leaving New York. Now, even though she had decided to shorten it, she realised with dismay that she would be finishing the last section in Santa Fe.

She had bought a book on fortune-telling by cards. After telling Asa's fortune and her own, she believed she had a talent for it. Asa's short visits were ideal, but other friends, with their invitations to go out, were a distraction she did not welcome. 'They don't seem to realise that a strong-looking, casual person like me can be so worn out that a social outing is the last straw. I cannot frankly see anyone.' With all the writing and marathon typing, the housework and visits to the dentist, packing and cleaning out closets, she acknowledged that a 'varmint' would have been 'utterly impossible'.

But there was one person she *did* want to see: Harry Bloom. His visits were rare these days. According to his wife Anne, he was 'working like a dog', and the long days on his feet left him tired and short-tempered.

> Anne is really suspicious (like any good wife!) & although he wants to come downtown & see me, he cannot do it openly ... You know it is not real love on his part for me, but only the desire to get away from the pharmacy and to expand a bit in different terms. This I know quite well & of course have never made the faintest disloyal move—but such are wives and so one can do nothing, though I know Harry is *suffering* because he could not see either of us before we left—perhaps for such a long time. He is the most affectionate guy.

When Stead collected their bank statement, she discovered that the account was down to $747.70. Deeply worried, she told Blake that the only certainty was $675 in July, as her advance from Viking.

Peter Neidecker ('Old Mercury') had phoned to see how she was. Asa, whom she saw for a few minutes each day, had registered for the army. Meanwhile, he had gone 'back to his old habits, sleeping till 11 or 12—in this awful heat too, in that filthy, smelly room with the windows closed'.

Two days before leaving for Santa Fe, at the end of June, she sat in a café with their Polish economist friend Henryk Grossmann, one of the 'revolutionary' friends she was planning to write about.

> Will tell you about Grossmann later on. Poor lost man. He cannot get over his insignificance here when he was such a figure, a celebrated scholar, in Europe ... What he misses most of all are his workshop of brilliant young men and the *café*.
>   ... Asked old Grossmann yesterday for some views on the revolutionary ... He does not think psychologically and what he said was utterly useless ... So all I can get out of him is *himself* as a revolutionary ... He does not give a

tuppenny damn for me and my affairs: nothing in the world counts but his work, 'Grossmann's Works' …

Until Wednesday, my dear boy … I have realised this month which has been so hard, what you mean to me. I would work without you, but not for long. I would go to pieces … What an extraordinary chance that I met you—I have met a few other men, of course, but only men who would have left me with a torn-up mind. I can't get over how cruel human beings, not are, but *must* be, to each other—for ever and ever, I suppose. It is a real inferno we are born into.

She finished cleaning the apartment. She packed up their books and papers. Asa Zatz lent her a small trunk for their typewriters and promised to accompany her to the station to help with the luggage. And—wonderful moment—dear Harry Bloom came 'sneaking in' to say goodbye.

IO

The Besieged Fortress

———— ❧ ————

July 1942 – December 1946

T
HE REST OF the summer of 1942 was spent in Santa Fe. Stead was enraptured by the fine mountain air and blue skies, the views of the sierras and sun-bitten plains. She tended to feel light-headed from the altitude, but her sinusitis and headaches disappeared completely, and she plunged back into *For Love Alone* without delay. A fortnight later, in mid July, she sent off the last third to Viking—a little too hastily, no doubt.

Her buoyant mood was thoroughly deflated in August. Viking publishers Pascal Covici and Marshall Best thought the final scenes 'quite impossible and unconvincing', and James Quick, the man who saves Teresa, 'a cardboard American'. Readers would understand that Australia was 'fifteen years behind the times', but the dialogue between Teresa and Quick could not possibly have occurred in London at that time. Stead was deeply stung. 'I have not told them the character is Bill, and the scenes ones in which I myself played a part,' she told Burnshaw. 'This is too juicy for them—and what difference would it make?'[1]

Covici infuriated Stead by holding up Viking's latest success, Steinbeck's war novel *The Moon is Down*, as a model of simple, understated writing. 'That brainless pamphlet of monosyllables!' she groaned to Burnshaw, bitterly recalling that six years ago Simon & Schuster were urging her to write like *Gone with the Wind*. 'This is the sort of nonsense I have to stand every time a book is a best-seller. May the word perish.'

She and Blake had become acrimonious about the 'weary hacks of the publishing trade', whose standard message was 'cut'. With their best-seller mentality, publishers were robbing literature of its most important characteristics: 'freedom, breadth and eloquence'.[2] Blake satirised American publishing in the novel he began that summer, *We are the Makers of Dreams*. And Stead's *Miss Herbert*, written in the late 1950s, would be a savage indictment of the publishing business.

With no income and no savings left as a buffer, they were in dire financial straits. They wondered whether to return to New York, and Stead asked Burnshaw, who as Editor-in-Chief at the Dryden Press had useful contacts, to let her know if he heard of an office job for her there. ('Not licking stamps.') At the end of the summer, they decided to head west.

Hollywood, 1942. The big lure for writers was money. Rumours of astronomical salaries circulated freely. Indeed, some screenwriters were paid $1200 or more per week, and income tax was low. But in reality, this talk amounted to Hollywood stardust. Writers were employed on week-to-week contracts, there was no security of income and the majority pocketed pay closer to the median weekly wage of $125. The Screen Writers Guild, not nearly as powerful as Blake had first thought, had only just won the battle for a minimum wage.

It sounded glamorous to be a Hollywood screenwriter: in fact, it was a hack job that merely entailed adapting and transforming material handed over by the story department. Producers wanted dramatic and entertaining scripts, and they wanted them fast. 'Scripters' had to clock in, work Saturday mornings and look busy. There was no room for originality, and they had no influence on the final product. It was no wonder that Hollywood writers looked forward to the non-salaried part of the year, when they could make for the mountains or return to New York and do *real* writing.

The writers, more than 10 per cent of whom were communists, formed the most radical group in the Hollywood film colony. This was the group Blake and Stead mixed with when they went out socially, though these occasions were rare. It was difficult for them to get around without a car:

distances were vast and residential areas remote. And they felt like outcasts in Hollywood, where even in communist circles the social hierarchy was rigidly based on salaries. Stead recalled: 'Even at gatherings of mostly communist writers, a fellow would be classified as a "$1000-a-week man", and therefore important, while another would be dismissed verbally as a "$150-a-week man".'

In late November or early December 1942, Stead landed a week-to-week assignment at Metro-Goldwyn-Mayer as a $175-a-week woman. Blake told Burnshaw: 'If she holds out a month, we shall clear all debts and have the return fare. If she holds out longer we might actually get ahead of the economic parade, for the first time in years. That remains for her producer to decide.'[3]

At the 'Lion's Roar', Stead's brain was 'racing with torpedo boats'. She was part of a team working on the film *They Were Expendable*. Directed by John Ford and released in 1945, it was to become a Second World War classic, starring Robert Montgomery and John Wayne. Hollywood was now turning out war films, many watched by the 12 million American servicemen stationed around the world. Even the radical Screen Writers Guild (to which Stead belonged) exhorted its members to produce 'fighting words' to spur on the struggle against fascism.

Next, Stead was put to work with a group of eight or so other writers on *Madame Curie*. Her boss, Sidney Franklin, had directed several successful films—*The Barretts of Wimpole Street*, *The Good Earth* and *Goodbye, Mr Chips*—and was now working for the first time as a producer. The film had a long history. Back in 1938, Aldous Huxley had been put to work on the script. He was paid $15000 for eight weeks' work, and Franklin had scarcely glanced at the script. Later F. Scott Fitzgerald had worked on a new script at $1000 a week; later still the Polish émigré actress and writer Salka Viertel wrote another. Originally, there had been talk of Greta Garbo for the title role; in the end, it went to the redhaired Irish actress, Greer Garson, famed for her role in *Mrs Miniver*, a moving propaganda film that Churchill said was worth one hundred warships.

Scriptwriting, Stead discovered, was 'a dreary sort of office job'. The absurdity of the work conditions irritated her: for hours on end the writers and advisers sat around feeling useless. Her employment lasted eight weeks. Blake did not land a Hollywood contract; nor did anything come of his George Graham Rice script. He gave some lectures at the Hollywood School for Writers. And he took advantage of his free time to finish *We are the Makers of Dreams*. As soon as he had sent it off to the Dial Press, he began a series of essays on imperialism, a subject on which he was exchanging a voluminous correspondence with Henryk Grossmann in New York.

Viking eventually rejected *For Love Alone* outright. The Dial Press also sent back Blake's novel. He would have to wait seventeen years to see it published.

Stead and Blake stayed in Hollywood for three or four months altogether. It was more than enough. For Stead, the only virtue of the place—apart from the clear air and mild weather that reminded her of Sydney—was that it made her appreciate New York.

It also gave her an impression of Hollywood communism, enabling her to set part of her future novel, *I'm Dying Laughing*, in the film colony. Her own impression of the wrangling, doctrinaire communist set with their vast mansions and Japanese butlers would be filled out the following year by Ruth McKenney, who spent twelve months there with her husband Richard Bransten and wrote to Stead regularly.

The communist scriptwriters liked to talk as if their films were a powerful weapon in the campaign to influence public opinion, but this was utterly illusory. John Howard Lawson, leader of the Communist Party in Hollywood, was exultant when he was asked to write *Blockade*, a film about the Spanish Civil War. But the producer stripped his script so successfully of political content that audiences were not even sure on which side the hero was fighting.

Influential or not, communists were irrevocably cast as 'baddies' by the House Un-American Activities Committee (HUAC). Though the Russians were America's wartime allies, Martin Dies, head of the HUAC, was convinced that communists posed a much greater threat to the nation's internal security than the Nazis or Japanese. His explanation for communist influence in Hollywood was that the producers were mostly Jews.[4]

When McKenney and Bransten were in Hollywood, from the summer of 1944 to May 1945, they made a considerable fortune as freelance scriptwriters and 'chummed around with the $2,500-a-week radical crowd'. In *Love Story*, her highly sentimental portrait of their marriage,

McKenney writes that she and Bransten collaborated on a movie script that sold for $25 000. This success was followed by others. They bought a house two doors down from Joan Crawford in the fashionable suburb of Brentwood and employed servants. McKenney and Bransten now had the care of Eileen's son Patrick, Bransten's son Tom, the issue of his previous marriage, and their own daughter Eileen. The children attended expensive private schools. *I'm Dying Laughing* depicts it all.

Yet their year in Hollywood was a 'low point' in the Bransten marriage. They were living so high that they were soon in debt. They fought incessantly. Ruth (like Emily Wilkes in *I'm Dying Laughing*) ate 'like a cormorant, an elephant, a pelican'. Richard developed severe ulcers. To readers of *Love Story* Ruth McKenney confessed that she and her husband were doomed to a tempestuous marital life. 'We are too passionate, and too blundering, to inhabit any safe and comfortable plateaus.'

Within the Communist Party, their comrades denounced McKenney and Bransten as 'renegades' or 'semi-Trotskyites'. Like Bill Blake, they disagreed with 'Browderism', which to them had come to mean capitulation to American capitalism. Ever since America and Russia had become war allies, Party General Secretary Earl Browder, following orders from the Comintern, had pursued a policy that aimed to reconcile the CPUSA with mainstream American politics. The Party persuaded the trade unions not to strike and asked blacks not to pursue their struggle for civil rights. Browder's book *Victory and After*, published in 1942, called for a truce between capitalists and workers.

In 1950, long after they had been expelled from the Party as 'renegades', Ruth McKenney would write about 'the little band of serious Hollywood thinkers' who gave them such a hard time. One memorable evening among the radicals, embellished by Stead in *I'm Dying Laughing*, was first described by McKenney in *Love Story*:

> Stacy ... was a big, leading writer and made $2,500 a week when he worked, which was fairly steady; his wife wore sables ... He always had a tendency to be domineering and loudmouthed, back in the old days of the League of American Writers. But in New York people used to sit on Stacy practically every time he opened his mouth. 'Oh, what bilge,' was the general cry when Stacy made deep, philosophical comments. The first time we went to a Hollywood party, we were flabbergasted to discover that now everybody formed a respectful, alert circle and listened to Stacy sound off, gruffly, on

purple thoughts like 'The Motion Picture Is the Art Form of the People,' or 'The Novel is Esoteric and Dead.'

... We were invited to a soirée at the great man's home—quite an honor, we gathered, although I cannot say we felt it keenly. The refreshments were a little buffet of champagne, lobster, and the like—not bad. But before we had half a chance to stuff ourselves on the goodies, Stacy called the party to order, whipped out a little leather-covered notebook and a Waterman pen, and drew up an agenda. This is an absolute fact. It was not a meeting, either, just a cheerful little gathering of higher-paid Hollywood gadabouts, the $2,000 a week set, in fact. Stacy Summed Up. Afterwards, as the jolly fête was breaking up, he took me aside and urged me to be psychoanalyzed before it was too late.

A comparison of *Love Story* and *I'm Dying Laughing* shows the resemblance between the voices of Ruth McKenney and Emily Wilkes. Stanley Burnshaw, who knew Ruth McKenney well, was 'astounded' when first reading *I'm Dying Laughing* in the mid 1960s, by the way Stead had captured her voice.

'Stacy Cresswell' in McKenney's story—Jay Moffat Byrd in Stead's— was John Howard Lawson, the unofficial leader of Hollywood's communists from 1937 until 1950, when he would be sent to jail as one of the Hollywood Ten. A doctrinaire and bullying character, Lawson would take it upon himself to explain sudden switches in the Party line, to settle internal conflicts, and summon wayward members for ideological 'discussions' at which he would 'straighten them out'. One such scene is graphically depicted in *I'm Dying Laughing*.

In February 1943, while Stead and Blake were still in Hollywood, Ruth McKenney's revolutionary novel *Jake Home* was published. Stead sincerely admired it. Israel Amter, reviewing it for the *Daily Worker*, deemed it an 'untimely' moment for a portrait of a flawed communist. Stead was dumbfounded by Amter's rigid righteousness and censoriousness, and courageously fired off an angry missive to the *Daily Worker*. A novel is not a pamphlet, she expostulated, and it cannot be 'timely', for the simple reason that it takes at least one year to write a book and a second year to see it in print.

I will say that *Jake Home* will probably outlast us; it has some of the spirit of Jack London's best proletarian novels, and I'm certain its author will write yet greater proletarian novels. She is probably the best writer of and for the left; and to discourage, insult, and attack such a fine writer is about the greatest disservice anyone could do to the left.

It was a passionate expression of solidarity with what Stead considered intelligent, rather than uncritical, leftism. At the time, she regarded McKenney as a great friend. By the time she came to write *I'm Dying Laughing*, ten years later, she had changed her mind. By then, it seemed to Stead that McKenney had no political integrity whatsoever—perhaps no integrity of any sort.

When Stead and Blake returned to New York, in March 1943, the Desert War in North Africa was raging and there was active engagement in the Pacific, but the tide of war seemed to be turning: the Germans had just surrendered in Stalingrad, the greatest battle in the war so far. American males under thirty-seven were being called to the armed services. Asa Zatz was about to depart for the Middle East; Ettore Rella had left to serve in the Pacific.

Their top floor apartment in Asa Zatz's house had been sublet to the Austrian playwright Ferdinand Bruckner and his wife, escapees from Nazism. Zatz did not want to throw out the Bruckners, and through a friend he found Blake and Stead an apartment nearby, at No. 21 E. 14th Street. It was spacious and modern and not so close to the El—though it turned out to be noisy just the same. On the street side, fire engines would tear up and down; on the courtyard side was the roaring ventilator of an all-night bakery. Stead never slept the night through. But they were to stay there almost four years, and later in life she would pride herself on being 'a tried and true 14th Streeter'.[5] She liked the old houses on 14th Street, the cosmopolitan flavour and its location at the edge of Greenwich Village.

Bill Blake had hoped that the shortage of personnel in civil employment might open up an opportunity for him in publishing. But no. He would find he had to resort to a number of short-term jobs—all unsatisfactory. He worked for Alf Hurst in his grain and fur business. Under the pseudonyms George B. Collingwood and George S. Kent, he wrote about finance and stock investment for *The Magazine of Wall Street*. Then, in the spring of

1944, Stanley Burnshaw as Editor-in-Chief of Dryden Press, came up with an idea to take advantage of Blake's prodigious research skills: *An Intelligent American's Guide to the Peace* would contain a potted history, geography and economic analysis of every major country in the world. The rationale was that better international understanding would lead to better international relations in peace time.

For the next few months, Blake worked at the Dryden Press offices on Fourth Avenue, hammering out 5000 to 7000 words a day. Since his name carried no weight outside communist circles, the book needed someone to give it public authority. Sumner Welles, former Undersecretary of State, whose book *A Time for Decision* made him a leading expert on international politics, was the perfect candidate.

Burnshaw edited Blake's draft, then sent it to Sumner Welles, who made numerous changes. The book came out in January 1945, with Sumner Welles' name on the cover. It sold extremely well—55 000 copies—and was widely praised for its vast and useful coverage, clear style and intelligent organisation. All praise and royalties went to Sumner Welles. Blake had been paid a fixed sum.

'Who Done It?' was the headline of a review by George E. Sokolsky, a notorious rightwing journalist, in the Hearst newspaper, the New York *Sun*.

> I recently received from the Dryden Press a copy of *An Intelligent American's Guide to the Peace*, a massive volume of what appears to be objective information. On the blurb the name of Sumner Welles appears in letters one and a quarter inches high. Above that name appears, in letters one-eighth of an inch high, the legend, 'Under the General Editorship of.' In a 'Publisher's Note' I came across the fact that 'the research and preparation of the material were entrusted to Mr. William J. Blake.' As the research and preparation of the material are the business of an author, it would seem that William J. Blake must be the author.

On close reading, Sokolsky found that the information was not 'objective' at all. The account of the depression in the United States was 'one-sided', and the section on Soviet Russia improbably rosy. Its bias notwithstanding, the journalist declared it an 'extremely valuable reference book':

> So as long as there is nothing better available—and there is nothing better available—this is the book for an intelligent American. And if the publisher

was afraid that I would shout 'Marxist!' if he admitted that Blake wrote the book, he might get over that inhibition and give the devil his due.[6]

Coming from someone known to attack anything even mildly liberal, Sokolsky's endorsement of the book undoubtedly helped to increase sales.

———— ✧ ————

Stead spent July 1944 at the Kotlarskys' rambling country house at Hunter in the Catskills, far removed from the terrible events of the world. The old house was surrounded by fields, fruit trees, rust-coloured barns; over the tool shed, and crawling towards the house, a sprawling wild hops vine strangled every plant in sight. Impressed by its indestructibility, Stead would use it, in *The People with the Dogs*, as a metaphor for the suffocating nature of family bonds.

It was an enchanting place. Every few days the air would become hot and steamy, the light would turn a supernatural pink, and an afternoon thunderstorm would break from the west. In the evenings Stead sat on the terrace with Aida and Max, looking across the valley to the mountains, watching the furtive shadows and darting fireflies. Nights on the mountainside were soft and cold, and for once, she slept soundly. To her, those weeks in the mountains were a 'midsummer night's dream'.[7]

Blake, working on the 'Sumner Welles book', had had to remain in the heat-struck city. He caught the bus up for the weekend before Stead's birthday, and stepped off looking pale and enervated. Stead kept trying to persuade him to come again later in July, but he was under too much pressure. 'I have already completed the physiography, resources, ethnology, economics of 46 countries but I have 22 to go and then I must write the political structure and history of 68 and all by August 15th,' he wrote to her from the city, adding that on unbearably hot days, he wrote about Greenland, Iceland, Norway or Antarctica.

Aida was the most hospitable of friends. Stead was left to write in peace, in a room with a view of the mountains. She liked to hear Max Kotlarsky practising his piano in another part of the house. In the late afternoon, the women would walk together, or swim in the small dam ten minutes from the house, returning with glowing skin.

The month at Hunter allowed Stead to observe the 'dog family' at close quarters, and though none of them knew it, she was taking voluminous notes. *The People with the Dogs* is full of humour, but not Stead's usual sharp satire. For once, the central character, Edward Massine, recognises himself more or less for what he is. And though there is plenty of talk in this novel, it is *conversation*—not manic wind-bagging, as in several other Stead novels.

The characters are not idealised. Oneida's love for her dogs is shown to be a substitute for adult love, a spiritual or professional life. Edward is affable and talented, but without purpose. After having tried in vain to throttle the massive hops vine at the country house, he sits back exhausted and angry, musing that it is a symbol of his life: 'the sloth that stretches back into my childhood'. He is unable to commit himself to Margot, the woman he has loved for twelve years. Walt, a happily married man (based on Bill Blake) consoles him, but with an edge of irony:

> 'You only understand the communal life, that's why you don't want to marry, isn't it? You don't see the reason for crawling into a corner with one woman and having one child. You need abundant multiple life around you like Whitehouse, like the Massines; the perfect still life, eh? Ha-ha. Fruitfulness with grapes and rabbits dropping over the edges of an oak table on a woven cloth—and many dogs and dishes and many children and many days? Isn't that you fundamentally?'

Edward Massine believes he cannot live for himself: he needs to live for others, and in the end he decides he wants commitment to one woman. This desire is seen, within the narrative, as a sign of his new maturity.

When Edward announces his impending marriage, his Aunt Oneida is distraught:

> 'Children are Frankenstein's monsters! They grow up and leave you: but dogs never leave you ... Edward, oh, Edward! Are you going to leave me?'
> 'Jesus!' said Edward getting up and strolling to the window.

Interestingly, in this book it is a man, not a woman, who feels unable to live for himself, and who finally discovers a point to his life in marriage. During his last hours as a bachelor, Edward feels 'Very happy that this arid stretch of his life was over, and excited, curious to know what the next would be like'. The journey imagery is similar to the ending of *Letty Fox*, though in Edward's case the reader feels optimistic. His marriage takes place on St Valentine's Day. Outside, there is 'the earliest, faintest intimation of spring'. In the final scene, the Massine tribe is gathered together: they are standing around, 'not especially arranged', on the stairs, round the long table, waiting patiently for the toasts. It is the 'perfect still life' Walt once described. But Edward has broken out of the closed circle. If the book has a message, it is that even benevolent, extended families such as this need to be left behind.

Stead had been revising *For Love Alone*. She paid Ruth Blake to type it professionally. Her new agent, Helen Strauss, who worked for the prestigious William Morris Agency, quickly sold the novel, arranging a three-book contract with Harcourt, Brace. It was Stead's third American publisher in eight years.

For Love Alone appeared on 6 October 1944, a cheap wartime edition. Its title did not do it a service. The jacket illustration, a drawing of a bare-breasted girl leaning out of her window on a starry night, reinforced the impression that this was a popular romance. As critic Jose Yglesias, one of Stead's admirers, saw it, the book was 'inevitably bound … for the 49c remainder counter at the Concord bookstores'. He wrote later that the small côterie of Stead admirers were beginning to feel 'like disappointed lovers'. 'We shook our heads about Christina Stead's shortsightedness in allowing her publishers to misrepresent her work.'[8]

Some twenty years later, Patrick White was to read *For Love Alone* for the first time. He thought the first half of the novel even more powerful than *The Man Who Loved Children*. 'It is a *remarkable* book,' he told a friend. 'I feel elated to think it is there.'[9]

But most reviewers did not understand the intense Australian heroine whose passionate Odyssey was a search for Cytherean love. The *New York Times* reviewer was more perceptive than most:

> It would be easy to be flippant about this book and miss its gravity, or be gross and miss its pathos. Christina Stead does not have the stature of D. H. Lawrence, but she has many of his qualities, and her new novel suggests his early and best fiction.[10]

Another critic dismissed it as 'five hundred morbid pages of lust and abnormality'.[11]

When Peter Davies published the novel a year later, the reception in England was similarly mixed. The most enthusiastic review for once came from Australia. For the first time since *Seven Poor Men of Sydney*, Stead had set her novel partly in Australia. The *Bulletin* only reviewed 'Australian' books and had not paid any attention to Stead's other novels. This time though, the anonymous reviewer was Douglas Stewart, the *Bulletin* literary editor and himself a distinguished writer. He wrote that the style of *For Love Alone* was 'unmistakably excellent', the delineation of character equalled Dostoevski and the novel had 'tremendous vitality'.

> There is a profoundly original talent speaking in *For Love Alone*, something wild and fierce and fearless that tempts one to use the word 'genius.' ... It is a work of the highest quality.

More typically, the Sydney *Daily Telegraph* claimed that the book 'just fails', adding, 'yet it is the profoundest book this most gifted and intellectually rich of Australia's contemporary novelists has produced'. The *Sydney Morning Herald*, in one small paragraph, called the 500-page novel 'an admirable little book', adding: 'All her books have been written since she went abroad to live in 1926, which is a pity, because we should be proud to call her an Australian novelist.'[12] It was not enough that Australians wrote about Australia: they also had to stay at home to do it.

Stead had taught a Workshop in the Novel from September 1943 until January 1944, one evening a week, as part of the New York University extramural program. She prepared the workshop with her usual thoroughness, typing pages and pages of notes, and calling on her thorough knowledge of nineteenth- and twentieth-century European literature as examples of narrative techniques. She was to repeat the course in 1944 and 1946 because she needed the income, but complained it was time-consuming. It always took her a whole day to prepare the two-hour lesson.

'People do not like originality,' she warned her students. Nevertheless, writers must have the courage to respect those 'ideas that rush up and force themselves into the story'. By the time she wrote *For Love Alone*, her sixth work of fiction, she was quite definite about what she was aiming for in her writing: '*intelligent ferocity*'.

> The sensuality, delicacy of literature does not exist for me; only the passion, energy and struggle, the night of which no one speaks, the creative act: some

people like to see the creative act banished from the book—it should be put behind one and a neatly-groomed little boy in sailor-collar introduced ... But for me it is not right: I like each book to have not only the little boy, not very neat, but also the preceding creative act ... Most of my friends deplore this: they are always telling me what I should leave out in order to have 'success.'[13]

Her aim was to disturb, even madden the reader, and she believed that a polished style reduced the force of the impact. She did not want to produce carefully wrought, well-balanced 'literature', with a neat plot and a tidy ending. She refused to tie together the loose ends of narrative. Characters are introduced in her fiction, never to reappear—just as this happens in life. Her endings are open; very often they circle back to the point of departure. The moral message is ambiguous, as it is in life. And her dialogue has the fractured syntax, repetition, colloquialisms, facetiousness and bullying of actual speech. As Angela Carter writes, it is 'that chaotic sense of flux that makes reading Stead somehow unlike reading fiction, that makes reading her seem like plunging into the mess of life itself'.[14] This quality of unpolished *rawness* is something Stead's readers either find immensely seductive or immensely irritating.

Stead greatly admired the nineteenth-century realists Balzac, Flaubert, Zola, Tolstoy, Gorki. For her, realism (or naturalism) was about objectivity. Like Flaubert, Stead aimed to rid her fiction of overt authorial judgement. Flaubert once said:

Human beings must be treated like mastodons and crocodiles; why get excited about the horn of the former or the jaw of the latter? Display them, stuff them, bottle them, that's all—but appraise or evaluate them: no!

This suited Stead: she believed herself to have 'a terribly strong moral streak'[15], but in order to immerse herself in her characters, she needed to engineer herself into a state of sympathetic identification. In not making her own moral viewpoint clear, the risk she ran was of being misunderstood, and she often was.

Susan Sheridan points out that Stead's 'lack of moral colouring' and 'dizzying lack of narrative direction' unsettle and disorient readers.[16] This sense of moral vertigo arises partly because Stead herself was often undecided about her characters. From her early childhood, love had been associated with resentment, even hate, and this is a terribly confusing foundation from which to establish emotional commitments. Her major love as a child—her father—was someone she also bitterly resented. Moreover, there was a disconcerting gap between the ideals he professed and his actual actions, and though he was puffed up with grandiloquent talk, his grasp on the real world was decidedly slippery. The other love of Stead's life was Bill Blake, a man full of passionately held socialist ideals, who constantly found himself pandering to self-serving capitalists. Alphendéry, in *House of All Nations*, is not a happy man, nor is he an admirable man, but we sense that the narrator loves him.

In a sense, writing lifted Stead out of her moral dilemmas. In her writing, she suspended judgement: her aim was to understand. Writing the 'truth', which she believed to be neither black nor white, made her feel a more moral person. In *I'm Dying Laughing*, Emily Wilkes speaks in this instance for Stead:

> I think a writer *has* a tremendous responsibility to tell the truth and tell it with all the skill and ability and experience—he has—to rise above himself … That's a funny thing, but every night I wake up and I think, I want to be better than I am by nature. To be a writer in an age when the truth will set us free—means to be a writer of the truth; or to be an utter, utter, decadent damned soul.

Stead lived for her writing. In describing Edward Massine, one of her writer-characters, she is no doubt describing herself:

> He had an effective method for getting to sleep. It was to piece together names, faces, backgrounds, times of day, temperatures and seasons, tones of voice, things that had been said to him that had caused him emotion. He tried to form an idea of any given person's character, temperament.

Another self-portrait is that of the Musical Critic in *The Salzburg Tales*, who tells the assembled group that he looks at life 'as a spectator who looks at a vast stage-setting'.

> If you have five minutes to observe a man, from a secret cranny, you will find out a great deal about him. Does he shake his head, loosen his collar, noiselessly gargle his throat and brush back his hair with his hand, does he take out his handkerchief and refold it, button and unbutton his coat? What is the colour of his eyes, hair, skin: what is the quality of the cloth in his coat, and of what cut is the garment? Is he fat or thin? What are his half-dozen tics?

... Does he look into jewellers' windows, or bars, or banks? Has he a stick or a bag: what paper does he carry? ... What is his gait, what his tread? There are a thousand things to observe which will give away the party he votes for and the amount of his bank-balance. And for this reason, I am an inveterate and shameless eavesdropper, I listen at the doors of rooms, I pussy-foot along the corridors, I read private letters and stare at people in their emotion. My own life is too calm for my energy, I suppose that is the reason.

How did Stead go about her writing? As she explained to her students, the germ of a story would 'exhibit' itself to her one day. The idea would nag at her. She would mull it over, usually for several years, read books on the subject, collect newspaper clippings, keep a notebook, talk to the people on whom she thought she would base her characters, make more notes. Generally, she tried to keep all this file-keeping and auxiliary writing to the afternoons and evenings: the mornings were reserved for serious writing.

The subjects she treated would always involve conflict: between a parent and a child, between a man and a woman, or a conflict of values within an individual. She never underestimated the passions these conflicts engendered. 'We have a society that believes in reason or that would like to, and for one reason or another we are obliged to ignore or suppress various human passions, but the novelist must know what they are.'

For any particular subject, she would read books that might help her focus on the social milieu she was delineating. She would choose characters—people she knew or amalgamations of people she knew—and make notes about their physical characteristics and their ages at various stages of the narrative. In the case of Letty Fox, mainly modelled on Ruth Blake, she 'studied' Ruth, asked her questions, examined the letters she had written to her father over the years, discussed her with Bill. In order to find out in what ways Ruth was representative or special, she talked to other young women of Ruth's age. Eventually, she would amalgamate and concentrate the various experiences of these young women. It was important that no one knew she was writing about them.

To inspire her, she would go back again to the great dramatists: Shakespeare, Ibsen, Chekhov. Reading them always taught her more about dialogue. Above all, she listened. She listened to her character model speak: she listened to friends talking, she listened to people talking in the street, in the trolley car. She made notes as soon as she could after hearing a conversation she wanted to remember. Though she had acquired an excellent verbal memory, she knew that speech was not something one remembered like faces, attitudes and characters.

Eventually, the 'depth charge' would occur that made her impatient, almost feverishly so, to start writing. She described it as an intense emotion, like a shock or the stab of love that grips the belly. When it worked best, she would write in a state of white heat, fast, obsessively and all day long—almost as if in a kind of trance. Some twenty-five years later, she would describe it in these terms:

> I'm a psychological writer, and my drama is the drama of the person. The start of a story is like a love affair, exactly. It's like a stone hitting you. You can't argue with it. I wait and wait for the drama to develop. I watch the characters and the situation move and don't interfere. I'm patient. I'm lying low.[17]

With her first draft, she allowed herself to write haphazardly, not necessarily in sequence. If she was blocked, held up in mid action, she would say to herself, 'Leave them alone for a few minutes and see what they will do'. This meant throwing herself on her bed and staring at the ceiling, while thinking about her characters. After she had completed her first draft, she would re-arrange the sequence. Chapter One might become Chapter Four or the ending. Usually she wrote (or re-wrote) the beginning last of all. At this stage a new art came into play: 'the art of throwing away'. She was cautious here: 'By throwing away I do not mean what is called "paring to the bone."'

Stead disliked revision. By then her passion was spent. For the most part, she preferred to re-write than revise. This meant rolling a fresh page into the typewriter and writing the page again, working alongside the old draft but altering as she went. Among Stead's papers are pages and pages of slightly different drafts, all typed single-spaced on flimsy paper (light for suitcases) and with numerous crossings out. It is usually quite impossible to tell which draft is which.

Not only did this method of revision involve constant typing: it also explains the appearance of spontaneity and the genuine carelessness in Stead's writing. Ironically, this effect of spontaneity, which made it seem as if Stead wrote almost effortlessly, was achieved by monumental hard work.

Stead had been frustrated by the reaction of American critics to *For Love Alone* and sincerely hoped that her current character—she had gone back to her manuscript *Letty Fox*—was a young woman Americans could understand. Letty was a tough-minded New Yorker, intelligent and cynical, who claimed to be a typical New York college girl. However, she is sexually promiscuous, and the picture of American society in the novel is hardly flattering. Once again, Stead had written frankly and daringly about subjects that were still taboo: female sexual aggression and male impotence. The novel, Stead was well aware, was likely to provoke outrage.

In *For Love Alone*, Teresa Hawkins is a heroic figure, with ideals, passion, moral integrity. With *Letty Fox*, Stead was entering a new phase: from now on, she would portray anti-heroines, anti-heroes—with varying degrees of sympathy. The portrait of Letty, while deeply ironic, is not unsympathetic. The sexual, social and political binds in which Letty is caught up are real.

Letty Fox was Stead's first truly American novel; *The Man Who Loved Children*, transferred from Australia, did not arise out of her American experience. This time, she could not risk being told that her characters were 'cardboard Americans'; her challenge was to capture American voices, American behaviour and preoccupations. In preparation for writing, she immersed herself in the world of New York women—their magazines, their talk.

Men's talk interested her too. At the beginning of *Letty Fox*, Stead acknowledges that certain jokes and stories in the novel were taken from conversations heard in midtown Manhattan. She relished the storytelling culture in New York. One evening, a friend had dropped in at the flat and recounted a series of horse stories currently circulating in New York. Stead typed them out the following morning from memory, and several appear in the novel.[18] Like James Joyce, T. S. Eliot and many artists, Stead was an indefatigable scavenger.

Ruth Blake, who was now twenty-three, lived in the Village and would often call in at their 14th Street apartment, and talk freely about her rather complicated love life, her reading, the political meetings she had attended. She was a lively young woman, and her father always invited her to their parties. Occasionally, when Bill was away on a business trip, Christina and Ruth would go out together for a meal or drinks. Since gaining her B.A. at NYU, Ruth had been working at various jobs. Stanley Burnshaw had employed her for a time at the Dryden Press, but he began to worry that she would 'corrupt' the other office girls with her stories of her sexual adventures. Now she was working for the Free Belgian and the Free French Movements in Exile, using her fluent French.

Stead had access to the letters Ruth had written to Bill over the years—an invaluable reminder of Ruth's evolving preoccupations. She had also seen quite a bit of Nadine Lewin, the daughter of a friend. Nadine, who studied French and art at Hunter College, was quite different from Ruth Blake. Sheltered and idealistic, she was eager to become an artist. She would be the model for Jacky, Letty's younger sister.

In the novel, the two sisters are polar opposites. They also represent the two sides of Christina Stead. Jacky, who cultivates Romantic agony (she even has tuberculosis, that Romantic disease), is 'wild about' Spinoza, Melanchthon, Shelley, Dostoevski, Napoleon, Goethe, Baudelaire. She is compared to Marguerite in *Faust*, whose 'grande passion' is for an older man. Letty, on the other hand, admires Marx and Hegel, distributes the *Daily Worker*, and aspires to write for the *New Masses*. She enjoys Odets' *Waiting for Lefty*, admires Dreiser and reads Milton's *Lycidas* alongside Barbusse's *Stalin*.

Edith Anderson was an aspiring writer in her late twenties when she and Stead became friends in 1944. The friendship began when Anderson wrote to Stead, whom she had heard read at the League, asking for advice on a writing project. Stead wrote back an encouraging three-page letter, and invited her to the apartment. Edith wrote her impressions in her diary:

> I met Christina Stead last night. She made me feel like a bumptious adolescent, crude, undeveloped and prudish. She is a strange-looking creature. She has a good nose—small light blue eyes with a reptilian glitter, and a mouth which invites peculiar speculation ... The conventional clothes in which all women disguise themselves succeed also in disguising her to the outsider who doesn't really look ... But if you care to look closely you may even be terrified. I don't think there is any thought that Christina is afraid to think. She thinks, she draws conclusions constantly. She is not unkind but she is truthful and this may hurt sharply.

Edith's admiration brought out the best in Stead: Edith believed her to be a great writer and a great woman—intelligent, mysterious, experienced. It made a welcome change; few of Stead's American friends had read her books. With Edith, a fellow writer, Stead could discuss her intense psychic life: the dreams she had had at the time of Ralph Fox's death, her intuitions, her telepathic insights. Ruth McKenney liked to talk; Edith Anderson was happy to listen.

Edith had worked for a time as an editor at the *Daily Worker*; now she was working on the railways, making her contribution to the war effort. She had just married for a second time. Her husband, Max Schroeder, was a communist activist who had fled Germany in 1933 and been in gaol in Paris and a concentration camp in Morocco before he made it to New York in 1941. Anderson had been intrigued by the tattered-looking foreigner who moved into her block of flats. Over time, Max and Edith would become firm friends of Bill and Christina's.

Edith found Christina extraordinarily generous and kind. Once she caught a severe dose of 'flu and happened to mention to Christina, during a phone call, that her flat was very dirty.

> What did she do but come over and clean the kitchen herself! I was in an agony of contrition and shame that this great woman was on her knees in my filthy kitchen. But there was no stopping her.[19]

On 12 April 1945, shortly after being elected for a fourth term, Franklin D. Roosevelt died at the age of sixty-three, with Allied victory only weeks away. Within a fortnight, Hitler committed suicide in his Berlin bunker and Mussolini was shot by Italian partisans. In May the Germans surrendered unconditionally. In July, a conference of the victorious powers at Potsdam had Churchill bitterly complaining that Stalin had erected an 'iron curtain' across Europe. On 6 August, the world's first atomic bomb destroyed Hiroshima, followed three days later by another dropped on Nagasaki. When Japan surrendered on 14 August, carnival broke out in allied cities. 'My guy's come back', crooned a popular American hit song.

But the 'Cold War' was under way. President Harry S. Truman showed none of Roosevelt's reluctance to prosecute communists. 'Red-baiting' and 'witch hunting' would dominate American political life for more than a decade and the Left would be relegated to the margins.

Inside that besieged fortress, the Communist Party, members were engaged in their own vilifications and expulsions. At the end of the war, 'rightwing revisionism' came to be associated with General Secretary Earl Browder, leader of the Party in America. In May 1945, the French communist leader Jacques Duclos wrote an open letter, published in communist newspapers around the world, which vehemently attacked Browder. This was the signal that Moscow wanted to remove Earl Browder from the American leadership. It was already clear that the Kremlin's main enemy in the coming years would be the United States: Browder's vision of post-war harmony between America and Russia now looked ridiculous. In July 1945, he was ousted from the leadership. At branch meetings all over the country, comrades stood up to confess that they had allowed themselves to be misled by Browder.

Bill Blake and his 'old-liner' friends, who had been against Browder's 'United Front' policy throughout the war years, formed a discussion group in 1944, composed of like-minded anti-Browderites. They met at Stead and Blake's 14th Street apartment. (Edith Anderson went along once with her husband and found the room full of 'brilliant people'.) At the same time, Blake kept up a demanding schedule of money-raising talks for the Party, and he and Stead were both members of the Joint Anti-Fascist Refugee Committee. In June 1945 they helped arrange a seventieth birthday celebration for Thomas Mann, the main spokesman for the anti-fascist émigré writers.

Blake's 'leftwing sectarianism' was not well regarded by the Party, even when Browder was no longer in favour. Like-minded thinkers Ruth McKenney and Richard Bransten (alias 'Bruce Minton') were expelled from the Party in September 1946. They were deemed guilty of advocating the petty-bourgeois notion of 'freedom of criticism' in order 'to facilitate their propagation of views hostile to the party'.[20] Horrified, Stead wrote to Edith Anderson:

> The statements even in the D.W. [*Daily Worker*] were the opposite of the truth. At a time like this a wretched clique can think of nothing better to do than make a stink and throw out good Bolsheviks; and lie!!—you should see what lies! ... My chief interest is to tell people that Ruth and 'Bruce' are innocent, absolutely innocent.[21]

It is this atmosphere of fierce recrimination, the 'besieged fortress' from within, that Stead portrays in *I'm Dying Laughing*.

⋯

Bill Blake went to Stanley Burnshaw with a suggestion for a possible money-spinner: an anthology of contemporary fiction about love, with an introduction by Louis Untermeyer, the New York poet and critic. Burnshaw, dubious at first, agreed, and Stead and Blake worked on it together. They selected a dozen short stories and forty-eight excerpts from novels (including the shotgun wedding scene in *For Love Alone*), and called the collection *Modern Women in Love*.

Louis Untermeyer wrote an enticing introduction: 'The pages run from the purest virtue to the most debased *voyeurism*, from natural fulfilment to almost insane frustration.' Three years later, Stead was to describe the book as 'an excellent ... anthology which bears my name too, but only because they had to have a woman on the title-page ... It was a charming bit of Bill's work.'[22] They found it satisfying to publish in joint names, and the volume did make them some money.

⋯

In the summer of 1946, Stead and Blake spent a week in the Catskills with Asa Zatz and the Kotlarskys, and then stayed some time with the Branstens in Westport, Connecticut. Stead took advantage of these visits to make notes for *The People with the Dogs* and her novel about revolutionaries (later called *I'm Dying Laughing*). Blake returned to New York alone in early August, to take up a new job. He was not enthusiastic, but Stead told Aida Kotlarsky: 'I am only wanting him to keep at it long enough to put awful Alf in his place. Awful Alf is batting about as large as life in Canada, at present.'

Bill Blake, famous among New York communists for his fund-raising prowess, had landed a job with the American Birobidjan Committee. His task was to promote and raise money for a Jewish settlement in Birobidjan, a province in Siberia set aside by the Soviet government for Jews already living in Russia. After the Holocaust, the American Jewish community was overwhelmingly in favour of establishing some sort of Jewish homeland.

Blake, like most of his Jewish communist friends, had never liked the idea of a Jewish homeland. Ruth Blake recalls that when she once wrote a short story about the Jews needing a home, her father had said to her:

'Beware of false sentimentality.' But during and after the war, Jewish national aspirations were encouraged by the Party. Indeed, the American Birobidjan Committee was openly a communist front.

Birobidjan was a swampy, mosquito-ridden terrain, with winter temperatures of minus fourteen degrees; however, Blake saw it as a wholly generous gesture on Stalin's part. In early September, he travelled around Michigan and Ohio, raising money for the scheme. The Zionists he encountered were not as conservative as he had feared, he wrote home.

But Birobidjan would prove a hopeless venture. After the establishment of the State of Israel in 1948, Stalin no longer attempted to conceal his anti-semitism. The Comintern, ruling that Jewish nationalism was anti-progressive and anti-Soviet, suppressed Jewish institutions in Birobidjan. Those who had settled there, and those who had sent money, were betrayed once again.

Stead left the Branstens' suburban home in mid August, but found the heat in New York unbearable. The cafeteria below their apartment had upgraded its airconditioning system and now sounded like a fleet of low-flying bombers. In desperation she wrote to Aida, still at Hunter:

> It gets me down: I don't work. I sit there and every fifteen minutes or so, heave myself out of my chair and write about four bad lines just to fool my typewriter. I have been thinking—who has a spare room in N.Y.?

She asked if she might leave her typewriter at the Kotlarskys' apartment and work there for six weeks, until their return to New York City. 'I would (if you permitted) arrive there about nine or ten, say, have a sandwich and milk lunch there and come home about four, doing my shopping on the way, or even at five, if busy … I hardly ever work at night anyhow.' Aida no doubt agreed to this.

In the evenings, too tired to work, Stead would play solitaire or double patience or embroider—the very things her stepmother had always done. She also enjoyed crosswords and puzzles. That summer she was enthusiastic about that bleak and despairing novel, *The Heart is a Lonely Hunter*, written in 1940 by the 22-year-old Southern writer, Carson McCullers.

She was learning Yiddish from Ber Green, one of the editors of the Yiddish-language communist daily, *Morgen Freiheit*. In return, she was helping him translate his Yiddish poems into English. She enjoyed her sessions with this scholarly and cultivated man.

When Bill was away on fundraising tours, she would occasionally go for evening drinks with Ber Green or Henryk Grossmann. When he was not in 'one of his black or silly moods', Grossmann was 'a marvellous companion'. As unhappy as ever in his New York exile, he was living for the day when he could return to Europe. Stead wrote to Blake wistfully: 'Why doesn't *Letty Fox* sell like mad and then we could all (three) be over there?'

The imminent publication of *Letty Fox* was making her anxious. Would it be considered scandalous? She thought she might run away to the Branstens in Connecticut when it came out. She was nervous about the communist reaction to her novel. It scarcely presented a flattering picture of communists, and from Letty Fox, a Young Communist Leaguer, comes the quip: 'Radicalism is the opium of the middle class.' Stead was worried about libel: what would Nadine Lewin say about a letter she had reproduced almost verbatim in the book? She must also have been uneasy about Ruth and Mollie's reaction to a novel in which, to all who knew them, they were recognisable as Letty and Mathilde Fox. Fortunately Mollie and Ruth were busy preparing to leave for France. When Ruth did eventually read it, she was very upset.[23]

Letty Fox was published in New York in early October 1946. Harcourt, Brace once again presented the novel like a cheap romance, with a soft cameo drawing of two pretty girls on the jacket. On the flap were the words of critic Harrison Smith: 'To read it is like listening through a keyhole to a conversation in a harem. There are no reticences. Miss Stead proves once more that she is one of the greatest novelists of our day.'

The novel caused quite a stir. Some critics were shocked; others were outraged. Letty's claim to be a typical New York college girl angered the locals: Mary McGrory in the *New York Times* accused Stead of 'serious misrepresentation': 'All is distorted, turgid and overblown in her world, with sex rampant and passion unbridled.'[24] The communists were predictably incensed.

Stead was grateful to Harrison Smith, who, reviewing the novel in the *Saturday Review of Literature*, found it 'something of a miracle that anyone who was not born in this country should be able to capture so accurately the American scene and the nuances of American speech'. He agreed that there were 'tens of thousands' of Letty Foxes in New York, and added that if Christina Stead was not accepted by 'comfortable people', it was 'because she has touched too closely and too sharply the nerve centres where our conscience lies'.[25]

Letty Fox, her best-selling book to date, sold well over 12 000 copies in the States alone. Stead had at least achieved a *succès de scandale*.

Stead now began something she intended to be a short novel, *The Blondine*. Later called *A Little Tea, A Little Chat*, it became a 400-page novel, and is a scathing portrait of Alf Hurst. Heartily tired of his endless empty promises, Stead told Aida Kotlarsky: 'We have not the slightest faith in him, but we play along with him, why not?' For years Blake had been struggling with this complicated love-hate relationship, but he could not risk cutting contact with Hurst altogether.

Blake was impatient to leave the US despite frightening stories of shortages in Europe. There seemed no choice but to go back into business, at least temporarily, but he believed he had sufficient contacts in Antwerp to make a decent living 'out of commerce and not out of favours'. He was sure he would not have to rely on Alf Hurst.

He left from Montreal in November 1946, crossing the Atlantic on a Victory Ship, as the makeshift converted troop ships were euphemistically known. From Antwerp he wrote to Stead on 26 November:

> The voyage was a beast. Five days of raging tempests and mountainous seas … The narrow seas are sickening: dozens of masts sticking out of the water … dead freighters and troop ships. The Nazis blew up the damned world. We had to have special pilots to sweep and indicate floating mines in the North Sea and the Scheldt …
>
> By this afternoon I am the happiest bugger in many lands. I wandered among the baroque stones and simply adored the city … Come over. We have a wonderful home, a beautiful office in which you can do your best work, a heavenly city, a true, if miserably poor, civilization. Oh, how rich America is!

His 'New York cobwebs' had completely blown away, he told her. 'I am full of ambition and a new youth.' He added: 'As to Alf, just keep him amused and fairly sweet for the present … In any event, in Europe, we will have practically nothing to do with him.' Blake was researching his book on imperialism in Brussels, only forty minutes from Antwerp by train.

'The documentation in Brussels is beyond comparison: for my work it is ten times that of New York, and in saying this I am not exaggerating.'

Stead had a name for Blake's hyperbolic enthusiasms: 'Blakery'. The home to which he referred was one room above Alf Hurst's office. And Antwerp, transformed by the war, was hardly 'heavenly'. Before the war, there had been 60 000 Jews; now there were 3000, Blake told Stead.

Blake had hoped that his friend Edgar Lallemand, previously the manager of Alf Hurst's grain firm and now Minister for Food Supplies in the socialist government, would prove a useful contact, but Lallemand was up to his neck in a ministerial crisis and under daily attack in the conservative press. To his chagrin, Blake found himself waiting for Alf Hurst to return from the States. Moreover, in the Brussels financial world, he kept running into former clients of the Travelers' Bank. (He still had not received a formal clearance from the French courts.)

Stead was tying up ends in New York, her home for the past nine years. She had intended to sail before Christmas, but in mid December Ruth McKenney developed septicaemia as a result of an abortion and was rushed to the Beth Israel Hospital in New York. For a time it looked as if she might not survive. Richard Bransten, hovering anxiously at his wife's bedside, rang Christina twice a day with progress reports. When Ruth eventually regained consciousness, Richard persuaded Christina to postpone her trip and spend Christmas with them at the hospital. She deferred her sailing date until 28 December. Over the next fortnight, she spent hours at Ruth's bedside, deeply moved. McKenney told her that it had been Richard's desperation that had pulled her through.

Stead was waking at 2 am and unable to go back to sleep till dawn. There was the business of packing up. (She sold some of their furniture and gave other pieces away.) She had to say goodbye to dozens of friends. ('We know too many people.') She worried about organising income tax payments before she left. They had money for once: Harcourt, Brace had forwarded her $2700 as an advance for her forthcoming novel *A Little Tea, A Little Chat*, and another $2500 in royalties for *Letty Fox*. (University lecturers averaged $3000 a year at that time.)

She was avoiding Henryk Grossmann (she called him 'Count Chatterbox'); evenings with him were exhausting. She was even avoiding

Ber Green, though she felt guilty about hurting him, for he had proved one of her most helpful friends. At night she was tossing and turning, and taking belladonna for nervous exhaustion. There was only one man she wanted to see, and that was Harry Bloom. He seemed to be avoiding her.

On Saturday, 14 December, the Blooms had a farewell party for Christina. Three days later, she wrote to Bill:

> Mr Bloom, Harry, was an amusing spectacle on Saturday night. He did not smile once, looked grave and even stolid, and did not look at me straight once: reason—he told me EVERYONE thinks he is in love with me and he cannot control his expression, so he did not look at all. It is amusing after all for a man of his age!

Five days after the party, Christina was in a terrible state, and admitted as much to Bill:

> Mr Harry, such a good friend, cannot find time to see me, what a shodheaded scrambled egg he is. He did not even take me to the movies and at the same time, love-love, flon-flon. How annoying he is.

The following day: 'I sent Bloom H. a sizzling letter about his goings-on and did not answer the phone, am angry with him. Harry has NOT come to help me.'

On a Monday evening, five days before Christina was due to sail, Harry Bloom finally turned up, looking like Abe Lincoln, 'a dark, tall man made taller by a dark, tall hat'.[26] He brought steel-strapping and a sealing-machine, and sealed her trunks. Peace was made.

> Poor old Harry—said he rang me 10x on Friday and 6x each other day but I was out. I WAS out—so all my tantrums were for nothing and he said the nasty letter I wrote him should result in my arriving in Antwerp black and blue only he always knew I was crazy.

On Saturday, the day of her departure, Harry Bloom turned up at the apartment one last time. Asa Zatz took Christina to Hoboken, New Jersey. They crossed the Hudson on the Christopher Street Ferry—a service that was to close forever in a few days' time.

In *The People with the Dogs* it is Vera Sarine, a concert artist, who is leaving for Europe just after the war, seen off by a small group of close friends:

> It was a bitter morning, with a fresh breeze sharpening the waves in the river. The ferry slid along by the moored ships and presently they saw the

Victory ship she was to sail on, the Blue Peter flying, faint smoke from the smokestacks. It was a sad gripping sight: for though each had made a promise to see Vera in Europe, part in joke, part in seriousness, and though Vera had promised to return to them next summer ... with the way things were shaping up, as they put it, both in Europe and at home, all felt they might never meet again. Madame Sarine was at home in Europe; and their home was here.

Stead was to travel on a cargo ship, the *Oglethorpe Victory*, with just two other passengers. They were to be at sea on New Year's Day. Just like Vera Sarine's Victory Ship, the boat's departure was delayed. Stead and Zatz went back to New York and spent the day in lower Manhattan, which felt like home to Stead by now. Together they walked the frozen, slippery streets. Asa took her for a last lunch at Luchow's, an old German restaurant she and Blake had always loved. Later that afternoon, at dusk, Asa watched as the ship pulled out into the river, 'black and smoking slightly against the wonderful brocade, the skyscrapers of the city'.[27]

Ellen Butters, Christina Stead's mother, at
first communion, *c.* 1890. (Gilbert Stead)

David George Stead, around the time of his
marriage to Ellen Butters, 1901. (Gilbert Stead)

Christina Ellen Stead, aged two, 1904.
(David Meale and The National Library of Australia)

Left to right: Fred, Peg, Weeta, David and Kate.
(Gilbert Stead)

Sydney Girls High School (1919). Left to right: (back row) Viola Bonnette, Margaret Faram, Florence Quodling, Ruth Hunt; (front row) Christina Stead, Freda Cavell, Tempe Datson. (*High School Chronicle 1919*, Sydney Girls High)

David Stead in Malaya, 1922.
(Thistle Harris)

William Blake (Blech), c. 1928.
(Gilbert Stead)

Christina Stead in the Paris years, 1929-35.
(Gwen Walker-Smith)

Walter George Keith Duncan, late 1920s.
(Duncan papers, courtesy of Hugh Stretton)

Gwen Walker-Smith and Florence Stead,
Sydney 1940. (David Meale)

Christina Stead, Brussels, c. 1937. Stanley
Burnshaw said of this photo: 'It must have been
taken by someone who specialised in making
women look appealing.'
(David Meale and The National Library
of Australia)

Ruth McKenney: Emily Wilkes in
I'm Dying Laughing.
(*Current Biography*, 1942)

Mike Gold, 'The Yankee "tribune of the people"',
c. 1938.
(Elisabeth Granich Humeston)

Ralph Fox — a lifelong passion of Christina
Stead. Fox believed in heroes: 'The heroic
must come back to the novel.'
(Marx Memorial Library)

Harry Bloom, 1950s. (Michael Bloom)

Christina Stead's favourite picture of the older Bill Blake, mid 1960s.
(Ron Geering)

Christina Stead in London, early 1950s. Her
cousin Gwen was shocked by her appearance.
(Ron Geering)

En route to New York and Puerto Rico on the SS *United States*, February 1966. Christina Stead was at the height of her fame. (Gilbert Stead)

Puerto Rico, 1966: Bill Blake was often ill; Christina Stead, bored, drank a great deal of Scotch. (Michael Bloom)

Christina Stead at Heather Stewart's house, January 1983.
(David Meale and The National Library of Australia)

II

From One Perch to Another

January 1947 – December 1951

Christina Stead, a British subject with permanent residence in the United States, was an outbound passenger on the SS Oglethorpe Victory of the Black Diamond Line from New York on December 28, 1946, bound for Antwerp, Belgium.

... A pretext interview with the doorman at 21 East 14th Street, New York City, reflects the information that CHRISTINA STEAD resided at that address until the latter part of December, 1946. She then sold some of her furniture and left for France, and it was the doorman's understanding that she would be gone about ten months. He said further, that she had retained the lease on her apartment ...[1]

For Bill Blake, departing from the States had been a great joy. Returning to the Old World at last, he had thought himself 'the happiest bugger in many lands'. Stead was more circumspect, painfully conscious that she was once again leaving part of her life behind: a pleasant flat in New York, a literary culture, Harry Bloom, friends. Nevertheless, she must have felt a sense of excitement as the boat tossed on the rough seas. She as much as Blake regarded Europe as her spiritual home. It was New Year and a new beginning. After nine years in the States, she was returning to the Europe she loved. The war was over.

But the Cold War had begun; and for Stead, Blake and their communist friends, the term would be terrifyingly apt. The warmth of anti-fascist solidarity was a thing of the past. Publishers were cold about their books; and poverty was chilling.

In the US, the House Un-American Activities Committee (HUAC) and J. Edgar Hoover's Federal Bureau of Investigation (the FBI) would create an atmosphere of subtle terror, menacing everybody who had ever been even remotely connected to the communist party. Leftists departed from the States in droves. Mike Gold, Richard Wright and their families headed for France. The Branstens and their three children sailed for Belgium in the spring of 1947. Henryk Grossmann left for Soviet-occupied Germany.

Stead was in Belgium by the time the FBI started to assemble a file on her in February 1947, after they read in the *New York Times* that the principal character in her novel *Letty Fox* was a young Communist Leaguer. Stead's case did not interest them for long: investigation of her activities ceased in 1948. But the file on Blake, opened in October 1943, when he was on the 'key figure' list in the New York area, was almost 200 pages by the time it was finally closed in 1962.

Replying to Mike Gold's news that her friend Ber Green, editor of *Morgen Freiheit*, was being hounded by the FBI, Stead remarked that Americans arriving in Europe 'draw a big breath, like former escapees from tsarist Russia'.[2] She believed they were fortunate to escape Hoover's frenzies. But she would have her illusions shattered: Europe did not provide the refuge American leftists hoped for. The US government's activities were transatlantic. It was not only in the US that the State Department withheld or revoked the passports of Americans suspected of Left leanings; Americans in Europe lived with the same threat. Stripped of their papers, they were ineligible for work and unable to travel elsewhere to look for work.

By 1947, the United States had assumed Britain's pre-war position of global eminence. The 'Truman Doctrine' made the United States the guarantor of the 'Free World'. America would support 'free peoples' against any 'aggression' that threatened their 'freedom'—an ambiguously formulated policy used to justify the ousting of communists from governments in Greece, France, Italy and Belgium. Similarly, the Marshall Plan, which installed a program of massive economic assistance in Europe, was used as a subterfuge for political interference. Some on the left, including Blake and Stead, were convinced that the 'frenzied American imperialists' were deliberately creating a food crisis in Europe to starve the Europeans into submission.[3]

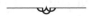

Christina Stead changed after they left the US. She lost something of her fire, her joy in life. From now on, her letters have a different tone: angry, bored, resentful. The expression is careless, as if written with a shrug. Her typing is worse than ever. Rarely do we glimpse the lively correspondent who once took such care over her writing. Occasional gusts of the old warmth blow through these pages, but mostly her letters to friends and family are disconcerting in their coolness.

Stead's fiction also underwent a metamorphosis. Apart from *The People with the Dogs*, a mellow novel conceived in a time of happiness, Stead's post-war fiction is fierce and bitter, devoid of the softer shadings that give relief to her earlier works. The satirical humour has a sharper bite to it. Stead's style, Angela Carter would observe, becomes 'craggy, unaccommodating, a simple, functional, often unbeautiful means to an end'.[4] This does not detract from the power of Stead's fiction. Carter considered that *A Little Tea, A Little Chat* and *Cotters' England* equal, and in some ways surpass, *The Man Who Loved Children*, and that Stead's two British novels, *Cotters' England* and *Miss Herbert*, with their astute analysis of post-war Britain, are far greater novels than Doris Lessing's *The Golden Notebook*.

Stead left the US as a mature writer with an international reputation. At forty-four, she had seven books to her name, which at least some reviewers had called outstanding. During their years in the US, Blake had established his literary career with a much-praised first book, rapidly followed by others. By 1947 (he was fifty-two), he had written three historical novels, an important textbook on Marxist economics and most of an encyclopaedia. However, his last publication in his own name had been *The Copperheads*, in 1941. And now he and Stead were about to have the humiliating experience of one rejection after another—as if they were unknown novices.

There was a book crisis; it was said that with the advent of television, people were reading less. There was a paper shortage. British publishers lacked capital. American publishers, investigated by HUAC and the FBI, had become conservative. Blake's name was tainted by communism. Neither his nor Stead's work was commercially promising. Stead's fiction, angrier, more relentless than ever, did not appeal to 1950s war-scarred sensibilities, which celebrated femininity, family and hearth. From now on, her fiction offered neither moral integrity nor hope. Instead, it confronted readers with poverty, corruption and self-deception—things they preferred to forget.

When they left the US, Stead became subject to a low-grade depression that would prove chronic. She would complain that she could not settle to her writing. She blamed her listlessness on the poor nutrition in post-war Europe, and on their wandering life, which she detested. Always on the move, they were eternally packing up papers and typewriters. They could accumulate nothing. They had no time to make real friends. Stead used her high blood pressure—which she also blamed for her violent blushing and furious angers—as an excuse to stay inside and conserve her energy, and she became housebound, isolated and bored.

Though she did not want to admit it to herself, Stead was profoundly disillusioned. Her thirst to write something so good that there would be 'no denying it on anyone's part' had remained unassuaged for two decades. Reviewers had not appreciated her: some had been extraordinarily harsh— worse, patronising. It hurt. Stead had begun to refer to her writing quite disparagingly, as she had done early in her career. Self-deprecation came naturally to her.

Nevertheless, the late 1940s and 1950s would be productive years for Stead. Despite the lack of recognition and their nomadic life, she could still enter into a state of excited immersion in her fictional world. She told a friend: 'I only think on … the typewriter: and while I foot it restlessly round I am longing to sit down on that little chair … the keyboard tugs deliciously at me and when I put my fingers on the keys I am childishly happy.'[5]

Why then did they spend the next seven years moving from hotel to hotel, if Stead felt she could not write properly in such circumstances? England seemed the logical place to settle; they had friends there and good libraries, and Stead would always feel the need after a time to be enveloped by the English language. But they had never really liked England—neither the English nor the climate. After the war, food rationing there was severe: one egg a week, one ounce of bacon, two ounces of butter, three ounces of potatoes per person. Stead, a committed carnivore who scorned vegetables, was tempted to write a 'heart-rending and very fervent' ode to meat. She was not good at making do with dried eggs and milk and off-ration meat—kidney, liver, heart and tripe. Though petrol and clothes rationing did not affect them, gas and coal rationing did. After a brief stay in London, they would tell themselves that such conditions made sustained work impossible and they would flee. Yet on the Continent they were always searching for cheaper and less dreary accommodation, milder winters, better food, good libraries for research. One after another, each place became an alibi, an excuse for their dissatisfaction. It was Blake who was a wanderer by temperament, not Stead, and it was a point of tension between them.

Stead no longer cared about new places: she wanted a congenial environment to write in, sufficient money to be able to write in peace, and some friends around her. But she had none of these. Blake went for long exploratory walks, sat in cafés and worked in libraries. Stead spent the days beside suitcases and behind her typewriter, 'wedged between the hotel bed and the hotel window', in a succession of tiny rooms all over Europe. She scarcely ventured out, except for evening drinks.

They were both sociable people in their different ways, and they were forced to depend on one another for company to an extent that was good for neither. Without the opportunity to make close friends whom she could love and hate as she needed to do, Stead's life lacked passion. For her this was a deathknell.

When Stead first joined Blake in Belgium, they lived in Antwerp. But they soon moved to Brussels, where they installed themselves in the dilapidated Hôtel George Scheers, near the station. They lived in one room, but were grateful that it was heated.

Blake had not intended to work for Alf Hurst again—Hurst's willingness to engage in war-profiteering had finally disgusted him—but he found himself once again playing Alf's factotum, his 'do-all and net-nothing'.[6] Stead, who had learned hard drinking from the New Yorkers, now resorted to it in earnest to calm her anxiety and keep the incipient dread at bay. Every morning she drank a glass of port and a Luxembourg beer in the hotel restaurant before she went upstairs at 9.30, when their room was done, to work on her novel. When Blake and Hurst arrived after work, they would go to a wine café: Stead would have several drinks, Blake would mostly drink coffee and Alf Hurst would excitedly arrange 'a little tea, a little chat' with some woman. Robbie Grant, in the novel Stead was writing, does the same: 'Ever since his early manhood, since his marriage, he had bought women; most had been bargains and most had made delivery at once. He never paid in advance: "I got no time for futures in women." ' Though Stead was making the most of her dismal circumstances by writing about this Don Juan (once again), she was monumentally bored.

She typed all day long. Her only other pastime was to teach herself Flemish from a conversation book. As she banged away on her large manual typewriter, the hotel cleaning-woman was heard to mutter: '*Est-ce une vie, ça—toute la journée à taper?*'[7] Blake was out all day, doing business with Hurst or examining documents at the Belgian Ministry for the Congo for his book on modern economic imperialism. Some months later, Stead told a friend that she had worked so hard in Belgium she almost had the DT's from writing, and that by the time they arrived in London, in May 1947, she was 'nearly at nervous breakdown stage'.[8]

A Little Tea, A Little Chat was Stead's angriest book to date. Robert Grant (Robbie), a middle-aged businessman who has made his fortune through cotton trading, pursues money and women with equal opportunism. He is arguably the most loathsome character in Stead's formidable collection of dangerous charmers: he certainly has none of the redeeming qualities of other characters based on Alf Hurst. Not a single ray of moral virtue penetrates this seamy narrative, set in New York in the early 1940s. Stead would tell Nettie Palmer defensively: 'I recognise it's not very "nice". It's merely true. Too bad. (New York City in wartime—everyone was not rolling bandages.)'[9]

The Belgian government was unstable. Fearing communist rule and government control, Hurst decided to give up his Grain Union in Antwerp. In May 1947, Blake and Stead left for England. They found London battered and impoverished. Many of the areas they had known and loved before the war—like the Jewish East End—were now desolate blitzed areas, with weeds growing on the bombsites. The railway porters looked so thin and weary that Stead felt ashamed to hand them her bags. Rents were high because of the housing shortage. After the resplendence of New York, London was a real shock.

Labour had won an overwhelming election triumph, but the working class struck Stead as lethargic, more interested in playing the horses, the dogs and football than in Home Secretary Herbert Morrison's announcement that England faced imminent starvation. The women all seemed to have heavy bellies as well as babies in prams.

Blake managed to organise a three-month sublet arrangement on a top-storey flat of a crumbling old house in Primrose Hill. It was close to Regent's Park and two minutes from the zoo, which Stead visited frequently in an attempt to find some inner peace. The shops were further away and Blake, the family shopper, sometimes had to take the bus several times a day to pick up their ration of eggs or meat that had not been available earlier. Feeding themselves was a time-consuming occupation.

Food parcels arrived from Kate and Gwen in Australia. From New York Stead's Spanish friend Pilar Libenson sent three pounds of coffee, though the parcel went astray, and Stead guessed that a customs officer had been lucky. She and Blake sent chocolate, English paperbacks and a subscription to the *Daily Worker* to Mike Gold in France.

London did not feel the same without Ralph Fox, but there were other old friends to see. Stead visited her cousins Jessie and Winnie Martin, now in their late sixties, still living in the same house at Streatham Common. Living in Primrose Hill were Anne and Patrick Dooley, old communist friends, as 'avid, lively, hungry for life' as ten years before.[10] Pat wrote for *Irish Freedom*; Anne, the thin, highly strung Tynesider whose accent fascinated Stead, had just lost her job on the *Evening Standard*; paper shortage forced newspapers to run on a tight budget. There was also Claud Cockburn and his wife Patricia. Cockburn's influential newsletter *The Week* had recently folded, and he was writing for the *Daily Worker* again.

Peter Davies, his wife Margaret and their three sons were living nearby in St John's Wood. Stead was shocked to find Davies pale and sick, suffering badly from the emphysema that had plagued him since he fought in the Somme trenches. It seemed an opportune moment for Stead and Peter Davies to go their separate ways, which they did amicably and to the relief of both. Stead was convinced another publisher would promote her books more effectively.

The Blakes struck up an acquaintance with their next-door neighbours, Mark and Miriam Risner, who would in time become friends. A tailor by profession, in his spare time Mark Risner worked with Unity Theatre, the workers' theatre established back in the Popular Front days. Stead became a supporting member. She was impressed with Roger Woddis' satirical play *Dragnet*, which ridiculed the 'Land of Freedom'.

———— ❧ ————

Edith Anderson had become Stead's keenest correspondent and closest confidante, though they had been only casual friends in New York. Anderson was about to leave for Paris, from where she would try to arrange permission to join her husband, Max Schroeder, in Soviet-occupied East Berlin. Schroeder was flourishing in socialist Germany. A cultivated, knowledgeable man, he had become literary editor at the Soviet-oriented Aufbau Press, and was busy publishing the best of the German exile literature: Heinrich Mann, Bertolt Brecht, Anna Seghers, Johannes Becher, Arnold Zweig.

With characteristic generosity Stead, who had recently received a cheque for the French and Italian translations of *For Love Alone*, sent Anderson $100 to help with her fare. She passed on Ruth Blake's address in Paris, and added that if Anderson should chance to meet Mollie Blech, who was living near Ruth on the Boulevard Raspail, she should not mention their names. 'She hates us both.'

Mollie Blech remained a thorn in Stead's side. She had returned to the Paris she loved, and was working for the Joint Anti-Fascist Refugee Committee—a relief organisation for Jewish refugees. When Stead heard that Mike Gold and Elisabeth had befriended her, she felt personally betrayed. 'I hear they are pals of Mollie now and all sit together in the Dôme: this "Sun Also Rises" set up bores me to rags.'[11]

Their sublet was due to run out at the end of August, and Blake went round to some twenty-five hotels looking for a cheap place to live. Stead was desperate to settle somewhere and do some serious writing. 'We have just hopped from one perch to another since we left the U.S.A.'

In September, they decided to head to southern Europe to avoid the English winter and the food rationing. Stead first went to Paris: she needed more dental work done—this time by their friend Fred Loeffler—and she wanted to see Edith Anderson. Blake had research to do in Basel, where they arranged to meet after a week or so.

It was ten years since either of them had seen Paris, and without telling Christina, Bill had written to Fred Loeffler and given him her arrival time. To Christina's surprised delight, Loeffler was at the station to meet her in his new Ford. She wrote to Bill from the Hôtel Alexandra:

> The last few days (week) of running about after all the formalities made you look tired. I was quite absorbed by that thought and no other and that

you wept, at the station, you know, and so the trip seemed short, for I was only thinking of you.

Entering France, one sees Boulogne ... a terrible sight of rubble; and the factories in all that part blown up, skeletons. All this first part of the trip I felt a sort of fixed horror ... I thought of you, too, all the time and felt a real—heart-pain you could call it—to think you were not seeing it. So I saw it with your eyes. ...

Last night after we had dinner Edith and I walked all through shining, sweet and lively Paris, all the parts we knew all those years and I felt so very gay and intelligent, simply tiptop ... I told Edith I didn't dare really think where I was and about it all for I should burst into tears that you were not there.

Blake and Stead were put off Basel by reports of the harsh winter there, and decided to spend winter in Montreux instead. By early October, they had found cheap and pleasant accommodation at a small hotel called the Hôtel de Londres, with a balcony looking over the lake. Stead was inspired by the thought that Byron and Shelley had lived in the region for a time.

The food, French-style fare, made them instantly feel stronger and fitter. By the end of the year, Stead had *A Little Tea, A Little Chat* ready for Harcourt, Brace, and Blake sent his imperialism book to Reynal & Hitchcock, where his friend Leo Huberman worked as an editor.[12]

At weekends they went on excursions, taking a tram to the Château de Chillon, Villeneuve, Clarens, and walking at the other end before stopping to sample the local wine. They took a steamer to St Gingolph and Evian-les-Bains. It was a beautiful part of the world. But Stead felt restless. She told herself that it was almost as if the place harboured a sinister spirit.

The climate does not suit me at all: it is dull, sedative, yet unnaturally stimulating in an underhand way ... This town creaks into bed at 9.30 ... Even after theatre they scoot home as if the Devil was after them ... I am having a dreadful séjour but can't put my finger on it. We are happy, we are working hard, everything is organising itself, as to work. Well, maybe when winter comes it will be better.[13]

In their isolation, they avidly devoured newspapers and letters from friends. Political news from the States was intensely depressing. A witch hunt had begun in Hollywood. Notable conservatives Walt Disney and Ronald Reagan, President of the Screen Actors Guild, had testified about the communist threat in the studios. Several of Blake and Stead's Hollywood acquaintances—Alvah Bessie, Herbert Biberman, John Howard Lawson and Dalton Trumbo, members of the so-called 'Hollywood Ten'—were fired from their jobs and would soon spend a year in prison for 'contempt of Congress'. Thomas Mann protested that the congressional hearings resembled the first measures undertaken by the Third Reich.

One weekend at the end of October, McKenney and Bransten flew from Brussels to see their adopted son Patrick (Eileen's child), now ten, at an exclusive boarding school in nearby St Prex. To Stead they seemed to have changed. Their rhetoric was as leftwing as ever, but Ruth and Richard had become obsessed with luxury and commercial success. In Belgium, they were living like princes, in a sumptuous house with servants, and had no compunction about buying blackmarket goods.

At Christmas, Patrick Bransten stayed overnight on his way to Brussels, and he and Stead had great fun playing with Nello. They had left their other puppets behind in London in various trunks and depositories, but Stead could not bring herself to part from Nello, the 'wonderful little wooden man' in the yellow pantaloon. In an amusing and ironic story 'Trains', probably written at this time, Joe, a 10-year-old American boy who attends an élite school in Switzerland, is coming to stay for the night with the narrator and her husband. His humorous, overbearing mother writes with detailed instructions.

When a Christmas card arrived from her 'little brother', Gilbert—the first sign of life from him for fifteen years—Christina wrote back, imploring him for details about the family. He and David Darwin had both divorced, but Christina had been told almost nothing. She only ever received polite little letters—'all except the Old Man who of course is a wretched hothead, but at least writes about something real'. These days, he tended to write about 'the Art of being Grandpa'.[14]

One cold day in late January, Stead and Blake returned from their apéritif outing to find a letter from England, which produced a 'wonderful amusing evening' of reminiscences. Stead replied the following day:

> Dear old Firenze, Well, by jove, you could have laid us out with a feather yesterday evening when we returned from cocktailing and discovered your letter. We didn't know it was your letter but as Bill tore the letter out of

my hands (he ALWAYS reads my letters first) your photo fell out and I
positively shouted, 'It's Florence.'

Florence was back in London with her girls, divorced from Pym Heyting.
During the war years in Australia, she and her friend Dymphna Cusack
had written a children's story, *Four Winds and a Family*. Now Florence was
trying to find a London publisher for their thick novel *Come in Spinner*,
set in wartime Sydney. Stead's comment on all this literary activity was
written as a postscript:

> The most important I left out. I am awfully excited about it and simply
> must get a copy of *Four Winds and a Family* ... And as for *Come In Spinner*, I
> know it is asking much, but could I get a copy in galleys? ... I am very much
> interested and fascinated in this; and I have not forgotten one day of your
> literary life in London. You worked so much and with such endurance, and
> hope too, now fully justified. You are really a woman I like, you kept it up
> in spite of family and all.[15]

Reynal & Hitchcock rejected Blake's book on imperialism. Blake was
dismayed: the book was the product of ten years' research and writing,
and he believed it by far his most significant work to date. He was obliged
to send it to Helen Strauss, their New York agent, to have it do the rounds.
Meanwhile, he went to Italy in March to do some preliminary research
for an historical novel on the *Risorgimento*, Garibaldi's movement for
Italian unification. His letters to Stead, still in Montreux, were full of
enthusiasm for Italian life. Hers reveal her concern for him, and express
the self-reproach that seemed to surface whenever she thought about
their relationship:

> Well, sweetie, it seems you are really having a good time for once, and I
> rejoice. You deserve it, you are a poor old mite and you don't have much
> of a good time; especially with the Australian Nasty you are tied up with. I
> hope you are eating something nice old boy, none of your Italian versions of
> hamburger and coffee.

For her own work, Stead was keen to spend time in England. She had been
wanting for years to write a novel about the English working classes, and

the desire was becoming more urgent. She planned to visit the coal-mining area in the north of England with Anne Dooley, 'a splendid girl and pal who knows the working class inside out'. Anne's family, 'pure grind-and-drudge working class'[16], lived in Newcastle-upon-Tyne, the coal town.

The obstacle to the trip was money, and prospects were not promising. A *Little Tea, A Little Chat*, which was due to appear in the States in September, was proving too strong a brew for English publishers, who were not interested in a grim novel about profiteering in wartime New York.

For the first time since 1925, Stead tried the Australian publishers, Angus & Robertson. All she had ever received from Australian sales of her books was the ludicrously small 'colonial fee' offered by British publishers for distribution of the book in Australia. But she had what she considered an 'impudent' reply from A & R editor Colin Roderick, and she was still indignant when she wrote to Nettie Palmer:

> A & R were offered my first book ... by my father ... about 1924 or 1925 ... and this firm has not yet made up its mind to take anything of mine: and who else is there? I consider it disgraceful, and the disgrace is not mine.[17]

Since she could not afford the English trip, Stead joined Blake in Bologna. They were enchanted with the mediaeval university town, where the politics were as red as the local brick. It was early April 1948: the spring was delightful. In Italy, with luxury leather and silk goods in the shops and the pastries in the cafés, it was almost as if there had never been a war. Living costs were about a third lower than in Switzerland, an important consideration. Nevertheless, Stead observed, though the rich were able to 'stuff themselves to death' in Italy, there was genuine poverty: the workers seemed to live on pasta and 'green stuff'.[18]

For the first month, she worked 'like old Nick' to learn some Italian. After that, she took it more calmly. Immersing herself in Italian literature in translation, she was impressed by Natalia Ginzburg, whose portraits of women and families she thought among the most poignant and penetrating she had ever read. She and Blake were elated by the colourful May Day procession, which reminded them of New York.

She had returned to the manuscript begun in New York, *The People with the Dogs*, inspired by Asa Zatz and the Kotlarskys. It bored her a little; she felt she had been 'dabbing' at it for years. But the more likely reason for her lack of enthusiasm was that this mild and affectionate novel did not tap into the stronger emotions—ambivalence and anger—that best galvanised her creative energies. Having finished *A Little Tea, A Little Chat*, she had told herself 'I can't go on criticising', but the truth was that she needed to be worked up in order to write. She told Florence James she was longing 'to get down to a big dramatic subject'. She did not yet know what.

At the beginning of summer they left for Basel, where Blake wanted to examine documents at the Bank for International Settlements. He was revising his imperialism book. Simon & Schuster had rejected it as too 'deep' for their readers. George Joel at the small Dial Press liked it, but decided the financial risk was too great. Angus Cameron at Little, Brown, had said he would perhaps be willing to publish if Blake made some revisions. But he too rejected it in the end. The book that Blake considered his most significant work was doomed never to find a publisher.

Meanwhile he was writing another historical novel, *The Angel*, a fictional biography of Tsar Alexander I of Russia, Napoleon's great antagonist. He sent the completed manuscript to Helen Strauss in September 1948, and this time, the manuscript was accepted in both the US and UK.

Their four-month stay at the Hotel Krafft-am-Rhein in Basel was not a particularly productive time for Stead, who was 'paddling along' with *The People with the Dogs*. She blamed the 'boorishness' of the Swiss-Germans, the endless rain that swelled the Rhine and the lack of meat. Their diet was mostly potatoes, with veal fry or pot-roast once a week.

She again attacked the local language with demonic energy, setting herself the task of learning 200 to 300 German words a day, 'hail or shine'. She was reading the contemporary Marxist critic Georg Lukács in German, and though she found the language a trial, she was pleased with her progress.

A Little Tea, A Little Chat was published in New York in August 1948, the third book in Stead's three-book contract with Harcourt, Brace. The chorus from reviewers was more or less unanimous: 'There are some individuals in whose company one can remain only to a point. Miss Stead takes the reader far beyond that point.'[19] *Time* commented: 'Christina Stead's prose is as hard and cold as a cake of ice. She specializes, with the murderous calm of a hangman slightly bored with his job, in dissecting egotists.'

In June, Florence James had written with the news that *Come In Spinner*, the novel she had co-written with Dymphna Cusack, had won the A£1000 Sydney *Daily Telegraph* literary prize. Stead sent warm congratulations, but she did not write to Florence James again that year. It was Blake who wrote in October, explaining that Christina was busy putting the finishing touches to *The People with the Dogs*. He added that his own book on imperialism had been turned down by several American publishers.

> At the moment in the States the censorship is so violent … that it is hard to place not merely a 'red' or a 'pink' book but any book critical of any value established in God's own country … The amount of liberty in our much touted Western democracies is such that we are seriously wondering whether it is possible for two people like ourselves, both working, and without family obligations, to make a mean living given these circumstances. I would hate to give up writing for a living …

Blake's *Copperheads* had finally been published in England, seven years after its American publication, and was well received by the British Left. But the income was small, and by now Stead and Blake were completely disillusioned with the publishing industry. As Stead explained to her cousin Gwen, English publishers waited to see if the book was a success in the States before committing themselves, and then at much lower author's rates. And the income from the 'colonial edition' was a scandal. Authors' royalties were halved for Australian sales, though the sales were just as lucrative for the publisher. Australian sales of *The Copperheads* had brought the British publisher Cassell almost £400, and Bill Blake a mere £3. Moreover, Stead complained, the publishing industry practised tacit censorship. The English were such 'daffodils' that they could not stomach *A Little Tea, A Little Chat*, and they would be sure to dislike the trenchant novel she planned to write about working-class England.

She and Blake left Basel for Lausanne, and at first were pleased to be back in French-speaking territory, with French cuisine. But Stead was soon bemoaning the dullness of the place. She longed for some interesting social connections to relieve the daily monotony of writing books and letters, cooking meals and feeding the sparrows on their windowsill. There were moments when she actually wished she had some housekeeping to do.

They left Lausanne and its 'milky spring' at the end of April 1949, having decided to give London another chance. Blake went first to Milan to research his *Risorgimento* novel, spending his days in the library of the ruined Palazzo di Brera and his evenings looking up Communist Party documents in the Casa della Cultura. He returned via Basel, where he checked more documents for his imperialism book. Stead went straight to London, taking cubes of sugar wrapped in paper as presents from Switzerland.

When Florence James was in hospital for several days, Christina looked after her daughters, Julie and Frances, now young adolescents. Julie, aged twelve, found her uncomfortable and aloof.[20] Florence herself found Christina much changed: colder, more brittle. For her part, Christina felt closer to Florence again now she was divorced. She told her brother Gilbert that Florence had 'tended to the suburban model matron for a while', but had remained 'one of the best of women' and 'a left type'.

When Blake arrived in London in mid May, he found them a ground floor flat in a large Victorian house at No. 6 Downside Crescent, Belsize Park. For once there was space for their trunks. From Belsize Park Station, it was a fifteen-minute tube trip into the centre of the city, and from their flat it was a short walk to Anne and Pat Dooley in Chalk Farm. The Branstens had left Brussels and were living in Chelsea, 'Hollywood style'. Richard Bransten had a modest job as an editor with a small English publishing firm, but they rented a large, handsome house, all white and gold inside and furnished with heirlooms; they paid exorbitant gas bills, imported extravagant food from the States, Denmark and Belgium, and mixed with the publishing crowd. Stead went there as rarely as possible; McKenney irritated her these days. Blake visited more often. From now on he often saw friends by himself.

Stead complained that London was 'oafish, suety' and 'dull', but she had no desire to leave it—at least not before the winter. She felt an urgent need to 'get some hold on life'.[21]

American publishers, one after the other, were turning down *The People with the Dogs*. Set in New York, it was Stead's most positive, benevolent book: why did they not want this one? Stead felt the despair rising. She told Florence James bitterly: 'I have been a writer, quite unsuccessfully for twenty years.' Yet she dreaded the idea of taking a dull office job, and wanted to make a start on her English working-class novel.

She accompanied Anne Dooley on a brief visit to Newcastle-upon-Tyne, staying with her family, the Kellys. Stead was intrigued by this eccentric working-class northern family who were always at each other's throats: alcoholic 'Pop Kelly' with his 'face of fire', timid and prematurely aged 'Ma Kelly' who had just had a stroke and their plump, dark daughter Zena, in her mid thirties. There was also Uncle Tom, 'a wee bowed man' of seventy-eight, and the black, hairy dog, 'foolish and noisome', who belonged to Zena. From Newcastle in June, Stead wrote to her sister Kate: 'It is a decaying family, you might say. The two lively ones, Anne and Peter, left home, went to London fifteen years ago … Both are now and have been for many years C.P. members.'

Anne Dooley, in her early forties, was tall, thin and garrulous. Her black hair was gathered into a topknot, and with her buck teeth and long legs, she reminded Stead of a marsh bird. She showed Stead the working-class suburbs of Newcastle, the little university town of Durham, the seaside at Tynemouth. After a few days among the Tynesiders, straining to catch every detail of the dialect, Stead was talking like a girl from Jarrow herself. In her letter to her sister, she repeatedly called Kate 'old girl', 'dear girl' and 'poor old girl'.

Stead took every opportunity to see the English working class. She accompanied Anne Dooley's brother Peter to Norfolk, where he was to be interviewed for an engineering job. He liked to talk to Christina about his family and his future, and she found his boyish face and open, caressing manner immensely appealing. She went with Anne to the London docks, where Anne was reporting on the Canadian seamen's strike for the *Daily Worker* under her maiden name Anne Kelly. To see more of the countryside, Stead joined McKenney and Bransten on a weekend car trip to King's Lynn and Norfolk. They were writing an American guidebook on South-East England, undeterred (Stead observed) by their almost complete ignorance of the country. For the most part, McKenney would write all day in their luxurious Chelsea house; she disdained public transport and ordered deliveries of food and library books over the phone.

It was McKenney who did the writing—in the jaunty, personal style her readers loved. She projected herself as a loud and pampered American who found England's smallness cute and its lack of good food and heating deplorable. It was as if she had never been a communist. Her former Hollywood comrades were in gaol, and she presented herself in her Introduction as a proud American citizen:

> *Here's England* is no mealy-mouthed, judicious guide-book; my husband and I are not in the least neutral. We love England; but love has not totally dewed over our approach. Richard and I are American tourists: we belong to the great Solidarity of the Green Passport, long may it wave.

'She got $5000 berries, five thousand, count them, for this bit of embroidery,' Stead told Edith Anderson with envy and disbelief, 'so this will keep the Branstens going for the next week.'

These days, Stead considered McKenney a traitor—politically and morally. As well as planning her novel about working-class England, Stead was now making detailed notes on 'Emily Wilkes' for the novel she was to call I'm Dying Laughing.

Stead had decided she need go no further than the Kelly family for her picture of English working-class life. The Kellys were not exactly *typical* of the English working class: on the contrary, they were 'far from repressed, not at all reticent, very unreasonable, very fantastic, emotionally turbulent and amazingly immoral in an old-fashioned sixteenth century style'.[22] They strangely aroused her emotions—perhaps because they reminded her of aspects of her own family.

No doubt Stead told Anne that she wanted to write about the English working class generally, rather than about the Kelly family specifically. Anne arranged for her to make another visit to Newcastle-upon-Tyne—for several weeks if necessary—to research her novel. Stead decided to go as soon as possible, not wanting to spend winter in that damp region, which had the highest rate of tuberculosis in the country. She left in late October, and stayed a fortnight. At first she enjoyed the family's abrupt manner and appreciated their 'decent simple manners' and cheerful generosity. But the house was cold, food was rationed and she soon found the constant family dramas degrading. The dog tore up a pair of her silk stockings. Zena, she told Bill angrily, was a pyromaniac, selfish and verging on insane. Brother Peter, who visited at weekends from Norfolk, was 'very sweet indeed, but too weak', and this made her 'really angry'. Anyone in their right mind would have fled from that family and that area, yet the parents and Zena considered Peter and Anne 'selfish' for escaping Yorkshire. 'This is insanity! Stupidity! I do despise families.'

Bill, who visited briefly, was worried about her. Back in London, he urged her:

Leave as soon as you think you have had whatever minimum experience you need. Your situation there is so miserable that unless you see a genuine fictional source in staying, come as soon as you can …

Get out of that icebox … Lastly, your old monk is ready to take care of you in every way you think you need him. I am your lover. That is my job in life.

But Blake knew by now that Stead *needed* to immerse herself in the family dramas and work herself up into a rage. It was the way she wrote best.

In London, Blake had given up the large Belsize Park flat and was staying with the Branstens. Even he, with his tolerance and golden heart, was finding 'Emily', as he and Stead now called Ruth McKenney, hard to bear. McKenney was eating ferocious quantities and, too fat to be comfortable in ordinary clothes, sat around all day in her dressing gown. Richard was ravaged and miserable. Blake, after working on his *Risorgimento* novel at the British Library during the day, spent the evenings correcting proofs for the McKenney-Bransten guidebook, *Here's England*.

He eventually found Ruth and Richard all too much and escaped to the Dooleys' attic flat in Chalcot Square. This was scarcely an improvement. Patrick Dooley had just left for Bucharest, where he was going to work for a time for the Comintern. Anne could not decide, from day to day, whether to join him. Blake commented that everyone but Anne herself could see that her marriage was in tatters. Stead returned from the North; Anne continued to dither. Eventually she left, going via Sofia, Bulgaria, from where she was to report to the *Daily Worker* on the trials currently being conducted there. There had been a wave of purges, trials and executions since 1948; Blake, Stead and their friends continued to view the thousands of political victims as ignominious turncoats.

The 'mad excitement and upset over getting Anne off to Sofia' exhausted Stead and 'quite broke Bill down'. Anne Dooley, Stead decided, was a 'human maelstrom'.[23] While the Dooleys were in Bucharest—seven months in all—Blake and Stead occupied their flat.

At her typewriter in the Dooleys' flat, Christina Stead's head was full of the Kelly family. She told Gwen Walker-Smith: 'I am (more or less) engaged in shaping them up for writing—of course at the other end they will come out quite different, but it doesn't matter.' It was rare for her to admit that the creative act inevitably transformed life.

She had set herself an awesome challenge: to capture the atmosphere of the Newcastle region, its physical qualities and, above all, the speech and preoccupations of the Tynesiders. It was her first wholly English novel, and she was plunging into a world as foreign as any she had encountered anywhere. Her interest in languages served her well. Ma and Pop Kelly were old-line Geordies, and Ma Kelly used a 'very complex old style English with pluperfects and conditionals' that Stead had thought occurred only in grammar books. Stead began by trying to record phonetically exactly what she heard, but soon gave this up as an absurdity. 'Dialect novels are a bore.'[24] She decided to aim for impressionistic veracity.

In 1982, British critic Rodney Pybus would claim that *Cotters' England* is one of Stead's great novels, its intense psychological power, dense texture and originality reminiscent of Dostoevski and Lawrence:

> As someone who was born in Newcastle and lived there for a total of more than 20 years I can vouch for the fidelity (more important in this context than literal accuracy) with which the harsh sounds, both guttural and flottal, and sing-song part-Scandinavian rhythms of Tyneside speech have been given form and resonance on the tongues of the Cotters ... All this ... enables Christina Stead to tap the energies of areas of English society still largely neglected in the novel.[25]

Peter Kelly, Anne Dooley's brother, now worked in Norfolk and often came to spend weekends at the Dooleys' London flat, with Blake and Stead. He was that powerful mix of political radicalism and masculine gentleness that always attracted Stead. She told Edith Anderson:

> When I see him on some weekends, I have a delightful feeling that my own brother is around the house. He behaves like a brother too: I mean unobtrusive and dependable and understands everything without being told, but just as if we had grown up together. Don't think I am saying something else: I am saying what is.[26]

Peter Kelly had a close relationship with his sister Anne, and Stead had always tended to idealise the brother-sister relationship. In *For Love Alone*, Teresa feels great tenderness for 'adorable' brother Leo. In *Seven Poor Men of Sydney*, Catherine and Michael are half-siblings who talk of fleeing across the world and living together as lovers. In *Cotters' England*, Nellie Cotter and her brother Tom are so close that neither can have successful relationships with others.

While writing her novels, Stead inhabited a world somewhere between reality and fiction. Now she was imagining Peter Kelly as *her* brother. In order to write about Nellie Cotter, she was projecting herself onto her, even talking like her. For Stead the process of creating fiction from life involved intricate psychological blurrings and layerings.

Christmas of 1949 was an Australian affair. Blake and Stead had a small Christmas Eve party in the Dooleys' flat, with Florence James and her two girls and Florence's co-writer Dymphna Cusack and her partner Norman Freehill. Florence Walker-Smith had sent a rich Christmas cake from Sydney. Nello the puppet distributed presents. The guests were in a buoyant mood: *Come in Spinner* had just been accepted for publication in the UK.

Stead was not impressed by *Come in Spinner*, written for a popular readership. She did not like Dymphna Cusack: neither her socialist moral righteousness nor her commercial success, nor the 'valueless clichés' in her fiction.[27] While she tried to be pleased about Florence James' success, she found it 'a boiling shame' that Blake should have such difficulty selling his 'serious book on imperialism and his good book on Alexander I'.[28]

McKenney and Bransten had invited them for Christmas Day in Chelsea. But Stead 'broke down' after their own party and refused to go. She told Aida Kotlarsky:

> How mean of me. I spent Christmas Day in bed or armchair—and why, goodness knows, there weren't any cocktails to account for it. But I actually had a good time. Bill went, said they had the biggest Christmas tree he has ever seen outside Radio City and Washington Square, also imported delicacies and lord knows what, lots of fun, great excitement. She raised a toast to herself: 'To Mummy who has sold two books!' What do you think of that?

Eighteen months earlier, Stead, writing to Florence James, had called Ruth McKenney her 'dearest American friend, female' and Anne Dooley her 'best English friend female'.[29] Now she was making detailed notes on their characters for novels in which she intended to portray them with all their flaws and contradictions. A few years later, she would be making notes on Florence James.

Stead's attitude towards the friends she wrote about was profoundly ambivalent: one minute admiring and the next vehemently antagonistic. Her oscillation from one pole to the other is reminiscent of the fervent adolescent who was driven to write out of both love and a desire for revenge. One day in January 1950, feeling bored with the 'doormat islanders' who surrounded her (she meant the English), Stead headed to Chelsea 'to see Mme. Gargantua perform'. She told Edith Anderson: 'I laugh at her—I like her, Edith. She is big, noisy, ravenous and alive ... I have a lot of fun when I visit Ruth'.

A year later, Stead and Blake went to see *Jericho*, a 1937 film starring Paul Robeson, about racism and the notion of being a traitor to one's country. Stead—who by then had begun to write *I'm Dying Laughing* in earnest—'wept like a fool'.

> I'd never known until then how far this 'traitor' theme I am treating had got under my skin ... I felt how dreadful dreadful dreadful it is for R McK (the only friend I have in that category) to betray. I never thought her anything but Gargantua, a crazy out-of-size drawing ... (Of course I'm writing about the whole thing, so I'm not normal about it.)[30]

What exactly had Ruth McKenney allegedly betrayed? McKenney was disillusioned with Soviet communism and the dogmatism of Party politics. In Europe, she and Bransten tried to organise an anti-Stalin opposition, which Blake and Stead certainly would have opposed. It horrified Stead that McKenney admired George Orwell, whose post-war novels *Animal Farm* and *1984* made him a treacherous renegade in the eyes of the Stalinists. And she was shocked to hear that Ruth's 'mamma-in-law'— Richard Bransten's wealthy mother—had demanded a list of their friends, wanting to check that no 'reds' were among them before she agreed to lend the couple money, and Bransten had obliged her with the list. In 1952, Stead would comment to Edith Anderson that the Branstens had managed to renew their passports, unlike many of their communist friends: 'I think I would be afraid to know what declarations were made by ONE of them, to get the passports. I have an idea.'[31]

In *I'm Dying Laughing* Stead has the fictional Stephen summoned to the American Embassy in Paris, in April 1950, to name names. He does so and goes home 'pleased because there is no more ambiguity'.

Seventeen years later, when Stead was revising *I'm Dying Laughing*, she equivocated as strongly as ever, commenting to Stanley Burnshaw, who had been a close friend of Richard Bransten:

> I'm re-reading material from the past—and it's borne in on me how much more brilliant Emily was than I make her ... She was very incisive, hardminded, and with—until the end—a high sense of integrity and what

people should be doing as opposed to what they do do. Part of her decline came from that terrific struggle.[32]

———————— ⚭ ————————

Stead was excited about *I'm Dying Laughing*. For the first time since *The Man Who Loved Children*, she allowed herself to hope it would be a great novel, even if she no longer dared hope for commercial success. The subject embodied the kind of conflict she thrived on in her writing: Emily Wilkes, strong and freckled, who likes to say she comes from 'Hix-in-the-Stix' (she is from a small town in Arkansas), marries Stephen Howard, tall, effete, peevish and rich. Both are 'pickled in contradictions'. Their marriage degenerates. Their socialism degenerates. Their preoccupation with money and success as well as freedom and individualism is portrayed as quintessentially American: Emily herself calls it the 'American dilemma'.

Stead told Edith about the 'queer problems' she faced in building up the character of Emily Wilkes: problems that stemmed from the contradictions in Ruth McKenney's own personality. 'They're all real, not invented by me in a nightmare moment.' McKenney believed hummingbirds came from the union of moths and birds, and she would talk of spraying American forests with DDT to kill off the bees, birds and butterflies. She disliked Nature, which she could not control. Although a communist, she loved splendour and high living; there was nothing she liked better than to stuff herself with food in the finest restaurants in Europe. Stead was intrigued by McKenney's 'tumbrils obsession', which seemed to reflect her guilt about her high living.

In the novel, Stead gives Emily Wilkes the same obsessions. The tumbrils image works beautifully as a metaphor: in post-war Europe, the Branstens' pampered existence did bring to mind Louis XVI and Marie Antoinette ensconced at Versailles, indifferent to the plight of the starving peasants.

As preparation for writing, Stead read all Ruth McKenney's letters to her, which dated from the late 1930s. When McKenney was in Connecticut, then Hollywood, she had written to Stead in New York; after the war, they kept in touch. Stead eventually destroyed these letters. We will never know to what extent McKenney's own words were incorporated into Stead's fiction. McKenney, like David Stead, revealed herself so brilliantly in her own writing that it would have been hard for Stead to resist letting her speak for herself.

In February 1950, Bill Blake made a trip to the German Democratic Republic, formally established by Stalin in October the previous year. Henryk Grossmann, now living in Leipzig, had nominated Blake for a lectureship in American literature to be created at the university there. East Germany was depressed and neglected, and controlled by Soviet troops and the Secret Police, but Blake fervently hoped the appointment would come off. He told his daughter Ruth that he was 'mad about living in a country directed towards socialism'.

Leipzig was in ruins, but Blake thought it a lively town, and told Stead he was sure they would find some intellectual life in Germany and that it would be good for their writing. She was willing to take his word for it; she even quite looked forward to it. They had a number of friends in East Germany—friends who had been in exile in New York or Hollywood during the war years. Blake would be in his element as a lecturer, paid to teach and write: he was already eagerly planning a Marxist-Leninist book on American literature. The salary, though modest—1200 Deutschmarks a month, the equivalent of $70 a week in the US—would solve their financial problems. But it all depended on the approval of the Soviet Occupation Authorities.

In East Berlin he stayed a few days with Edith Anderson and Max Schroeder. They lived on the outskirts of the city, and Edith was suffering from the isolation of motherhood in the suburbs. She was unhappy, trying unsuccessfully to write fiction. Max Schroeder was about to bring out Blake's novel *The Copperheads* with the Aufbau Press, and Blake spent his evenings cutting it in preparation for the German translation, called *Maria Meinhardt*. His friends told him the German publication would surely swing his case.

He gave seminars in Berlin and Leipzig—one in English, on Cotton Mather and Puritan American literature; the other in German, on the Italian *Risorgimento*. He wrote to Stead: 'My German is fluent—few grammatical errors. Within a month's study I should be able to lecture better in Gm than I did in Lausanne in Fr.'

But it was a sad trip for Blake. Henryk Grossmann, who had been appointed Professor of Marxian Economics at the Planned Economy Institute in Leipzig, was in hospital, with cancer of the prostate. At the age of sixty-eight, he was prematurely worn out. The years of neglect in New

York had been followed by the shock of Europe after the Holocaust. Blake told Stead: 'When he came back to Europe, he found his ex-wife had been murdered by the Nazis, and son (of 16, of whom we never heard) had been barbarously killed.' While in Leipzig, Blake visited his friend in hospital every day, and came away crying.

By the end of Blake's sojourn in East Germany, the Leipzig lectureship looked doubtful. He did not lose hope for several more months, but in October 1950, the East German authorities finally sent word that although he was a comrade they greatly honoured, the widespread poison injected by the US government had forced them to make a general ruling: not to employ Americans.

———————— ✧ ————————

At the beginning of June 1950 Christina received a tentative letter from her sister Kate. She was planning a six-month trip to Europe the following year, but knew that her elder sister was always on the move and was not wanting to be an imposition. Christina was offended that her hospitality was in question:

> Dearest Kate, Well, thanks for your funny letter. You're very welcome, wherever we may happen to be. I have only had one place in my life where there wasn't a spare bed, it's a cult with me to have a spare bed and an extra plate. So once you get here, we'll take care of you. I only got your letter last night and my first thoughts were, 'Oh, gosh, where are my bachelor friends?' For in New York, where we had a regular plunder of friends ... I always had four or five bachelors ... to get into parties, and even kept one or two as pets—but here![33]

Stead was somewhat unbalanced by the news that after twenty-one years a member of her own family was at last crossing the seas. Her letter must have seemed offputting to Kate, who was now forty-two and had never been a good-time girl. Nor was Stead's reaction to Kate's 'funny letter' entirely reasonable: despite her protestations of hospitality, she and Blake had not had a spare bed for years on end, and when Kate eventually arrived, she would find herself staying in a hotel. In truth, Stead was not good with guests: she desperately needed her own space. She told Nettie Palmer she had become a hermit. 'Friends cause me to scowl for the most part, "get out of my life while I WRITE." You see how disagreeable I am.'[34]

The demands on one's time were something she discussed with Edith Anderson, who was finding that her baby daughter made progress on her novel almost impossible. Stead agreed that it was not easy for women, particularly mothers.

> I guess I wouldn't know how to do it myself. We always talk about having a home when we get to the hotel stage—it's cheaper, it's nicer, it's more fun for me, cooking, than just sitting on a threadbare hotel carpet and tapping away: but the fact is, the minute I'm surrounded by 'the home', even with a man who is not overwhelmed with his own preoccupations in the evening and who even—in one way very surely—lives for me more than for himself, even so, once in 'the home' I get practically nothing done.[35]

The summer of 1950, spent in London, was a trial. After being scratched by a cat, Stead felt exhausted and suffered heart palpitations. She wondered whether it had anything to do with the tetanus injection; only later did she learn that cat scratches can cause debilitating viral diseases. Blake, who had rheumatism, patiently nursed her for two months. By the end of summer, he wanted to go to Belgium, where the food and climate were better. In London, they were about to face the prospect of flat-hunting again: after seven months, the Dooleys were returning from Eastern Europe. ('They don't get on too well abroad—no languages, for one thing. And NO TEA!'[36]) An acquaintance in Brussels had offered them half her house for a time, free of rent. This was lure enough. But Stead regretted leaving London.

> I like it here, I have had some pleasure, some personal approaches, have begun to feel my way about … On the continent, I am in that lonely life which deprives me of that casual contact of friendship which I like and of the intense contact of character-hunting which is everything to me. Bill does not understand this at all.[37]

Once again, they had to store clothes, books and other belongings. Stead hated having to leave her reference books and dictionaries behind, but now that they had decided to move, she was anxious to get it over with. The one good thing about going to Brussels was that McKenney and Bransten had lived there for some months, and Stead would be setting part of *I'm Dying Laughing* in that city.

The Angel, Blake's fictionalised biography of Tsar Alexander I, was published by Doubleday, New York, in June 1950, the week the Korean crisis flared up. Blake was sure this was the reason it did not sell well. In England, it was published the same year by Cassell. Angus Cameron at Little, Brown had accepted *The People with the Dogs*: Stead was sent an advance for which she had waited three years, and they could at last buy some warm winter clothes. There were some changes to make to one section ('A Night in Town'), which Stead had feared might have to be cut. 'Bill is manfully holding back his shrieks while I re-hack Section III. (He doesn't believe in rewriting: it's my only religion.)'

Before they left England, they struck up a warm friendship with Jack Lindsay. Stead had first heard of this *Wunderkind* back in her twenties. The eldest son of painter Norman Lindsay, he had been one of the editors of *Vision*, the Dionysian magazine that had so inspired her in her Teachers' College days. He had left Australia two years ahead of her, and in the late 1930s they had met briefly in the offices of the *Left Review*. Over the years he had proved an extraordinarily prolific writer—of fiction, biographies, books on literature and art.

Stead initiated the contact, asking Lindsay to include her name on a list of Australian expatriate writers protesting against Prime Minister Menzies' new Bill to outlaw the Communist Party in Australia. In mid July they met Jack Lindsay in Lyons Corner House, and talked for hours, over prodigious quantities of red wine.

Lindsay was active in the newly formed Writers' World Peace Appeal, which Stead and Blake had also signed. The Peace Movement, officially not associated with any political movement, was in fact Moscow-inspired, and rapidly achieving the status of a global crusade. Lindsay had just returned feeling very positive from a trip to the USSR. (He had no inkling, he said later, of the Stalinist repressions behind the scenes.) Now he and his wife, Ann Davies, an actress from Unity Theatre, were on the point of leaving for a holiday in Czechoslovakia.

'Is he a lovable chap!' exclaimed Stead, who thought him very like Bill Blake in many ways.[38] They met several times in the next weeks. Stead, walking with Ann Davies behind the men, was warmed by the sight of the 'two short energetic polymaths, excited scholars, borne along rapidly by their legs and whirling arms and their hot exegetics'.[39] She and Blake would write several affectionate letters to Lindsay and would see him again on their return to England, but the first flush of friendship was not maintained.

Blake went by himself to the Peace Demonstration in Trafalgar Square on 23 July 1950. That evening he visited Dymphna Cusack and Norman Freehill to say goodbye before he and Christina left for Belgium. Stead was still feeling weak from her virus, and ventured out only rarely. She did go to Chelsea to say goodbye to Ruth McKenney, who, despite the love for England she had professed in her guidebook, had finally had enough of its hardships. The family was going back to Connecticut.

> She's too tired to fight all the day. Of course, poor us: only central heating, hot and cold, refrigerator, fully furnished with carpets, broadloom style, diamond-cut glass, Belgian wine glasses, pink-bordered and embroidered linen sheets, servant daily etc.—all in—what a pity, we're not in the U.S.[40]

It was, Stead sensed, the end of their friendship. However, Ruth McKenney—with all her brilliance, quirks and hypocrisies—was to loom large in Stead's mental universe for years to come.

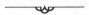

They left for Brussels at the beginning of August 1950. Their apartment was in a house belonging to Miss Hitchcock, an English friend of Mitzi Enders, the one woman for whom Hurst had once seriously thought of divorcing his wife. The affair had eventually gone the way of his others. One day Mitzi, whom they saw from time to time, asked to borrow *A Little Tea, A Little Chat*; she had heard it was based on Alf Hurst. Stead told Edith Anderson: 'She knows "Grant"—knows more than anyone about certain aspects and again less than anyone about others. It's quite a story, I can't tell you in writing.'[41]

What did Mitzi Enders think of the novel? We will never know, but the effect may well have been powerful. In the novel, her fictional counterpart, Myra Coppelius, a small, honest and genteel brunette, humiliated by her physician husband's numerous affairs, falls for Robbie Grant, who is full of promises about a possible future together. When she discovers just how false these promises are, she throws herself out of a seventh floor hotel window. One or two years after reading Stead's novel, Enders too would commit suicide.

Stead had still not completely recovered from her cat-scratch virus, which had been like a severe bout of influenza. When they first went to Brussels, she could do little more than move herself from chair to chair.

After a while, she started to work again. At the end of August, she sent her revised manuscript, *The People with the Dogs*, to Little, Brown. Angus Cameron, her publisher, had written them a woeful letter about the political situation in America. (He himself would be grilled by the House Un-American Activities Committee the following year and forced to resign from his job.) Stead was horrified by it all—and disgusted that Australia under Menzies was following the same path. 'I used to be proud of being an Australian with industrial action and political freedom. Imagine that they now take passports away and threaten jail for mere opinion ... What have we come to?'[42]

Having sent off *The Dogs*, Stead went back to reading and taking notes for *I'm Dying Laughing*. All she wanted was to immerse herself in it properly, but for this she needed to be settled. It would require her complete concentration. The other problem was that a novel about communists (even if the characters were bad communists) was not likely to sell in the United States, so that it was a luxury to spend time on it. She really needed to move on to a less angry and more marketable subject. Blake's novel *The Angel* had brought in a small sum, and the Norwegian translation of his novel *The Painter and the Lady* netted $500, having been voted a Norwegian Book Club choice. But their financial situation was grim.

After two months in Belgium, she still felt weak, and Blake wanted to try the famous healing properties of Swiss air. The trip, via Paris, was tiring. In Paris, Stead, to her chagrin, was constantly taken for a German. Her sedentary life had caused her to put on weight: tall and fair, she did not look like a half-starved *Anglaise*. She solved the dilemma by wearing a pin with an Australian flag.

When Kate heard that Christina had been ill for so long, she offered to give up the money she had saved for her fare to Europe, so that Christina could have a holiday in Australia instead. This generous gesture greatly touched Christina, who was not entirely looking forward to her sister's visit.

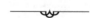

Blake and Stead stayed in the Hôtel Metropole in Montreux, then moved round the lake to Lausanne, where library resources were better. Both needed a good library; they had no reference books at home. Their living conditions were good: two heated rooms on top of a modern apartment house, with a view of the misty lake and the Alps across the water in France. Stead cooked their meals in the kitchen they shared with the landlady. The winter was exceptionally harsh that year, and the landlady kept turning off the hot water. Truman was shamelessly rattling the atomic bomb over Korea, and everyone was worried about a Third World War.

Stead was working on *I'm Dying Laughing*, and managed almost to complete a first draft within the next year. It entailed massive research: reading documents, personal letters and books on contemporary American history, including the recently published and controversial book *The God that Failed*, six accounts by disillusioned former communists including André Gide and their old friend Richard Wright. It did nothing to shake her own faith in communism, but it was useful to know the renegades' viewpoint.

At the same time Stead was taking notes for a short novel based on their experience of the international rightwing expatriates they had met in Swiss hotels. Blake continued to nurse her as if she were 'a sort of hothouse product'. In an attempt to shake her out of the doldrums, he took her to see some plays and films. She told Edith Anderson, 'Dear old Bill is trying to pull me over the rough spots. I expect it's good for me to be treated this way: I expect I'd be climbing the walls in a padded cell if not.' She consoled herself: 'Dostoevsky had a *TERRIBLE* time in Switzerland, and so did Lenin.'[43]

Blake's spirits were untamed and there were times when Stead wondered what strangers must think of them.

> You know him, imitating Senator this and Congressman that, imitating an angry husband and a lying tradesman, and all in the first person … Bill was followed around the street the other night, it was the night when the Truman gang spoke of using the atombomb first—because he was imitating 'an American talking to his wife'—oh boy. I hustled him round the corner: look out, you're going to get HIT … Ai-ai-ai! But I'm fairly hardened to living with 64 plays, all written, produced and acted, and even applauded by Little B.B. I must have NO stage ability at all, for with this life I ought to have written dozens.

So worried was she about *I'm Dying Laughing* never selling that she was working on several things at once. As well as occasional short stories, she was continuing to make notes and plan her novel on England's industrial North-East. Her loneliness and intense immersion in her fictional world plunged her into a strange emotional state. She reproached herself for drinking too much. But she was waiting for a letter from a man. Her diary gives him the code-name 'Elie' and Bill is called 'Walt'—the name of his fictional counterpart in *The People with the Dogs*. She noted that she thought of Elie every day, longing for him—'though without reason'. The object of her obsession was Peter Kelly, Anne Dooley's brother. On 16 January 1951, she noted in her diary:

> In night, sickening feeling of doubt about Elie, why do I send cards he doesn't answer? Felt his sister controls him, must have made mischief, yet all may be sick. He's really only a boy nonentity. Wish I had more friends to forget this maternal obsession, yet misery of their lives bothers me.

On 3 February, she wrote:

> Said to Walt, 'It wasn't the cat that hurt me, it was Elie, he withers and blasts all the women he's close to.' Walt said, 'Cut out that Elie stuff and stick to me, I never did you any harm.' I came back and said 'I love you,' he put his hand on his heart sincerely and said, 'Thank you.' I said 'Are you surprised?' 'Very surprised,' said he, but he kept his hand on his heart.

In December 1950, Blake heard within the space of a week that he had lost two fathers. He had written to his father for the first time in years to congratulate him on his eightieth birthday. Eventually a reply came from his wife in Chicago: Gustavus Blech had died more than a year before, in August 1949, and had been buried in Arlington Cemetery among the national war heroes. Stead mused that physically Gustavus and William were similar, though the father's eyes were 'uncompromisingly field-Marshal blue' and the son's 'Latin brown'. Intellectually, they could not have been more different: General Gustavus Blech had written books about supply-lines and the organisation of field hospitals; his son, also a writer, was a Marxist and pacifist.

The real loss was Henryk Grossmann, who had died in November 1950. 'A release,' his doctor wrote. Bill wept. Christina stayed awake all night, angry with the world. She thought of the tragic lives currently being led by former communists and resolved to show all this in *I'm Dying Laughing*. And she reproached herself for not treating Grossmann as well as she might have. 'Thought of the ugly things I had done to him incidentally, the day he was very wet, I let him stay in the lobby because the flat was untidy, and so on. Horrible. I really have no heart.'[44]

Blake wanted to put together a volume of Grossmann's writings, which he proposed to translate from German. He wrote to Leipzig to ask for information about Grossmann's literary estate. In time, the reply came from Leipzig. The next day, the Lausanne security police, in contact with the FBI, arrived and questioned both Blake and Stead about their 'extremist political frequentations'. What had Blake earned as editor of the *Magazine of Wall Street*? What had Stead been taught in her history class at school? Stead explained that all she did was sit at a typewriter. But she was so dumbfounded and intimidated by the whole affair that she answered politely—much to her regret when she thought about it afterwards. After this episode, they both heartily disliked Lausanne. Before, it had been a 'dull town'; now they were keen to 'quit the wretched village'.

In March 1951 they went to Paris, and from there to St Germain-en-Laye, an old cavalry town, half an hour away by train. Near the huge château, where Louis XIV lived until he moved to Versailles in 1682, was a large forest. Blake and Stead found themselves a modest but warm two-room flat, in a villa owned by an old French army officer, who lived there with his daughter, his servant and her little daughter and a boisterous dog called Yac. But they had to produce three months' rent in advance, and it was more than they had intended to pay.

They worked. They took daily walks along muddy tracks in the forest, with Stead pointing out the early spring flowers. From the upstairs window, she liked to hear the forest 'sigh and rustle' at the onset of evening.[45] At first Blake disliked the large exuberant Greenland dog, Yac—he did not think much of animals—but after a while he took to feeding him remnants of their dinner. Stead wrote a story set in that place called 'Yac, Yac'.

Another story, 'The Captain's House', also gives a good impression of the old royal town that spring, the cobbled streets and high-walled houses. The characters Aldo and Laura are English-speaking guests staying in the Captain's villa: after dinner they go to a café and return about eleven. One night Aldo slips on the stairs and hurts himself: the Captain does not want to call a doctor, because if it becomes known that he has tenants, he will have to pay tax.

Blake was delighted to be back in the vicinity of Paris. After spending spring in the countrified outskirts, he and Stead intended to move to

Paris permanently. 'It's Bill's favourite spot,' Stead told Aida Kotlarsky. 'He really doesn't feel at home elsewhere. I must admit he's tried a lot of other places.' Ruth Blake, thirty that year, and well established as a simultaneous interpreter, regarded Paris as her home, as did her mother. The surprise, when Bill visited Mollie, was that after all this time—Bill had lived with Christina for twenty-two years now—Mollie finally agreed to a divorce.

But Stead was worried about Blake. For once it was he who was tired and depressed. Every day he went into Paris to organise papers for the divorce, trudging from office to office to obtain the stamped approval of various departments. He was anxious to get the case through before Bastille Day, when the courts would go into recess. Stead noted in her diary:

> It is twenty minutes over cobbles to station, he insists on doing all the shopping before he goes, and he walks back at night and I suspect walks all over Paris to save fares and does not eat much.

One evening in a café he almost wept after a liqueur. Alcohol tended to upset him when he was tired. At night he would groan and snore.

In mid March, a general transport strike put a halt to his trips to Paris. Then, at the end of the month, just as the strike was about to be resolved, Blake was incapacitated by a fall. One night, he was 'on his way to the antique invention they think here is a toilet'—in stockinged feet so as not to wake the house—when he fell down the polished wooden stairs. He was in bed for a week and still not quite fit when he resumed his Paris trips in mid April.

Stead was frustrated by the transport strike for another reason. They now heard that Janet Bloom, Harry and Anne Bloom's 22-year-old daughter, had been living in Paris for the past month. For Stead, she was a precious link with Harry, from whom letters came all too rarely. Back in the days when the Blooms had lived at Brighton Beach, Janet had been impressed by Stead and Blake's enthusiasm for French culture. She had ended up majoring in French at NYU.

Stead and Blake invited Janet out to St Germain-en-Laye one Sunday early in April. They were waiting on the platform when the Paris train came in. Stead scanned each passing face. She was looking for Harry's features, and she found them.

A remarkable figure, very tall, slender, dark crop, black sunglasses, flat shoes, graceful large steps … Eyes made up. She looks older than 22, beautiful eyes, colour of her father's, but bigger, husky pure variable voice like H's.[46]

Young women always interested Stead. She told Edith Anderson:

I have been lonely, my loneliness is maternal. I like all kinds of stray young sad people … Daughter of an old friend of mine has escaped to Paris for the old America escape—she's really a nice brave attractive funny naive type … One of my consolations in life is to meet the youngsters of the men who once loved or might have loved me—this letter is not for general use, you see—and to feel very happy when I am with them, because these kids in a way either know or sense that I liked their papa and vice versa and they're so kind to me—it's strange, it's the modern world: I think it very nice of them.[47]

Stead often spoke of her 'maternal' love for others—including grown men like Peter Kelly, or even Bill. She seems to have meant there was an element of tenderness in her affection, an empathy with the person's vulnerability. For her part, Janet Bloom was intimidated by Stead, whose empathy was more a writer's than a mother's.

Later, Stead would hatch the idea of a collection of novellas about 'stray, young sad' women. It would become *The Puzzleheaded Girl*, a collection of four novellas, eventually published in 1968. One of the stories, 'Girl from the Beach', is about 22-year-old Linda Hill, who is modelled on Janet Bloom in the spring of 1951.

The irresponsible children of Stead and Blake's radical friends were the new 'lost generation'. When Janet lived at the Beach in her early childhood, everyone seemed to be a communist, but by the time she was in her late teens, Cold War fever had hit America. Janet, at twenty-two, was something of a dislocated drifter. She felt she did not belong in America, and yet abroad she was totally the American girl. She was wary of French food; her parents sent her provisions from the States. She had been earning money by playing guitar and singing in bars, and when her repertoire of folk songs ran out, she sang the old union songs her father had taught her in her childhood.

That first day, she told Blake and Stead matter-of-factly that she stole 'creamers' (little silver or metal cream pots) from cafés or hotels. She hid them in the deep pockets of her full pleated tartan skirt, intending to take them back to the States. Stead did not say much at the time, but she woke up in the night and said to Blake: 'My gosh, what a bandit!' Eventually Janet's landlady discovered the hundreds of creamers hidden in her room and told the police. Blake and Stead vouched for her, and Janet was fortunate to escape with a reprimand.

Stead did not realise it at first, but modern girls did not like their father's girlfriends any more than girls in her own generation had done. She was to discover that Janet Bloom resented her complicity with Harry. Before leaving for France, Janet had come across several letters from Christina to her father, in which Christina made a casual reference to his female friends. For Janet, it had been a terrible shock to discover that her father had dallied with someone other than her mother. She 'adored' her father, finding him more interesting than any of her boyfriends.[48]

According to Janet Bloom, the details in the novella are extraordinarily close to the facts. Her mother, Anne Bloom, was outraged. Janet herself was flattered by the attention: Stead's knowledge of her, she admits, was astounding. She showed the story to her psychiatrist, who was equally awed by Stead's perceptiveness.

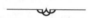

Stead, always interested in the relationship between fathers and daughters, was disconcerted to discover the power her own father could still exert from across the world. It all came back when she saw her sister Kate.

At the end of May 1951, Stead and Blake returned for a few weeks to Brussels—probably for residence reasons. Kate arrived in London and stayed with Florence James and her daughters; then in early June, she took the boat to Antwerp. Christina had sent her three closely typed pages of instructions about currency, tipping, food on the train, how to reply in French to the customs officers. One paragraph was 'How to recognise us'.

> A smallish roundish whitehaired man with big brown eyes, and me, same brown wig, same smallish suspicious greyish eyes as before. I'm a bit taller than Bill. Will probably wear a brown suit of British cut (feel like saying alas to that) and a very colourful large scarf which I may wave, if I think it right. Bill has a big big grin, me a strained expression.

Kate was nineteen when Christina left Australia, but on the railway platform in Brussels, Christina recognised her sister instantly. Small, thin, wiry and dark-haired, she looked just like her mother. Ada had been forty-nine when Christina left Australia: Kate was now only seven years younger. Christina told Gwen, who was very close to Kate:

> The old Kate was not there. She is someone different, altogether different, with a number of Mother's traits—it's quaint. Kate spent a few days with us here and then went off to Switzerland, having so much to do and see in so short a time and so short a purse. But she is managing very well, quite unusually so, is very self-reliant and quick: she seems to have a taste for language: it is a pity she had not learned one or two. Certainly she has no foolish embarrassment, but is quite lively and comes forward, smiles, makes a pleasant impression and is quick to make friends.

Kate spent a few days in Brussels, staying in a hotel nearby. Then she left for Montreux, with two more pages of typed instructions. The three had arranged to meet in Paris in July.

Soon after Kate's departure, Christina had a letter from Gilbert announcing that Ada had died. Christina worried that Kate would want to catch the first boat home. They decided that Bill should go on ahead and break the news to her. When Christina arrived later, she also fussed over Kate. But Kate took the news with fortitude, saying she had almost expected it.[49] Ada was seventy-two and had always been frail: her children never thought she would reach that age. Moreover, she had been ill and mentally confused for some time.

The Paris holiday was not a success. Bill so wanted Kate to love Paris that he flooded her with explanations and details. The sisters were tense with one another from the outset. They had no interests in common. Kate was unmarried and worked as a machine telegraphist at the Sydney GPO: Christina could regard her 'spinster-dom' only as a 'defeat', and her letter the previous year about not knowing available bachelors suggests that she would not have been entirely tactful on this score. Kate's lack of curiosity about European history appalled her. And she was irritated (according to the fictional notes) when Kate, sitting in a French restaurant, would say things like: 'I'm waiting to go back to England to have some oats, some porridge. I miss my oats.' She and Blake wanted her to dislike England and love France, just as they did.

Kate was also not without ambivalence towards her sister: she disliked Christina's books ('terribly wordy') and had not been at all happy about some of the family details in *The Man Who Loved Children* and *For Love Alone*—and no wonder. In *The Man Who Loved Children*, dark-eyed Evie, modelled on Kate, is the one child Louisa openly dislikes. Evie is her father's pet, and Louisa cannot stand the feminine wiles and the 'dolly voice' that the little girl cultivates to please him. In *For Love Alone*, Kitty, younger, prettier and more docile than Teresa, is once again the daughter their father prefers.

From thinly fictionalised accounts among Stead's surviving papers it is clear that Kate was impatient with Blake. She disliked his loudness, his verbosity, his mini-lectures. In Stead's notes, Meg hurts her older sister Sally (a writer) by telling Sally that her companion Tony is just like their father.

> He's like Dad because he's always saying a thing's the best in the world, the finest in the world, the greatest in the world … I can't stand it when someone is always boasting that something is the best in the world. It makes me boil.[50]

Later there is a bitter exchange between the two women:

> 'He's just like Father and that's why you yes him. You yes each other. You have no independence.'
> 'Well, I didn't yes Father.'
> 'Oh, you understood each other.'[51]

If this conversation ever took place, Christina would have found the situation very painful. She was fiercely proud of Bill, and she depended on him heavily to act as social mediator between her and the world. It is significant that he was the one to go ahead and tell Kate the news of her mother's death. But Christina herself must have realised that Bill had several of her father's qualities. Both were autodidacts with extraordinary energy and enthusiasm; both shared a love of language, both had fine, melodious voices, both had a tendency to be know-alls, both exaggerated. Bill dominated conversations; his need for attention drove even Christina mad at times. So the spectre of their father came between the two sisters in the form of Bill Blake.

Moreover, in the fictional notes, Meg tells her older sister: 'You went off without thinking of us. I could have done what you did but I was not so selfish. Poor mother slaved for you and you went off like that.'

After Kate left Paris, Stead was still tossing at night in anguish. In her notes, 'Sally' says to 'Tony' in bed: 'I am living through agony: why is it?' A few weeks afterwards, Stead confided to Edith Anderson: 'I was heart-sick,

sick, and feverish for ten days. What a haunt! To no one but you and Bill would I dare declare this effect of a sister.'[52]

Stead and Blake stayed on in Paris for several months, living in a series of hotels. Stead had completed a first rough draft *of I'm Dying Laughing,* but calculated that she needed at least a year to revise it. She felt obliged to put it aside now and write something that might sell. But it was like putting aside a love affair: it meant losing the original rapture. When she did eventually return to the novel, it had gone slightly stale.

Stead dreaded taking a job and rationalised that her real earning power lay in writing: the sale of a book could keep them for almost a year. She was working on novellas, hoping to finish a volume more quickly this way. But *The Puzzleheaded Girl* would not be published for another fifteen years.

From Australia came the news, in June 1951, that communist writer Frank Hardy, author of *Power Without Glory,* a semi-fictional novel about the millionaire Melbourne businessman John Wren, had just been acquitted after a nine-month court case for criminal libel. The case had caused a national sensation. Jack Lindsay and Dymphna Cusack, who supported Hardy's case, sent the book to Stead. She admired it and was delighted that Hardy had defeated the libel laws, 'the gag that has ruined English and Australian literature, the privilege of the propertied and the corrupt'.[53] Since she herself risked libel charges with almost every novel she wrote, Stead was adamant that libel laws were a sham.

There was family news from Australia too. On 30 June 1951, the same month that Ada died, David Stead married Thistle Harris at Boongarre. He was seventy-four; Thistle was forty-nine, the same age as Christina.

In her will, Ada Stead had left her children £300 each—her *own* children, that is. There was nothing for Christina. It was a cruel gesture, for Christina had never enjoyed any benefits from her own mother, and it provides a glimpse of the exclusion to which she had been subjected as a child. Kate Stead, who had just returned from her trip abroad and could doubtless have done with the money, immediately offered to share her inheritance with her sister. Stead was all for turning it down, but she and Blake needed the money so badly that she was obliged to swallow her pride and accept the offer. Kate sent the money to England. As a British resident, Stead was not allowed to take money out of the country. And so, in December 1951, feeling as emotionally buffeted as ever by her family, Stead once more left with Blake for London.

12

Literary Hacks

December 1951 – December 1959

B ACK IN LONDON, they stayed two months with Mark and Miriam
Risner, generous communist friends who had a spare room at the
top of their house in St John's Wood. 'A dark, dank weary town it
is,' Stead told Gwen Walker-Smith.

Money was so short they felt they could hardly even afford to see
friends. 'Friendship is next to impossible in London—it takes half the
night and too much money for anyone to travel to dinner.'[1] McKenney
and Bransten had returned to the US. Stead had fallen out with Anne
Dooley, who had implied that her writing was 'trivial paperwasting'.
Peter Kelly had told Stead things that did not warm her to Anne. Later
she would tell Ron Geering (using the fictional name as she always did):
'Nellie [Cotter] seduced her brother and sister to sex, when they were
little.'[2] Rightly or wrongly, she had decided that Anne was a lesbian,
and she did not conceal her irrational animosity towards homosexuals,
particularly women.

In January, they went to dinner at Jack and Ann Lindsay's and met Guy
(R. G.) Howarth, a visiting Australian from the Department of English
at the University of Sydney. He was the founding editor of *Southerly*, a
quarterly literary journal that since the war had focused on Australian
literature. Not having access to the magazine, Stead would not have read

Howarth's recent (1950) review of Patrick White's novel, *The Aunt's Story*, which concluded:

> Christina Stead having committed formal suicide, Patrick White challenges Kenneth Mackenzie as the most expert Australian stylist in the novel … It is gratifying to know that, after his war service and European wanderings, White has now returned to settle down in his native country.

That January evening, Howarth, moved by Stead and Blake's obvious financial hardship, encouraged Stead to apply for an Australian Commonwealth Literary Fund Fellowship, worth up to £600. He even checked that she was eligible, residing as she did in England. She was, for she still had an Australian passport. He also asked her for a story, and a few months later published 'The Hotel-Keeper's Story' in *Southerly*. Stead was grateful for speedy payment.

The friendship with Guy Howarth would become strained in 1958 when Howarth, who by then was Professor of English at the University of Cape Town, wrote a chatty article on Stead for *Biblionews*, the magazine of the Book Collectors' Society of Australia. In this he wrote that he had met Stead and Blake in London and discovered they were puppet enthusiasts. He understood that they assembled their cast of puppets 'to act the plot out' before Stead started writing—an approach that might explain the 'relative planlessness and formlessness' of her novels. He added: 'Any such composition of course benefits from the jolly or caustic contributions of the irrepressible Bill.' Stead would write back in high dudgeon:

> The notion that I just sit down and write my novels without knowing what I am going to do next, is so untrue, and even ridiculous, especially to me, considering how I sweat blood over them and write and rewrite and rewrite and that I make for each one a thousand plans … that I feel quite annoyed.[3]

In February 1952, not wanting to impose on the Risners any longer, Blake and Stead moved to a cheap room in nearby Woronzow Road. The house looked pretty enough from the outside—painted white, with a little green balcony, and just around the corner from exclusive St John's Wood villas. Inside, it was 'a disgusting slum', with 'the dirt of generations'. The landlady was a 'frightful old monster' who looked capable of murder. The carpet reeked of her tomcat.[4] The thin blankets were dirty. (Stead and Blake had left their bed linen and typewriters in Paris.) For water, they had to go upstairs to a freezing bathroom, and they were forever putting shillings in the meter for gas and electricity.

An Australian journalist friend, Anne Matheson, who worked for Consolidated Press, arranged for Stead to work in a heated office in Fleet Street during the day. 'By the time I got there,' Stead told Edith Anderson afterwards, 'I felt as if I could not live any more; the old sinking feeling.'

It was while they were living in that dismal 'hole', with Stead fighting off severe depression, that Blake and Stead eventually married. The bitter irony of it all would not have been lost on Stead. She had waited twenty-three years for this divorce—for years she had longed for it—and now, when the final decree came through from Paris, their conjugal life had sunk to its lowest ebb ever. The French divorce proceedings had been slow. The non-conciliation order had gone through in June 1951; the Prefecture de la Seine ruled the divorce on 17 October (naming Mollie Blech as the wronged party), but the certificate was not finally signed and stamped by the French Civil Authorities until 14 February 1952. Soon after receiving it in the mail, Blake and Stead went off to the St Pancras Registry Office. They were married on 23 February 1952. The groom was fifty-seven; the bride was forty-nine. The witnesses, G. Banks and A. Oxley, were probably Registry Office employees.

Six years earlier, Stead had portrayed the wedding of Teresa Hawkins and James Quick in *For Love Alone*. It was prescient writing: the fictional marriage is described as one of those 'lonely distant unions known to wanderers'.

> The wedding ceremony means nothing, the man is there before and there after, he and she have looked after everything themselves. The witnesses are two street cleaners and a messenger boy. They take a bus or taxi and eat their wedding breakfast alone ... The whole move is made in the heart of a great city, where no one knows whether they were united yesterday or last year.

What did marriage mean to Stead after all this time? She did not mention the ceremony in her letters; it no longer had any romantic connotations. She had become a married woman too late to enjoy the psychological security marriage would once have brought her. Mollie Blech was no longer a threat. Children were now out of the question. She was beyond caring about the social stigma of separate passports in hotels. There was a time when marriage to Bill Blake would have facilitated her residence status in the States, but she had no interest in an American passport now, and as a communist, Blake himself was in danger of losing his American citizenship. On the other hand, Stead's Australian passport, which gave her automatic British residency, conferred residency rights on her husband.

The marriage in *For Love Alone* is a cheerful, even if anonymous occasion. Was theirs? On that drab February day, as they returned to their dreary lodgings without so much as a marital bed, a cosy lamp or a writing desk to call their own, Mrs Blake, as she liked to call herself, must simply have had a leaden heart.

She was torn apart to see 'poor dear Bill ... calling round hopelessly to 101 places' looking for work and getting nowhere.[5] As a foreigner, he was not legally entitled to work in England. And when Stead scrutinised the jobs for women her age, she despaired.

> England is stuffed with very well-educated women, Cambridge, Girton, all that, who are struggling for the meanest jobs: there's a terrible unemployment of that sort. You can get matron's jobs etc. but very often it's next door to au pair and always live-in. But I'm a married woman.[6]

Because social security premiums were higher for older people, employers preferred applicants below forty. Stead was about to turn fifty. And though they dyed Blake's hair to make him look younger, they could not conceal the reality. Their only consolation was the bitter one that their situation was shared by thousands of talented Americans both at home and in Europe—'really brilliant people who were best-sellers who now do not know where they can eat'.

Stead advertised herself in a newspaper as a writer looking for work. Not surprisingly, it produced nothing. Blake believed they should stretch their money for a few more months and try to write something that would sell. Stead retorted, 'That is what has ruined us!'

As Stead told friends, she could have produced much faster if only they could afford a professional typist to do the final draft. She saw the issue as one of speed, but in fact the constant rejections she was now encountering from publishers may have been due in part to the dreadful presentation of her manuscripts. Viking publishers had had to re-type *For Love Alone* before they could read it. Stead was terribly impatient with what she considered a vacuous obsession with presentation. To her, publishers seemed 'like schoolteachers' when they returned her manuscripts with the comment that the typing made a bad impression. She felt like retorting: 'But what about the BOOK, you nitwits!' When she asked for her manuscript back after the publication of *The People with the Dogs*, an editor at Little, Brown had the 'insensate pertness' to write to her: 'Your MS. is in a very dirty condition and I hardly think it is worth keeping.'

Typists were expensive; furthermore, they were 'so spoiled' these days that one or two had even refused to work from Stead's drafts. This problem was a constant lament in letters. She told Edith Anderson: 'I've got such stacks of stuff, but by James, they want everything so beautifully typed these days that I don't really know what we are going to do. Look at the outlay before we can even send things in for their lordly approval!'

She and Blake talked of escaping to the Australian sun, but they did not have the means. The fare was high, and so was the cost of living there. Australian law, unlike British, discriminated against women in that marriage to an Australian woman did not entitle her foreign spouse to Australian nationality or right of residence. As an American, Blake needed £400 and a return ticket in order to stay six months, as well as a clean bill of health— which also had political implications. (Kate Stead's political credentials had been checked by ASIO before she was granted leave of absence to go overseas in 1951.) Stead was not convinced that Blake would like life in Australia. She told Nettie Palmer, 'He even gave up USA for Europe so I don't believe all my charm stories about Manly and Newport etc. would compensate. Besides, how would we make a living? It's impossible. It's a pity though. I'm getting tired of this lifelong wandering.'[7]

She herself had mixed feelings about Australia, which was scarcely surprising, since Australia felt the same about her. She found the country parochial and culturally on the defensive, yet she angrily repudiated any notion of an Australian sense of inferiority. Nettie Palmer had recently sent her two 1950 issues of the cultural and literary magazine *Meanjin*, thinking they might be of interest to her. Stead wrote to thank her, but confessed she was irritated by Arthur Phillips' article 'The Cultural Cringe', which argued that Australian writers and artists suffered from 'the centrifugal pull of the great cultural metropolises'. Stead told Nettie Palmer that in her early years in Australia she had only ever encountered 'an honest ... hatred and contempt for the seat of a vicious Empire'. If the 'cultural cringer' really did exist, was he perhaps 'the Menzies type of Australian?' she asked. But she was missing the point.

In the same letter, she had asked Nettie Palmer if *Meanjin* would be interested in a regular 'Letter from Paris', where they would soon be living again. (Dymphna Cusack's recently published 'Letter from London' had made Stead ashamed of her own inertia.) Nettie Palmer replied that she had no formal connection with *Meanjin*, so Stead should write to the editor, Clem Christesen, but she suspected there might not be space for a regular Paris Letter. Stead (who had just railed against the idea of European cultural metropolises) privately thought this 'silly and even mean'. Furthermore, she was insulted by Nettie Palmer's comment: 'I always meant to write something about you, but never seemed to get round to it, though I do sometimes unexpectedly drop a mention of your books into the middle of one of my lectures.'[8]

Stead was angry about many things these days, and would have been even more upset had she read Nettie Palmer's account of their 1935 Paris meeting in *Fourteen Years*, Palmer's diary, recently published by the Meanjin Press in Melbourne. Palmer made it seem as if the elegant Christina Stead was obsessed with hats and fashion. This was a tragic irony: Australian readers could scarcely have been given a more false impression of her current circumstances. How far away the Parisian Christina Stead seemed now!

In early March 1952, the Blakes left for Paris, buoyed by hopes that Stead was to be given work at UNESCO. In three months in London they had had no success with finding work, and had merely spent Kate's precious inheritance. But they had been introduced to an Australian, Mr Bellew, who worked in the cultural section of UNESCO, and he had assured them that 'nothing would be easier' than finding Stead work at UNESCO in Paris. It was arranged that they should come and see him in March, when he would be back from a holiday in Australia.

They crossed the Channel thinking their troubles were over. But Mr Bellew did nothing for Stead: he merely palmed her off on to someone else who also could not help. 'Bill was terribly upset,' Christina told Edith Anderson. 'Me too. We were ruined.'[9] Every expense was now 'lifeblood'.[10] They spent the next few months in Paris moving from one cheap hotel to another—a 'shifty life' brought about by a new rental law that, aiming to protect tenants, decreed that hotel rates should be lowered for clients staying longer than a month. In practice, it meant that hotels accepted clients only on a short-term basis.

Ruth Blake thought she could find them enough translation work to keep them going, but she managed to find only two small jobs for her father. In their anxiety about money, Blake and Stead were overworking: it was not proving productive. Unable to concentrate with Stead banging away on her typewriter in the same room, Blake worked at Ruth's during the daytime.

Friends of Ruth sublet their apartment cheaply to the Blakes for the three summer months. It was in a working-class district in the east of Paris. Stead was overjoyed to have a 'home' again, and admitted to Florence:

> I spent two and a half blessed days doing housework, cooking, washing, and all the other things that you itch for when cooped up in one small bedroom in a hotel, the rest of the time tramping the streets or sitting in cafés, to pass the time until lunch or dinner or bed.

Food was plentiful again in France. On fine summer days, they would sometimes walk to the nearby park, taking a picnic with the treats they so missed in England: ham, pâté, black olives, brie.

Blake had two manuscripts doing the rounds of publishers in the US. The problem, as he saw it, was that if a book contained 'even contingent praise of any communist character' or if it did not show 'intense enthusiasm for the American way of life', it was not acceptable to publishers. Several publishing houses had been 'assailed by the McCarthyite barbarians', and most had become conservative and censorious. Yet—he told himself— Arthur Miller and Nelson Algren were still managing to be published: it was not completely impossible for left wingers.[11] However, neither his imperialism book nor his *Risorgimento* novel would ever find a publisher.

Stead admired Blake's courage. He rarely descended into self-pity, and he never stopped working. She was finishing the short novel she had begun in Lausanne in 1950, *Mrs Trollope and Madame Blaise* (later *The Little Hotel*). Set in a modest Swiss hotel in the late 1940s, the narrative focuses on an eccentric group of characters, a 'sad lot of scarecrows', trapped by their fear of commitment. (The mature Stead was no longer celebrating the unattached, free and easy wanderer.) Mrs Trollope complains to her companion Robert Wilkins, 'At times you seem to me a complete stranger. I am living with a stranger.' He replies: 'We all are.'

Mrs Trollope and Madame Blaise was close to completion in May 1952. 'Perhaps Little Brown won't take it,' Stead told herself anxiously. 'They're so very moral … And who cares about Switzerland anyway?'[12] It was probably an untidy manuscript that she sent to Helen Strauss, who wrote from New York that she did not much like the novel and doubted whether publishers would be interested.

In July 1952, Clem Christesen wrote to Stead inviting her to write a Paris Letter for *Meanjin*. She had offered it, in need of money, but it was not the sort of article she liked to write. Stead left it until the September deadline fell due before eventually sitting down at her typewriter and producing two and a half untidy pages. She told Christesen that since her letter was late, he should take it as a personal letter to him. Christesen, who had no time to clarify what she meant by this, plucked out a lengthy extract and printed it in his editorial column as a letter he had received from abroad, without attaching her name to it. He wrote and thanked her warmly and suggested she write another—next time an open letter that he could attribute to her. Stead was dismayed at not being paid. She was not to know that *Meanjin*, regarded as a socialist journal, had its government subsidy cut in half that year and that Christesen had already put in £2000 of his own money.

Stead's 'Letter from Paris' was such uninspired polemic that it is surprising Christesen asked for another. She wrote mostly about the Camus–Sartre controversy—the talk of Paris that summer. But the article was muddled, and too prejudiced to be good journalism. It expressed impatience with the 'backyard quarrel' of the two Existentialists—both of whom she regarded as anti-communist.

This was quite misguided. Indeed, the issue of communism was at the heart of the feud. In his latest book, *L'Homme révolté*, Camus had taken a stand against Stalinism and condemned Western intellectuals who remained silent about the Soviet forced labour camps and the show trials in Eastern Europe. Sartre, on the other hand, had moved toward the Communist Party and his journal *Les Temps Modernes* advocated solidarity with Soviet communism.

Stead explained none of this. She merely scoffed that Existentialism was a 'middleclass movement', representing 'normal postwar pessimism'. She had nothing good to say about Jean-Paul Sartre:

> Sartre is a smart pedlar with a few varied goods in his pack, he is not selling any of them particularly, till he sees which line takes, and so he offers tears

for the poor, home-truths, the wickedness of French colonial policy, Soviet oppression of the Turkmens, and so on, a remarkable stream of bright rubbish.

Camus, she grumbled, was leaning towards mysticism.

Arthur Levy, an Australian working in UNESCO in Paris, told Clem Christesen that Stead's piece was 'hopelessly inaccurate', whereupon Christesen asked Florence James: 'By the way, could you tell me what are Christina Stead's politics?'

Stead had not yet registered the strength of anti-communism in the post-war world. She did not seem to realise that a pro-communist 'Letter from Paris' would reflect badly both on herself and on *Meanjin*. Her naivety in this respect is surprising, for along with Jack Lindsay, Florence James and Dymphna Cusack, she had become a member of the newly formed Australia & New Zealand Civil Liberties Society in England, in which anti-communism was frequently discussed. The Society made formal protests about such matters as censorship, the position of Aborigines and Maoris and the confiscation of alleged communists' passports. Meetings were usually held in the congenial atmosphere of the Bull and Mouth, in Bloomsbury.

In September 1952, just three days before she sent her Paris letter to Clem Christesen at *Meanjin*, Stead sent off her application to Australia for a Commonwealth Literary Fund Fellowship. She could not have applied at a worse time. In February that year, Robert Menzies had instructed the Australian Security Intelligence Organisation (ASIO) to investigate the political colouring of all writers applying for grants. ASIO had opened files on numerous writers—Katharine Susannah Prichard, Vance Palmer, Judah Waten, Eric Dark, Frank Dalby Davison, Jean Devanny, Stephen Murray-Smith (editor of *Overland*), Nina Christesen (Clem Christesen's Russian wife) and Christina Stead.

Stead heard in November that her application had not been recommended. Neither her communist politics nor her residency abroad would have helped her case. But the more likely reason for being knocked back was that her application simply had not impressed the committee. She had sabotaged her chances of success with an extraordinarily badly presented application, obviously written in haste. Her project outline, typed onto the official Commonwealth Literary Fund form, was inchoate notes, marred by clumsy expression and crossings-out. Although the subject she proposed was extremely interesting—a novel about immigrants to Australia, set in Europe and Australia—she portrayed herself as a kind of dilettante.

Her referees further weakened her case. She had nominated her old Psychology supervisor, Dr Gilbert Phillips, now Principal of the Sydney Teachers' College, but he was ill and told the committee he would forward his reference later. Another referee was Stead's old university friend Marie Byles, a well-known Sydney barrister, who told the Committee that she was aware of Stead's international reputation, but she herself was no novel reader and had scarcely read Stead's work. Only their 'onetime friend' E. W. MacAlpine, now Editor-in-Chief of the conservative Sydney *Daily Telegraph*, produced a reference that was at all persuasive. Faced with this embarrassing situation, Thistle Harris, whom Stead had asked to collate the application, hastily asked Sydney author Eleanor Dark for an additional reference. Dark wrote a brief but generous reference; however, it would not have helped that her husband Eric was listed by ASIO as a leftwing subversive.

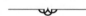

When the Paris sublet ran out in September, Stead and Blake moved to Brussels. These days, in order to stay longer than six months in France, they needed residence cards. For this they had to prove financial resources, which they could not do.

In Brussels, they had hoped to stay a second time in Miss Hitchcock's house, but in winter, with the high price of coal, she had to charge more than they could afford. They found accommodation at the Hôtel Junon. On the front door was a lead-light picture of Juno, 'powerful and half naked'. The ground floor was a tavern with drawn curtains. They did not at first realise that it was a 'half and half place'. But the amorous goings-on did not affect them. The hotel was quiet and warm, and the furnishings—dark blue velvet curtains and peacock blue wallpaper—were sumptuous. There was stout clean linen every two days, and it was cheap. Stead made friends with the room-maid, Louise, a young Jewish woman from whom she heard the 'inside stories'.

Stead's English agent, David Higham, wrote to say he could not sell *The People with the Dogs* in England. (British publishers were put off because *The People with the Dogs* had sold badly in America—fewer than 3000 copies—even though it paid affectionate tribute to New York City.) Stead was disgusted: 'What a jellyfish he is.' She felt like reminding him that she had published nine books in the States and seven in England, and that the two not published in England were the two he 'shepherded to a miss'. Nor had he been able to find a publisher for *Come in Spinner*, which had since sold upwards of 48 000 copies. But what was the use of saying so?

Brussels was a lively city; Stead liked it, but the autumn days seemed grey that year. In Belgium, the 'two months rule' applied: after this time they either had to leave or acquire official residency papers. In November, an old friend of Blake's, Arnold Spur, visited from Holland. Shocked to find them living above a brothel, he pressed them to move to The Hague, and found them first-rate accommodation in an inexpensive hotel opposite the Peace Palace, where they had a fine sitting room with a large balcony, and a bedroom in the attic. Hot baths were readily available. The meals were heavy but nourishing Dutch-style food. And there was no housework to do. Stead and Blake gratefully moved there in late November 1952.

Stead's agent, Helen Strauss, had predicted correctly: Little, Brown did not like *Mrs Trollope and Madame Blaise*. Since *The People with the Dogs* had not sold well, they now wanted to cancel their three-book contract with Stead. It was one blow after another. With no money either for typing or the luxury of spending time on manuscripts that would not sell, Stead had begun several projects that she had put aside. Several short stories were lying around 'half-dead', and she was still lugging about a complete first draft of *I'm Dying Laughing*, which needed 'such heavy work' that she could not face it just then. She was waiting until she had money and strength. These days, she would often begin letters then put them aside, sometimes to be finished weeks or months later, sometimes to be abandoned altogether.

Now she decided to have a run at *Cotters' England*. She had been reading and drafting bits for months: it was ripe for writing. There was no desk in their sitting room: Stead was obliged to type on her lap supported by cushions and books. Nevertheless, the first few months in Holland were a period of intense productivity reminiscent of the summer in Ronda, Spain, seventeen years before, when she worked on *House of All Nations*.

Stead seldom breathed fresh air, except to feed the sparrows on their balcony or visit the American Library. Blake, happy to have a new city to explore, went for long walks by himself. They knew no one except Arnold Spur, who had once been a successful Berlin wheat merchant. As a Jew, he had fled in the mid 1930s to Paris, then to Belgium, where their mutual friend Mitzi Enders had hidden him throughout the German occupation. Stead rarely joined the men for evening drinks; Arnold liked to 'talk wheat' in fast Berliner German and she became 'hard of hearing' after half an hour of this. For company she had only Nello, whose wise sayings were cited in letters to friends, and Corrie the hard-working young maid, with whom she spoke German.

By mid January 1953 Stead had written more than 100 pages of *Cotters' England*, and was greatly encouraged when Blake pronounced it her best novel to date. 'It's a pretty little Strindberg type of comedy, filled with tears of blood,' she told Florence James sardonically, 'but Bill likes it, I think he really does, it's not just the kindness of a husband.'

She was excited by *Cotters' England*. This time her egocentric monster was a woman, Nellie Cotter. One of Stead's manipulative charmers, she— like Sam Pollit, Robbie Grant and Emily Wilkes—is dangerous enough to precipitate suicide by someone close to her. Nellie's brother Tom is another of Stead's seducers: 'a queer character who entangles all the women by suggesting that he can't make good as a lover: they're fascinated'. She was worried that American publishers would not be interested in a novel set in working-class England. 'As for the wretched British publishers, they don't publish anything now unless it's published first in U.S. and then they don't.' She thought she would try Australia, which had just set up a Left Book Club. [13]

Cotters' England caused Stead 'weeks of moral struggle'. She asked herself: 'Is it fair to show the good so bad? Is it not sentimentality to show the bad so good?'[14] It is a question others have asked in relation to Stead: was it fair to take a real-life individual who is both 'good' and 'bad' and create a fictional fiend? Was it moral to use details from life to enhance the reality-effect, and at the same time to transform and distort reality? Stead often complained that the libel laws made writing burdensome, but she never wanted to change the minor details that made real people recognisable.

The German classics that lined their mantelpiece, and the long dresses and picture hats of Dutch society women reminded Bill Blake of the backwater German culture of his childhood, and he was inspired to write a novel set in turn-of-the-century New York about the love between an elderly German doctor and a middle-aged Viennese lady, living in Brooklyn. His novel *Evergreen* would be rejected in America and England. Jonathan Cape found the story 'charming', but regretted that no one was interested in old people. That it was a serious study of old age and class was only recognised by the East Germans: Aufbau would publish the novel as *Späte Liebe*. The translation added to Blake's store of Ostmarks, but (except for occasional cheques that came through in pounds sterling) this money could be spent only in East Germany. In a mood of desperation, he dashed off a sequel to his 1938 best-seller, *The World is Mine*, but it aroused no interest from publishers.

In January 1953, hurricane winds and high tides created havoc in Europe. In Holland, dykes burst, causing more than 1000 deaths. Bill Blake answered Florence James' concerned letter:

> The crisis is, of course, the one talk of the country. I am afraid it is being used to cover up secret military deals with the U.S ... Every time I see the newspapers obsessed by one subject I ask what is missing from their columns.

He trusted only the communist press.

On 6 March 1953 the flags in The Hague were at half-mast. The editorial in the British *Daily Worker* proclaimed: 'Long live the immortal memory of the greatest working-class leader, genius and creative thinker that the world has ever known!' Shortly afterwards, Stead wrote to her brother Gilbert and his new wife Sylvia:

> As to the death of Stalin, that was a very great event, so strange and so close to millions! Lenin established the Revolution but the socialist state has lived and firmly been founded with Stalin ... It will take a *long time* for Stalin to leave the world; he is so firmly fixed in it ...

Liberal newspapers noted that Stalin might well have been responsible for more deaths than any man in history, with the possible exceptions of Genghis Khan and Hitler. Nevertheless, Blake's faith in Stalinism never wavered, and if Stead had private doubts, she would never say so publicly. But she became very worked up about the terror in the anti-communist West. She was haunted by the trial in New York of Julius and Ethel Rosenberg, faithful communists of Jewish immigrant backgrounds, accused of transmitting atomic secrets to the Soviet Union. 'I dream about the Rosenbergs every night,' she told Edith Anderson in February, 'that I am visiting them in jail.'

On 19 June 1953 the Rosenbergs were executed in the electric chair at Sing Sing prison. Stead was horrified. 'This *will out*,' she told Ettore and

Jessie Rella. 'It was the knockout blow of America's prestige: but they don't care, do they?' She added that most of their other American friends no longer even mentioned politics in their letters. 'They are afraid if they say "it's damn hot weather," they will be taken (by the censors) for Reds.'

By the end of the summer, Stead had finished *Cotters' England* and felt stale. She wondered whether she had exhausted herself by writing so fast at the beginning of their stay in The Hague. Florence James had found her an inexpensive typist in England, and for once Stead sent off a neat manuscript to Helen Strauss. But it was greeted with silence. The novel did the rounds of publishers unsuccessfully, and eventually was added to the pile of abandoned manuscripts in trunks. Stead would not touch *Cotters' England* again for twelve years—not till 1965.

In The Hague they enjoyed a level of luxury they knew they would never find in England. But they now found the town dull, and told themselves they were tired of the 'soggy sort of over-steamed potato-bolstered cooking'.[15] Most of all, they were sick of being so cut off from friends. And there was an immediate reason for going back to England: Ruth Blake's wedding at Aldershot, Hampshire.

Ruth married Laurence Hall, an Englishman working in Civil Aviation, on 23 September 1953. Bill and Christina hurried over to England for a wedding to which Christina was not invited. Even though she was now Bill's legal wife, it remained the rule, twenty-five years after Mollie and Bill's separation, that Christina's name was never mentioned in front of Mollie.

It must have hurt Christina that she was not invited to the wedding. Earlier that year, Ruth had travelled to Australia as interpreter at an International Civil Aviation Organisation Conference in Melbourne. Afterwards she had gone to Sydney and met the Stead family. She went to Boongarre; Christina's father had shown her his snake collection and terrified her by placing a snake on her shoulder; she had been entertained by Thistle, Kate and Gwen. 'Everyone liked everyone,' Christina told Florence James, 'quite a surprise.'

***

In London, the Blakes were again living in a one-room flat. This time it was a large attic room in a condemned house at No. 103 Broadhurst Gardens, in West Hampstead, a narrow, tree-lined street with the railway line across the road. The house was so dilapidated that friends wondered whether it would hold up, but it was cheap.

Housing was still in short supply in London. Old houses were divided up and partitioned off to cram in boarders. These cold, bleak rooming houses recur in Stead's late fiction. In a short semi-fictional piece, '1954: Days of the Roomers', the middle-aged Watsons are 'literary hacks' who type most of the day on a rickety table on the bare floor, ashamed to disturb the people below with the banging. When they walk around the streets to feel the weak rays of sun on their faces, they are always on the lookout for a better place to live. But everywhere is the same.

Ruth and Laurie Hall lived in a two-storey house at Willesden Green, two stations away on the tube. It was in this thin-walled 'draft-catcher' that Blake and Stead spent Christmas 'toting large bronze scuttles up and down steps', while Laurie and Ruth were in Paris. Christina, who had been immobilised for a while with a sprained ankle, told Gwen that they felt like 'crabbed old people' beside the blooming couple. Ruth was looking 'remarkably beautiful' and Laurie, 'tall, very blond with a fascinating stammer and a lively mind', was 'simply madly insanely in love'.[16]

By November 1953, Stead had begun to realise the full implications of being stereotyped as a communist in the Cold War world. Several of their American acquaintances had had their passports withdrawn. The 250 or so blacklisted Hollywood writers and actors were having difficulty scrabbling together a meagre income, whether in America or England. There had been breakdowns and suicides.

Stead became very nervous when Dal Stivens, a fellow Australian writer in London and member of the Australia & New Zealand Civil Liberties Society, called on them and in the course of his visit intimated that he knew Blake was a communist. Shortly after this, a journalist from the Sydney Morning Herald asked Stead if she and Blake had left America because of political pressures. Stead suddenly started to worry. How had Australians heard that Bill was a communist? Had Florence James (who was in contact with the Australian literary set) said something? She sent her a semi-accusatory letter, saying she was 'rather hesitant about how to put something'.

What's strange is that the Australians ... think that Bill is a Communist. How would they get that idea? He's quite unknown to them. ... I don't know whether you ever have occasion to discuss my (our) political attitudes with anyone, but if it ever crops up, I hope you would do your best to remove any such ideas.

Florence James replied patiently but firmly:

Chris dear,
... You write as though you were a couple of nonentities whom no-one would be likely to speculate about, which is very far from the case. Bill's brilliant talking is enough to set him upon people's tongues and your own light doesn't hide naturally under a bushell; it doesn't take much speculation to place either of you on the extreme left with or without labels ... Your place in Australian letters would make Bill interesting to them even if he weren't already so as a writer. And he's personally known to quite a few people in Australian journalism.

I'm sorry it's distressing you, but the fact that two cases have come to your notice needn't mean anything sinister at all.

Stead's reply two days later, still tetchy, shows how defensive and jittery she had become. Florence had said nothing about England being a 'free country' nor had she called Stead 'nervous', but she was accused of both:

Dearest Florence,
... Please don't brush away the difficulties of this time for many people by saying I am nervous: or that we live in a free country. As Nello said about another and greater land—'You can say anything you like in this country if you keep your mouth shut.' True this is a free country for, say, my aged cousins who regard the royal family as sacred and spend their time at church bazaars.

In the rest of the letter, Stead railed against a second Australian journalist (an 'impudent, brassy dame') who, when Stead had said she could not afford to return to Australia, had suggested the Ten Pounds Immigrant Scheme. Stead felt humiliated.

Two established writers ... are to go out there in their middle-age as charity cases—my revolt at such shameful treatment is physical. The bourgeois and the philistine has always loved to see the 'artist in the garret.'

A few days later, Stead apologised to Florence for her 'hotheaded note':

> You see I have cooled off. I don't know why I got so choleric—I AM choleric to begin with and then this enforced inaction—and I should be writing, all this messing about is no good. However, I must make a humble apology and beg some more of your infinite goodness and patience. Love, as ever, Christina.

⸎

'My last manuscripts and Bill's haven't had a nibble, and we are really on the beach,' Stead wrote to Edith Anderson in September 1953.

> I hope to get a job at the minimum wage anyway, but not office work I hope and literary devilling is getting to be the lowest paid of all possible jobs ... I hope I can get a job say in a parrot and monkey shop or something like that. Bill can't get a job here.

Florence James' experience of 'literary devilling' had removed any illusions they might have had about this way of life. She worked at home as a reader for Constable, reading manuscripts seven days a week, often till midnight, and scraped together about £6 a week. (Bus conductors and ticket collectors were paid £8 or £9 a week.)

Whereas Florence James had exceptional physical stamina, Stead and Blake did not. Stead tired easily these days and Blake had started to hold books three or four inches from his eyes. His trouble would later be diagnosed as glaucoma.

Stead had practised her shorthand in preparation for work, but her typing was neither accurate nor fast. An employment agency found her work as a domestic to a 'hoity-toity TV and radio family' but Blake would not hear of it. For a few weeks that winter she worked in the office of a hospital on the other side of Hampstead Heath, catching a bus across Hampstead in the mornings. One memorable day in February, there had been rain, and a sudden freeze had caused an ice-storm: 'Every trunk, branch, twig and fibril was coated in thin glass and shining in the sun—a woodland in glass.'[17]

Max Schroeder, at Aufbau, had managed to send Blake £250 as royalties for *Späte Liebe*: it had been quite a feat to get the money out of East Germany. This unexpected cheque saved them for a time. Stead wrote to the *Times Literary Supplement* asking for review work that required her to swallow her pride, since the *TLS*'s reviews of her own books, except for *The Salzburg Tales*, had been singularly ungenerous. They did not send her anything. Things had come to such a sorry pass that Stead—once the prestigious author—found herself turning to Peter Davies to ask whether he would recommend her as a publisher's reader.

Literary hackwork seemed the least unpleasant of the available jobs, and at first, Blake and Stead went at it with their usual determination and energy. There were two of them, they reasoned, and they had no dependants. Surely they could make enough to live on?

Blake had acquired a temporary work permit, and soon they had a stream of editing and translating jobs. It was irregular work and badly paid. They reported on books in German and French for Frederick Muller, Hutchinson and Cassells, and took on some translating—Stead from French, Blake from French and German—and editing work and proofreading. Translations were preferable in that they provided work for several months, but they had to wait until the job was finished for payment. Blake was pleased when Muller commissioned him to write a light, humorous book about Americans for a series on different peoples of the world. But he dismissed *Understanding the Americans*, published later that year, as a 'sorry tidbit'. In 1954, Stead edited a book of short stories set in the South Sea Islands and translated a reportage on the Far East by a Swiss-French journalist, but told Gwen despairingly: 'It really won't do—they do not pay enough to feed a small louse.'

They had little time and no energy in reserve for any writing of their own. With both of them working flat out, they were managing to scrape together a living equivalent to the wage of one skilled worker: about £10 a week. But the pay was irregular and it was 'hackwork pure and simple'.[18]

Their demeaning situation gave Stead insight into a new and shabby world: Grub street, 'where you grub in the garbage of literature for a living'.[19] It was this world of drafty rooming houses, humiliating job interviews and the wretched struggle for money by sweated and inky labour that Stead would portray in her next novel, *Miss Herbert*.

Food rationing had just ceased in 1954, but the life and spirit seemed to have gone out of England. Nevertheless, as Blake pointed out, the country was at least humane compared to 'the silent land beyond the seas'.[20] Their American friends were saying almost nothing about the activities of that 'unconscionable egocentric' Senator McCarthy[21], though communists were hunted, oaths of loyalty imposed, university professors ousted, welfare benefits denied to communist veterans and their widows, and passports confiscated. Confronted in court by the House Un-American Activities Committee, members of the Old Left usually dodged the questions—afraid of losing their livelihood. In that atmosphere of terror, everyone distrusted everyone else. The FBI suspected all communists of being Soviet agents; leftists suspected new acquaintances of being FBI informers masquerading as communist sympathisers.

In June 1954, Blake's application for a renewal of his American passport provoked renewed FBI investigation. In September, he was obliged to submit a sworn affidavit to the United States Embassy in London about his communist past. In it he declared that he had written articles and reviews for the *New Masses* until 1942, but had never been on the magazine's editorial board. He had been a member of the Communist Party in New York for one year, from March 1938 to April 1939. He concluded:

> I am not now in politics, have no political affiliations, belong to no organizations whatever, have not for many years. I am not and was not a member of the Communist Party except for the period mentioned above.

On 19 October, he was called back for more details. This time, in a second affidavit, he named the branch of which he had been a member: 'To the best of my recollection, it was the James Connoly Branch on Upper Broadway, New York City.' He stated that he had attended only three or four meetings during the whole year, because he had mostly lived outside New York. 'Under the circumstances I had almost no contact with the Branch aforementioned except that I believe its Chairman was William Browder, a brother, I think, of Earl Browder.' He had decided that his best strategy was vagueness.

Two months later, the State Department informed him that it was still not satisfied with his affidavits: its officials wanted 'further details regarding the members of the unit with which he was connected'. On 20 December 1954, Bill Blake submitted a third affidavit. This time, he had had enough of the humiliation.

> With reference to my membership in the Communist Party during parts of the years 1938 and 1939, I am astonished that you have impeached the completeness of my affidavit upon no evidence whatsoever except your own assumptions. I have sworn to the truth and the whole truth and stand to face the consequences of this veracious statement, and I regard as a personal insult your statement that it is incomplete.

I repeat that I attended only three or four meetings casually, scarcely remembering them. I do not remember what persons were in the unit. It is immaterial to me whether you believe or not, this is the fact.

With respect to my own activities there, all I can say is that I was present and I remember once being asked to deliver a speech, but I could not as I was going to the country. If there were any other information to give in this matter I would furnish it, but there is no more.

His boldness worked. On 11 January 1955, the Department authorised a passport valid for one year. Subsequently it was extended to the full two-year period. And when Blake applied to renew his passport again, two years later, the FBI did not object. By 1957 that particular form of government harassment was coming to an end.

Mark and Miriam Risner had introduced the Blakes to the Friedmanns, who became the Blakes' closest friends. The Friedmanns were South Africans who had come to England in 1949. Boyce Friedmann (known to his friends as 'Boy'), a biochemist by profession, was very interested in politics and economics. Years before, he had used Blake's book on Marxism when he taught evening classes at the Left Book Club in Johannesburg. Boy Friedmann was another talented raconteur. He was dark and Jewish; his wife Tella, blonde and lively, was of Dutch Huguenot origin. She worked as a dress designer at Marks and Spencers, and she also had a flair for colourful storytelling. Tella was the only one of their friends who actually read Stead's books.

The Branstens also were back in London, and they spent Christmas together. Ruth and Richard were quite neurotic these days, with no friends left. Stead and Blake felt they could not desert them, despite 'their false position'. It would have been 'too upstage'.[22]

In 1955, Stead translated from French one humorous book, *The Candid Killer*, one children's book and a scientific book, *In Balloon and Bathyscaphe*, by deep sea explorer Auguste Piccard.

She was attending German classes, with the idea of translating from German as well. Blake was talking of a holiday in East Germany, which would enable them to spend his pile of Ostmarks and live in luxury for a time. He was translating a German book on Albert Schweitzer. But he hoped to do research work for the American television producer Hannah Weinstein, who had recently formed a London company, Sapphire Films Ltd, with the intention of employing blacklisted Americans as screenwriters.

Professionally, the bright spots of the year were two articles by American critics. Well-known poet and critic Randall Jarrell briefly mentioned *The Man Who Loved Children*, 'a wonderful novel', in the *New York Times* in July 1955:

> I've been getting people to read it for ten years, with the most dazzling results; so many have bought it for themselves that Simon & Schuster wrote one a letter saying: 'Would you be kind enough to tell us how you happened to order this particular book? In recent years there has been a small but steady demand for it.'

Then in a three-page article in the August issue of *New Republic*, Elizabeth Hardwick, wife of the poet Robert Lowell, reminded readers of the existence of a remarkable author who had been unfairly neglected.

> The dust seems to have settled rather quickly upon the works of Christina Stead. Her name means nothing to most people ... At the present time none of Christina Stead's work is in print ... The dust, grimly, meanly collecting, has fallen upon a work of sheer astonishment and success.

Coming when it did, when Christina Stead had almost been forgotten, Hardwick's appraisal of the 'truly radical power and authenticity' of Stead's fiction was like rain in a desert. Stead and Blake were touched by the article, and Blake proudly sent it to friends.

They moved twice in 1955, once to a squalid basement flat at No. 10 Primrose Gardens in Hampstead, where they put up with all sorts of discomfort simply because the landlady was in the Peace Movement. They washed with a bowl on a chair in the freezing cellar-kitchen, and by the beginning of winter Stead was putting on a dressing gown, sweater and topcoat to make a cup of coffee. Every morning, they would wake up with back or neck ache from draughts.

In December, a friend of a friend offered them a groundfloor flat in an old whitewashed cottage at low rent. Tella Friedmann, who was there with Christina waiting for their boxes to arrive, thought it a nice place. But there was a problem. In the sitting room was a small fireplace, in which a sheet of newspaper had collected some drops of soot. Tella, who until then had not been aware of the extent of Stead's superstitiousness and occultist learnings, recalls:

> Chris was restless, pacing up and down. She said: 'This will never do. We can't stay here.' I asked her why, and she said:
> 'Can't you see the soot? Don't you know what that means? This woman is in her menopause and she has got it in for me.'[23]

Stead refused to stay there. The next move was to a Dickensian rooming house in Adelaide Road, Hampstead. This time the house was inhabited by night workers, and the Blakes felt mortified to be typing during the day when through the thin walls their neighbours were trying to sleep. The common bathroom and toilet were next to their room, and the noise of people coming and going kept Stead awake most of the night.

In July 1955, Gwen Walker-Smith made a long-planned trip to the northern hemisphere. Christina, who once had been so keen for her favourite cousin to share the delights of her European life, must have been profoundly embarrassed to be seen in such poverty. And there was no question of Gwen staying with them.

Gwen was shocked by the Blakes' living conditions. She was also taken aback by her cousin's appearance and evident poor health.

> She had changed so much I could scarcely recognise her. Her hair was a different colour. It had been fair, and now it was dyed almost black. And she'd put on such a lot of weight. She was a big woman now, and she'd been so painfully thin when she left Australia.[24]

Photographs from this time confirm that Stead had put on weight. It did not suit her. Her hands and wrists were puffy. The keen, hooded eyes, arched eyebrows and knowing mouth were padded by plump cheeks. Her short hair was tightly permed in an unflattering 1950s style. She looked weary, sad. The American writer Hortense Calisher, who arranged a meeting with Stead around this time, thought she looked like a country matron in town for the day.

In December 1955, Richard Bransten gassed himself in his car. Only a few days earlier he had been talking to Bill. A week later, Blake told Max Schroeder:

> Richard Bransten ('Bruce Minton') ... committed suicide last week. Whatever our sharp differences on politics (he never abjured his faith and yet did not maintain it: this twilight caused him intense pain and wrecked his life), I simply had to take care of the children and speak to his widow, despite the fact that I have a real dread of her: she is a demon of verbosity, vanity, and, although she was very much in love with her husband, had that sort of love that can express itself only by mad quarrelling, mad gadfly bites.

A month later, Stead commented to Edith Anderson that Ruth was 'in a very strange state of mind', and it was not caused by Richard's death. Ruth McKenney had begun to lose her mind. In the next few years, she would be in and out of mental asylums.

Bransten's suicide did not soften Stead's attitude to Ruth McKenney. In November 1956, McKenney, back in the States, sent her a pre-publication copy of *Mirage*, a book about Napoleon's campaign in Egypt that she and Bransten had written in collaboration. Stead told Edith Anderson furiously that McKenney, 'that greedy pig', had written 'a monstrous prefabricated best-smeller':

> It's got lush sex scenes and summer-tourist French and all kinds of Hwd [Hollywood] garbage about the French Revolution and absolutely hackneyed types and comic-strip conversations and it was all done purposely, every word done purposely to make a best seller, done by Richard and Ruth consciously, with the intention of *being* garbage but just the right sort to appeal—not too low, mind you.

McKenney's sell-out as a writer irritated Stead even more than her political sell-out. For Stead, writing involved honesty, probing beyond the surface; this was what gave writers their moral integrity. She once told an interviewer: 'I'm not moral when I'm not writing. When I'm writing ... I'm a thoroughly moral being.'[25]

The idea that writing which merely caters for the market is a form of prostitution, with literary agents and publishers acting as treacherous pimps, is one of the themes of *Miss Herbert*. In 1955, Stead was embarking on this novel, which gave vent to her bitterness and humiliation about their situation as hack writers, the new educated proletariat. As usual, minor characters in the novel are based on herself and Bill Blake, and for the first time in her fiction, the portrait is a bleak one.

The Blackstones, two middle-aged writers, are living in a foul bed-sitting room in a side street of St John's Wood, with a 'bachelor's oven' in the fender. The bed is made with the landlady's coarse, patched and grimy bedclothes, thin, old blankets, yellow and gray. The couple translate from French and German, and read books in foreign languages for publishers. Millia Blackstone works in a hospital in the mornings and writes reviews for the *Times Literary Supplement* in the afternoons. Ben Blackstone is 'a very gentle soul' whom people 'can't help liking'.

The main character, Eleanor Herbert, is inspired partly—but only partly—by Florence James. For the rest the fictional character is an amalgamation of various women, including the landladies Stead had met as a 'roomer'. Eleanor epitomises the Cold War conservatives whom Stead had already portrayed in *The Little Hotel*. Stead would later tell a friend she also had Dymphna Cusack vaguely in mind. (In real life, Cusack was a committed socialist; Florence James, a liberal, mistrusted the Left.)

Eleanor Herbert despises the Blackstones for their poverty. As she tramps from one job interview to another, she tells herself proudly: 'I won't go so low as Millia Blackstone, I'm no defeatist.' The remark reveals Stead's utter sense of humiliation.

A pragmatist, Eleanor Herbert considers the Blackstones partly responsible for their fate; they are Reds, after all. As a publishers' reader, she identifies with the interest of publishers: 'You can hardly blame people, publishers and editors for not paying for unpopular minority opinions.'

Eleanor Herbert is shamefully exploited: her long hours of work for a pittance constitute sweated labour, no less. Even so, she has a slight edge over the writers on whose material she is dependent. In one job interview, she tells the publisher savagely:

> I love to rip into manuscripts, tear them to pieces, rip out the flummery, show them the top-heavy stuff that simply has got to be jettisoned … and tell them that writing is guts, nothing but guts.

The chief editor looks pleased at this, and she continues 'more sweetly':

I never lose sight of the publisher's point of view. I consider a writer, once
he has written something and offered it for publication, has formed a kind
of unwritten pact with the publisher to conform to the rules.

As a Marxist, Stead was attuned to the issues of production, exploitation
and power involved in the publishing industry. Indeed, it is surprising that
so few novels treat this crucial aspect of the production of literature. *Miss
Herbert*, with its sombre vision of commercialised culture, stands with
Balzac's *Illusions Perdues* and Gissing's *New Grub Street*. It was time for a
twentieth-century novel on the subject.

But Stead's novel is more than a satire on publishing: its other interest is
the complex character of Miss Herbert, who in some ways also represents
struggling, rightwing post-war Britain.

Exceptionally beautiful, Eleanor Herbert (reminiscent even in name of
narcissistic Elvira Western in *The Beauties and Furies*) sees her life in terms
of the clichés of women's magazines and acts out two contradictory roles:
the old-fashioned 'lavender and musk' romantic virgin, and the 'modern
woman' who has 'the right to have fun'.

Eleanor Herbert's marriage to a Swiss reactionary is miserable, but
Eleanor tells herself she is 'radiantly happy'. She works hard at making a
success of their boarding house, even deciding, for the sake of respectability,
that she will exclude dark-skinned foreign students. (Her prejudices against
blacks, Jews and displaced persons represent post-war England generally.)
However, she cannot avoid being exploited herself. Legally, her earnings
belong to her husband. When they eventually divorce, he becomes an
'alimony-skipper', and with two children to support, Eleanor joins the
ranks of penurious hack writers living in mean, drafty rooming-houses.

The fictional Miss Herbert has a number of real-life models, as Stead
herself admitted, but again there were enough similarities between fiction
and life to make Stead worry about libel, and it seems she did not want
the book to be read by Florence James, who had once protested about the
way Stead interwove real life with fictional fabrication to create hurtful
caricatures. When the book was accepted for publication in the States
in 1976, Stead asked for it not to appear in England or Australia. It did,
nevertheless, and Florence James was duly hurt.

David Darwin Stead was coming to London on business in the spring of 1956. He was almost bald these days, he warned his sister. For his part, he had been forewarned by Gwen that Christina and Bill were living in grim conditions. Still, he was shocked by what he saw. Their poverty was so palpable that when Bill and Christina once gave him sardines on toast, he suspected they were depriving themselves of their own lunch.[26]

He talked to them about the prospect of going out to Australia, suggesting they could live with Gilbert and his wife for a time, and that the family as a whole would keep them until they were established. 'How's that,' wrote Christina, deeply moved. 'And I have been squalling and yelping because they didn't seem to know I was a writer.'[27] In early October, she wrote to Gilbert and put it to him straight:

> I am putting it simply because I feel embarrassed about it and I should like you to say yes or no ... We wouldn't want to put off going to Australia too long, if we were really going. Australia attracts us, not only because it's my country and I feel (even now) I understand Australians, what they are up to, mentally and temperamentally, but because of the climate. Against this we must put a. the question of getting a living, b. where to live, c. the fact that Bill is an outlander. However, he isn't at home anywhere, so why not Australia where the climate would be good for him.

Gilbert replied that he and Sylvia would be moving the following year to a house in Mortdale, in Sydney's western suburbs. He offered to build an extension for them, saying he would be happy with a nominal rent to cover costs.

The letter brought Blake and Stead back down to earth. Mortdale was a long way from the city centre. And they did not want Gilbert to make alterations that would tie them down. Then, in December, they heard that Bill would qualify for an old-age pension if he remained a British resident and paid social security contributions for three more years. It seemed a poor thing to stick around for, but they had become more practical these days. They would think again about Australia in three years' time.

In the immediate future, their break from poverty and England would take the form of a three-month holiday in East Germany, to spend Blake's accumulated Ostmarks. It was planned for autumn of the following year, and Blake talked of little else. Stead was reading Goethe's *The Sorrows of Young Werther*, and was pleased to be able to appreciate its beauty in the original. In September 1956, they saw the Berliner Ensemble performance of *Mother Courage*, in German, with Helene Weigel as Courage. The Friedmanns had booked front row seats weeks ahead. Shortly before the British tour, Bertolt Brecht had died, but Weigel, his widow, performed nonetheless. She was given a roaring ovation. Stead was disappointed to understand as little as she did, but the performance turned her into an admirer of Brecht.

In mid September, they spent two weeks on a farm in Devon, their first real holiday for a long time—and cheap. The farmers were a delightful young couple, who took boarders in the summer months. The wife was a regular Mrs Beeton cook, and the Blakes enjoyed elderberry wine, homemade bread, giblet pie and clotted cream. Stead read, made notes for *Miss Herbert*, and dug in the garden. She and Blake went for walks in and around Dartmouth and the beautiful Dart Valley. Back in London, feeling stronger after the holiday, Blake told a friend he had been truly exhausted by the unremitting hard work: 'I just about had to go to Devonshire before I fell into the arms of Jesus but right now it looks as though the Nazarene's kisses are a long way off.'[28]

The year 1956 was a watershed for communism. In February, Khrushchev, successor to Stalin, revealed to the Twentieth Congress that the rumours of frame-ups, torture and murder in Stalinist Russia were substantially true, and that no less than 70 per cent of the members of the Central Committee elected in 1934 had been eliminated on anti-revolutionary charges. Stalin, it transpired, was a brutal despot and criminal murderer.

The speech caused havoc. There was a mass exodus from the Communist Party throughout the Western world. Those who left declared themselves disgusted at having been unwitting apologists for tyranny. Those who stayed saw Khrushchev's speech as grounds for optimism that Soviet Russia was undergoing genuine liberalisation. But then came 4 November 1956, when Soviet tanks rolled into Budapest, crushing the Hungarian workers' movement for democracy. Soon hundreds of Hungarians were facing death penalties for distributing leaflets or carrying arms. When the major European communist parties defended the Soviet invasion, there was a second mass exodus from their ranks.

Ten days after the invasion, Stead wrote to Edith Anderson, who, living behind the Iron Curtain, had reason to be anxious:

> Don't let politics faze you, is Bill's opinion: he doesn't think the present crisis will be 'historically significant' however much of a 'hurly-burly' ... it looks now ... Many intellectuals who regard party activities as 'part of my picaresque life,' are jumping off the train at this station. It's quite a clean-out of the soft element ... Bill and I were discussing the curious traits of intellectuals, the liberal bourgeoisie—why are they so immoral? For they are. To jump off every time you're threatened is immoral.

It was, Stead admitted, Bill's opinion, and in politics she would only ever echo him. To regard those who jumped off the locomotive of history as immoral was understandable in previous years (though a bit preposterous coming from someone who had never clambered on to the train), but after 1956, it was difficult to defend this position. Yet until the end of their lives, Blake and Stead would be impatient with those who criticised the USSR.

At the end of 1956, Hannah Weinstein, the American television director, gave Blake a job researching the fifteenth-century Siege of Florence for a television script, *The Sword of Freedom*. It was the sort of project he enjoyed, but it was still piecemeal work and underpaid, and it ran out after six months.

They moved again—a few blocks away, to No. 14 Glenmore Road. They considered themselves fortunate because the rent was below the market rate. Stead liked the 'funny little Hanseatic doll's street', and here they had a separate kitchen where Stead worked, near the oven for warmth, her large typewriter on the kitchen table. She hoped to be able to get some real work done at last. She was still writing *Miss Herbert*.

Boy and Tella Friedmann wanted to buy a small weekend house in the country, and they discussed the possibility of buying a house as a foursome. The Blakes could live there permanently, and the Friedmanns at weekends. The prospect of getting out of London appealed to Stead, and the communal aspect appealed to Blake. The problem was that the house would have to be on the main transport line for Blake, not too far from London's libraries, and yet it would have to be cheap. In the spring and summer of 1957 they piled into the Friedmanns' car at weekends and motored all over the countryside looking at houses in various stages of dilapidation. Stead told Edith Anderson:

> We saw some old bush shanties, with kerosene lamp (one) and tarpaper toilets and marsh-grass a yard high and one string of wire in the fence last weekend—you'd think such places were only in the upcountry of South Africa or the Never-Never of dear old N.S.W.

One of the bonds Stead enjoyed with the Friedmanns was that they too came from a southern continent with vast spaces and blue skies. None of them felt at home in England.

On 2 August 1957, Christina's father died at Watson's Bay. He was eighty. His life, ever since being thrown out of the Civil Service and losing the pension that was due him, had been difficult. In addition to arthritis and poor eyesight, he had been seriously ill following a prostate operation. Christina had empathised with his plight in the last years. Bill's life, and her own, in some ways resembled her father's. Most importantly, her father's death freed her from her anger towards him—something that writing *The Man Who Loved Children* had not achieved. From now on, she would talk of him quite affectionately to friends. In the short pieces she was still to write about her childhood, the portrait of her father is gentle and loving.

They had planned their trip to East Germany for months. Blake was longing to travel again. It was Stead's first visit to a socialist country. They both badly wanted a holiday: Blake's eyes were weak and Stead, with her high blood pressure, was feeling tense and lethargic.

Blake had accumulated nearly 30000 Ostmarks in East Germany. *Späte Liebe* had done quite well, and *Maria Meinhardt*, the translation of *The Copperheads*, had been reprinted five times and sold 10000 copies—partly because it explored the role of German immigrants in the American Civil War. (There would be a sixth edition of 10000 copies in 1962.) Blake planned to spend two-thirds of his Ostmarks and leave the rest intact; from time to time Aufbau managed to send him a cheque in sterling, and it often proved a life-saver. They were hoping, while in socialist Germany, to place several of Stead's books for translation. As she explained to Edith Anderson, it would mean 'small regular money from HONEST people'.

They arrived at Friedrichstrasse, the border station, on 30 August 1957, and stayed a few days with Max Schroeder and Edith Anderson, who were living in a large apartment ten minutes from the centre. The atmosphere in the house was heavy. Max, always a gaunt figure, was fatally ill with lung cancer. He was to live only five more months.

Edith Anderson recalls that she and Christina got on well, though they never had an intimate conversation, despite the years of letters. When it came to tête-à-tête conversations, Stead was reserved. Her last truly intimate friendship had been with Florence James, back in the 1930s; now Stead was transforming her old friend into 'Miss Herbert'.

It was the second time Blake had come to East Germany to find a friend dying, and it cast a pall on the holiday. Nevertheless, they had a wonderful break. For once they had plenty of money. They had friends, who made them welcome. They found the countryside beautiful and the socialism admirable.

They went to Schierke in the Harz Mountains, where they stayed in the elegant Heinrich Heine Hotel, and told each other wryly that the bathroom alone was the size of their Glenmore Road flat. Stead found the regional German 'delightful'. She loved the ubiquitous chime of cowbells. And she was fascinated by the ancient pagan traditions and legends of the Harz region—the origin of the famous Walpurgis Night legend. Edith and Max Schroeder joined them there. Max was in pain and his voice was almost inaudible, but he had retained his sharpness and his wit, and his pithy remarks delighted the Blakes, who admired his fortitude.

They made the most of the opportunity to buy things: Stead bought herself a winter coat, a suit, Czech shoes, blouses, a nightdress, stockings, underwear. They bought four puppets. And a typewriter.

They made arrangements to have a thorough medical examination by a senior doctor, Professor Tietze. Stead and Blake had great faith in socialist medicine, particularly in Germany. Stead was told she suffered from hypertension, with dangerously high blood pressure. The doctor, who must have presumed they were wealthy, prescribed a 'cure' in Bad Tölz, West Germany. Stead told Edith Anderson: 'I hope the *Oberarzt* Tietze can suggest some simple line for me to follow until I graduate as a West German millionaire.' He did, and Stead was horrified:

No meat, fish, eggs, no protein of any kind, and I have always lived on protein! No tea, coffee—it goes on and on. But he says four strict months and then Bad Tölz (I don't know how we'll do it) and one year altogether plus taking RAUWULEIN and other things and I will be able to work properly for a long time. And that is consideration number one.

He recommended an eyewash for Blake's bloodshot eyes and told him he might have a tendency to cataracts. (This would prove correct.) And he told Blake to give up coffee. That was a rude shock—Blake was as dependent on coffee as Stead was on alcohol—but he cut back his intake radically and eventually gave it up altogether, drinking strong black tea in its place. Tietze also told him he had poor circulation and needed regular massages—an equally unaffordable cure. The Blakes would return to England very impressed with the holistic approach of socialist medicine.

Before they left Leipzig, they visited Henryk Grossmann's grave, now seven years old. Blake was upset all over again.

Early in November they went to Weimar, at the edge of the Thuringian Forest, and stayed a week in the luxurious Hotel Elefant, with a balcony overlooking the city square. They went for daily walks in the pine forests, devoured the art museums and historic buildings, visited Goethe's house and saw Schiller's Räuber at the Weimar Theatre. On a bitter foggy day they went on a tour to the remains of the concentration camp at Buchenwald. Over the large entrance gates was the sign '*Arbeit macht frei*'. Inside, they saw 'all the horrors ever mentioned'. Blake was unable to complete the tour. Stead stayed on. She wanted to experience that reality.

Finally they returned to Berlin for two more weeks, staying this time in a hotel in the centre. They had no luck placing Stead's books for translation. But at the end of the trip, Stead told Edith Anderson:

I feel Bill and I *owe* it to the Republic to write something about our visit: we have had such a good time; and (I know this will seem perhaps infantile to you) we have been so happy to be in a socialist state.

It was to be their last happy holiday abroad together.

Tella Friedmann organised a welcome home party in London in early December. She remembers thinking that Christina and Bill looked wonderfully well and refreshed. The returning travellers were proud of having kept to Dr Tietze's rigorous diet for two months, though Christina complained that it took her far longer to prepare a 'carrot toothsome' than to fry a juicy steak.[29]

They returned to a cramped room and the London winter. Stead found it depressing to take up *Miss Herbert* again: the novel had definitely reached the Albatross stage. Jonathan Cape had seen part of the manuscript and expressed cautious interest; Stead hoped he would become her next English publisher.

Christmas that year was spent with the Friedmanns in Hampstead, and soon afterwards, they resumed country-house hunting. But by February 1958, the Friedmanns were beginning to realise the idea would never work. Friends declared they must be 'daft': 'Chris would be hell to live with.' And it did not seem likely that the Blakes would be able to borrow enough money for a mortgage, though the money question was never properly discussed. The dilemma was solved when Hannah Weinstein, the American television producer, offered the Blakes free accommodation at Foxwarren Park, her country estate at Cobham, Surrey.

The Blakes left the city in March 1958 without regret. Foxwarren marked the end of their days as London roomers.

———— ❧ ————

Foxwarren Park was one of England's large estates. The Victorian Tudor-style manor in which Hannah Weinstein lived with her companion, John Fisher, and her three adolescent daughters from a previous marriage, boasted fifteen bedrooms and numerous ornate reception rooms. The Blakes moved into the adjoining cottage, once the stables, and were merely obliged to pay the cost of fixing the place up. For them it was wonderful to have more than one room again, even if it meant buying furniture and doing housework again.

The grounds, tended by a team of gardeners, were magnificent. The hyacinths, daffodils, azaleas and rhododendrons were just coming into bloom, and beyond the gardens stretched the woodland and heath of Wisley Common, once the haunt of highwaymen. This was the view from their windows. Stead, who thought herself in paradise, was not surprised when a young man called at their door and asked: 'Is this Shangri-la?' It transpired that a cottage down the road had that name.

Stead made a point of learning the names of the flowers, ferns and fungi. Outside their kitchen window was a large holly bush where she spread crumbs for finches, robins, blackbirds and sparrows. Occasionally she would see cock pheasants. And she was very excited when one evening she heard a nightingale for the first time.

It was a lively place. Gardeners cut hedges, pathmakers tarred paths, horse-sellers brought horses. When the Blakes took a walk they were likely to meet Robin Hood, Little John or the Sheriff of Nottingham in full dress. For the past four years, Hannah Weinstein had been producing the highly successful series *Adventures of Robin Hood* for American television, and the estate was full of film sets, including a two-dimensional baronial castle. Richard Greene, the boyishly handsome British actor who played Robin Hood, would be seen in the distance riding his horse up to the gallows to rescue a condemned man, or scaling a high wall and shooting an arrow at the same time.

The historical research Blake was doing for Weinstein required him to make regular trips to the British Library, and in this respect, their rural retreat was far from ideal. Foxwarren was twenty miles from London, on the road to Portsmouth, and poorly served by transport. The bus trip took fifty minutes and cost almost six shillings return. Even the local Cobham shops involved a bus, which meant planning the shopping carefully. Nevertheless, Blake, in particular, enjoyed the communal life at Foxwarren. Apart from the staff who lived on the property, there were constant American visitors: Weinstein commissioned scripts from a number of talented writers on Hollywood's blacklist and would always be inviting the Blakes for 'high tea' or drinks to meet them. Some were communist screenwriters the Blakes had met in Hollywood: Jerome Chodorov, Albert Maltz, Adrian Scott. The last two had since served a year in prison as members of the Hollywood Ten.

Early in May, a few weeks after they had moved to Foxwarren, Stead was distracted from the daily grind on *Miss Herbert*. Harry and Anne Bloom were in London for a few days.

It had been eleven years since Stead had said goodbye to Harry Bloom in New York; she had left the States in love with him. In Europe, restless and unhappy, she had at first been hurt that he had not written. Eventually she and Bill had heard from him, and he proved as lively in letters as in the flesh. In the mid 1950s, the Blooms had moved to Puerto Rico, where

Harry Bloom had opened an electrical goods business—mostly selling lights. He was doing very well these days. He had taken up sculpture as a hobby, and sent them a photo of himself at his art class, his long hands dripping with clay. Stead thought them beautiful hands.

She and Bill were at Waterloo Station to meet Harry and Anne, their arms full of spring flowers from Foxwarren. Stead described the scene in her diary. Harry Bloom leapt out of the first carriage and hugged them 'in his graceful style'. He had the same animated face; he even wore the same hat. Anne looked older and had adopted a 'mid-western' style of dress. Bill had booked the Blooms in at the Cumberland and had arranged for him and Christina to sleep at the Risners that night. But Harry would not hear of it, and insisted on getting them a room at the hotel. They had dinner in a French restaurant and went for a walk. The city was 'splendid and bright'. Stead hardly slept. (In her diary she attributed it to the overheated room.) The following morning, she accompanied Anne Bloom to the American Embassy to make visa arrangements; Harry and Bill walked the streets of London together. That afternoon, Ruth Hall joined them all for drinks at the hotel. To Stead's acute embarrassment, Harry Bloom was paying for everything.

Over the next few days, Bill caught the train into London to spend as much time as possible with Harry; Christina stayed at home, broodily writing in her diary: 'Two's company, four's none.' On Sunday, the Blooms came to Foxwarren for a picnic with the Friedmanns and the Risners. 'Harry with cold. No chance to talk,' Stead noted cursorily. The next day Bill went to London to see the Blooms off to Paris; Christina did not go. 'Letter from him [Harry]. Regret I felt too,' writes Stead briefly. But if Harry regretted they had not had time to talk, he was being careful about Anne.

The following Saturday morning, Christina and Bill were out walking in the Foxwarren grounds when they were handed a telegram by the stable master. Harry Bloom was inviting them to Paris. France was in crisis: they must be there.

The issue of Algerian independence from France had come to a head. De Gaulle had just been recalled from his retreat at Colombey-les-Deux-Eglises to take power. Harry knew how Bill would enjoy witnessing the making of history.

Bill and Christina were touched, but Bill left for Paris on his own the following morning. Christina told herself she did not want 'one of those sleazy foursomes'.[30]

Blake left on Sunday, 1 June 1958, the day de Gaulle was voted into office. The Left held a massive demonstration opposing him. Policemen were everywhere. De Gaulle's investiture as Premier took place the following evening: the National Assembly gave him full powers for six months. France's Fourth Republic was dead.

The three stayed at the Lutétia, where Bill and Christina had honeymooned some thirty years before. While in Paris, Bill did some research at the Bibliothèque Nationale. For him, the 'bourgeois cowardice' of the French over Algeria called to mind Germany in 1933. He did not mention the political situation in his brief letter to Christina, merely telling her that the cost of living in France was hugely high and to expect him back on Sunday evening, the day after the Blooms were to sail home. He signed off: 'xxxx to my own dearest girl from her petit Willy.' It is the last surviving letter between them.

After Blake's return, Stead noted in her diary: 'We were talking much of Harry, how unusual for a man to keep on developing; Bill said he … really got to know him for the first time, he is a big man in all ways, he fell in love with him.'

She had just begun to recover from Harry's visit and the subsequent nights of restless insomnia when a spring storm flooded the cottage. It created mayhem and her work was held up again. Stead eventually sent *Miss Herbert* to Jonathan Cape in July 1958.

After their 1958 reunion, Harry Bloom would correspond regularly with the Blakes. Some of their letters to him have survived—written sometimes by Blake, sometimes by Stead, with the other invariably adding a note at the end. They are the most consistently affectionate letters Christina and Bill ever wrote to anyone.

Other handsome American leftists made fleeting appearances at Foxwarren that year. It is amusing to think that *Robin Hood*, a series that everyone thought so very British, about that gentlemanly British outlaw who robbed from the rich and gave to the poor, was written mostly in New York by two blacklisted American communists. They wrote under the pseudonym 'Oliver Skene', though they even had to change this name from time to time. Ring Lardner Jnr had been one of the Hollywood Ten. He had not been able to leave the US until 1958, when the Supreme Court declared it unjust to withhold passports on political grounds, and Lardner finally obtained a passport. One day he turned up at Foxwarren with his co-writer, Ian McLellan Hunter, who had been issued with a passport in 1955 and had been commuting in the last few years between London and New York, acting as the liaison.

Stead was impressed by Ring Lardner Jnr, whom she described in her diary as dark and tall, with a lank, Indian-looking face. At the age of thirty-one he had earned $2000 a week; now, at forty-four, he was struggling to support his wife and five children. (He would later script *The Cincinnatti Kid* and *M.A.S.H.*) Stead had already encountered Lardner in the mid 1940s, when he had written a screenplay for *The Man Who Loved Children*; but with the advent of the blacklist, nothing had come of it. Stead had not been entirely sorry about that; she disliked the liberties Lardner had taken with her text.

Another visitor to Foxwarren in 1959 was Paul Robeson. After nine years, the State Department had finally given back his passport; now he was in England to play *Othello* at Stratford-on-Avon. His life had been savagely affected by the blacklist: whereas writers could take on pseudonyms and still attempt to scrape together a living from writing, singers and actors could not conceal their identity.

The Blakes had a three-year rental lease from Hannah Weinstein, but her company, Sapphire Films Ltd (which owned Foxwarren Park) looked as if it were heading for bankruptcy, and they feared they might have to leave the cottage at any time. They did not want to accumulate furniture they could not use in the future, and so the stone cottage remained rather bare. In winter, it was cold and damp. But it was a pretty cottage and in magnificent surroundings, and for the first time in eleven years they had a spacious dignified home. They ended up staying 'three blissful years'.[31]

They would seem blissful in retrospect, but in fact, all the old problems remained. Stead, who had been dabbling with *Miss Herbert* for five years now, had hoped that the country air would cure her writing lethargy. It did not. After finishing *Miss Herbert*, she intended to complete her collection of short stories. But instead, she became entangled in a novel based on Hannah Weinstein and John Fisher that eventually led nowhere.

Later, Stead would resort to the old excuse: 'I had no place to write.' But the conditions for writing were fine. Moreover, in the past Stead had written some of her best work on kitchen tables, squashed in bedrooms, even writing on her lap. In their cottage, she and Blake shared a magnificent hand-carved oak partners' desk, which he had bought at an auction for £12. It was not the physical conditions, it was the motivation that was lacking. It had been lacking ever since they came back to England in 1952, and Stead tended to blame England. She had not enjoyed writing *Miss Herbert* (though the novel does not seem to suffer from this). And now she became thoroughly worked up about the Hollywood-style goings-on in the manor house. She maintained her rage for three years, but for once it did not result in a book. It ate her up, but unproductively.

From the beginning of March 1958 to January 1959, Stead kept a handwritten diary, a secret notebook. She destroyed it the following year, but not before she typed out a second version of it. (No doubt she omitted the more intimate entries, just as she had in the revised version of her Belgian diary.) The typed diary has survived, and although the badly typed single-spaced text is difficult to decipher, the 'Foxwarren Hall' diary, as she called it, gives a sense of their daily life there, and Stead's obsessive involvement in the characters around her. Hannah Weinstein and John Fisher had something of the crazy qualities of the McKenney-Bransten ménage. Hannah was charming and hardworking, tiny and full of energy, but she had an 'unquestioning egotism' and a weakness for luxury. John Fisher was empty, authoritarian, fraudulent and an incurable spender. He was to bring about their financial ruin.

Hannah Weinstein married John Fisher soon after the Blakes moved to Foxwarren. The Blakes attended the wedding: a Jewish ceremony, with readings in Hebrew. Hannah's father, 'Papa Dorner', and her three daughters were present. No expense was spared on the wedding attire, and the banquet afterwards was sumptuous.

Stead soon decided that John Fisher was a sadist and an extortionist. He squandered money on himself, yet was astoundingly mean with others: 'Bill says he'll soon begin to look into how many nails the workmen use.' He was imperious and dominating. 'He said to servants immediately after marriage, if you call her Mrs. Weinstein, I'll dock you two weeks' salary.' Stead wondered why Hannah was so blind to his flaws: 'She's going down with him, down, down to the devil.' She mused: 'He may be very sexy, can be with some insane criminal types. (Also *undersex* has great value in attracting women.) *I feel no sex in him.*' For Stead, the sexual drive was a crucial aspect of personality.

Stead's opinion of John Fisher is supported by Ring Lardner Jnr: 'Fisher was obviously a phony, full of bluff. Anyone could see it except Hannah, who was completely taken in.' He adds: 'Fisher was an even bigger spender than she was. He ran the business into the ground. Everyone was completely confused as to what was spent on the film business and what on the estate.'[32]

Robin Hood had made huge profits, but Weinstein's other swashbuckling productions—*The Buccaneers, The Adventures of Sir Lancelot, The Sword of Freedom* and *The Four Just Men*—were running at a loss. Soon after the marriage, everyone associated with Sapphire Films was expecting black disaster.

Hannah Weinstein saw herself as a communist; was she being philanthropic or exploitative in the Foxwarren days? According to Ring Lardner Jnr, she was both. If Weinstein provided employment for blacklisted writers, the benefits were mutual. She was taking a risk. As an independent producer she had no formal connection with Hollywood, but would have found herself in severe trouble had it become generally known that she employed blacklisted writers. She was paying highly talented writers Screen Writers Guild wages; it was a mere fraction of their former earnings, but then again, she was not Hollywood, and no one else would employ them.

Bill Blake certainly considered himself exploited, despite the free accommodation. He did considerable research for Sapphire Films: Weinstein's movies all had historical settings, and his knowledge and research were invaluable. Stead's notes for her novel *Fan Pearl* show that she certainly did not see Weinstein as entirely altruistic. 'Fan Pearl', in these notes, is Hannah Weinstein:

> The persecutors had done her a favour: they had thrown these brilliant talents on the labour market and denied them all employment: they had once worked for fantastically high wages, now they must work for nothing and find doors shut, or must work under assumed names ... These highstarred gentry found in her a foster-mother; they were anxious to work for reduced wages.

Miriam and Mark Risner sometimes visited Foxwarren with their two children, who liked riding the horses. Mark Risner, a tailor, would give the Blakes clothes his clients had ordered but never claimed. In this way, Stead acquired a smart winter coat and Blake some new suits, but they never quite fitted him, despite the alterations.

It was through the Risners that Bill and Christina met the Harveys. Leah Harvey was Miriam Risner's cousin; Philip, her husband, was Senior Resident at St Stephen's Hospital. Politically active, extroverted and goodlooking, Philip Harvey rapidly became Stead's favourite man in the circle. She disliked Leah Harvey.

The Risners, the Harveys and Boy Friedmann were all Jewish—and all communists, though none were still active Party members. They were delighted when the Russian rocket 'Lunik' flew past the moon in January 1959, putting Russia ahead in the space race, and demonstrating what a workers' state could achieve. There was heated discussion in the group about Boris Pasternak winning the 1958 Nobel Prize in literature for Dr Zhivago—a novel hostile to Soviet communism. Stead followed the newspaper controversy with interest, and read a wealth of material on the book. At first she could not help being impressed by the power of Pasternak's writing. He was 'a real poet', she told Neil Stewart, an Australian communist they had befriended in London. She added dutifully: 'Many good poets are very very weak in the head.'[33]

Politics was the passionate topic of conversation among the men. Apart from Miriam Risner, the women were less devoted to political talk, though they were more vocal about current affairs than Christina. According to Tella Friedmann, when Christina made a comment, it was invariably about personalities. It was people who captured her imagination.

The Blakes saw the Friedmanns most often. Boy and Tella had eventually found a pretty country house at Braughing, thirty miles from London, and Bill and Christina would sometimes go to their Hampstead flat on a Friday evening and drive out to the house with them for the weekend. 'They were easy guests,' Boy Friedmann recalls, 'though they never partook in the renovating and gardening. Bill was happiest sitting and talking. Chris would read or play patience.' Sometimes the Friedmanns would arrange a lunch party on Sunday. 'Bill loved these occasions,' Tella says. 'By 11 am he would be pacing up and down saying, "When are they coming?" '

It was Bill this group of friends loved. They found Christina difficult, odd, self-contained and awkward. Whenever the Blakes entertained at

Foxwarren, Christina spent most of the time in the kitchen preparing food. Bill used to boast that she was a marvellous cook, but guests never sat down to full meals; Christina would make an array of little courses—things like pickled oysters and curried eggs. Tella Friedmann imagines that she was happier fussing in the background than sitting down and talking. Stead admitted as much to Edith Anderson:

> I have been with too many great talkers in my life and it gives me the heeby-jeebies … I need much quiet, a lot of quiet and after a certain time with people I get 'removed'—I do not hear them.

Quite often Bill would turn up to lunches or dinners by himself, saying 'Chris sends her apologies: she's crashed', or 'Chris is totally exhausted'. There was never any forewarning and Bill never said more.

They were all aware that Stead prided herself on her psychic powers. At Foxwarren too, it became known that Mrs Blake could tell fortunes. In her diary, Stead mentions reading Hannah Weinstein's hand and, on another occasion, telling her fortune with cards. Talk of communication with the dead or with alien worlds fascinated Stead as much as it appalled Blake. Stead told friends: 'He would not like, really, anything to crop up that is not accounted for by Hegel and Marx.'[34]

From East Germany Aufbau had managed to send Blake £617—more royalties for *Späte Liebe*. Victor Gollancz in London and Simon & Schuster in New York were now expressing interest in *We are the Makers of Dreams*, the novel Blake had written in Hollywood in 1942. Blake was dismayed by the exploitative deal offered him by Gollancz, the notoriously tight Left Book Club publisher of old days. 'That Christian Yid offered me the sum of 100 pounds on *publication* and, in the meantime, insisted on cutting over a third of its length as otherwise he couldn't sell it at 18 shillings,' Blake told a Jewish friend in New York.[35] 'Simon & Schuster paid better, but they also wanted changes, *different* changes. It all took time'. This was Blake's first publication in nine years, and it was to be his last.

Jonathan Cape turned down *Miss Herbert*. Stead, bitterly disappointed, wondered if it was because of its grim portrayal of the British publishing industry. Blake joked that it was 'like sending ethical tracts to whorehouse proprietors'. In the US, her agent Helen Strauss liked the novel, but for more than eighteen months—from October 1958 to April 1960—the manuscript went from publisher to publisher without success. Stead had come to detest the book, a symbol of her failure. She told Edith Anderson: 'I can hardly face Bill, when I think of him struggling away at research at his age and with his poor eyes.'

Bill tried to console her. He was convinced that the resistance to *Miss Herbert* was because it was saying something important—both about publishing and about women. He told Stanley Burnshaw that Stead revealed female experience in a way no female writer had dared to do before her. Despite his faith in it, Bill Blake would not live to see the publication of *Miss Herbert*, sixteen years later. And neither he nor Stead would see *I'm Dying Laughing* in print—a book Blake had vigorously championed.

Blake's eyesight was getting worse, and he worried about Christina, who had lost her optimism, her spark. He refused to see it as depression; to him, ever the stoic, this would signify defeat. When Stanley Burnshaw enquired after Stead's health in 1959, Blake attributed her problems entirely to physical causes—hypertension, causing a lack of strength. He clearly found it hard to contend with his companion's bitterness and disillusionment. When *We are the Makers of Dreams* came out in England, he had asked Gollancz to send advance copies to certain friends. Stead told Edith Anderson:

> Bill's book came out Monday. He sent copies to best friends. No acknowledgments. He got hot in the collar. I said, 'Pooh, that's human nature. Writers pull it out of the air; why thank them!' Bill said, 'You're beaten, that's all.' I said, 'I know Marxists ought to believe in changing the world but I know a few corners it will be hard to dust out and this is one of them! I'm just a realist.'

Their disappointments and struggle were taking their toll.

13

'Bill, My True Companion'

June 1960 – February 1968

B Y MID 1960, Hannah Weinstein and John Fisher were on the verge
of bankruptcy, and the Blakes were expecting to have to leave
their Foxwarren cottage at any time. In August, the tranquillity
of the estate was disturbed by a deluge of photographers, reporters and
'transatlantic snoopers': Elizabeth Taylor was in England to play in the
Twentieth Century Fox blockbuster *Cleopatra*, and she and her husband
Eddie Fisher were going to rent the manor, at a phenomenal price, while
Weinstein and Fisher were in the US for six months. But the actress changed
her mind, claiming the security was not tight enough, and Foxwarren was
left empty when Weinstein and her husband left in November. 'We are so
rural,' Blake told friends, 'that we will soon hear only the Pipes of Pan.'[1]

Culturally, the Western world seemed to reflect their dreary personal
circumstances. Marxists were now 'a despised minority'. Only the anti-
nuclear campaign in Britain attracted any sort of mass following. Blake
bemoaned the absence of politics in contemporary British writing: where
were the larger social questions? Where was the passion? The French literary
scene was more lively, especially in the theatre—but French universities
were bitten by an arid new 'fad', structuralism. 'The intellectuals having
decided that all values are "unprovable" are pretty much out of it,' Blake
lamented.[2]

The previous year, when he turned sixty-five, Blake had managed to obtain some financial relief. Though he was not technically eligible for it, with the help of Harry Bloom (who may have put him on his payroll at some point), he received an old-age pension from the United States. (From July 1964, when she turned sixty-two, Christina, as his wife, would also receive an American pension—about A$90 a month.) In addition, Blake had been making small payments to a British social security fund since 1953, and he now received a monthly payout. Though a bare minimum, these pensions at least provided a regular income.

Blake's eyes had become a serious problem: he had developed chronic glaucoma and a cataract. His sight had degenerated rapidly. It was too blurred for proofreading, and his typing was full of errors. His London eye specialist did not want to operate. Stead bought a tape recorder and tried to persuade him to work by dictation; but Blake, concerned about the effect this would have on his style, refused to use it. Still an omnivorous reader, he held the pages a few inches from his nose, sometimes using a magnifying glass.

Though he rarely complained, he, too, was depressed these days. His spirits would not have been lifted by his wife's growing obsession with their medical friend, Philip Harvey—which he could hardly have failed to know about. The Harveys were the focal point of their group of friends. Energetic, sociable people, they had a large, pleasant house and garden in Roehampton, and an Austrian housekeeper who would do the catering for lunch and dinner parties. At forty-four, Philip Harvey was in his prime. He worked five and a half days a week as a senior consultant physician at St Stephen's Hospital, Fulham, seeing patients and lecturing to medical students. In the evenings he regularly studied for three to five hours, to keep abreast of medical developments. A committed communist, he was active in organising medical aid to Castro's Cuba, and had even learnt Spanish to lecture to Cuban medical students.

Christina Stead, her English friends observed, was capable of substituting fantasy for reality with quite extraordinary blindness. Philip Harvey had known his wife Leah since their schooldays. The friends in the circle, who were all aware of Stead's passion, wholeheartedly agree today that the Harveys' was a happy marriage and that Philip did not have a roving eye. Leah Harvey was a calm, confident and compassionate woman, with a busy life of her own and many friends. Over the years, Stead would come to detest her with an ardour almost equal to her infatuation for Philip. Leah

Harvey, she would tell friends, was a lesbian. This fictional embellishment enabled her to construct the myth of a long-suffering Philip, whom only she, Christina, knew how to love. A few years later, she would tell Norman Rosten, an American poet with whom she had struck up a friendship by correspondence:

> When you love several people truly, there is always one who is La Traviata (and a man can be too) … I think these are the people we love most. They need us, our love, and we cannot do the slightest thing for them: that is very troubling.[3]

Some time during 1960, the Blakes had a visit from Edith Anderson, whom they had last seen in 1957, in East Germany. After the death of her husband, Max, early in 1958, Edith had wanted to return to the US, and she and their 12-year-old daughter Cornelia had just been to New York for three months to assess their situation. But Cornelia did not like it, and did not want to leave her friends in East Germany. Conscious that Cornelia had already suffered the trauma of her father's death, Edith had decided not to uproot her. They returned to Berlin via London, and stayed overnight at Foxwarren.

To Edith it seemed a happy reunion, though Stead made one comment that (she recalls) 'went through me like a knife'. When they were preparing for bed, Christina admired Edith's white satin peignoir. Edith told her that it was synthetic and cheap: she had bought it in the US for six dollars. Christina said, 'I wish I had six dollars.' Only then did it dawn on Edith just how poor the Blakes were. The cottage was pleasant, but it was very bare.

Later that same year, Edith experienced a rather unpleasant, though seemingly trivial, incident. In December, Philip Harvey made a trip to East Berlin with a medical colleague. At the Blakes' instigation, he contacted Edith, and spent an evening at her flat. On his return, he reported that she was lonely and still grieving for her husband. Did the comment suggest a familiarity that piqued Christina, who was aware that Edith was attractive to men? Or was she annoyed by Edith writing that she had found Harvey bourgeois and cold? When Philip, Leah and their two sons came to Foxwarren on Christmas Eve, Christina told Philip that Edith had described him as 'an English middleclass bourgeois doctor'. Then, in her next letter to Edith, she told her she had passed on this comment, adding (in a voice strikingly reminiscent of her manipulative character Nellie Cotter): 'This was just to cut you out, pet: knowing your penetrating charm.' Anderson was 'puzzled and discomfited' by Stead's behaviour—though she chose not to make anything of the incident.

That winter, the South of England was swept by violent gales and storms. The Blakes' Foxwarren cottage had cold cement floors and plenty of spaces for draughts, and they could afford to heat only two rooms. Weinstein and Fisher returned from the States early, declared bankrupt.

While the receiver showed potential buyers around Foxwarren, the Blakes looked for another place to live. Ruth Hall drove her father around in her Ford jalopy, looking at flats in the Aldershot area where she lived. Bill was keen to live close to Ruth and his two young grandsons, Louis-Antoine and Nicholas.

It was Ruth who secured them a flat in Hawley, near Camberley, five miles from where she lived. The flat was light and airy, occupying the entire upper floor of an old villa, and though the views did not compare with Foxwarren's glories, they overlooked trees, a green common and a farm courtyard. Stead thought it a great improvement on their 'Foxwarren stables'.[4] Since they were thirty-three miles out of London, the rent was low.

They had dreaded a return to inner-city rooming houses. But this was a different hell: this was the dreary outskirts. Stead had no need to complain of the noise here. However she would soon be complaining about the deadly dullness of 'Hawley, Queen of the Yawnies'.[5] It was poorly served by public transport, and with the last bus at 8.30 pm, an evening in London meant staying overnight with friends. For groceries they depended on deliveries from Camberley. The one shop within walking distance was a nightmare for Blake to reach, with his poor eyesight. There were no footpaths on the road; pedestrians had to hug the hedges as the traffic whizzed past.

The Blakes spent four years in Hawley—four years of isolation from the literary world, London and friends. Outings to the theatre or cinema were too expensive and complicated. And Stead complained that having friends to stay at Hawley for the weekend involved so much cooking, cleaning and serving meals that the pleasure evaporated. 'Ruth lives a few miles away and she and the grandchildren toddle over often: that is our company,' Blake told the Burnshaws.

> The butcher's boy wears the traditional straw hat and advises us on our gardens, the grocer's boy approves of us, says our orders arc 'jolly good', the milk boy likes us, the 'dustmen' (Garbage collectors to you Yankees) speak happily to us already anticipating their 'Christmas box.' ... Not since Virgil has a more imbecile life been led in the countryside but we are, Thank God, remote from the lunacies of American city life with its emphases on psychic 'problems.' Nary a problem seems to bother the various human fauna about here.

They had no car, no radio and not even a newspaper, and when after a few months friends gave them a television set, the Blakes were delighted with this breeze from the outside world.

In the summer of 1959, on their way to France, Stanley and Leda Burnshaw passed through London. Burnshaw, who had not seen the Blakes since they left New York in 1946, was appalled by their poverty. He promised himself that he would do his best to persuade his publishing firm—he had sold the Dryden Press to Holt, Rinehart & Winston—to re-issue some of Stead's work. He decided to begin with *The Man Who Loved Children*.

Negotiations were long and tiresome. Burnshaw wrote to the Blakes asking for details of Stead's contracts with previous publishers, print runs and sales figures. Blake, who acted in all business matters as Stead's literary manager, did his best. But the saga had its ups and downs. The Blakes relied too heavily on Burnshaw, their sole friend in the New York publishing world: they were always asking advice, information and favours. On one occasion Burnshaw received a letter from Blake, asking him to please contact so-and-so and do such-and-such. The letter was typed by Stead (Burnshaw knew her typewriter, which had smaller print), but there was no word of greeting from her. Burnshaw was a crusty character, as blunt as Stead was tactless, and he told them what he thought of being treated as a secretary. Stead hurriedly apologised.

Soon after this incident, Burnshaw invited them to join him and his wife Leda on a short trip in France and Italy, all expenses paid. Stead did not like the idea of being beholden. ('I WON'T go around as a poor relation picking out the cheapest dish—or the one next to the cheapest to make it nice,' she told Edith.) It fell to Blake, who would dearly have loved to go, to write back with an excuse. Burnshaw made it clear that he was piqued.

Though Blake was sixty-nine and half blind, he still saw himself as the indefatigable researcher he had always been. To Burnshaw he proposed various projects that he thought might make money. All involved vast research. One suggestion (a decade in advance of the times) was a Women's Encyclopaedia. Another, which interested him less but which he thought would appeal as a gift item, was a Jewish guide to Europe. A third proposal was a biography of Engels.

He was being optimistic, as always. The fact was, he was now typing by touch, so that even his typed letters were difficult to decipher. Every four hours, he put drops in his eyes for his glaucoma. If he was in London for the day, he would call in at his friend Paul Koston's bookshop, on Newman Street, to administer the drops. But his visits to London were rare. The English winter of 1962–63 was the most severe in more than eighty years: birds froze in the trees. Even when spring came Blake scarcely ventured into the city, except for visits to the Royal Eye Hospital. Stead worried about him.

And Blake worried about her. She sat at the typewriter and typed furiously, just as she always had, but she never finished anything. A number of full-length manuscripts in first draft form were packed away in trunks; she had lost interest in them. Most days, she admitted to Edith Anderson, she felt 'lazy, soggy, even weak'. Though she herself never admitted as much, there is little doubt that she was chronically depressed.

Blake was a staunch old-fashioned stoic. He would often make some disdainful comment about the American preoccupation with self and with popular psychology. A very private man, he rarely talked about himself or others. He considered it 'gossip' to air people's private lives. He did not even like to mention to friends if he or Stead were ill. In this too, he influenced Stead. If they commented at all on one another's health, it was done almost stealthily, as if they were breaking a pact by disclosing their private suffering. Blake told Burnshaw:

> Chris has been quite poorly lately—her hypertension has resulted in dizziness and even staggering so I am taking her to London soon for a checkup. Do not refer to this in answering.

In later years, when Blake was seriously ill, Stead would write to her editor at Secker & Warburg:

> Bill has been quite sick. (In hospital, which means trouble for him and many visits to town for me, but I am not complaining.) ... Do not write about this.[6]

This fierce sense of privacy was linked to their wretched situation, which they saw as fallen. They did not want others to see them in this state. For Blake it was less a question of pride than a refusal of self-pity. But Stead was deeply humiliated by their poverty. As a romantic and ambitious adolescent, she had envisaged a very different future for herself.

Left to herself, Stead tended to give psychological explanations for things. As a younger woman, when she had fallen ill on her visits to London for the Travelers' Bank, she believed that London's soot and greyness had affected her, when in fact she had appendicitis. Blake was the opposite. He did not like to probe the psychological sphere. Thus he preferred to believe that Stead's depression and lethargy had a purely *physical* origin. Whether or not she privately thought otherwise, Stead outwardly adopted Blake's view. Apart from anything else, it provided an excuse to visit her favourite doctor.

Dr Philip Harvey suggested Stead should come in for observation at St Stephen's Hospital. For her it was a welcome rest, and pleasant to have her indolence regarded as a physical illness. She told Edith Anderson: 'Dr. Harvey inspires a childlike trust in me.'

Harvey and his medical team found no physical cause for Stead's listlessness. They observed a mild post-menopausal hormone imbalance. Harvey also noticed signs of her once having had tuberculosis, which had obviously cured itself. He privately believed that Stead's main problem was alcohol, and he tried to suggest that she abstain. This was not a suggestion she appreciated.

Neither Stead nor Blake ever seemed to consider her dependence on alcohol a problem. It is possible that Blake was privately concerned, and that it was not the sort of thing he would mention to others. More likely, he closed his eyes to it. Perhaps he did not even realise the extent of her private drinking, which began in the mornings.

Stead's drinking was never an embarrassment. On social occasions friends noticed that she drank 'like a fish', but no one ever saw her unsteady on her feet. Leah Harvey and Pera Koston both recall that Stead would always turn up to parties with a carton of cream, which she would drink before she started imbibing in earnest. They presumed she thought it would cushion her stomach. (She also believed that cream gave her skin a flattering glow, but they did not know this.) Philip Harvey comments that Christina's facial colour was always ruddy; when she had drunk too much, her skin would become mottled and her nose would shine.

After her stay in hospital, Stead joked that Harvey had given her pills to make her 'tick faster'. A few weeks later, she told Harvey she was suffering from terrible insomnia. Worse still, she said to him pointedly, was the randiness—with no one to fix it on.

∿

As always, she and Blake were feeling 'dank' about Britain. 'If only the country were vital enough to be *hated*, that would be something,' Blake would grumble.[7] They became quite excited when they received an unexpected letter from Peter Neidecker, head of the old Travelers' Bank, hinting that they should join him in foreign purlieus. Neidecker had retired to Nice after two serious motor accidents severely curtailed his financial and sporting adventures.

But the free health services kept them in England. Moreover, despite Stead's complaints about dreary England, it was really only Blake, the more dedicated Gallophile, who wanted to 'fly the coop' and move permanently to France. Stead was still haunted by the memory of 'those frightful years going from hotel to hotel'. And she was too tired and lethargic to contemplate moving.

When the Bakwins (wealthy American friends who owned a gallery in New York) invited them for a trip to Europe in the summer of 1963 (all expenses paid), she again refused. Harry Bakwin persevered, saying he wanted Bill to bid for him at art auctions in Paris, and eventually Blake took the train to Paris. He came back sparkling. Paris made him so happy. He and Harry had had wonderful gourmet meals; he had seen old friends, and enjoyed several Montparnasse lunches with Ben Shahn, the socialist-realist painter, an old friend from the 1930s. And he would have seen Mollie. Whenever she came to England to stay with Ruth, he always visited her.

He did some research at the Bibliothèque Nationale, and after he returned to England, he started work on a novel, Balzacian in scope, about the scurrilous activities of the bankers during the French Revolution.

Stead shared her inner world with nobody. She prided herself on being 'more silent than the grave (for posthumously how many silly secrets come out!)'. But there was something in her life she finally had to tell a friend. She chose Edith Anderson:

> I *had* to mention that thing to someone … I'm not going soft in the head either. It's just that—you'll have to take my word for it as I can't go into it—this is real. And I sound like Letty Fox, don't I? 'This is it.' I assure you I'm blushing from embarrassment and probably shame.

Letty Fox was twenty-three: Stead was sixty-two. Stead was in love with Philip Harvey, as she continued to be for the next ten years. Edith Anderson would not be the only one to know. Stead's infatuation became an open secret.

Any social occasion without Philip Harvey seemed dull. One week before Bill's seventieth birthday party, organised for his actual birthday, 28 July 1964, Stead told Edith Anderson: 'Many people, too many, are coming; I hope I get through it, but no one I love among the guests, too bad. I won't have time to love anyway.'

In December that year, she told Edith, 'I know you are shocked at my loving anyone besides Bill—but you don't know anything about me really, do you? It is no underestimation of Bill. Nothing to do with it.'

That year, Paul Koston became a confidant. The Blakes had met Paul and Pera Koston through the Harveys. Paul Koston, originally a New Yorker of Latvian Jewish parentage, and his second wife, Pera, had come to England from South Africa in the mid 1950s. Koston managed Hatchard's bookshop in Piccadilly before he set up his own business, a bookshop dealing mostly with international mail-orders, on Newman Street, off Oxford Street. He was one of those inestimable booksellers who read voraciously and know their books.

Koston, himself a frustrated writer, was fascinated by writers and the 'spring of creativity'. He admired Stead and Blake, and he (like Tella Friedmann) was one of the few friends who had actually read their fiction. His other passions were food and gambling. A generous fellow, who prided himself on his gallantry, he liked nothing better than to invite Christina and Bill, together or singly, to lunch in a restaurant near his bookshop.

He could also be irascible and difficult—though this was a side of him the Blakes rarely saw. On social occasions, when he had drunk too much, Paul, a Trotskyist, would berate Blake and Harvey for being 'Stalinists' who were preventing the Workers' Revolution.

Christina flirted with Paul Koston, though not seriously; she thought him physically unprepossessing. The perception was mutual: Koston found her *interesting*. He comments: 'There's nothing like plainness to sharpen a woman's wits.' [8]

In November 1964, Stead and Koston enjoyed a well-lubricated lunch of oysters and steak, and Stead found herself confessing her passion for Philip Harvey. With Koston, she could say what she liked. Indeed, he rather encouraged a comradely lewdness. In the note she wrote afterwards to thank him for the meal, she told him she intended to buy Harvey a present of a little Chinese box. 'Being the straightforward wholesome type he is, he won't start to wonder why I am always giving him lovely little boxes.'

Throughout 1963 and 1964, Stead was working on four novellas. Three of them were about young American women and their inconsistent attitude to sex. Stead was interested in a phenomenon she called the 'Diana complex'. In several young women she had observed a kind of chastity complex, a 'tug-of-war between wanting and not daring'. [9] The novellas would eventually be published under the title *The Puzzleheaded Girl*.

As she reflected on the young women she had known, Stead reread the letters she had received over the years from Edith Anderson. She had kept them all in a file, chronologically arranged. Struck by their frankness and lively tone, she wrote and told Edith she would like to write about her, asking permission to use her letters. She posed the delicate question clumsily:

> I have a question to ask, and want to formulate it, put it the right way. No, with this introdn I will put it badly; will you mind if I use your letters as a source? I wish they could be printed as they are: they are unusual (with your frankness and gift of forcible and personal expression) and they give an excellent purely personal idea of Berlin in the early days. But that cannot be, I expect; my idea is not to use them for that, in any case. I hope you will say yes. (Not to print them, I don't mean that, good gracious.)

Though it was not quite clear what Stead *did* mean, Edith was flattered, and consented. That was August 1963. A year later, when the signs all pointed to a cooling in Stead's affections, Edith changed her mind and asked to have the letters back, saying she might use them in a novel herself. Stead returned them in November 1964. 'I have no other correspondent now,' she told Edith (meaning no other close woman friend). About the letters, she commented: 'When I read through them with an eye to story-writing, I saw that I could not use them—they are too much yours; it would be quite wrong.' In fact, she kept a thick bundle—almost a hundred.[10]

At Christmas in 1964, Anderson made an impetuous visit to England. Her meeting with the Blakes was not a success. Afterwards, Stead felt contrite for appearing so ungrateful for Anderson's little gifts.

> I am sure we let you go without saying thankyou properly.
>
>   I don't know why we were so *rough*. And I am sure you were not happy about the visit. But what can one do, short visits at such long intervals? Unhappy things.

For six months they did not write to one another. In mid July 1965, it was Bill who wrote to Edith. In September 1965 Stead wrote one last amicable letter. Then, in November, Stead wrote a tirade about the evils of bohemia. She added:

> I was not going to write to you. I was very angry with you for coming into my affairs; and for taking advantage of a confidence, you should not have done it. But you would do it again! You can't help it ... You are so girlish. You'll never grow up.

Anderson, flabbergasted, asked what she was supposed to have done. A week later, on 8 December 1965, came the 'terrible letter' (Anderson's words) in which Stead 'lowered the portcullis with a crash'.[11]

> You have asked me what it is that you have done that has made me angry. I am sure you know. I won't elaborate. We have jogged along a considerable time with a very vast disagreement between us over things that cannot be reconciled.

Edith Anderson claims she does not know to this day what she was supposed to have done. She was devastated.

Though Anderson did not know it, she was not the only woman friend of Stead's to receive this treatment. She had lasted longer than any of

Stead's other female correspondents. Florence James, Anne Dooley and Ruth McKenney, once intimate friends, had all been written off—literally. All three were now hanging in Stead's fictional gallery of monstrous characters.

Stead's difficult relationship with women reflected her uneasy relationship with herself. Elvira Western, Letty Fox, Nellie Cotter, Eleanor Herbert and Emily Wilkes all contain aspects of herself. Deep down, she raged at one person: herself. She upbraided Edith Anderson for betraying a confidence, but this was something she herself had done five years earlier, when she told Philip Harvey what Edith had said about him. She accused Edith of being 'girlish', yet she admitted she herself had begun to sound like 23-year-old Letty Fox. Her tirade against Edith was in the very voice that Stead, eternally plagued by self-recriminations, used in relation to herself.

Among Stead's papers are notes for a story based on Edith Anderson. They include passages that have been copied from Anderson's letters to Stead, though Max Schroeder has become Ernst, and Edith is Agnes. Stead would later refer to Edith and Max as 'dreadful bohemians—the real Berlin Bohemia'.[12] To friends she would say that she once knew a woman living in Berlin who was a 'horrid horrid lesbian'.[13] It was a bizarre conclusion to draw, considering Edith's obvious liking for men.

In the winter of 1964–65, Stead put aside her novellas about young women and sex, and returned to an old manuscript, *Cotters' England*, in order to develop the picture of Nellie Cotter as a bohemian and a lesbian. Nellie Cotter, Stead wrote to Burnshaw, is 'married to a husband she admires'. She added: 'This is very typical of aggressive lesbians. They use the husband in many ways … This kind of "male" Lesbian does not hate men, she uses them, when she is tired of the perverted practice.'

Stead's imaginative world was once again impinging on her perception of reality. Eventually, her fictional characters became more 'real' to her than the flesh-and-blood individuals on whom they were based.

She told Paul Koston she was worrying about the morality of *Cotters' England*. She had first raised the issue when she drafted the novel in the 1950s, but it was never quite clear what she meant. Was it the way she manipulated reality that worried her? Did it trouble her that Nellie Cotter *appeared* (to all who knew her) to be based on Anne Dooley, whereas she was in fact a mixture of different women, and heavily laced by Stead's imagination? To portray Nellie's brother Tom, Stead studied Freud on impotence. Though she claimed to have little time for Freud, she certainly embraced his central thesis: that sexual behaviour is a major determinant of personality.

She commented that the novel was meant to be 'an attack on mental moral and physical squalor enjoyed in Bohemia, an attack on bohemia which I detest'.[14] In 1967, she would tell Ron Geering, in response to a letter he wrote her about *Cotters' England*, 'I detest lesbians'. In her fiction lesbians are always portrayed as aggressive and predatory.

It seems as if a deep, repressive pathology was at work here. Why was Stead—who had always vigorously championed sexual freedom—so hostile to lesbianism and bohemia? Why did she react so violently to something that surely did not threaten her? Or did it? She had left Australia precisely to avoid the suburban life she now found herself living. She had fallen in love with an erudite cosmopolitan, who now seemed weak and dull. Did she rail against unconventional lives because she was appalled at how boring her own had become?

Stead saw herself as ugly, something of a monster. Unable to come to terms with the monster within herself, she made her characters monsters. In their manic talk and manipulative behaviour there is both her father and her own fragmented identity. Her characters reflect the irresolvable tensions within Stead between the self and other.

She had long ago internalised her father's misogyny. In 1973, at the age of seventy-one, she would tell a female interviewer that she disliked women because of their smell. Her biologist father looms large:

> There is something (it's purely physical, I think a sense of smell is very strong in our make-up, especially some of us), there's something about women's skirts, I mean there's too, much smell of material, I don't know what it is, something like that—I don't like it. Whereas, well this is a purely sexual thing, you see, I'm sure that the men we like … I'm sure there's something—we're animals after all—that attracts us … Now I'm sure that the reason I don't like women is that I don't get this particular stimulation, you see.[15]

In her adolescence, Stead had written love poems to women, though later she would shrug this off as immaturity. Most of her novels are about women. She spent years of her life musing about women: their bodies, minds, needs, desires. How could she maintain so emphatically that she did not like them?

Naturally, Stead's protestations about disliking women made her friends wonder. Ruth Hall comments that her father would sometimes tell friends, in front of Christina, that Christina seemed to attract women: 'There would be great gusts of laughter from him and Christina.' Their wealthy friend Ruth Bakwin (probably the model for the lesbian, Lucy Headlong, in *Letty Fox*) gave Stead one of her mink coats in the early 1930s, and was thought to be keen on Stead. Stanley Burnshaw recalls that his late wife Leda was convinced that Christina had lesbian proclivities. She and Christina were sitting on a sofa and playing with a puppet in the Burnshaws' New York apartment one night in the 1940s, and Christina— Leda was sure she was not imagining it—began to flirt with her in an intense, rather uncomfortable way.

Pera Koston remembers a bizarre incident at one of the Blakes' parties in Surbiton in the mid 1960s. Christina was in the kitchen and Pera went to ask if she could help. Christina ignored the question, walked over and shut the kitchen door, leaned against the sink and said to her: 'You know, you have a beautiful body.' Pera (who intensely disliked Christina) made for the door, embarrassed.

Stead described Pera Koston to her cousin Gwen as 'a magnificent woman' with a 'physique of the sort loved by Henry Moore'.[16] Certainly, Stead was extremely conscious of beauty in women; she profoundly envied it. But it is interesting that she appraised beautiful women with the sexualised gaze normally associated with males. A scene in *The Beauties and Furies* is particularly striking in this respect. Elvira, alone in her Paris hotel room, is contemplating her body as another might look at her. She does not know it, but her lover Oliver has come in, and is gazing at her from the doorway. It is one of the most overtly erotic passages in Stead's fiction.

Along with the often expressed hostility towards lesbians and, increasingly, towards women in general, went Stead's often expressed liking for men. It is scarcely surprising, since she openly flirted with their husbands, that Leah Harvey and Pera Koston never much liked Christina Stead. 'If she hadn't hung out for the admiration of men, she would have been more relaxed,' says Pera, who sensed that Stead was 'very knotted inside'. She adds:

> Christina would adopt a coy manner with men. It was a coyness that seemed to go along with her liking for frills and lace and crêpe de chine blouses with bows. She lived in a kind of time warp as far as women were concerned.[17]

There was a desperation in Stead's behaviour—a terrible insecurity about her own appearance that left her with a lifelong need to convince herself she was attractive to men. Her preference for men was so often and so emphatically stated that plainly it had to do with her self-image. It was more about power (or, rather, powerlessness) than sex—though she always expressed it in blatantly sexual terms. Significantly, the men she loved—with the exception of Harry Bloom—were all passions of the head.

———— ꝏ ————

By the end of 1963, Stanley Burnshaw had finally persuaded Holt, Rinehart & Winston to re-issue *The Man Who Loved Children*. It was to be in hard cover instead of the paperback Burnshaw had envisaged, and he was embarrassed that Stead's advance was a token $250, but he was determined to make this as successful an exhumation of a buried author as possible. He had arranged for the distinguished poet and literary critic Randall Jarrell to write an introduction. (He would be paid $300 for this.) The re-issue was due to appear early in 1965.

In England, no publisher was prepared to re-issue the book. Peter Davies, Stead's sole champion in the British publishing world, had committed suicide four years before. Secker & Warburg considered it, and the reader they sent it to (writer and critic James Burns Singer) commented: 'she could easily have the kind of success which Lawrence has had ... I think her a much better and more central writer than Lawrence', but Fred Warburg would only be persuaded when he saw the good sales in the US.

Publishers on both sides of the Atlantic believed that a serious attempt to launch Stead again would require a new book as well. Fortunately, Stead had two manuscripts almost ready for publication, *Cotters' England* and *The Puzzleheaded Girl*.

———— ꝏ ————

'It is a small edition,' Blake told a friend at the end of 1964, referring to the forthcoming re-issue of *The Man Who Loved Children*, 'but one hopes a harbinger of better things'.[18]

The galleys of Randall Jarrell's Introduction, entitled 'An Unread Book' (it would also appear in the *Atlantic Monthly*), arrived at the end of 1964, a few weeks before the book was due out. Several days passed before

Stead sat down to read it. She dreaded the feeling of 'quiet nausea' that nearly always overcame her when she read criticism of her books. But she was overwhelmed by Jarrell's 'wonderful sympathy' and 'profound understanding'.

He rated it highly:

> Where *The Man Who Loved Children* is concerned, I can't help myself; it seems to me as plainly good as *War and Peace* and *Crime and Punishment* and *Remembrance of Things Past* are plainly great.

With Jarrell, Stead had found her 'perfect reader'. She told people that when she read his Introduction the same delightfully warm feeling would creep over her that she had when she felt loved. When she read it a third time, slowly this time, to savour it, she wept and wept, 'a regular fountain'.[19] She found it difficult to write to Jarrell about it. Four months later she managed to thank him. 'It is quite the loveliest thing that ever happened to me in "my literary life." '[20]

In February, several copies of the book arrived in a large airmail parcel from the States. It was a handsome edition. The jacket was illustrated by Milton Glaser, the most fashionable book designer around, and on the back were tributes from Hortense Calisher, Robert Lowell, Elizabeth Hardwick, Jean Stafford and Peter Taylor. Stead told Burnshaw gratefully: 'It is a miracle to have a book reprinted after 25 years.'

Randall Jarrell made Stead able to read again a book she had not opened for twenty-five years. For the first time she could see it 'not as a miserable story, but as it looked to a sympathetic outsider'. But there was one thing Jarrell said that hurt her to the quick:

> *The Man who Loved Children* was a failure with critics and the public. It has been out of print for many years, and Christina Stead herself is remembered by only a few readers. When the world rejects, and then forgets, a writer's most profound and imaginative book, he may unconsciously work in a more limited way in the books that follow it; this has happened, I believe, to Christina Stead. The world's incomprehension has robbed it, for twenty-five years, of *The Man Who Loved Children*; has robbed it, forever, of what could have come after *The Man Who Loved Children*.

Jarrell's statement basically nullified Stead's writing after 1940. As he saw it, the world had been robbed, forever. Stead protested, but only halfheartedly:

I do not think the absence of appreciation of *TMWLC* stopped me writing. I have grit. But you may be right after all. Perhaps you are. You are on the outside and see.

He did not see. No one on the outside saw. Jarrell had presumably read the four novels published after *The Man Who Loved Children*, and not been impressed. But he had no idea about the other books, which had not seen the light of day because one publisher after another rejected them. If he had known the facts, a more tactful Jarrell might have mused to himself that if Stead had received the recognition she deserved, her later fiction would perhaps have been more mellow. But what's the point of telling a writer she could have written different books?

In April 1965, while the New York literati were all discussing the Stead novel Randall Jarrell had championed, Jarrell was in hospital, having slashed his wrists. It was there that he received Stead's first letter, thanking him profusely.

Six months later, on a mid October night, Jarrell was struck by a car in North Carolina and killed. It was the tragic end, at fifty-one, of a 'noble, difficult and beautiful soul', as Robert Lowell described his friend.

Jarrell's death made Stead feel sad and guilty. She believed they could have been friends, at least by correspondence, and she felt sorry that she had never been able to do anything for him. In September 1966, she wrote to Jarrell's widow: 'About that Introduction, allow me to say one word. It is so extraordinarily friendly and close to me that if I ever need encouragement I just look at a little part of it and I feel ready to work again.'[21]

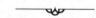

'How does it feel to be famous?' Stanley Burnshaw asked Stead, in March 1965. Harry Bloom wrote: 'You must be walking on air. Floating. Do you talk to people?'

This time round, American reviewers raved about the novel. The *Saturday Review* called it a 'long-neglected masterpiece'. The *New York Review of Books* termed it 'a marvelous neglected novel'. The *Nation* pronounced it 'a funny, painful, absorbing masterpiece'. In a single week in April, the book sold almost 1200 copies. There were several reprintings. In Australia, Patrick White read Christina Stead for the first time, and commented:

> In *The Man Who Loved Children* Christina Stead has written a book as chock-a-block and as recognisable as private memory. The humiliating part of the whole business is that most of us overlooked her genius till Randall Jarrell fought the battle for it.[22]

It is significant that it was the burst of recognition and the pressing requests of publishers for more work, rather than Philip Harvey's pep pills, which revived her spirits and made her eager to write again. She still lacked physical energy, and would complain that she was easily exhausted (especially if she had to entertain people or go into the city on some errand), but she had a new lease on life. For the first time, she felt the impulse to polish all her unfinished manuscripts. 'Now I am being pursued by myself,' she told Burnshaw.

Meanwhile, Blake was having no success whatsoever with publishers. He was elated that Stead had at last been recognised as one of the twentieth century's major writers, but he himself had been doggedly working for years entirely in vain. His last publication, *We are the Makers of Dreams* (written in 1942), had been in 1959. He would never have another publication.

Yet he never stopped working. In 1965, he took time off his French Revolution novel to produce another college students' guide to Marxism, which his friends Leo Huberman and Paul Sweezy, editors of Monthly Review Press, had asked him to write. He worked hard on the project, which strained his eyesight, and when he finished, he thought it 'a damned good book'. However, after some prevarication, Monthly Review Press rejected it as too deep for American students. It was worse than the usual rejection because Monthly Review Press was a last bastion of Blake's kind of accessible, non-academic Marxism.

By 1965, at the age of seventy-one, his health was flagging. He had always prided himself on being able to walk for miles and work late into the night without noticing it. Now he was distressed by his declining energy. With the aid of a strong light and magnifying glass, he still spent most of the day reading and writing, but he had become more dependent, and Stead was not patient. Now that she was motivated to work on her old manuscripts, she resented demands on her time. In April Blake had influenza and became so despondent that Stead felt quite 'harassed'.

> I had rather a bad time with Bill—had a touch of 'flu and it looked to me like a touch of something like hypochondria which as you know is a disease: I don't want him to get it.[23]

She could not bear it when Blake was not cheerful: he had always been the one to rally her when she was depressed. She was terrified of losing him. When Max Kotlarsky died in 1960, she told Aida, 'I am afraid to think what it is to lose a life companion'. Christina's insistence that Bill's problems were psychosomatic made her a harsh and patronising nurse, and her unsympathetic attitude shocked her friends on occasion. Tella and Boy Friedmann recall a dinner just before they left England to live in Italy, in 1967. Blake, by this time, was seriously ill with stomach cancer, though no-one knew it. In the middle of the meal, he abruptly got up and went out. Stead made no move to follow him. The Friedmanns wanted to go after him, but Stead held them back, explaining that he felt nauseated and that it was psychological: he was jealous of her literary success and not finding it easy to adjust. 'This was the only time she appeared to us unfeeling about Bill,' says Tella Friedmann, but they saw the Blakes seldom these days.

Philip Harvey recalls Blake and Stead quarrelling late one evening, when he was taking them home after dinner at his house. Christina flung at Bill that he had hindered her as a writer; Bill sat on the edge of his seat, his hands gripping the leather tightly, and said nothing. Harvey also recalls another occasion when Bill kept saying to Christina, apparently trying to justify himself: 'It was all for you, Chris, you know. I did it all for you.' There seems little doubt that Stead had begun to blame Bill for their problems. Their wandering life in Europe now seemed a terrible waste. Perhaps, in bitter moments, she also blamed him for the grim poverty of their last twenty years.

In early May 1965, Harry and Anne Bloom visited London again from Puerto Rico. A photograph from this visit, presumably taken by Stead, shows Bloom and Blake standing under the imposing head of Karl Marx at his tomb in Highgate Cemetery. Blake, grey and fragile, looks stiff and sad; Harry Bloom is tall, loose-bodied and strong-looking.

Christina Stead had allowed herself to become painfully distracted by her completely unrealistic infatuation for Philip Harvey. Because she no longer had a confidante, her fantasies tumbled around crazily in her own head. She did not dare to tell Philip Harvey her feelings about him. And she could not talk to Bill about it. They no longer shared their intimate thoughts. So it was a relief to be able to tell Harry Bloom. At the same time, it enabled her to show Harry that he was not the only love in her life. When it came to promoting jealousy, Stead was an able strategist.

Later, she would describe that period to Leda and Stanley Burnshaw:

> I had AN AWFUL time. Comes along my big brudder Harry Bloom (who fights people for me) and I felt better ... Alas, his years and terribly hard work are telling and he has *angina pectoris*. It is strange to see a big tall strong man, a fighter—he was a terror with his fists, a union organiser in NY and I can't say blacker than that!—and also an artist, a humane, reasonable and intensely keen man—to see such a man getting older, beginning to crumple. It makes me feel so bad.[24]

Three weeks later, a second letter to the Burnshaws reveals the same proclivity for mythologising.

> I had a big skyride with my mad passion, Mr. X. [Philip Harvey], all in the air, too—I was so entangled I sent for (well, all but) my old friend and cobber (Australian for the closest and best friend) Harry Bloom. He came from P.R. I am still humble, I can tell you, at this devotion: I really am. I am thinking over human life and love. I couldn't tell him all; it hurt him too much; but the fact that he was there, enabled me to see things in a normal way. It was very necessary, I assure you.

The Halls had recently moved to the South London suburb of Surbiton. They now had a third son, Simon, who was the image of Bill: small and rotund, with dark, animated eyes. Bill missed the contact with Ruth and his grandsons, and he and Christina decided to move to Surbiton themselves. Ruth found them a flat at No. 12A Elmers Court, Avenue Elmers, and Laurie Hall covered over the grime on the kitchen walls with a fresh coat of paint.

They moved at the beginning of June 1965. The flat was in a dilapidated tenement building, a fifteen-minute walk from the Halls and just sixteen minutes from Waterloo by express train. It was smaller, much less pleasant and more expensive than the Hawley flat and up three flights of stairs, but after seven years in the remote countryside and London's suburban outskirts, they were relieved to be closer to libraries and friends.

June was taken up with settling in. Perhaps it was this drudgery, so soon after the excitement of Harry Bloom's lightning visit, that prompted Stead to remark to an Australian journalist that when she was writing she sometimes wished she were not married. ('Only then, mind you.')[25] These days she was impatient with her married life.

Throughout July, Blake was obliged to do everything in the house. Stead had slipped, breaking a bone in her foot. Told not to put any weight on it for a fortnight, she walked with crutches, and after this had her foot in a reinforced cast for several more weeks. It did not improve the state of her nerves. She admitted to Burnshaw she was 'mad as a hornet all day long with being thwarted' and kept blowing up 'like a volcano'.

Bill wanted them to take a holiday. They had some money now— though they cautiously regarded the recent windfall as no more than a lucky break. The hardcover re-issue of The Man Who Loved Children sold 20000 copies, and an editor who was then at Holt estimates that Stead would have made about $25–30000 from it—enough to live modestly on for two years.[26] Holt also paid her $19000 as an advance for Cotters' England and The Puzzleheaded Girl, which seemed to Stead a phenomenal sum. (In England, Seeker & Warburg's advance for the same two books was £1000.)

Stead finally agreed to a fortnight's holiday in Yorkshire in September. Blake looked forward to exploring old villages, Norman castles and ruined abbeys. They booked an inexpensive bed-and-breakfast (abstemiousness had become a habit) and travelled north by train. Three days later they were back in London. The cold damp climate of Yorkshire had given Blake such painful lumbago and fibrositis that he was almost crippled, and they had had to come home. Stead had not wanted to be there in the first place.

Stead was trying to persuade Blake to make the trip to Puerto Rico. Harry Bloom wanted them to go for a visit, and it was warm there. For once, it was Bill who was hesitating: Puerto Rico was a long and expensive trip, and he was feeling ill. He suggested the South of France instead, but Stead baulked at this. She confessed to Burnshaw: 'I could not tell him that the idea of a S. of France holiday à deux, more little cafés, little hotels, cosy walks, talks would SUFFOCATE me.'

She was making it more and more plain to a number of their friends—and doubtless to Bill as well—that his company no longer excited her. To Harry Bloom she sighed:

I am so horribly lonely! My books are coming out all over the place in reprint and new; and it doesn't mean anything to me. I mean it. I need 'a drinking companion' as you said. I thought that very cute: since neither of us drinks more than 2 at a sitting.

By October 1965 they had decided to go to Puerto Rico early the following year and see the Blooms. Stanley Burnshaw suggested they go via New York, making it partly a business trip for tax purposes, as well as to meet Holt publishers and Stead's agent, Cyrilly Abels. This seemed a good idea, though Stead felt shy at the thought of the publicity. The English re-issue of *The Man Who Loved Children* was to appear while they were away.

They sailed on 27 February 1966, travelling tourist class on the SS *United States*. It was a rough crossing, and they had scarcely recovered when they were plunged into the whirl of New York literary society. 'The first time I ever rated a literary New York life,' Stead told Paul and Pera Koston, evidently rather pleased by it all. They were in New York for twelve days, staying with their friends the Steinbergs, and had an enjoyable time, with a very full calendar. Stead was blooming, rejuvenated by her success.

Holt, Rinehart & Winston threw a party for their brilliant and neglected new protégée. Stead bought a cream ribbon dress and fluffy little jacket for the occasion. Ettore and Jessie Rella organised a cocktail party for Stead in their split-level 14th Street apartment. Ettore, still a devoted puppeteer, manipulated his three-headed puppet, the Three Fates, for Stead, who was so gripped by the performance that she felt 'quite scared'. Robert Lowell was there, but he had a 'dull effect' on Stead, who conjectured that he was temperamentally unsuited to his position of 'grand man of letters'. The poet and playwright Norman Rosten, a young man when the Blakes first met him in New York political circles in the early 1940s, enjoyed a playful conversation with Stead. It was the beginning of a warm, flirtatious friendship.

The Blakes left for Puerto Rico on 16 March 1966. It was the first time these seasoned travellers had ever flown in an aeroplane. Blake, who suffered from vertigo, had always been convinced that flying would terrify him, but he was persuaded to try it by the Steinbergs, who accompanied them on the flight, to spend a few days with the Blooms. It was 'fair sailing' all the way, and Stead was absolutely thrilled by the views. Even Blake was converted to flying—though this was to be his only flight.

The Blooms lived on the top floor of a modern penthouse flat in Hato Rey, a suburb of San Juan. The weather was hot, humid and sleepy. It was the rainy season, and it rained and rained. Puerto Rico was having a building boom, and the bulldozers started up at 6 am, even on weekends. Stead slept badly. Blake had no energy. Harry Bloom was preoccupied with his electrical business. In the evenings, his angina left him tired.

Stead, bored, drank a great deal of scotch. In the first few days she occupied spare moments by checking the galleys of *Dark Places of the Heart*, due out in September. When she finished this task, she wrote to Burnshaw (in Florida for the winter): 'Am already showing signs of violence, so must do *something*.' According to Michael Bloom, who heard about the visit later from his parents: 'There was a bit of a set-to in Puerto Rico. Chris told mother she was not the woman she used to be—meaning she'd become conservative.'

The Blooms must have hoped that their guests would be more independent and energetic than they turned out to be. Bill had never been so lacklustre. Public transport was difficult. And the price of everything horrified the Blakes. They tended to rely on Harry and Anne taking them around in their car. When they got out, they were charmed by the pastel-coloured Spanish-style bungalows with their ornate grilles, the banana and coffee plantations, and the bright blue ocean. But it was a long seven weeks.

The days before their departure brought the sort of drama Stead seemed to have been wanting. She and Harry Bloom spent some passionate time alone together. By the time she stepped aboard the *Flandres*, a French liner destined for Le Havre, Christina was in quite a state. Eighteen months later, she gave an oblique account of her departure to the Burnshaws:

> My *Orlando Furioso* in P.R. who has been so close to me for over 30 years, suddenly got into a passion and said he would kill me if I left him and he would do such and such and I would never get on the boat. Ungrateful for this, I made up my mind to get on the boat, even with four broken limbs (which he promised—you think it's a joke? No.). But he did manage to stab me to the heart the morning I left and I did not get over it for many months.

She added, in the margin: 'Don't refer to this when writing back. Of course, Bill, my true companion, knows something, but I managed to make it fairly light-hearted.'

After the large glass windows and oceanic views at San Juan, they had been dreading the dark little flat in Surbiton. But it was a splendid summer afternoon when they arrived in London. The trees were flowering, and Ruth Hall had filled their refrigerator with supplies. They were relieved to be home.

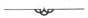

Blake was not at all well, and Stead was miserably unhappy. Her only chance, she thought, was to try to write herself out of her gloom, and she returned to the big project that had been hanging over her for sixteen years, *I'm Dying Laughing*, based on the turbulent lives of Ruth McKenney and Richard Bransten. A year later, she told the Burnshaws that the circumstances had been 'something like those that made me write *TMWLC* in a very bleak period … I hauled myself out of that Slough of Despond with my hand round my own neck'. Her fame did not help: she felt there was nothing in her life. Harry Bloom was the other side of the Atlantic with his wife Anne. Philip Harvey, in London, was equally inaccessible. For months she mooned about Harry Bloom. Eventually, after 'a lot of stiffneckedness and courage and whatnot', she told herself: 'I am never going to get over this!' and she began to improve. She told the Burnshaws: 'I'm much better now, though I won't get over it! I guess there's no age at which all passion is spent, after all.' She was sixty-five.

Without sexual passion, Stead had no passion for life or writing. Nevertheless, she was eager to deliver *I'm Dying Laughing*, and she put in one final intense burst. In the evenings she read it to Bill, who thought it magnificent.

By the beginning of November 1966, Stead had the revised manuscript ready to send to Stanley Burnshaw. Ruth McKenney was still alive, and Stead may have been worried about libel. She wanted Burnshaw to read it before she officially submitted it to Holt. 'You are the only person I know who knows part of the story,' she told him.

She knew that a book about communists during the McCarthy period would not be seen as 'timely', but she told Burnshaw: 'No matter—it is there. And I felt I had to write "the truth"—and this is it, expressed in my own way.'

Burnshaw was awe-struck by the way Stead had captured Ruth McKenney and Richard Bransten; the characters' voices were 'uncannily real'. But he thought she should change some of the details for fear of prosecution for libel. Did Stephen Howard have to commit suicide just like Bransten? Could she not invent an illness for him? Burnshaw, though he was very impressed with the novel, again recommended considerable pruning. He also wanted Stead to build in more information about the political atmosphere of the late 1940s.

> The whole Hollywood situation sounds incredible today, and so does all the kowtowing to the party hacks through the forties and fifties. The CP and the radical movement are absolutely nil here; you wouldn't believe it. And your novel will come upon a reading public that regards the American experience with the CP and the radical left as nonsensical, idiotic, meaningless.

Stead's agents and publishers all agreed that the novel had great power, but everyone wanted changes. Stead agreed to revise, but the barrage of advice quite paralysed her. Nevertheless, it was understood that the novel was almost ready for publication. By mid 1967 Stead's American and English publishers were discussing the possibility of a co-production. Yet the novel was not published for almost twenty years—not until after Christina Stead's death.

I'm Dying Laughing clearly presented libel problems and Holt could not have published it as it was. Emily Wilkes was instantly recognisable to those who knew McKenney. But Stead could have changed personal details easily enough (though she would have hated the idea). It was the request for more political detail that bogged her down: building in explanations went against her grain. The 'fling' of writing the first draft was behind her, and she was not at all convinced by the revisions requested. Over the next few months she wrote three totally different bridging chapters ('to bring back the past to those who have forgotten') and did not like any of them. *I'm Dying Laughing* would become her worst albatross ever.

Dark Places of the Heart was published in New York in September 1966. The reviews tended to be halfhearted, and sales would not have been lifted by Joseph Mathewson's damning review in the *New York Times Book Review*: 'The reader is Nellie's victim … a blurry-eyed victim, with hands too weak to support … so leaden a volume.'

But Stead had conquered the literary establishment, and an Australian academic, Ron Geering, was writing the first analytical study of her work. On study-leave in London in 1966, he made several visits to Surbiton to talk with her. He was depressed by the dismal flat, and though he found Blake charming and animated, he was frustrated that Blake dominated the conversation, making it difficult for him to ask Stead questions about her work.

In later years, Geering and Stead would become firm friends. Eventually, he was to be her literary executor.

Bill Blake had done vast quantities of work on his French Revolution novel, but his eyesight made progress depressingly slow. And now he was having trouble swallowing food. Thinking that a change might help to restore his spirits, he tried to persuade Christina to take a holiday with him. She told him she could not face the packing. She suggested that he go and stay with Alf Hurst in Paris, but he refused to go without her. Eventually, in September 1967, she agreed to go away for a week to the Midlands. They caught trains and buses to Leamington Spa, Warwick, Coventry and Stratford-upon-Avon and visited old castles and cathedrals.

Back in London, Bill's discomfort in swallowing became acute, and he began to panic. Christina did her best to make special mashed dishes or broth, and he would eat a few spoonfuls, and say, 'It's very nice, but that's all I can take now'. Stead, describing herself to friends as 'half-wild with the work and anxiety'[27] persisted in believing that the problem was psychological. She observed with impatience that Bill was behaving exactly like his mother in the years before she died, when Rosa had been falsely convinced she had tuberculosis. Friends were told that his illness was a rejection of age, and a form of depression.

Because she regarded Blake's problem as 'a refusal to eat' and a form of 'hypochondria', Stead acted like a harried mother with a recalcitrant child of seventy-three. A constant refrain in her letters was her lack of time: Bill's perversity made it impossible for her to get on with her writing. She told Aida Kotlarsky: 'Bill knows he is taking all my time and energy, he regrets it, constantly mentions it—but his own need is greater than his conscience; so it is with sick people.' She added: 'Bill wants to believe there is something serious that is taking his appetite ... No one wants to think he is a hypochondriac.'

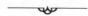

Life is certainly a lottery. The $10000 Britannica Australia Award for Literature was Australia's most generous literary prize. Sponsored by the Encyclopaedia Britannica company since 1964, the award was presented annually for the most outstanding contribution to Australian literature. Winners had been Judith Wright in 1964, R. D. FitzGerald and A. D. Hope in 1965, and Hal Porter and Randolph Stow in 1966 (after Patrick White had turned it down).

In September 1967, the committee's unanimous vote was for Christina Stead, 'the outstanding Australian novelist of this day'. On 27 October, the decision was overturned because Stead had not lived in Australia for forty years and 'on available information it was also doubtful whether the proposed candidate's contribution to literature was of sufficient and specific relation to Australia'.

There were protests, including from members of the committee. The most outspoken critic was Patrick White. He had suffered as much as Stead from his compatriots' obsession with 'Australianness', and now he wrote an enraged, mocking letter to the *Sydney Morning Herald*:

> Sir,
>
> If the Higher Junta of Australian Intellect considers a novelist of genius like Christina Stead ineligible for its much-juggled American award, it helps explain to me why, for some time past, I have felt a foreigner in this pathetically chauvinistic parish.
>
> And what about Sidney Nolan? Ineligible too, because he doesn't squat around the pump along with the other blokes?
>
> Patrick White.
> Centennial Park.

(Sidney Nolan, the eminent Australian painter, was frequently abused for spending most of his time in London and New York.)

It was fortunate that Stead knew nothing about the whole affair until afterwards. She would always be impatient with the notion of 'cultural cringe', but this was an unmistakable instance of it. There was a long tradition of resentment in Australia about its overseas talent drain. As much as possible, expatriates were punished for living abroad. This made it extraordinarily difficult for Australian expatriate artists to find funding, since America and Britain (which tended to patronise colonials) looked after their own citizens first—though that year the British Arts Council put Australia to shame by awarding a grant to Stead (the equivalent of a good year's salary) as well as to Jean Rhys, born in Dominica.

Had Stead received the Australian prize, it would have been the first time she had in any way been honoured by her own country in thirty-three years as a published writer. Not until 1965 had Angus & Robertson decided to publish two of her books. Even then, the company was only interested in the novels set in Australia.

Stead would later express impatience with the notion of 'Australianness'. 'Would you call Byron an expatriate writer because he wrote in Italy?' she asked. 'He's English. I am Australian.'

But she dismissed the whole affair with a shrug. She had more serious concerns on her mind. In retrospect, these make the Council's decision even more tragic.

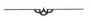

At the beginning of November 1967, Philip Harvey had Blake in hospital for three days for a series of tests. His stomach cancer was diagnosed. Blake was not told, but Harvey is convinced that he made it clear to Stead at this point that Bill might not have long to live.[28]

In mid November, in a letter typed by Christina, Bill described the tests to Harry Bloom. It was, he said, a 'science fiction run of x-rays'.

> I was tilted, spun about, forced to lie recumbent, suddenly jerked up, and felt like a 21st century robot. These technicians found out that my neck-bones, owing to age, impinge on the oesophagus (or gullet), thus making swallowing difficult. There is nothing any doctor can do about this; and so I have to adapt myself and I am doing so. It takes some of the fun out of living; but once you live with it, you forget about it.

A few days after Christmas, in 1967, Philip Harvey rang and asked to speak to Bill. The patient was in bed and told Christina he felt too weak to go to the phone. Harvey was surprised. 'If he's too weak to come to the phone, he ought to be in hospital.' He called for Bill the following morning, 30 December, and took him to St Stephen's Hospital in Chelsea.

Left by herself, Stead collapsed with the 'flu. She was exhausted. 'I have not the strength for this enormous effort of care,' she told Aida Kotlarsky. For four days she was confined to bed, and for another week she scarcely went out. She wrote tender letters to her 'darling boy', in which she told him how much she loved him—something she could only ever do in writing. Bill rang her when he could, and told her he loved her.

Blake was in St Stephen's Hospital for three weeks. Paul Koston called in every day. Alf Hurst wrote and rang from Paris. Blake, a much-loved man, had no shortage of visitors. His Texan friend, Bill Ash, thought he looked 'terribly wasted' but was impressed that he had not lost his spirit. Blake joked about the humiliation of taking weak tea by the spoonful. They discussed 'the financial crisis of British imperialism and the opportunity this presented for a genuine Marxist-Leninist party to provide revolutionary leadership for the British working class'. Blake also spoke of death, Ash recalls, but 'lightheartedly, as a matter of no concern to a convinced materialist'.[29]

On 19 January 1968, Blake was moved to the care of a specialist surgeon at Westminster Hospital. Stead appeared to believe—as Blake himself did—that he had a severe ulcer. She told her sister Kate that he looked thin and old, but was 'quite cheerful, considering', and that she was hoping surgery would restore him to a normal living. She wrote to Aida that Bill had a stomach ulcer:

> It never crossed my mind that Bill, always the good eater, always the eupeptic, might have a thing like that. He foresaw it—no one believed him. It seems we do know our own bodies. (And our nearest and dearest misunderstand us!)

It is possible that Stead could not bear to 'know' what she really knew. She had to steel herself, not allow herself to think about the future, so that she could face Bill in hospital without breaking down. Before Bill was moved to Westminster, Philip Harvey had told her that tests revealed cancer of the upper stomach and lower oesophagus, and that he did not have long to live. Bill himself knew he might die. In the last weeks, he told both Ruth and Christina that he wanted his ashes scattered to the wind—no funeral.

When Christina brought him a book by Che Guevara sent by his friend Leo Huberman and held it close to his eyes for him to see, Bill told her he did not want to look at it just then. 'I've been thinking only about myself,' he told her. 'I haven't thought about anything outside.'[30] This was quite unlike him.

It was Philip Harvey who persuaded Professor Ellis to perform surgery. Ellis was not keen: Blake was very weak. But Harvey knew it was his only chance. Ellis operated on 26 January, removing part of Blake's stomach. Afterwards, Christina hung over his bed, watching Bill 'reaching out feebly for life, almost like a sea-animal attached to a rock'.[31] It seemed that he would not survive. Christina and Ruth expected to be called at any time during the night.

Five days later, there were flickers of his old spirit, and Stead began to hope again. Bill, once so proud of his powerful voice, asked her in a frail whisper: 'Do you think my voice is getting stronger?'

When Philip Harvey called in that day, fussed over him and gave him a kiss, Bill gave him 'a bit of a grin'—his feverish eyes seemed to be twinkling—and he whispered: 'Hey Philip, we're going to beat this, 'aint we?'

On 1 February, Bill asked for the newspaper. The Vietnam War was at its height and the Viet Cong had just attacked Saigon in the Tet Offensive. That evening Stead spoke to Bill for the last time—a visit she would later describe to Burnshaw:

> He was lying down on a couch in the corridor-end they used as a sitting-room (nicely furnished). I hung over him, holding his hand and saying those things I knew to be untrue but that would help, for instance that he would soon come home to me. He looked at me with such a 'trusting believing' sweet expression and smile—it was about to be our anniversary and that made it easier for him to believe.

It would be the thirty-ninth anniversary of their life together that year. Bill was seventy-three.

Christina left the hospital when Ruth arrived. Ruth and her father talked briefly about the war in Vietnam. An interpreter friend had just given Ruth a Spanish bible, which she showed Bill. They smiled about Saint John being 'San Juan'. She tucked him in and put drops in his eyes. He told her she did it better than the nurses. He never woke up.

The hospital rang Christina at 5 in the morning, on 2 February 1968. Bill, who had developed a major pulmonary embolism as a result of surgery, was close to the end. Ruth and Laurie rushed over to collect Christina.

While Laurie was parking the car below, the two women watched Bill take his last breath. They just had time to kiss him. He was unconscious, but Stead thought it was 'as if he had waited' for them.[32]

14

Hundred Thousand Regrets

FEBRUARY 1968 – AUGUST 1974

'B ILL'S DEATH WAS just like a heart attack,' Stead would tell friends
ten years later. 'Part of me died.'[1] Over the years, she had often
dreamt about a little boat that would determinedly travel on,
whatever the elements. When Bill became seriously ill, the little boat
sailed into her dreams and sank. 'I see now the little boat was Bill,' she
wrote to Stanley Burnshaw.

> Did I tell you that after travelling a long way suddenly the little boat sank on
> Thames-side? I called it and called it—all the fleets came, liners, warships,
> but it did not come, Did I tell you that?

Bill was cremated at Golders' Green on the afternoon of 5 February.
According to his wishes, there was no funeral service—no one was present.
Christina was glad to be spared that harrowing ceremony. The Harveys
thought a funeral might have helped her come to terms with the death.

On the day Bill died, Stead went to stay with the Harveys for a few
days, and for the next few weeks she would go there for weekends. Leah
Harvey remembers a sad, lonely figure staring out of the windows for
hours on end.

In her bewilderment, Stead wrote twice to Aida Kotlarsky announcing
Bill's death—on 3 February and again two days later. 'I am tempted to say

to myself, "He is only away for a long time",' she told Aida, 'but that is a wrong attitude. I must not do that.' She kept saying to herself: 'I must get organised and then decide what to do.' She thought she might not stay in that cold country that neither she nor Bill had ever liked. But where would she go? She knew only that she must not think about Bill for the moment. It hurt too much. She told Stanley Burnshaw:

> He telephoned me every day from the hospital while he could and kept saying 'I love you so much'; and I ask myself and I did ask then, who else ever was so good to me? Or ever will be? I didn't deserve it. But then I know that none of us deserves the gifts of that sort that are carelessly and without any reason thrown at our feet. No more. I am trying to avoid this kind of thinking.

Kind letters arrived from the family in Australia. Thistle Harris told her the family would like to have her home again. Tella and Boy Friedmann invited her to stay a while in Tuscany. When Stanley Burnshaw, in London for a brief visit, suggested she make a trip to the US to see old friends again, Stead knew that was what she wanted to do. She could not face the Friedmanns, who would remind her of Bill and, being a couple, of all she had lost. She was afraid she would do nothing but weep. More than anything, she wanted to see Harry Bloom. She thought vaguely that she might move to the States, but she needed to see Harry first. By early March she was making travel plans. At least it gave her something else to think about.

⤜⤛

A week after Bill's death, Stead and Ruth Hall quarrelled bitterly. The issue was Blake's novel about financiers in the French Revolution. Both women were pained, as Blake himself had been, that he had not been able to bring to fruition the solid work of several years. In his last weeks, lying in his hospital bed, Bill had wondered whether Ruth might finish the novel, and he asked her to write a summary of the events he had described to her over the years. He seemed pleased with the four pages of notes she produced.

When her father died, Ruth asked Christina for the manuscript. The task was virtually impossible. Blake's typing was full of mistakes, with his sight so poor, and there were hundreds of pages of notes in his almost illegible handwriting. The book was Bill's vision alone; and then there was the problem of continuity of style. Moreover, Ruth, as a part-time interpreter and mother of three, had very little time.

Stead handed her the manuscript on a five-year loan, and as soon as she had done so, worried that she might never see it again. For Bill's sake, she even entertained the idea of trying to finish the novel herself. Ruth resented what she considered Christina's patronising attitude towards her; Christina thought Ruth grasping. Eventually Stanley Burnshaw stepped into the breach. He wrote to Ruth that publishers in the States were interested in the manuscript: would she please lend Christina the manuscript to bring with her to the States? (In the States, Burnshaw would make a copy of it. The era of photocopies had dawned at last.)

A year later, Christina angered Ruth by writing to ask for a progress report. Ruth complained that Stead was harassing her, and asked for their 'vague' arrangement to be clarified.

Dear Ruth,
Thank you for your letter.

There is nothing vague about Bill's French Revolution MS. and you. I am Bill's executor and gave you this MS. on loan, at your request, a week after Bill's death, to see what you could do with it. At the end of one year (in February this year), I asked you what progress you had made. I have not harassed you in any way. (If you think authors do not get constant queries about the progress of their work, you do not know their life; there is nothing at all humiliating about it.)

At the end of the second year, February 1970, I will find out what progress you have made and if it is not satisfactory, we will have to think what to do.

If within that time, you have finished a MS. acceptable to a publisher and which is in agreement with Bill's ideas (which are known to me), and you have been offered a suitable contract (and you would be wise to employ a good agent), then, if I am satisfied, I will consent to your having complete rights.

You do not know the literary world and do not understand that this is a generous offer. I told you, I think, that I had two offers from two friends of Bill, both established authors, just after his death, offering to work on this same MS. These authors would have naturally made an arrangement with me, financial and otherwise, and giving Bill all credit for the remarkable and dense groundwork done by Bill. All this is not required of you; but you must show that you can do suitable work on the MS.

That is how it stands at present.

Kind regards and I trust you all are well,

Sincerely,

Christina Blake

Relations between the women would remain strained—though both made token efforts at friendship.

Before he died, Blake, who may have foreseen the rivalry between his wife and daughter, asked Bill Ash to be an unofficial literary executor. Over the next few years, Ash, who wrote an effusive two-page obituary in the *Monthly Review*, tried unsuccessfully to interest a number of publishers in Blake's unpublished manuscripts. In the end, Blake's book on imperialism, his novel about Garibaldi's 'Mille' and his unfinished French Revolution novel were relegated to packing boxes to gather dust.

Soon after Bill's death, Stead received a letter from Florence James. Back in Australia, Florence had heard nothing of Blake's sudden illness and death, but she *had* heard about the Britannica Award fiasco, and told Stead she was pleased Patrick White's scathing comments had put the record straight. She was now a doting grandmother, she reported.

Stead wrote to her niece in Sydney, asking *her* to reply to Florence's letter. 'I do not feel I can prick this great healthy jolly bubble of her joy in life by saying Bill is dead. So would you write for me—or ask someone?'[2]

Florence James had been with Christina when Bill began to court her thirty-nine years earlier. With Florence, Christina had excitedly shared her 'dearest secrets' about her cultured, cosmopolitan boss. Now Christina could not bring herself to write Florence a short note.

As usual, anger served to deflect Stead's anguish about herself. Haunted by her uncharitable behaviour towards Blake in his last few years, she was suffering agonies of self-reproach. 'I have very little to console myself with,' she told Ettore Rella six months after Bill's death. 'We always look back and think, "I should have noticed this and that, I who knew him so well"; and you think, "And so how well did I know him?"' Three years after Bill's death, she wrote to the Burnshaws of the '100,000 regrets' of her 'recent life':

In fact, everything is a regret, until I say to myself, 'But surely I must have done something kind for Bill?' and I try to think of something—but then at once clouds of vicious little black birds with beaks and wings assail me, quite visible to me though not to others—remorse, regret.

Throughout her life, Stead had only ever been able to express powerful or convoluted emotions through the medium of fiction. Now her tragedy was that not only had she lost Blake, her muse had deserted her too. She had written very little in the past ten years, and she would write almost nothing after Blake's death. She *wanted* to write: indeed, when she was not writing, she did not feel 'moral'. She would not feel quite moral for the last fourteen years of her life. Not a day would pass without her talking about writing and worrying about not writing. But her motivation, drive, willpower were gone. Like many writers abandoned by their muse, she relied heavily on drink to assuage her frustration. But it brought only temporary relief.

Though she tried not to complain, her thoughts from now on were to be one long lament. She missed Bill, she was lonely, she was frightened to live alone, she was repelled by women living on their own, she wanted to be loved, she wanted a man, she was not working, she felt lazy, she hoped to start writing again soon.

She was sixty-five when Bill died. Alone, Stead was beset by the same panic she had felt as a young woman; the prejudices of her childhood had not weakened over time. Women on their own were pathetic creatures, devoid of dignity.

While other widows could take comfort from female friends, Stead all too frequently reiterated her negative views about her own sex. To journalists and friends, she would make swaggering comments such as: 'I adore men. While there is a man left on earth, I'll never be a feminist.' Where her friends were couples—the Rellas, the Burnshaws—it was the men she loved, as their wives well knew. She told Ettore Rella she would hate to go on a holiday with a woman. 'Must be something wrong, a hormone deficiency ... I love men.'

She was vehemently opposed to the burgeoning Women's Liberation Movement. As a socialist, she had to admit that women lacked certain rights, and she was particularly sympathetic to the lonely plight of suburban mothers. But she insisted that the women's movement was 'purely middle class' and a 'waste of time'. Men and women complemented each other, and that was that.

The worst thing about some of the so-called women's liberationists is their hatred of men, but men and women are made to love each other. It's only by loving each other that they can achieve anything. This separation of women from men is the most disgraceful thing and disorderly thing in the movement, and that's why I'm against it.[3]

Several female friends eventually grew tired of Stead's misogynist ways. After Bill's death, Pera Koston, fed up with seeing Christina openly flirt with her husband, while she herself was ignored, refused to have her in their house again. Anne Bloom put up with Christina's rudeness during the Puerto Rico visit in 1966. But when Stead's novella *Girl from the Beach* appeared in 1967 (in which Anne Bloom's fictional counterpart is a mindless housewife), Anne wanted nothing more to do with her. No doubt she sensed the affection between Christina and Harry, and guessed that Christina would happily have taken her husband.

On 5 February 1968, Stead wrote to Anne and Harry Bloom, who had already heard the sad news from Ruth Hall. Harry Bloom rang Christina from Puerto Rico. A week later, Stead wrote him a letter, evidently passionate, and sent it to his post office box. He replied on 14 February:

Dear Darling,

I've reread your letter many many times. For now better left unsaid all the things I would want to say. Of course you are constantly in my thoughts.

I know you pretty well. I'm afraid you will do something impulsively now. Please wait a little while. Things have changed for you. Let raw edges heal a bit.

In one of your letters you said that you may come to the States in the spring. Will you be coming? If you do I want to be there when you come. I want to see you so much and its much too long since I've last been with your great tenderness and that great volcano inside of you.

Over the next few years, Stead's days would revolve around the postman's early morning visit and the hope of a letter from Puerto Rico. The 'clandestine correspondence' with her 'lover-brother' made her feel alive. Not that it was very clandestine. She told Burnshaw:

He goes to the P.O., memorises my letters and then tears them up leaving them in the trash-basket there. It is all very funny, I laugh at us, he is very funny, and yet such romances are quite romantic, too, if you're thinking of lifetimes.[4]

Bloom's letters brought Stead back from the dead. And she took them much more seriously than she let on to Burnshaw. The trip to the States was principally to see 'dear Harry'. She allowed herself to hope that he would come up with some proposal that would make sense of her life. She hesitated to travel just then: the arrangements tired her. In the past Blake had always dealt with these. There were all sorts of formalities: she needed permission from the Bank of England to take money out of the country, and the American Embassy wanted evidence that she had sufficient capital to cover her stay. It seemed foolish to spend so much just then. But she had to see Harry.

At the end of April, a cryptic letter arrived from Puerto Rico:

Darling Christina,
We will be coming to N.Y. about May 15th.
    ... I reread your letters about 4 or 5 times. Sort of devour them and commit them to memory and then destroy them. All at the Box.
    ... The doctor gentle soul told me a tale; 'beware of the Wild Cats but a pussy is allright.' So bring me kitten like the one that we had in P.R. or when you were on 14th St. Crazy?
    Love, Harry.

Aida Kotlarsky had invited Christina to spend the summer in the Catskills. It had been a firm invitation for two years now, and Bill had talked of their going there that summer. Kind Aida wrote to say she had borrowed two typewriters, one electric and one manual, in preparation for Christina's visit. She even pressed her to move permanently to the States: she could live half the year at Hunter free, Aida suggested, and the rest of the year she could live in a studio in downtown Manhattan. Stead was moved, but reasoned that the offer was made because Aida was lonely. 'Youngest of a big family, mostly gone, even her dogs and cats are gone—and a widow some years since.'[5]

Before she left for the States, Stead wrote a will in which she made Stanley Burnshaw her literary executor. It was not entirely sensible, she realised. He was only three years younger than she was, and she warned him that her family had a proclivity for living well into their nineties. But she felt she owed him a great deal. She bequeathed him her published and unpublished works as 'an absolute gift', though she expressed the hope that if the money ever justified it, Burnshaw would 'set up a fund for money to be given to writers who need it, whether young or old'.[6]

She put Bill's clothes in mothballs, thinking she would give them away when she came back. The sad task made her reflect all over again that she had not given the 'dear boy' enough affection; she had been 'too unbending'. She felt terribly tired: tired of sadness, tired of being stoic. 'To be honest with you,' she told Burnshaw in mid May, 'if the Little Bill came through the door, put out his hand and said "Come with me", I would gladly go with him to the land of shades.'

> I know I'll keep going, but really my life was for that, wasn't it? To live with Bill. I didn't know that was it, but it was. I'm glad to say I told him so just before the end and he liked it. Must stop: of course, I'm crying my eyes out.

Her days, only rarely lightened by a letter from Puerto Rico, were lonely, sad, and full of self-reproach.

Paul Koston was a comfort, giving her avuncular advice and inviting her to lunch in the city at least once a week. She looked forward to his company and the good wine that temporarily restored her spirits. And Philip Harvey did his best to help where he could. When he went on holiday in April, she suffered from nervous stomach pains—an old complaint that seemed to occur when she felt she was entirely on her own. She told Burnshaw:

> I rang Philip (doctor friend) the other day. He said, 'Come over for supper and stay the night' (which I often do) but later I rang again saying I was too tired; and he said, 'Are you in a state? Because if so, I'll come over and hold your hand,' (meaning have a talk). I said, 'I am not in a state and am never in a state.' But he said, 'You are always in a state, and so you don't know when you're in a state.' A highly medical conversation. But oddly enough, I think he is right.

She crossed the Atlantic by ship early in June 1968. Harry Bloom did not meet her. Stead stayed alone in the Burnshaws' 11th floor apartment, at No. 32 Washington Square West. Stanley and Leda were at their summer house on Martha's Vineyard, where Christina was to visit them later.

Bloom was stuck in Puerto Rico with bad angina. He wrote to her: 'I think of you in the daytime and dream of you at night.'

New York was steamy, and Washington Square was noisy, full of brightly dressed hippies playing guitars until the early hours of the morning. The newspapers were full of Vietnam and anti-war demonstrations. Earlier that year, there had been riots at Columbia University. In April, Martin Luther King had been assassinated in Memphis. In June, Senator Robert Kennedy had been fatally shot in Los Angeles, after winning the Presidential Democratic primary election in California. It was a different country from the one Stead had known in the 1930s and 1940s.

Her letters did not mention political events. She was absorbed by her own problems that year. The days yawned ahead. Stead had brought *I'm Dying Laughing* with her, but she was in no mood for work. Instead, she read her way through Burnshaw's library and saw friends: Ettore and Jessie Rella, Isidor and Polly Steinberg, her agent Cyrilly Abels, her Holt editor Charlotte Mayerson, her writer friend Norman Rosten. But she was terribly restless.

She took the bus to Hunter on 2 July, and told Aida everything. Aida pressed her to invite Harry to Hunter. Stead wrote to his post office box on 15 July, and Aida, an enthusiastic matchmaker, hatched all sorts of plans for when Harry would come. But there was silence from Puerto Rico. At the beginning of August, Stead wrote a curt four-line letter to his house. (She probably arranged to have it posted in England. Anne Bloom must not know she was in the States.)

At Hunter Stead had a large studio room with a balcony. Red squirrels clambered around on the roof, and tame chipmunks sat on her shoulders. Aida was generous and affectionate ('an unadorned good heart'), and Stead loved to hear her beautiful piano playing. The women went for walks together. Yet Christina was far from calm. She attacked the garden vigorously. And she spent hours each day cooking—so obsessively that she apologised afterwards to Aida, explaining that her cooking mania was probably due to having spent so many hours preparing food for Bill at the end of his life. 'I expect it set up an obsession in me, I am sure it did … It must have annoyed you. Blessings on you for all your human understanding.'

The days were hot and steamy, punctuated by dramatic Catskill downpours, but the nights were cool, and she slept a great deal. In the evenings, they would sit in white rocking chairs on the verandah, looking out at the wooded mountains. They would sip 'sours', and discuss life, love and men.

One evening they rang Asa Zatz, who now lived in Mexico City with his Guatemalan opera singer wife and their two sons. Asa was a translator from Spanish. There had been an earthquake in Mexico, but Asa reassured them: 'It just rocked me to sleep.'

Stead felt cooped up in Hunter. By mid August, when she took the rickety plane to Martha's Vineyard to stay with the Burnshaws, she was extremely tense. Later she would tell the Burnshaws that staying with them on that beautiful New England island had enabled her to calm down and remember Aida's many good points. But with them, too, she could be irritable and contrary. It became a joke with Stanley and Leda to count the number of times she said, 'My dear, you're wrong'.[7]

Life on the Vineyard was sociable. Fashionable New York leftwing society formed a colony there in the summer months. Lillian Hellman owned a house on a bluff overlooking the water; Cyrilly Abels and Jerome Weinstein rented a cottage and Leo Huberman, Bill's friend from the Monthly Review Press, came to dinner one evening. At a big party Burnshaw held for her, Stead was delighted to meet people who had actually read her books. It was a blow to the Left when Soviet tanks moved into the Czech capital in late August, crushing the 'Prague spring'. But Stead made no mention of it in her letters.

Back in New York, Stead still waited for Harry Bloom. It turned out that he had not picked up her 15 July letter from his post office box until 5 August—by which time it was too late for him to go to Hunter. He had been seriously ill, in hospital. His angina, which he referred to, mock-lovingly, as his 'Angelina' or 'Angina Doll', had occasioned several stays over the years in intensive care wards. Now he told Christina that he planned to come to New York early in September, alone or with Anne. ('I'm not pressing her to come,' he added.)

Stead tossed and turned at night, and changed rooms several times in her attempt to escape the noise of the street and the neighbours' air-conditioners. During the day, the heat confined her to the apartment. She told Jonah Raskin, who interviewed her over gin and tonics the day before she left, that she had read more than a hundred books in the three months she had been in the States. Malcolm Lowry was a 'genius', she ventured. She admired Joseph Heller's *Catch 22* and Gunter Grass' *The Tin Drum*. And she was impressed with Thomas Berger's *Little Big Man* and Wallace Stegner's *Wolf Willow*—recent American novels that reappraised the myths of the old frontier. She had been reading works by American blacks. James Baldwin played up to whites, she thought, but Eldridge Cleaver's *Soul on Ice* 'gives an outsider a lot of inside'.[8]

She spent two pleasant evenings at the Rellas' W. 14th Street apartment. They sat outside in the small terrace garden on the roof of a Spanish bar, the Oviedo, and chatted over 'Manhattans'. Stead was not impressed when Cyrilly Abels and her lawyer husband Jerome Weinstein took her to a wineless restaurant in the Village, and she made up for it by doing some serious drinking in a bar in the Village with Charlotte Mayerson, her editor at Holt. Mayerson, a much younger woman, thought Stead 'rather forbidding looking, but striking'. She dressed in a 'conventional, dowdy, British way', but carried herself well. To Mayerson's surprise, they talked like old college chums—about men and sex. Stead told her she was worried that her life from then on would be spent among women. When Mayerson outlined her own relationship troubles, Stead joked that Mayerson's problem was that she liked tall men. She should try little men, she told her. The implication, Mayerson recalls, was that little men like Bill were lusty. Stead gave her the impression that 'she got around quite a bit'.[9]

Stead's return to England was scheduled for 12 September; it was early September and Harry Bloom still had not appeared. It was hurtful, terribly disappointing. Stead may have been reminded of another fateful trip across the world, forty years before. To Philip Harvey she wrote bitterly that her 'mythical friend Harry' had not appeared. Their romance was 'just a fable and a myth together'.

And then the phantom turned up. He had been in New York for some days, but had been ill. His wife was with him—they were staying at their son Mike's—and it was difficult for Harry to phone. It was a tender meeting. Afterwards, Bloom wrote to her: 'It was so short ... I was so overwhelmed. All the things I wanted to ask you ... It was wonderful.' They hoped to meet again, but Harry was too ill. Stead summed up her American sojourn as a 'curious mellow season in hell'.[10]

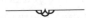

Stead disembarked in Southampton early in the morning on 17 September. Miriam Risner drove down to meet her. There had been floods in the south of England. It was cold and windy and the streets were like rivers.

The trip to the States had made her more realistic about Harry Bloom. He had wanted her to move to New York, but she told him she was put off by the cost of living. She did not tell him that she did not want to be a 'floater', living in a modest one-room apartment, waiting for him to visit. His 'noble affection' and 'romantic visits' would make her ill, she was sure. In a mood of grim realism, she told Aida: 'To tell the truth, whatever he may think, Harry cannot do anything for me that would suit both him and me. (It's a beautiful dream!)' Evidently, it was a dream she had often dreamed.

Her fantasies now settled again on Philip Harvey. 'We're devoted to each other in a nebulous romantic genuine manner and in the manner described by the inimitable D. H. Lawrence, "every friendship is a kind of marriage".'[11]

Soon after her return, Ettore and Jessie Rella visited London, and Stead had them to dinner in Surbiton with Philip and Leah Harvey. Jessie Rella recalls: 'It was clear that something was going on there.' Later, Stead would tell the Rellas: 'That fatal dinner was a sort of turning-point.' She implied that Harvey was jealous of her friendship with Ettore Rella.

In her acute loneliness and distress, Stead was building up a picture—in her own mind as well as in her friends'—of a complicated love-life, beset with rivalries and jealousies. Harry Bloom encouraged this propensity:

> My darling Chris,
> I miss you dreadfully. You're a great woman. Really very strong and some of it seeps into me. You have verve and it sets off vibrations. Of course I'm jealous of the bookman and the postman and the tailor and all the other men that even look at you. I'm pretty tough and I was smacked from the first time I saw you.

When Aida Kotlarsky wrote, making coquettish mention of her admirers, Stead replied with enthusiasm:

> How are you, my dearest girl, and all your boyfriends! My goodness what a roll call! And to think you have kept them all from your girlhood. 'Aida keeps her men.' This makes me like you even more than before. I respect such women. No matter if we can't marry them all. It's a pity.

Stead was flattered when Ettore Rella (in his mid sixties and 'apparently happy with an understanding wife') told her he loved her. She took Rella's effusiveness as a serious declaration, and spent many pleasant hours musing why it was that men liked her. It seemed to her that her male friends—with the exception of Harry Bloom—regarded her as an elder sister or mother figure.

Paul Koston was one of her brother figures. In the brief notes Stead wrote him, usually to thank him for an extravagant and boozy lunch, he had become 'darling Pauli'. At her request, he would often act as host at the lunch parties she felt obliged to organise when Australian and American acquaintances came to London. (She was very embarrassed when he insisted, as he sometimes did, on paying for everyone.) Occasionally she would even shop for clothes with 'Pauli' in attendance, providing 'a man's eye'. According to Koston, Stead once asked him over lunch why he never 'made a pass at her'. She patted her hips and said: 'I'm not fat.' For his part, he insists, he was never interested in her in that way, but he enjoyed her company—'in small doses'.

In February 1969 Stead was bold enough to write a note to Philip Harvey asking if she might join him on an excursion he was about to make to the country, to give a speech on behalf of the Medical Aid to Vietnam Committee. ('If Leah sees no objection.') She explained that it was just to see the sights, adding: 'I may after all quit the country sooner or later.'

Harvey willingly agreed, thinking it would help her to take her mind off her grief. Indeed, it was the beginning of a new interest. Harvey lent her books on Vietnam; Stead kept a file of newspaper cuttings. Over time, they would make more than twenty trips together.

In the spring of 1967, Harvey had gone to North Vietnam as a medical witness with the International Association of Democratic Lawyers and was horrified by what he saw. The US Defence Department denied using plastic-coated fragmentation bombs: Harvey created a scandal by bringing one back and showing it to the British Press. (Harry Bloom even saw him on the American television news.) Ever since, Harvey had been giving lectures all over the country, decrying America's use of chemical and bacteriological warfare, and raising money for medical supplies to North Vietnam.

In May, they went to Porthcawl for the day, where Harvey addressed Welsh miners. They made day trips at weekends—to Coventry or Manchester. Usually they went to evening meetings in the London area. Harvey lectured to universities, schools, charities and trade unions. For Stead, these trips in the car were precious—when she and Harvey were alone together. She would have her hair set in the morning, and look forward all day to the evening adventure. For his part, he enjoyed her company. 'You could have a really good conversation with Chris, an *excellent* conversation, when she was on the reality plane—provided you were determined not to let things stray out of control.'

He was aware of her interest in him, and probably flattered. But he claims that though she would have loved physical contact, he would have 'run a mile'. One evening, according to Harvey, Stead 'made a pass' at him in the car, stroking his cheek and trying to kiss him. He said, 'Please Chris, don't.' She withdrew and said, 'All right, no sex'. He discussed the incident afterwards with Leah. They thought it best to act as if nothing had happened.

Harvey's brilliance as a speaker must have reminded Stead of her father and Bill. As a young girl, she had often gone with her father when he lectured. She told Aida Kotlarsky that Harvey was no 'dingdong rabble-rouser'.

> He is a most serious speaker, with those details only a doctor could give (he was in Hanoi under the bombing, to inspect the devastation and war-wounds) and speaks quietly and dispassionately just because he is fully passionate about this business. It makes a tremendous effect.

In 1970, Michael Wilding, an English lecturer at the University of Sydney, would ask Stead, as an Australian writer, to contribute to an Australian anti-war anthology he was co-editing. It was published the following year. Stead liked the idea. In her essay, 'What Goal in Mind?', she condemned the American involvement in Vietnam and sang the praises of the paramedical services in 'democratic Vietnam', paying special tribute to the work of the Medical Aid to Vietnam Committee and the 'socialist doctor' Philip Harvey.

At first she thought of calling the piece 'Doctor in Vietnam', and her rough jottings were about Harvey the man. ('The doctor, a burly powerful person in his fifties, amiable and at times much like the medical student he must have been, gay, rough, argumentative, resolute and with that particular subtlety of observation which comes from a passion for the truth, appears defenceless against private criticism.')

Though she was more interested in the man than the cause he espoused, Stead eventually realised this was scarcely appropriate material for the anthology and, after several drafts, she cut out the character sketch of Harvey. Her published article merely quotes Harvey, and presents a passionate indictment of American war crimes.

Clem Christesen, editor of *Meanjin*, had nominated Christina Stead for a Creative Arts Fellowship at the Australian National University in Canberra. Stead explained to Laurence Pollinger, her English agent, that the Britannica Award saga had caused 'a lot of sore feelings' in Australia, and that in the end the publicity had done her a service. *Meanjin* and *Southerly* had requested stories from her, and she asked Pollinger not to quibble about the low fees she would be receiving. Australian journals could not compete with American rates.

Early in 1969 Stead heard that the Creative Arts Fellowship at the Australian National University had come off. She was offered a short-term 'B class' fellowship: a category for Australian expatriate artists of international repute. The lump-sum stipend, $5000, was to cover her fare and expenses. The only previous Fellow had been artist Sidney Nolan, in 1965.

The letter from the university stated that there was 'no obligation to give lectures or talks', but it was hoped that fellows 'would meet and talk, at least informally, with members of the academic staff and students'. Stead would be given an office in the English Department.

Stead, more nervous than excited, tried to postpone the trip until 1970, thinking she would try to finish *I'm Dying Laughing* before she left. But a deferral was not possible, since the budget had been planned for the year. After that, it seemed like the hand of fate. She told Harry Bloom: 'I am at a Whistle Stop ... waiting for the first express to take me somewhere, I don't know what will be the destination, but I will take it.' She opted for four months, rather than the full term of six. It was an opportunity to see something of Australia, and to make up her mind whether, eventually, she could live there.

Feeling guilty that she had done nothing for a whole year, she resumed desultory work on *I'm Dying Laughing*, still hoping to have the manuscript ready before she left for Australia, but it had become 'a large albatross' and she 'a reluctant sailor'.[12] The Secker & Warburg files contain numerous letters from Fred Warburg to Christina Stead asking about her progress with the novel. In March 1969 she told him: 'Oldfashioned people would say laziness, Americans would (and do) say "a block"—and the British say it's "the weather"—and it may be a combination of these three.' He then asked her to aim for delivery by 30 June 1969. She replied: 'Dear Fred: You were right, no doubt, to give me a dead-line. Perhaps the old firehorse will now snort and gallop. We'll see.' It did not.

Anxious about the prospect of being a visiting literary expert, Stead spent the next months devouring contemporary fiction. She read Updike's *The Centaur* and Mailer's *An American Dream* and was surprised how good they were. Günter Grass' *Dog Years* she thought 'first rate, wonderfully good'. She was less impressed with *Herzog* than with Saul Bellow's earlier novels. And was no one except Norman Mailer prepared to criticise America's foray into Vietnam?

———— ⌘ ————

Stead left for Australia on the evening of 28 July 1969. Philip Harvey drove her to Heathrow. She had left instructions that if anything should happen to her, there was a suitcase in her flat marked Paul Koston, which contained love letters and 'a lot of manuscripts' to be destroyed.

After forty-one years she was going home, alone. Bill Blake had always wanted to see Australia and meet her family and friends. They had talked of retiring to Australia. She felt terribly sad to be making the trip without him.

She had left Australia at the age of twenty-six, a budding writer. Now she was sixty-seven, a writer with an international reputation. In Australia, however, most of her books had been out of print until 1965, when there were re-issues of *Seven Poor Men of Sydney*, *For Love Alone* and *The Salzburg Tales*. Several of her books remained virtually unobtainable, even in libraries.

The trip was long and tiring. First, the departure from Heathrow was delayed. Then there was a seventeen-hour delay at Bangkok. The plane was 'close-packed as a crate of eggs'. Sitting next to Stead was a Greek-born mother who talked across the aisle to her friends about 'the good life in Australia'. Mentally picturing the woman delivering this 'rich boast' to the grandparents somewhere outside Athens, Stead looked out of the window, fascinated by the 'distant earth, every spine and wrinkle visible in the dry air'.[13]

They stopped in Darwin at 3 am, and eventually arrived at Sydney airport twenty-four hours late. Stead felt like a rag. To her horror, a sprinkling of reporters and press photographers were at the airport to greet her, as well as a small crowd of family members. Wanting only to run away, Stead was obliged to give a short interview in the airport press room.

The journalists pressed her about her feelings towards Australia. 'No, no! I didn't go to England full of resentment that my great talents weren't being recognised in parochial Australia,' Stead told them. And when asked about her reaction to the withholding of the Britannica Award, she assured them, 'I didn't mind. After all, it was only fairy money, wasn't it?'

Stead had arranged to spend the first few days with her maternal cousin Elsie Ford, rather than with her immediate family. Elsie and her husband Robert had visited her and Blake in London in 1967, and the two couples had formed an easy friendship. Elsie Ford believes Stead wanted a 'breathing space' before more emotional meetings with the family.

'I had forgotten the Australian splendour, the marvellous light,' Stead would write later. The Fords lived in Pymble, on Sydney's North Shore. Where once there had been green hills, there was a rash of red roofs. But trees were everywhere, and glimpses of blue harbour. The following year, she would write her impressions in an essay, 'Another View of the Homestead'.

> The most exquisite thing in my recent life was a giant eucalypt on the North Shore as we turned downhill, the downward leaves so clear, the bark rags, so precise, the patched trunk, so bright. 'Look at that tree!' It was outlined in light. It was scarcely spring, but the lawn outside the house was crowded with camellias, magnolias in bloom, even falling; at both dawn and dusk the kookaburras thrilling high in the trees, the magpies—I had quite forgotten those musicians and their audacity ... Too long in London! Everything was like ringing and bright fire and all sharpness.

Culturally, everything had changed. Modern Australia was only twenty-four hours from Europe. The post-war influx of European immigrants had created cosmopolitan cities: the choice of food was as great as in New York. Driving into the city over the Harbour Bridge (opened in 1932, after she had left), Stead looked at the skyscrapers and thought to herself: 'Is this Sydney? This is New York.' Much of the early colonial architecture had been destroyed, and the electric trams were no more. Instead there were buses, an overhead railway station at Circular Quay and the Sydney Opera House at Bennelong Point.

Christina called to see Florence Walker-Smith. Her favourite aunt was very frail now at ninety, and was living with Gwen in a flat in harbour-side Cremorne. Gwen was at work that afternoon, but she gathered the meeting was slightly strained. Six weeks later, in September, Christina would be back in Sydney for Florence's funeral. Gwen would never forget that moment: in the middle of the service, during a violent thunderstorm with torrents of rain and flashes of lightning, Christina suddenly appeared, and thrust some beautiful flowers into her hands.

Christina was awkward with her family, and though she was painfully shy about meeting Australian literati, she was relieved to leave Sydney for Canberra. A. D. Hope and Dorothy Green, well-known writers from the English Department, met her at the airport and drove her to University House, a residential college for academics and postgraduates.

The 'bush capital' had been officially declared the federal capital in 1927, the year before Stead left Australia. The city, which had sprung up behind her back, was a dramatic reminder that she had been out of the country a long time.

Surrounded by hills and mountains, Canberra struck her as beautiful. The air was crisp, clear and dry—quite different from Sydney's humidity. The nights were cold, and in the mornings the grass was covered in frost. The campus had only native trees, between which flitted multicoloured rosellas. Some mornings there would be a 'dawn chorus of hellish laughter' from the kookaburras.[14]

The flat in University House comprised a living room, bedroom and bathroom: Stead had not expected such comfort. There was a large wooden desk, but she sensed she would not be able to write there. She had told the Creative Arts Fellowship Committee, as well as the press at Canberra Airport, that she was going to work on Bill Blake's French Revolution manuscript during her four-month term. But if she lacked energy for *I'm Dying Laughing*, she certainly lacked energy to work on a novel that was not her own. She read a great deal: she made notes on Patrick White's *The Living and the Dead* and *Voss*, neither of which filled her with enthusiasm. She wrote letters. She was lonely, she told the Harveys.

> It is not hard to think of you, for I really have no links here. Sydney is jewelled, a wonderful city, (though smog) and full of friends and relations— but I don't at the moment contemplate settling there—all alone. This 'all alone' business when you have had someone to understand, 'to forgive' (to forgive the ineptitudes, etc.) is a new state, an odd state.

Australians, seemingly obsessed with being 'cut off', talked incessantly about the 'cultural cringe'. It irritated her, yet she told Paul Koston: 'I hear words, names, I haven't heard for 40 years. But no feeling of nostalgia ...

One could not live here—some do and like it, but it is "erewhon" and "never-never-land".'

Australians were curious about this famous writer, briefly back from her long exile. All sorts of people wrote her letters: people who wanted to meet her, people she had known in the past. Her telephone rang with requests for talks or interviews. Interviewers were struck by the musical intonation of her voice and her slight American accent. 'It is a mellow contralto, deep for a woman, yet not too deep,' a male journalist commented. 'A beautiful instrument, beautifully used.'[15] In the *Australian Women's Weekly*, Anne Matheson commented on Stead's 'soft, well-modulated voice', and gave a flattering description of her appearance:

> Christina Stead is a handsome woman. Her hair is strong, short, and only touched with grey. Her eyes are blazing blue, yet soft. She has an upright figure that looks so well in tailored clothes that I was not surprised to learn she wore trousersuits from the moment Paris decreed pants.

Stead would have been delighted by such comments, for the official photographs taken in Australia caused her great distress. Old age suited her: her craggy features lent her a noble profile. But she was as painfully self-conscious as ever about her appearance, and vehemently resented the airport photographs. Cruelly, fate afflicted her with a skin problem throughout her stay. Near the end of her trip, she admitted to the Burnshaws:

> I have stacks of 'official' photographs taken with a wen on the very end of my nose, nothing could be more noticeable … I suffered tremendously in my shyness having to appear as a special 'Fellow' before all sorts of curious and talented audiences.

Unused to being treated as a celebrity, she encountered it at a time when she had neither Bill nor current writing projects to make her feel good about herself. She worried that she was not carrying out her obligations satisfactorily. 'I have a dreadfully immoral feeling that I am worse than chaff,' she told Harvey.

She made two trips to Melbourne, a city she had visited only briefly in her student-teacher days, and made several trips to Sydney, where she was invited to talk at a meeting of the radical writers' group, PEN, and at a meeting of the Fellowship of Australian Writers. At this meeting, she exchanged passing greetings with Florence James, but left without saying goodbye. Nor did she answer a letter from Florence inviting her to stay a few days in the Blue Mountains.

Patrick White invited her to lunch, which passed very amicably. When she told him she was vaguely thinking of returning to Australia to live, White told her she should 'give it plenty of thought before burning her bridges'.[16]

In Sydney the family treated her with 'extraordinary courtesy', yet for some reason she avoided Thistle Harris, and never once visited the house at Watson's Bay, which Thistle shared with Christina's brother Kelvin and his family. She was uncomfortable with her two sisters, Kate and Doris (Weeta), and much preferred the company of her brothers, David and Gilbert. In letters to 'dear, dear Philip' she grumbled: 'I don't care to remember how I'm filling in this dreadful time ... It's long and dreary.'

Nevertheless, there were moments of genuine pleasure. She drove to Melbourne and back with Dorothy Green, poet and critic, who lectured in English at the ANU and was writing a book on Henry Handel Richardson. (Stead grumbled to Burnshaw that 'HHR' might as well be 'Her Highness Royal' in Australia, adding: 'They dislike her best book about her musical time in Leipzig, *Maurice Guest*.')

Dorothy Green had been married to H. M. Green, the eminent critic of Australian literature. Now a widow, Dorothy was a 'sweet, pure, serious and absolutely darling little creature', who dressed 'charmingly' and drove with 'great competence'.[17] What won Stead over—even more than her generosity and kindness and the detours she took to show Stead the countryside—was that she said there were one or two men whom she loved.

Stead enjoyed lunch with Dr H. C. Coombs, Chancellor of the ANU, whom she had once met in London. She was hugely taken by this 'small sunbaked personage' with his nuggety build, widely known by his West Australian nickname 'Nugget'. One of Australia's most impressive public figures, Coombs, who had a doctorate from the London School of Economics, had played an active role in Australia's post-war financial policies. He was an enthusiastic patron of the arts and Chairman of the Council for Aboriginal Affairs. In 1972, when she met him again in London, Stead would send him a copy of *House of All Nations*, and it was his turn to be impressed.

She rang an 'old boyfriend', Colin Kenneth Lawson, who had managed Henderson's hat factory where she once worked, and brought her roses, calling her his 'Tosca'. Later, he had given up business and become the manager of the Sydney Symphony Orchestra. Stead commented: 'It was as if we had met only yesterday—although he is twice the size.'[18]

A less welcome, totally unexpected confrontation with her past occurred when Stead found herself sitting at the same table as Professor G. W. Keith Duncan at dinner. He was in Canberra for a conference, and was staying at University House. Stead, sitting with the Geerings, left straight after dinner, embarrassed. According to Duncan, when his wife (who knew virtually nothing of the whole story) asked him why he did not speak to his old friend, he retorted: 'I will never talk to that woman!'[19]

Stead left Australia on 3 December 1969, flying to London via Rome. She was going to spend a few days with the Friedmanns, near Florence. But now she was anxious to be home again—Australia definitely was *not* home—and Florence seemed like another hurdle to cross.

Tella and Boy met her at Rome airport, a three-hour drive from where they lived in Greve-in-Chianti, north of Florence. It was the beginning of winter and there was snow on the Apennines. Their renovated Toscana villa, 200 years old, was in the middle of rolling hills of vineyards. Stead privately thought it too lovely —like a dream.

In 1967 when the Friedmanns left England, Bill had seen them off with a bouquet of violets in his hands and tears in his eyes. They still found it difficult to accept that he was gone. Stead told them that she did not want to talk about Bill; it would upset her too much.

Stead did not sleep in Italy. She was plagued by an urgent feeling, 'Get on, you must be getting on'. For the first time, Tella Friedmann found Stead's drinking excessive. She would have several hard drinks in the middle of the day—gin, martini or dry vermouth—and again in the evening. At dinner they drank the local chianti.

Stead had always thought Boy Friedmann a 'lovable man', though he was not one of the men with whom she flirted. She had once written affectionate letters to Tella, but now she felt strangely hostile. Perhaps it was jealousy: Tella, after all, had what she most wanted—a loving male companion.

One morning they had a row. According to Tella Friedmann, they were talking in the kitchen while Tella was cooking. 'For something to say', Tella asked Christina: 'How do you create characters? How does one set about making a character in a novel that is not recognisable to others?'

The ensuing argument was reminiscent of a heated one Stead had once had with Florence James over *Power Without Glory*, when James argued that it was wrong of Frank Hardy to create recognisable characters. It rapidly escalated into a full-scale row. Tella, almost fifty, took the opportunity to tell Christina she did not appreciate being referred to as a 'sex kitten'.

The friendship between the two women more or less died after this visit. It was the last time Stead ever saw the Friedmanns.

When Stead had written from Australia saying she felt inadequate and harassed in her role as an 'Official Personage', Harvey reassured her. It did not matter; she was timid, that was all. Stead found this verdict strangely comforting—perhaps because, in one small domain, it allowed her to accept herself. Before, her timidity had been partly concealed by Blake's sociability. After her return from Australia, she embraced her 'timidity', using it as an excuse. She told Burnshaw in January 1970:

> I had a severe shock from that Australia visit—still get a violent headache from 'society', 'company', can hardly endure more than half an hour of the company even of my dear Doc. It just shows what a timid person I really am.

In January 1970 she was working on the essay about her return 'home', commissioned by *Hemisphere*, and finding it 'strangely difficult'. How could she explain that she had never had a home other than Bill?

Later that year she began work on a short piece about her father, 'A Waker and Dreamer', commissioned by Stephen Murray-Smith, editor of the socialist literary magazine *Overland*. At first she was not enthusiastic—she felt she had said everything in *The Man Who Loved Children*—but she asked Gilbert Stead for some material about their father's family, and in the end she enjoyed imagining her grandfather coming to Australia, and her own father's childhood. Looking back this time, she saw her father as 'an unusually gifted man', with 'great courage'.

Over the next years, Stead revised old short stories for various Australian and American magazines. She did not touch *I'm Dying Laughing*, but it remained a burden on her mind. She believed it was preventing her from writing other things. She toyed with other ideas, at times thinking she would like to write a book about Bill. But guilt and affection were not emotions that stoked her creative fires. Her anger, one of the important sources of her creative vitality, had subsided into depression.

She read a great deal. Having made her way through the French books in the local Surbiton library, she started on German. She particularly enjoyed historical nonfiction. To Alexander Solzhenitsyn's *The First Circle*, a blistering portrait of Stalin and the Soviet treatment of dissidents, her reaction was much the same as it had been to Pasternak's *Dr Zhivago*. 'Though written with a lot of eagerness, skill, imagination … and you are carried along by his energy, you keep saying, "How many? Where? Prove it." ' It seemed to her 'very saleable' these days to run down Stalin and the Soviet Union.[20]

Stead heard almost monthly from 'dear Harry', though he was often laid low with his angina. He was full of plans, but nothing much came of them. Either he was ill, or his wife was. Disappointing though it was to have her hopes constantly dashed, Bloom's letters went some way towards filling the emotional void in Stead's life. His letters were passionate, warm and tender. He wrote as he talked—in colourful, racy American. He told her about their mutual friends, the political situation. He related amusing anecdotes. He worried about her. He encouraged her. He missed her. He wished he could hold her hand and talk to her. When the press reported heavy snowfalls in England, he worried that her flat would not be warm enough. Was she managing to shop? 'Why couldn't I snuggle in bed with you and let all those cold winds blow as much as they wanted to?'

He even made her feel desirable. 'Nobody I can think of can fill your shoes, your heart, your mind and your beautiful body,' he told her. 'Much love and kisses I send to you my darling.' Five days later, he assured her: 'Think of me as always loving you. I live on it.'

Stead still thought of Harry Bloom as the 'Faithful Henry', the King's loyal servant in the Grimms' tale 'The Frog Prince'. She thought she would like to write about him. 'I have not told him,' she confided to Burnshaw, 'since I don't want to make it difficult for him to write freely.' However, she could not. Although she spent her last years wishing she could write about the men she loved, to please them, she could not.

———— ✧ ————

Stead did not complain about ageing; she accepted it with the rationale of a good naturalist: it was natural. Her existence was a 'thin grey soup', and she longed for a 'richer brew'[21], but her health was good at sixty-eight. She was too heavy, and conscious that she ought to lose weight, but she did nothing about it. Her staple diet was steak and alcohol.

But late one Sunday night in October 1970, she suffered a mild heart attack. Philip Harvey was away at the time, but when he returned, he took her to hospital for observation. Tests revealed she had had a coronary. She spent three weeks in a private room at St Stephen's Hospital, 'treated like a princess'. With 'almost daily views and news of that nutty Doc. I am so fond of', she enjoyed her stay, though she felt 'quite a fake'.[22] Paul Koston brought her a 'ravishing nightgown' and slippers with roses on them. (Stead told this with great delight to all her friends.) And the 'Doc' would come to see her—'all instruments and horse-laughs'.[23] She felt much loved by her men.

However, the reality—and she knew it—was less cheerful. Back in Surbiton, she conjectured that the heart attack might have been caused by the bottling-up of her feelings. There was now a new dimension to her life: fear. She became more sedentary than ever, afraid that exertion might cause another attack.

———— ✧ ————

The highlight of the following year—at least Stead *thought* it would be— was a two-week trip to Albania, in an organised group with the Harveys. In May 1971 she received a royalty cheque from the United States for $1200—*The Man Who Loved Children* was still enjoying steady sales—and she felt able to treat herself to the trip in August. Excited letters were posted to Ettore Rella, her 'Albanian friend'. Where was his father born? ('I should like to see it—then I could tell you; I know how you miss your ancestors.') The only book about Albania she could find in the local library was *Illyria Reborn*, by Dymphna Cusack, who had visited the country in 1965. Stead told Rella that Cusack was 'a facile enthusiastic journalist' who tended to greatly praise 'leftist countries', but did not 'dwell on the shadows in the picture'.

Stead herself was not known for dwelling on the shadows when it came to socialist countries. Once in Albania, she would have several arguments with Leah Harvey, who was critical of the Stalinist-style regime, whereas Stead opined that repressive measures were necessary for the country's development. It was *other* shadows that would haunt Stead. Though she was never prepared to elaborate, she made it clear to all her friends that the two-week trip was an unmitigated disaster.

The party of sixteen left for Albania on 21 August, among them several archeologists from Cambridge. The group flew to Dubrovnik, the seaport in Yugoslavia, and after that, they travelled over rough, cliff-hanging roads in a bus decked with photographs of Lenin, Stalin, Marx, Engels and Enver Hoxha, the Albanian head of government. As musical accompaniment there was the horn, blown as they approached each turn.

The tourist industry was newly emerging. Americans were still not permitted into the country. The visitors were confined to special locations. ('I am not one to complain about that,' Stead told friends. 'Would we allow ignorant visitors to roam around our factories and workshops, without guides and with cameras?') The hotels were primitive, the food was undistinguished, but the beer and raki, a potent kind of slivovitz, aided its digestion.

Physically, the country was extraordinarily beautiful, with steep, rocky mountains and a narrow, ancient coastal plain. Stead was struck by the 'old yellow cities, mud-coloured and as old as Mud', and the 'dark, thronging people' in traditional dress.

But she was bitterly unhappy. Back in England, she told Burnshaw she felt 'sick' when she thought about the trip. 'I will never forget it or get over it.' She added: 'It is perhaps too private, can only be said *in public* (writing).'

What happened in Albania? Remaining remnants of Stead's Albania story, entitled 'On the Beach', suggest that Stead was offended that the Harveys went their own way, leaving her to make friends among the group. She felt lonely and abandoned. Instead of being one of a trio, she felt that she stood out in the group as a pathetic figure, a woman on her own.

Leah Harvey was studying at that time to become a barrister, and was preparing for her final exams. She would sit on the beaches and study. Philip Harvey was preparing for his next term's medical teaching. Another of his favourite pastimes was to swim to the point of exhaustion. These were not sociable pursuits.

Stead's fictional notes are written in the first-person. 'Marigold' and 'Reed', old friends of the narrator, invite her to accompany them on their holiday to Albania. Though Stead changes minor details, it is quite clear whom she is describing:

> He is tall, muscular, burly, once an athlete; he has tender dark shortsighted eyes, a pale skin, a big nose and chin and he is quite well known in his profession ... he's a physicist with a laboratory in his charge. He's about 55.
>
> Marigold is younger, middlesized, dark ... with the ... colouring of an antique Graeco-Roman painting on wood ... She has fine white teeth which she has been told to show and she does so continually, when talking, in a strange wolfish manner ... and her voice, usually coarse and dull, then takes on a ringing precision, with the tone of the bell in the committee rooms she is fond of.
>
> In the airport, Reed, who calls himself 'a chronic swot' sat at a small table studying physics, while Marigold hurried about collecting our allowances of dutyfree liquor and cigarettes, which she intended to carry all through the trip to bring back home.

One evening, at some coastal town—it seems to be the ancient Adriatic town of Durres—the three of them go for a walk. Then comes the first hint of crisis:

> Next morning I was early on the beach waiting for my friends and was presently breath-taken to see them lying ready for the sea under an umbrella.
> I stared. I was sitting on a tussock, easy to see. Mortified, I returned to the hotel to sit under an oleander.

It is obvious that she resented Leah Harvey throughout the trip, and was furious with Philip Harvey for ignoring her. Writing about it afterwards was Stead's way of coming to terms with anger and pain. (If she could publish it, it would also be a means of revenge.)

Stead, it seems, made up for Philip Harvey's obvious preference for the company of his wife by throwing herself at the other men in the group. Two months later, when she wrote to Burnshaw about the Albanian trip, she could not bring herself to say exactly why the trip was so infernal. Like Burnshaw, we are obliged to read between the lines:

> I was sick in bed for six days after I returned and for four or five weeks after (morally sick only); and I can say now that I am better, but it took

the same amount of froth and foam and sweat that a hurdle race takes. There was I in full public, making friends with one chap after another, for company—and all very nice, mind you, all splendid 'shipboard' friends, all inveterate travellers who knew their way about and how to behave on a package trip or any other trip in fact—I would go with them to the moon, these unknown blokes I will never see again—but the despair, horror of it! Each single day a new thought struck me and then I realised it was always the same thought: 'This is Hell.'

As a postscript she added:

I felt sucked down hopelessly in a suffocating thing, maybe like the caves, those frightening caves in 'Passage to India' (Malabar Hills) [sic]. It was SO dreadful; I tremble now when I write about it. Must not. Must one day write a long-short for myself and so cure myself.

If the trip constituted a terrible crisis for Stead, it was in all likelihood because she, who liked to think of herself as a 'man's woman', who painted herself in this light to all her friends, including the Harveys, felt she had been exposed. It made her feel 'morally sick'. The 'very severe "rejection" anxiety' Stead had once analysed in herself (attributing it to her childhood, when her love and her appearance were constantly rejected), caused her intense distress.

How interesting that at such a time Stead should think of the dark, echoing Marabar caves in *Passage to India*, the climactic scene in which young Adela Quested imagines herself attacked by her Indian friend Dr Aziz. For Adela, the novel implies, the caves were frightful because it was in those pitch black caves (her unconscious?) that her repressed sexual desires took the form of hysterical hallucination. Later, Adela feels terribly guilty as she begins to think she imagined the whole incident. Stead was certainly aware of the ambiguity of the caves scene in E. M. Forster's novel. For her to make the comparison was tantamount to an admission that she could not bring herself to face the indignity of her sexual desire and emotional desperation. Albania had become her Marabar cave.

Unable to write her long-short story, she could not cure herself. She could not rid herself of the feeling that she had degraded herself. She struggled with the story for weeks, but could not finish it. The only other way she knew to relieve the pain and embarrassment of the memory was her standard ploy: to repress it.

The *Sydney Morning Herald* had asked her for a story. As she could not write the Albania story, finally, on the day of the deadline, she switched to a story based on herself and Bill in their old age. A sentimental story about the romantic love between Jenny (a tall fair woman) and Gill (a square-cut, dark man) after forty years of marriage, she called it 'Street Idyll'. It was the kind of thing Stead had never written before, and if she wrote it now it was because she felt the need to purify herself, as it were, to revive the memory of her love for Bill, to lessen the guilt she felt toward him, to eradicate the memory of her recent desperate behaviour and to bring back some dignity into her life. Having sent it off, Stead felt embarrassed by it, thinking it coy and weak. But the newspaper liked it, and published it in January 1972. It gave Sydney readers a highly romanticised view of Stead's relationship with Bill Blake in their last years together.

Stead avoided the Harveys for several months, 'not having quite digested their behaviour in Albania'.[24] Over time, she came to the more digestible conclusion that her misery in Albania was due to the depressant drugs she had been taking to keep down her blood pressure, and that she had missed Bill, who had always been her travelling companion. However, the trip marked a turning point in her relationship with Philip Harvey. Things would never be quite the same again. By 1973 she scarcely saw the 'splendid fellow' any more; she was no longer invited on his lecturing trips.

The disappearance of the Harvey factor in her life badly affected her morale. She felt old now. 'My affection for the good Doc. filled in the cracks and puttied the falling panes of the old building. Now that does not work.'[25] It was the lack of romance, more than any other factor, which prompted her to think of leaving for Australia after all.

The building metaphor was not a random image: her mind was on old buildings. The old tenement houses in her street were being demolished all around her, to be replaced by modern high-rise flats. The building next door was almost down. Her own, a rambling brick house, was due to be wrecked within a year or so and already had an enormous crack from attic to basement. Stead's downstairs neighbour, Marjorie Way, a retired nurse who would call in each day for a chat over a drink and a few cigarettes, used to lie awake imagining the chimney falling through her flat. The other occupants of their building had gradually found somewhere else to ive. Stead and Marjorie Way were hanging on, partly because they had not decided what to do next, and partly because they had heard that the landlord was obliged to pay substantial compensation to evicted tenants. Stead was hoping it might be enough to pay her fare to Australia.

'I am basically awfully lonely my dears,' Stead told the Rellas. After the mailman passed, at 7.30 or 8 am, the day stretched wearily ahead. The highlight of her week was Thursday morning, when Hilda Adamson, a Durham girl, arrived to clean the flat for two hours. Stead usually detained her for a sherry afterwards.

She was not well. She had had another scare in the night in the summer of 1971, just nine months after the first. In August 1973, she suffered a more serious attack. The fear was making her into a cautious valetudinarian. The hill on the way to the shops worried her, so did the steps up to her flat. She even worried about serious mental exertion. Ruth Hall did her shopping once a month with the car—and her 'huskies', as Ruth called her three boys, were there to help if necessary. The Halls, Stead had to admit, were remarkably good to her, inviting her to dinner on Bill's birthday and at other times. But they were not intending to remain in England permanently. Ruth, like her mother (who had died in Paris in February 1971, three years after Bill), was happiest in France, and she and Laurie were buying a house in the south, in the hills near Nice.

Harry Bloom still wrote, though less often. His health was very poor. After a bad attack early in 1972 and another stint in an intensive care ward, he told her: 'I had made up my mind that this is it and I only came out of it because I thought, I mustn't die, Chris needs me.'

Later that year, he planned to visit Switzerland, then come to her in London. Christina wrote to Gwen, enclosing a letter to the Blooms, and asked Gwen to post it from Sydney. This ruse was Harry's idea: if his wife believed Stead was in Australia, he would be let off the leash for a visit to London from Switzerland. He did get to Switzerland, but he did not manage to make it to London after all.

As the buildings around her came down, and a return to Australia became almost a certainty, Stead was going through her papers: 'big dollops of paper, hundreds'. It was probably at this time that she destroyed a vast quantity. At her death, she would leave behind complete files of correspondence from Ettore Rella and Stanley Burnshaw, beginning in the 1930s, and all the letters she had ever received from Philip Harvey, a friend since 1952. There were letters from Bill and from Harry Bloom.

But there were none from the people on whom she had modelled her major characters: Keith Duncan, Florence James, Anne Dooley or Ruth McKenney.

During the sorting process, Stead came across *Mrs Trollope and Madame Blaise*, the short novel about British expatriates in Switzerland that she had written in Lausanne in 1949. Little, Brown had rejected it back then. Early in 1967 she had given it to her new agents in New York and London, but again, there had been no interest. Now Stead decided to give it to her friend Oliver Stallybrass as a 'token of esteem'. She sent it to him on 14 February 1972, jokingly telling him it was a Valentine gift.

Stallybrass liked it very much, and though he no longer worked in a publishing house, he told her he would try to have it published. He edited it carefully, suggested minor changes, altered the title to *The Little Hotel* (which Stead never liked), and sent it around to publishers. This time, it was accepted by Angus & Robertson in London and Sydney, and published in 1973. Two years later, Holt published it in the US. Its reception was remarkably positive in all three countries.

In 1972, Holt sent Stead an advance of $4000 for the re-issue of *House of All Nations*. In early 1973 she decided to abandon *I'm Dying Laughing* for good. Quite firm this time, she told Burnshaw:

> My 'forthcoming novel' is now in the dustbin or as good as. I ploughed it under—instead of dying laughing it was dying of boredom and overwork and what Bill used to call ree-search. It is not my métier and it got me down, so low I could not even read a book—any book.

Ruth McKenney had died in July 1972, after years of mental instability. When she heard the news, Stead, who had spent twenty years, off and on, musing about McKenney's strengths and weaknesses, wrote to Harry and Anne Bloom:

> What a wonderful personality she had; what a marvellous friend she was! I never met anyone like her, gay, clever, astute, and pithy: as well as pithy, she could be a torrent, an endless talker—a phenomenon. You couldn't always endure it—but it was unique—(probably led to her mental disorders; there was no limit) ... Then how charming, cunning in her impulsiveness! I have had few women friends: she was the best, wisest, and as a personality, much the most gifted ... Her generous and politically sensitive nature made her a communist: she WAS a rebel; she was in nature great.

There was no mention of McKenney being a 'traitor'; there was no sign of any anger at all. Stead's judgements could be as whimsical as they were intransigent.

In August 1972 she was asked by the New York journal *Nation* to review Quentin Bell's biography *Virginia Woolf*, just published by the Hogarth Press. She had never liked Woolf's fiction, nor did she have much time for literary biography, but she agreed to take on the review. She thought Bell's biography good, like an interesting novel—but instead of discussing it on its own terms, she started to make notes on Virginia Woolf as if she were a character in her own fiction. And in a sense Stead made her into one. She read all Woolf's essays and several of her novels; she read Roger Fry's recently published *Letters*; she even went so far as to steep herself in the 'unreadable' Jane Austen (that 'tiresome chronicler of the country marriage-hunt') to try to understand why Woolf so admired her. She was following far too many tangents, and felt inadequate, wishing she had the 'brilliance, thoroughness' and 'good sense' of her scholarly Canberra friend Dorothy Green. She told herself she was going mad with it all.

Virginia Woolf became the new target of her anger. The beautiful Woolf was a 'beast' when it came to remarks about the appearance of other female writers. Woolf was a terrible snob. Her feminism was a 'narrow and savage passion'. *A Room of One's Own* was 'ridiculous even when it appeared in 1929, with its notion that to equal men in fiction … a woman must have not only a room of her own but £500 yearly. (Ben Jonson was a brick-layer, Keats a clerk.)' *Three Guineas* was a 'bitter, and intolerable attack on men'. Virginia Woolf 'had no notion of history'. Worst of all, *The Years* revealed a 'coarse and unnecessary anti-Semitism' that made Stead 'absolutely furious'.[26] She also took it as an indication of outrageous anti-semitism that Woolf told Violet Dickinson she was going to marry 'a penniless Jew'. She ignored the next line in Woolf's letter, quoted in Bell's biography: 'I'm more happy than anyone ever said was possible.'

Stead's behaviour was no longer rational: she had become one of the Furies. She wrote to Burnshaw:

> Well, I said to myself, when I saw my furious red face in the looking glass, 'You are right but calm down' and I was surprised at my intense feeling.

In December 1972 she abandoned the review, asking her agent Cyrilly Abels to make some excuse to the *Nation*. Not only did she feel a miserable failure, she simply could not understand why she had had 'to fight 100 devils', why the whole thing had upset her so.

Yet she did have some idea. In a letter to the book editor of *Nation*, she tried to explain why she felt unable to write the review:

> I took it harder than necessary perhaps, because I too married a Jew (though I would never have thought of saying so), I married a fine man who in a sense was my creator too: he did everything for me, as L.W. did for V.W. You see, I could not bear her mean behaviour.

To her cousin Gwen she wrote:

> I was held up three months on a piece about Virginia Woolf, got snarled up horribly, because of the dreadful subject (as I saw it eventually). She was mad and tortured her husband in every way (partly through her own agonies)—he was a Jew as you know and she was beastly about it ... and I became very upset about her horrible behaviour: so it all fell through ... Naturally, V.W. who had been mad all her life, and cottonwooled all her life, was extremely spoiled and thought she could do and say anything. Well, no more of that.

Clearly, Woolf's aristocratic upbringing, snobbery and alleged anti-semitism were not the issue. Her sin was that she was 'unbalanced, strange, unreliable, malevolent as the sick are, especially to those closest to them who are caring for them'.[27] In other words, the *real* issue was that Stead unconsciously identified with Woolf. Reading about Woolf, a female writer with whom she had several things in common, from a deep insecurity to a Jewish husband, had brought all the remorse she felt about Bill to the surface again. It caused her agony. Stead was dealing with her self-hatred in her habitual way: she deflected it into fury against others. 'Virginia Woolf'—a very different figure from Quentin Bell's Virginia—nearly became one of Stead's fictional creations.

By the end of 1973 she was making plans for her return to Australia. Winter was approaching; she hated the cold, and there was a world oil crisis. She did not want to return to Australia at seventy-one: it was more a question of having nothing to live for in England. Under Gough Whitlam's new Labor government, the country was flourishing culturally, and Patrick White had just won the Nobel Prize for Literature. But Stead was obsessed with one thing only: finding a companion. For a while she hesitated: should she go to Australia via the States? She was frightened by the stories of hijackings. But she decided she wanted to see Harry Bloom one more time. Since he had not come to her, she would go to him. She knew it would probably be the last time she ever saw him. Her plan was to go to New York for three weeks. To Aida Kotlarsky she wrote wryly that she and Harry Bloom would probably meet in a Greenwich Village café over glasses of tomato juice—since they both had heart trouble and angina.

Uprooting herself from England made her anxious, and she suffered from 'the three a.m. worries'. She went at the task slowly: she had to give away her furniture, sort through remaining papers, pack trunks, farewell friends. 'It is only now that I know all that Bill did for me, for us,' she told Aida Kotlarsky. Paul Koston arranged for her books to be packed up and sent off. The Halls helped with the heavy work.

On 2 May 1974, Philip Harvey and Ruth Hall accompanied her to Heathrow. Stead was flustered and nervous. She was leaving for good the country in which she had arrived, full of hope, almost exactly forty-six years ago. There was nothing to stay for; she felt an outsider in these people's lives. But they had known her for years. They had loved Bill. And now she was going to a country where only a handful of people had ever set eyes on the man she had lived with for almost forty years. She was cutting herself off from her past as radically as she had done at the age of twenty-six.

She guessed she would never see Ruth or Philip again. She and Ruth had never loved each other. But they had both loved Bill, and this had created a significant bond. It was touching to watch Ruth walk along beside her. Ruth, short and plump with smiling eyes and animated gestures, looked just like her father. The burly, cheerful man cajoling her and carrying her luggage was another man she had loved—for more than a decade now. It had been a painful passion, a 'great waste of time and heart'.[28] But he had been good to her.

Only Bill had ever given her the greatest gift a man could give her: his love. She had scarcely been able to believe in it at first. And England was the country, London was the city, where it had all begun.

Stead spent a miserable time in the air. Once through the barrier, she lost her boarding card. She eventually found it in her handbag. Over the

Atlantic she worried about the whereabouts of her health card. Surely she would be asked to produce it in New York. Eventually she found that it was in 'the right place', and they did not even ask for it.

In New York she stayed with Ettore and Jessie Rella in the downstairs section of their double-storey apartment. Full of plants and flowers, the Rellas' world always seemed magical to her. Hidden away in their cupboards and drawers was a 'secret life': the fine glove puppets they had made together over the years. (Ettore did the 'beautiful faces' and 'fine long elegant hands'; the dressing was done by Jessie, a skilled dressmaker.)[29] Over the furniture stalked their haughty Siamese cats. Stead called them the 'aristo-cats'.

She wrote to Philip Harvey meaningfully: 'NY is very dear; but pleasant. I am very much at home here, much more than in London and much much happier. Thank goodness.' He answered her from Corsica, where he and his family were on holiday.

> You lived in close association with all that is best in the American character for many years … Your present environs must be striking answering points that have not sparked since Bill died. Fancy living with 10 million Bills around you, not but that the lovely man was not unique & not really capable of being duplicated. But one friend will hint at his level of generosity of mind & Spirit, another will smack of his bubbling humour, a third will whisper of his scholarship & profundity & perhaps most will reflect his optimism & vigorous affirmation in their joy of life & for the human scene.

Stead was profoundly moved by his letter. She liked American male voices, and she would often hear traces of Bill's rich accent. She *was* partial to Americans because of Bill, Harvey was right. And for the same reason, she felt particular warmth towards Jewish people. She also liked to speculate that small men were more likely to show geniality and brilliance.

Harry Bloom had written: 'Darling Xris, Now soon I will see you in the flesh and hear your lovely voice and touch you!' He had told her he would be in New York on 10 May, one week after her arrival. But he had been ill again, and his wife Anne had had a heart attack. For the moment he was stuck in Miami, and once again, Stead found herself waiting for Harry Bloom.

By 6 June, around the time Stead had planned to leave for Australia, there was still no sign of Bloom. She told herself 'it would be useless to come here and go off without seeing him, after all this'.[30] She sent telegrams to Australia. When Aida Kotlarsky went to Hunter for the summer, Stead moved into her twelfth-floor apartment on E. 18th Street. She had always liked Aida's furnishings: the carved ebony chairs, oriental lamps and rugs, the brocades from ancient China, the handsome pianos. This time Aida's apartment seemed 'faded, as a pale story'.[31]

Eventually, on 12 June, Harry arrived in New York. His wife had come with him, and they were staying with their son Michael, so once again, his movements were restricted. He managed a brief visit. When he stood at the door in the half-light, Stead was shocked by his appearance: she imagined she had seen the Egyptian horror 'Thoth' at the door.

Bloom arranged to have lunch with her at Luchows, a favourite old restaurant of hers, but then he telephoned to say he was ill. For the first time, Stead, in a letter to Aida Kotlarsky, expressed irritation. But even now she took out her annoyance entirely on Anne Bloom, fabricating a picture of a wicked wife that smacked of fairy tale:

> If this goes on, though I am truly anxious for Harry's health and good spirits, I will have to think of moving on. She (the wife) does not know I am here— but she is suspicious of any trip Harry makes … She doesn't want him to see anyone, any old friends; for she has got a mania about his MONEY. She wants to be a rich widow and does not want him to give presents etc. maybe to old friends (like me, eh?). That is the sordid fact. And that is why she keeps him under lock and key … I am not telling this to the Rellas—it is too sordid, and makes this whole thing, which was a blessed thing, a real tender farewell between two old lovebirds, old lovers, something unpleasant. Well, let us hope things will improve in a few days.

Two days later she apologised to Aida for her badtempered letter. She was happy; she was buoyant. She even felt like writing fiction again, and had already written a funny piece based on a story Harry had told her the day before. He had eventually turned up at the apartment and they had 'a fine long time together'. He looked a little better. She was planning a story called 'Lover's Meeting'. She told Aida: 'Suddenly you see I have begun to see everything as a story; and that is why we get on. Not only does he love me but he turns me into a Scheherazade; which is what by nature I am.'

She would stay in New York as long as Harry was there; when he went south to Miami, she would leave for Australia. In the meantime, she decided she was enjoying New York. 'If it were possible for me to live here, I feel I would be happy here; many very good old friends. But that cannot be.'

Harry's return to Miami was delayed, but not because of Christina, as she would have liked. Soon after his visit, the 'honeytongued' Harry was admitted to the coronary division of St Luke's Hospital. He sent her a letter via a nurse. Once, Ettore Rella telephoned the hospital on Christina's behalf. When he started to improve, Harry rang her. On one occasion he even arranged for her to visit him in hospital. Three weeks passed. Stead was having nightmares. She told the Harveys: 'Harry ... gets his night nurses (noy-ses) to telephone me and tell me how he is; but though I am sure he loves this cloak-and-dagger work, I am quite tired of it; no one's fault.'

In Australia the family had planned a birthday party for 17 July. Stead sent another telegram and spent her seventy-second birthday with the Rellas at the Plaza Hotel. She was waiting for Harry Bloom to come out of hospital. The nurses told her he should be out in three or four days. She saw friends. The Rellas were 'great comforters'.

But when Bloom came out of hospital in late July, he was 'under observation' by his family, and they had no opportunity to meet. Stead had been in New York three months, not three weeks as planned, and had seen Harry Bloom just three times. From Australia she would write to Aida that the trip to New York had been worth it to see Harry, but it was not what either of them had expected.

> It seems certain that I will not see him again; so it was well that I managed to see him those few times. Things end—one knows it; but it is an odd experience to feel.

A few months later, living at her brother's house in Sydney's dusty western suburbs, she called her New York sojourn 'a sort of heaven-haven ... between the limbo of London and this strange little suburban wilderness'.[32]

15

Humping Her Own Bluey

AUGUST 1974 – MARCH 1983

C HRISTINA STEAD WAS tired. She was tired, in particular, of loneliness. At the age of seventy-two, after forty-six years in the northern hemisphere, she had returned to Australia to live in her brother Gilbert's house in Hurstville, just one suburb down the railway line from Bexley, where she had spent her first fifteen years. From her 1969 visit she remembered Hurstville as a dreary, hot and dusty suburb, a long way from the city. She knew there was no deep affinity between her and her family. But with her heart condition, she was so frightened of living alone that she had paid approximately A\$7000 for an extension to be built at the back of Gilbert's house.

Hurstville, thirty minutes from the centre of Sydney by train, epitomised working-class Australian suburbia. It had few trees; the corner shops were going broke. 'New Australians' (as European immigrants were called) had settled in the area, their brick-veneer houses sporting white doric columns and newly concreted backyards. The sky roared with the sound of jets boring in and out of Sydney's Kingsford Smith Airport to the north-east—a far cry from the beginning of the century when Christina Stead had lived there.

Christina's new quarters comprised a long, narrow room, much like a barn, with a small bedroom off to the side. A large sliding aluminium window at the eastern end looked out onto a small backyard with a lemon tree, banana-palm, pepper tree and ferns. Stead would sit by the window and watch the birds come for the birdseed she put out. At night, she derived some comfort from the patter of birds on the tin roof and the ping of berries as they dropped from an overhanging tree.

The ceiling was unfinished: Stead looked up at silver lining and rough wooden beams. The light was a naked bulb hanging from the rafters, and the furniture was cheap. But she hardly noticed these things any more. For years her surroundings had been austere, often grim. Dorothy Green had been shocked by Stead's dingy flat in Surbiton, especially when she saw pigeons strolling around in the kitchen.

Gilbert took a week off work to help his sister settle in. She paid for, and he installed, an electric stove, television, refrigerator and filing cabinets for her papers. Christina felt immense relief at being looked after by her 'baby brother', strong at fifty-six, though he too had suffered a heart attack. They had a congenial relationship. When Gilbert came home from work, he would join Christina for evening drinks. Betty, his third wife, worked long hours in a catering business, often at night as well. Their two boys bore the traditional family names: David was twelve; little Gilbert, a spoilt, cheerful fellow, was seven. For the first two or three weeks, Christina sincerely believed her loneliness was over.

It was wishful thinking. In all Stead's fiction (behind her now), there is no glimpse of cosy family life. Christina had almost nothing in common with her half brothers and sisters. After a month in Australia she wrote to Rella: 'I am very welcome and well-received here, Ettore, but they are not "my own." They are not the brothers and sisters I picked up along the way of my life, whom I miss.' When Stanley Burnshaw asked if she was beginning to feel at home in Australia, she replied emphatically: 'I left my life lying on the shores of other countries and I came to Australia. No question of coming back—you can't come back ... I am not home.'

Kate lived alone in a flat in harbour-side Cremorne, not far from Gwen Walker-Smith, with whom she was close friends. Weeta had converted to Catholicism when she married a Catholic (to her father's horror) and had four children, now grown up. She lived in Wollongong, on the south coast of New South Wales. Christina was happier with her brothers: they were men, they enjoyed drinking, they appeared more broadminded. Gilbert was a finance officer at the Metal Workers' Union; for relaxation he made endless alterations to the house in Hurstville. David, a metallurgist, lived on the affluent North Shore in a house set in bushland. Christina saw nothing of Kelvin, the middle brother, whose family shared Boongarre, at Watson's Bay, with Thistle Harris. (Thistle lived at the back, quite independently.) David and Gilbert had read Christina's books and were proud of their famous sister; the two sisters could not quite forgive her for what she had written about the family. To Ettore Rella Christina mused about the neuroses of the 'Pollit family', as she called them. Convinced that their peculiar childhood had scarred her and all her siblings, she made notes, 'The Bones the Parents Left'. She believed she herself had been wilful enough to stand up to her father, but some of her siblings were less forceful. ('If it did that to me, what did it do to certain gentler members?') All seemed 'marked with the iron ring.'[1]

Over the years, Stead had occasionally written to Thistle Harris from the northern hemisphere, but now that she was back in Sydney, Stead ostentatiously avoided her—just as she had in 1969. Thistle never knew why. Only once did Christina go back to Boongarre. It was in May 1976, two years after her return. *Miss Herbert* had just appeared in the States and *Time* magazine's article would praise it effusively. Their photographer, David Austen, rang Stead and suggested he come out to Hurstville to photograph her in her home environment. Gilbert Stead was in the throes of renovations and the house was dusty and noisy. Austen came up with the idea that they should go out to her childhood home at Watson's Bay. Stead concurred, admitting she had not seen 'the old patriarchal hut' for forty-eight years. Watson's Bay had changed dramatically. In Christina's youth there had still been large areas of dirt road and bushland; now the harbour-side settlement was filled with the houses of the well-to-do. She and Austen walked down the drive of Boongarre, and through the garden to the harbour beyond. He photographed her walking on the jetty in front of the house. Thistle came out and spoke to them, but Christina was distant and awkward. The incident left Thistle dumbfounded.

Ettore and Jessie Rella, in 'lovely New York', became Stead's confidants; she wrote to them at least fortnightly, sometimes more often. To friends she spoke of Ettore Rella as her 'Albanian boyfriend'. As summer approached, she would type letters during the night, sometimes at 3 am, or 'nightride' through a book. She liked the early mornings, the coolest hour of the day, when she could watch the dawn come up through the window. Writing letters made her feel less alone. Her thoughts were often with Harry Bloom, but he could not keep up with the Rellas' letter-writing pace. Invariably, he was too ill to fetch her letters from his post office box.

It was a twenty-minute walk up a slight incline from Gilbert Stead's house at No. 10 Donald Street to Hurstville's main street and railway station, and Christina no longer walked that far. She found it a strain to take a taxi to the station and the train into the city, and preferred, despite the expense, to take a taxi straight to the city. She made the trip once a week or so—necessary, she was soon telling herself, for her sanity. She would meet David at The Green Jade, his favourite restaurant in Chinatown. They both liked food and enjoyed a good bottle of wine. Or she would meet Gwen or Kate, who would help her shop for an item of clothing or a present, before having lunch in a café.

Gradually Stead made friends. Ron Geering, who had visited her in Surbiton in 1966 when he was researching his book, *Christina Stead*, invited her to lunch at his house in the leafy North Shore suburb of Gordon, and Stead met his wife Dorothy, a lecturer in Early Childhood Training. Geering, a warm, unpretentious man with a keen sense of humour, taught English at the University of New South Wales. He soon found himself playing the avuncular role men so often assumed with Christina. He and Dorothy regularly had her to lunch at Gordon: they would sit on the terrace overlooking their magnificent garden. Sometimes they invited Christina to stay for the weekend. They celebrated her birthday, invited her for Christmas. With 'Ron-Ron', as she called him, Stead could talk about books and nature: she could relax, joke, grumble about her family. She flirted with him, of course—and he indulged this, kissing her hand and fussing over her—but above all, she treasured him as a kind, brotherly friend. 'Doro' was a 'sweet person' and a 'great cook', but it was to Ron that Christina wrote letters.

Through the Geerings, Stead was re-acquainted with the novelist Elizabeth Harrower, whom she had met several times in 1972 in London. Harrower was close to Patrick White and his companion, Manoly Lascaris, and occasionally they would meet as a foursome.

In mid October 1974, Harrower rang to invite herself out to Hurstville on a 'mysterious mission'. On arrival, she announced to Stead that she came as Patrick White's emissary: he wanted her to receive the first Patrick White Literary Award. Would she please accept? The $6000 award came from a trust fund that White had set up when he won the Nobel Prize for Literature the previous year. Now that the Britannica Award had ceased, it was the richest annual award open to Australian writers. White stipulated that he particularly wanted to help older writers who had not received the critical acclaim they deserved, and he and his fellow judges agreed that Christina Stead was 'the most brilliant and deserving of any Australian writer'.

The prize brought a brief burst of publicity, but Stead did not even mention it in a letter to Stanley Burnshaw later the same month. It made her feel more comfortable financially, for she still regarded herself as poor—more from habit, these days, than from necessity.

With her customary helplessness, she had handed her financial management over to her brother David, who says today that she had little idea about the state of her finances though she did complain, probably influenced by him, that the 'income-tax crows' picked her bones.[2] Apart from occasional cheques from royalties or lending rights, she lived quite well on three different pensions: an Australian old-age pension, the British one to which she and Bill had made small payments and an American widow's pension. She rarely touched the capital she had amassed in recent years, and at her death she would leave more than $70000—a considerable amount in the currency of the day. She remained impulsively generous: she was always buying gifts for the family, her friends and their children. When Ettore Rella had a stroke the following year, she sent him and Jessie $2000.

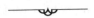

Patrick White had championed Stead since the re-issue of *The Man Who Loved Children* in 1965, when he had first discovered her writing. No other Stead novel had quite the same impact on him, but he thought *For Love Alone* remarkable, and when he read *Letty Fox*, he remarked to Geoffrey Dutton: 'It's quite extraordinary to think of that quiet, sedate woman writing anything so hilarious.'[3] Stead was always nervous about their social encounters. White had invited her to lunch during her 1969 visit and afterwards told Geoffrey Dutton that they 'got on very well'. He commented: 'Christina Stead's characters ... are all people she has known. She wasn't prepared to believe that mine, the important ones anyway, are latent bits of myself.'

To talk to her is more like talking to a man than a woman, although there is
nothing overtly masculine about her, and I shouldn't think anything lesbian.
Her marriage seems to have been one of the best kind.[4]

In that short encounter, Patrick White had been quite mystified. He did
not know it—perhaps she did not either—but her characters, as much as
White's, contained latent bits of herself.

Stead sensed that White listened and observed with the same sharp-eyed
awareness that she did—and she feared it. When, soon after her arrival in
Sydney, he and Lascaris invited her to lunch at their house in Centennial
Park, Stead kept postponing it, pleading dental troubles. To add to her
shyness, her skin problem had returned: several keratoid spots had appeared
on her face, and she turned down most social engagements that summer.

Embarrassed that she had read so little of White, her patron (as she saw
it), that summer she was 'stuffing' and 'cramming' herself with his work.
It was not the ideal frame of mind in which to read White, and it left her
unenthusiastic.

Patrick White was impeccably polite to her, but privately she thought
him 'a courteous and friendly cuss'.[5] Moreover, Stead was convinced that,
as a homosexual (which she saw as being 'anti-woman'), White would
look upon a plain woman without generosity. She described one of his
'delectable lunches' with more admiration than warmth:

> Everything is perfect, he is perfect, the long room where one sits and dines
> is delightful—all the paintings chosen by one man—and one cannot help
> feeling the stage-man in him, who gets everything to a pitch of perfection
> for the performance ... He must be a *cordon bleu*—his cooking is also
> perfection.[6]

***

It was not easy to start all over again, in a new place, with new friends,
at the age of seventy-two. 'Fact is,' she told her friend Dorothy Green in
Canberra, 'I have to build up a new world, I suppose ... What remains is
ancient history, barrel-scrapings.' That first summer the roar of the planes
overhead drove her mad. To add to her misery, the family had purchased
a portable swimming pool and the backyard was full of the 'demoniac
shrieking' of young Gilbert and his friends. A sulphur-crested cockatoo
hung around the 'hellish pool' and shrieked in imitation. 'I'm of strong

nerve, good heart and indifferent spirit,' Stead grumbled to the Rellas, 'but tomorrow, no later, I'm buying some ear stopples.'

She found preparations for Christmas 1974 at Hurstville tiring. In honour of her return, there were to be twenty-six guests, two turkeys, six chickens and one ham. Christina was put in charge of the drinks. She had a brief moment of pleasure when buying plastic beakers in the local hardware store. Hearing them speak Italian, she said something in Italian herself, and was promptly 'smothered' with 'celestial storms' of the language. She had already fished out her Greek dictionaries to exchange words with the Greek owners of the corner shop, but some months later, to her dismay, her friends went bankrupt.

Early in 1975 came the blow she had been expecting for some time: Harry Bloom died. Fearing he would not survive heart surgery, he had written to Christina on 21 January from a cardiac unit in Miami. After that there was silence. She was filled with dread, but dared not write to his wife for news. Eventually Polly Steinberg wrote to say that Harry had died on 6 February. Stead was quite stricken. She told friends it was as if she were widowed a second time. She told Stanley Burnshaw:

> I would tell him all sorts of things, for he always responded and we spoke the same language. An *amitié amoureuse* which went on for just on 40 years, one way and another. I am only just now getting over my habit (of which I was unconscious) of saying to myself (inside the head), 'Harry would laugh at that' and 'I'll tell Harry that.' He wrote to me every year on the anniversary of Bill's death saying something like 'I stayed awake nearly all night, I could not sleep for thinking of Bill and what is lost.'

The Little Hotel, written in the early 1950s, came out in the States in April 1975—two years after England this time. It received enthusiastic reviews in both countries. Lillian Hellman bought the option for a screenplay. In New York, Holt, Rinehart & Winston had just re-issued *House of All Nations* in paperback, and Angus & Robertson published it in Australia in 1974. On the strength of all this, Cyrilly Abels, Stead's American agent, encouraged her to take *Miss Herbert* out of its box. Gwen Walker-Smith re-typed the manuscript, untouched for more than a decade, and it was sent off to the US.

Random House paid Stead an advance of $5000. (Charlotte Mayerson, previously Stead's editor at Holt, now worked at Random House.) Stead dedicated the novel to Cyrilly Abels, who was seriously ill with lung cancer.

Harry Bloom had died; Cyrilly Abels was dying. Aida Kotlarsky had serious osteoarthritis; in July 1975, Ettore Rella had a stroke. Stead told Ruth Hall: 'He used to fly up and down the stairs and round the town and come back with extraordinary amusing Commedia dell'Arte stories, about nothing, about incidents—it was his Italian theatre—and now he can't.' It would be months before he could even manoeuvre himself downstairs. Faced with these sobering reminders of human mortality, Stead arranged for her papers to go to the National Library of Australia, in Canberra, after her death.

'Politicians battle and do murder to each other,' Stead told the Rellas in October 1975. It was a time of great political tension in Australia: the Senate was blocking supply, making the government's position untenable. But no one was prepared for the events of 11 November 1975, when the Governor-General, Sir John Kerr, sacked Labor Prime Minister Gough Whitlam and dissolved Parliament, and within the hour, Liberal leader Malcolm Fraser announced that he had been commissioned as Caretaker Prime Minister. Stead was as disgusted as her friends that a representative of the Crown had the power to dismiss an elected Head of Government.

Few believed that the coup would come off. However, on 13 December 1975, Malcolm Fraser won the general election. Long gone were the heady Whitlam days of the early 1970s; the Liberal–National Country Party Coalition was again in power.

Herbert Cole ('Nugget') Coombs wrote to Stead in March 1976, inviting her to lunch with him and his daughter-in-law. Stead had first met Coombs, then Chancellor of the ANU, in London in 1968. She saw him in Canberra in 1969, then again in London in 1972. From their first meeting, Stead had been charmed by the wiry, boyish-looking, short man with the sharp blue eyes, gravelly voice and mischievous smile. Despite his prominent status in Australian political and cultural life, he was devoid of airs and graces. In June 1976, Stead wrote to him from Newcastle, telling him that he ('King Cole') and 'dashing Don' (Dunstan) were her heroes. By June 1977 she was addressing letters to 'Darling Cole'. Coombs' replies were friendly but reserved.

That Stead admired Nugget Coombs is not surprising. He was her type of man: intelligent, fiery, energetic. He was no leftwing radical, but he was committed to good causes, a man of astounding diversity and energy. He had made his mark in Australia during the 1940s as Director-General of Post-War Reconstruction, doing much to establish the welfare state. When the Reserve Bank was established in 1959, he became its Governor. From the 1950s through to the 1970s he played a major role in persuading the government to support the arts. An omnivorous reader, he admired Stead's work. As an economist, he was hugely impressed with *House of All Nations*.

Coombs had been concerned about Aborigines since his school-teaching days in Western Australia in the 1920s, and more than anyone else in Australia, he was responsible for establishing Aboriginal Land Rights. For months each year he would go 'on walkabout', as Stead called it: travelling with Aborigines in tribal areas in the outback. He became recharged in the bush, which, he told friends, generated a powerful spiritual energy. He was also an outspoken conservationist. In 1977, he would be elected president of the Australian Conservation Foundation—a society that owed a great deal to Stead's father, David G. Stead.

Coombs was a busy man. When he was not away in the desert, he was writing books, giving speeches, chairing committees. Stead saw him only occasionally, either in Sydney or Canberra, but she thought about him a great deal.

To friends, Stead also made much of her admiration for another highly talented man, 50-year-old Don Dunstan, Labor Premier of South Australia. This time, her crush was more playful than genuine. She had been told he preferred men. To Stead, he was 'the most colourful and unusual personage' in Australian politics. She admired his 'immense voice of bronze'[7], and called him Demosthenes, after the Greek orator. Dunstan was hardly a typical Australian politician. He was interested in the classics and gave public poetry readings. Under his influence, Adelaide, 'the Athens of the South', had entered a new era of cultural libertarianism.

Stead heard Don Dunstan speak on the steps of Parliament House after Whitlam's dismissal, and was deeply moved. They had dinner together in August 1976. The Premier found her charming, a delightful conversationalist. He recalls discussing Greek and Latin poetry and the influence of Cicero's speech 'Pro Caelio' on Shakespeare.[8] He encouraged her to write some short stories for the South Australian Film Corporation he had founded, with the idea that they could be used for scripts. For a while, Stead thought she was at last inspired to write again. She typed out a cover page for a book of short stories, 'The First Hundred Tales', and dedicated the manuscript to Dr H. C. Coombs. But she needed more than distant muses.

———————

In April 1976 Stead was invited to the English Department of Melbourne's Monash University for a week. The trip was a strain. Recently, she had had all her teeth removed and new dentures fitted. From now on, her gums were often ulcerated, and she could eat only soft things—painstakingly slowly. Her staple food had always been steak; now it became steak tartare. When she had her own cooking facilities, she would buy fillet steak, singe it rapidly in a frypan, then cut it up with nail scissors. She was embarrassed to eat in public, and when asked out to dinner, would think to herself: 'Oy, another hungry night.' At Mannix College, where she stayed that week, she sat in a corner and ate with her back to the throng. If somebody joined her, she left her food untouched.

For Easter she went to Clem and Nina Christesen at their beautiful old house in Eltham, in bushland on the outskirts of Melbourne. They celebrated with Russian Easter bread, painted eggs, sweet delicacies and plenty of drinks. Nina, born in St Petersburg, had come to Australia with her family at the age of thirteen and later introduced Russian Studies to Australian universities. Small and roundfaced, goodhearted and hospitable, she reminded Stead of Aida Kotlarsky. Nina and Clem were gracious and thoughtful hosts, and Stead loved the cosy house, with its redwood panelling, embroidered cushions, books and nicknacks.

At the beginning of June 1976, Stead went for a nine-week term to the University of Newcastle. She was their second Writer-in-Residence; Xavier Herbert had been there the previous year. She stayed in a hotel near the campus, and this time, because it was only a few minutes' walk from shops, she managed to eat properly. Evening meals in her room were steak tartare with a raw egg on top, and several drinks. The problem was the twenty-minute walk (through pleasant bushland) to her office in a building without lifts. She walked slowly these days. She had become quite weak.

At weekends Stead was entertained by colleagues and shown the surrounding Hunter Valley and coastal region—an area she had often visited in her childhood. In company, her spirits would lift and she would sparkle and joke, but her letters were as desolate as ever. While Stead was in Newcastle, *Miss Herbert* appeared in the States. The *New York Times Book Review* hailed her as 'one of the most distinguished novelists writing in English'. A more general article on Stead in *Time* (with David Austen's photograph of Stead at Watson's Bay) alluded to Stead's 'extraordinary craftsmanship' and 'the touch of the sadist' in her characterisation of Miss Herbert.

Stead had decreed that the novel should not be published in England and, therefore, not distributed in Australia (where people might recognise Miss Herbert), but it turned out that American Random House copies were freely available in Australian bookshops. She told interviewers she had been carrying the manuscript around in a trunk for thirty years. It made everyone wonder what else was at the bottom of her suitcases. Several articles referred to her 'new novel,' *I'm Dying Laughing*. She told herself she really should return to it.

There was domestic tension at Hurstville—Gilbert and Betty were on the brink of a divorce—and Stead now referred to the place as 'Curstville'. In March 1977, when she left for ten weeks as Writer-in-Residence at Monash University in Melbourne, she resolved never to go back there. It meant leaving her manuscripts, most of her books and some clothes behind; a couple of years later, Ron Geering would take four filing cabinets full of papers to his house. At seventy-five, without Bill, and in fragile health, Stead was a wanderer again. From March 1977 until her death in March 1983—six years in all—she would be 'map-hopping', restlessly moving from place to place. The constant moving was exhausting, mentally and physically. She decided to take a trip to New York in October, at the end of the northern summer, but this left several months to fill between Monash and New York. From now on, she was forever worrying about where she would be staying in a few weeks' time.

Monash would become her favourite Australian university. The campus was lively and friendly. She lived in Mannix College, across the road from the university. Every morning she walked to the Menzies Building, ten minutes away, and took the rattling escalators to her office on the seventh floor. Her window overlooked many kilometres of flatlands, with the Dandenong ranges in the distance. Monash's heyday as a radical university was over, but Stead liked to see the communist booths in Orientation Week. Less pleasing were the 'outrageous raging ridiculous feminist rampages', in which female students carried notices declaring: 'All men are complicit in rape'. She was horrified.

She enjoyed meeting new people. Her door was always open, and when students called to see her, she was welcoming and helpful. Afterwards, in a letter to Michael Costigan, the Director of the Australia Council, which had arranged the Writer-in-Residence program, she claimed the main purpose of a resident writer was to undo the negative effects of literary studies at tertiary level:

> I may have helped one or two confused and hesitant young writers by talking over their hesitations—but I don't know. My feeling still is that the gifted student does not need help—except in only one particular: He needs to have it confirmed that literature is by writers and not by critics, that critics should be thrown out the window ... In any case, the gifted student will soon come to the conclusion that criticism has nothing to do with creative writing, but he may waste some time before that.

Stead (like Patrick White) was openly scathing about academics, whom she tended to regard as uninspired dullards. But several of her colleagues in the English Department were affable and hospitable. There were dinners, parties and weekends away. Mary Lord, a lecturer, proved a particularly kind and caring friend.

While in Melbourne Stead renewed contact with Judah and Hyrell Waten, who had visited her and Blake in Surbiton in 1966. Judah, in his mid sixties, was the type of man Stead most missed in her life. A Russian-Jewish Australian, Judah loved conversation. Like Bill, he was self-educated and astonishingly erudite. He too was a passionate communist. And his main interest was one that Stead shared: Jewish migrant life in Australia.

Waten also provided a precious link with Stead's past. Not only had he met Bill and liked him; when he was in London in the early 1930s, he had met Ralph Fox.

For the second year in a row, Stead spent a 'marvellous Russian Easter' with the Christesens at Eltham. 'Christina was the most uncomfortable guest we have ever had,' says Clem Christesen candidly. He and Nina were used to house guests, and they were genuinely fond of Christina, but there were moments of exasperation. On the second day, she asked to borrow Clem's typewriter: to his annoyance she kept it for her own use for five weeks. After breakfast, she would type letters. Between ten and eleven she had her first gin and vermouth. Initially, Clem gave in to her entreaties to join her, but soon admitted defeat. In the afternoons she would usually squat in an armchair in the lounge, her legs drawn up to her chest, and watch television at high volume. Clem would occasionally try to persuade her to talk about her past, her travels. Once he suggested taping a discussion and she allowed him to set up the tape-recorder and record the identification of tape message, but the interview went no further. She would answer his questions with three words. To his frustration, if she ever talked about her past, it was over the television, in her low, husky voice.

Clem and Nina agree they never had a 'profound talk' with Christina. She was 'earthy' rather than analytical or introspective, happiest when exchanging stories about people and their lives. She got on well with Nina's mother Tatiana (Tanya) Semeonovna Maximov, who lived in a little white cottage up the drive. At eighty-eight she was frail but still full of vitality. She and Nina's father had loved each other from childhood, and Stead was charmed by this romantic story.

Stead would ask Nina questions about *her* past: Nina had worked at two jobs during the Depression, supporting her mother who had tuberculosis, before she established the Department of Russian at the University of Melbourne. Nina was both merry and earnest, and her earnestness, Stead told the Rellas, had the virtue of not making her feel guilty. Clem was 'excitable, friendly, hot-tempered but engagingly humane and kind'.[9]

Stead enjoyed speaking French and learning Russian phrases. Nina was impressed with her smattering of Russian. Stead spent quite a bit of time in the kitchen and would show Nina how to make little things. Her omelettes were the best Clem had ever eaten.

Nina believes that she and Christina got on well because Christina did not see her as a competitor for male attention. When they entertained,

Nina would deliberately sit her beside some charming man. 'I would tell him beforehand: "For goodness sake, kiss her hand. She likes it."'

The Christesens witnessed a couple of 'uncomfortable' dinners, when Christina seemed to want to dispute every remark anyone made. 'She would point-blank contradict you,' Clem recalls. ' "No, no, you're wrong," she would say, and then she would contradict herself after fifteen minutes, no less dogmatically.'[10]

Stead turned seventy-five while in Melbourne, and Stephen Murray-Smith, editor of *Overland*, hosted a party on her birthday. Stead particularly liked Nita Murray-Smith, her Russian-Jewish hostess. Twenty or so people came—some close friends, some strangers. Coombs was invited, but he had caught 'flu in Central Australia. (He was 'probably wearing a fringe of leaves' with his tribe, Stead joked.) Stead cut the cake and went home laden with gifts. The occasion had been 'very pleasant' and 'very soothing'. She felt she had made some real friends in Australia at last.

She was leaving for the US on 8 October 1977, arriving a month before Ettore Rella's seventieth birthday. To Dorothy Green she explained she had to see Rella: 'We have an old fond friendship with love mixed in it.'

A brief return to 'Curstville' was necessary to pack for the trip. Back in her old quarters, she was wide awake at 2 am with 'the horrors and anxiety'. The American trip worried her: arrangements were still up in the air. Neither the Rellas nor Aida Kotlarsky had extended an invitation to stay, and only three weeks before she left, Stead was obliged to write to the Rellas asking tentatively if she might stay with them, 'for a short while at least'. Kindhearted Jessie Rella, fully occupied with looking after Ettore, had been ill herself, with suspected breast cancer, and surely did not relish the idea of a tense Christina under their roof, but she wrote a welcoming letter back. Stead was grateful. 'On this ticket I have, I can stay away a year—so no hurry.'

Two weeks before her departure Stead flew to Melbourne for one night to attend the National Conference for a Democratic Constitution. In the wake of Whitlam's dismissal, leftwing intellectuals were to debate the issues of political rights and democracy and how these could best be incorporated into a new Australian constitution. Stead was on the list of sponsors, with, among others, H. C. Coombs, historian Manning Clark, Patrick White, writer Frank Hardy and Bob Hawke, then President of the Australian Council of Trade Unions. It was not the conference that interested Stead so much as H. C. Coombs, who was chairing the opening session. She wanted to write a story about him and she needed 'to penetrate his system'. She told Coombs: 'I want to know you, I don't feel I do know you; I feel you are unique.'[11]

The trip to the States, Stead's last trip abroad, was a catastrophe. She had overestimated her strength. Too embarrassed to eat on the plane in company, she arrived weak and wobbly. Her chronic anxiety did not go away at the Rellas: despite her overwhelming jet fatigue, she lay awake in a state of nervous agitation. She had been shocked to find Ettore so helpless, much more so than she had imagined from his letters, and only now was she conscious of the extra burden she placed on Jessie. Perhaps, too, it pained her to see the contrast between Jessie's devoted nursing of her husband and her own behaviour when Bill was ill. After a fortnight at the Rellas during which she scarcely went out, unable to walk more than two blocks, she moved for a few days to Polly and Isidor Steinberg's small studio apartment. From there she wrote her first letter in three weeks, to her brother David:

> Since Jessie has everything to do for Ettore who has NOT recovered (though mentally all there) and though I was in the downstairs flat, not in their way, I thought it wiser to go elsewhere for a while. Ettore tries to get downstairs, almost every day … but only with real difficulty, wheelchair to top of stairs, handing himself down on handrail installed for him and then that 'spider' sort of walking-stick to the downstairs flat and if possible (more great difficulty), out on to their terrace, which they have made into an Italian garden.

The next month saw her 'to-ing and fro-ing between kind friends'. Aida could not accommodate her in her small studio apartment. Stead had dreamt of basking in the love of New York friends, and instead she felt an imposition, 'an all-out nuisance'.[12] On 26 November, she was back at the Rellas when she woke up at 4.30 am, feeling she was about to suffocate. She struggled and panicked and eventually summoned Jessie on the intercom system to the upstairs apartment. Two days later, it was from bed in St Vincent's Hospital that she wrote to David Stead:

I began to sniff the pearly gates it seemed to me and a very bad smell I thought it—so unwilling, at last, I buzzed poor dear friend Jessie (at about 4 a.m.)—the good girl came downstairs, went up, rang the police & ambulance (it's the system) dressed, went with me to hospital, waited & returned that same day—& next day.

It was a frightening experience to be put on a stretcher and rushed to hospital with the siren screeching. Perfectly alert, Stead knew she was being given oxygen and morphine. It was congestive heart failure, brought on by water in the lungs. At the hospital she underwent a series of electrocardiac tests. She had no medical insurance and Joan Daves, the agent who had taken over at Cyrilly Abels' death, was obliged to advance her hospital fees—almost $3000—before Stead could be discharged. Stead wired David, in Sydney, to send the money urgently from her Australian account.

The New York episode left her more afraid of being alone, and with a new fear of drowning in her own fluids, for the doctors told her that Jessie Rella's quick action had saved her. When, after four days, she was discharged, she was told not to get over-excited or strained and to limit her fluid intake. Since fluids included soups and stews, among the few things her dentures allowed her to eat, she felt uncertain about any food. What *could* she eat? Joan Daves' mother was away in the country and so Stead was taken to her apartment on E. 55th Street, where she lay around miserably until 9 December, when she had her next appointment with the doctor. She was anxious to get back to Australia, but where would she live back there? It worried her terribly. She was upset by a letter from Betty Stead, which made it plain she was no longer welcome at Hurstville. When Ron Geering wrote to New York inviting her for Christmas, Stead accepted with relief. She had asked Dorothy Green to enquire about residential colleges in Canberra. She had friends in that city, and her 'preux chevalier', Nugget Coombs, was there, when he was not in the outback. She thought that having her own room in a communal college might be the solution to her problem. 'I do think, that in view of my having become a water-drunk and having to be careful about that, I had better be in a place where people can look out for me and say, "What happened to our beautiful neighbour today?"' Joking aside, she hated the idea of being discovered 'out cold on the coir matting'.

Stead was far too weak to attend a dinner party at Lillian Hellman's, and was glad of the excuse. What with her timidity and her embarrassment about eating in front of others, the dinner had given her the horrors. Though they never met, Hellman was a loyal admirer. That December, she was asked by the *New York Times Book Review* which writers she most admired:

> Of the older generation I have long believed that Christina Stead is first rate. … If ever the Nobel Prize Committee could get off the highwire of trying to balance world literary opinion with the diplomatic consideration of which-country-should-it-be-this-year, they will give her what she deserves.

When Saul Bellow was awarded his Nobel Prize for Literature in November 1977, he had said he would like to see Christina Stead receive the laurels.

The heart attack in New York left Stead considerably weakened. When she returned to Australia in mid December 1977 and stayed at her brother David's, she felt so unsteady she would not walk without someone at her side.

Dorothy Green had enquired about Stead living in Bruce Hall, a residential college at the ANU in Canberra. An undergraduate college, it accepted a small number of senior academics and was considerably cheaper than University House, which catered exclusively for postgraduates and academics. Bruce Hall also had a reputation for the best food among the undergraduate colleges.

In early February 1978, Ron Geering drove Stead to Canberra, along with her huge electric typewriter, some books and a large suitcase. She was installed in Room 40, slightly bigger than the standard tiny undergraduate cell, with her own telephone and a balcony overlooking Mount Ainslie. The bathroom was shared with the inhabitant of Room 41—at that time a male professor in economic history.

Stead was pleased with the arrangement. In her red brick college under Black Mountain, she was not 'degraded by domestic conflict' and was close to intellectual life. The warden, Bill Packard, an energetic, kind man, had hoped she would occasionally eat at the High Table and contribute to the intellectual tone of the college, but she always ate in her room. In 1969, when she had lived briefly on campus, she had walked into town to the shops; now she had to order a taxi, and even this 'short sally' left her 'knocked out.' An obstacle she had not anticipated was that University House, where Nugget Coombs lived, was across the campus, too far for her to walk. Being near Coombs had been an important reason for coming to

Canberra. She saw him one morning in the distance, jogging in a tracksuit. At seventy he still jogged or swam every day.

At the end of March, 'Eponym', as she called him—referring, presumably to his nickname 'Nugget'—was officially invited, as patron of the college mountaineering club, to dinner at Bruce Hall. He rang Stead the day before and said he would call in for a drink. She rushed out in a taxi and bought expensive French champagne and two champagne glasses. Then Coombs rang back and invited her to join the dinner party. They did not drink the champagne. She sat among the 'comely' climbers at the High Table, feeling terribly self-conscious about the keratoses on the end of her nose, but happy to be among the men. The food was good and the wine plentiful. 'Eponym', though he seemed tired, was 'burning hot with energy and zeal'.[13] Just back from three weeks in northern Australia, he talked mostly about the Aboriginal question.

Shortly afterwards, Stead spent four days in hospital having her 'sunburnt nose' repaired. For some years now, she had had trouble with cancerous spots on her face. The spots were removed and skin was grafted from the delicate, white skin behind her ear. It created a white patch on her otherwise rather red nose, which she, disgusted, compared to a strip of bacon. Afterwards she hid herself from view at Dorothy Green's. Green comments: 'She set a lot of store by her appearance. She could look enormously impressive even in her old age, but her father had hammered it into her that she was ugly. So Chris told me.'

Dorothy Green invited Stead to stay on a number of occasions. Christina 'got on her conscience'.

> I'd have her here to stay, thinking it would be peaceful, and thinking that, like most writers, she'd most like tranquillity and peace to read and write. At the time I was enormously busy, lecturing, and writing. I'd be in my study and waves and waves would come at me. When I went out of the study she would trap me, want to talk. She was desperately lonely.[14]

Christina Stead stayed eight months at Bruce Hall, but soon realised that an undergraduate college was really not suitable for her. 'I felt and looked an anachronism beside that moiling, toiling, ambitious young lot.'[15] She was sorry to leave Canberra and friends, but she had seen very little of Nugget Coombs; and Mary Lord, from Monash, had invited her to live with her in Melbourne. Mary, fifty that year, divorced with four grown-up children, was about to have her large house at No. 28 Wilmot Street, East

Malvern, to herself, and she told Stead she would welcome the presence of an interesting female friend. Christina was 'a sunrise to sunset person'; she herself was 'a sunset to sunrise person', so they ought to be able to keep each other company without getting in one another's way.

Stead stayed twenty months with Mary Lord. It was one of the paradoxes in her life that she vastly preferred the company of men and fervently hoped that the end of her isolation would come from them, yet the closest she came to escaping isolation in her last years was with female friends, especially with Mary.

> She is a warmhearted lively soul, loves Mozart (like me, but she is a natural musician) and a practised Mamma; hence, does not worry very much about housepride and is a great hand at looking after people, while not knowing the word coddle. She is a good companion.[16]

Mary Lord was busy with teaching, administrative matters and a book on Australian writer Hal Porter that she was editing, but Lord was a sociable woman, who disliked the idea of living on her own as much as Stead did. In other ways too, she and Stead were alike. Lord was large-boned and practical, with a reputation for being forthright, tactless and difficult. Both women enjoyed stimulating company; neither suffered fools gladly. Both could be scathing about academics. They both liked to laugh. Moreover, Mary was tolerant and patient with Christina. Looking back, she describes herself as 'Christina's nurse, mother and servant'. According to her friends, Mary did things for Christina in such an unobtrusive, natural manner that neither she nor Christina was fully aware of the extent of Christina's dependence. Mary's friends and children called in frequently; it was a lively household, and Stead welcomed the change from life in an institution.

For the first time in years, she wrote and completed a story—the last complete piece she would ever write. 'The Old School' was based on her experiences at Bexley primary school, below Lydham Hill. This poignant story, which describes the way underprivileged children were cruelly scapegoated by the others, reveals an older, mellow Stead reflecting on her past.

Since her bedroom was too small for a desk, Stead's typewriter was kept on a table at one end of the living room, in front of a picture window looking onto the garden. It was a choice location but in time the arrangement became an excuse for not writing: when visitors or children came, there was no peace or privacy.

Some weeks passed before Mary Lord became conscious of Stead's eating problems. 'Chris was vain,' she explains, and 'very proper, modest, in a Victorian kind of way.'[17] Christina liked to eat by herself, and because she ate inordinately slowly, eating took up several hours each day. Breakfast—bread soaked in milk with sugar, or packaged desserts with cream—was eaten in her dressing gown, sitting at her desk watching the birds attack the birdseed she had spread in the garden. Before lunch and dinner she would have what she called her 'poison': equal quantities of gin and cinzano rosso, with double the amount of water, and ice. At dinner, which she usually ate sitting in an armchair, she would drink red wine or rosé. If there were guests, or if Mary had cooked something Christina particularly liked, she would join the table, but it meant that she hardly ate anything: she ate so slowly. Mary persuaded her to see a dentist only with great difficulty; Christina hated the idea of a male dentist seeing her without her teeth. The new set of lower dentures he provided made no difference to her ulcerated gums.

On Boxing Day, Stead found herself gasping for breath, and was taken to Moorabbin Hospital with pulmonary oedema. When she came out twelve days later, she was given an oxygen tank to keep in her room for emergencies. She no longer walked more than a few metres, and relied on Mary to drive her to the shops, to the post office, to friends. A doctor, a large, big-hearted man, called at the house every second Wednesday morning. Dr Donald Macdonald, a family friend, was even known to bring his boys round to attack Mary's garden, and he was always ready to attend in emergencies, at any time of night. Stead found him a reassuring, calming presence.

One night Mary, still up working at 3 am, came out of her study to find Christina walking around looking upset. She told Mary her 'Artie' (heart) was playing up. Mary rang Dr Macdonald there and then. On another occasion, Stead thought she was suffocating. She panicked, gasped and drew deep breaths from her oxygen tank. Dr Macdonald, when he arrived, told her she had been hyperventilating, and advised her, if it should happen again, to sit and listen to Mozart and take shallow breaths. It was a very frightening condition.

In July 1979, Stead stayed a week with the Geerings, and during this time she asked Ron Geering to be her literary executor. Fifteen years younger than Stanley Burnshaw, whom she had appointed ten years before, Geering lived in Sydney, where her papers were. He had done a great deal to promote interest in her work in Australia and struck her as the ideal person for the job.

Stead had become totally dependent on her, but Mary Lord claims she did not want her to leave, despite the moments of irritation. On Sundays the women would go to friends' for lunch or entertain at home. They often went to Box Hill to visit the Watens, Stead's closest friends in Melbourne. 'Judah would tell Russian-Jewish jokes; Christina would chortle.' They would visit the Christesens at Eltham, or other Monash friends. Stead would arrive armed with exquisitely wrapped presents: scents, liqueurs, flowers. Before social occasions, she would apply perfume to the back of her hand, telling Mary: 'You never know when a fella will kiss your hand!' (The way she held out her hand was a sign for men to do so.)

Occasionally, Stead would back out of something at the last minute, invariably because she was feeling fluttery in the heart. Whenever they had guests to the house, she would ask Mary in advance to 'rescue' her (let her disappear to her room) after a certain time.

Stead seldom reminisced, but Lord remembers one occasion when she talked about Bill and suddenly burst into tears. 'Something swept over her. She told me she hadn't been good enough to Bill. "Poor darling Bill. I was not kind to him." ' It was the only time Mary Lord ever saw Stead weep.

More often, she talked about Ralph Fox. He was the other half of herself, her twin, and she never quite believed he was dead, even though she knew he was. She told Mary Lord, Ron Geering and the Watens: 'I firmly believe that he will turn up at the door, the day before I take off for some other planet.'

In December 1978 a letter came from the Official Secretary to the Governor-General offering to make Christina Stead a member in the General Division of the Order of Australia. The honours were to be announced in the press on Australia Day, 26 January 1979. Stead declined. She had never been impressed by the monarchy, and the memory of 11 November 1975 still stung. Patrick White had withdrawn from the Order of Australia in 1976.

In 1981, Virago re-issued *A Little Tea, A Little Chat* and *The People with the Dogs*, making these American publications available to readers in England and Australia for the first time. The following year, the same firm re-issued *The Beauties and Furies*, long out of print, and *Miss Herbert*.

Whatever Stead's qualms about a publishing house focusing exclusively on women's writing, Virago did a great deal to restore her stature. For the first time ever, most of her work was available in paperback.

———— ✺ ————

H. C. Coombs wrote to Stead to say he would be visiting Melbourne in September 1979, on his way to Yugoslavia. Stead and Mary Lord invited him to dinner. Stead still talked a great deal about Coombs. She carried a picture of him in her wallet, and told him so. Every so often, she would say to Mary, in that clairvoyant way of hers, that she sensed 'Cole' was back from a trip to the Centre: the air felt warmer.

Over dinner, Coombs asked about her work, and Stead admitted she was not writing. Coombs, concerned about her, may have intimated that University House in Canberra might suit her better. He could not have known—on social occasions no one ever knew—the extent of Stead's physical frailty. After his visit, she developed the fantasy that Coombs wanted her in Canberra. Mary Lord comments: 'She was fantasising what she would like things to be. I found it terribly sad and terribly moving.'

With the air of helpless passivity she tended to cultivate where men were concerned, Stead told the Rellas that Coombs was now taking her in hand.

> He wants me to go to Canberra, University House, where he thinks (I know) I will have more creative quiet than here. He didn't say all that; but I know what the Nugget is thinking ... Mary is a dear, very kind, and but for the In-and-Outs and the considerable traffic at Grand Central East Malvern, I would not think of moving. ... Well, never mind—I was born under a wandering star, that is more than clear.

The Australia Council for the Arts gave Stead an 'Emeritus Fellowship'—a recently coined term for a literary pension that would be paid for the rest of her life, in monthly instalments. Stead was convinced that Coombs had arranged the Fellowship. Mary Lord said to her, mildly: 'I don't think he did. It's a Literature Board thing.' But Stead replied: 'Oh, yes he did, dear.' Having persuaded herself that Coombs wanted her in Canberra, she was looking forward to his 'dear company', but she was terribly anxious about the coming move. During the last few months at Mary Lord's she felt 'rattled', slept badly and was 'under the queerest gloomspell'. Her courage was failing her along with her strength. Leaving Mary, being on her own again, was frightening. 'I am so lonely you wouldn't believe!' she wailed to the Rellas. She continued to hate herself for not writing: writing had always been her weapon against despair.

In February 1980, Rodney Wetherell interviewed Stead on ABC radio—one of the most nerve-wracking interviews in his life. Stead showed just how contrary and dogmatic she could be. Various exchanges:

Q: There must have been a great restlessness in you … right from early days.

A: No, not at all.

Q: You were very determined to leave Australia, for example.

A: No, not at all.

Q: Do you have a professional sort of writer's interest in psychology?

A: No, I was never a professional writer, and I am not now. This is quite true. It's a thing I do, but I'm not a professional.

About *House of All Nations*:

Q: It's a very glittering world you portray in that book, very sophisticated, and corrupt, I suppose.

A: Well, corrupt is the way you may see it. If you have very strange ideals about any kind or part of the world, you don't know it. You've got to be in it to know it.

Q: Would you say there was a definite political intention behind that book?

A: None whatever.

The Australia Council for the Arts wanted to include Stead in their series of video interviews with Australian writers, and Stead, as a recipient of one of their Emeritus Fellowships, felt she could not refuse, though she hated the idea. A young woman came to see her at Mary Lord's to discuss how they would proceed. She wanted Stead to talk in the film about her attitude to the women's movement and Marxism; Stead refused point blank. It took her three days to recover her nerves after this preparatory interview, and she worried that she would not be able to cope with two days of filming. Mary Lord promised to take the film crew away for lunch so she could rest between shoots.

The video was filmed on 10 April and 11 April 1980, partly in Mary Lord's garden, partly in the house. Elizabeth Riddell asked the questions.

Stead gave one word answers: twice Riddell gave up in despair. It was the cameraman, Haydn Kernan (a 'nice-looking young fella'[18]) who eventually got Stead to thaw.

The forty-minute video, carefully edited, shows none of this. As posterity's only glimpse of Christina Stead talking, moving and laughing, it is a precious documentary. In still photographs, Stead tends to look austere; it is in movement that she charms. The video captures her whimsical humour and the mischievous glint in her keen blue eyes. Her most striking feature is her voice: soft, sing-songish, the voice of a skilled storyteller. She is shy, nervous, dressed in an elegant trouser suit. Talking about Bill and Paris and the writing of her early books, she almost becomes young again. She is close to tears when she tells how she lost consciousness at the very moment when a friend of hers was killed in Spain. Then she makes a joke, covering up her emotion. The image she projects is that of an easy-going wanderer.

> I never think about my life. The idea of death was never present to me, because of the fossils in the rocks. We are probably taught a fear of death …
> I don't expect anything, because I don't care. I take everything as it comes.

By mid April 1980 Stead was back in Canberra, installed in University House. The fellowship covered most of the cost, but she was nevertheless worried about the expense and had decided to take a small flat without a kitchen. It was an impractical decision: she knew she would not go to the dining room for meals. But the most important thing for her was that she lived close to H. C. Coombs. And as it happened, their flats were on the same stairwell in the north wing: hers on the second floor, his on the first. Opposite her, on the same landing were former Prime Minister Gough Whitlam, now a University Fellow, and his wife Margaret. They exchanged friendly words when they met. Stead liked to think of herself surrounded by illustrious presences.

Her balcony looked onto the Fellows' Garden below. From the window she could see over the treetops to the Telecom tower on the top of Black Mountain. Lit up at night, this 'Arabian Nights tower' was strangely comforting. It reminded Stead of Watson's Bay Lighthouse, which she had seen from her window at Boongarre. She never pulled her curtains.

Friends rallied round. The poet Rosemary Dobson became one of her 'collectors'—picking her up from the hairdresser, doctor or dentist. Then they would go to lunch. Dobson was embarrassed that Christina never ate anything, but she found her humorous, meandering conversation quite wonderful.

Clare Golson, an ex-nurse, partly assumed Mary Lord's role of nurse and mother. Clare worked at the University crèche and would call in on Stead on her way home. She took her cooked food, and lent her a crockpot, encouraging her to make nourishing soups and stews. It was obvious that Stead was not eating properly.

Clare's husband, Jack Golson, Professor of Archaeology, dropped in after work, sometimes with his colleague Douglas Yen. 'The boys drink deep,' Stead told Burnshaw, 'and I am not opposed to the stuff as you know.' The evening drinks were the highlight of her day. It pleased her to think she was once again among scientists, 'the most humane of people'.

Dr Coombs was rarely around. Stead told Philip Harvey, a little pointedly: 'I don't see him often—he's far too busy saving the Aborigines where the foreign industrialists are trying to grab their land for mining … But he lights up the landscape for me—you know me.' She admitted to Geering: 'I'm so lonely that when I know for sure that Dr. H.C.C. is not in (I can look through the brick screen down on his place) … I telephone him. No answer. But I know that.' Coombs did call in for a sociable drink every so often. Once or twice he asked her to dinner in his flat—he was a good cook—but he found it disconcerting that she ate almost nothing. He enjoyed their conversations, but found her difficult. 'There were times when she was quite intolerant,' he recalls. Once he invited her for a drink without explaining that he had invited another female writer whom he thought she would like to meet. 'It was an absolute disaster. Christina was obviously annoyed that another woman was there. She was pretty rude.'[19]

Stead soon realised that she had deluded herself about Coombs' desire for her presence in Canberra. After a few months there, she was wishing herself back with Mary Lord again. Mary Lord had resigned from Monash University and was moving to Sydney at the end of the year to work as a freelance writer.

Stead fell in love with men who seemed to have infinite reserves of energy, but she herself had none any more. Now her terrible lassitude never left her. Mornings were the worst time. The diuretics she took to control the excess fluid in her system—combined with her diet of meat and alcohol, without fruit or vegetables—brought on an attack of gout. Her foot was inflamed and painful. Then the antidote pills caused digestive problems: pills were a risky business. The only reliable relief was her 'therapeutics'. She told the Rellas: 'At least the docs, all say—no exception, that alcohol is good for you.'

Her letters ached with self-reproach. From University House she wrote to the Rellas:

> I'm lonely and I'm wasting my time—and get up in the morning seeing all the usual things ahead and think 'another wasted day— I'm a shame and a disgrace'—for I have a sort of bursary to this cursory nursery, as it were—and I'm doing nothing in return.

One morning early in February, Stead was walking to the postbox, waving cheerfully to a room-maid, when she tripped on the broken cement path. She heard a cracking noise as she fell. The maid and a young man helped her to her feet. To her surprise, no bones were broken and she was able to continue on her way. She noticed nothing for a few days except that she tended to forget the names of her visitors, but after a week she developed a bad backsprain. For weeks it hurt her to sit at the typewriter to write letters, and a year later, she still complained of backache. It was a stumble toward death.

Stead was probably as happy in University House as she would be anywhere, under the circumstances. In the first half of 1982, her heart played up on two more occasions, and she spent some days in Canberra Hospital. The second time, in May, the doctors agreed that the problem was partly alcohol. University House had a bottle shop on the premises, and the cleaners complained about the number of empty bottles in Stead's flat. Stead was pressured to return to her family in Sydney. H. C. Coombs, who had thrilled Christina by visiting her in hospital, was 'terribly angry' about the decision. He could not see that she was doing anyone any harm.

After Stead's departure from Canberra, her life darkened. Back with her family, she was 'shovelled about', as she put it, from one relative to another. She felt she was a burden on them all. First she stayed with David and Doris, then she was passed for two months to her sister Weeta, recently widowed, who lived in a small brick house in Wollongong, an hour from

Sydney. Though Weeta was kind and her grown-up children called in often, Stead felt 'all but a prisoner'. She missed friends with whom she could have 'a little booze, a little chat'.[20] When she had the strength, she typed desolate letters to friends in Canberra, pleading with them to get her back there. In more realistic moments, she told herself she was about to turn eighty. 'I can't keep on humping the bluey, carrying my tent along the track can I?'[21]

No one in the family wanted to have Christina permanently; she was not an easy companion. She could be quite demanding and imperious, and would ring Ron Geering or her siblings with constant requests to take her here or there. One Sunday morning, early, Ron had been urgently summoned to her sister Kate's: Christina, in a kind of delirium, kept saying that Ralph Fox had come for her.

At one point, Christina asked Thistle Harris if she could live at Boongarre. Her brother Kel was ill at the time, and Thistle (whom Stead had ignored all these years) had no illusions about Christina; she said no, and felt bad about it for years. Stead also asked Elizabeth Harrower if she could live with her. Harrower liked to live alone, and felt she needed her house to herself in order to write. She also felt terrible about saying no.

From the Rellas came the news that Aida Kotlarsky had collapsed and died during a walk. Stead was becoming used to friends disappearing for good, but she was sad to lose this 'best of friends'. It impressed her that Aida had adoring young men in her life, around her piano, to the end. Aida's loving companion in her eighties was Don Shaw, a talented concert pianist in his late twenties.

When the writer Barry Hill came to interview her in Wollongong, in honour of her eightieth birthday, it brightened up Stead's day. She found him charming, and their impressions were mutual:

> We sat in the sunroom. Her sister's African violets were in bloom. Christina Stead found a shawl, because the radiator had to give up its plug to the tape recorder. She is an exquisitely frail woman these days, and not at all like those plump, sporty shots of her with her husband, taken on cosmopolitan

jaunts. Her fingers in the morning light were translucent and coral pink, like the bow of her blouse.

But when she spoke, the frailty disappeared. Her features sharpened, and the New York timbres of her voice deepened. When she got up to pour vermouth, her step, in the fawn slacks and black kid pumps, had a snap to it; one could imagine her clicking her heels as she left the room—cocktails, olé![22]

Patrick White saw Christina Stead as Australia's literary giant. He and Manoly Lascaris befriended her, inviting her usually with Elizabeth Harrower to their house. Lascaris used to give Stead friendly advice about denture problems. When she left for Melbourne, the two men sent her an electric blanket: a thoughtful gift, it was perhaps also a pointed joke about the winters there. They were concerned about her, and Stead was touched.

Over time, White lost patience with Stead. He was unimpressed by her restless moving about and her almost boastful drinking; above all, he was impatient with the way she depended on others and yet blamed them for her inability to write. Elizabeth Harrower comments that White 'liked people to be in control of their own lives, to "front up" to adversity and soldier on'. His 'slow turning-away' from Stead was 'part of a general attitude: he admired extravagantly and was extravagantly disappointed'.[23]

It came, one day, to 'words'. Stead had been invited to lunch at Centennial Park with Elizabeth Harrower. Stead arrived in a taxi, with a bag of empty bottles that she asked White to put in his rubbish bin. Later, over lunch, she boasted, 'I've always humped my own bluey'. White snorted, 'Like hell you have.' He made some sharp comments about her living arrangements and her dependence on others. According to Harrower, 'Christina defended herself in a dignified and calm manner.' The storm passed, and they adjourned to the sitting room for coffee. Afterwards, sharing a taxi with the loyal Harrower, Stead tactfully attributed the outburst to White's bad health.

It was to be the last encounter between White and Stead. After her death, Patrick White would send David Stead his condolences, with the comment: 'I'm sorry I did not know her earlier on when she was at the height of her powers.'

As well as the losses, there were new friendships in the last months of Stead's life. One was Jonathan LaPook. A 29-year-old gastroenterologist from Columbia University, he came bearing gifts to Stead from his close friend Lillian Hellman. One was *Pentimento*, a volume of Hellman's memoirs, with the inscription: 'To Christina Stead. Perhaps her greatest and oldest admirer, Lillian Hellman.' The other was a cheque for $10000.

Stead was very uneasy about accepting the cheque, says LaPook. She protested that she did not need it; she even offered to give it to him. 'In the end, she accepted it only with the logic that it would become part of her estate which she could then give to somebody else.'[24]

LaPook was working at the Royal North Shore Hospital in Sydney for three months, and he and Stead saw quite a bit of each other during that time. Stead was proud of her new friend, nearly two metres tall, and 'very humane'. She told Burnshaw that when he heard about her difficulties in finding a home, this 'attractive' and 'delightful' man had offered to share his flat in New York with her. 'Remember he is twenty-nine, I am eighty.'

Then there were honours. In September 1982 Stead was awarded a NSW Premier's Award for her services to literature. Feeling fragile, she asked Elizabeth Harrower to attend the ceremony on her behalf.

A more prestigious honour was being made an Honorary Member of the American Academy and Institute of Arts and Letters. Honorary Foreign Membership of the Academy, intended to strengthen cultural ties with other countries, was limited to seventy-five. The other new member that year was Chinua Achebe from Nigeria. Famous Academy members, past and present, included Isak Dinesen, T. S. Eliot, Doris Lessing, Bertrand Russell, Alexander Solzhenitsyn and Rebecca West.

The Academy award presentation was at the American Consulate in Sydney on 24 November 1982. Heather Stewart, the Cultural Affairs Adviser, collected Stead from David Stead's house in Lindfield, and drove her to the Consulate. In the car, Stead told her that she hated living with relatives and was looking for somewhere to live. Heather, who had a large house in inner-city Glebe, said 'I have a room—you might like it.'

In conversation, Stead appeared quite vigorous. Stewart had no idea what she was offering to take on.

After the ceremony, there was lunch at the Washington Club, attended by Consul General Horowitz and his wife, Justice Harold Glass and his wife, and Heather Stewart. Amid these Jewish New Yorkers, with 'pics of George on wall and menus' and a 'huge bust of Old Abe' in the foyer, Stead sparkled.[25] Afterwards, Heather Stewart said to her, 'We must have lunch again.' Stead answered, 'What about tomorrow?' She came in to the city the very next day by taxi, wanting to talk seriously about the house proposition.

They walked one block from the Consulate to a restaurant, and Stewart noticed that Stead was gasping for breath. Stewart then broke the news that she did not live alone at Glebe. 'What's his name?' 'Archibald.' 'Congratulations!' Stead exclaimed. 'You won the Archibald Prize!'

To Stead's dismay, she was not able to move in until after Christmas: there was work to do on her room, which had damp patches and needed painting. 'At New Year, then?' Stead asked. Heather Stewart agreed. A month later, Stead told Rosemary Dobson: 'If all goes well, I shall have a home there. How I hope for it! I can't tell you how bad this has been.'

It was a strange existence for a woman of eighty. Stead had met Heather Stewart twice before she moved into her house. Only after her new acquaintance moved in, did Stewart realise that she was considerably more helpless than she had seemed.

The house, at No. 17 Wigram Road, Glebe, was a beautiful three-storey terrace, but it was the hottest time of the year, inner-city Sydney was plagued, as usual, with summer cockroaches and Heather's partner Archibald Zammit-Ross was hammering loudly on the roof. Stead left again, saying she would stay at Kate's until the repair work was finished. While at Kate's in Cremorne, she had another heart attack and was back in hospital. It did not stop her from moving to Glebe in the middle of January.

The arrangement was utterly impractical. Heather Stewart worked full-time at the Consulate and, a violinist in her spare time, rehearsed with the Macquarie University Orchestra two evenings a week. Stead's room downstairs was next to a toilet and basin, but the bath was upstairs, and she had to be helped up the stairs and helped into the bath. She would not let Heather Stewart do this, so David, Gilbert or Kate had to come to help her. Stewart, who had fondly imagined Stead could walk to the shops, had to do the shopping on Saturday mornings. Stead hardly ate anything, she recalls, except steak tartare. She drank—sometimes fortified milk, mostly alcohol. She was lonely, there all day on her own, and was pleased to have company in the evenings. She warmed to Zammit-Ross, a goodlooking sculptor whom she called Archimedes.[26]

———— ❧ ————

Stead had been writing to Coombs about her will. She wanted to leave her money to a good cause: what did he suggest? His passion was Aboriginal rights: should she leave her money to an Aboriginal organisation? 'Anything you say,' she told him. Coombs found it difficult to counsel her: Aboriginal organisations tended to be shortlived. He advised the Australian Conservation Foundation, and suggested that she specify the money should be used (in consultation with Aborigines) for national parks in Aboriginal land.

In the end, Stead kept to the will she had made on 2 August 1979. In it she left $3000 to each of her five siblings, as well as her cousins Gwendolin Walker-Smith and Elsie Ford. She gave another $3000 to David for being her executor, and she 'forgave and released' Gilbert from a total debt of $7800 for the annexe at No. 10 Donald St, Hurstville. Her books and paintings were to go to David Stead and Ron Geering, Bill Blake's manuscripts to Ruth Hall and all English royalties from Stead's own books were to go to Ruth. The residual estate and royalties or film rights other than in England were to go to the Australian Conservation Foundation—an ongoing bequest.

She loved nature, but conservation had never been one of Christina Stead's passions. Her first will, made in England in 1969, had decreed that her money should be given to writers in need and this would seem to reflect her own interests more accurately. However, in her will as in life generally, she was her father's daughter. Politically and intellectually, she always allowed herself to be guided by the man she loved.

———— ❧ ————

When Mary Lord called to see Christina in Glebe in late January 1983, she was shocked by her condition and immediately rang her doctor friend, Helena Berenson, who admitted her to Balmain Hospital for several days of tests. Stead had a history of ischaemic heart disease, myocardial infarction, cardiac failure and longstanding hypertension. Now, at eighty and an alcoholic, she had gouty arthritis and severe swelling round the ankle joints, due to an accumulation of uric acid. She was short of breath and unsteady.

Helena Berenson, in her early thirties, had a talent for bringing home stray people and caring for them. Stead could not have fallen into better hands. Berenson, who regarded her as 'a very great lady', collected her things from Heather Stewart's and took her to the rambling Victorian home on Johnson Street, Annandale, where she lived with her husband, Geoff Davis, also a doctor. Like something out of a fairytale, The Abbey, as it was called, was a High Gothic castle, with a Gothic spire, Gothic church windows and gargoyles guarding the tower. Stead had always had a taste for the Gothic: now she was entering the castle of her imagination.

Her tiny groundfloor room, the size of a monk's cell, was formerly the butler's pantry. Next to it was the dining room—or, rather, the banquet room. On the heavy wooden table, Stead had her typewriter. On one wall was a Gothic fireplace; on the other a large traceried bay window, through which filtered light fell on the patterned floor. Propped against the wall was a series of grotesque Charles Blackman paintings, belonging to a friend. A door opened to the outside verandah, where Stead would sit and watch the birds. Sydney was particularly humid that summer. It rained and rained.

Geoff Davis was gradually restoring the house, and the place was chaotic. Planks of wood and lumps of marble and building materials were piled all over the garden. In the house, books and paintings were stacked beside antiques from the Davis family estate. Cats and dogs chased each other through the house; Geoff Davis' young children from a previous marriage regularly came to stay. It was not unlike the atmosphere in *The People with the Dogs*.

Helena Berenson was home during the day; she ran an after-hours practice, in Leichhardt, from 6 pm till midnight. Geoff Davis worked during the day and was at home in the evening. Consequently, Stead was never without a doctor in the house.

In this Gothic mansion, her past unreeled before her. Her childhood had been spent at Lydham Hill, with visits to Dappeto—both grand old Sydney houses. She was ending her days at The Abbey, featured in the book *Fine Houses of Sydney*. Lydham Hill had been owned by Frederick

John Gibbins, Ada Stead's father; his wife's family, the Picketts, were related by marriage to the Davis family, from the Gosford area. This was Geoff Davis' family. Things have a strange way of coming full circle.

Helena Berenson supplied the European element in Stead's life. Most of Stead's northern hemisphere friends had been Jewish: Berenson's family was Polish Jewish. As a child Helena had spoken Yiddish before she learnt English, and Stead liked to get her to speak a few phrases of Yiddish. And then, like Aida Kotlarsky, Berenson was a gifted pianist—in her teens, she had regularly beaten Roger Woodward in competitions at the NSW Conservatorium of Music—but finally she had chosen medicine as her career.

Berenson became Stead's nurse, doctor and friend. When Stead got up in the morning, Berenson would wash her—either helping her upstairs to the bathroom or bringing a bowl downstairs. (Very modest, Stead had never allowed anyone such intimacy before.) Berenson supervised her pill-taking—there was a row of pill bottles by now—then helped her into the lounge. While Stead sat on the sofa with her feet up, Berenson played to her—mostly Mozart, by request. When she stopped playing, after an hour or so, Christina, whose thoughts had been wandering with the music, would talk in her low voice. She mentioned a great romance across a crowded room, a romance with a man who was killed in the Spanish Civil War. Berenson never knew whether it was fiction or fact, but she was just as enthralled as Geoff Davis' children were when Stead told them a story. It all sounded very beautiful and mystical. Though she longed to, Berenson never broke the spell by asking questions.

In the afternoons Stead would nap; in the evenings she would type in the dining room. The household went to bed at odd hours and Stead, probably woken by the strange noises, would be wandering around in the early hours of the morning, drinking, or making steak tartare in the kitchen. She had a supply of 1½-litre bottles of cinzano rosso, and got through one and a half of these a day. Berenson and Davis did not interfere.

One night in mid March, they were woken by the sounds of clattering and banging downstairs. Geoff Davis hurried down to find Stead stumbling around the dining room in her nightdress. She looked extraordinarily excited. Her face was shining, she was quite unco-ordinated, but she was not drunk. (They never saw her drunk.) To Davis' amusement, she had put her foot right through one of the Charles Blackman paintings. 'He's here! He's come for me!' she kept saying. She hardly registered Davis' presence, and struggled when he tried to take her back to her room. 'You don't understand! He's come for me!'

Davis had seen delirious patients before, but never like this. It could have been a combination of fever, dehydration and alcohol consumption, he says, but there was something else. 'It was', says Davis, 'very, very impressive.'[27]

They took her to Balmain Hospital the following day. Stead's condition rapidly worsened. From the ulcerated gouti tophi on her feet and ankles she developed septicaemia, and though she was given massive doses of intravenous antibiotics, nothing worked. She refused to eat, and she complained of chest pains and shortness of breath. She had difficulty remembering recent events, and she showed signs of dementia. The nursing staff thought her a cantankerous old woman. Helena Berenson was sad to observe their hostility.

Stead was able to register that the University of New South Wales was offering her a doctorate. 'They're making me one of you,' she joked to Ron Geering, meaning the dreaded category of academic drones. She told him she was anxious to leave the hospital as she had an idea for a story she wanted to write.

When Mary Lord visited Christina for what turned out to be the last time, she seemed at first to be asleep. Mary sat quietly by the bedside. After a while, Christina opened her eyes. 'It's lovely to open my eyes and see your face, you dear thing,' she told her. Then she said: 'He came for me.' Mary knew whom she meant.

Easter was early in 1983. On Maundy Thursday, 31 March, Ron Geering went to see Stead in the early afternoon. He had retired, but he still gave occasional lectures at the University of New South Wales, and he had just been lecturing on *The Man Who Loved Children*. He found Stead in a terrible state, distressed and in pain, finding it hard to breathe. Drawn and haggard, her face looked like a skull. She was in a panic, convinced the nurses were not giving her the heart tablets she needed. She put her thin hands on Geering's and looked at him wildly: 'Unless I get the tablets this will do for me.' He rushed out to fetch the nursing sister and doctor: they brought in an oxygen cylinder. Christina Stead lost consciousness. Ron Geering stayed for an hour or so, listening to the sound of her wheezing breathing. Then Kate Stead arrived and he left.

That same afternoon, Helena Berenson was at the Easter Show with Geoff's children. She watched them go down the big dipper, and suddenly went quite cold. She immediately rang Balmain Hospital. Christina Stead had just died.

Stead died at eighty, the same age as her father. There was no announcement in the press until after the burial, and because of the Easter holiday, the obsequies had to wait until 6 April. The body was cremated at the Northern Suburbs Crematorium: there was no ceremony, there were no speeches. Just seven people witnessed the coffin sliding into the flame: David and Doris Stead, Gilbert Stead, Ron and Dorothy Geering, Mary Lord and Elizabeth Harrower. Stead's sisters were not there: David Stead had told them that Christina did not want them to attend. They were extraordinarily hurt, and out of loyalty, Gwen Walker-Smith, Christina's 'sister-cousin', also stayed at home. The women, who had done so much for Christina, were dismayed by this last gesture from the grave.

After the ceremony, there were drinks at David and Doris' home in Lindfield. Christina's name was barely mentioned. Her friends were mortified by the utter bleakness of the occasion.

Forty years earlier Christina had written to Bill, 'Marriage for us has very little meaning, except that if we pass out, we will be buried as "Munx & Mrs. Munx" and that is worth something.' It was not to be.

On another occasion Christina had told her brother David she would like her ashes to be scattered in Botany Bay. But her final will left no instructions, and after a year, when the family had not come to collect them, the ashes were tossed by an official onto the grounds of the crematorium.

Epilogue

CHRISTINA STEAD NEVER thought death the end of everything. As the daughter of a naturalist, she always knew she would go the way of 'the coral-insects, ... the ancient leaves and saurians that had left only a small imprint in the kerosene shale'.

Like dreams, Stead's books do not have definite endings; they leave us with a sense of recurrent patterns, endless cycles, 'terrestrial eternity'. Christina Stead thought of herself as a Scheherazade, conscious of 'the powerful story rooted in all things', and forever spinning tales. Scheherazade, the legendary queen in the *Arabian Nights*, told stories to retain the interest of the man who held her life in his hands. By telling stories, she held life in *her* hands.

Christina Stead's natural habitat was the 'ocean of story'. As she once said, 'It is the million drops of water that are the looking-glasses of all our lives'.

Notes

Abbreviations

Note: Source details are given in the Bibliography.

Anderson	Edith Anderson
Beauties	*The Beauties and Furies*
Blech/Blake	Bill Blech/Blake
Burnshaw	Stanley Burnshaw
Coombs	H. C. (Nugget) Coombs
Cotters'	*Cotters' England*
CS	Christina Stead
DDS	David Darwin Stead
DGS	David George Stead
Dogs	*The People with the Dogs*
FJ	Florence James
FW-S	Florence Walker-Smith
Geering	Ron Geering
GW-S	Gwen Walker-Smith
Herbert	*Miss Herbert*
Hotel	*The Little Hotel*
House	*House of All Nations*
Laughing	*I'm Dying Laughing*
Letty	*Letty Fox: Her Luck*
Love	*For Love Alone*
McKenney	Ruth McKenney
The Man	*The Man Who Loved Children*
NLA	National Library of Australia
NSW	New South Wales
Ocean	*Ocean of Story*
Poor Men	*Seven Poor Men of Sydney*
Puzzleheaded	*The Puzzleheaded Girl*
Rella	Ettore Rella
Salzburg	*The Salzburg Tales*

SL	Selected Letters
Tea	*A Little Tea, A Little Chat*

Prologue

1 Stead's notes on Quentin Bell's biography of Virginia Woolf, NLA, Box 7, folder 53.
2 *Beauties*, p. 159.

1. Ocean of Story

1 The details are reconstructed from Stead's unpublished piece, 'Lydham Hill'. NLA, MS 4967, Box 6, folder 38.
2 'A Waker and Dreamer', *Ocean*; Preface to *Ocean*.
3 Elsie Ford to me, 23 iv 1988. (Elsie's father, Duncan Cameron Butters, was Ellen's brother.)
4 The house at 18 Lydham Avenue, Rockdale, later renamed Lydham Hall, was one of the few original stone houses in the area to survive. It was bought by the Rockdale Municipal Council in October 1970, and is now open for public inspection at weekends. The brochure advertises it as the 'childhood home of the authoress Christina Stead'. The land around was sold off. Christina Stead visited in 1979 and found it greatly changed.
5 'A Waker and Dreamer', *Ocean*.
6 CS to FJ, 2 xii 1933 (FJ papers).
7 CS interview with John B. Beston, September 1975, *World Literature Written in English*, vol. 15, no. 1, April 1976.
8 This is actually Louisa's memory of Henny, but it is likely to have been Christina's own memory. She was five when David Darwin was born.
9 These trials are recalled in the story 'The Milk Run'. Matthew, who goes to fetch milk at Dappeto, is based partly on Stead and partly on her brother David, who later took over the errand. (*Ocean*.)
10 CS to Burnshaw, 5 iii 1981. (SL)
11 *The Man*, p. 421. It is actually Miss Aiden who thinks this, but plainly CS did too.
12 CS to Nadine Lewin, undated, 1938.
13 This and the next few observations come from my conversation with DDS, Sydney, 9 i 1987.
14 'A Waker and Dreamer', *Ocean*.
15 CS to Thistle Harris, 7 vii 1939. (SL)
16 Unpublished draft of 'A Waker and Dreamer', NLA, Box 10, folder 75.
17 'We men are all weak as water before the primitive devices of Eve,' Sam Pollit complains. (*The Man*, p. 160.)
18 Thistle Harris interviewed by Chris Williams for an ABC Radio documentary on David George Stead in the *Sunday Feature* series, broadcast on 1 and 8 June 1986. The text appears in *Meridian*, vol. 8, no. 2, October 1989, as 'David Stead: The Man Who Loved Nature'.
19 CS to the Rellas, 3 iii 1980.
20 CS to Burnshaw, 15 i 1981.
21 Unpublished notes for 'A Waker and Dreamer', NLA, Box 10, folder 75.
22 The play's Oedipal undertone is reinforced by the use and reversals of classical mythology. Antaeus (as it is usually spelt) was a belligerent giant, ultimately strangled by Heracles, who, in a fit of madness, also killed his own children by Megara, his wife, one of the Furies.
23 CS to Thistle Harris, 7 vii 1939. (SL)
24 Holman's unpublished reminiscences, quoted in H. V. Evatt, *Australian Labour Leader*, A & R, Sydney, 1940, p. 506.
25 Unpublished draft of 'A Waker and Dreamer', NLA, Box 10, folder 75.
26 'A Waker and Dreamer', *Ocean*, p. 490.

27 CS, 'A Writer's Friends', *Ocean*, p. 495. Stead's unpublished novel, *The Wraith and the Wanderer*, written in the early 1930s, contains this poem, called 'Green Apricots', probably reconstructed from memory, and perhaps improved slightly. (NLA, Box 6, folder 40.)

28 Angela Carter, Introduction to the Virago edition of *The Puzzleheaded Girl* (1968), London, 1984.

29 Conversation with GW-S, 24 ix 1991.

30 CS interview with Rodney Wetherell, broadcast 24 February 1980. Published in *Australian Literary Studies*, vol. 9, no. 4, October 1980, pp. 431–8.

31 CS interview with Joan Lidoff, Surbiton, England, June, 1973. In Joan Lidoff, *Christina Stead*, Ungar, New York, 1982, pp. 182–3. Also: CS to Nadine Lewin, undated, 1938.

32 At fifteen, Jessie was sent to teach in a country town in western NSW. It was a stark, lonely life for young female teachers. (Conversation with DDS, 20 ix 1991.)

33 CS interview with Ann Whitehead (1973), *Australian Literary Studies*, vol. 6, no. 3, May 1974.

34 CS interview with Rodney Wetherell (1980), *Australian Literary Studies*, vol. 9, no. 4, October 1980.

35 Mary McCarthy, 'Framing Father', review of *The Man*, *New Republic*, vol. 104, no. 2, 13 January 1941.

36 Clifton Fadiman, review of *The Man*, *New Yorker*, 19 October 1940.

37 Charles Poore, review of *The Man*, *New York Times*, 18 October 1940.

38 Randall Jarrell, Introduction to *The Man*, Holt, Rinehart & Winston, New York, 1965.

39 CS to Thistle Harris, 7 vii 1939.

40 Conversation with GW-S, 24 ix 1991.

41 The term is used by B. K. de Garis in *A New History of Australia*, ed. Frank Crowley, Heinemann, Melbourne, 1974, p. 258.

42 CS interview with Joan Lidoff (1973).

43 Dappeto was bought by the Salvation Army and used as a children's home until 1968. Now called Macquarie Lodge, it is a home for senior citizens.

44 H. V. Evatt, *Australian Labour Leader*, p. 389. See also pp. 505–6.

45 *Poor Men*, p. 17. Stead was probably thinking of Nietzsche, whose refrain this is: 'One has still to be as close to the flowers, the grass and the butterflies as is a child.—He who wants to partake of all good things must know how to be small at times.' (*Human, All Too Human.*)

2. Embarkation for Cythera

1 *Poor Men*, p. 1.

2 Conversation with DDS, 27 ix 1991.

3 Peggy Stead, 'The Hill', *High School Chronicle*, October 1918, p. 7. (Sydney Girls' High School papers.)

4 CS to Thistle Harris, 7 vii 1939. (SL)

5 Weeta Stead to Dorothy Green, 9 v 1983.

6 I owe several of the details about the school to Lilith Norman's book *The Brown and Yellow*, Oxford University Press, Melbourne, 1983.

7 Kathleen Grieves (née Nyman) to CS, 3 vi 1976. (NLA, Box 7, folder 51.)

8 *Poor Men*, p. 54.

9 CS interview with Rodney Wetherell (1980).

10 CS, 'A Writer's Friends', *Ocean*, p. 496.

11 Conversation with Tempe Mann (née Datson), Sydney, 25 i 1987.

12 Mary Gilmore to Hugh McCrae, 22 ix 1936. Cited in *Letters of Mary Gilmore*, selected and edited by W. H. Wilde and T. Inglis Moore, Melbourne University Press, Melbourne, 1980.

13 CS interview with Ann Whitehead (1973), p. 234.

14 CS interview with Robert Drewe (1982), *Scripsi*, vol. 4, no. 1, July 1986.

15 Unpublished notes for 'A Waker and Dreamer', NLA, Box 10, folder 75.

16 DGS wrote his columns well in advance, for they continued to appear at weekly intervals for the thirteen months he was away in Malaya. The articles—from 25 September 1921 to 8 April 1923—are among the David G. Stead papers, Rare Books Collection, Mitchell Library, MS 5413.

17 DGS to Tan Kah Kee, 6 xi 1922. David G. Stead papers, MS 5413 1.

18 DGS to CS. (Handwritten at top: 'First six lines for Woit and the rest for Pedler [sic.].') Singapore, 5 vii 1922. [Woit is Weeta.] Christina Stead included this letter almost verbatim in *The Man*. There are minor changes—mostly improvements to his style, or to make Sam Pollit convincing as a contemporary American. For example, she altered the last sentence to 'Let's strip Jack naked!'—which DGS, who clung ferociously to his puritanical Victorian upbringing, would never have said.

19 These observations are based partly on photographs of Duncan at the time and partly on FJ's description. (Conversation with FJ, 3 vii 1989.)

20 Unpublished notes for *Love*, NLA, Box 1, folder 2.

21 CS to NSW Education Department, Superior Public School, Darlinghurst, 21 February 1923. NSW Archives, Darlinghurst School files, 1917–1926, S/15655, B.

22 CS interview with Joan Lidoff (1973).

23 *Love*, p. 81.

24 Dr John A. O'Keefe opined that Miss Stead would be unfit to resume her ordinary duties for at least a month. Medical report, 24 June 1925. (NSW Archives, William Street Public School files. S/18122.1 B.)

25 *Love*, p. 136.

26 Medical report from Dr O'Keefe, 5 October 1925. William Street Public School files.

27 S. H. Smith, Director of Education, 14 October 1925. William Street Public School files.

28 Conversation with Thistle Harris, Watson's Bay, 15 i 1987. According to Harris, she met Ada Stead only once, and it was nothing like the meeting described in 'About the House', in *Ocean* (probably written in the early 1930s, after Thistle Harris moved in with David Stead). Interestingly, the narrator of this story understands both women: there is no judgement.

29 H. D. Black, 'An Australian Institution or "If I could a tale unfold" ', *Economic Review* (Sydney University Economics Society), vol. 15, 1969.

30 'Mr. Duncan ... dwelt for a moment on his beloved Russia ... Fortunately time prevented an exposition of his usual panacea.' *Union Recorder*, 10 July 1924. Other details come from Herman Black and also *Union Recorder*, 26 July 1923 and 29 April 1926.

31 *Union Recorder*, 19 July 1923. In the US, in the 1940s, Stead would defend the notorious White Australia Policy for the same reason.

32 H. D. Black, *Economic Review*, vol. 15, 1969.

33 FJ to me, 2 iv 1992.

34 CS interview with Joan Lidoff (1973).

35 George Robertson to DGS, 21 vii 1925. (A. W. Barker, *Dear Robertson*. A & R, Sydney, 1982.)

36 DGS to George Robertson, 1 x 1925. A. W. Barker, *Dear Robertson*.

37 CS to Nettie Palmer, St Germain-en-Laye, 9 v 1951. (Palmer papers.) (*SL*)

38 John Beaglehole to his family, 30 viii 1926 and 18 ix 1926. (Tim Beaglehole's unpublished article about his father: '"Home"? J. C. Beaglehole in London, 1926–1929' shown me by Hugh Stretton.)

39 CS interview with Joan Lidoff (1973).

40 It is possible that Stead included passages from Duncan's actual letters (vaguely altered and embellished) in the novel. There is evidence that she made use of real letters in her fiction on more than one occasion.

41 GW-S and Jean Saxelby, *Biblionews*, vol. 2, no. 14, December 1949.

42 It is one of the stories she rewrote partly from memory and included in *Salzburg*.

43 In 1922, CS wrote contemptuously to her father (in Malaya) that her maternal cousin Edna, from Narara, was marrying the neighbour's son. Her father replied: 'Don't be too hard on the people who marry their next doors.' (DGS to CS, undated, 1922.)

44 NLA, Box 4, folder 24.
45 These are books mentioned in *Poor Men* and *Love*. Considering Duncan and Stead's interest in psychology and philosophy, it is likely that this was her own reading matter—as well as a great deal of fiction, drama and poetry.
46 *Poor Men*, p. 207.
47 Friedrich Nietzsche, *Human, All Too Human*. (Aphorism 422) tr. R. J. Hollingdale, CUP, Cambridge, 1986.
48 Jean Williamson, 'Christina Stead Tells of Her Latest Book!', *Australian Women's Weekly*, 9 March 1935.
49 In *Love*, the *Quarterly* is an allusion to *Vision*: a magazine 'written and illustrated by the young artistic set in Sydney ... in which, with imitations of Marlowe and Shakespeare, Donne, and free verse, it was chiefly a question of free love and naked women; on each page were drawings of voluptuous, fat-faced, naked women, running away from a crowd of satyrs, carried off by centaurs or tempted by evil-eyed fauns.' *Love*, p. 209.
50 See Jack Lindsay, *Life Rarely Tells* (1958, 1960, 1962), Penguin, Harmondsworth, 1982.
51 Diana Brydon makes this point in *Christina Stead*, Macmillan, London, 1987.
52 *Poor Men, Love, Beauties, The Man.*
53 NLA, Box 4, folder 24.

3. Port of Registry: London

1 'A Night in the Indian Ocean', *Ocean*, pp. 53–66. The manuscript is typed on the back of 'American & Foreign Discount Corporation' paper, Stead's Paris office between 1929 and 1932.
2 *Love*, p. 189.
3 Henry Handel Richardson, *Myself When Young*, Heinemann, London, 1948, p. 87.
4 Jack Lindsay, *Life Rarely Tells* (1958), Penguin, Ringwood (Victoria), 1982.
5 CS to Nellie Molyneux, 1 iii 1929. (SL)
6 Several of the following details are taken from 'J. C. Beaglehole in London, 1926–1929'. (Tim Beaglehole papers, Wellington, New Zealand.)
7 Stead describes it thus in *Love*, p. 305.
8 CS interview with Joan Lidoff (1973), in Lidoff, *Christina Stead*, Ungar, New York, 1982. The opening of the novella 'The Puzzleheaded Girl' is based on this scene, transferred to New York. Augustus Debrett, 'a stubby dark man with large hazel eyes, ... round head ... pale face' interviews a diffident, plain young woman carrying a book (on French symbolism!). Debrett is a 'married bachelor' who feels that 'he was not loved and never had been'.
9 CS to FW-S, 17 vi 1928. (SL) Many of the following details are taken from Stead's letters to Gwen and Florence Walker-Smith.
10 Conversation with Jack Bermond (Alfred Hurst's son-in-law), London, 17 x 1988.
11 *House*, p. 7. According to Jack Bermond, the description of Henri Léon is an accurate, if slightly amplified, description of Hurst.
12 'Why I am an Expatriate', NLA, Box 15, folder 113.
13 CS to GW-S, 1 i 1929.
14 FJ says the portrait of Jonathan Crow in *Love* made her sorry for Duncan. 'Everyone at uni. knew it was him.' She added: 'Chris had a cruel streak, a lack of compassion.' (Conversation with FJ, Sydney, 11 vii 1987.)
15 Nora Ephron, 'Revision and Life', *Nora Ephron Collected*, Avon Books, New York, 1991, pp. 213–16.
16 'Why I am an Expatriate', NLA, Box 15, folder 113.
17 CS interview with Rodney Wetherell (1980), p. 447.
18 Portrayed as shadows of each other, they recall their tragic precursors, Catherine and Heathcliff.
19 CS interview with Rodney Wetherell (1980).

20   CS, *Christina Stead* (video), Australia Council Archival Film Series (1980).
21   Blech mentions these Corner House meetings in an undated letter to CS, May or June 1942. (NLA, Box 16, folders 119–20.)
22   Conversation with Professor W. G. K. Duncan, Adelaide, 27 ii 1987.
23   Hugh Stretton to me, 26 vi 1990.
24   FJ to her mother, 8 xi 1928. (FJ papers.) Many of the following details are taken from Florence James' letters to her mother over the following months.
25   CS to GW-S, 1 i 1929.
26   Unpublished paper, NLA, Box 10, folder 73.
27   CS to GW-S, 25 v 1930: 'Few Jews like their race being mentioned, Wilhelm [William] being quite exceptional in his enthusiasm for his race.' (*SL*)
28   Blech refers to the incident and to the snows near Canterbury and Peterhouse in an undated letter to CS, May or June 1942. NLA, Box 16, folder 119.
29   CS to Dorothy Green, 3 x 1976. (Green papers.) The general parallels between the two couples are striking. Blech and Stead would live together out of wedlock for twenty-three years.
30   FBI file on William James Blake: File no. 100–236179. The file was opened on 1 October 1943.
31   I owe most of the following details about William Blech's family to conversations with Mrs Ruth Hall (née Blech) at Chateauneuf-de-Grasse, France, in October 1987 and September 1988.
32   CS wrote a short story based on Rosa Blech's life called 'Life is Difficult'. Included in the posthumous collection *Ocean*, it was probably written in the late 1960s or early 1970s. Stead calls the character Emma—perhaps because of the parallels with that other dreamer, Emma Bovary.
33   CS tells this story in a letter to E. F. Patterson, 16 v 1975. The Goldsmith poem is 'The Deserted Village'.
34   CS to E. F. Patterson, 16 v 1975. (SL)
35   Conversation with Ruth Hall, 5 x 1987.

4. La Parisienne

1   CS to Burnshaw, 30 iv 1974. (SL)
2   CS to Rellas, 16 xii 1979.
3   FJ to her family, 14 ii 1929.
4   Dora Russell, *The Tamarisk Tree*, Virago, London, 1975, p. 69.
5   Rebecca West to Dora Marsden, late 1913, in Victoria Glendinning, *Rebecca West*, Weidenfeld & Nicolson, London, 1987, p. 51.
6   These phrases come from *Beauties*. William Blake would refer nostalgically to their 'first week at the Aigle Noir and at Moret ... and all the little incidents of courting and honeymoon' in a letter to CS, undated (May or June 1942).
7   *Love*, p. 73.
8   CS to Kate Stead, 14 ii 1951.
9   CS to Nellie Molyneux, 2 iv 1929. (*SL*)
10   ibid., 1 iii 1929. (*SL*)
11   Putnam is probably the model for the translator in *Salzburg*, and for Laban Davies, the alcoholic translator in the novella 'The Right-Angled Creek', in *Puzzleheaded*.
12   'Lost American' gives a fictionalised portrait of Townsend's oddities and his strange marriage. Townsend was also the model for Tom Withers in *Poor Men*, and Andrew Fulton in *Beauties*. In her non-fictional piece, 'A Writer's Friends', Stead paid tribute to Townsend's friendship, leaving out most of the negative details.
13   Frederick Sard was the model for the 'Centenarist' in *Salzburg* and Marpurgo in *Beauties*—a cabbalistic character with *Arabian Nights* colouring. Letters from Sard published in *Transition* show the dogmatic and eclectic style of his diatribes, captured by Stead in *Beauties*.
14   'Lost American', p. 137.
15   CS to GW-S, 25 v 1930. (*SL*)

16 'In Paris, Our Bistrot', NLA, Box 11, folder 79.

17 CS to GW-S, 3 vii 1929. (SL)

18 Noel Riley Fitch, *Sylvia Beach and the Lost Generation*, W. W. Norton & Co., New York, 1983, p. 72. Stead would have heard these stories. Years later, in *Cotters'*, she had lesbians dancing in the moonlight, though she made them grotesque figures.

19 CS to GW-S, 25 v 1930. (SL)

20 Conversation with Ruth Hall, 5 x 1987.

21 Conversations with Nadine Lewin, New York, 12 x 1987 and 6 vii 1988.

22 CS to GW-S, 18 ix 1929. (SL)

23 CS to GW-S, 11 i 1932 and 22 vii 1929.

24 ibid., 30 ix 1929 and 26 vii 1932. In later life Stead would denigrate Joyce.

25 The term is Patrick White's. See 'The Prodigal Son' (1958), in *Patrick White Speaks*, Primavera Press, Sydney, 1989, p. 16.

26 FJ to her mother, 5 xii 1929.

27 FJ to me, 15 v 1992.

28 In Bill Blake's novel *We are the Makers of Dreams*, written in 1942 and published in 1959, this is what Peggy Hume (modelled loosely on Christina Stead) says of Jim, her husband: 'I tremble at Jim's humanity. One of these days it is going to blow up our marriage, which, silly as it sounds, is the most beautiful union I know. He will think that deep as his love for me is, he has purchased it too dearly, for it has been paid for with cruelty. And so he will be cruel to me. That woman who dulled his wife, waits, waits.' (Simon & Schuster, New York, p. 147)

29 'A Writer's Friends', *Ocean*, p. 500.

30 Conversation with FJ, Sydney, 3 vii 1989.

31 CS to GW-S, 25 v 1930.

32 FJ comments: 'I have no detailed memory of the early draft. My general impression is that it was not altered substantially, but was put on "hold" while she wrote *Salzburg*.' (FJ to me, 15 v 1992.)

33 Dorothy Green, obituary for Christina Stead, *Sydney Morning Herald*, 8 April 1983.

34 CS to GW-S, 5 viii 1930.

35 Blech to CS, 6 viii 1930.

36 James Quick says this in *Love*.

37 Jean Williamson, 'Christina Stead Tells of Her Latest Book!', *Australian Women's Weekly*, 9 March 1935.

38 NLA, Box 6, folder 38.

39 CS to FW-S, 26 vii 1932.

40 CS to GW-S, 20 vi 1931.

41 Nietzsche wrote about the 'Wanderer and his Shadow' in *Thus Spake Zarathustra* and *Human, All Too Human*.

5. In the Phantom Buggy

1 Peter Neidecker is the model for the 'banker' in *Salzburg*, Antoine Fuseaux in *Beauties* and Jules Bertillon in *House*.

2 Stead liked this image of recklessness. Emily Wilkes in *Laughing* also says she wants to go out 'looping the loop'.

3 Blake to CS, 1 vi 1942.

4 Adam Constant is an imaginative blending of Stead, Stanley Burnshaw, and the man she had come to regard as her spiritual soulmate, Ralph Fox, who in real life had nothing to do with the bank.

5 CS to FJ, 17 x 1935.

6 ibid., 23 viii 1933. The Centenarist tells several Jewish tales. There is also 'The Amenities', told by the Solicitor, and 'The Prodigy', told by the Musician.

7 ibid., 13 v 1933.

8   ibid., 8 xii 1933.

9   ibid., 20 xii 1933.

10 Jacques Coe, a financier friend of Blech's, mentions Blech's Kreuger windfall in his book *Fame, Fraud and Fortune, 74 Years in Wall Street*, Exposition Press, Smithtown, NY, 1983.

11 William Blake, *We are the Makers of Dreams*, Victor Gollancz, London, 1959, p. 14.

12 Much of the information in this section comes from French and English newspaper articles from July 1935, when the bank crashed.

13 CS to FJ, 12 xi 1933.

14 Ruth remembers long walks over the West Sussex downs with Bertrand Russell, and Dora Russell's natural history lessons in which she had the children put their hands on her pregnant belly and feel the baby move. The children could choose not to go to lessons; in summer they played in the nude.

15 In *Salzburg*, 'The Little Old Lady', 'Poor Anna' and 'The Wunder Gottes' are all loosely based on Rosa Blech.

16 CS to FJ, 2 xii 1933 and 16 v 1934.

17 CS to Anderson, 5 i 1965.

18 CS to FJ, 2 ii 1934.

19 ibid., 22 xi 1934.

20 ibid.

21 Mulk Raj Anand, Preface to *The Novel and the People* (1937), Cobbett Publishing Co., London, 1944.

22 Huxley to Victoria Ocampo, June 1935, *Letters of Aldous Huxley*, ed. Grover Smith, Chatto & Windus, London, 1969.

23 Nettie Palmer, 'A Reader's Notebook' in *All About Books*, vol. 7, no. 2, 11 February 1935.

24 Palmer papers, MS 1174/16/1935–39. This and several other passages about Stead were not included in the published version of her diary, *Fourteen Years*.

25 CS to Dorothy Green, 17 iii 1971. Green papers, MS 54678, Box 6.

26 Patrick White, *Flaws in the Glass*, Jonathan Cape, London, 1981.

27 CS to Hal Porter, 12 vii 1982. (Unsent letter.)

28 *Le Matin*, 25 July 1935.

29 Unpublished notes, 'America', NLA, Box 11, folder 79.

6. Manhattan Peaks

1   CS to Burnshaw, 23 vii 1973. (*SL*) She mentions the episode in 'America'.

2   'America'.

3   CS to FJ, 29 ix 1935.

4   ibid., 31 xii 1935.

5   ibid., 4 ix 1935.

6   ibid., 31 xii 1935.

7   In *Laughing*, Emily and Stephen (who are otherwise not modelled on the Golds) meet on the ship going to France. Stephen is heading for the 1935 Paris Writers' Congress.

8   CS to Gilbert Stead, 30 viii 1938.

9   Joseph Freeman, *An American Testament*, Victor Gollancz, London, 1938, p. 225.

10 Stanley Burnshaw to me, 18 ix 1992.

11 Phone conversation with Elisabeth Granich-Humeston (San Francisco), 18 vii 1988.

12 Bloom's son, Michael, comments that his parents' was 'hardly a monogamous marriage, though it was supposed to be'. Conversation with Mike Bloom, New York, 5 viii 1988.

13 Max Eastman, *Love and Revolution*, Random House, New York, 1964.

14 Stead's article on Burnshaw was eventually published after her death, in *Agenda* (London) vol. 21, no. 4–vol. 22, no. 1, Winter–Spring 1983–84, Special Issue on Stanley Burnshaw.

15 Mike Gold, *New Masses*, vol. 6 (September 1930). Blake and Stead never had a good word to say for Proust either.

16 CS to Burnshaw, 2 x 1936.
17 ibid., 8 i 1936; 13 viii 1936.
18 CS to Nettie Palmer, 8 i 1936. (SL)
19 CS to FJ, 31 xii 1935.
20 ibid., 20 iv 1936.
21 Extract from Clifton Fadiman's letter to me, 15 vii 1988.
22 Handwritten notes of Max Lincoln Schuster, Schuster Collection, Rare Book and Manuscript Library, Butler Library, Columbia University.
23 Harold Strauss, review of *Beauties* in the *New York Times Book Review*, 3 May 1936.
24 Clifton Fadiman, review of *Beauties*, *New Yorker*, 25 April 1936.

7. 'A Harmless Affair'

1 CS alludes to the banana seller in her diary, Algeciras, 4 June 1936.
2 CS to FJ, 15 vi 1936.
3 CS diary, Ronda, 4 June 1936.
4 CS to Burnshaw, 2 x 1936.
5 CS, 'Journal of *The Blackmailer*', in Geering, 'The Bank Novel: *House of All Nations*', *Southerly*, no. 4, 1990.
6 CS, 'Uses of the Many-Charactered Novel', Paper delivered at the Third American Writers' Congress, 4 June 1939. Rare Books and Manuscripts, Bancroft Library, University of California.
7 Harold Strauss, 'A Novel of Frenzied Finance', *New York Times Book Review*, 12 June 1938.
8 Stead's Spanish diary, 30 July 1936. NLA, Box 15, folder 112.
9 Spanish diary.
10 Stead's original diary, August 1936. NLA, Box 15, folder 112.
11 CS to FJ, 27 viii 1936.
12 Interview with Jacques Coe, New York, 19 July 1988.
13 CS to FJ, 13 viii 1936.
14 These books are in the private collection of Jack Bermond. In *Modern Women in Love* (1945) Bill called Alfred 'our beloved friend'. The dedications stop around this date.
15 CS to FJ, 13 viii 1936.
16 This passage is in the revised diary—the only intimate comment she makes here about Bill's defects.
17 'A Harmless Affair', *Ocean*.
18 Conversation with Ruth Hall, Châteauneuf-de-Grasse, 5 x 1987.
19 CS to Blake, 24 vi 1942. Jack Goodman was a senior editor at Simon & Schuster, a leftist, who was destined to appear before the House Un-American Activities Committee in the early 1950s. Clifton Fadiman comments: 'Jack Goodman was head of advertising during my tenure as editor at Simon & Schuster. A most attractive, indeed a brilliant young man, he may well have been fancied by Christina, as he was by many other ladies.' (Clifton Fadiman to me, 22 i 1991.)
20 CS to Geering, 14 xii 1980. (SL)
21 Judith Cook, *Apprentices of Freedom*, Quartet Books, London, 1979.
22 Edith Anderson, *Love in Exile*, Vermont, Steerforth Press, 1999.
23 *Christina Stead*, Australia Council Archival Film Series, 1980.
24 CS to Gilbert Stead, 25 i 1937.
25 CS to Burnshaw, 2 x 1936.
26 Blake to 'Cosette, Mike and Nikolai' (Elisabeth and Mike Gold and their son Nicholas), 11 vi 1937. (Mike Folsom papers, University of Michigan, Ann Arbor.)
27 CS to Burnshaw, 2 x 1936.

8. The Battleground of Life

1 CS to FJ, 13 xii 1937.
2 CS to Kate Stead, Lambertville, summer, 1938.

3   'Shiksa' is a derogatory Yiddish term for a gentile woman.
4   CS to Harvey, November 1969. (*SL*) For the same conversation, see *Letty*, p. 203.
5   Jacques Coe mentions the incident in his book *Fame, Fraud and Fortune*, Exposition Press, Smithtown, NY, 1983.
6   CS to FJ, 13 xii 1937.
7   In March 1943, DGS donated the book to the Mitchell Library in Sydney.
8   CS to FJ, 13 xii 1937.
9   CS to Burnshaw, 7 vi 1938.
10   CS to Burnshaw, 13 vii 1938.
11   The novella was not published until 1967, in the collection *The Puzzleheaded Girl*.
12   Conversation with Ruth Hall, 25 ix 1988. Samuel Putnam (1892–1950) was known for his translations from French, Spanish, Italian and Portuguese.
13   CS to Maurice Temple-Smith, Secker & Warburg, 19 viii 1967. (Archives & Manuscripts, University of Reading.)
14   CS to FJ, 12 xii 1938.
15   Peter Davies to CS, 7 ix 1938. NLA, Box 7, folder 51.
16   Private comment. Simon & Schuster papers.
17   *Saturday Review of Literature*, 6 August 1938.
18   Fred Stead had worked in a motorcycle factory, and when he was stood down during the Depression, he organised political resistance at the factory. He did not play the guitar. (Conversation with Gilbert Stead, 2 ii 1990.)
19   CS to Gilbert Stead, 30 viii 1938.
20   CS to Blake, 15 vi 1942.
21   Conversation with Burnshaw, New York, 29 vi 1988.
22   CS to Burnshaw, 29 ix 1938.
23   CS to FJ, 12 xii 1938.
24   H. M. Green, 'Australian Literature, 1938', *Southerly* 1939.
25   Palmer papers, MS 1174.
26   Mitchell Library, Rare Book Collection.
27   CS to Thistle Harris, 7 vii 1939. (SL)
28   Mariann Heimans, 'Christina Stead ... Writer Courageous', *Sun* (Melbourne), 11 April 1977.
29   CS to Blake, 14 vi 1942.
30   Conversation with Thistle Harris, Sydney, 15 i 1987.
31   Jose Yglesias, 'Marx as Muse', *Nation*, vol. CC, 1965.
32   Mary McCarthy, 'Framing Father', *New Republic*, 13 January 1941, p. 61.
33   CS to Eldon Branda, 2 iii 1965. (*SL*)
34   CS to Thistle Harris, 7 vii 1939. (*SL*)
35   Clifton Fadiman, *New Yorker*, 19 October 1940, p. 84. The critics did not agree on this. Charles Poore declared Sam Pollit's letters 'spectacularly dull'. (NYT, 18 October 1940.)
36   CS interview with Joan Lidoff (1973). *Christina Stead*, Ungar, New York, 1982.
37   CS to FJ, 15 vi 1940.
38   Conversation with Ruth Hall, 5 x 1987.
39   *Letty*, p. 231. The same detail recurs in the short story 'Life is Difficult,' in *Ocean*.
40   CS to FJ, 15 vi 1940.
41   *Nation*, 26 August 1939. That Christina Stead signed the letter is noted in her FBI file.

9. Dearest Munx

1   CS to FJ, 15 vi 1940.
2   Conversation with Asa Zatz, New York, 14 x 1987.
3   Aida Kotlarsky died on 2 January 1982. Asa Zatz wrote her obituary in the *New York Times*: 'She lived a long life but never aged. A beautiful, caring adult who remained always a wide-eyed elfin child, she found joy always in her music, her mountains and in those she loved. She brought

fantasy, delight, humor, warmth to many lives. All who knew her will miss this irreplaceable spirit.'

4   CS to Thistle Harris, 6 iv 1942. (*SL*)
5   CS to Isidor Schneider, 7 xi 1940. Schneider Collection, Rare Books and Manuscript Library, Butler Library, Columbia University.
6   Pearl K. Bell, 'A neglected master', *New Leader*, 11 December 1972.
7   Mary McCarthy, 'Framing Father', *New Republic*, vol. 104, no. 2, 13 January 1941.
8   Clifton Fadiman, review of *The Man*, *New Yorker*, 19 October 1940.
9   The letter has not survived. I am surmising the content from CS's letter to Blake.
10 Louis B. Salomon had written in the *Nation*: 'While I have every reason to hope that Sam Pollit is an exaggerated figure, he is drawn convincingly enough to make a lot of men want to crawl away into a corner and die. But of course the Sam Pollits never know when a barb is aimed at them.' (26 October 1940.)
11 Blake to Burnshaw, 1938.
12 CS to Rella, 30 vi 1953. (*SL*)
13 Rella is the model for Roselli in *Dogs*.
14 CS to Burnshaw, 19 ii 1965. (*SL*)
15 Ruth McKenney, *Love Story*, Harcourt, Brace & Co., New York, 1950.
16 Burnshaw to me, 31 vii 1992.
17 In *Laughing*, Emily Wilkes says this.
18 *Current Biography*, H. W. Wilson, New York, 1942.
19 CS to Walter Stone of the Book Collectors' Society of Australia, 24 iii 1958. (Walter Stone papers, NLA, MS 9093.)
20 CS to Burnshaw, 18 xi 1941.
21 John Simon Guggenheim Memorial Foundation, New York.
22 Diana Trilling, 'Women in Love', review of *Love*, *Nation*, 28 October 1944.
23 CS to Blake, undated. (June 1942.)
24 CS to Elizabeth Harrower, 21 vi 1976. (*SL*)
25 Conversations with Michael Bloom and Janet Ladenheim (née Bloom), New Jersey, 17 viii 1988, and with Michael Bloom, New York, 5 viii 1988.
26 CS to Thistle Harris, 6 iv 1942. (*SL*)
27 Marion McDonald, 'Christina Stead: the exile returns, unhappily', *National Times*, 22–27 November 1976.

10. The Besieged Fortress

1   CS to Burnshaw, 31 viii 1942. (*SL*)
2   CS, 'Workshop in the novel', NLA, Box 11, folder 84.
3   Blake to Burnshaw, 9 xii 1942.
4   Otto Friedrich, *City of Nets*, Harper & Row, New York, 1986.
5   CS to Rella, 31 v 1979. (*SL*)
6   George E. Sokolsky, 'Who Done It?', *Sun* (New York), 30 December 1944.
7   *Dogs* has strong echoes of Shakespeare's play. There is even a country wedding, in which the bridal pair appear from the wood. Two of the characters' names, Lydia and Leander, evoke Hermia and Lysander in *A Midsummer Night's Dream*.
8   Jose Yglesias, 'Marx as Muse', *Nation*, 5 April 1965.
9   Patrick White to Geoffrey Dutton, 5 ii 1967. Dutton papers.
10 Ruth Page, *New York Times*, 29 October 1944.
11 Katherine Shorey, *Library Journal*, 15 October 1944.
12 *Sydney Morning Herald*, 30 December 1944.
13 CS to Thistle Harris, 6 iv 1942. (*SL*)
14 Angela Carter, *Expletives Deleted*, Chatto & Windus, London, 1992.
15 CS to Anderson. Undated. (End of March or early April, 1961.)

16   Susan Sheridan, *Christina Stead*, Harvester Wheatsheaf, London, 1988.
17   CS interview with Jonah Raskin, 'Christina Stead in Washington Square', *London Magazine*, vol. 9, no. 11, February 1970.
18   The friend was Phil Shahn, brother of Ben Shahn, the socialist-realist painter. The notes, called 'Zany Department', are dated 21 November 1939. (NLA, Box 6, folder 44.)
19   Anderson to me, 8 vii 1988.
20   Irving Howe & Lewis Coser, *The American Communist Party*, Frederick A. Praeger, New York, 1962.
21   CS to Anderson, 20 ix 1946.
22   CS to FJ, 1 ii 1948.
23   Conversation with Ruth Hall, 5 x 1987.
24   Mary McGrory, *New York Times*, 6 October 1946.
25   Harrison Smith, review of *Letty* in *Saturday Review of Literature*, 12 October 1946.
26   This detail is taken from the story 'Girl from the Beach'.
27   *Dogs*, p. 329.

11. From One Perch to Another

1   CS's FBI file No. 100-82232, opened New York, 18 February 1947.
2   CS to Mike Gold, 24 vii 1947. (Folsom papers.)
3   CS to Nadine and Lina Lewin, 1 ix 1947. (*SL*)
4   Angela Carter, 'Unhappy Families', *London Review of Books*, 16 September–6 October 1982. Carter writes that the change of style occurred after *The Man*. In my opinion, it occurred after *Love*.
5   CS to Anderson, 7 ii 1950.
6   CS uses the term to describe David Flack in *Tea*.
7   CS, 'Les Amoureux. (Life of Two Writers)', *Ocean*. The maid's comment was: 'Is that a life, typing all day?'
8   CS to Anderson, 8 vi 1947.
9   CS to Nettie Palmer, 5 xii 1950. (Palmer papers.) (SL)
10   CS to Mike Gold, 13 vii 1947.
11   CS to Anderson, 10 ix 1947.
12   In 1949, Leo Huberman set up the *Monthly Review* with Paul Sweezy. In 1952 he established the Monthly Review Press, for books that would not otherwise find a publisher in the era of McCarthyism.
13   CS to Anderson, 13 xi 1947.
14   CS to Gilbert Stead, 12 iv 1949.
15   CS to FJ, 1 ii 1948. (FJ papers.)
16   *Cotters'*, p. 231.
17   CS to Nettie Palmer, 9 v 1951. (SL)
18   CS to Pilar Libenson, 10 v 1948. (Unsent.) NLA, Box 7.
19   Robert Knittel, 'Unpleasant little group', *New York Times Book Review*, 22 August 1948.
20   Conversation with Julie James Bailey, Sydney, 4 iv 1988.
21   CS to Anderson, 27 viii 1949.
22   CS to Gilbert and Sylvia Stead, 24 vii 1950.
23   CS to Aida Kotlarsky, 29 xii 1949. (Don Shaw papers, Shaw private archives.)
24   CS to Rodney Pybus, 16 xi 1968. (Unsent—at least in this form.) (*SL*)
25   Rodney Pybus, '*Cotters' England*: In Appreciation', *Stand*, vol. 23, no. 4, 1982.
26   CS to Anderson, 20 i 1950.
27   CS to Dorothy Green, 14 iii 1976. (Green papers.)
28   CS to Anderson, 6 ii 1951. Unsent. (NLA, Box 7, folder 50.)
29   CS to FJ, 10 vi 1948.
30   CS to Anderson, 13 xii 1950.
31   ibid., 25 x 1952.

32   CS to Burnshaw, 6 iii 1967. (*SL*)
33   CS to Kate Stead, 2 vi 1950. (Kate Stead papers.)
34   CS to Nettie Palmer, 5 xii 1950. (*SL*)
35   CS to Anderson, 14 xi 1950.
36   CS to Gilbert Stead, 24 vii 1950.
37   CS to Anderson, 20 vii 1950.
38   CS to Gilbert Stead, 24 vii 1950.
39   CS, 'A View of Australian Fiction', *National Times*, 18–23 October 1976.
40   CS to Anderson, 21 viii 1950.
41   ibid., 11 x 1950.
42   CS to GW-S, 12 xi 1950.
43   CS to Anderson, 27 xii 1950.
44   CS, diary, 'The Travellers' Bed and Breakfast', 7 November 1950. NLA, Box 15.
45   CS, 'The Captain's House', *Ocean*.
46   CS, diary, 17 April 1951.
47   CS to Anderson, 16 iv 1951.
48   Conversation with Janet Ladenheim (née Bloom), New Jersey, 17 viii 1988.
49   Conversation with Kate Stead, Sydney, 20 i 1987.
50   'The Oats Fantasia', NLA, Box 5.
51   'The Lodger in the Bones', NLA, Box 5.
52   CS to Anderson, 23 ix 1951.
53   ibid.

12. Literary Hacks

 1   CS to GW-S, 16 vii 1952.
 2   CS to Geering, 13 vii 1967. (*SL*)
 3   CS to Walter Stone (editor of *Biblionews*), 24 iii 1958. (*SL*)
 4   CS to GW-S, 16 vii 1952.
 5   CS to FJ, 18 iv 1952.
 6   The next few quotes are taken from letters from CS to Anderson.
 7   CS to Nettie Palmer, 5 xii 1950. (SL)
 8   CS quotes Nettie Palmer in a letter to FJ, 16 vi 1952.
 9   The humiliation of the UNESCO incident is transposed into fiction in *Miss Herbert*. Bob Standfast (note the irony of the name) tells Miss Herbert 'it would be easy for a girl like her' to find work in UNESCO. She pays the fare from London to Paris in vain.
10   CS to FJ, 16 vi 1952.
11   Blake to FJ, 9 ii 1953.
12   CS to FJ, 18 iv 1952.
13   CS to Anderson, 17 ii 1953.
14   CS to FJ, 20 iii 1953.
15   CS to Anderson, 25 viii 1953.
16   CS to GW-S, 31 xii 1953.
17   CS, '1954: Days of the Roomers'.
18   Blake to Anderson, 2 vii 1954.
19   *Herbert*, p. 229.
20   Blake to Anderson, 2 vii 1954.
21   CS, '1954: Days of the Roomers'.
22   CS to Anderson, 28 x 1954.
23   Conversation with Tella Friedmann, 29 ix 1988.
24   Conversation with GW-S, Sydney, 16 i 1987.
25   CS interviewed by Joan Lidoff (1973), *Christina Stead*, Ungar, New York, 1982.
26   Conversation with DDS, 9 i 1987.

27   CS to Anderson, 9 viii 1956.
28   Blake to Murray Teigh Bloom, 9 x 1956. (Murray Bloom papers, Bloom private archives.)
29   CS to Neil Stewart, 22 xii 1957.
30   CS to Anderson, 23 ix 1963.
31   ibid., 7 iii 1961.
32   Conversation with Ring Lardner Jnr, Lorne, Victoria, 23 iii 1991.
33   CS to Neil Stewart, 31 i 1959. (*SL*)
34   CS to Anderson, 11 xii 1964.
35   Blake to Murray Bloom, 21 ii 1959.

13. 'Bill, My True Companion'

1   Blake to Burnshaw, 31 viii 1960.
2   ibid., 17 xii 1960.
3   CS to Norman Rosten, 7 viii 1967. (NLA, Box 14.)
4   CS to Doris and David Stead. The letter was begun on 14 i 1961, continued on 31 i and completed on 29 iii. (Gilbert Stead papers.)
5   CS to Anderson, 9 iii 1963.
6   CS to Maurice Temple Smith, 31 i 1968. (Secker & Warburg papers, University of Reading.)
7   Blake to Burnshaw, 28 ix 1962.
8   Conversation with Paul Koston, Brighton, England, 8 xi 1988.
9   CS to Rodney Pybus, 16 xi 1968. (*SL*) 'The Girl from the Beach' was based on Janet Bloom; 'The Dianas' was based loosely on Nadine Lewin (also part model for Jacky in *Letty*).
10   These letters were in Stead's possession at the time of her death.
11   Anderson to me, 3 xi 1988.
12   CS to Barbara Baer, 7 x 1972.
13   CS to Dorothy Green, 31 iii 1970. (NLA, MS 54678.)
14   CS to Burnshaw, 14 ix 1965.
15   CS interview with Ann Whitehead (1973), *Australian Literary Studies*, vol. 6, no. 3, May 1974.
16   CS to GW-S, 13 vi 1972. (GW-S papers.)
17   Conversation with Pera Koston, Oxford, 27 x 1988.
18   Blake to Murray Bloom, 1 xii 1964.
19   CS to Burnshaw, 23 ii 1965.
20   CS to Randall Jarrell, 16 iii 1965. (Jarrell papers.)
21   CS to Mary Jarrell, 15 ix 1966. (Jarrell papers.)
22   Patrick White provided this quote for publicity purposes. (Secker & Warburg papers.)
23   CS to Burnshaw, 26 iv 1965.
24   ibid., 18 v 1965.
25   R. J. Scholfield, *Bulletin*, 22 May 1965.
26   Conversation with Charlotte Mayerson, New York, 26 vii 1988.
27   CS to Aida Kotlarsky, 8 i 1968. (Shaw papers.)
28   Conversation with Philip Harvey, London, 20 ix 1987.
29   William Ash, 'In Memory of Bill Blake', *Monthly Review*, June 1968.
30   CS to Burnshaw, 22 iv 1968.
31   ibid., 10 ii 1968. After Blake's death, Stanley Burnshaw sent Stead a poem, 'Friend Across the Ocean', dedicated to Bill, which Stead found deeply moving. It begins:

> I go to my quiet bed, put out the light, prepare to sleep
> And my friend across the ocean lies in his sickbed
> waiting.
> Dying with nothing more to reach for ...

The poem is included in Stanley Burnshaw, *In the Terrified Radiance*, George Braziller, New York, 1972.
32   CS to Aida Kotlarsky, 5 ii 1968.

14. Hundred Thousand Regrets

1 CS to Hyrell and Judah Waten, 24 xi 1978. (Waten papers.)
2 CS to Margaret Hanks (née Stead), 19 ii 1968. (Margaret Hanks papers.)
3 Interview with Rodney Wetherell (1980), *Australian Literary Studies*, vol. 9, no. 4, October 1980.
4 CS to Burnshaw, 2 v 1968.
5 ibid., 6 v 1968.
6 ibid., 7 v 1968.
7 Conversation with Burnshaw, New York, 5 vi 1988.
8 'Christina Stead in Washington Square'. Interview by Jonah Raskin, September 1968. *London Magazine*, February 1970, and CS to Burnshaws, 24 viii 1968.
9 Conversation with Charlotte Mayerson, New York, 26 vii 1988.
10 CS to Burnshaws, 24 viii 1968.
11 ibid., 23 ix 1968.
12 CS to Clem Christesen, 17 i 1969. (SL)
13 'Another View of the Homestead, *Ocean*.
14 CS to Harveys, 11 viii 1969. (SL)
15 Stuart Sayers, 'Books you just listen to', *Age*, 23 August 1969.
16 Patrick White to Geoffrey Dutton, 22 ix 1969. (Dutton papers.)
17 CS to Burnshaw, 7 viii 1973.
18 CS to Philip Harvey, 16 x 1969.
19 Conversation with G. W. K. Duncan, 27 ii 1987; and conversations with Geering.
20 CS to Philip Harvey, 17 iii 1970.
21 CS to Geering, 14 i 1974.
22 CS to Burnshaws, 9 xi 1970.
23 CS to Paul Koston, 29 x 1970. (*SL*)
24 CS to Burnshaws, 9 i 1972.
25 ibid., 18 x 1973.
26 ibid., 6 ix 1972.
27 Notes on Woolf, 'Spectral Presences', NLA, Box 15.
28 CS to Rella, 20 viii 1974. (*SL*)
29 ibid., 8 x 1974.
30 CS to Burnshaw, 5 vi 1974.
31 CS to Rella, 8 x 1974.
32 ibid.

15. Humping Her Own Bluey

1 CS to Rellas, 29 vi 1977.
2 CS to Ruth Hall, 15 viii 1977.
3 Patrick White to Geoffrey Dutton, 13 i 1975. (Dutton papers.)
4 ibid., 22 ix 1969.
5 CS to Rellas, 20 ii 1975.
6 CS to W. H. Pearson, 3 ix 1975. (NLA, MS 7570.)
7 CS to Rellas, 14 i 1976.
8 Don Dunstan to me, 13 ix 1991.
9 CS to Rellas, 8 vii 1977.
10 Conversation with Clem and Nina Christesen, Eltham, Victoria, 24 vi 1991.
11 CS to H. C. Coombs, 14 vii 1977. (Coombs papers.)
12 CS to DDS, 4 xii 1977.
13 CS to Rellas, 5 iv 1978.
14 Conversation with Dorothy Green, Canberra, 9 iv 1988.
15 CS to Philip Harvey, 22 xi 1978.

16 CS to Burnshaw, 31 viii 1978.
17 Conversation with Mary Lord, Melbourne, 26 vi 1991.
18 CS to Geerings, 9 vi 1980.
19 Conversation with H. C. Coombs, Cremorne, Sydney, 8 i 1987.
20 CS to Rellas, 19 v 1982.
21 CS to Rosemary Dobson, 2 vii 1982. (Dobson papers.) 'Humping the bluey' is Australian slang for carrying one's pack on one's shoulders.
22 CS interview with Barry Hill, *Sydney Morning Herald*, 17 July 1982.
23 Elizabeth Harrower to me, 8 x 1991.
24 Jonathan LaPook to me, 6 xii 1991.
25 CS to Rosemary Dobson and Alec Bolton, 21 xii 1982.
26 Conversation with Heather Stewart, Sydney, 13 vii 1987.
27 Conversation with Helena Berenson and Geoff Davis, Sydney, 26 ix 1991.

Bibliography

Works by Christina Stead

Fiction

The following are first publications; the modern editions cited in the endnotes are given last.

The Salzburg Tales. Peter Davies, London, 1934; D. Appleton-Century, New York, 1934; Sun Books, Melbourne, 1966.

Seven Poor Men of Sydney. Peter Davies, London, 1934; D. Appleton-Century, New York, 1934; A & R, Sydney, 1965.

The Beauties and Furies. Peter Davies, London, 1936; D. Appleton-Century, New York, 1936; Virago, London, 1982.

House of All Nations. Simon & Schuster, New York, 1938; Peter Davies, London, 1938; A & R, Sydney, 1974.

The Man Who Loved Children. Simon & Schuster, New York, 1940; Peter Davies, London, 1941; Penguin, Harmondsworth, 1970.

For Love Alone. Harcourt, Brace, New York, 1944; Peter Davies, London, 1945; A & R, Sydney, 1966.

Letty Fox: Her Luck. Harcourt, Brace, New York, 1946; Peter Davies, London, 1947; A & R, Sydney, 1974.

A Little Tea, A Little Chat. Harcourt, Brace, New York, 1948; Virago, London, 1981.

The People with the Dogs. Little, Brown, Boston, 1952; Virago, London, 1981.

Dark Places of the Heart. Holt, Rinehart & Winston, New York, 1966; *Cotters' England.* Seeker & Warburg, London, 1967; A & R, Sydney, 1974.

The Puzzleheaded Girl. Holt, Rinehart & Winston, New York, 1967; Secker & Warburg, London, 1968; Virago, London, 1984.

The Little Hotel. A & R, London and Sydney 1973; Holt, Rinehart & Winston, New York, 1975.

Miss Herbert (The Suburban Housewife). Random House, New York, 1976; Virago, London, 1979.

Anthologies and Translations

Modern Women in Love: Sixty Twentieth-Century Masterpieces of Fiction. Edited by Christina Stead and William Blake. Dryden Press, New York, 1945.

Great Stories of the South Sea Islands. Selected with a foreword by Christina Stead. Muller, London, 1955.

Gignon, Fernand. *Colour of Asia*. Muller, London, 1955.

Giltène, Jean. *The Candid Killer*. Muller, London, 1956.

Piccard, Auguste. *In Balloon and Bathyscaphe*. Cassell, London, 1956.

Posthumous Publications

Ocean of Story. The uncollected stories of Christina Stead, edited with an afterword by R. G. Geering. Viking/Penguin, Ringwood, Victoria, 1985.

I'm Dying Laughing: The Humourist. Edited with a preface by R. G. Geering. Virago, London, 1986.

The Palace with Several Sides: A Sort of Love Story. Limited edition, edited by R. G. Geering. Officina Brindabella, Canberra, 1986; repr. in *Southerly*, no. 2, 1987, pp. 115–25.

A Web of Friendship. Selected Letters (1928–1973). Edited with preface and annotations by R. G. Geering. A & R, Sydney, 1992.

Talking into the Typewriter. Selected Letters (1973–1983). Edited with preface and annotations by R. G. Geering. A & R, Sydney, 1992.

Dearest Munx: The Letters of Christina Stead and William J. Blake. Edited by Margaret Harris, The Miegunyah Press, Melbourne, 2005.

Selected Articles

(This list does not include pieces re-published in *Ocean of Story*.)

'The Writers Take Sides', *Left Review*, vol. 1, no. 2, July 1935, pp. 435–63, 469–75.

'America' (1935), *Australian Book Review*, June 1992.

'About Woman's Insight, There Is a Sort of Folklore We Inherit', Contribution to a symposium on 'Women's Intuition', *Vogue* (US) vol. 158, no. 5, 15 September 1971, pp. 61, 130.

'What Goal in Mind?' in Shirley Cass, Ros Cheney, David Malouf and Michael Wilding (eds), *We Took Their Orders and Are Dead*. Ure Smith, Sydney, 1971, pp. 119–30.

'On the Women's Movement', *Partisan Review*, vol. 46, no. 2, 1979, pp. 271–4.

'Some Deep Spell: A View of Stanley Burnshaw', *Agenda* (London) Special Issue on Stanley Burnshaw, vol. 21, no. 4, vol. 22, no. 1, 1983–4.

Selected Interviews

Beston, John. 'An Interview with Christina Stead' (September 1975), *World Literature Written in English*, vol. 15, no. 1, April 1976, pp. 87–95.

Chisholm, Anne. *National Times*, 29 March–4 April 1981, pp. 32–4.

'Christina Stead', *Wilson Library Bulletin*, vol. 13, no. 4, December 1938, p. 234.

'Christina Stead', Australian Writers series, Program Two, Australian Broadcasting Corporation, 23 March 1976. Copyright No. 76/AW/2.

Drewe, Robert. 'Christina Stead' (1982), *Scripsi*, vol. 4, no. 1, July 1986.

Guiffré, Giulia. 'Christina Stead', in *A Writing Life*, Allen & Unwin, Sydney, 1990.

Hill, Barry. 'Christina Stead at 80 says love is her religion', *Sydney Morning Herald*, 17 July 1982, p. 33; *Age*, 17 July 1982, p. 2.

Keneally, Thomas. 'Conversation Piece', *Vogue Australia*, vol. 21, no. 4, May 1977, pp. 91–3.

Kinross Smith, Graeme. 'Christina Stead—A Profile', *Westerly*, no. 1, 1976, pp. 67–75.

Lidoff, Joan. 'An Interview with Christina Stead'. Surbiton, England, June, 1973. In Lidoff, *Christina Stead*, Frederick Ungar, New York, 1982, pp. 180–220.

Raskin, Jonah. 'Christina Stead in Washington Square', *London Magazine*, vol. 9, no. 2, February 1970, pp. 70–7.

Riddell, Elizabeth (interviewer). *Christina Stead* (1980), Australia Council Archival Film Series. Producer: Haydn Kernan.

Wetherell, Rodney. 'Christina Stead: An Interview', *Australian Literary Studies*, vol. 9, no. 4, October 1980, pp. 431–48.

Whitehead, Ann. 'Christina Stead: An Interview' (1973), *Australian Literary Studies*, vol. 6, no. 3, May 1974, pp. 230–48.

Williamson, Jean. 'Christina Stead Tells of Her Latest Book!', *Australian Women's Weekly*, 9 March 1935.

Manuscript Sources

Christina Stead's manuscripts, diaries and miscellaneous correspondence are held in the Manuscript Collection of the National Library of Australia, Canberra. This contains family correspondence, as well as the important correspondence with Edith Anderson, Philip and Leah Harvey, Ettore and Jessie Rella, and Gwen Walker Smith. The NLA also has the 'Hazel Rowley papers', material to do with this book: MS 9244.

Some of Stead's correspondence remains in private hands. The public collections are listed below:

Stanley Burnshaw papers, Harry Ransom Humanities Research Center, University of Texas at Austin.

Clem Christesen papers, Meanjin Archives, Baillieu Library, University of Melbourne.

H. C. Coombs papers, NLA, MS 802, Box 49.

Rosemary Dobson papers, NLA, MS 4955.

Geoffrey Dutton papers, NLA, MS 7285.

Dorothy Green papers, NLA, MS 54678.

Guy Howarth papers, HRHRC, University of Texas at Austin.

Charles Humboldt papers, Manuscripts and Archives, Yale University Library.

Florence James papers, State Library of NSW.

Randall Jarrell papers, Henry W. and Albert A. Berg Collection, New York Public Library.

Stephen Murray-Smith papers, Overland Collection, La Trobe Library, State Library of Victoria.

Palmer papers, NLA, MS 1174.

W. H. Pearson papers, NLA, MS 7570.

Isidor Schneider papers, Rare Books and Manuscripts, Butler Library, Columbia University.

Neil Stewart papers, Rare Books, Fisher Library, University of Sydney.

Judah Waten papers, NLA, MS 4536.

I also drew on the following manuscript sources:

ASIO file on Stead, Australian Archives, Series A 6119 XRI, Item 231.

Aufbauverlag papers, Berlin.

Australia Council Emeritus Fellowships, Australia Council, Christina Stead file.

Creative Arts Fellowships, Australian National University, Chancellery, ANU.

FBI files on William James Blake and Christina Ellen Stead.

Literature Censorship Board, Canberra, regarding *Letty* and *Tea*, Australian Archives, Canberra.

Little, Brown collection, regarding the publication of *Dogs*, Special Collections, Boston University, Massachusetts.

Secker & Warburg files, Archives & Manuscripts, University of Reading.

Simon & Schuster collection, Rare Books & Manuscripts, Butler Library, Columbia University.

Stead, 'Uses of the Many-Charactered Novel', Paper delivered at the Third American Writers' Congress, 4 June 1939. League of American Writers papers, Rare Books and Manuscripts, Bancroft Library, University of California.

Stead's 1941 application for a Guggenheim Fellowship, John Simon Guggenheim Memorial Foundation, New York.

Woolf, Cecil and John Bagguley, (eds). *Authors take sides on Vietnam*. Correspondence with Christina Stead, Astor, Lenox and Tilden Foundations, New York Public Library.

Acknowledgements

Throughout the six years I was involved in this project, I had assistance and encouragement from three continents.

The biographical trail has its dramatic ups and downs, excitements and frustrations. Stead's old friends, Edith Anderson, Stanley Burnshaw, Ron Geering, Florence James were all cautious at first, neither encouraging nor discouraging. Later, their generous assistance and encouragement seemed to have no bounds.

I am above all indebted to Ron Geering, Stead's late literary executor, for his trust in me, and for generously allowing me to see and quote from Stead material that was closed at the time (until 2001), and for granting me world rights to quote from Stead's unpublished papers and letters.

Edith Anderson, hurt by Stead's behaviour towards her, at first refused my entreaties. After more correspondence came the reply, covered with East German stamps: 'Dear Hazel Rowley, what a temptress you are!' The four days spent perusing letters in her flat were a source of invaluable material and seeded a warm friendship.

I owe special thanks to Gwen Walker-Smith, with her astounding recall and affectionate insights into the Stead family. I am indebted to Gilbert Stead, whose family archives were a rich source of material. These people, and many others (below) whom I spoke to in the 1980s, have since died.

For interviews in Australia, England, France, Germany, Italy and the United States, I thank: William Ash, Barbara Baer, Julie James Bailey, Phyllis Barnett, Cedric Belfrage, Helena Berenson, Jack Bermond, Norman Berry, Geoffrey Blainey, Michael Bloom, Murray Teigh Bloom, Alec Bolton, Phil Brown, Clem and Nina Christesen, Axel Clark, Jacques Coe, H. C. Coombs, Margaret Coombs, Beatrice Davis, Geoff Davis, Rosemary Dobson, W. G. K. Duncan, Don Dunstan, Geoffrey Dutton, Ralph Elliott, Clifton Fadiman, Mike Folsom, Elsie Ford (née Butters), Boyce and Tella Friedmann, Judith Kegan Gardiner, Dorothy Green, Ruth Hall (née Blech), Margaret Hanks (née Stead), Thistle Harris, Elizabeth Harrower, Philip and Leah Harvey, Shirley Hazzard, Mark Higgie, Shirley Hokin, Edward Huberman, Elisabeth Granich Humeston (Gold), Yvonne Kapp, Graeme Kinross Smith, Hortense Kooluris, Richard Kopley, Paul Koston, Pera Koston, Janet Ladenheim (née Bloom), George Lanning, Jonathan LaPook, Ring Lardner Jnr, Pilar Libenson,

Mary Lord, Donald and Wendy Macdonald, Margaret Mackie, Harry Magdoff, Tempe Mann (née Datson), Charlotte Mayerson, Nadine Mendelson (née Lewin), Stuart Monro, Nita Murray-Smith, Pauline Nestor, Neil and Peggy O'Connor, Bill Packard, Jenny Palmer, E. F. Patterson, Gerald Pollinger, Betty Lewis Reid, Ettore and Jessie Rella, Elizabeth Riddell, Miriam Risner, Betty Roland, Norman Rosten, Albert Rubin, Kel Semmens, Clement Semmler, Don Shaw, Gunnwor Stallybrass, David D. Stead, Gilbert Stead, Ivy and Kelvin Stead, Kate Stead, Miriam Stern, Heather Stewart, Jean Stone, Hugh and Pat Stretton, Helen Thomson, Pat Waddington (Coontz), Patricia and Donald Walker, Gwen Walker-Smith, Enid Wall, Noel Warry, Michael Wilding, Marguerite Young and Asa Zatz.

I am grateful to the Institute for Research on Women and Gender at Columbia University for providing excellent working conditions for my three-month stay in New York in 1988, and to the Humanities Research Centre at the Australian National University for enabling me to enjoy a productive two months there in January to February 1990.

It was a pleasure to work on Christina Stead's papers in the manuscripts and archives room of the National Library of Australia in Canberra, and I thank Marlene Bonny, Elizabeth Penc, Graeme Powell and Pam Ray for their helpfulness and efficiency.

I thank the Estate of Christina Stead, Harcourt Brace and Co., Henry Holt and Co., Martin Secker & Warburg Ltd, Random House Ltd and Virago Press Ltd for permission to print material from Christina Stead's novels, Angus & Robertson for permission to include material from *Seven Poor Men of Sydney*, *For Love Alone*, *House of All Nations*, *The Salzburg Tales* and *Letty Fox*, and Penguin Books Australia for permission to use extracts from *Oceans of Story*.

For their valuable assistance, I thank the following institutions and their librarians: Baillieu Library, University of Melbourne; La Trobe Library, State Library of Victoria; Fisher Library, University of Sydney; Aufbauverlag papers, Berlin; Special Collections, Boston University, Massachusetts; Bancroft Library, University of California; Irene Stevens at the Australia Council; the Australian Archives in Canberra; the Australian Conservation Foundation; the Berg Collection in the New York Public Library; Jean Rose at the Reed Consumer Books Library, Rushden, Northants; Michael Bott for photocopying the Secker & Warburg papers, Archives and Manuscripts, Reading University Library; Bernard Crystal in the Rare Book and Manuscript Library, Butler Library, Columbia University; the Harry Ransom Humanities Research Center, University of Texas at Austin; the State Archives of New South Wales; the Mitchell Library, Sydney; the Yale University Library, New Haven, Connecticut; the Mugar Memorial Library at Boston University; Jim Fletcher, Historical Research Officer in the Department of Education, New South Wales; Sydney Teachers' College; the John Simon Guggenheim Memorial Foundation; the William Morris Agency, New York; the Federal Bureau of Investigation, US Department of Justice, Washington.

I will always remember the afternoon of 15 February 1986, when I was walking on Phillip Island with Alex Coram, and he convinced me to take on a project that then seemed too difficult. Damien Broderick encouraged me to dance across the page. Lynn Buchanan read through my manuscript at different stages, and offered helpful comments and suggestions. Ann Timoney Jenkin read three drafts of the book, and provided that sustained, concentrated and altruistic editorial assistance that writers rarely find.

I am touched that it was Louise Adler who published this book in 1993 (the launch at Miettas, in Melbourne, was a magical occasion) and that fourteen years later, Louise is bringing it back into print. I well remember her reaction back in 1992, when I handed her the completed manuscript—a vast tome of 290000 words. Dismay? She published it anyway, whole. Fourteen years later, I'm the one who insisted that I return to this narrative with a sharp scythe. I hope this abridged edition is sharper, and even more savoury. My thanks to Elisa Berg and the MUP editorial team.

Index

G L N Si Jo